THE BIBLIO FILE

THE BIBLIO FILE

An Index of Prose Passages

COLIN AND SUSAN
SWATRIDGE

BASIL BLACKWELL · OXFORD

ISBN's 0 631 92640 2 (cased)
0 631 92620 8 (paper)

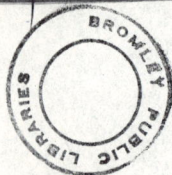

Set and printed in Great Britain by Billing & Sons Limited
Guildford, London and Worcester
Bound by Kemp Hall Bindery Ltd., Oxford

Contents

General Introduction

The Biblio File is a thematic guide for teachers, and others, to two hundred and twenty-five novels, collections of short stories, and works of autobiography. The books have been chosen either because they are well-established or modern 'classics', or because they lend themselves to use in schools by reason of their style, subject-matter, or presentation. All are such as might be found in department stock-rooms, and libraries, in upper primary, middle, and secondary schools. References throughout are to standard, or school editions, and where possible, both hardback and paperback editions have been included.

Passages have been selected from the books according to two fundamental criteria: firstly, a passage had to be self-sufficient and comprehensible out of context (to be, in short, the sort of passage that might appear in a good prose anthology); and secondly, it had to be susceptible to being given one or more subject-labels of a kind that might correspond to project-titles, or teaching-themes. The subject-headings have been suggested by the passages themselves, and are therefore original; however, it is hoped that, by means of the network of cross-references, passages will be found, directly or indirectly, under whatever subject-name the inquirer might use.

The authors have refrained from grading the books according to pupil age-groups, since in many cases passages have been chosen which might be thought suitable for, say, third or fourth year secondary classes, from books which, in their entirety, would be better suited to study at the sixth form level. It has not been considered wise to attempt to classify individual passages, in this way; however, it is the authors' hope that the brief synopsis of each of the passages will be a sufficient indication of the age-group for which it might be most appropriate.

The subject-index occupies the major part of the work. This consists of more than two thousand main references, and several hundred cross-references, to passages clearly defined by page and chapter (where applicable). Each main reference is supplied with a synopsis of the subject-content of the passage in, as a rule, between forty and fifty words. The author-index which follows sets out the publication details of the books, and lists all the passages that have been chosen from each book, as they appear in the subject-index. Finally, a brief anthology-index lists more than twenty prose-anthologies in common classroom use which contain passages, in whole or in part that have been chosen and defined in the subject-index.

Instructions for its use are given in more detail at the head of each index.

Subject Index

Introduction

Passages are ordered alphabetically by subject name. Where there are subheadings, and in some cases sub-subheadings, (e.g. ACCIDENTS – ROAD, ACCIDENTS – ROAD – DRUNKENNESS), these too are in alphabetical order. Connecting words in brackets (e.g. ACCIDENTS (at) WORK) do not affect this order; they merely define the relationship between the heading and its subheading. Where there is more than one passage under a subject-heading, entries are ordered alphabetically by author. Where possible, defining sub-headings have been used to prevent the accumulation of undifferentiated entries under one main heading. All entries are numbered so that cross-references can be made to main headings from one or more alternative subject-names.

Page and chapter references follow the author's name and book-title. Where both hardback and paperback editions are referred to, page and chapter references to the former are placed first. This order corresponds to the order in which the editions are cited in the author-index; it is there that full details of the editions to which reference is made are to be found.

When a passage that has been selected appears in whole or in part in one of more than twenty prose anthologies in common classroom use, the title of the anthology and the page – reference of the passage are given in brackets.

The first and last four or five words of the passage follow the above page-references. Where possible, chapter and other 'natural' breaks are used, to make it easy to isolate the passage; otherwise the first and last words are taken from the beginnings, and to the ends, of paragraphs.

A brief synopsis of the 'action' of the passage, in about forty or fifty words, is the final component of each entry. It is the authors' hope that this synopsis will enable the teacher to determine the suitability of the passage for a particular class or teaching-theme. Further, it is hoped that the summaries will be sufficient to remind the reader of books and passages dormant in the memory, or perhaps to open up books hitherto unread, and therefore unexploited.

In addition to the main entries, there are many hundreds of cross-references of three different kinds: first of all there are 'see' references from one subject-heading to another under a particular author's name and book-title; secondly there are 'see also' references from one subject-heading to other more general or specific subject-headings on related themes; and thirdly, there are 'see' references to used, from unused headings. By means of this network of cross-references it should be possible to unlock a secret passage with one of a number of different keys.

Subject Index

ABORTION

1. SILLITOE, Alan
   Saturday Night and Sunday Morning
   pp. 70–72 (Part 1, Ch. 5)
   'While Arthur looked ... the kid, that's all.'
   Arthur asks his Aunt Ada, in the professed interest of 'a friend', how an unwanted baby might be prevented. Ada is guarded, and then specific: the mother should bath in hot water for two hours, and drink quantities of gin.

ACCIDENTS

see also: DROWNING;
FLYING – ACCIDENTS;
HORSES – RIDING – ACCIDENTS;
ICE-SKATING – ACCIDENTS;
INJURIES;
MINING – ACCIDENTS

ACCIDENTS

1. BERNA, Paul
   A Hundred Million Francs
   see GAMES – RACES 1
2. CANAWAY, W.H.
   Sammy Going South
   see BLINDNESS 1
3. CHURCH, Richard
   The White Doe
   see TREES – FELLING 2
4. THOMAS, Leslie
   This Time Next Week
   pp. 33–35 (Ch. 3)
   'Half-way down Fore ... merrily on High.'
   It is Christmas Eve. The author and his best friend are required to pump the organ for the midnight service. Leslie loses the rhythm of the handle, loses hold of it, and is knocked out, in mid-carol.

ACCIDENTS – FALLING

1. KING, Clive
   Stig of the Dump
   pp. 7–10 (Ch. 1)

2

'If you went too near ... my neck if I hadn't.'
Barney knows the edge of the chalkpit is not safe, but he still goes to look over, into the rubbish tip. The ground gives way and he lands tangled in creepers, but unhurt, at the bottom of a pit.

2. KNOWLES, John
   A Separate Peace
   see DEATH (of) FRIEND 2

ACCIDENTS (at) HOME

1. BARSTOW, Stan
   A Kind of Loving
   pp. 228–234 (Part 2, Ch. 7, Sn. 1)
   'I get back from the shop ... trembling and empty and cold.'
   On his arrival home from work, Vic learns that his wife has fallen down the stairs and been taken to hospital. The neighbours give him a cup of tea and run him to the hospital, where he finds out that their baby has miscarried, and that Ingrid has lost a lot of blood.
2. NESBIT, E.
   The Railway Children
   (i) pp. 151–159 (Ch. 10), (ii) pp. 166–173
   'They had not been a week ... not see the trains.'
   The children are cultivating a patch of garden each, but Bobbie and Peter argue over the rake. When Bobbie finally leaves go, Peter falls over onto the rake, which spears his foot. The Doctor is called, and Bobbie is full of remorse.

ACCIDENTS – ROAD

1. DICKENS, Charles
   A Tale of Two Cities
   pp. 114–117 (Bk. 2, Ch. 7)
   'He was a man of about ... ran their course.'
   The carriage of a French Aristocrat knocks down and kills a child in a poor quarter of Paris. He fails to

understand the grief, and thinks only of his horses.

2. HARDY, Thomas
Tess of the D'Urbervilles
(i) pp. 35–39 (Ch. 4); (ii) pp. 40–44
'Left to his reflections ... of a murderess.'
Tess and her young brother Abraham are taking the hives to market. Both are lulled to sleep by the movement of the waggon. As they sleep, the lantern goes out, and they are hit by the speeding mailcart. Their horse is impaled on the latter's shaft, and dies.

3. NAUGHTON, Bill
The Goalkeeper's Revenge
see COMPETITIONS – RACES 2

4. NAUGHTON, Bill
Late Night on Watling Street
pp. 15–18 ('Late Night on Watling Street')
(Crime and Punishment pp. 30–34)
'Suddenly, ahead down the road ... the egg and chips ready.'
Jackson engineers what appears to the police to be an accident. He catches sight of a police-car tailing him. He jumps on the brakes, knowing the car will go under his tail-board, and the witnesses against him on a charge of dangerous driving, will be silenced.

5. WOODHOUSE, Martin
Tree Frog
pp. 48–51 (Ch. 6)
'Somewhere, somebody blew out a tyre ... I'd remembered right.'
A tyre bursts, the windscreen shatters, and Giles Yeoman loses control of the car. He and his passenger scramble out with nothing more serious than cuts. What is serious is that Giles suspects the tyre has burst, because it was shot at. The evidence later bears out his suspicion.

ACCIDENTS – ROAD – DRUNKENNESS

1. BARSTOW, Stan
A Kind of Loving
pp. 243–245 (Pt. 2, Ch. 7, Sn. 3)

'How're you feeling–... long, long time.'
Vic is being driven home after a pub crawl, by an old friend. Both are quite drunk. Vic has forebodings of trouble, and sure enough, his friend miscalculates on a corner, and the car grates against a stone wall. Happily, neither of them is injured.

2. BRAINE, John
Room at the Top
pp. 217–220 (Ch. 30)
'He gave me the folder ... bones sticking through.'
Joe is told about the death of his one time mistress in a car-crash; she had been drinking to help her to forget his faithlessness. Joe reconstructs the event in his mind, until the horror of it is too much for him.

3. FITZGERALD, F. Scott
The Great Gatsby
pp. 60–62 (Ch. 3)
'But as I walked ... "in trying" he said.'
After one of Gatsby's parties a car is discovered in the ditch not far from the house. The passenger emerges, is mistaken for the driver, who eventually climbs out, drunk and uncomprehending.

ACCIDENTS (at) WORK

see also: MINING – ACCIDENTS;

ACCIDENTS (at) WORK

1. GORKY, Maxim
Childhood
(i) pp. 62–68 (Ch. 3); (ii) pp. 55–59
'It happened like this ... buried unnoticeably, unobtrusively.'
The broad-shouldered young apprentice, Tsiganok, carries a massive oak cross to the cemetery. Yakov and Mikhail help him, but when he stumbles, they jump out of the way, and he takes the full weight of the cross in the back. He is brought back

to the house, vomiting blood, and he dies, lit by candles, on the floor.

2. NAUGHTON, Bill
   One Small Boy
   pp. 269–273 (Bk. 3, Ch. 8)
   'He waited for the water ... for thy mam.'
   A man comes from the foundry where Willie works to report that Willie has received a nasty blow at work and is in the infirmary. Michael and his mother go with the man in the company car; but before they have a chance to see Willie, a doctor pronounces him dead.

ACTING

see also: AMBITIONS – ACTING

ACTING

1. ALCOTT, Louisa M.
   Little Women
   see ENTERTAINMENTS 1
2. STREATFEILD, Noel
   Ballet Shoes
   pp. 92–99 (Ch. 8)
   'On the day of the matinée ... the matinée was over.'
   Pauline and Petrova are both very nervous about the play they are in, and are glad to be kept busy the morning before. Once on stage after the first few lines, they settle down and really 'act'.

ACTING – AUDITIONS

1. STREATFEILD, Noel
   Ballet Shoes
   pp. 118–126 (Ch. 10)
   'She looked so anxious ... the money so dreadfully.'
   Pauline and Winifred are auditioned for the part of Alice, and the latter is very anxious to get it to earn some money. Pauline recites, sings and dances and although she makes small mistakes she is chosen because she looks right.

ADOLESCENCE

see also: COURTSHIP;
CRIME – JUVENILE;
GANGS – YOUTHS;
VANDALISM

ADOLESCENCE – BOYS

1. BALDWIN, Michael
   Grandad with Snails
   pp. 166–170 (Ch. 20)
   'He had pimples ... I did the railway bridge.'
   Michael's friends climb over the parapet of the railway bridge, and they dare him to do the same. He pretends to have better things to do, when a pretty girl passes. He and Tony chase her, excited, uncertain. They are churlish and gallant by turns.
2. BENTLEY, Phyllis
   Gold Pieces
   pp. 88–94 (Ch. 6)
   'I don't know how ... great ears, for company.'
   Dick Wade has made friends with Jamie Hartley. Jamie is a practical joker, and many of his pranks are cruel, but Dick enjoys the feeling of being grown-up that his involvement in them gives him. His parents disapprove, and matters come to a head when he throws a stone at John Wesley.
3. SALINGER, J.D.
   The Catcher in the Rye
   pp. 22–25 (Ch. 3)
   'Anyway, I put on my ... back again, and relaxed.'
   Ackley is an awkward, spotty, interfering 18-year-old. He noses about Holden's study bedroom, picking things up, sneezing, and ignoring Holden's heavy hints.
4. ibid.
   pp. 32–34 (Ch. 4)
   'Anyway, I was sitting ... crumby old razor.'
   Holden watches his room-mate

shaving. Holden fools about, while his room-mate dolls himself up for his date.
5. ibid.
   see FIGHTING (by) BOYS 4
6. THOMAS, Dylan
   A Portrait of the Artist as a Young Dog
   pp. 52–56 ('Extraordinary Little Cough')
   'One afternoon ... go down patiently.'
   Dylan and his friends meet three girls on Rhossili sands. Dylan sets his cap at one of them, but his cap falls off, so he extracts what satisfaction he can from casual mockery of those of his friends whose advances are encouraged.
   see also: CHALLENGES 9

ADOLESCENCE – BOYS (in) LOVE

1. WELLS, H.G.
   Kipps
   pp. 18–21 (Bk. 1, Ch. 1, Sn. 4)
   'They proceeded to the question ... talk to, and all that ...'
   Kipps and Sid exchange dreams. Sid's tale of his courtly affection for the vicar's daughter, whets in Kipps an appetite for love.

ADOLESCENCE – GIRLS

1. FRANK, Anne
   The Diary of Anne Frank
   see PARENTS 2
2. ibid.
   see MOTHERS (and) DAUGHTERS 1
3. ibid.
   pp. 143–146 (7.3.44)
   'If I think now ... perish in misery.'
   Anne looks back to the gay thirteen-year-old of 1942, and reviews her path to the present day 'Anne who has grown wise within these walls.' She has come to terms with herself, her family and their miserable existence, and still remains optimistic.
4. ibid.
   pp. 187–190 (5.5.44–7.5.44)

'Daddy is not pleased ... I will improve.'
Anne is annoyed with her father for virtually forbidding her to visit Peter in his room. She sends him a letter explaining how she has grown up and become independent. He is extremely upset by it, and she realises that it was a very selfish letter.
5. ibid.
   pp. 215–219 (15.7.44); 220–222 (1.8.44)
   'We have had a book ... carry them out'; 'Little bundle ... living in the world.'
   Anne looks at the two very different sides of herself, extravert or introvert, and how she has come to terms with them. She also looks at her relationships with her father and Peter, both of them disappointments to her.
6. HITCHMAN, Janet
   The King of Barbareens
   see MENSTRUATION 1
7. HUGHES, Richard
   A High Wind in Jamaica
   (i) pp. 134–140 (Ch. 6, Pt. 1); (ii) pp. 94–98
   'The weeks passed ... really want her.'
   Emily realises who she is and what she is. She indulges a new passion for introspection up on the masthead. She toys with the thought that she might be God.
8. LAWRENCE, D.H.
   The Rainbow
   see HERO-WORSHIP 2

ADOLESCENCE – GIRLS (in) LOVE

1. FRANK, Anne
   The Diary of Anne Frank
   pp. 131–138 (13.2.44–28.2.44)
   141–143 (3.3.44–6.3.44)
   150–151 (16.3.44)
   153–154 (19.3.44)
   161–162 (28.3.44)
   'Since Saturday ... Oh, help me!'
   'When I looked ... attracts me.'
   'The weather ... put into words.'

'Yesterday ... glorious times together.'

'I could write a lot ... he would speak.'

Anne is lonely, and feels the need of a friend. After 18 months Peter van Daan suddenly becomes interesting to her – she feels he suffers in the same way. Her thoughts revolve around him for nearly a month as they get to know each other better.

2. ibid.

pp. 164–165 (1.4.44)
177–179 (16.4.44–17.4.44)
182–185 (28.4.44–2.5.44)

'And yet everything ... he'll understand.'

'Remember yesterday's date' ... profit by it.'

'I have never forgotten ... No, I'm going.'

Having found a friend in Peter, Anne longs for a kiss from him. After the first kiss, they spend more and more time together, but Anne does worry about their physical contact, and seeks her father's advice.

ADOPTION

1. LEACH, Christopher
   Answering Miss Roberts
   pp. 9–11 (Ch. 1)
   ' "At any other time ... "He is."
   Katie's mother has been called away urgently, and Katie is with a neighbour. Worried as she is she cannot concentrate on the photos she is shown, until she hears the words 'like your mother adopted you.'

2. ibid.
   pp. 11–14 (Ch. 1)
   'The day of the funeral ... I wept.'
   Having discovered she is adopted, Katie looks back to her suspicions that she was not her parents' child.

3. ibid.
   pp. 39–42 (Ch. 4)
   'He picked up his cup ... acting for certainty.'
   Katie's mother is about to be married

again, and in the discussions about this finally tells Katie about her adoption.

4. STREATFEILD, Noel
   Ballet Shoes
   pp. 9–13 (Ch. 1)
   'I have travelled a lot ... speaking plain, sir."
   Great-Uncle Matthew, a great collector, manages to 'collect' a baby-girl on a sea-voyage when the ship is wrecked. His niece and her Nurse to whom he presents the baby are taken aback, but accept her.

ADVENTURE

see ESCAPADES

ALCOHOLISM

see also: DRUNKENNESS

ALCOHOLISM

1. BALCHIN, Nigel
   The Small Back Room
   pp. 105–107 (Ch. 8)
   'Whatever else you could ... I felt like a limp rag.'
   Sammy has a drink problem. After a hard day's work, it's the easiest thing in the world to toss off a glass of whisky. But he fights the urge, and wins by a whisker.

AMBITIONS

see also: CHILDREN – AMBITIONS;
DAYDREAMS;
SOCIAL CLASS – CLIMBING

AMBITIONS

1. CHURCH, Richard
   Over the Bridge
   pp. 144–146 (Ch. 13)
   'It was, of course ... than he could comprehend.'
   Father is utterly without ambition (whether from modesty or defeatism),

so Mother pins her hopes on her boys. But even for Jack – a boy with undoubted talents – she dare not hope beyond his, and her, proper station.

2. MAUGHAM, W. Somerset
The Moon and Sixpence
pp. 180–184 (Ch. 50)
'I told Tiaré the story ... argue with a knight?'
Two doctors and two definitions of happiness and success. The one realises his ambition to reach the top in his profession; and the other lives in poverty and simple satisfaction.

3. TROLLOPE, Anthony
Barchester Towers
pp. 5–11 (Ch. 1)
'In the latter days ... the glories of a bishopric.'
Archdeacon Grantly's father, the Bishop, is dying, and the Archdeacon hopes to be named as his successor. An imminent change of government, however, threatens his chances.

AMBITIONS – ACTING

1. HITCHMAN, Janet
The King of the Barbareens
pp. 202–209 (Ch. 9)
'All the time ... theatrical business is done.'
The writer frequents the Old Vic and Open Air Theatre in Regent's Park. She spots the rising stars, and writes to them in the hope that they will help her on to the stage. But when she does work in a theatre it is not as an actress.

2. MANSFIELD, Katherine
Bliss and Other Stories
see WORK – SEEKING 2

AMBITIONS – PAINTING

1. CARY, Joyce
The Horse's Mouth
see MOTHERS 2

2. MAUGHAM, W. Somerset
The Moon and Sixpence
see PAINTING 6

AMBITIONS – PROPERTY DEVELOPING

1. TOWNSEND, John Rowe
The Intruder
pp. 49–54 (Ch. 8)
'It's a great day ... helpless again.'
The stranger returns to Skirlston, and outlines his wild dreams for 'developing' the village, to Arnold, who is secretly afraid of him. His plans are totally unrealistic, but he defends them, even to the point of hitting a sceptic.

AMBITIONS – WEALTH

1. BRAINE, John
Room at the Top
see MATERIALISM 1

2. FITZGERALD, F. Scott
The Great Gatsby
pp. 104–108 (Ch. 6)
'About this time ... misconceptions away.'
The wealthy, but mysterious, Gatsby reveals his life story, to Nick, the narrator. He had always believed himself destined to a great future, although of poor background, and a chance meeting with a rich man helped him on his way.

3. STOREY, David
This Sporting Life
see MATERIALISM 4

AMBITIONS – WRITING

see also: WRITING (and) WRITERS

AMBITIONS – WRITING

1. JOYCE, James
Dubliners
pp. 70–71; 79–83 ('A Little Cloud')
'Little Chandler quickened ... to Gallaher about it'; 'Little Chandler sat ... started to his eyes.'
Little Chandler feels poetry welling up inside him. He must leave Dublin and write Celtic verse for those who

will appreciate his gifts. But Little Chandler, the romantic, succumbs to Little Chandler the family man with a screaming baby in his arms.

2. THOMAS, Leslie
This Time Next Week
pp. 122–124 (Ch. 12)
'He was a serious and mild ... not becoming a waiter.'
Leslie has written a story to pass the time. A master who reads it tells him he ought to be a writer. Leslie is fired by the thought, but he is not at all sure how he can get people to take him seriously.

AMERICA

see AMERICAN CIVIL WAR;
RACISM – AMERICA;
SECOND WORLD WAR – AMERICA
see also under books by particular American authors

AMERICAN CIVIL WAR

1. CRANE, Stephen
The Red Badge of Courage
passim.
The youth, Henry Fleming, fights for the Union Army. He fears that he will run from his first battle – and he does. Thereafter he seeks after the glory of a wound to efface his sense of shame.

AMERICAN CIVIL WAR – BATTLES

1. CRANE, Stephen
The Red Badge of Courage
pp. 42–46 (Ch. 5)
'There were moments ... upon the ground.'
The Youth finds himself in his first engagement. His mind is as confused a battle-field of conflicting ideas as that into which he and his comrades direct their fire. Men fall and shout. Everywhere, is smoke.

2. ibid.
see COWARDICE 1
3. ibid.
pp. 148–152 (Ch. 23)
'The colonel came ... slung high in the air.'
The youth bears the standard in a last desperate, do-or-die charge. The grey line of the enemy breaks and runs. Just one knot of determined men resist, but they, too, are overcome by the sheer speed and fervour of the onslaught.

ANIMALS

see also: ANTS; BEARS; BIRDS; CATS; CHIMPANZEES; CRUELTY (to) ANIMALS; DEATH (of) ANIMALS; DEER; DOGS; FIGHTING (by) ANIMALS; GOATS; HORSES; HUNTING; INSECTS; LEOPARDS; LOCUSTS; OCTOPUS; PIGS; PLATYPUS; RABBITS; RATS; RESCUE (from) ANIMALS; RESCUE (of) ANIMALS; SCORPIONS; SHARKS; SHEEP; SNAKES; TOADS; TORTOISES; TURTLES

ANIMALS – CATCHING

see also: BIRDS – CATCHING
RABBITS – CATCHING
RATS – CATCHING
SNAKES – CATCHING

ANIMALS – CATCHING

1. THOMPSON, Flora
Lark Rise to Candleford
(i) pp. 159–162 (Ch. 9); (ii) pp. 152–155
'After they reached ... followed his work-mates.'
The boys rob birds' nests for insensitive fun, the young men go 'spadgering' for pudding sparrows, the women lay traps in their gardens, and the men know where to go for a game bird when they want one.

ANIMALS – EXPERIMENTS

1. O'BRIEN, Robert C.
   Mrs Frisby and the Rats of NIMH
   see CONDITIONING 4, 5

ANIMALS – MATING

see HORSES – MATING;
SNAKES – MATING;
TORTOISES – MATING

ANIMALS (of) PREY

1. LONDON, Jack
   White Fang
   see FIGHTING (by) ANIMALS 3

ANIMALS – SLAUGHTER

1. GOLDING, William
   Lord of the Flies
   see HUNTING 1
2. HEMINGWAY, Ernest
   The Old Man and the Sea
   pp. 71–72; 77–78
   'Just before it was ... and was still';
   'Back in the stern ... his right hand.'
   The old man catches a dolphin. It
   writhes in panic at the bottom of the
   skiff until he clubs it. He opens it up
   and deguts it, efficiently, with no
   excess of sentiment.
3. ibid.
   see DETERMINATION 4
4. ibid.
   see SHARKS 7
5. MANSFIELD, Katherine
   Bliss and Other Stories
   pp. 45–48 (Sn. 9, 'Prelude')
   'Pat came swinging along ... she
   asked huskily.'
   The handy-man slaughters a duck for
   his master's dinner. He takes the
   children along to watch, and he shows
   them how, when he has cut the duck's
   head off, it continues to run about.
6. SPERRY, Armstrong
   The Boy who was Afraid
   see COURAGE 17

7. STEINBECK, John
   The Grapes of Wrath
   (i) pp. 89–90 (Ch. 10); (ii) pp. 96–98
   'And then, all of a sudden ... he said
   uneasily.'
   Before their departure for California,
   the Joad family, kill their two pigs, to
   salt. The process is swift and efficient,
   with each person knowing their job
   exactly.
8. THOMPSON, Flora
   Lark Rise to Candleford
   (i) pp. 10–13 (Ch. 1); (ii) pp. 24–27
   'The family pig was ... meat to be
   had.'
   The family pig is killed, in what is a
   primitive, carnivorous ritual. It is a
   spectacle to be enjoyed by all present,
   adults and children. The 'noisy,
   bloody business' give place to the
   annual feast of plenty.
9. WOOD, James
   The Rain Islands
   see WHALES (and) WHALING 1

ANIMALS – TRAPPING

1. ADAMS, Richard
   Watership Down
   pp. 119–124 (Ch. 17)
   'He turned and dashed ... snickering
   behind it.'
   Bigwig is caught in a trap. The others
   try to dig up the peg holding the wire,
   while one runs to their new friends for
   help. Help is refused but Bigwig is
   freed.
2. SOUTHALL, Ivan
   Josh
   pp. 56–58 (Ch. 14)
   'Harry crashing up the track ...
   letting it happen.'
   Josh has no sooner heard a weird cry
   in the brush, than local boys rush up
   to see what they've caught; it's a
   rabbit. Harry has borrowed Josh's
   stick to kill it. Josh weeps for the
   rabbit, and for his having abetted the
   kill.
3. WILLIAMSON, Henry
   Tarka the Otter

(i) pp. 55–58 (Ch. 4); (ii) pp. 56–60
'While he was enjoying ... picked out its eyes.'
The otter family run to watch a fight between two weasels, but one cub is attracted by the smell of meat in a trap. She is caught, and although she manages to drag the trap away, the trapper finds and shoots her.
4. ibid.
(i) pp. 116–119 (Ch. 11); (ii) pp. 119–122
'Greymuzzle walked ... that never came.'
Tarka is caught by a gin. He manages to wrench himself free but leaves two toes behind. As he and Greymuzzle try to escape, a farmer finds them and kills Greymuzzle.

ANTIQUES

1. JEROME, Jerome K.
   Three Men in a Boat
   see ART 3
2. MANKOWITZ, Wolf
   Make me an Offer
   see BUYING (and) SELLING (by) DEALERS 2

ANTS

1. LESSING, Doris
   Nine African Stories
   pp. 39–42 ('A Sunrise on the Veld')
   'At the edge of the trees ... rustling of cast snake skin.'
   A boy out in the early morning with his gun, comes upon a buck being eaten alive, screaming and kicking mechanically, by armies of whispering ants. The boy is powerless to help it. His gun lies heavy in his hand.

APPRENTICESHIP

see WORK-APPRENTICESHIP

ARGUMENTS

see DISMISSAL;
FAMILY – QUARRELS;
MARRIAGE – QUARRELS;
QUARRELS;
REVENGE;
RIVALRY

ARISTOCRACY

see GOVERNMENT – ARISTOCRACY

ARITHMETIC

see SCHOOL – SUBJECTS – ARITHMETIC

ARMY

see also: TANKS

ARMY

1. HOLBROOK, David
   Flesh Wounds
   pp. 28–30 (Ch. 1)
   'Here they were introduced ... rough shoddy blankets.'
   Paul and his squad are introduced to army jargon, army food, and bull.
2. ibid.
   pp. 52–55 (Ch. 1)
   'Miffin sat with him ... moan if I was you.'
   Two soldiers on brief leave, discuss army life. Miffin accepts it uncritically, and Paul, the undergraduate, dismisses it, uncritically.
3. SERRAILLIER, Ian
   The Silver Sword
   (i) pp. 99–101 (Ch. 16); (ii) pp. 82–83
   'They crossed the Elbe ... low Cossack horses.'
   Four Polish refugee children watch the spearhead of the Russian army, bound for Prague, marching over a bridge. It is a long and impressive procession.

ARMY – DEMOBILIZATION

1. HOLBROOK, David
   Flesh Wounds
   pp. 235–237 (Ch. 8)
   'Paul found a possible ... in the drizzle.'
   Being an undergraduate, Paul is eligible for early demobilization. But when it comes, the anonymity of his civilian suit, and the loss of respect accorded his rank, combine to rob the moment of magic.

ARMY-DISCIPLINE

1. BOULLE, Pierre
   The Bridge on the River Kwai
   (i) pp. 2–5 (Part 1, Ch. 1); (ii) pp. 9–12
   'In the past, Colonel ... rifles on to the truck.'
   Colonel Nicholson sees it as his duty, and that of his men, to surrender to the advancing Japanese, in as dignified a manner as possible. He refuses to hand the battalion arms to an enemy N.C.O. It is fortunate for his men that a Major arrives to whom the Colonel deems it fitting to make the act of surrender.

2. ibid.
   (i) pp. 19–23 (Part 1, Ch. 4); (ii) pp. 26–31
   'At one moment Clipton ... was completely deserted.'
   Once again, the Colonel's honour is to the fore. He has refused, on his own, and his brother officers', behalf, to do manual work. Now, he flourishes the Hague Convention in the Commandant's face, and is brutally assaulted for his pains. Clipton's intervention saves them all from possible massacre.

3. REMARQUE, Erich Maria
   All Quiet on the Western Front
   pp. 26–29 (Ch. 2)
   'By threes and fours ... out of the war-comradeship.'
   The author and his friends are sub-jected to considerable physical and psychological hardship by a martinet of a corporal. But they find a way of obeying his orders, and at the same time, making nonsense both of them, and of him.
   see also: REVENGE 21

4. ibid.
   see FIRST WORLD WAR – DESERTION 1

5. TREVOR, Elleston
   The Flight of the Phoenix
   pp. 130–134 (Ch. 16)
   'He told them his plan quietly ... wasn't free; he was lost.'
   A band of Arab tribesmen have stopped within sight of the wreck. Harris decides to approach them for help. He orders his sergeant to accompany him, but Sergeant Watson, for the first time, refuses the order. He is cutting loose, at the risk of court-martial, making up for years of subservience to Harris and his like.

ARMY – ENLISTMENT

1. CRANE, Stephen
   The Red Badge of Courage
   pp. 10–13 (Ch. 1)
   'He had burned ... deeds of arms.'
   The youth leaves his mother to join the Union Army against the Confederates. His mother delivers a homespun homily to keep back the tears, and when the Youth leaves, it is with some relief. He feels good in uniform: a decided cut above his college friends.

2. KNOWLES, John
   A Separate Peace
   pp. 229–232 (Ch. 13)
   'We went downstairs and found ... sometimes included his parents.'
   Gene meets Brinker's father, a man of the old school, for whom the war is a boy's finishing school. He disapproves of Gene's and Brinker's lighthearted attitude, and exhorts them to enlist in a branch of the services from which they will see some action – action that will earn them respect and honour.

3. LAWRENCE, D.H.
   Sons and Lovers
   (i) pp. 179–182 (Ch. 8); (ii) pp. 222–225
   'Arthur finished ... public house that evening.'
   Arthur, the third of Mrs Morel's sons, enlists in the army. She is very angry that he has gone to be a 'common soldier'; and Arthur, himself, repents his move at leisure. He writes to Mrs Morel to bail him out. She makes the attempt but fails.

4. REMARQUE, Erich Maria
   All Quiet on the Western Front
   pp. 24–25 (Ch. 2)
   'Once it was different ... for such distinctions.'
   Twenty young men enlist in the German army at the outbreak of the First World War. They learn to unlearn all that school has taught them, and to subordinate the world of ideas, to that of orders that are beyond question.
   see also: ARMY – DISCIPLINE 3

5. SASSOON, Siegfried
   Memoirs of a Fox-hunting Man
   pp. 261–267 (Part 9, Sn. 4)
   'It is ten years since ... mind to write my own.'
   George joins up. He reports as a second lieutenant to Clitherland Camp near Liverpool. Arrangements have a makeshift air. Drafts are sent to the front, with a speech and a prayer. G. Vivian-Simpson is killed by a sniper's bullet half way through his breakfast. George pauses for thought.

6. SHOLOKHOV, Mikhail
   Fierce and Gentle Warriors
   see CHILDREN – AMBITIONS 1

ARMY INSPECTION

1. HOLBROOK, David
   Flesh Wounds
   pp. 37–40 (Ch. 1)
   'The squad came together ... between her sheets.'
   There is little to do in off-duty moments, but clean the hut until it shines. The squad does this with a vengeance, and earns a weekend's leave for its pains.

ARREST

1. BALDWIN, James
   Go Tell it on the Mountain
   see RACISM – AMERICA 1

2. BENTLEY, Phyllis
   The Adventures of Tom Leigh
   pp. 128–131 (Ch. 9)
   'It was evening light ... "Well done, Tom".'
   Mr Gledhill and Tom go to Skipton to find the accomplice in the cloth-stealing plot. They mistake their man, but the guilty man bolts and gives himself away – to the intrepid Tom.

3. BENTLEY, Phyllis
   Gold Pieces
   pp. 134–137 (Ch. 9)
   'Yes, this is the Old Cock ... from the pain.'
   Mr Kay, who has seen a coiner at work, and been attacked by him, recognises the man in a pub. The coiner tries to escape, but is stopped by Mr Kay's dog, who was also injured in the original incident.

4. DEFOE, Daniel
   Moll Flanders
   see PRISON 2
   see also: TRIALS 4

5. DICKENS, Charles
   Bleak House
   (i) pp. 620–624 (Ch. 49); (ii) pp. 620–624
   'This sparkling stranger ... up the turnings.'
   The detective, Mr Bucket, joins a birthday party attended by his acquaintance George. He makes himself very agreeable to the family, and enters the festive spirit. On their way home, he arrests George for murder.

6. FORSTER, E.M.
   A Passage to India
   see RACISM – INDIA 2

7. GREENE, Graham
   The Power and the Glory

(i) pp. 112–116 (Part II, Ch. 2); (ii) pp. 115–122
(Themes in Life and Literature pp. 181–182)
'The beetles had disappeared ... in jail before?'
The runaway priest is arrested by a zealous Red Shirt for carrying spirits. He narrowly escapes being recognised, and tried, for being a priest in a persecuting state, but he is imprisoned on the lesser charge.

8. GRIMBLE, Sir Arthur
A Pattern of Islands
pp. 34–39 (Ch. 3)
'It was nearly midnight ... Government maneeba.'
Arther is commissioned to arrest one William Clarence, a burly, mad mutineer. William refuses to come quietly. He comes – but noisily; nevertheless, he distinguishes himself as a life-saver, and wins his case in default of prosecution witnesses.

9. KAFKA, Franz
The Trial
pp. 7–11 (Ch. 1) (The Receiving End, pp. 17–19)
'Someone must have been ... insist on playing it to the end.'
K is arrested one morning, in his lodging. He is detained by two warders, who eat his breakfast, on an unspecified charge. K is unsure whether he should take his confinement seriously.

10. KOESTLER, Arthur
Darkness at Noon
(i) pp. 3–6 ('The First Hearing' Parts 1 and 2); (ii) pp. 9–12
'The Cell door slammed ... on his door went on.'
Rubashov, ex-Commissar of the People, is arrested in the night, and taken away to prison in the manner foreshadowed in his recurring nightmare.

11. LEACH, Christopher
Answering Miss Roberts
pp. 99–107 (Ch. 8)
'Leading it were a group ... You do that.'

Katie joins a protest march, for want of anything else to do, on a warm London evening. She finds herself charging a line of policemen and is arrested. Her mother refuses to come and collect her, so she is sent to a remand home.

12. ORWELL, George
1984
(i) pp. 227–230 (Part 2, Ch. 9); (ii) pp. 176–179
'Do you remember ... Thought Police.'
Winston and Julia are surprised in their hideout, by a hidden telescreen, and a troop of Police, who wind Julia and carry her off, before taking Winston away.

ART

see also: MUSIC;
PAINTING;
SCHOOL – SUBJECTS – ART;
SCULPTURE

ART

1. BRONTË, Charlotte
Villette
p. 180 (Ch., 19)
'One day, at a quiet early hour ... name "Cleopatra".'
Lucy Snowe, a practical young lady, visits an art exhibition and describes the painting of a near-nude, very much with her tongue in her cheek.

2. ELIOT, George
Middlemarch
pp. 215–217 (Bk. 2, Ch. 22)
'You seem not to care ... put on the wall.'
Dorothea sees through much of the pretension of art, and wishes people's time and money could be more profitably spent.

3. JEROME, Jerome K.
Three Men in a Boat
pp. 54–54 (Ch. 6)
'To go back to the carved ... as Ancient English curios.'

J. reflects upon the art and artefacts of the past and wonders what, from among the common impedimenta of his own day, will be considered beautiful and artistic in the future.

4. MAUGHAM, W. Somerset
The Moon and Sixpence
pp. 131–135 (Ch. 39)
'When I left him ... discovery of new mysteries.'
Stroeve returns to his empty studio. There, he comes across a canvas of his late wife, as a reclining nude. He is about to vandalize it, when he forgets his hatred of the artist, in appreciation of the art.

ART – MODERN

1. HILDICK, W.E.
Birdy in Amsterdam
pp. 70–79 (Ch. 9)
'At first Birdy ... Suddenly it Clicks!'
Fixer, and Birdy, the Pop Whistler, visit a modern art museum in Amsterdam. Fixer tries to explain all the strange exhibits for his slower friend, but is apparently making little impression. Only in the final room where sound and rhythm are involved, does Birdy show any appreciation.

ASSAULT

see also: RESCUE (from) ASSAULT

ASSAULT

1. FALKNER, J. Meade
Moonfleet
pp. 69–72 (Ch. 6)
'There were a half-dozen ... in front of his desk.'
One morning in school, Mister Maskew settles a difference with Parson Glennie. Maskew takes exception to an epitaph the latter has written, and directs that the headstone should be removed. When the parson stands his ground, Maskew hits him across the face with a fresh fish.

2. FIELDING, Henry
Joseph Andrews
pp. 260–262 (Bk. 4, Ch. 7)
'Fanny was now walking ... so well provided for.'
The fair Fanny is accosted first by a young gentleman, and then by his servant. Each in his turn roughly demands favours of her, which the servant is near to enjoying, when the gallant Joseph runs to his beloved's rescue. He grapples with the servant and fells him, to Fanny's infinite relief.

3. LAWRENCE, D.H.
The White Peacock
see POACHING 3

4. NAUGHTON, Bill
One Small Boy
see PUNISHMENT – CORPORAL – SCHOOL 7

5. REMARQUE, Erich Maria
All Quiet on the Western Front
see REVENGE 21

6. TATE, Joan
Whizz Kid
pp. 103–107 (Nibs Ch. 3)
'I remember being hit ... broad daylight.'
Nibs is hit on the head in a dark wood – he sees all the stars and bright lights of the comic stories, but it is regaining consciousness which is the most painful and distressing experience.

7. WOOD, James
The Rain Islands
pp. 92–94 (Ch. 5)
'I stood watching ... quite unruffled.'
Leaving a dance, Major Scott is attacked by two men in a dark street – he is helped in beating them off by a small man he had noticed at the dance.

ASSAULT (by) BROTHERS

1. GORKY, Maxim
Childhood
(i) pp. 258–263 (Ch. 11); (ii) pp. 187–191

'One year the cold was so bad ...
quite shameless ... so they left ...
and that's all.'

Gorky's Uncle Mikhail bears a grudge
against his father Maxim. He and
Yakov, both drunk, throw Maxim
into a frozen pond, stamp on his
hands, and pelt him with broken ice.
They leave him for dead; but Maxim
manages to crawl out to safety and
searching questions.

ASSAULT (by) GANGS – YOUTHS

1. BARSTOW, Stan
   The Human Element
   pp. 123–125 ('The Desperadoes')
   'Vince waited for a moment ... worth
   the risk.'
   Vince and his gang intimidate a
   middle-aged man in the street. They
   tease him into thinking they will let
   him go, then they lay into him
   together, and leave him lying on the
   pavement with his broken spectacles.
2. ibid.
   see KILLING (by) GANGS – YOUTHS 1
3. LEE, Laurie
   Cider with Rosie
   see KILLING (by) GANGS – YOUTHS 2

ASSAULT (by) HUSBANDS

1. LAWRENCE, D.H.
   Sons and Lovers
   see DRUNKENNESS 7
2. SILLITOE, Alan
   *The Loneliness of the Long-Distance
   Runner*
   see MARRIAGE – QUARRELS 7
3. THOMPSON, Flora
   see MARRIAGE – QUARRELS 8

ASSAULT (by) RIVALS (in) LOVE

1. HARDY, Thomas
   The Mayor of Casterbridge
   (i) pp. 309–314 (Ch. 38); (ii) pp.
   293–297
   'Nobody was present ... died on his
   ear.'

Henchard seeks his revenge on Farfrae. He waits for him in the corn-
stores, meaning to throw him from
the open door three floors up. When
Farfrae comes, Henchard closes with
him and manoeuvres him to the
opening – but he cannot bring himself
to kill his one-time friend.

2. LAWRENCE, D.H.
   Sons and Lovers
   (i) pp. 364–367 (Ch. 13); (ii) pp.
   443–447
   'One night he left ... the journey
   home.'
   Baxter Dawes finally catches up with
   Paul. He kicks and punches him into
   instinctual, and very effective, fury.
   Paul, who is no fighter, gives a good
   account of himself and is beaten into
   near insensibility in the process.

AUCTIONS

see also: BUYING (and) SELLING;
MARKETS

AUCTIONS

1. FALKNER, J. Meade
   Moonfleet
   pp. 74–80 (Ch. 7)
   'One evening in March ... the *Why
   Not?* was lost.'
   The bailiff comes, as he does every
   year, to auction the 'Why Not?'
   public house. It is a formality, since
   Elzevir Block is the only bidder, and
   the rent never varies. But this year,
   Maskew bids against Block, out of
   spite, and secures possession of the
   inn at a grossly inflated rent.
2. THACKERAY, William
   Vanity Fair
   (i) pp. 156–159 (Ch. 17); (ii) pp.
   204–208
   'If there is any exhibition ... it's
   Captain Dobbin.'
   Thackeray describes London house
   sales in general, with the inquisitive,
   disrespectful buyers, and one sale in

particular, that of the Sedley household.

AUNTS

see also: DEATH (of) AUNT;
FAMILY;
RELATIVES

AUNTS

1. LEE, Harper
   To Kill a Mockingbird
   (i) pp. 83–87 (Ch. 9); (ii) pp. 82–87
   'Jem and I viewed ... much the way I was.'
   Christmas at Aunt Alexandra's: despite the excellent food, this is something of a trial, particularly for Scout, because her boyishness is an object of disapproval.

AUSTRALIA

1. MARSHALL, James Vance
   Walkabout
   passim.
   Two white children, survivors of an aircrash in the Australian outback, fall in with an aboriginal boy, and learn a lot about themselves, and Australia, before their return to civilisation.

AUTHORITY

see also: GOVERNMENT;
KINGS

AUTHORITY

1. GOLDING, William
   Lord of the Flies
   (i) pp. 26–30 (Ch. 1); (ii) pp. 20–24
   'Within the diamond ... to offer something.'
   Two kinds of authority: the arrogant, self-importance of the 'obvious leader' Jack, and the impressive 'stillness' of Ralph. Ralph is elected chief 'to decide things.'

2. ibid.
   (i) pp. 114–117 (Ch. 5); (ii) pp. 100–103
   'I'm chief. I was chosen ... powerless to help him.'
   Ralph's authority is slipping. Fear is gaining ground. The adult world of tea and discussion shimmers like a mirage, tantalizing. Piggy and Simon try to persuade Ralph to re-assert his authority.

3. ibid.
   see HUMILIATION 7

4. ibid.
   (i) pp. 195–199 (Ch. 10); (ii) pp. 175–178
   'When Roger came ... swelled and died away.'
   Jack's new authority over the boys is the product of a healthy respect for his brand of punishment, and of a carefully nurtured fear of the beast. Roger, a newcomer, assimilates 'the possibilities of irresponsible authority.'

5. LESSING, Doris
   The Grass is Singing
   pp. 133–137 (Ch. 7)
   'The compound was built ... sambok jauntily on her wrist.'
   Mary supervises the natives while her husband is sick. She passes among their mud huts, and summons them peremptorily to work. They come, with very bad grace. All day, she moves with them, along the maize rows, swinging the sambok that is the symbol of her authority, and the source of her confidence.
   see also: RACISM – RHODESIA 2

6. ibid.
   pp. 144–147 (Ch. 7)
   'Down in the vlei ... seen in the man's eyes.'
   One of the natives stops working to rest and drink. Mary orders him back to work. She forbids him to speak to her either in his own language, or in hers, and when he smiles, she interprets it as insolence. She strikes him, drawing blood, and barely keeps control of herself, and the situation.

7. MORROW, Honoré
   The Splendid Journey
   pp. 15–16 (Ch. 2); 84–87 (Ch. 6)
   'No matter how hurried ... the story
   of the ten lepers'; 'John and Francis,
   long since ... silently put it away.'
   When John is slow to join the family
   for the day's Bible-reading, Henry
   Sager drags him forcibly into the
   circle. Now that his father is dead,
   and it is his turn to wield authority,
   John forces his brother to a family act
   of Sunday observance.
8. SAINT-EXUPERY, Antoine de
   Night Flight
   pp. 23–27; 32–35 (Chs. 4, 6)
   'The inspector seemed ... his mouth
   to speak'; 'Informed that he was
   wanted ... were zealously scrubbed.'
   The Director, Rivière, keeps M.
   Robineau, his dull but dutiful inspector on a tight leash. Rivière does not
   seek to be loved by his pilots, but to
   be obeyed by them. To this end, he
   exercises an iron discipline over all his
   personnel, and it is the luckless
   Robineau who is its agent.
9. STEINBECK, John
   Of Mice and Men
   (i) pp. 34–37 (Ch. 2); (ii) pp. 31–34
   'From the washroom ... went out the
   door.'
   Slim, the jerkline skinner, is a man
   with a naturally dignified bearing,
   and authoritative manner, whom all
   men respect. He gives his opinion
   unassumingly, and it is taken for
   gospel.

AUTOMATION

1. ORWELL, George
   1984
   see CAPITALISM 2
2. STEINBECK, John
   The Grapes of Wrath
   (i) pp. 28–32 (Ch. 5), (ii) pp. 33–37
   'The tractors came ... after the
   tractor.'
   The small tenant farmers are turned
   off their land, which is to be farmed

on a large scale, with machines. The
tractors are driven by men who care
nothing for the land or the farmers,
only the wage they badly need.

BABIES

see also: ABORTION;
BAPTISM;
BIRTH;
DEATH (of) BABY;
DEATH (in) CHILDBIRTH;
MEMORIES (of) BABYHOOD;
STEALING (of) BABIES

BABIES

1. LAWRENCE, D.H.
   Sons and Lovers
   (i) pp. 36–37 (Ch. 2); (ii) pp. 49–51
   (Themes in Life and Literature pp.
   83–86)
   'The Sun was going ... darkening
   all.'
   Mrs Morel has not wanted a second
   baby; and it looks up at her so
   knowingly, that she feels guilty. She
   determines that she will make up to
   it, for having brought it into the world
   unloved.
2. LEE, Harper
   To Kill a Mockingbird
   see SEX – EDUCATION 2
3. TATE, Joan
   Clipper
   pp. 25–28 (Ch. 3)
   'After we'd had Clipper ... the subject again.'
   Clee and Nibs, very young and
   recently married, find their son, Clipper makes quite a difference to their
   lives. Clee is a very unorthodox
   mother, who follows no advice but her
   own instincts. Nibs is, at once, very
   proud, and jealous.

BAPTISM

1. BALDWIN, James
   Go Tell it on the Mountain
   pp. 75–76 (Part 2, 'Florence's Prayer')

'One Sunday at a camp-meeting ... Deborah looked away.'
Gabriel is baptised, much against his will, by total immersion in a filthy river. What should be a moving sacrament, to the accompaniment of prayer and singing, is made undignified by Gabriel's howling – not to say, his near-nakedness.

2. HARDY, Thomas
Tess of the D'Urbervilles
(i) pp. 118–122 (Ch. 14); (ii) pp. 112–115
'The baby's offence ... or for her child.'
Tess's illegitimate baby is on the point of death. Prevented from fetching the parson by her father, and afraid that it might go to hell through no fault of its own, she improvises a baptismal service in the company of her awestruck brothers and sisters.

3. NAUGHTON, Bill
One Small Boy
pp. 185–190 (Bk. 2, Ch. 8)
'She wasn't there ... "Give me a carrot".'
Michael and Ella take a picnic on the moors. Ella takes very seriously the catholic Michael's statement that she will have to be baptised before they can marry. Accordingly, she talks him into administering an impromptu baptism before letting him kiss her.

4. WRIGHT, Richard
Black Boy
see METHODISTS 2

BATHS

1. MANKOWITZ, Wolf
A Kid for Two Farthings
pp. 80–81 (Ch. 8)
'Moishe, the cap-maker ... another vapour bath.'
The Russian Vapour Baths. Lemon tea, fierce argument, and the feeling of well-being after the heat.

2. SILLITOE, Alan
Saturday Night and Sunday Morning
see ABORTION 1

18

BATTLES

see also: AMERICAN CIVIL WAR – BATTLES;
FIRST WORLD WAR – BATTLES;
PENINSULAR WAR – BATTLES;
SECOND WORLD WAR – SEA BATTLES;
SIEGES;
WAR

BATTLES

1. CHURCHILL, W.S.
My Early Life
pp. 143–154 (Ch. 11)
'Our march to the ... honour was satisfied.'
A bloody skirmish on the Indian frontier. Churchill comes near to death. Houses and crops are burnt in reprisal. British honour is satisfied.

2. FORESTER, C.S.
The Gun
(i) pp. 190–193 (Ch. 20); (ii) pp. 160–162
'The victors rejoined ... called into being.'
When his regiment is ambushed by a band of guerilleros, Lieutenant Aubard loses contact with his comrades. As he sees them defeated, he rides away, to seek refuge in a nearby French stronghold.

3. SEWELL, Anna
Black Beauty
pp. 150–153 (Ch. 34)
'I, with my noble master ... one in four that returned.'
Old Captain describes his experiences of the battle-field. He often went into action without any mishap, until one particularly fierce charge when his master was shot. He was immediately taken over by another soldier, but soon the whole army was on the retreat.

4. SUTCLIFF, Rosemary
The Eagle of the Ninth
pp. 44–48 (Ch. 3)
'Open up!' he ordered ... closed over him.'

Marcus leads a phalanx of Romans, enclosed by their shields, right into the mass of British warriors. The surprise gives them the advantage in the skirmish that follows; but Marcus has reckoned without enemy chariots.

5. TREECE, Henry
   Hounds of the King
   pp. 126–136 (Part 3, Ch. 16)
   'Shortly after dawn, the trumpets ... lay in a sleep of exhaustion.'
   The forces of Harold Godwinson ride out to meet Hardrada and Tostig. Far from receiving the hostages they have expected, the latter are killed in circumstances far from chivalrous. It is a messy battle, and a sad one for both Harold and Beornorth.

BATTLES – HASTINGS – 1066

1. TREECE, Henry
   Hounds of the King
   see INVASIONS – NORMANS 1

BATTLES – OMDURMAN – 1898

1. CHURCHILL, W.S.
   My Early Life
   pp. 195–201 (Ch. 15)
   'Everyone expected ... quarter of its strength.'
   A cavalry charge against the Dervishes at Omdurman. Churchill kills a man. Unaware of the danger he is in, he keeps a cool head, and really rather enjoys himself.

BATTLES – SOMME – 1916

1. FORESTER, C.S.
   The General
   (i) pp. 193–199 (Ch. 20); (ii) pp. 188–194
   'As the winter ended ... Hudson, "is attrition".'
   The excitement of the big push, following the longest and heaviest bombardment there has ever been, is dashed by the realization that the old

strategy is failing. Only superior numbers will now tell.
see also FIRST WORLD WAR 2

BATTLES – WATERLOO – 1815

1. Thackeray, William
   Vanity Fair
   (i) pp. 226–268; 269–271 (Ch. 28); (ii) pp. 324–326; 328–329
   'But it may be said ... Get some more beer'; 'Those who like ... most generous of men.'
   The British army and many civilian followers arrive in Belgium, to defeat Napoleon, and take over Brussels. Few thoughts are spared for the war as the social life is so brilliant and gay.

2. ibid.
   see LEAVE-TAKING 12

3. ibid.
   (i) pp. 316–323 (Ch. 32); (ii) pp. 379–386
   'It grew to be broad daylight ... bullet through his heart.'
   After a day of distant cannon-fire and confused reports of English defeat, the wounded are brought back to Brussels. Amelia takes charge of a young Ensign of her husband's regiment, and the occupation takes her mind off the further audible fighting. The day of the battle is spent in flight, and prayer, until suddenly the cannons cease.
   N.B. In the Penguin Edition this passage begins 'It began ...'

BATTLES – YPRES

1. FORESTER, C.S.
   The General
   (i) pp. 39–43 (Ch. 5); (ii) pp. 38–42
   'There go the Surreys ... quarter of an hour to occupy.'
   The Twenty-second Lancers, under the redoubtable Colonel Curzon, are caught off-balance by the German advance. But the regiment digs a

shallow trench with whatever comes to hand, and resists.

BEARS

1. SCHAEFER, Jack
   Old Ramon
   see DOGS 10

BEAUTY

1. JEROME, Jerome K.
   Three Men in a Boat
   see ART 3
2. LEE, Laurie
   Cider with Rosie
   see MOTHERS 11
3. MACKEN, Walter
   God made Sunday and other Stories
   pp. 39–41 ('God made Sunday')
   'I am aware ... pales in your eyes.'
   Colmain, newly married, is responsive to beauty. A simple fisherman, he is nonetheless alive to beauty in ordinary, as in conventionally beautiful things.

BIRDS

1. GALLICO, Paul
   The Snow Goose/The Small Miracle
   (i) pp. 12–16 ('The Snow Goose'); (ii) pp. 19–23
   'One November afternoon ... fair hair streaming out behind her.'
   A wild young girl brings an injured snow goose to the hunchback hermit on the marsh, believing that he will heal the bird. He bandages it, feeds it, and gives it a name.
2. GOLDING, William
   Pincher Martin
   pp. 56–58 (Ch. 1)
   'He lay with the pains ... and without offence.'
   The castaway is disturbed by roosting gulls. When he moves, they scatter; but it is their rock, so they return and flap about the flailing castaway, until he is more of a threat to them, than they are to him.

BIRDS – AUSTRALIA

1. MARSHALL, James Vance
   Walkabout
   (i) pp. 58–60 (Ch. 12); (ii) pp. 76–77
   (Young Impact 2 pp. 31–33)
   'Half-way through ... rose and gold.'
   The bush boy stops the children so that they might witness a performance of song and dance by a lyre bird. What at first sight is a rather dull-looking bird, turns out to have a captivating voice and striking plumage.
2. ibid.
   (i) pp. 86–88 (Ch. 17); (ii) pp. 111–113
   'They had gone first ... the hovering bird.'
   The children are entertained by the assorted songs and colours of Australian birds in the wild. They are as varied as they are numerous; and as fearless as they are exotic.

BIRDS – CATCHING

1. HINES, Barry
   A Kestrel for a Knave
   (i) pp. 51–54; (ii) pp. 41–44
   'The moon was ... himself all the way home.'
   Billy goes out in the night to a Kestrel's nest that he has found, high in a ruined monastery wall. He chooses the most developed of the young kestrels in the nest, and takes it home in his pocket.

BIRDS – NESTING

1. BURNETT, Frances Hodgson
   The Secret Garden
   pp. 222–225 (Ch. 25)
   'And the secret garden ... come into the garden.'
   A robin and his mate have built their nest in the secret garden, and are anxious about the presence and activities of the three children. As time passes, and they see there is no

threat, there is nothing to spoil the pleasure of sitting on the eggs.

2. DURRELL, Gerald
    My Family and other Animals
    pp. 106–108 (Part 2, Ch. 7)
    'Under the eaves of the villa ... black-and-white bomb earthwards.'
    The family life of swallows closely observed. The females have trouble with their mates: one does not take his role as a builder at all seriously; the other brings all manner of useless material. Fatherhood transforms both husbands.

BIRTH

see also: BABIES;
DEATH (in) CHILDBIRTH;
HORSES – BIRTH

BIRTH

1. ALAIN-FOURNIER
    Le Grand meaulnes
    pp. 181–184 (Part 2, Ch. 12)
    'School was to open ... swallowing my tears.'
    A baby girl is born to Yvonne; it is a forceps delivery, and Yvonne is laid low by it. Seurel visits mother and baby. The baby is well, and engaging, but Yvonne fails fast. As Seurel leaves, he passes a tell-tale priest.

2. BANKS, Lynne Reid
    The L-Shaped Room
    pp. 258–261 (Ch. 24)
    'I withdrew ... I hope so.'
    Jane's baby is born, unexpectedly, a month early. She is only dimly aware of what is going on, feeling withdrawn into a strange world of pain.

3. CHAPLIN, Sid
    The Leaping Lad and Other Stories
    see MEMORIES (of) CHILDHOOD 2

4. DURRELL, Gerald
    Birds, Beasts and Relatives
    pp. 84–87 (Part 2, 'The Myrtle Forest')
    'Presently we came to the low ... gleaming trophy inside.'

Gerald is visiting Katerina. He finds the house full of people, and Katerina's bedroom full of women, and screams. The object of his visit is supine on the bed at the height of her labour pains. Gerald has a front circle view of the emergence of the baby's head, and subsequently, of the swaddling.

5. LAWRENCE, D.H.
    The Rainbow
    see CHILDREN – TANTRUMS 3

6. MACKEN, Walter
    God made Sunday and other Stories
    pp. 45–49 ('God made Sunday')
    'I heard a girl's voice ... be her last born.'
    A complication sets in at the birth of Colmain's baby son, and the midwife is powerless to correct it. Colmain would go across to the mainland to fetch the doctor, but the sea is too rough, and his friends hold him back. By the time the doctor is brought, it is too late.

7. PEYTON, K.M.
    Flambards in Summer
    (i) pp. 68–71 (Ch. 7); (ii) pp. 95–98
    'Four days later Christina ... 'Why can't we call it Boxer?'
    The birth of a girl is the pleasantest of a number of crises punctuating Christina's new life as a landowner. She calls the doctor at the onset of pains and then waits while he reads *The Times* for news of the war. An argument follows with her adopted son, as to a suitable name.

8. SHOLOKHOV, Mikhail
    And Quiet Flows the Don
    pp. 183–185 (Part 1, Ch.12)
    'The summer was dry ... bleeding end with cotton.'
    Aksinia's baby is due, but she goes to the fields with her husband. When pains come on, she pleads with Gregor to take her home in the wagon. He drives at speed, but by the time they arrive, the baby is born, and it only remains for Gregor to wipe up the mess.

9. THOMPSON, Flora
Lark Rise to Candleford
(i) pp. 390–392 ('Over to Candleford'
Ch. 25); (ii) pp. 347–349
'Before they had been ... all the
world.'
Laura's mother has a baby while she
and her brother are staying in
Candleford. Sex education is non-
existent in the 1880's, and numerous
euphemisms are employed.
10. WELLS, H.G.
Kipps
pp. 371–372 (Bk. 3, Ch. 3, Sn. 5)
'Amidst all this bustle ... Kipps out
of the room.'
Mrs Kipps bears a son. Mr Kipps is
as proud and as mystified as any
father.

BIRTHDAYS

1. BENNETT, Arnold
Anna of the Five Towns
pp. 38–43 (Ch. 3)
'The next morning ... 'wi' them
potatoes.'
Anna is twenty-one – her birthday is
marked by a posy of flowers from her
12-year-old sister, and the signing
over to her of her mother's fortune.
Her father is business-like and totally
unsentimental about this momentous
step.
2. DICKENS, Charles
Bleak House
see FAMILY – PARTIES 1
3. NESBIT, E.
The Railway Children
(i) pp. 61–65 (Ch. 4); (ii) pp. 70–74
'Phyllis and Peter met ... end to the
birthday.'
The children and their mother have
been reduced to poverty, but they still
manage a party for Roberta's birthday, even though it is a very simple
affair.

BIRTHDAYS – GIFTS

1. LAWRENCE, D.H.
Sons and Lovers
(i) pp. 268–270 (Ch. 10); (ii) pp.
327–330
'When he celebrated ... his heart
ached so.'
Fanny the Hunchback gives Paul
('from us all') tubes of paint for his
birthday. Fanny is emotional in the
giving, making Paul embarrassed in
the receiving.
2. NESBIT, E.
The Railway Children
(i) pp. 132–147 (Ch. 9); (ii) pp.
146–162
'It was breakfast time ... as what you
mean.,'
The children determine to celebrate
Perks', the porter's, birthday, because
he doesn't usually do so. They amass
presents from the villagers and add
their own. Mrs Perks is surprised and
delighted, but Perks is furious at
receiving 'charity' until he realises
how everyone meant well.

BLACKMAIL

1. DICKENS, Charles
Bleak House
(i) pp. 530–534 (Ch. 41); pp. 605–607
(Ch. 48); (ii) pp. 530–534; 605–607
'I will not trouble you ... your
fidelity, sir'; 'But he wishes ... I am
going home.'
Mr Tulkinghorn knows the secret of
Lady Dedlock's youthful love affair
and illegitimate child. At first he
wishes just to torment her with this
knowledge, but he then threatens
betrayal to her husband, not for
money but for power over her.

BLINDNESS

see also: SIGHT

BLINDNESS

1. CANAWAY, W.H.
   Sammy going South
   pp. 25–28 (Ch. 5)
   'In the morning ... the Syrian's wounds.'
   Sammy is being taken south by a Syrian, who stops one day to bake bread on flat stones. One stone explodes in the Syrian's face: he is blinded.
   see also: SNAKES 1
2. LESSING, Doris
   Nine African Stories
   see MEDICINE – PRIMITIVE 2

BOARDING-SCHOOLS

see SCHOOLS - BOARDING

BOATS (and) BOATING

see also: CANOEING;
RIVERS – CROSSING;
SAILING;
TRAVEL (by) BOAT

BOATS (and) BOATING

1. CHURCH, Richard
   Over the Bridge
   pp. 148–150 (Ch. 13)
   'Another colleague of my father ... celebrate our survival.'
   A champion oarsman takes the young Richard's health in hand. Sunday after Sunday, he takes him sailing on the Thames. But it is when he drags a boat from its moonlit ignominy on a sand-bank, that he shows himself a hero to the boy.
2. JEROME, Jerome K.
   Three Men in a Boat
   pp. 86–89 (Ch. 9)
   'I remember being terribly ... time for supper after all.'
   J. is rowing his cousin on the Thames. She is anxious to get home, but J. is disturbed that they can't account for a lock that is marked on the map.

Just when they have given themselves up for lost, a party passes and tells them the lock has been removed long since.
3. ibid.
   pp. 149–150 (Ch. 15)
   'George never went near ... to really like boating.'
   George and his friends go rowing on the Thames. They underestimate the strength of the elements, and overestimate their own. They make a spectacle of themselves before a large crowd of onlookers.
4. STEVENSON, R.L.
   Treasure Island
   pp. 146–151 (Ch. 24)
   'it was broad day ... on the Hispaniola.'
   Jim is drifting in a coracle, with no knowledge of how to handle it. By frightening experiments he learns to paddle, but soon despairs of reaching land as the sun burns down and he is intolerably thirsty. However he finally reaches the 'Hispaniola.'

BOER WAR

1. CHURCHILL, W.S.
   My Early Life
   see ESCAPE (from) PRISON (of) WAR 1–3
2. FORESTER, C.S.
   The General
   (i) pp. 8–13 (Ch. 1); (ii) pp. 8–13
   'Troop Sergeant-Major ... on Bournemouth Promenade.'
   More by luck than good judgement Lt. Curzon, commanding a troop of cavalry, surprises entrenched Boers from behind. Curzon charges, redeems the day, and earns himself promotion.

BOMBING

see SECOND WORLD WAR – BOMBING;
WAR – BOMBING

BOMBS

1. BALCHIN, Nigel
   The Small Back Room
   pp. 50–58 (Ch. 4)
   'I had meant to stay ... expect much detail.'
   A girl has been blown to pieces by an unusual German bomb. Her brother was a witness of the incident, but he cannot be of much help in the subsequent enquiry.

BOMBS – DISPOSAL

1. BALCHIN, Nigel
   The Small Back Room
   pp. 197–200 (Ch. 14)
   '0645 hrs wire tested ... the cap in his hands.'
   The radio-record of a bomb-disposal officer's last thoughts and actions. In spite of all his meticulous care, the bomb carries a sting in its tail for which he is unprepared.

BOREDOM

1. ALCOTT, Louisa M.
   Little Women
   pp. 152–154 (Ch. 11)
   'You may try ... pleasure, fretting and ennui.'
   The March sisters, used to a very regular working day, decide to take a complete holiday and enjoy themselves. The unaccustomed idleness soon palls.
2. ALMEDINGEN, E.M.
   Little Katia
   pp. 1–5 (Ch. 1)
   'The Forecourt ... there were many such.'
   Katia is ignored by her father, her Nanny and the servants. She lives in an immense house, but has nothing to do. Even when she tries to help with her baby brother, she does wrong and is scolded.
3. BAWDEN, Nina
   On the Run
   pp. 9–16 (Ch. 1)
   'There are two things ... higher and higher.'
   Ben is staying with his father, while his brother and sister have measles at the house of the Aunt with whom they all live. His father's fiancée is spending the afternoon with them – Ben is hot, bored and embarrassed, and goes reluctantly into the garden to leave the other two alone.
4. COLLINS, Wilkie
   The Moonstone
   pp. 60–61 (1st Period Ch. 8)
   'Gentlefolks in general ... that they must do.'
   The house-steward of the Verinder family writes of the biggest problem facing gentlefolk – idleness – and the peculiar means by which they make themselves feel busy and useful.
5. POINTON, Barry
   Break-in
   see SCHOOLS – SECONDARY 2
6. SILLITOE, Alan
   The Loneliness of the Long-Distance Runner
   see FAMILY 11
7. STEINBECK, John
   The Red Pony
   pp. 43–45 (Ch. 2)
   'In the humming heat ... never to mention it.'
   Out of long-summer-holiday boredom Jody teases his dog. Then he returns his attention to his catapult, and a group of thrushes. He kills one of them and pulls it to pieces. He throws it away, conscious of what his parents would say if they knew.
8. WELLS, H.G.
   The History of Mr Polly
   see FRUSTRATION 7
9. WRIGHT, Richard
   Black Boy
   pp. 1–4 (Ch. 1)
   'One winter morning ... prepare it for my back.'
   Four years old Richard is bored and resentful. He burns straws in the fire, then sets the curtains on fire, innocent of any desire to destroy. Horrified by

this result of his curiosity, he hides from his mother, underneath the house.

BORSTAL

1. SILLITOE, Alan
    The Loneliness of the Long-Distance Runner'
    (ii) pp. 9–12 ('The Loneliness of the Long-Distance Runner', Part 1)
    'I'm in Essex ... "Like boggery, I will".'
    Smith is in an Essex Borstal, finding that the life is not as tough as he had imagined it would be. He is allowed to go out cross-country running on his own. But he is under no illusions about whose side he is on.
    see also: RUNNING 1

BOWLS

1. NAUGHTON, Bill
    Late Night on Watling Street
    see GAMBLING 7

BOXING

1. ALLEN, Walter
    All in a Lifetime
    pp. 145–146 (Ch. 12)
    'It was tough going ... his own strength.'
    The boys at the All Saints Club make a mockery of the slight, bespectacled Billy, until he challenges the biggest of them to a boxing bout. He makes a fool of the boy, and wins the Club's respect.
2. BRAITHWAITE, E.R.
    To Sir with Love
    see CHALLENGES 2
3. LLWELLYN, Richard
    How Green was my Valley
    pp. 329–335 (Ch. 37)
    'I had never been ... savage againt the world.'
    Huw acts as second for Dai, his trainer, at a prize-fight. His opponent is massive and Dai takes some fierce

punishment, finally losing his sight. However he still manages to knock his opponent from the ring.

BOYS

see also: ADOLESCENCE – BOYS;
BULLYING (by) BOYS;
FIGHTING (by) BOYS;
FRIENDS – BOYS;
GANGS – BOYS;
PRANKS;
RIVALS – BOYS

BOYS

1. LAWRENCE, D.H.
    Sons and Lovers
    see PUNISHMENT 11
2. BARSTOW, Stan
    Joby
    see PUNISHMENT 4
3. THOMAS, Dylan
    A Portrait of the Artist as a Young Dog
    see CHALLENGES 9
4. THOMAS, Dylan
    Quite Early One Morning
    see MEMORIES (of) CHILDHOOD 10
5. TWAIN, Mark
    The Adventures of Huckleberry Finn
    see GAMES 13
6. ibid.
    see SMOKING 1
7. WRIGHT, Richard
    Black Boy
    see INITIATION 11
8. ibid.
    see FIGHTING (by) BOYS (at) SCHOOL 7

BREAKFASTS

see MEALS – BREAKFASTS

BRITISH EMPIRE – INDIA

1. CHURCHILL, W.S.
    My Early Life
    see BATTLES 1
2. FORSTER, E.M.
    A Passage to India
    see RACISM – INDIA 1, 2;
    TRIALS 7

BRITISH EMPIRE – NIGERIA

1. ACHEBE, Chinua
   Things fall apart
   see MISSIONARIES 1
2. ibid.
   (i) pp. 161–164 (Ch. 21); (ii) pp.
   161–164
   'There were many men and women ...
   religion and education went hand in
   hand.'
   Mr Brown, the white missionary in
   Umuofia, is a persuasive spokesman
   for his religion. Belief is a part of the
   governing apparatus of the white
   man, and a path to success for the
   ambitious Ibo.
3. ibid.
   (i) pp. 173–176 (Ch. 23); (ii) pp.
   173–176
   'For two days after ... Okonkwo was
   choked with hate.'
   The leaders of Umuofia are brought
   before the Commissioners to account
   for the burning of the White Man's
   Church. But before they have a
   chance to state their case, they are
   seized and insulted. Okonkwo burns
   with hatred and desire for revenge.
4. ibid.
   (i) pp. 180–187 (Chs. 24, 25); (ii) pp.
   180–187
   (Themes in Life and Literature pp.
   15–18)
   'The market-place began to fill ...
   Tribes of the lower Niger.'
   Okonkwo, consumed with hatred for
   the white man, kills a high-handed
   District Commissioner's messenger.
   The commissioner and a party of
   soldiers come to apprehend Okonkwo,
   but they are too late. He has hanged
   himself.

BROTHERS

see also: ASSAULT (by) BROTHERS;
DEATH (of) BROTHER;

FAMILY;

QUARRELS – BROTHERS (and) SISTERS

26

BROTHERS

1. ELIOT, George
   The Mill on the Floss
   p. 43 (Ch. 5, Part 1)
   'So ended ... she did wrong.'
   Maggie adores her older brother
   Tom. He thinks she is silly, but feels
   strong and protective towards her.
2. HINES, Barry
   A Kestrel for a Knave
   (i) pp. 9–11; (ii) pp. 7–9
   'There were no curtains ... a warm
   place.'
   Jud and Billy sleep together. Billy is
   his older brother's keeper inasmuch as
   he has to ensure that he gets up in
   time for the pit. Jud is rough, and
   bullying, so that the two of them are
   always at daggers drawn.
3. ibid.
   (i) pp. 27–28; (ii) pp. 21–23
   'Jud was having ... round at the sky.'
   Billy breakfasts with Jud. Jud is off to
   the pit, and Billy is going nesting.
   They argue, and only Billy's agility
   saves him from a drubbing when Jud
   discovers Billy in his package of sandwiches.
   see also: FAMILY – QUARRELS 3
4. SHOLOKHOV, Mikhail
   And Quiet Flows the Don
   pp. 78–81 (Part 1, Ch. 5)
   'The Melekhovs set out to begin ...
   your head clean off.'
   Gregor and his brother Piotra have a
   row out in the fields, about Gregor's
   philandering. The latter, maddened,
   goes for Piotra with a pitchfork. They
   are seen, and their father is called.
   But by this time the brothers are
   reconciled.

BULL-FIGHTING

1. HEMINGWAY, Ernest
   For Whom the Bell Tolls
   pp. 176–178 (Ch. 14)
   'He wasn't much of a matador ... is
   my life passed now!'

A reminiscence of a matador, Finito, a man petrified of bulls before the corrida, but assured in the ring. Pilar recreates all the details of a fight.

2. ibid.
   pp. 344–346 (Ch. 34)
   'He loved the bull-baiting ... he would not have to do it.'
   Bull-baiting in a Spanish village. Each year, a bull is let loose in the square, and Andres makes it his job to subdue it. His hallmark is to bite its ear.

BULLS

1. HARDY, Thomas
   The Mayor of Casterbridge
   (i) pp. 234–237 (Ch. 29); (ii) pp. 229–232
   'Lucetta, in spite of her ... there with a stake.'
   Lucetta and Elizabeth are chased into a wayside barn by a runaway bull. Elizabeth manages to scramble to the 'top of a clover stack, but Lucetta is in real danger, until Henchard happens by, and secures the bull to the barn-door.

2. MACKEN, Walter
   God made Sunday and Other Stories
   pp. 152–153 ('This was my day')
   'After that I turned ... man to be careless.'
   The farmer is hand-milking a cow, when a bull charges him. The farmer uses the cow as a shield, and edges towards the gate. He escapes but resolves to master the bull. He manoeuvres a pole into the bull's nose ring, and walks him round the field, until he is subdued.

BULLYING

see also: FEAR (of) BULLYING; FIGHTING

BULLYING (by) BOYS

1. BRONTË, Charlotte
   Jane Eyre
   (i) pp. 1–6 (Ch. 1); (ii) pp. 9–14
   'There was no possibility ... I was borne upstairs.'
   Banished from the drawing-room for some slight misdemeanour, Jane is reading quietly and contentedly on a window-seat. She is rudely interrupted by her cousin John Reed who drags her out and torments her, till she can no longer contain her bitterness against him.

2. HINES, Barry
   A Kestrel for a Knave
   see FIGHTING (by) BOYS (at) SCHOOL 2

3. ibid.
   (i) pp. 95–98; (ii) pp. 77–80
   'Enter Mr Farthing ... began to cry again.'
   Mr Farthing breaks up the fight between Billy and MacDowall, and listens to their explanations and mutual accusations. It is plain to him that MacDowall has been bullying Billy, so he gives him a dose of his own medicine by overbearing him, to the point of tears.

4. HUGHES, Thomas
   Tom Brown's Schooldays
   see SCHOOLS – BOARDING – FIRST DAY 4

5. ibid.
   pp. 143–147 (Part 1, Ch. 8).
   'The Hall was full ... the evil with the good.'
   Flashman and his fifth-form cronies try to intimidate Tom into giving up his lottery ticket. When he refuses they roast him in front of the Hall fire. Tom lives but does not tell the tale.

6. KIRKUP, James
   The Only Child
   see SCHOOLS – INFANTS 1

7. THOMPSON, Flora
   Lark Rise to Candleford
   (i) pp. 186–188 ('Lark Rise' Ch. 11); (ii) pp. 174–176

'It has been said ... she was still outside.'

On the way to school, some of the less 'civilised' children select one of the younger children going their way, to be the victim of a short sharp persecution. Laura's little brother is set on one morning, and he quits himself much better than she would have expected.

8. WATERHOUSE, Keith
   There is a Happy Land
   pp. 77–82 (Ch. 11)
   'Get back into our ... hen, then?"
   "Hen." '

   The boy has fallen out with the rest of the gang – he meets them on the way home from the fair and they bait him. He tries to laugh it off, then appeals to a neighbour for help. Finally he has to answer 'Hen' (yellow) to their repeated 'Cock or hen?'

9. WRIGHT, Richard
   Black Boy
   see COURAGE 20

BULLYING (by) BOYS (and) GIRLS

1. HITCHMAN, Janet
   The King of the Barbareens
   pp. 53–56 (Ch. 3)
   'I have not been ... fight any of them.'

   The boys of the village, rough and rangy, mock and play practical jokes on outsiders. The writer, an offcomer, is the victim of these, and of bigger girls, until she learns to defend herself adequately.

2. SHOLOKHOV, Mikhail
   Fierce and Gentle Warriors
   pp. 19–20 ('The Rascal', Ch. 2)
   'The kids at the pond surrounded ... slowly wandered into his yard.'

   The village children taunt Mishka because his father is a communist. Vitka, the priest's son, is foremost among them. The taunting turns to kicking and beating. Mishka crawls away bloodied and tearful.

BULLYING (by) GIRLS

1. GODDEN, Rumer
   The Diddakoi
   pp. 89–91 (Ch. 4)
   'The short cut ... Fraser, the headmaster.'

   It's fourteen against one; fourteen girls against a half-gypsy girl who doesn't belong. Miss Brooke intervenes in time to prevent serious harm.

2. THOMPSON, Flora
   Lark Rise to Candleford
   (i) pp. 359–361 ('Over to Candleford' Ch. 23); (ii) pp. 321–323
   'There was one girl ... make a request.'

   Laura's life at school is made a misery by Ethel Parker, who forces her into all sorts of painful situations. When she meets Ethel years later, she is very friendly, but she notices her old bullying manner to her dog.

BULLYING (by) TEACHERS

see also: PUNISHMENT – CORPORAL

BULLYING (by) TEACHERS

1. BRAITHWAITE, E.R.
   To Sir with Love
   see REVOLT (at) SCHOOL 1

2. HINES, Barry
   A Kestrel for a Knave
   (i) pp. 127–133; (ii) 103–108
   'He was slipping ... staining it charcoal.'

   Mr Sugden, the games teacher, is as unremitting a bully as MacDowall. He obliges Billy to take a shower for little other reason than that Billy let in the winning goal; but he does not content himself with ensuring that Billy goes home clean; he sees that he goes home cowed.

BUSES (and) TRAMS

see TRAVEL (by) BUS;

TRAVEL (by) CHARABANC;
TRAVEL (by) TRAM

BUYING (and) SELLING

see also: AUCTIONS; JUMBLE SALES;
MARKETS; PAWN-BROKERS;
PEDLARS; SHOPS;
SALESMEN

BUYING (and) SELLING (by) DEALERS

1. CARY, Joyce
   The Horse's Mouth
   pp. 137–142 (Ch. 18)
   'But when I went ... for an under-coating.'
   Gulley Jimson is looking for a canvas to start a new picture. He tries an 'Antique' shop where he haggles with the dealer over a large painting he plans to re-use.
2. MANKOWITZ, Wolf
   Make me an Offer
   pp. 59–68 ('Make me an Offer')
   'The arrangement was ... when he left.'
   The narrator, a dealer, bids for the panelling of a room, is pushed up quite high, and then sells it in a second sale with two other dealers. He gains a handsome sum.
3. MOORE, John
   Portrait of Elmbury
   pp. 97–100 (Part 3)
   'The dealers of course ... blush to tell you.'
   'The dealers couldn't afford to be honest.' The author reveals some of the tricks of the antique trade as practised by two dealers in Elmbury.
4. STEINBECK, John
   The Grapes of Wrath
   (i) pp. 51–55 (Ch. 7); (ii) pp. 57–62
   'In the towns ... clean, runs good.'
   The evicted farmers of Oklahoma need cars to make the journey to California and the Used Car salesmen see and seize their opportunity. They

make a fortune from the ignorant and gullible.
5. STEINBECK, John
   The Pearl
   pp. 40; 44–50 (Ch. 4)
   'It was supposed ... lowest prices.'
   'The news of the approach ... trotting after him.'
   Kino goes to the town to sell his enormous pearl. The dealers, in league with each other, claim it is too large to be of any value, but Kino does not believe them.

CAMPING

1. JEROME, Jerome K.
   Three Men in a Boat
   pp. 19–21 (Ch. 2)
   'It is evening ... the whole of breakfast time.'
   An evocation of some of the drawbacks of a camping holiday: the fighting to get the tent up; the rain that makes a misery of supper; and the night that ends in a mêlé of bodies and blown tent.
2. SOUTHALL, Ivan
   Ash Road
   see FOREST – FIRES 3
3. TWAIN, Mark
   The Adventures of Tom Sawyer
   See STORMS 12

CANNIBALS

see also: PRIMITIVE PEOPLES;
RESCUE (from) CANNIBALS

CANNIBALS

1. DEFOE, Daniel
   Robinson Crusoe
   (i) pp. 120–122; (ii) pp. 163–164 (Ch. 15)
   'When I was come down ... would have been my lot.'
   Crusoe comes upon the remains of an inhuman feast on human flesh on the

shore of his island. He is amazed, terrified, and indignant at once.
see also RESCUE (from) CANNIBALS 1

2. SPERRY, Armstrong
The Boy who was afraid
pp. 65–69 (Ch. 5)
'A chill sweat ... toward the barrier-reef.'
The eaters-of-men come to their Sacred Place on the island where Mafatu has been ship-wrecked. He watches their celebrations in horror, and then has to run very fast to escape them.

CANOEING

1. SERAILLIER, Ian
The Silver Sword
see TRAVEL (by) BOAT 4

CAPITAL PUNISHMENT

see EXECUTION

CAPITALISM

see also: MATERIALISM;
SOCIALISM;
WEALTH

CAPITALISM

1. BRAINE, John
Room at the Top
see SOCIAL CLASS – CLIMBING 1
2. ORWELL, George
1984
(i) pp. 193–196 (Part 2, Ch. 9), (ii) pp. 153–154
'The primary aim ... continuous warfare.'
A pessimistic look at the future of the present economic situation-mechanisation produces too much and the surplus must be used for war.
3. GREENWOOD, Walter
Love on the Dole
see SOCIALISM 2
4. PATON, Alan
Cry, the beloved country

(ii) pp. 145–148 (Bk. 2, Ch. 6)
'There is little attention ... that name impossible?'
Gold has been discovered in a new area in S. Africa, and there is great excitement among white speculators. Paton conveys this excitement very ironically, illustrating their grasping selfishness.
5. STEINBECK, John
The Grapes of Wrath
see EVICTION 3
6. ibid.
(i) pp. 201–202 (Ch. 1); (ii) pp. 212–213
'Once California ... farms they owned.'
Farming in California has changed from a labour of love to a profit-making concern, controlled by men at desks who have never seen their land.
7. ibid.
(i) pp. 246–248 (Ch. 21); (ii) pp. 259–261
'And then suddenly ... began to ferment.'
With the inflow of hungry migrants from the East, the Californian land-owners see their opportunity for using very cheap labour, and making vast profits. There is great bitterness and resentment.

CAROL-SINGING

see CHRISTMAS – CAROLS

CARS

see ACCIDENTS – ROAD;
TRAVEL (by) CAR

CASTAWAYS

see also: RESCUE (from) ISLANDS;
SURVIVAL (on) ISLANDS

CASTAWAYS

1. BOMBARD, Alain
The Bombard Story

pp. 191–194 (Ch. 13)
'Problem for the day ... some sort of coastline!'
Things look desperate. Alain is running short of fresh water, his health is deteriorating, he is lost and giving way to despair. He writes his last will and testament.

2. ibid.
   see SHIPWRECKS 2
3. CALDWELL, John
   Desperate Voyage
   see SHIPWRECKS 3
4. DEFOE, Daniel
   Robinson Crusoe
   see SHIPWRECKS 6
5. ibid.
   (i) pp. 44–46; (ii) pp. 61–63 (Ch. 7)
   'My thoughts were now ... cellar to my house.'
   Crusoe sets about building himself a house-cum-fortress to protect him from both the elements and from the savages and beasts he supposes to be on the island. He describes its building in loving detail.
6. GOLDING, William
   Lord of the Flies
   passim.
   A party of boys of all shapes and sizes shifts for itself on an uninhabited island. They eat, make rules, kill and break the rules. They are rescued, fewer in number, and wiser.
7. GOLDING, William
   Pincher Martin
   see SHIPWRECKS 10
8. ibid.
   see SURVIVAL (on) ISLANDS 2
9. ibid.
   pp. 75–80 (Ch. 5)
   'The papers and booklet ... listens to him or not.'
   The castaway surveys his rocky islet and takes stock of his position. He strikes dramatic poses, and declares to the Atlantic that he will survive.
10. ibid.
    pp. 81–87 (Ch. 6)
    'The end to be desired ... declare to be a thinking day.'

The castaway resolves to remain sane, and await rescue. He gives familiar names to the cliffs and gullies of his mid-Atlantic rock, in order that he should impose his personality on it, and thereby feel at home.

11. SPERRY, Armstrong
    The Boy who was afraid
    pp. 27–30 (Ch. 3)
    'On his left hand ... the barrier-reef.'
    Mafatu has been ship-wrecked on an apparently uninhabited island, and he explores. It is an extinct volcano, whose lower slopes are covered in jungle.

CATS

1. DE JONG, Meindert
   The Tower by the Sea
   see CONDITIONING 1
2. FOAKES, Grace
   Between High Walls
   pp. 42–45 (Ch. 21)
   'I suppose I must ... longer to eat it this way.'
   Cats overrun the tenements, so no-one but the author is inclined to be sentimental about them. Some she takes to a cats' home; others, less fortunate, she mourns.

CAVALRY CHARGES

1. CHURCHILL, W.S.
   My Early Life
   see BATTLES – OMDURMAN – 1898 1
2. FORESTER, C.S.
   The General
   see BOER WAR 2
3. SHOLOKHOV, Mikhail
   And Quiet Flows the Don
   see FIRST WORLD WAR – BATTLES 4

CAVES

1. COOKSON, Catherine
   The Nipper
   pp. 78–87 (Ch. 6)
   'There was another silence ... me ma'll be worried.'

Sandy visits a one-legged tramp who lives in a cave. The tramp has something to show him: a hidden trap-door opens onto long dark passages, which lead to a priest's hole in the Manor House.

2. KING, Clive
   Stig of the Dump
   see INGENUITY 7

3. TWAIN, Mark
   The Adventures of Tom Sawyer
   (i) pp. 209–211 (Ch. 32); (ii) pp. 191–193 (Visions of Life 1 pp. 38–40)
   'Now to return ... thought of the dreadful posibilities.'
   Tom and Becky leave the rest of the party to explore alone in McDougal's Cave. They go farther than Tom has gone before, but apprehension seizes them only when a bat strikes out Becky's candle.

4. ibid.
   see; LOST (in) CAVES 1

CELEBRATIONS

see also: BIRTHDAYS; CHRISTMAS;
DANCES; HOMECOMING;
PARTIES; WEDDINGS

CELEBRATIONS

1. BRONTË, Charlotte
   Shirley
   see CHURCH – FESTIVALS 1

2. BRONTË, Charlotte
   Villette
   pp. 411–415 (Ch. 38)
   'I took a route well-known ... but could see little.'
   Lucy Snowe, unable to sleep seeks coolness and peace in the park, only to find a National Festival in progress. She is swept along by the crowds, and finds herself spectator of celebrations and decorations.

3. FOAKES, Grace
   Between High Walls
   pp. 18–19 (Ch. 9)
   'I have fond ... end in such a way.'

The red-letter days in May: May Day between high walls, Empire Day with its flag-waving, and the Catholic Procession with its fascinating rituals and drunkenness.

4. KIRKUP, James
   The Only Child
   see EASTER 1

CELEBRATIONS – NEW YEAR

1. ACHEBE, Chinua
   Things fall apart
   (i) pp. 42–46 (Ch. 6); (ii) pp. 42–46
   'The whole village turned out ... to fight for us.'
   On the second day of the New Year Festival, there is a great wrestling match in the village compound. The atmosphere is tense and exciting. To the throb of the drums, everyone awaits the climax of a good throw.

CELEBRATIONS – PEACE

1. LEE, Laurie
   Cider with Rosie
   (i) pp. 10–12 (Ch. 1, 'First Light');
   (ii) pp. 21–24
   'I was not at all ... to see another day.'
   When the war ends, Mrs Lee is away, and the sisters take the little children to the impromptu village peace celebrations. They see drunken men, and the school house chimney on fire.

2. ibid.
   (i) pp. 140–143 (Ch. 11, 'Outings and Festivals'); (ii) pp. 184–187
   'The first big festival ... say PEACE.'
   Peace Day 1919 – fancy dress and a procession. Laurie tries to make a five year-old angel fly, and is furious when his John Bull gaiters fall off.

CELEBRATIONS – ROYAL JUBILEE

1. BALDWIN, Michael
   Grandad with Snails
   pp. 51–59 (Ch. 6)

'One day I went home ... I had to go back to school.'

All the children at Michael's school are given Jubilee mugs, in 1935. They arm themselves, with flags for the arrival of the King and Queen to the town. Michael's is the biggest so he has to lead the school in the procession. He does not regard this as in any sense a privilege.

2. THOMPSON, Flora
   Lark Rise to Candleford
   (i) pp. 266–270 (Ch. 15, Lark Rise); (ii) pp. 242–246
   'The great day dawned ... "God Save the Queen".'

   To celebrate Queen Victoria's Jubilee, three villages join in 'tea and sports and dancing and fireworks' in the park of a local magnate. Laura has a good look at all the sideshows and chooses to see a tightrope dancer. This novelty becomes Laura's chief memory of the Jubilee for years afterwards.

CHALLENGES

see also: COMPETITIONS; COURAGE; DARING; FIGHTS; INITIATION

CHALLENGES

1. ALLEN, Walter
   All in a Lifetime
   see BOXING 1
2. BRAITHWAITE, E.R.
   To Sir with Love
   pp. 80–83 (Ch. 11)
   'On Thursday morning the class ... we'd talk about many things.'

   Things came to a head in the relationship between Braithwaite, and the boys of his class. Denham, the most outspoken of them, with a reputation as a boxer, challenges Braithwaite to a bout. The latter is stung into inflicting a low, wounding blow on Denham, and the fight is over.

3. DICKENS, Charles
   Great Expectations
   (i) pp. 99–102 (Ch. 11); (ii) pp. 85–87
   'When I had exhausted ... Same to you.'

   Pip meets a pale young gentleman in the grounds of Satis House, and is challenged to a fight. Pip is nothing loth, though he is astonished by the lack of any obvious motive, or pretext.

4. DOSTOYEVSKY, Fyodor
   The Idiot
   see TEMPTATION 2
5. GOLDING, William
   Lord of the Flies
   (i) pp. 146–149 (Ch. 7); (ii) pp. 129–133
   'Jack – that time you ... fear, enraged him.'

   Jack dares Ralph to join him in a twilight hunt for the 'Beast' on the mountain. Ralph knows it to be a foolish quest, but he agrees so that he will not be thought 'windy'.

6. HUGHES, Ted
   The Iron Man
   pp. 47–56 (Ch. 5)
   'There was no time ... but not the sun again.'

   The Iron Man challenges the space monster to an ordeal by fire. He lies above a bath of burning fuel oil, until the oil is all used up. Then he defies the monster to lie on the sun. The monster does so, twice, before capitulating.

7. LONDON, Jack
   The Call of the Wild
   see GAMBLING 6
8. MADDOCK, Reginald
   The Pit
   see MOORS 3
9. THOMAS, Dylan
   A Portrait of the Artist as a Young Dog
   pp. 56–61 ('Extraordinary Little Cough')
   'Look at Little Cough ... touching the flames.'

   George Hooping is teased by his

friends, and challenged by the school's bullies, to run the length of Rhossilli sands. He accepts the challenge in order to prove himself; but all that he proves is that he is gullible.

10. TWAIN, Mark
The Adventures of Tom Sawyer
see RIVALS – BOYS 3

CHARITY

see also: GIFTS;
SELF-SACRIFICE;
SELFISHNESS

CHARITY

1. ALCOTT, Louisa M.
Little Women
see CHRISTMAS 1
2. BRONTË, Charlotte
Shirley
(i) pp. 110–111 (Ch. 7); (ii) pp. 134–135
'And now Caroline had to ... it's your turn now.'
The Jew-basket, or Missionary-basket, by means of which the genteel convince themselves that they are doing their duty to the poor.
3. ibid.
see POVERTY 3
4. ibid.
see PRIDE 1
5. DICKENS, Charles
Bleak House
(i) pp. 33–38 (Ch. 4); (ii) pp. 33–38
'Mrs Jellyby, whose face ... overturned them into cribs.'
Mrs Jellyby is so preoccupied with her good works for Borioboola-Gha that she neglects her children who run wild, her husband who sits with his head against the wall, her household which is chaotic, and her guests who have to fend for themselves.
6. ibid.
(i) pp. 97–99 (Ch. 8); (ii) pp. 97–99
'I was glad ... with demonstrative cheerfulness.'
Mrs Pardiggle, with Esther, Ada, and

her children in tow, descends upon the brick-makers' house, ignores their ungracious reception, and delivers a moral lecture and leaves behind a great deal of ill-feeling.

7. ibid.
see MOTHERS 4
8. FIELDING, Henry
Joseph Andrews
pp. 46–49 (Bk. 1, Ch. 12); (Impact 1, pp. 30–32)
'Nothing remarkable happened ... parted with his money so easily.'
Two ruffians strip Joseph of all his belongings and leave him for dead. But Joseph revives and begs to be taken into a passing stagecoach. A lady protests that she will not sit with a naked man, the coachman demands a fee, the footman will not bloody his coat. Farther along the road, the same ruffians hold up the coach and enjoy further plunder.
9. FORSTER, E.M.
Howard's End
pp. 119–120 (Ch. 15)
'How ought I ... those up for himself.'
Helen and Margaret, with some friends, discuss 'How ought I to dispose of my money?' They put forward various schemes for helping the poor, both culturally and practically, but none, but Margaret, suggests giving the money itself.
10. GRICE, Frederick
The Bonny Pit Laddie
pp. 88–90 (Ch. 11)
'The Rushy Field ... the women were crying.'
The evicted miners of Branton, and their families, pitch union tents on common land. Their morale is raised, when almost every woman in the village not under canvas, shows sympathy for the miners' cause, by giving them fresh-baked loaves of bread.
11. HAUGAARD, Erich
The Little Fishes
pp. 6–11 (Ch. 1)

34

'In the Church of St.—— ... and entered the church.'

Guido takes a boy as hungry as himself to the Saintly Father Pietro. He counts on the priest's reputedly soft heart, and he is not disappointed. The priest gives him a fresh loaf of bread received a moment before as a thank-offering.

12. SERRAILLIER, Ian
   The Silver Sword
   (i) pp. 117–123 (Ch. 19); (ii) pp. 98–103
   'There were queer noises ... the farmer had his way.'
   Four Polish refugee children are found hiding in a barn by a Bavarian farmer. Despite his gruff exterior, he is sympathetic and allows them to stay.

13. SHUTE, Nevil
   A Town like Alice
   (i) pp. 106–111 (Ch. 4; (ii) pp. 101–106
   'The death of the sergeant ... or more.'
   The Japanese guard of the English women prisoners dies as they are marching to a prison camp. They manage to persuade the headman of a Malayan village, and then the Japanese occupying army, to allow them to stay in the village if they work for their living.

14. ibid.
   (i) pp. 124–128 (Ch. 4); (ii) pp. 118–122
   'She had a talk ... the work in hand.'
   Jean, one of the English prisoners, returns to Malaya after the war. She has inherited some money, and proposes to build a well and washhouse for the village which supported the prisoners for three years.

CHEESE

1. JEROME, Jerome K.
   Three Men in a Boat
   pp. 31–35 (Ch. 4)

'I remember a friend of mine ... there for years afterwards.'

A friend has asked J. to convey two noxious cheeses by train from Liverpool to London. The cheeses clear the carriage, and put the friend's wife to flight; but they come into their own when they add to the tang of the seaside.

CHILDREN

see also: BOYS; DEATH (of) CHILD; FEAR (of) DARK; FEAR (of) GHOSTS; FRIENDS – CHILDREN; GAMES; GANGS – CHILDREN; GIRLS; MEMORIES (of) CHILDHOOD; SONGS (and) RHYMES

CHILDREN

1. GROSSMITH, George and Weedon
   The Diary of a Nobody
   (i) pp. 162–163 (Ch. 22); (ii) pp. 261–263
   'We went to Sutton ... That is my opinion.'
   The Pooters visit friends and are disgusted by the self-possession, arrogance and insolence of their curly-headed son. Opinions are expressed about the proper bringing up of children.

2. MANSFIELD, Katherine
   Bliss and Other Stories
   pp. 165–172 ('Sun and Moon')
   'In the afternoon ... off to the nursery.'
   The children enjoy the preparations for their parents' elegant party. They stare open-mouthed at the sumptuous food, and are briefly displayed in their best before being packed off to bed. They are heart-broken, later, when they see the unmagical remains on the ravaged table.

3. MANSFIELD, Katherine
   The Garden Party
   pp. 21–25 ('At the Bay', Part IV)
   'Wait for me, Isa-bel! Kezia ... and far more beautiful.'

Three children are off to the beach. The youngest, Lottie, gets stuck on a stile, and requires patient instructing. The Samuel Josephs are playing organized games under the baton of the lady-help; and the Trout boys are digging in the sand, for treasures of coloured glass.

4. ibid.
   see GAMES 6

5. 'MISS READ'
   Village School
   (i) pp. 175–178 (Pt. 3, Ch. 19); (ii) pp. 175–178
   'In the infants' ... she was right.'
   Joseph Coggs has broken his yellow crayon. Eileen won't lend him hers. She holds it aloft, he bites her, she screams – and Joseph gets a wigging from everybody.

CHILDREN – AMBITIONS

1. SHOLOKHOV, Mikhail
   Fierce and Gentle Warriors
   pp. 32–34 ('The Rascal', Ch. 4)
   'Next morning, as they all ... tramp of the soldiers' feet.'
   Ranks of Red Army men march through Mishka's village, led by a military band. Young Mishka's blood is fired. He says he wants to join up. The commander tricks Mishka into returning home first, and by the time Mishka comes back, the men have gone.

2. TWAIN, Mark
   The Adventures of Tom Sawyer
   (i) pp. 60–62 (Ch. 8); (ii) pp. 60–61
   'Tom dodged hither ... start the very next morning.'
   Crossed in love, Tom daydreams. He drops his idea of being a clown, toys with thoughts of soldiering, and hunting buffalo with Indians, and settles for piracy, the more to impress his church-going St. Petersburg friends.

CHILDREN (in) LOVE

1. JOYCE, James
   Dubliners
   pp. 27–33 ('Araby')
   'North Richmond Street ... anguish and anger.'
   The author is in love with a girl across the street. In a foolish moment he says he will buy her something at the Saturday evening bazaar. But his uncle keeps him waiting for the money for the fare, and by the time that he gets there, the stallholders are packing up, and there is nothing for a lovesick boy to buy.

2. TWAIN, Mark
   The Adventures of Tom Sawyer
   (i) pp. 49–52 (Ch. 6); (ii) pp. 50–53 (Conflict 1, pp. 119–120)
   'When Tom reached ... ostentation for months.'
   As a punishment for being late at school, Tom has to sit with the girls. But he sits with Becky Thatcher to whom he makes a confession of love, and her acceptance of his suit makes of punishment a pleasure.

3. ibid.
   (i) pp. 55–59 (Ch. 7); (ii) pp. 56–59
   'When school broke up ... exchange sorrows with.'
   Tom and Becky meet in the schoolroom during the lunch-break. They exchange small-talk until Tom proposes that they should be engaged. Then he mentions Amy Lawrence and the spell is broken. Becky sobs and repels further advances.

4. ibid.
   (i) pp. 141–146 (Ch. 21); (ii) pp. 130–135
   'There was something about ... you be so noble!'
   Becky tears a page in the teacher's own book, in her haste not to be seen with it. When the teacher questions the class, Tom takes the guilt upon himself to save his beloved from being beaten.

CHILDREN (as) SAVAGES

1. GOLDING, William
   Lord of the Flies
   (i) pp. 79–80 (Ch. 4); (ii) pp. 68–69
   'There was a pool ... the mask compelled them.'
   Jack paints his face and becomes
   another, more compelling, more fearsome kind of person.
2. ibid.
   (i) pp. 139–143 (Ch. 7); (ii) pp.
   124–127
   'The bushes crashed ... everybody
   laughed.'
   What begins as an innocent hunt for
   wild pig, becomes a murderous,
   frenzied game. Robert, the victim, is
   badly frightened by the savagery of
   his friends, and Ralph surprises himself.
3. ibid.
   (i) pp. 187–189 (Ch. 9); (ii) pp.
   167–169
   'The hunters were looking ... staining
   the sand.'
   Jack invites his hunters to enact a
   ritual killing, a war-dance. In their
   frenzy the gang of boys fall on the
   defenceless Simon. They beat him
   and spear him until he is dead.
4. ibid.
   (i) pp. 235–246 (Ch. 12); (ii) pp.
   211–220
   'He was awake ... cry for mercy.'
   Jack and his hunters smoke Ralph out
   of the lair to which he has been
   reduced, and chase him across the
   island with the intention of killing
   him, and his kill-joy rules.

CHILDREN – TANTRUMS

1. BURNETT, Frances Hodgson
   The Secret Garden
   pp. 150–155 (Ch. 17)
   'She thought it was the middle ...
   You can go if you like.'
   Mary and Colin have argued – he
   works himself into a tantrum in the
   middle of the night, and the adults

appeal to Mary to deal with him. She
is furious with him, shouts at him and
thus shocks him to his senses.

2. ELIOT, George
   The Mill on the Floss
   pp. 28–29 (Part 1, Ch. 4)
   'Maggie, Maggie ... the dog for it.'
   Maggie is reprimanded for running
   away from her mother while her hair
   is being curled. She is furious, and
   retreats to the attic which sees all her
   rages, and where she works out her
   ill-humour.
3. LAWRENCE, D.H.
   The Rainbow
   pp. 75–78 (Ch. 2)
   (Visions of Life 3, pp. 9–13)
   'He went upstairs to her ... one
   breathed darkness.'
   Brangwen tries to get Anna ready for
   bed, but Anna wants to be with her
   mother. Brangwen can do nothing
   against her sobbing hysteria. At first
   it irritates him, then he is dazed into
   passivity by it.

CHIMPANZEES

1. SERRAILLIER, Ian
   The Silver Sword
   (i) pp. 92–96 (Ch. 15); (ii) pp. 76–79
   'Later that week ... a chain of office.'
   A British officer in Berlin at the end
   of the war writes to tell his wife of an
   encounter with a chimpanzee, which
   had escaped from the zoo. It 'com-
   mandeered' his jeep, and was only
   persuaded to leave by a ragged Polish
   refugee boy.

CHRISTIANITY

   see also: BAPTISM; CHURCH;
   CHRISTMAS; EASTER;
   HELL; METHODISTS;
   MISSIONARIES; RELIGION;
   ROMAN CATHOLICS

CHRISTIANITY – CONVERSION

1. BARNES, Ron
   A Licence to Live
   pp. 58–61 (Ch. 7)
   'One summer dinner time ... he is a blood brother.'
   There is a West Indian, a Christian, at work, to whom Ron feels drawn. They go to church together, and Ron is the only white man there. Within a few weeks of his introduction to his friend's persuasive brand of Christianity, Ron testifies to his own conversion.

2. 'MISS READ'
   Village School
   (i) pp. 85–89 (Pt. 2, Ch. 10): (ii) pp. 85–89
   'It was during this bleak ... out into the night.'
   Arthur Coggs imagines himself to have been saved. Drunk with enthusiasm, and with what he claims will be his last drink, he gets Mr Willet – an old faithful – out of his bed, to do a spot of evangelism.

CHRISTIANITY – EVANGELISM

1. BENNETT, Arnold
   Anna of the Five Towns
   pp. 66–72 (Ch. 5)
   'Anna had meant ... one shilling each.'
   The Bursley Wesleyan Methodists hold 'A Revival' to win more souls to God. The preacher is a fiery, histrionic figure and the atmosphere is soon tense and emotional. Anna suffers torments but remains unconvinced.

2. BUTLER, Samuel
   The Way of all Flesh
   pp. 215–217 (Ch. 58)
   'Next day he felt ... this was what he did.'
   Ernest decides it is high time he set about converting the poor among whom he lodges. He hopes to throw a little light in the way of Mr Holt, who

beats his wife, but his courage fails him at the tailor's threshold.

3. COLLINS, Wilkie
   The Moonstone
   pp. 227–228 (Second Period, Ch. 3); pp. 237–239 (Second Period, Ch. 4)
   'Little did my poor aunt ... the window of the cab.' 'You might feel stronger ... like a child again.'
   Miss Clark learns that her aunt has only a few weeks to live – instead of sorrow and sympathy she feels thankfulness that she has found a soul to be saved at the point of death. She distributes religious tracts about the house.

4. DICKENS, Charles
   Bleak House
   (i) pp. 241–243; 248–249 (Ch. 19); (ii) pp. 241–243; 248–249
   'Mr Chadband is a large yellow man ... the works cease.'; 'Mr Chadband at last ... cow-like lightness.'
   Mr and Mrs Chadband visit friends, where Mr Chadband's every utterance is a sermon on its own, whose meaning is tortuous and contrived. He attempts to make an impression on Jo, a poor crossing-sweeper, but fails.

5. WRIGHT, Richard
   Black Boy
   see METHODISTS 2

CHRISTMAS

1. ALCOTT, Lousia M.
   Little Women
   pp. 34–38 (Ch. 2)
   'Where is mother ... "a perfect fit".'
   Mrs March persuades her daughters to give their Christmas breakfast to a poor starving family. Even present-giving is delayed until they return home.

2. ALMEDINGEN, E.M.
   Little Katia
   pp. 57–62 (Ch. 6)
   'Christmas Eve came ... fast asleep.'
   Christmas in a large, aristocratic, mid-nineteenth century Russian

family – candle-lit tree, extravagent presents and tremendous excitement.

3. DICKENS, Charles
    A Christmas Carol
    pp. 47–49 (Stave 1)
    'A merry Christmas ... Good afternoon! said Scrooge.'
    Scrooge's nephew wishes Scrooge a happy Christmas, and Scrooge flings the compliments back with a sneer.

4. ibid.
    pp. 75–77 (Stave 2)
    'Why, it's old Fezziwig! ... without a stagger.'
    The ghost of Christmas past has Scrooge relive a happy Christmas he had as an apprentice of old Fezziwig. Scrooge is made to realize how much power a man has to make others happy – or unhappy.

5. ibid.
    pp. 89–91 (Stave 3)
    'Holly, mistletoe ... the bakers' shops.'
    A Dickensian Christmas in the streets of the City of London. The shops are stuffed to their ceilings with honest fare, English and exotic.

6. FOAKES, Grace
    Between High Walls
    pp. 57–59 (Ch. 27)
    'In the very earliest ... be the better buy.'
    It's a poor Christmas, but a happy one. Father takes the children to Smithfield market on Christmas Eve. The girls wake up to a doll, nuts, chocolate, and a bright new penny in their stockings, and go to bed on chestnuts and 'Happy Families'. Then, all that's left is the pantomime.

7. KIRKUP, James
    The Only child
    pp. 165–167 (Ch. 13)
    'On Christmas Eve ... were taken down.'
    The writer catalogues the sensations of a child's Christmas. He holds firmly to a belief in Father Christmas, but he wonders how he can have been so omniscient all the same.

8. LAWRENCE, D.H.
    Sons and Lovers
    (i) pp. 79–82 (Ch. 4); (ii) pp. 101–105
    'He was coming at Christmas ... loved him passionately.'
    William comes home for Christmas. The whole family is a-flutter waiting for him. The children meet him at the station while Mr and Mrs Morel fret at home. He brings expensive presents from London for everyone and is 'such a gentleman'. A very good time is had by all.

9. MOORE, John
    Portrait of Elmbury
    see MARKETS 6

10. STREATFEILD, Noel
    Ballet Shoes
    pp. 62–65 (Ch. 6)
    'Perhaps because they ... a lovely finish to it.'
    The Fossil sisters enjoy Christmas at home with their guardian, Nurse and the boarders. Church, Christmas Dinner, an enormous jig-saw in the afternoon, then a glittering tree and presents. Carol singers complete the day.

11. THOMAS, Dylan
    A Prospect of the Sea
    pp. 97–103 ('Conversation about Christmas')
    'Small Boy. Years and Years ... it is Christmas now.'
    Dylan talks about Christmases when he was a boy, to a young sceptic. It is a kaleidoscope of a Christmas with its food and drink, and Uncles, and snow. It is all one, like a full stocking in the memory.

12. THOMAS, Dylan
    Quite Early One Morning
    pp. 21–25; 27–28 ('Memories of Christmas')
    (Impact Two, pp. 61–62)
    (Young Impact 3, pp. 164–169)
    (Come Down and Startle, pp. 46–48)
    'Our Christmas ... dinner was ended.'; 'And I remember that ... we did that.'

Christmas is a snowball of memories. Dylan thrusts his hand in, and pulls out uncles and aunts who sing, play games and eat a great deal; and a Mr and Mrs Protheroe whose parlour catches fire; and Christmas carols and jelly.

CHRISTMAS – CAROLS

1. BARSTOW, Stan
   The Human Element
   see OLD AGE 3
2. HARDY, Thomas
   Under the Greenwood Tree
   pp. 35–40 (Part 1. Ch. 5)
   'When the expectant stillness ... murmured Mr Spinks.'
   The Mellstock church choir goes carol-singing. One young swain, Dick Dewy, falls in love at first brief sight with the new school-mistress. While the rest of the choir serenade the village, Dick steals off back to the schoolhouse hoping he might see her again.
3. LEE, Laurie
   Cider with Rosie
   (i) pp. 106–110 (Ch. 8, 'Winter and Summer'); (ii) pp. 142–148
   'Later towards Christmas ... gifts for all.'
   The choir go carol-singing on a blowing, snowing evening. They visit all the rich houses, receive money and food, but, except for the Squire, they never see the owners. A lot of singing, walking and fighting.

CHRISTMAS (in) CHURCH

1. STOLZ, Mary
   Ready or Not
   pp. 109–113 (Ch. 8)
   'It was Christmas Eve ... getting sore, sitting here.'
   Julie is at an age to be touched by the magic of the Christmas story. She sits with her brother Ned in a pew, enjoying the uplift afforded by the candles and the quiet. Ned is less impressed.

2. THOMAS, Leslie
   This Time Next Week
   see ACCIDENTS 4

CHRISTMAS – DINNERS

1. CHURCH, Richard
   Over the Bridge
   pp. 114–116 (Ch. 11)
   'Although he was still sleepy ... and the job was done.'
   It is a small, family Christmas. Father spends all morning working on the new bicycles, but he comes in in time to carve the beef with characteristic panache. Christmas pudding, crackers, nuts, and port succeed in their turn, mother retires to bed, and the boys wipe up.
2. DICKENS, Charles
   A Christmas Carol
   pp. 93–97 (Stave 3)
   'Then up rose ... the last of all.'
   Christmas Dinner with the Cratchits: the good cheer, warmth, and excitement as each course is served, and the sincere delight in each other's company.
3. JOYCE, James
   Dubliners
   pp. 193–199 ('The Dead')
   'At the moment Aunt Kate ... white field of Fifteen Acres.'
   Aunts Kate and Julie mount a sumptuous Christmas Dinner for family and friends. Gabriel carves, and is pleasant to everybody. Conversation ebbs and flows, until the company is full, glasses are topped up, and Gabriel prepares to make the customary speech.

CHRISTMAS – GIFTS

1. NAUGHTON, Bill
   The Goalkeeper's Revenge
   (i) pp. 71–77 ('Skinny Nancy'); (ii) pp. 71–78
   'We moved to Lancashire ... "out of sight," she said.'
   Young Bill, with money to spend,

makes frequent visits to a shop fascinating to boys. He joins the Christmas club and saves up for a pair of beautifully-turned Indian Clubs. He hasn't enough money, though, when Christmas comes, so the shopowner makes him a gift of them.

2. STOLZ, Mary
   Ready or Not
   pp. 114–116 (Ch. 8)
   'On Christmas morning ... look at this, Geoff.'
   The exchange of presents. Julie can't find anything from her older sister, Morgan, but she doesn't say anything. The doorbell rings, and their friends from the top floor come in with a big box. It's a kitten for Julie, from Morgan, with love.
   see also: CHRISTMAS (in) CHURCH 1

CHRISTMAS – NATIVITY PLAYS

1. STOLZ, Mary
   Ready or Not
   pp. 100–102 (Ch. 8)
   'Up the iron stairway ... the air with spice.'
   It's almost Christmas. Morgan skips school one afternoon to see her young brother act the part of one of the three kings in a nativity play. Carols are sung, and a few private tears are shed at the simple beauty of it all.

CHRISTMAS – SHOPPING

1. FORSTER, E.M.
   Howard's End
   p. 77 (Ch. 10)
   'Her name remained ... our daily vision.'
   Margaret Schlegel and Mrs Wilcox go Christmas shopping, and Margaret is amazed by the commercialism of Christmas in London.

CHURCH

see also: CHRISTMAS (in) CHURCH;
METHODISTS;

RELIGION;
ROMAN CATHOLICS

CHURCH – FESTIVALS

see also: CHRISTMAS;
EASTER

CHURCH – FESTIVALS

1. BRONTË, Charlotte
   Shirley
   (i) pp. 299–300 (Ch. 16); pp. 301–303 (Ch. 17); (ii) pp. 297–298; 300–302
   'Mr Helstone produced his watch ... God also reform it!'; 'Mr Helstone here spoke ... was none of their managing.'
   It is the day of the school-feast. The Rev. Helstone leads twelve hundred Sunday School children, their teachers, and bands, on the annual parish procession. They confront a procession of Nonconformists in a narrow lane. The Church stands its ground.

CHURCH – SERVICES

1. BALDWIN, James
   Go tell it on the Mountain
   pp. 6–9 (Part 1, 'The Seventh Day'); (Impact Two, pp. 122–124)
   'The Sunday morning service ... moaning filled the church.'
   A Sunday morning service in a packed down-town chapel. It is an act of worship in which everyone in the congregation heartily joins. There is singing, clapping and beating of tambourines. All lend their power sympathetically to any among them who might witness to God's presence in a solo performance of song and dance.
   see also: SIN 1

2. LAWRENCE, D.H.
   The Rainbow
   pp. 109–112 (Ch. 4)
   'They were on the highroad ... both reddening.'
   Anna makes an exhibition of herself

in church. Her cousin's singing is so loud, and his manner is so novel to her that she cannot help snorting with laughter. She tries to disguise it in a cough, but with no great success.

3. LEE, Harper
   To Kill a Mockingbird
   (i) pp. 125–129 (Ch. 12); (ii) pp. 123–126
   'With that, Calpurnia ... and church was over.'
   Calpurnia, the black housekeeper, takes Scout and Jem to her church. They are fascinated particularly by the singing of the hymns, and by the fact that the preacher is no respecter of persons in his pulpit.

4. LLWELLYN, Richard
   How Green was my Valley
   pp. 127–129 (Ch. 15)
   'There is good ... looking in the book.'
   Huw remembers childhood Sundays, when the world seemed beautiful and secure. The family went together, the chapel was always the same, the singing and the organ were wonderful, and Mr Gruffyd was a stirring preacher.

5. SASSOON, Siegfried
   Memoirs of a Fox-hunting Man
   pp. 137–140 (Part 5, Sn. 2)
   'A tenor bell in Hoadley ... old one for wet days.'
   George and his friend Stephen attend the village of which Stephen's father is incumbent. Colonel Hesmon reads the lesson at a brisk pace, and Mr Colwood preaches about giving to the missions overseas. The service fails to uplift George.

6. THOMPSON, Flora
   Lark Rise To Candleford
   (i) pp. 228–231 ('Lark Rise', Ch. 14); (ii) pp. 210–213
   'Clerk Tom' as he was ... had as yet no use.'
   The Hamlet goes dutifully to church. For the children, especially, the long prayers, psalms and sermons are very tedious. The minister preaches drily

about the rightness of the ordained social order; only once does he get 'worked up', and that about Liberalism.

CINEMA

1. BALDWIN, Michael
   Grandad with Snails
   see FEAR 1
2. BARSTOW, Stan
   Joby
   see PUNISHMENT 4
3. NAUGHTON, Bill
   One Small Boy
   pp. 47–49 (Bk. 1, Ch. 6)
   'He pulled open ... we'll miss Dad.'
   Michael goes to the pictures with his friend and big brother. They fight for cramped places in the front stalls, then sit through the advertisements, the news, a Chaplin comedy, and a western, forgetting for a while, their acute discomfort.

CINEMA – FUTURE

1. HUXLEY, Aldous
   Brave New World
   pp. 134–136 (Ch. 11)
   'The House lights ... sudden nervous start.'
   Lenina takes the Savage to a Feely – a film with synchronized sensations, giving the audience as total an experience of events as possible at second hand. Lenina loves it, but the Savage is unnerved by so complete an appeal to the senses.

CIRCUS

1. MACKEN, Walter
   God Made Sunday and Other Stories
   see CRUELTY (to) ANIMALS 3
2. TWAIN, Mark
   The Adventures of Huckleberry Finn
   (i) pp. 158–161 (Ch. 22) (ii) pp. 210–212
   'I went to the circus ... all of my custom, every time.'

Huck crawls under the circus tent, and is enthralled by all that he sees therein; dancing, riding, and clowning. He is taken in, along with everybody else, by a dare-devil drunkard, who turns out to be a stunt horseman.

CITIES

see TOWNS (and) CITIES

CIVIL SERVICE

1. CHURCH, Richard
   Over the Bridge
   see WORK – FIRST DAY 1

CLIMBING

1. CHURCH, Richard
   The White Doe
   see COURAGE 3
2. GRAVES, Robert
   Goodbye to all that
   pp. 57–60 (Ch. 9)
   'I spent a season with George ... hold and join him.'
   Graves goes climbing with Mallory and others in Snowdonia. He explains some climbing terms, and savours some rockface moments of particular danger.
3. MACKEN, Walter
   God made Sunday and Other Stories
   see RESCUE (of) ANIMALS 5

COLLECTING

1. LEE, Laurie
   Cider with Rosie
   (i) pp. 94–96 (Ch. 7, 'Mother'); (ii) pp. 127–130
   'Not until I left ... asked them double.'
   Mrs Lee is an inveterate collector, but her great love is china. She hunts it for miles around, and occasionally manages to get a good piece, even if it is in two pieces and with a load of junk.

COMMUNISM

see also: SOCIALISM

COMMUNISM

1. KOESTLER, Arthur
   Darkness at Noon
   For communism under Stalin in Soviet Russia
   see ARREST; EXECUTION;
   PRISON; TORTURE
2. ORWELL, George
   Animal Farm
   passim.
   Orwell satirises the collapse of revolutionary ideals in Stalinist Russia, and the emergence of naked police power.
3. SHOLOKHOV, Mikhail
   And Quiet Flows the Don
   pp. 135–138 (Part 1, Ch. 9)
   'During the winter evenings ... not to be repulsed.'
   Stockman has gathered about himself a group of local young men who relish his anti-Tsarist literature, and the stimulus of advanced ideas.
4. ibid.
   pp. 397–402 (Part 3, Ch. 3)
   'In Listnitsky's company ... middle of the street.'
   Communist ideas are spreading in the ranks. Listnitsky the company commander canvasses the opinions of a known sympathiser, Lagutin, but is provoked by his 'Bolshevik' ideas to such an extent that he can barely refrain from shooting him down.
5. SHOLOKHOV, Mikhail
   Fierce and Gentle Warriors
   pp. 35–37 (Ch. 5)
   'A couple of days later ... better watch out!'
   Red Army Soldiers search the houses of the village for grain. Mishka's father gives willingly for the cause, but the priest's wife holds back. Mishka reminds her that she has a cellar, thereby informing on her (in

all innocence), to the Soldiers, who find the cellar full of grain.

COMPETITIONS

1. HUGHES, Thomas
   Tom Brown's School Days
   see FIGHTING (by) MEN (with) STICKS
   1
2. LAWRENCE, D.H.
   Sons and Lovers
   (i) pp. 252–254 (Ch. 10); (ii) pp. 309–311
   'When he was twenty-three ... as if it were nothing.'
   A letter arrives by post informing Paul (and his mother) that he has won a painting competition, and that his work has been bought by a local worthy for 20 guineas. Mrs Morel is immoderately proud of her son; her husband reflects upon easy money.
3. TOLKIEN, J.R.R.
   The Hobbit
   (i) pp. 66–81 (Ch. 5); (ii) pp. 66–81
   'Deep down here by the ... we hates it for ever!'
   The Hobbit falls in with the slimy, carnivorous Gollum deep underground, and engages in a gruesome competition with him. Riddles are exchanged for high stakes: escape or death. By dint of borrowed magic, the Hobbit wins his freedom.

COMPETITIONS – RACES

1. HILDICK, E.W.
   Louie's Lot
   pp. 46–57 (Chs. 8, 9)
   'The crowd had been very quiet ... it's the savage dog.'
   A race is held to simulate a milk delivery. The contestants, competing for a job with Louie, are required to deliver milk to a row of imaginary houses. There is a sting in the tail of the race, when each boy has to read a note pushed too far down in a milk bottle.

2. NAUGHTON, Bill
   The Goalkeeper's Revenge
   (i) pp. 20–30 ('Spit Nolan'); (ii) pp. 20–30
   'Spit Nolan was a pal ... dead and gone for ages.'
   The lads of Cotton Pocket race homemade trolleys down a steep hill. The one-lunged Spit Nolan is pitted against Ernie Haddock, on his new works-made trolley. The excitement of the race is turned to tragedy when Spit's trolley collides with a charabanc.

CONCERTS

1. FORSTER, E.M.
   Howard's End
   see MUSIC 1
2. THOMAS, Leslie
   This Time Next Week
   see COURTSHIP – DATING 5

CONDITIONING

1. DE JONG, Meindert
   The Tower by the Sea
   pp. 15–25
   'With the growing kitten ... She had won the battle.'
   The wise old woman teaches the white cat to co-exist with, if not to learn to love, the magpie. She does this by attaching thorns to the magpie's cage. Thus, a leap at the bird is associated in the cat's mind, with a pain in the paws.
2. HUXLEY, Aldous
   Brave New World
   pp. 16–18 (Ch. 1)
   (Themes in Life and Literature, pp. 111–112)
   'I shall begin at the ... the use of that?'
   The Director leads an impressionable group of students round the Central London Hatchery and Conditioning Centre. He explains how biological engineering makes for stability in the World State.

3. ibid.
pp. 27–30 (Ch. 2); (Impact 1, pp. 65–67); ('That once was me,' pp. 32–33)
'Mr Foster was left ... lost in admiration.'
Students are shown how low-caste babies are conditioned by association of books and flowers, with shock and pain, to reject what the Brave New World state requires them to reject.
4. O'BRIEN, Robert C.
Mrs Frisby and the Rats of NIMH
pp. 98–100 (The Maze)
'During the days ... triangle and so on.'
Dr Schulte is experimenting, with certain injections on rats to speed up their learning. Nicodemus one of the rats, explains the learning processes.
5. ibid.
pp. 106–110 (A Lesson in Reading)
'The one important phase ... understood the sign.'
The rats are taught to read – first they recognise letters, then words with pictures. However they are quicker than the humans realise, and can soon read notices in the laboratory.
6. WYNDHAM, John
The Day of the Triffids
pp. 52–53 (Ch. 3)
'I stood there indecisively ... lying on the counter.'
In spite of the catastrophe that has overtaken the world, Bill Mason is too conditioned by an honest upbringing to take food from a shop without paying for it.

CONFESSION

see ROMAN CATHOLICS – CONFESSION

CONFIDENCE-TRICKSTERS

1. TWAIN, Mark
The Adventures of Huckleberry Finn
(i) pp. 141–144 (Ch. 20); (ii) pp. 191–194

'When we got there, there warn't ... to wind a camp-meeting with.'
One of Huck's new passengers turns out to be a confidence-trickster. He persuades a revivalist meeting that he is a reformed pirate, and that if they will take a collection, he will use it to convert Indian Ocean pirates to the true path.

CONFLICT

see DISMISSAL; FAMILY – QUARRELS;
LOVE – DISILLUSIONMENT;
MARRIAGE – QUARRELS; QUARRELS;
REVENGE; RIVALS

CONSCIENCE

1. ALCOTT, Lousia M.
Little Women
see ICE-SKATING – ACCIDENTS 1
2. CHAPLIN, Sid
The Leaping Lad and other Stories
pp. 138–142 ('Bread')
'And now it was over ... himself from bread.'
Danny listens to the Rev. MacPherson's sermon, and it stirs his conscience. He is alive, but Joe, his pit marrer, a friend from whom he concealed his last piece of bread, is dead.
3. DU MAURIER, Daphne
Jamaica Inn
see GHOSTS 2
4. GOLDING, William
Lord of the Flies
(i) pp. 192–195 (Ch. 10); (ii) pp. 171–175
'At last Ralph ... "We left early".'
Ralph, Piggy, Sam and Eric try to justify, and then to forget the part they have all played in killing Simon. It is on their collective conscience, but they do not wish to talk about it. The subject is taboo.
5. HUGHES, Thomas
Tom Brown's Schooldays
see PRAYER 2
6. JOYCE, James

A Portrait of the Artist as a Young Man
pp. 111–113; 115–116 (Ch. 3)
'As he walked home ... howling into hell.'; 'Every word of it was ... condensed within his brain.'
Stephen proves to be very fertile ground for the preacher's words. He has lain with prostitutes. He reproaches himself with his foulness, and reflects upon how near he is to hell.

7. ibid.
pp. 128–130 (Ch. 3)
'The second pain which will ... they cannot evade.'
The preacher describes the torments that will be suffered by those with guilty consciences, in the everlasting fires of hell. Here, in all its relentlessness, is the Jesuit definition of sin and conscience.

8. ibid.
see ROMAN CATHOLICS – CONFESSION 1

9. NESBIT, E.
The Railway Children
see; ACCIDENTS (at) HOME 2

CONSCIENTIOUS OBJECTION

see FIRST WORLD WAR – CONSCIENTIOUS OBJECTION

CORPORAL PUNISHMENT

see PUNISHMENT – CORPORAL

COUNTRY – LIFE

see also: FARMING

COUNTRY – LIFE

1. HARDY, Thomas
Far from the Madding Crowd
passim.
Farming life in Dorset at the end of the nineteenth century.

2. HARDY, Thomas
Under the Greenwood Tree

passim.
A Dorset village, its choir, its courtly rituals, its English seasons.

3. LEE, Laurie
Cider with Rosie
passim.
Life in a Gloucestershire village between the wars.

4. ibid.
(i) pp. 166–167 (Ch. 13, 'Last Days');
(ii) pp. 216–217
'The last days ... as lusty as ever.'
Lee looks back over the years covered by the book – from the peaceful rural horse-drawn days to the age of the motor-car.

5. 'MISS READ'
Village School
passim.
Village life from the benevolent point of view of the spinster school mistress. A year of fêtes, and jumble sales, snow and unseasonal heat.

6. THOMPSON, Flora
Lark Rise to Candleford
passim
A portrait of life in an Oxfordshire hamlet in the 1880's.

COUNTRYSIDE

see LANDSCAPE

COURAGE

see also: CHALLENGES;
DARING;
DETERMINATION

COURAGE

1. BATES, H.E.
The Purple Plain
pp. 125–131 (Ch. 14)
'They began to walk ... It can't talk.'
Forrester, carrying the injured Carrington on his back, and Blore, set out to walk along the dry river bed in Burma where their plane has crashed. Forrester tries not to think about the difficulties of the walk, and is full of

ideas for improving their lot, and of good humour.

2. ibid.
pp. 144–151 (Ch. 15)
'It was four o'clock ... You'll beat us yet.'
Forrester now has Blore with a broken rib to cope with, as well as Carrington, but he refuses to be depressed or disheartened. He keeps up the joking, with Carrington, and organises the two men to carry on with their walk.

3. CHURCH, Richard
The White Doe
pp. 175–180 (Chs. 22, 23)
'Tom, suddenly calm ... some unlucky chance.'
Tom's enemy, Harold Sims, has fallen over the edge of a cliff. Tom forgets his enmity and climbs down to the ledge where Harold is held up by a hawthorn bush.

4. COOKSON, Catherine
The Nipper
pp. 118–124 (Ch. 9)
'Sandy felt the blood ... and talk and argue.'
Sandy and Stan overhear that Stan's father plans to blow up the mine-owner's house. Stan defends his father, but Sandy tries everything he can to warn the potential victims.

5. ibid.
see HORSES – RIDING 1

6. DE JONG, Meindert
The Wheel on the School
see FRIENDS 2

7. ibid.
(i) pp. 69–74 (Ch. 6); (ii) pp. 70–74
'Aw you clumsy fathead ... you were so strong.'
Jella is trying to retrieve a wheel from the canal when one of the pieces of wood he is hanging from comes away. Eelka remembers a rope nearby and hauls his friend to safety. Usually the slow one of the gang, he has proved his strength.

8. LLWELLYN, Richard

How Green was my Valley
see LOST (in) MOUNTAINS 1

9. MACKEN, Walter
God Made Sunday and Other Stories
see SUPERSTITION 9

10. ibid.
see RESCUE (of) ANIMALS 5

11. MORROW, Honoré
The Splendid Journey
see EXPEDITIONS 5

12. NESBIT, E.
The Railway Children
(i) pp. 90–99 (Ch. 6); (ii) pp. 96–113
'The Russian gentleman ... rather heartless.'
On a search for wild cherries, the children see a landslide, which blocks the railway line. Realising a train is due, they tear up the girls' red flannel petticoats to signal with, and a serious accident is avoided.

13. ibid.
see FIRE 2

14. SASSOON, Siegfried
Memoirs of an Infantry Officer
pp. 63–68 (Part 4, Sn. 3)
'There wasn't much wire ... worrying about souvenirs now.'
One of Sherston's colleagues is hit in an attack that he is leading. He is incensed. With a primed Mills bomb in each hand, he rushes on the enemy trench, throws his bombs, and finds himself the sole occupant of a trench from which his lone action has scared some forty Germans.

15. SPERRY, Armstrong
The Boy who was afraid
pp. 33–38 (Ch. 3)
'Mafatu decided that ... the jungle stillness.'
Mafatu, shipwrecked on an apparently uninhabited island, finds a man-made trail, which leads him to a clearing in the jungle dominated by huge idols. It is the Sacred Place of a cannibal tribe. Overcoming his fear, he steals a spear from the sacred platform, and feels he has won a great victory over himself.

16. ibid.
    see SHARKS 10
17. ibid.
    pp. 52–54 (Ch. 4)
    'This day ... return to Hikueru.'
    Mafatu is surprised by a wild boar,
    and kills it as it charges him. He
    cooks the meat, and makes a necklace
    of its teeth, to prove he has killed it.
18. ibid.
    see SEA – DIVING 1
19. STEINBECK, John
    The Grapes of Wrath
    (i) pp. 195–199 (Ch. 18); (ii) pp.
    207–210
    'On the back of the truck ... I'm
    awful tar'd.'
    Ma gets the truck through the Cus-
    toms Post and into California without
    an inspection by showing the Officer
    Granma, who she says is sick. They
    continue to drive all night, and are
    overjoyed to see the green fields at
    dawn. Only then does Ma reveal that
    Granma died before the border.
20. WRIGHT, Richard
    Black Boy
    pp. 13–15 (Ch. 1)
    'One evening my mother ... streets of
    Memphis.'
    His mother forces Richard out on to
    the street to face up to a gang of boys
    who have beaten and robbed him. She
    arms him with a stick, and a desperate
    courage, with which to win freedom
    from fear, and his independence.

COURTSHIP

see also: LOVE;
MARRIAGE;
WEDDINGS

COURTSHIP

1. AUSTEN, Jane
   Pride and Prejudice
   (i) pp. 17–19 (Ch. 6); (ii) pp. 19–21
   'The ladies of Longbourn ... in this
   way yourself.'
   The growing attachment of Jane and
   Mr Bingley is observed by all those
   around them. Elizabeth and her
   friend Charlotte discuss how Jane
   should go about securing his affections.
2. BARSTOW, Stan
   The Human Element
   see DANCES 2;
   HUMILIATION 1
3. DEFOE, Daniel
   Moll Flanders
   see WOMEN – RIGHTS 1
4. ibid.
   (i) pp. 66–72; (ii) pp. 83–89
   'The captain's lady, in short, ... of
   being ill-used afterwards.'
   An agreeable, and not impecunious
   gentleman is secured as a husband.
   He has been artfully persuaded that
   Moll is worth far more than she is.
   Only when they are married, does
   Moll acquaint him with the truth.
5. DURRELL, Gerald
   My Family and Other Animals
   pp. 86–90 (Part 1, Ch. 6)
   'I'm very sorrys to haves ... fearful
   enough', said Larry.'
   Margo is courted by a boastful Turk.
   The rest of the family is put off him
   from the first; and Margo herself is
   disenchanted by his inept over-acting,
   when he takes her (and Mrs Durrell)
   to the cinema.
6. FORESTER, C.S.
   The General
   see SOCIAL CLASS – SNOBBERY 6
7. HARDY, Thomas
   Far from the Madding Crowd
   see SHOWING OFF 3
8. HARDY, Thomas
   Under the Greenwood Tree
   pp. 67–69 (Part 1, Ch. 9)
   'The early days of the year ... and
   turned away.'
   Dick pays his first call on Fanny Day,
   the young lady of his dreams. His
   excuse for calling is that he has to
   return a lost handkerchief. He fulfils
   this obligation but has not self-confidence enough to press home his
   advantage.

9. HUXLEY, Aldous
Brave New World
pp. 149–152 (Ch. 13)
'The bell rang ... he had been mistaken.'
The Savage professes his love for Lenina, and he explains to her that where he comes from, some act of chivalry would be required of him, before he could win her. But in the Brave New World, chivalry is dead. Lenina responds to his profession by undressing.

10. JAMES, Henry
Washington Square
pp. 50–53 (Ch. 10)
'What Morris had told Catherine ... the fountain in Washington Square.'
Catherine is taken by surprise when Morris declares his love so soon, but accepts it as a 'priceless treasure'. She remembers, however, her duty to her father, but cannot believe he will disapprove.

11. LAWRENCE, D.H.
Sons and Lovers
(i) pp. 9–11 (Ch. 1); (ii) pp. 16–19
'When she was twenty-three ... she was very happy.'
The sensitive, subdued Gertrude Coppard meets the boyish miner Walter Morel, at a Christmas party. They have little in common beside the warmth of this first meeting.
see also: MARRIAGE –
DISILLUSIONMENT 2

12. ibid.
see SHOWING-OFF 5

13. LEE, Laurie
Cider with Rosie
(i) pp. 172–175 (Ch. 13, 'Last Days');
(ii) pp. 224–228
'Now the last days ... absence of us entirely.'
Laurie's half-sisters all acquire young men, who spend evenings with them, terminating in a rota of long good nights; go on an unsuccessful picnic; and in one case, have a violent argument with Mother.

14. SALINGER, J.D.
The Catcher in the Rye
pp. 81–84 (Ch. 11)
'The way I met her ... it just about kills you.'
The girl next door. Holden falls in a kind of love with her. They play checkers on the porch and hold hands in the cinema.

15. THACKERAY, William
Vanity Fair
(i) pp. 102–105 (Ch. 12); (ii) pp. 146–148
'We must now take leave ... good deal of easy resignation.'
Thackeray looks, with an ironic eye, on the attractions that gentle, demure young ladies have for the opposite sex, and the judgements other women make upon them. George's sisters do not understand his love for Amelia.

16. THOMPSON, Flora
Lark Rise to Candleford
(i) pp. 176–179 (Ch. 10, 'Lark Rise');
(ii) pp. 166–169
'With the girls away ... sight was too familiar.'
With their girlfriends away in service for fifty weeks of the year, the young men of the hamlet must either pine, or seek out a substitute among the local dairy maids, or underservants. When the children do not have young lovers to watch and harry, they follow the fortunes of a patient, middle-aged pair, Chokey and Bess.

17. ibid.
(i) pp. 592–598 (Ch. 38, 'Candleford Green'); (ii) pp. 517–522
'She went in and out ... so I gathered.'
Laura meets a young game-keeper on her post round, and subsequently sees him every day. She supposes they are sweethearts, but doesn't really like him as he is too self-centred. The affair comes to an abrupt end, when he asks her directly 'You are my girl, aren't you?'

18. WATERHOUSE, Keith
Billy Liar
pp. 54–62 (Ch. 4)

'The point about ... oranges," I said.'
Billy is engaged to Barbara, but
dislikes everything about her. When
they meet they go through an
elaborate pretence of being in love,
and planning for the future, but
occasionally the true situation
becomes apparent.

19: WELLS, H.G.
The History of Mr Polly
pp. 84–94 (Ch. 5, Part 5)
'And then it happened ... from slight
abrasions.'
Polly falls in courtly love with a
pretty schoolgirl who sits remotely on
the school wall and listens raptly to
his chivalrous badinage. His hopes of
her are cruelly dashed when it
becomes plain that she is enjoying a
magnificent joke at his expense.

COURTSHIP – DATING

1. BARSTOW, Stan
'A Kind of Loving
pp. 49–55 (Part 1, Ch. 2, Sn. 3)
'But course I do, and now here ...
think about you walking.'
It's the evening of Vic's first date
with Ingrid. They go to the pictures
together. Vic is self-conscious about
doing the right thing. They have a
kiss in the back row, nothing improper. He misses his chance to kiss her
goodnight, at her gate, but things are
very promising.

2. BRAINE, John
Room at the Top
pp. 70–74 (Ch. 8)
'Waiting for Susan ... for matches
any more.'
An evening at the ballet. Joe is on his
best behaviour, because Susan has
more class than the usual run of his
escorts. He is charmed by her, and
she is as impressed as he could have
wished, by his urbanity.

3. STOLZ, Mary
Ready or Not
pp. 80–82 (Ch. 6)

'Rumble of music and voices ... 'Oh,
I'd love.'
Verna arranges a blind date: she pairs
Morgan with a gangling youth who
can't dance, but who can dive, and
who talks about diving ad nauseam.
When Morgan does get to dance, it is
with Pete, who can dance, and doesn't
talk about it.

4. THOMAS, Leslie
This Time Next Week
pp. 153–157 (Ch. 14)
'Boz and I, and some ... mud patch
towards the dormitory.'
Leslie makes a date with Helen, and a
blind date for Frank, with her friend.
They sell their crystal radio set to
finance the venture. But the girls
don't turn up, so the boys blow five
and twopence in a café, and drown
their sorrows in tea.

5. ibid.
pp. 164–169 (Ch. 15); (Conflict 2, pp.
11–15)
'Some evenings in a week ... wasn't it
murder with women.'
An evening of exquisite anxiety.
Leslie takes a young lady from Sur-
biton to an Albert Hall concert. She
is scathing about the music, and
demanding in a way that has Leslie
nervously counting his pennies. But
she almost pays for her gin and tonic
when she calls him darling.

COURTSHIP – ENGAGEMENT

1. BARSTOW, Stan
A Kind of Loving
pp. 199–203 (Part 2, Ch. 5, Sn. 1);
(Conflict 1, pp. 66–70)
'I watch the water ... go and get my
coat.'
Vic breaks the news to his parents
that he is going to marry a local girl.
His mother quickly tumbles to it that
it's a 'forced do', and she lets her
annoyance and disappointment spill
out. Vic's father is more understanding. He placates his wife.

2. LAWRENCE, D.H.
Sons and Lovers
(i) pp. 114–120 (Ch. 6); (ii) pp. 144–151
'William was engaged ... any sort of conclusion.'
William brings Gyp, his fiancée, home to meet his parents. Everyone defers to this refined young lady from London. William tires of her airs, and of her shallowness, but he loves her all the same.

COURTSHIP – PROPOSALS (of) MARRIAGE

1. ACHEBE, Chinua
Things fall apart
see MARRIAGE – ARRANGED 1
2. AUSTEN, Jane
Emma
pp. 77–82 (Ch. 7)
'The very day of Mr Elton's ... the idea of Mr Elton.'
Harriet has received a proposal of marriage from a farmer. She would like to accept, but Emma skilfully persuades her against it on the grounds of social standing. She has other plans for Harriet.
3. AUSTEN, Jane
Pride and Prejudice
(i) pp. 95–100 (Ch. 19); (ii) pp. 91–96
'The next day opened ... coquetry of an elegant female.'
The ridiculous Mr Collins proposes to Elizabeth, making much of the social and financial advantages of the match. He will not believe that her refusal is other than coquetry.
4. BRONTË, Charlotte
Jane Eyre
(i) pp. 300–309 (Ch. 23); (ii) pp. 247–254
'The moth roamed away ... good night my darling." '
Jane believes Mr Rochester is about to marry Blanche Ingram, as he talks to her about his marriage. When at last, he ceases his pretence, and pro-

poses marriage to her, she is only with difficulty persuaded of his earnestness. Soon however the situation is clarified, and both are ecstatic.
5. BUTLER, Samuel
The Way of all Flesh
pp. 36–40 (Ch. 11)
'The next morning ... was to accept.'
The newly-ordained Theobald Pontifex is snared by Mr and Mrs Allaby as a suitor for one of their many unmarried daughters. After some months, Theobald proposes by letter to Christina, in the belief that he does so of his own free will.
6. DICKENS, Charles
Bleak House
(i) pp. 114–116 (Ch. 9); (ii) pp. 114–116
'You wouldn't allow me ... passed the door.' •
Mr Guppy, a somewhat naïve solicitor's clerk, makes a proposal of marriage to Esther, having seen her once, and been impressed by her looks. He makes it sound like a commercial proposition.
7. ibid.
(i) pp. 791–794 (Ch. 64); (ii) pp. 791–794
'He was embarrassed ... we should get out.'
Having once withdrawn his proposal, Mr Guppy tries once again to make an impression on Esther. He is accompanied by his mother and his friend, who are both astonished, and the former annoyed, by her refusal.
8. DICKENS, Charles
David Copperfield
pp. 542–550 (Ch. 33)
'I have set all this ... and I were engaged.'
David Copperfield is invited to his idolised Dora's birthday celebrations. He spends the day in a state of bliss, and finishes it by declaring his love. They are immediately engaged.
9. HARDY, Thomas
Far from the Madding Crowd
(i) pp. 30–36 (Ch. 4); (ii) pp. 36–42

'Bathsheba was out ... ask you no more.'

Gabriel Oak is in love with Bathsheba Everdene. He visits her aunt's cottage to ask for her hand in marriage. She plays hot and cold for a while, then, when Gabriel paints the picture of his rural idyll, to tempt her, she excuses herself on a number of disqualifying grounds.

10. LAWRENCE, D.H.
The Rainbow
see JEALOUSY 7

11. LAWRENCE, D.H.
The Virgin and the Gipsy
pp. 47–50 (Part 5)
'The next day, at the party ... to single her out.'

One of her regular escorts, Leo Wetherall suddenly suggests that he and Yvette should become engaged. Yvette is so astounded that she all but laughs. She has admired the manliness of the gipsy. Leo is a mere 'house-dog' in comparison, whose suit is unthinkable.

12. MANSFIELD, Katherine
The Garden Party
pp. 120–132 ('Mr and Mrs Dove')
'Of course he knew – no man better – ... came slowly across the lawn.'

Hoping against hope, Reginald nerves himself to propose to the object of his courtly love, the wealthy talented Anne Proctor. She finds his suggestion more laughable than inspiring, but she is not prepared for his evident dejection. This arouses her sympathy and conscience.

13. PEYTON, K.M.
Flambards
(i) pp. 174–182 (Ch. 13); (ii) pp. 212–222
'William came with some ... "It's a splendid horse." '

Christina is with William at the Hunt Ball. In the conservatory, Mark takes advantage of William's momentary absence, to propose marriage. He does it roughly and unfeelingly. Christina tells William what has

happened, and he, no less ineptly in some ways, but palpably sincere, makes a counter-proposal, which is accepted.

14. TATE, Joan
Clipper
pp. 5–10 (Ch. 1)
"Senior' he said ... two of us at it.'

Clee and Nibs don't discuss a great deal, so she is somewhat surprised when he suddenly asks her mother if they can get married. The request is accepted quite calmly, and Clee and Nibs settle the matter in very few words, later.

15. TROLLOPE, Anthony
Barchester Towers
pp. 352–357 (Ch. 40)
' "That which has made them ... the path to the house.'

The odious Mr Slope contrives to lead Eleanor into the shrubbery, where ignoring her coldness, he proposes to her. She is disgusted, and boxes him on the ear. He is mortified.

16. WATERHOUSE, Keith
Billy Liar
pp. 47–50 (Ch. 3)
'Arthur slumped himself ... gum-chewing nonchalance.'

Billy makes a date with Rita who serves in a coffee bar. They exchange clichés over the counter, and he suddenly slips an engagement ring across to her. The moment passes quickly, and she returns to her banter with the customers.

17. WELLS, H.G.
The History of Mr Polly
pp. 101–105 (Ch. 6, Part 2)
'When, after imperceptible ... said Miriam firmly.'

Polly finds himself sitting on a park bench with his cousin Miriam. He thinks aloud about himself and her, man and wife, with a shop and a cat; and he finds he has proposed marriage to her.

18. WELLS, H.G.
Kipps
pp. 180–183 (Bk. 2, Ch. 3, Sn. 2)

'Helen sat fearlessly ... obscurity of their descent.'

Kipps, and the goddess Miss Walsingham, are alone. He has so much on his mind and so much to say, but he is awkward, almost apologetic, in his approaches. It is she who has to coax him to his question.

19. ibid.
pp. 301–304 (Bk. 2, Ch. 8, Sn. 5)
'The basement door opened ... Artie, on the stairs.'

Since his first proposal, to Miss Walsingham, Kipps has learnt a lot about himself. His proposal to Ann, a desperately sincere plea, is an acceptance of how things are, not of how they might be.

COUSINS

see also: FAMILY;
RELATIVES

COUSINS

1. WELLS, H.G.
The History of Mr Polly
pp. 75–81 (Ch. 5, Parts 2, 3)
'The street was a little ... 'Right-o' said Mr Polly.'

Polly visits his Larkins cousins on his bicycle. He amuses them and appreciates being the centre of attention in female company. Half-seriously, he weighs up the possibility of marrying one of the Larkins 'gals'.

COWARDICE

1. CRANE, Stephen
The Red Badge of Courage
pp. 50–52 (Ch. 6)
'The youth turned ... there was a race.'

The youth has imagined that the enemy would not return after their first repulse. When they do, and the youth sees some of his comrades running from the line, all his fears are recollected, and he runs too.

2. SALINGER, J.D.
The Catcher in the Rye
pp. 93–95 (Ch. 13)
'You wouldn't even have ... I'm not kidding myself.'

Holden reflects on his 'yellowness'. He has lost his gloves. He imagines himself confronting the school-mate who had stolen them, and being too yellow to challenge him.

3. WRIGHT, Richard
Black Boy
see COURAGE 21

CRABS

1. DURRELL, Gerald
Birds, Beasts, and Relatives
pp. 54–55 (Part 2, 'The Bay of Olives')
'It was in this bay ... perched on top of it.'

Gerald observes the means by which the spider crab camouflages itself. It secretes a glue with which it attaches seaweed to its shell. Gerald scrubs one clean and places it in a pool innocent of seaweed, and awaits events.

CREATION

1. ADAMS, Richard
Watership Down
pp. 37–40 (Ch. 6)
'Long ago, Frith made ... can never be destroyed.'

The Creation story, as seen through rabbit eyes. All animals were created equal, and friendly to each other, but the rabbits annoyed the Creator. He bestowed gifts on the others, to help them hunt rabbits, but relented and gave rabbits the skill to escape.

CRICKET

1. GRIMBLE, Sir Arthur
A Pattern of Islands
pp. 27–32 (Ch. 2)
'The beginnings of cricket ... beyond all argument.'

The game according to the Polynesians. It began as an extension of island rivalries, and developed as an expression of Gilbertese good humour. Arther is called up to serve as a coach.

2. LEE, Laurie
   Cider with Rosie
   (i) pp. 134–135 (Ch. 10, 'The Uncles'); (ii) pp. 178–179
   'Uncle Sid's story ... on occasions.'
   Laurie's Uncle Sid was a champion cricketer – he was at his prime during the Boer War, where he worked havoc among the officers.

3. SASSOON, Siegfried
   Memoirs of a Fox-Hunting Man
   pp. 60–63; 72–74 (Part 2, Sn. 3)
   'Butley had lost ... thinks it hasn't done badly.'; 'Next moment I was ... Flower Show Match.'
   George plays for the Butley eleven against the village of Rotherden. It is a close-fought match, and its climax, its winning run, is authored by George himself.

CRIME

see also: CONFIDENCE-TRICKSTERS;
FORGERY;
HIGHWAYMEN; KIDNAPPING;
KILLING; PICKPOCKETS;
ROBBERY; SHOPLIFTING;
SMUGGLING; STEALING

CRIME

1. ALLEN, Walter
   All in a Lifetime
   pp. 223–226 (Ch. 15)
   'It was Tom who was ... cross to be borne.'
   Tom, Billy's son has grown into a regular sponger and confidence trickster. Billy can't imagine how it can have happened. Tom merely smiles.

2. DEFOE, Daniel
   Moll Flanders
   see SHOPLIFTING 3

3. ibid.
   see STEALING 1

4. ibid.
   see SHOPLIFTING 4

5. DICKENS, Charles
   Great Expectations
   (i) pp. 387–390 (Ch. 42); (ii) pp. 332–334
   'Dear boy, and ... afore mentioned.'
   Abel Magwitch gives an account to Pip and Herbert of his life as a 'warmint', of his hard, predisposing background, his numerous jail-sentences, and his ill-use at the clean hands of a smooth operator.

CRIME – DETECTION

1. ELIOT, George
   Silas Marner
   pp. 68–71 (Ch. 8)
   'The next morning ... who remembered it.'
   Silas's gold has been stolen, a tinder box has been found, mention has been made of a pedlar with a tinder box, and immediately a number of people remember suspicious circumstances concerning this pedlar. The story grows.

2. TOWNSEND, John Rowe
   Gumble's Yard
   pp. 67–72 (Chs. 6, 7)
   'We had wandered some distance ... then what would happen?'
   Kevin and Dick watch two men piling packing cases in an empty house. When the men have gone, they hide one of the cases in the interest of crime detection. Later, Kevin sees the same two men loading the cases on to a canal barge.

3. TOWNSEND, John Rowe
   The Intruder
   pp. 93–96 (Ch. 16); 100–106 (Ch. 18)
   'Peter felt silly ... the end cottage.'; 'There was nothing ... were so weak.'
   Arnold suspects that the man who has come to live at his house, claiming to be a relative, is lying and pursuing

possibly criminal ends. He follows him, by train and bus to his home, a derelict cottage in a city, but is there trapped by the man.

CRIME – JUVENILE

see also: ASSAULT (by) GANGS – YOUTHS;
GANGS – YOUTHS;
KILLING (by) GANGS – YOUTHS;
VANDALISM

CRIME – JUVENILE

1. BRAITHWAITE, E.R.
   To Sir with Love
   pp. 111–120 (Ch. 15)
   'One morning in October ... for nearly six hours each day.'
   One of Braithwaite's pupils knifes a boy by accident, out of school. Braithwaite sees the boy's parents and attends the juvenile court. The cases he hears there compel him to appraise his influence on the lives of the young people he teaches.
2. LEE, Laurie
   Cider with Rosie
   see PUNISHMENT 13

CRUELTY

see also: HATRED

CRUELTY (to) ANIMALS

1. LONDON, Jack
   The Call of the Wild
   see DOGS – TRAINING 1
2. ibid.
   pp. 62–66 (Ch. 5)
   'From every hill slope ... Buck licked his hand.'
   The dog-team has been grossly overworked and mismanaged. When the feckless drivers announce their intention to press on, John Thornton tries to dissuade them. Buck can go no further. He lies down and suffers a rain of blows for his obstinacy.

Thornton saves him from being beaten to death.
3. MACKEN, Walter
   God made Sunday and Other Stories
   pp. 195–206 ('The Lion')
   'Jim stood patiently ... said the Inspector.'
   Jim takes pity on a mangy lion in the circus, who is tormented by his keeper. Jim lets the lion out, intending to lead him to freedom. But the authorities put a stop to his plans – and to the keeper's cruelty.
4. SEWELL, Anna
   Black Beauty
   pp. 44–46 (Ch. 8)
   'The next time ... I was sold again.'
   Ginger suffers the pain of a sharp bit and a very tight bearing rein. Her discomfort prevents her doing her best, and she is then punished in an attempt to force her on.
5. ibid.
   see FASHION 1
6. STEINBECK, John
   The Red Pony
   see BOREDOM 7
7. WRIGHT, Richard
   Black Boy
   pp. 8–11 (Ch. 1)
   'One morning my brother ... never see another kitten.'
   Richard wilfully hangs a kitten to revenge himself on his father. His mother teaches him a lesson and brings home to him the full force of what he has done, by having him bury the corpse in the night.

CRUELTY (in) WAR

1. FORESTER, C.S.
   The Gun
   (i) pp. 124–125 (Ch. 13); 135–136 (Ch. 14); (ii) pp. 105–106; 115–116
   'So it was done ... he had to govern.';
   'That was not the only ... at a stroke.'
   Having captured Leon, O'Neill, the guerilla leader, has no mercy on those accused of being traitors – there are

no trials, only executions. The war and its strain have brought out a terrible vein of cruelty in O'Neill.

CUNNING

see INGENUITY

CUSTOMS

see BIRTHDAYS; CELEBRATIONS;
CHRISTMAS; COURTSHIP;
EASTER; ETIQUETTE;
FUNERALS; RELIGION – RITES;
WEDDINGS

CYCLING

1. CHURCH, Richard
   Over the Bridge
   pp. 32–33 (Ch. 3)
   'It was impossible ... displayed on a greasy duster.'
   Father is an enthusiastic cyclist. He keeps his pampered machine in a big shed in the garden, and reads avidly about all the latest machines.
2. ibid.
   pp. 123–126 (Ch. 11)
   'Leaving the park, by an eastern ... over Battersea Bridge.'
   It is Boxing Day, and Father takes his family out on the new tandems. He has relished this prospect for so long, that he overdoes it. The boys, tired and cold, fall off, and Mother gives Father publicly a piece of her mind.
3. THOMPSON, Flora
   Lark Rise to Candleford
   (i) pp. 280–281 ('Over to Candleford' Ch. 16); (ii) p. 255
   'But although it was ... would have said.'
   Bicycles make their first appearance in Lark Rise, and are considered fast and dangerous. Nobody believes they are more than a passing craze.
4. ibid.
   pp. 543–546 (Ch. 35, 'Candleford Green'); (ii) pp. 476–478

'The sound of a bicycle ... the bicycle bell.'
Cycling at first is the pastime of smart young men from the towns, but it soon spreads, although considered 'unwomanly' for some time. Even women take it up finally, with a liberating effect upon their clothes.

DANCES

see also: PARTIES

DANCES

1. AUSTEN, Jane
   Emma
   pp. 322–325 (Ch. 38)
   'Emma could hardly understand ... very good-natured, I declare.'
   The Westons hold a dance for the 'society' of Highbury. It is difficult to please everyone with their partners, and Harriet Smith is slighted by Mr Elton.
2. BARSTOW, Stan
   The Human Element
   pp. 126–128; 131–132 ('The Desperadoes')
   'They edged their way through ... all over your feet.'; 'They sat in silence ... a bit too much.'
   Vince meets at a dance, the girl he had met earlier, and been impressed by, in the street. He dances stylishly with her, tells her about himself, and steers her outside when the hall gets too hot.
3. GROSSMITH, George and Weedon
   The Diary of a Nobody
   (i) pp. 39–46 (Chap. 4); (ii) pp. 65–74
   'Perfectly astounded ... first consulted Carrie.'
   Mr Pooter and Carrie are invited to the Lord Mayor's Ball at the Mansion House. The honour of the invitation is diminished when, certain, rather unfashionable acquaintances are found to be there. The Pooters go for a burton in the Waltz.

4. MANNING, Olivia
The Play Room
pp. 116–120 (Sn. 2, Ch. 3)
'The Band started up ... had treated her.'
Laura and Vicky go for the first time to a factory-dance in a working-class area of the town. The noise and the freedom amaze Laura who throws herself into the dancing with enthusiasm.

5. MANSFIELD, Katherine
The Garden Party
pp. 192–202 ('Her first ball')
'Exactly when the ball ... even recognize him again.'
The country cousin is taken to her first ball. Leila is diffident, but determined in her shy way, to enjoy herself, and learn the ropes. She dances dutifully with all the men who sign her card, she is rather put out by a worldly wise, fat man, but she doesn't let him have the last word.

6. STOLZ, Mary
Ready or Not
see COURTSHIP – DATING 3

DARING

see also: CHALLENGES;
COURAGE

DARING

1. KNOWLES, John
A Separate Peace
pp. 11–15 (Ch. 1)
'The tree was tremendous ... "You're goofy!" '
To cement their friendship, Phineas proposes to Gene that they, and any other who dares, should jump into the river from a tall tree. Gene feels honour-bound to comply, but no-one else takes up the challenge.

2. ibid.
see SWIMMING 4

3. SOUTHALL, Ivan
Josh
pp. 70–77 (Ch. 17)

'Josh, what have you done? ... on his back, exhausted.'
No sooner has Josh been kind to the uncomely Laura, than she declares she will jump off the railway bridge into the creek. Josh is powerless to stop her. He knows she is trying to prove something to him – and she does.

4. SPERRY, Armstrong
The Boy who was afraid
pp. 10–12 (Ch. 1)
'The boys disappeared ... and followed.'
Mafatu is mocked by the other boys of his Polynesian tribe because he is afraid of the sea. He decides that he must prove himself to them, so he leaves his island in a canoe to brave the sea.

DARKNESS

see FEAR (of) DARKNESS

DATING

see COURTSHIP – DATING

DAWN

see also: MORNING

DAWN

1. GREENWOOD, Walter
Love on the Dole
pp. 13–15 (Part 1, Ch. 2)
'5.30 A.M. ... over the Two Cities.'
Salford, first thing in the morning. Blind Joe Riley wakes up the Hardcastles at No. 19, and sneers at the policeman's easy money.

2. HEMINGWAY, Ernest
The Old Man and the Sea
see SEA 2

3. HILDICK, E.W.
Louie's Lot
see WORK – FIRST DAY 2

4. HINES, Barry
A Kestrel for a Knave

57

(i) pp. 9–13; (ii) pp. 7–10
'There were no curtains ... crossed the road.'
Billy's sleep is rudely interrupted. When his miner brother has gone, he gets up, and out of the house in the half-light. Jud has robbed him of both his breakfast, and his bike. He does not feel well-disposed to the grey-wash world.

5. LESSING, Doris
    The Grass is Singing
    pp. 237–239 (Ch. 11)
    'She got out of bed ... heat and haze and light.'
    Dawn over Rhodesia. It is compounded of creeping colour, a marvellous peace, of shrilling birds and cicadas, of spreading red, and of the sudden onset of heat.

6. STEINBECK, John
    The Pearl
    pp. 1–4 (Ch. 1)
    'Kino awakened ... that was conversation.'
    Dawn in a village on the Gulf of Mexico – the scene, and the activities of one household are described.

7. THOMPSON, Flora
    Lark Rise to Candleford
    see FARMING – HARVEST 2

8. TWAIN, Mark
    The Adventures of Tom Sawyer
    (i) pp. 101–103 (Ch. 14); (ii) pp. 96–97
    'When Tom awoke ... fluttering upon the scene.'
    Dawn comes up over the island where Tom and his friends are sleeping in the open. Tom watches insects going about their business, and other animals minding the business of these 'intruders'.

DAYDREAMS

1. BARSTOW, Stan
    Joby
    pp. 42–44 (Ch. 3)
    'The Fashists had gone ... thinking about something.'

Joby is at the barber's. He is so busy repelling the 'Fashists' on the school playground, and impressing the headmaster, and Elsa Laedeker, with his gallantry, that he is unaware of the barber's questions.

2. DE JONG, Meindert
    The Wheel on the School
    (i) pp. 43–46 (Ch. 5); (ii) pp. 46–49
    'It seemed that even two ... do things alone.'
    Pier and Dirk are looking for spare wagon wheels – Pier, left to himself, quickly tires, and sits down. His imagination takes over, and he pretends he has no legs, like a man in the village. The feeling is so real he is quite scared, and very relieved when Dirk reappears.

3. NAUGHTON, Bill
    Late Night on Watling Street
    pp. 70–75 ('Tom's Sister')
    'One evening, about ... fastening itself to me.'
    Tom catches his workmate's interest, as they work together, late, at their machines, by talking to him about his sister, Mary. His work-mate looks forward to meeting her, and buys himself a new suit for the occasion. Then, one evening, Tom tells him he does not have a sister after all.

4. TWAIN, Mark
    The Adventures of Tom Sawyer
    see CHILDREN – AMBITIONS 2

DEATH

see also: ACCIDENTS; DROWNING; EXECUTION; FUNERALS; GRIEF; KILLING; SUICIDE; WAR

DEATH

1. ALLEN, Walter
    All in a Lifetime
    pp. 214–215 (Ch. 15)
    'Once upon a time ... in another room.'
    An old man contemplates his end. He

does not view its certainty with calm equanimity; rather, he is appalled by it.

2. ibid.
   see LIFE 1

3. DICKENS, Charles
   A Christmas Carol
   pp. 113–117 (Stave 4)
   'They left the busy scene ... Ha, ha, ha!'
   Scrooge sees himself on his death-bed, and the ungrieving glee of poor people profiting from his death, in the distribution of his effects. Scrooge is appalled that his death causes nobody to be in the least way melancholy.

4. DICKENS, Charles
   A Tale of Two Cities
   pp. 339–342 (Bk. 3, Ch. 13)
   'In the black prison ... turned to walk again.'
   In the condemned cell Darnay prepares himself for death, passing from despair to resignation and calmness.

5. FORSTER, E.M.
   Howard's End
   pp. 83–84 (Ch. 11)
   'The funeral was over ... in his pocket.'
   After Mrs Wilcox's funeral, the villagers pass the grave – Forster describes how they are excited by death, especially among the upper classes.

6. HUXLEY, Aldous
   Brave New World
   pp. 157–158 (Ch. 14)
   'The Park Lane ... she was asleep.'
   Linda, the Savage's Mother, lies on the point of death in the Park Lane Hospital for the Dying. The Savage visits her there, and is amazed to find all the patients looking so young. All are lulled to death by airy words and music. All die smiling.

7. JOYCE, James
   Dubliners
   pp. 213–220 ('The Dead')
   'A ghastly light ... living and the dead.'
   Gabriel is feeling loving towards his wife after the dinner-party; but she is abstracted. She tells him that she is thinking about a man who died for love of her. Gabriel is fiercely jealous at first, but by degrees, he falls to thinking about death, and its claims on his old aunts and, in time, on himself and his sleeping wife.

8. MANSFIELD, Katherine
   The Garden Party
   pp. 37–40 ('At the Bay', Part VII)
   'Kezia and her grandmother were ... what the 'never' was about.'
   Kezia teases herself with the thought of death. She gets her grandmother to tell her about her Uncle William's death. She asks what would happen if she were to refuse to die; then, in face of the inevitability of death, she is alarmed at the thought that her grandmother might die, and leave her.

9. ibid.
   pp. 74–87 ('The Garden Party')
   'Sadie brought them in and went ... 'Isn't it darling?' said Laurie.'
   Overshadowing Laura's enjoyment of the garden party, is the knowledge that a poor man has died in an accident a few yards down the lane, leaving a family fatherless. She takes a basket of food to the house, and is anxious to leave even before she arrives. Nearness to death in poverty disturbs her.

10. MARSHALL, James Vance
    Walkabout
    see FAITH 7

DEATH (of) ANIMALS

see also: ANIMALS – SLAUGHTER; HUNTING

DEATH (of) ANIMALS

1. LESSING, Doris
   Nine African Stories
   see ANTS 1

2. ibid.
   pp. 192–194 ('The Antheap')

'One day his mother ... some bushes and return whistling.'
A native friend of Tommy's brings him a baby buck whose mother he has shot. He gives Tommy the buck as a pet; but it is much too young, and it does not respond to forced feeding. It dies. Tommy is half desolated, and half angry.

DEATH (of) AUNT

1. ALMEDINGEN, E.M.
   Little Katia
   pp. 106–110 (Ch. 11)
   'We never knew ... to the nursery.'
   Katia's Aunt Marie, the mother of her three beloved cousins, dies after a long illness.

DEATH (of) BABY

1. ALCOTT, Louisa M.
   Little Women
   pp. 237–238 (Ch. 17)
   'So Beth lay down ... I'd have the fever."'
   Although she feels unwell herself, Beth visits the Hummel family, whose baby is ill. While she is left in charge of it, the baby dies, and the doctor pronounces the cause to be scarlet fever.

DEATH (of) BROTHER

1. JOYCE, James
   Dubliners
   pp. 11–16 ('The Sisters')
   'In the evening my Aunt ... gone wrong with him.'
   The Rev. James Flynn is dead and coffined. Visitors see his body and drink sherry with his sisters. The latter deal kindly with his memory, but permit themselves the observation that 'poor James' has not always been in his right mind.
2. LAWRENCE, D.H.
   Sons and Lovers

(i) pp. 133–136 (Ch. 6); (ii) pp. 166–169
'When they were going ... off for his father.'
William, almost predestinedly, dies. Death, has been in his conversation and on his gaunt face, for many weeks. Now, in rooms in S.E. London, he dies of pneumonia, and a curious, discolouring inflammation caused by chafing.
3. ibid.
   see FUNERALS 7

DEATH (of) CHILD

1. DICKENS, Charles
   Bleak House
   (i) pp. 595–596 (Ch. 47); (ii) pp. 595–596
   'After watching him closely ... around us every day.'
   Jo, the crossing-sweeper, lies dying, comforted by Allan Woodcourt, the doctor, and George, who has taken him in, wretched and ill. He thinks of the cemetery, and knows the end is near. Allan has him repeat the Lord's Prayer.
2. NAUGHTON, Bill
   see COMPETITIONS – RACES 2

DEATH (in) CHILDBIRTH

1. ALAIN-FOURNIER
   Le Grand Meaulnes
   see BIRTH 1
2. BRONTË, Emily
   Wuthering Heights
   (i) pp. 52–53 (Ch. 8); (ii) pp. 65–67
   'On the morning ... she was dead.'
   Frances, Hindley's young wife, dies of 'a consumption' soon after the birth of her child. Her death renders Hindley desperate, and dissolute.

DEATH (of) FATHER

1. LAWRENCE, D.H.
   The White Peacock
   pp. 179–182 (Part 2, Ch. 2)

'Some four or five days ... had over-taken the keeper.'

The gamekeeper, Annable, has been crushed to death by falling stones in the quarry. It is his young son, Sam, who finds him. Sam is terrified, only half knowing, and accepting that his father will not waken.

2. MORROW, Honoré
   The Spendid Journey
   see ILLNESS – DYSENTERY 1

3. SHOLOKHOV, Mikhail
   Fierce and Gentle Warriors
   pp. 37–40 ('The Rascal', Ch. 6)
   'One day Mishka came home ... his head into the sand.'
   Mishka's father goes off to fight for the cause. His mother and grand-father try to dissuade him, but he is resolute. That night shots are heard near at hand. In the morning, grand-father goes out to fetch in the sabre-slashed body of his son, Mishka's father.

4. TROLLOPE, Anthony
   Barchester Towers
   see AMBITIONS 3

DEATH (of) FATHER (and) SISTER

1. GASKELL, MRS
   Cranford
   (i) pp. 23–29 (Ch. 2); (ii) pp. 55–59
   'Captain Brown called ... or murmur more.'
   Captain Brown, whose elder daughter is dying, is killed in a railway accident. His younger daughter con-ceals it from her sister until almost the very last moment.

DEATH (of) FRIEND

1. BRONTË, Charlotte
   Jane Eyre
   (i) pp. 92–95 (Ch. 9); (ii) pp. 82–84
   ' "Helen" I whispered softly ... the word "Resurgam." '
   Jane visits her friend Helen, who she knows is very ill. Helen tells her that she is about to die, and why she is

very happy to do so. Jane lies down with her as they talk, and the following morning they are found together, Jane asleep, Helen dead.

2. KNOWLES, John
   A separate Peace
   pp. 206–208; 222–225 (Ch. 12)
   'Everyone behaved ... plunged into darkness.'; 'The rest of the day ... cry in that case.'
   Finny has fallen down a marble stair-case and broken his leg a second time. But Dr Stanpole assures Gene that it's a simple, clean break. Gene calls in at the infirmary later in the day to see his friend; he is numbed by the news of Finny's death.

DEATH (of) GRANDPARENTS

1. STEINBECK, John
   The Grapes of Wrath
   (i) pp. 116–124 (Ch. 13); (ii) pp. 124–133
   (Young Impact 3, pp. 103–108)
   'Ma came out ... strew stuff over her.'
   Grampa has a stroke, just as the Joad family have made their first camp on the way west. Death comes quickly, and he is laid out with the help of kind neighbours. Although it is illegal they have no choice but to bury him there, with a simple service.

2. WATERHOUSE, Keith
   Billy Liar
   pp. 165–169; 170–172 (Ch. 13)
   'The old man ... only as a listener.'; 'The swing doors ... down the corri-dor.'
   Billy goes to the hospital, and is regaled by his mother with a minute-by-minute account of his grand-mother's last 'attack'. He can feel no emotion, even when his mother re-appears and announces her death.

DEATH (of) MOTHER

1. DICKENS, Charles
   David Copperfield

pp. 175–183 (Ch. 9)
'I pass over … held her hand.'
Copperfield is called out of class to be told of his mother's death. He returns home from his boarding-school immediately, is measured for mourning clothes, to the accompaniment of the hammering together of his mother's coffin. His step-father and aunt are as distant as ever, but he shares his grief with his old nurse.

2. ibid.
pp. 185–187 (Ch. 9)
'She was never … on her bosom.'
Peggotty describes David's mother's death.

3. GORKY, Maxim
   Childhood
   (i) pp. 326–328 (Ch. 13); (ii) pp. 232–233
   (Impact Two, pp. 161–162)
   'She died at about noon on a Sunday … and stumbling like a blindman.'
   Having wasted for many months on a bed in the corner, Gorky's mother dies quietly and uncomplainingly. Gorky watches the transfiguration and knows it is death; but Grandfather does not believe him.

4. LAWRENCE, D.H.
   Sons and Lovers
   (i) pp. 390–399 (Ch. 14); (ii) pp. 474–485
   'He was not tired when … and went upstairs.'
   Mrs Morel slowly and painfully, dies. Her tumour gives her pain, and her tenacity tempts Paul and Annie to ease her passing by increasing the morphia dosage. Her death leaves a hole in Paul's life that is never filled.

5. O'BRIEN, Edna
   The Country Girls
   see GRIEF 5

DEATH (in) OLD AGE

1. BARSTOW, Stan
   The Human Element
   see OLD AGE 3

2. BRONTË, Emily
   Wuthering Heights
   (i) pp. 32–35 (Ch. 5); (ii) pp. 48–51
   'In the course … there safe together.'
   Old Mr Earnshaw dies quietly in his chair leaving a family of troubles behind him: Heathcliff, the adopted urchin, his father's favourite, Hindley the embittered heir, and Cathy, the mischievous beauty. With Earnshaw's death, the flood-gates open.

3. THOMPSON, Flora
   Lark Rise to Candleford
   see OLD AGE 18

DEATH (in) WAR

1. CANAWAY, W.H.
   Sammy going South
   see WAR – BOMBING 1

2. CRANE, Stephen
   The Red Badge of Courage
   see HORROR 5

3. SHOLOKHOV, Mikhail
   Fierce and Gentle Warriors
   see DEATH (of) FATHER 3

DEATH (of) WIFE

1. DICKENS, Charles
   David Copperfield
   pp. 834–839 (Ch. 53)
   'I must pause … out of my remembrance.'
   David Copperfield's young and ingenuous wife Dora is gradually growing weaker. Her decline is mirrored by that of her beloved dog, Jip. She distresses her husband by talking of how their marriage might have gone wrong, then dismisses him and calls for their friend Agnes. Jip dies at the same moment as his mistress.

DEER

1. CHURCH, Richard
   The White Doe
   pp. 108–111 (Ch. 13)

'Out where the thinning trees ... no longer visible.'

As the light fades on a winter's afternoon Tom and his father see a grey doe and her newly-born white fawn. Tom is entranced.

see also: HUNTING – DEER 1

DEMOCRACY

1. GOLDING, William
   Lord of the Flies
   see AUTHORITY 1, 2
2. ROBINSON, Rony
   A Walk to see the King
   see KINGS 3

DESERTION

1. CRANE, Stephen
   The Red Badge of Courage
   see COWARDICE 1
2. ibid.
   see HORROR 4
3. FORESTER, C.S.
   The Gun
   see BATTLES 2
4. REMARQUE, Erich Maria
   All Quiet on the Western Front
   see FIRST WORLD WAR – DESERTION 1

DESERTS

see also: LOST (in) DESERTS;
SURVIVAL (in) DESERTS

DESERTS

1. GUILLOT, René
   Kpo the Leopard
   pp. 90–96 (Ch. 9)
   'Once on the sands ... Azalai went by.'
   The cheetah family and their adopted leopard daughter take up life in the deserts, a life of gazelles, oases, onyx, ostriches, and distant camel trains.
2. SCHAEFER, Jack
   Old Ramon
   pp. 39–42 (Ch. 5)

'The land stretched away ... had brought it to the water.'

Old Ramon tells the boy how he and the boy's grandfather, herding sheep westwards to California, are caught in the Mojave Desert without water. The watering-places are dry, and the men are almost mad – but they find water at last, and their loyal dog has followed them with the sheep that have survived.

3. TREVOR, Elleston
   The Flight of the Phoenix
   pp. 26–30 (Ch. 4)
   'Their eyes were red ... edges of the silk. 'Sarnt Watson!'
   Captain Harris is determined to leave the aircraft wreck, and his co-survivors, to march across the Libyan Desert, in search of water and help. Moran, the navigator, describes to him what he would be up against in the desert, but Harris is adamant.
4. ibid.
   pp. 89–93 (Ch. 11)
   'They had begun work again ... the sky beautiful and meaningless.'
   Guided by the smoke signal, Captain Harris finds his way back to the wreck, grossly dehydrated. He has lost Roberts in the desert and seen Cobb picked clean by vultures. He describes his ordeal through cracked lips.
5. ibid.
   pp. 107–110 (Ch. 14)
   'Somewhere in the middle ... the moon, drew over them.'
   The survivors of the plane-crash know they are near the end. The water is running out, and with it, their will, and strength to work for their survival. Each hides his head in the sand of a private, distracting obsession.
6. ibid.
   see SURVIVAL (in) DESERTS 2

DETECTION

see CRIME – DETECTION

DETERMINATION

1. ACHEBE, Chinua
'Things fall apart
see FARMING – HARVEST 1

2. BATES, H.E.
The Purple Plain
pp. 167–170 (Ch. 17)
'Carrington confronted Forrester ...
went straight ahead.'
Blore has committed suicide, and
Forrester must continue alone with
Carrington on his back. Having made
all the preparations, he almost finds
the effort of starting again too much
for him.

3. HEMINGWAY, Ernest
The Old Man and the Sea
pp. 60–66
'Then, with his right hand ... must be
very strange.'
The giant Marlin pulling the old man
in his skiff, rises to the surface as if to
show the old man what he is up
against; but the old man is determined to prove himself, to it, to his
friend the boy, and to all other fishermen.

4. ibid.
pp. 86–94
'It is a vey big circle ... floated with
the waves.'
The old man pits himself against the
biggest fish he has ever seen in all his
years of fishing the Gulf. His reason
is clouding with his vision after so
many hours of holding the line. The
fish has to die; there are moments
when it seems that he will take the
old man with him. But he perseveres,
and harpoons his quarry at last.

5. JAMES, Henry
Washington Square
see DOCTORS 1

6. SCHAEFER, Jack
Shane
pp. 32–38 (Ch. 3)
'It was no fun watching ... into each
other's eyes.'
Shane and Joe Starrett uproot a huge
oak-stump after hours of determined

axe-work. They do this, in token of
their new friendship and understanding, because they find it easier
than words.

7. STEINBECK, John
The Pearl
pp. 50–54 (Ch. 4)
'In his house ... sleep a little, he
said.'
Kino, having refused the derisory
offers of the local pearl dealers for his
enormous pearl, resolves to take it to
the capital. He dreads this, his
brother tries to dissuade him, and he
is injured while fighting off a potential thief – however, he is still determined to go.

8. TREVOR, Elleston
The Flight of the Phoenix
see DESERTS 3

DICTATORSHIP

see GOVERNMENT – DICTATORSHIP

DINNERS

see CHRISTMAS – DINNERS;
MEALS – DINNERS;
PARTIES – DINNERS

DISASTERS

see also: ACCIDENTS ; DROUGHT;
EARTHQUAKES; FLOODS;
MINING – ACCIDENTS;
SHIPWRECKS; STORMS

DISASTERS

1. WYNDHAM, John
The Day of the Triffids
see LONDON 10

2. ibid.
pp. 185–189 (Ch. 11)
'From our road we had ... the inn at
Steeple Honey.'
The countryside has been overrun by
Triffids. An isolated, frightened man
in a wayside pub is struck down by a

waiting Triffid within a few feet of rescue.

3. ibid.
see LONDON 11

DISCIPLINE

see ARMY – DISCIPLINE;
AUTHORITY;
CONDITIONING;
LEARNING;
NAVY – DISCIPLINE;
PUNISHMENT;
TEACHING – DISCIPLINE

DISEASES

see ILLNESS

DISHONESTY

see HONESTY

DISILLUSIONMENT

see LOVE – DISILLUSIONMENT;
MARRIAGE – DISILLUSIONMENT

DISMISSAL

1. ALLEN, Eric
The Latchkey Children
see TRADE UNIONS 1

2. BUTLER, Samuel
The Way of all Flesh
pp. 137–139 (Ch. 38)
'Ernest used to get up ... being driven to the station.'
Ellen, the Pontifexes' pretty housemaid, is found to be pregnant. Lest any taint of immorality be attached to a clerical household, she is given her marching orders within two hours of the doctor's diagnosis.
see also: GIFTS 2

3. DICKENS, Charles
Hard Times
(i) pp. 141–148 (Bk. 2, Ch. 5); (ii) pp. 152–158
'Well, Stephen ... he departed.'
Stephen Blackpool who has already

been ostracized by his workmates for not joining their union, is summoned by his employer to give an account of the complaints of the workforce. In all humility, Stephen advises against using 'the strong hand' against the malcontents. For this advice, he is summarily sacked.

4. LAWRENCE, D.H.
Sons and Lovers
(i) pp. 347–349 (Ch. 13); (ii) pp. 422–425
'He did not see Dawes ... thought him a skunk.'
Dawes, itching to get his hands on Paul for going out with his wife, seizes his opportunity at the office. He threatens Paul and when Mr Jordan, his employer intervenes, Dawes throws him down the steps. He is thereupon dismissed for rowdyism.

5. NAUGHTON, Bill
Late Night on Watling Street
see DRUNKENNESS 12

6. PEYTON, K.M.
Flambards
(i) pp. 112–117 (Ch. 8); (ii) pp. 141–147
'Mark put a splash ... 'You make me tired.' '
Dick, the Groom, has connived with William and Christina at preventing a horse from being killed and given to the hounds to eat. The turbulent Russell finds out that his orders have been disobeyed: he dismisses Dick, thrashes William, and even fells Christina in his overmastering rage.

7. WELLS, H.G.
The History of Mr Polly
pp. 24–31 (Ch. 2, Part 1)
'Suddenly Parsons ... sobbing for breath.'
Polly's friend Parsons has a revolutionary scheme for window-dressing. His employer is not amused. He orders Parsons to leave the window, which he refuses to do. There ensues an unseemly public struggle for territorial possession. Parsons is dismissed.

DIVING

see SEA – DIVING

DIVORCE

see also: MARRIAGE –
DISILLUSIONMENT;
MARRIAGE – SEPARATION

DIVORCE

1. DICKENS, Charles
   Hard Times
   (i) pp. 71–76 (Bk. 1, Ch. 11); (ii) pp. 75–81
   'The work went on ... dead the better.'
   Stephen Blackpool wishes to be divorced from his slatternly wife. A humble and conscientious weaver, he applies to Mr Bounderlay, his employer, for his advice. He is assured that divorce is not a resort for the working class. He is reminded that he took his wife 'for better or for worse'.

2. HARDY, Thomas
   The Mayor of Casterbridge
   (i) pp. 8–13 (Ch. 1); (ii) pp. 40–44
   'For my part ... rustics near the door.'
   Michael Henchard, addled with rum, auctions off his wife for a joke. His wife is not amused. Thus, when a passing sailor pays cash on the nail, she takes to the road with him, hopeful of better fortune.

DOCTORS

1. JAMES, Henry
   Washington Square
   pp. 5–8 (Ch. 1)
   'During a portion ... fear of losing her.'
   Doctor Sloper, a New York physician, enjoys a very high reputation, based on an even balance of learning and skill. He has devoted all his time and energies to being successful, and even

the death of his baby son, and later his wife have not swayed him from his purpose.

2. 'MISS READ'
   Village School
   (i) pp. 160–162 (Part 3, Ch. 17); (ii) pp. 160–162
   'Dr Curtis arrived ... our pleasures variously.'
   The school doctor arrives and sets up her medical room in Miss Read's office. She appears to be particularly zealous about flat feet on this occasion, and is clearly gratified when her last patient has the flattest feet she has ever seen.

DOGS

1. DE JONG, Meindert
   The Wheel on the School
   see FEAR (of) DOGS 1

2. DURRELL, Gerald
   Birds, Beasts and Relatives
   pp. 25–28 (Part 1, 'A Brush with Spirits')
   'So at nine o'clock we ... into the bowels of the earth.'
   The family is delivering a litter of Bedlington puppies to their new owner. They go by underground train. Their leads wind round people's legs, they hold up a mob of irate passengers at the top of the escalator, and their plaintive squeals in the gusty warmth of the platform, excite sympathy and clucking from passing ladies.

3. DURREL, Gerald
   My Family and Other Animals
   pp. 247–250 (Part 3, Ch. 16)
   'Dodo was a breed known ... with a raging headache.'
   Mother acquires a bitch-puppy, like a dachshund; Dodo has a weak hindleg, a weak mind, and a weak resistance to the lusty advances of one of Gerald's dogs.

4. LEE, Harper
   To Kill a Mocking bird
   see FATHERS 7

5. LONDON, Jack
   The Call of the Wild
   see FIGHTING (by) ANIMALS 2
6. ibid.
   pp. 46–49 (Ch. 4)
   'It was a hard trip ... the belt of river trees.'
   The dog team is overworked pulling the Yukon mail, but they all pull their weight doggedly. Dave is far too weak to go on. The drivers unfasten him from his traces, but Dave's pride won't let him run behind the sled. Finally, he has to be shot.
7. ibid.
   see GAMBLING 6
8. LONDON, Jack
   White Fang
   pp. 82–84 (Ch. 9)
   'It was at the cutting-up ... his bleeding wounds.'
   White Fang and Baseek fight over a shin-bone. White Fang is no longer an innocent cub, and Baseek is no longer quick and strong enough to bully other dogs into submission. White Fang's speed forces him to abandon his claims to the bone.
9. MACKEN, Walter
   God made Sunday and Other Stories
   pp. 140–149 ('Light in the Valley')
   'The March sun ... valley with light.'
   A boy proves his faith in his sheepdog, accused of killing sheep, by running away with him. By the time his father finds them, the real culprit is discovered.
10. SCHAEFER, Jack
   Old Ramon
   pp. 88–91 (Ch. 11)
   'Slow moments moved ... And Pedro lived ...'
   Old Ramon tells the boy how the brown dog Pedro once fought a grizzly bear, and saved his life. Old Ramon had tripped and dropped his gun, and Pedro occupied the bear for long enough, suffering an awful wound in the process, for Old Ramon to shoot the bear.

DOGS – LOYALTY

1. LONDON, Jack
   White Fang
   pp. 109–116 (Ch. 11)
   'Grey Beaver refused to sell ... every whim and fancy.'
   White Fang is the property of the Indian Grey Beaver until Beauty Smith fuddles his mind with drink. Twice, Beauty drags off White Fang, and ties him to a stake, and twice, despite savage beatings, White Fang returns to his old master.
2. ibid.
   see RESCUE (from) INTRUDERS 1

DOGS – TRAINING

1. LONDON, Jack
   The Call of the Wild
   pp. 8–10 (Ch. 1)
   'Four men gingerly carried ... the struggle for mastery.'
   Buck is loosed from his crate, maddened by his long and unaccustomed captivity. He jumps at the man who lets him out, ignorant of the language of the club. He is beaten unconscious, to wake a wiser dog.

DRAGONS

1. TOLKIEN, J.R.R.
   The Hobbit
   (i) pp. 195–198 (Ch. 12); (ii) pp. 195–198
   'The stars were coming ... price and count.'
   At considerable peril of his life, the Hobbit steals into the dragon's mountain lair. He finds him asleep, guarding ill-gotten treasures of a magnificence beyond a hobbit's dreams.
2. ibid.
   (i) pp. 226–230 (Ch. 14) (ii) pp. 226–230
   'The men of the Lake-town ... but not of Bard.'
   The dragon, Smaug, is on the rampage. He reckons without the redoubt-

able Bard, who stands his ground, and looses an arrow into the one unprotected patch on Smaug's breast.

DREAMS

see also: DAYDREAMS

DREAMS

1. DOSTOYEVSKY, Fyodor
   The Idiot
   (i) pp. 373–375 (Part 3, Ch. 5); (ii) pp. 427–429
   'It puzzles me much to think … and the Prince entered the room".'
   The consumptive Hippolyte recounts a bad dream that he has recently had, in which a scorpion-like creature crawled about his bedroom putting him in considerable fear. He tells how his (dead) Newfoundland dog came in and seized the reptile, crushing it in her teeth, and being bitten by it in her turn.

2. GROSSMITH, George and Weedon
   The Diary of a Nobody
   (i) pp. 148–149 (Ch. 19); (ii) pp. 236–237
   'I am getting quite … to the horse.'
   Charles Pooter recounts one of his 'extraordinary' dreams to his family and friends. They are unimpressed. They call it nonsensical. Charles is well and truly snubbed. He promises never to talk about his dreams again.

3. WELLS, H.G.
   Kipps
   see WEALTH 8

DRINK

see FOOD (and) DRINK

DROUGHT

1. ACHEBE, Chinua
   Things fall apart
   see FARMING – HARVEST 1

2. PATON, Alan
   Cry, the beloved country
   (i) pp. 157–160 (Bk. 3, Ch. 2); (ii) pp. 195–199
   'Kumalo began to pray … I commend Ndotsheni.'
   Ndotsheni is suffering from drought, and poor overworked soil. Rev. Kumalo approaches first the chief, then the headmaster to argue them to get something done. Both are unhelpful.

3. ibid.
   (i) pp. 183–186 (Bk. 3, Ch. 6); (ii) pp. 225–227
   'There is ploughing … white man's milk.'
   With the help of an agricultural demonstrator provided by a sympathetic white landowner, the people of Ndotsheni begin, in a small way, to improve their land.

4. STEINBECK, John
   The Grapes of Wrath
   (i) pp. 1–3 (Ch. 1); (ii) pp. 5–7
   'To the red country … thinking-figuring.'
   In Oklahoma, there is drought – the earth dries, the dust rises, the wind whips up the dust, and the crops die.

DROWNING

1. HARDY, Thomas
   The Return of the Native
   (i) pp. 438–442 (Bk. Fifth, Ch. 9); (ii) pp. 386–390
   'At this moment a footstep … put into warm beds.'
   Yeobright, in search of his wife, meets Wildeve, who is waiting with a carriage to take her away. They hear the splash of a body in the weir, and both run to the rescue. It is dark, and in the confusion, both get into difficulties themselves in the strong current of the stream.

2. LAWRENCE, D.H.
   The Rainbow
   see FLOODS 9

3. LEE, Laurie
   Cider with Rosie
   see SUICIDE 7

DRUNKENNESS

see also: ACCIDENTS – ROAD –
DRUNKENNESS;
ALCHOHOLISM

DRUNKENNESS

1. DEFOE, Daniel
   Moll Flanders
   see PICKPOCKETS 3
2. DICKENS, Charles
   David Copperfield
   pp. 419–424 (Ch. 24)
   'One of Steerforth's friends ... a day
   it was.'
   David Copperfield, newly arrived in
   London, entertains three friends: the
   wine flows freely, and cigars are
   passed round. David is used to neither
   and soon loses track of what is
   happening. They visit a theatre, where
   he meets Agnes, whom he admires for
   her purity – he is deeply ashamed.
3. DU MAURIER, Daphne
   Jamaica Inn
   pp. 36–40 (Ch. 4)
   'They came singly ... bleating like a
   sheep.'
   Mary Yellan has to help behind the
   bar on one of the rare opening nights
   at the inn, and witnesses the arrival of
   some very rough characters, and their
   drunken excesses.
4. GOLDING, William
   Pincher Martin
   pp. 134–136 (Ch. 9)
   'No thanks old man ... You a member?'
   A scene in a pub at closing time. The
   drunken Pete declaims at the top of
   his voice about (inter alia) Chinese
   maggots, until his companions bear
   him off.
5. GORKY, Maxim
   Childhood
   see FAMILY – FIGHTING 3
6. ibid.
   see ASSAULT (by) BROTHERS 1
7. LAWRENCE, D.H.

The Rainbow
see FLOODS 9
8. LAWRENCE, D.H.
   Sons and Lovers
   (i) pp. 37–40 (Ch. 2); (ii) pp. 51–55
   'Walter Morel was ... and lock the
   door.'
   Mrs Morel is nursing baby Paul,
   when the oblivious Morel arrives
   home drunk, and demands something
   to eat. He loses his temper when she
   refuses to wait on him, and throws the
   cutlery drawer at her. He injures her,
   and is as wretched and loving as he
   can be.
9. ibid.
   see FATHERS 4
10. ibid
    see MARRIAGE – QUARRELS 5
11. 'MISS READ'
    Village School
    see CHRISTIANITY – CONVERSION 2
12. NAUGHTON, Bill
    Late Night on Watling Street
    pp. 78–81 ('Boozer's Labourer')
    'Another habit I took up ... in the
    four-ale bar.'
    An assistant barman is sent into the
    cellar for bottled beer. He is tempted
    to have a drink, so starts on a big
    bottle of stout; too late, he realises
    that having started it he must finish
    it. Back in the bar, he finds himself
    saying things he had not planned to
    say.
13. SASSOON, Siegfried
    Memoirs of an Infantry Officer
    pp. 136–138 (Part 8, Sn. 2)
    'Before dinner Ralph ... clear-headed
    and alert.'
    Sherston joins a couple of comrades-
    in-arms in a behind-the-lines carousal.
    They put war-thoughts away at a
    wine-merchant's house, drinking,
    'bubbly' and singing maudlin songs.
14. SEWELL, Anna
    Black Beauty
    see HORSES – RIDING – ACCIDENTS 6

DYSENTERY

see ILLNESS – DYSENTERY

EARTHQUAKES

1. HUGHES, Richard
   A High Wind in Jamaica
   (i) pp. 20–27 (Ch. 1, Part 3); (ii) pp. 17–22
   'The cavalcade mounted ... film of dust.'
   The Thornton and Fernandez children picnic on the beach. Everything is still and superheated. A mild earthquake ensues which goes to Emily's head and remains there for a long long time.

EASTER

1. KIRKUP, James
   The Only Child
   pp. 153–156 (Ch. 13)
   'Palm Sunday was ... new aspirations.'
   On Good Friday, all South Shields foregathers in the Square. The Sunday School children sing under their banners, and the colliery bands play. Everyone wears something new. Then, on Easter Sunday, there is the 'jarping' of the eggs, and the bowling of the hoops.
2. 'MISS READ'
   Village School
   (i) pp. 150–152 (Part 2, Ch. 16); (ii) pp. 150–152
   'In the infants' room ... free for a fortnight.'
   The school is a-bustle with end-of-term festivities. The Vicar arrives to tell the children about Palm Sunday and Easter Day, and eggs are handed round. The atmosphere is of spring, and of promise.
3. SASSOON, Siegfried
   Memoirs of a Fox-hunting Man
   see FIRST WORLD WAR – TRENCHES 4
4. THOMAS, Dylan
   A Prospect of the Sea

pp. 42–50 ('The Tree')
'Rising from the house ... the palm of his hand.'
A disturbing story, about a credulous boy, a tale-spinning gardener, and a wandering idiot called by fate to be a Christ. There is more than a single meaning of Easter here, in a religious setting that is primitive and stark.

ECCENTRICS

see also: MADNESS;
OLD AGE;
RELATIVES

ECCENTRICS

1. DICKENS, Charles
   Bleak House
   (i) pp. 106–107 (Ch. 9); (ii) pp. 106–107
   'We have been misdirected ... infinitely rather.'
   Mr Boythorn arrives late at Bleak House. He has been misdirected and proceeds to describe his informant in extremely exaggerated terms, declaring he should be shot. His conversation continues in similar vein.
2. ibid.
   (i) pp. 265–266 (Ch. 21); (ii) pp. 265–266
   'At the present time ... Such is Judy.'
   Grandmother Smallweed chatters nonsense, Grandfather is enraged and thows a cushion at her. This reduces him to a shapeless mass, whence he is rescued and shaken up by his old/young granddaughter Judy.
3. DICKENS, Charles
   Great Expectations
   (i) pp. 61–67 (Ch. 8); (ii) pp. 53–58
   'At last we came ... Go, Pip.'
   Pip meets Miss Havisham for the first time. She is a recluse living amid the trappings of what was to be her wedding. She asks a lot of confusing questions before she dismisses him, and puts him in the care of the proud and beautiful Estella.

4. ibid.
   (i) pp. 230–234 (Ch. 25); (ii) pp. 197–201
   'At first with ... of the Stinger.'
   Mr Wemmick favours Pip with an invitation to spend the night at his house. It is in the form of a little gothic castle, with a draw-bridge, turret, and lattice-work gun-stage. Wemmick shows Pip his collection of curiosities, not the least of which is his Aged Parent.

5. DURRELL, Gerald
   My Family and Other Animals
   pp. 43–46 (Part 1, Ch. 3)
   'During these trips Roger ... bagpipes beneath their bellies.'
   Gerald makes friends with three of the natives: a mentally defective youth, an old peasant woman with whom he sings emotional Greek love-songs, and a shepherd who gives him kindly, superstitious advice.
   see also: PEDLARS 1

6. TROLLOPE, Anthony
   Barchester Towers
   pp. 64–68 (Ch. 9)
   'But the two most prominent ... the men of Barchester.'
   The beautiful Madeline Stanhope returns to her father's house, a cripple, after a disastrous marriage to an Italian. She determines to lead as full and glittering a life as possible.

7. ZINDEL, Paul
   The Pigman
   pp. 31–37 (Ch. 5)
   'One-ninety Howard Avenue turned out to be ... Mr Pignati, we get it.'
   John and Lorraine call on a lonely old man to collect his contribution to an imaginary charity. It turns out that he visits the zoo every day, plays memory games, and keeps toy pigs in a curtained room.

EDUCATION

see also: CONDITIONING; LEARNING; READING; SCHOOL: SCHOOLS; SEX-EDUCATION; TEACHING

EDUCATION

1. DICKENS, Charles
   Great Expectations
   (i) pp. 48–50 (Ch. 7); (ii) pp. 41–43
   'One night I was ... certainly poor Joe.'
   Pip questions Joe about his education. He learns that Joe cannot read, and he learns why.

2. DICKENS, Charles
   Hard Times
   (i) pp. 7–14 (Bk. 1, Chs. 1, 2); (ii) pp. 9–16
   'Now what I want ... and distort him!'
   Mr Gradgrind 'murders the innocents'. His facts-based schoolmastering leaves no room in young imaginations for fancy. Definition is all. Exactitude is of the essence.

3. STREATFIELD, Noel
   Ballet Shoes
   pp. 52–55 (Ch. 5)
   'The Fossils became ... their white sandals.'
   The three Fossil sisters lead extremely busy lives. They do not go to an ordinary school, but have lessons at home, between walks and dancing practice. Every day except Sunday they also attend an Academy of Dancing for very rigorous training.

4. TWAIN, Mark
   The Adventures of Huckleberry Finn
   see FATHERS 10

EDUCATION – FUTURE

1. HUXLEY, Aldous
   Brave New World
   pp. 129–132 (Ch. 11)
   'At Eton they alighted ... It was all arranged.'
   Bernard, who is charged with showing the Savage the civilised world, takes him to Eton, where they are taken on a guided tour. They look in on a

lesson on elementary relativity, learn the principle of sleep-teaching, and hear tell of death-conditioning.

ELECTIONS

see POLITICS − ELECTIONS

ELOPEMENT

1. ELIOT, George
   The Mill on the Floss
   see RUNNING AWAY 2

EMBARRASSMENT

see also: HUMILIATION;
SHAME

EMBARRASSMENT

1. GRIMBLE, Sir Arthur
   A Pattern of Islands
   pp. 40–44 (Ch. 3)
   'Every Gilbertese village ... recruiting business.'
   Arthur is called upon to give a speech in Gilbertese, a language of which he has but tenuous grasp. He says the wrong thing, but the Islanders' sense of humour being what it is, it becomes the right thing, and Arthur's face is saved.
2. HARDY, Thomas
   Far from the Madding Crowd
   see ENCOUNTERS 2
3. KIRKUP, James
   The Only Child
   pp. 37–39 (Ch. 2)
   'But one afternoon ... shame and embarrassment.'
   Young Jim is upstairs with his blousy neighbour, Mrs Battery. Three of Mrs Battery's friends come in, full of their bargains bought at a sale of cloth remnants. Without ado, and quite without any consideration of Jim's finer feelings, Mrs B. Hoists up her skirt and shows off her home-made bloomers.

4. LAWRENCE, D.H.
   The Rainbow
   see CHURCH − SERVICES 2
5. MARSHALL, James Vance
   Walkabout
   (i) pp. 39–41 (Ch. 7); (ii) pp. 49–52
   'They cooked the yam-like ... to dressing-up.'
   Mary is grateful to the aboriginal boy for saving their lives, and she appreciates that it is not his fault, but she cannot blink the fact that he is naked. She sees it as her missionary duty to give him her pants, so that he shall be decently clothed.
6. 'MISS READ'
   Village School
   see JUMBLE SALES 1
7. SASSOON, Siegfried
   Memoirs of a Fox-hunting Man
   see HUNTING − FOXES 4
8. ibid.
   pp. 80–83 (Part 3, Sn. 2)
   'It was a wet and windy ... one does not forget.'
   George's Aunt Evelyn boils up a pot of tea in a first-class railway carriage. The overt disapproval of two fellow passengers makes George uncomfortable, to the point of disowning his aunt.
9. WATERHOUSE, Keith
   Billy Liar
   pp. 67–69 (Ch. 5)
   'One of the habits ... in an embarrassed way.'
   Billy is waiting for his boss, who wishes to see him about his resignation from the firm. He fills in time by talking, and then shouting, nonsense, a kind of verbal doodling. He is shocked to find his boss has been there, and listening, all the time.
10. WAUGH, Evelyn
    Scoop
    pp. 200–205 (Bk. 3, Ch. 2, Part 3)
    'It was eight o'clock ... Where is William?'
    The travel-stained and weary Mr Salter from London, arrives at remote Boot Magna. He can raise no-one

until he hammers on the front door, he sinks, exhausted, in the first chair he can find, only to be taken for drunk, by the ladies of the house.

EMIGRATION

1. ALLEN, Walter
   All in a Lifetime
   pp. 90–91 (Ch. 9)
   'I didn't write ... I saw the defeated.'
   The lure of America to the working-man. Billy is realizing a dream. He has saved and planned, but he reckons without the tears of parting, and the sudden loneliness.
2. ibid.
   pp. 92–94 (Ch. 9)
   see VOYAGES 1
3. GRICE, Frederick
   The Bonny Pit Laddie
   pp. 128–131 (Ch. 15)
   'Mr Fairless and Mr Allathorne ... hands from the windows.'
   Two families emigrate to Australia. All their friends see them off at the local railway station, with good wishes, confused tears, small gifts, and a hymn.

EMPLOYMENT

see INTERVIEWS;
UNEMPLOYMENT;
WORK

ENCOUNTERS

1. BRONTË, Charlotte
   Shirley
   see CHURCH – FESTIVALS 1
2. HARDY, Thomas
   Far from the Madding Crowd
   (i) pp. 185–189 (Ch. 24); (ii) pp. 181–185
   'Her way back to ... his coat no longer.'
   Bathsheba meets a tall dark stranger in unwonted circumstances. Her hem is caught in the rowel of his spur, and

he is so forward as not to want to sever the connection.
3. LEWIS, C.S.
   Out of the Silent Planet
   see LANGUAGE 3
4. TOLKIEN, J.R.R.
   The Hobbit
   see COMPETITIONS 3
5. TREECE, Henry
   Hounds of the King
   see KINGS 5
6. TWAIN, Mark
   The Adventures of Tom Sawyer
   see RIVALS – BOYS 3

ENCOUNTERS – SEXUAL

see SEX – ENCOUNTERS

ENGAGEMENT

see COURTSHIP – ENGAGEMENT

ENTERTAINMENTS

see also: CHRISTMAS – NATIVITY
PLAYS;
CIRCUS;
CONCERTS;
DANCES;
PARTIES

ENTERTAINMENTS

1. ALCOTT, Louisa M.
   Little Women
   pp. 38–43 (Ch. 2)
   'No gentlemen were admitted ... walk down to supper.'
   The March sisters perform an opera on Christmas night, to an audience of friends. Despite scenery, and the audience seating collapsing it is a great success.
2. LEE, Harper
   To Kill a Mockingbird
   (i) pp. 262–265 (Ch. 28); (ii) pp. 260–263
   'When we reached the auditorium ... the audience left.'
   Scout takes part in a Hallowe'en

Show designed to foster county pride in the people of Maycomb. Children are dressed up as agricultural products. Scout is a ham; and she misses her cue.

3. O'BRIEN, Edna
   The Country Girls
   pp. 44–47 (Ch. 5)
   'We mounted ... voices on the stage.'
   Caithleen, Baba, and Baba's mother go to a show at the Town Hall. The audience provides quite a lot of interest for them, the show is hardly a polished affair, and the two girls are asked to sing to Caithleen's embarrassment.

4. THOMPSON, Flora
   Lark Rise to Candleford
   (i) pp. 213–217 (Ch. 12, 'Lark Rise'); (ii) pp. 197–200
   'Squire himself called ... enjoy the cinema.'
   The Squire organizes a concert to take place in the schoolroom. The whole village assembles to hear his Negro Minstrel Troupe, several piano pieces, and communal songs. As the villagers disperse, they rehearse the finer points and belabour the weaker.

5. WATERHOUSE, Keith
   Billy Liar
   pp. 112–121 (Ch. 9)
   'The New House ... cup of cocoa!" '
   Billy arrives at the pub where he does a Saturday night turn. The Public Bar is full of men who taunt him, the concert-room is full of large gin-drinking women. He is thrown off-course by seeing his father by the bar and makes a mess of his act.

ESCAPADES

see also: PRANKS

ESCAPADES

1. GRICE, Frederick
   The Bonny Pit Laddie
   pp. 48–56 (Ch. 7)
   'It did not take ... correct she was.'

Dick and Kit venture down an old pit shaft. The last ladder breaks under them, and it would seem they are trapped, but they explore the workings and grab a lone miner's pick, to make footholes in the brickwork of the shaft.

2. LEE, Harper
   To Kill a Mockingbird
   (i) pp. 57–61 (Ch. 6); (ii) pp. 57–61
   'Dill stretch, yawned ... he bawled after us.'
   Jem and Dill are determined to look through the windows into the Radley's mysterious house. They are scared into a flight that costs Jem his trousers.

3. ibid.
   (i) pp. 61–63 (Ch. 3); (ii) pp. 61–63
   'Had Jem's pants ... him stir again.'
   At the risk of his life, Jem retraces his steps, so as to retrieve his trousers, and prevent any news of his nocturnal misdoings from reaching his father.

4. LLWELLYN, Richard
   How Green was my Valley
   pp. 24–26 (Ch. 4)
   'That night, after I had ... hedge in front of us.'
   Huw and a friend are going to a Union meeting outside the village, at night. Huw has to get out of the house without being heard, and suffers all the agonies of creaking boards, stiff window and a steep drop to the ground, followed by an eerie walk in the dark.

5. ibid.
   pp. 27–29 (Ch. 4)
   'I had forgotten ... he had known and seen.'
   Having attended the Union meeting Huw finds he cannot get back in the house. He falls in the water-barrel he has to stand on, and is met by his father, who, however, is not angry.

6. NAUGHTON, Bill
   Late Night on Watling Street
   pp. 62–65 ('The bees have stopped working')

'Ned was standing ... simply poured off me.'

A chorister prepares himself to sing a solo, by drinking some of his mother's bee wine. His friend has some too. Then they top up the bottle with water.

7. NESBIT, E.
The Railway Children
(i) pp. 28–36 (Ch. 2); (ii) pp. 36–44
'Mother had told them ... cared to own it.'

The children are not allowed to light a fire on a cold day because their mother says they cannot afford the coal. Peter has an idea, and suddenly they have plenty of coal. The supply does not last however, when he is caught by the station-master, stealing it from the station yard.

8. ibid.
(i) pp. 66–72 (Ch. 4); (ii) pp. 74–82
'The very next morning ... an Engine-burglar.'

Bobbie wants to get Peter's engine mended, because she has been kind to her. She takes it to an engine-driver, but while she is trying to attract his attention, the engine moves off with Bobbie on the footplate. The driver and fireman are surprised but helpful, and her mission is successful.

9. PICARD, Barbara Leonie
The Young Pretenders
pp. 53–57 (Ch. 5)
'She had already put out ... silver-leaved world, Bella thought.'

Bella and Francis secretly leave the house late at night to visit the wounded Jacobite they are helping. They each make their own preparations, and slip out together into the strange moonlit world.

10. SILLITOE, Alan
The Loneliness of the Long-distance Runner
(i) pp. 43–48 ('Noah's ark'); (ii) pp. 95–99
'Colin took Bert's arm ... earth might surround him with.'

Colin and Bert are at the Goose Fair.

Their ambition has been to go on the Noah's Ark, but they have no money left, so they steal a ride. Colin enjoys himself until he is caught, and cuffed, by the attendant.

11. THOMAS, Leslie
This Time Next Week
pp. 99–102 (Ch. 9)
'After the Autumn had ... life now and again.'

One Saturday afternoon, Leslie and Boz do a bunk. They take the bus to Swaffham and do the only thing there is to do there; they go to the cinema. They stay longer than they intend and miss the last bus back. They have to pay for their escapade, but it's worth the price.

ESCAPE

see also: HIDING;
HOME – LEAVING;
RUNNING AWAY

ESCAPE

1. ADAMS, Richard
Watership Down
pp. 221–227 (Ch. 25)
'Bigwig and Blackberry found ... after Hazel into the farmyard.'

A group of wild rabbits free four tame ones from their hutch on a farm. The escape is complicated by the tame rabbits having no idea of moving in the open.

2. ibid.
pp. 247–249 (Ch. 27)
' "That night, when we ... we shall ever know.'

Holly and his companions escape from the police-state burrow of Efrafa. They trick the captain, overpower the sentries and are saved from pursuers by a train which knocks them down.

3. CANAWAY, W.H.
Sammy going South
pp. 147–151 (Ch. 25)
'The train ran along ... in his imagination.'

A reward of £1,000 is offered for Sammy. A fellow-traveller in the train, on the last stage of his journey, suspects his identity and questions him closely, until he is convinced. Sammy escapes at the last moment.

4. STEINBECK, John
   The Pearl
   pp. 61–64 (Ch. 5)
   'In a few moments ... thou also with God.'
   Kino has killed a man who tried to steal his enormous pearl. He and his wife and child hide in his brother's house till nightfall when they can escape.

5. TOLKIEN, J.R.R.
   The Hobbit
   see COMPETITIONS 3

6. WOODHOUSE, Martin
   Tree Frog
   pp. 198–205 (Ch. 27)
   'The truck rolled to a halt ... hot exploding stones.'
   Alone in the desert, with a top-secret aeroplane, Giles is awaiting a search-party. Instead, his old adversary Pzenica homes in on him, inspects the plane, and waves Giles into his truck with a gun. Giles resists, there is a fight, Pzenica is pizioned by the tilting plane, and burnt to death when it explodes.

ESCAPE (from) FIRE

1. GUILLOT, René
   Kpo the Leopard
   pp. 22–30 (Ch. 3)
   'Chirgu and Abga had ranged ... taste of blood.'
   The leopard parents, returning from the hunt sense danger, and then see that the forest is ablaze. Man is trying to burn the animals out. They quickly snatch up their cub, and after a desperate flight, during which the mother is wounded, reach safety.

ESCAPE (from) FLOODS

1. BERNA, Paul
   Flood Warning
   pp. 77–83 (Ch. 4)
   'It was eight o'clock before ... There were seven, himself included.'
   The floods have reached a crucial stage. Majority opinion is for evacuating the school without delay. Accordingly, staff and pupils dress warmly and take their bedding with them. They go by car in relays. The last is cut off when the road is submerged.

2. ibid.
   pp. 92–98 (Ch. 5)
   'From the gathering dusk outside ... those in the hull of a sinking ship.'
   Vignoles builds a rough bridge of ladders to span the twelve feet between the school building, and a mill tower. One by one, the seven evacuees cross over, inches above the flood waters to safety. Chomel, scared beyond self-help, has to be hauled across in the water, at the end of a rope of knotted sheets.

ESCAPE (from) KIDNAPPERS

1. BAWDEN, Nina
   On the Run
   pp. 79–82 (Ch. 8)
   'I am betrayed ... on the garden wall.'
   Thomas, son of an African chieftain exiled in London, fears he is about to be kidnapped by his father's enemies. Aided by Ben, an English boy, he escapes from his house late one evening – but his sheltered existence has not prepared him for such impromptu, unorthodox action.

2. WOOD, James
   The Rain Islands
   pp. 116–125 (Chs. 6, 7)
   'Dill woke me ... down to him carefully.'
   Major Scott, a prisoner on the boat of a criminal, manages to escape over

the side and swim to a small island nearby. His captors follow by boat, do not find him, but leave one of their number behind to deal with him, when they leave. Scott easily overcomes him.

ESCAPE (from) MONSTERS

1. WELLS, H.G.
   The Time Machine
   see HORROR 18

ESCAPE (from) POLICE

1. MANKOWITZ, Wolf
   Make me an Offer
   pp. 102–106 ('The Day Aunt Chaya was buried')
   'So it was with ... look after cats better.'
   The police come to arrest Aunt Chaya for throwing a bomb, but her brother pretends that a wooden box containing a smelly dead cat is her coffin, and she escapes arrest.

ESCAPE (from) PRISON

1. LONDON, Jack
   White Fang
   see RESCUE (from) INTRUDERS 1
2. WOODHOUSE, Martin
   Tree Frog
   pp. 110–118 (Chs. 13, 14)
   'I woke up again. I felt much better ...
   'Excuse fingers,' I said.'
   Giles takes his warder by surprise, and takes his gun. He has him release Binnie, and the two of them find a window from which to jump into the snow. Giles takes a few shots at faces at other windows before scrambling after Binnie to the cover of trees.

ESCAPE (from) PRISON (of) WAR

1. CHURCHILL, W.S.
   My Early Life
   pp. 274–278 (Ch. 21)

'During the first three weeks ... the want of either.'
Churchill is held as a prisoner-of-war by the Boers. He makes an early resolve to escape. A mixture of desperateness and sheer youthful audacity is enough to ensure success.
2. ibid.
   pp. 284–290 (Ch. 21)
   'During the day ... he has won the Derby.'
   Churchill's plan to reach the Portuguese frontier by train, falls through. He is reduced to aimless walking, and wondering, until he decides to try his luck at a kraal fire. Providentially, he is taken in hand by a willing Briton.
3. ibid.
   pp. 299–304 (Ch. 22)
   'At two o'clock ... and Christmas Eve.'
   The final leg of Churchill's escape from the Boers. He is well hidden among bales of wool on a train bound for Lourenço Marques in Portuguese territory. Either the train is not searched or he is not aware of a search at the frontier. He is fêted on his return to Durban, and the war.
4. SERRAILLIER, Ian
   The Silver Sword
   (i) pp. 15–19 (Ch. 1); (ii) pp. 11–14
   'Very carefully ... he walked on.'
   Joseph determines to escape from his prison camp in Nazi-occupied Poland. Having got himself into solitary confinement, he knocks out the guard who brings him his meal, takes his uniform and leaves the camp with the other guards.

ESCAPE (from) PURSUERS

1. PICARD, Barbara Leonie
   The Young Pretenders
   pp. 15–17 (Ch. 2)
   'She was roused ... the gate, and was gone.'
   Bella is waiting for her brother by a gate in the wall of their father's

estate. She is surprised to see a man come through the gate, and terrified when he holds her tight to stop her screaming, until the voices of his pursuers have faded away.

2. SUTCLIFF, Rosemary
   The Eagle of the Ninth
   pp. 236–240 (Ch. 17)
   'Three more days, ... the hunters of souls.'
   Marcus and Esca are on the run, hunted by clan-warriors. They are spotted, and wring the last atom of energy out of their ponies, before flinging themselves into a beck, in the hope that the hounds will be distracted from them by the scent of stags.

3. TOWNSEND, John Rowe
   The Intruder
   pp. 160–166 (Ch. 26)
   'I'd like to have a look ... to the stranger.'
   Arnold has brought an official to investigate the stranger who has moved into their house. While the official goes out to the phone, the stranger attacks Arnold, and then pursues him as he runs away across the sands. Arnold's knowledge of the sands and tides saves him.

ESCAPE – SECOND WORLD WAR

1. BATES, H.E.
   Fair stood the Wind for France
   (i) pp. 123–128 (Ch. 12); (ii) pp. 125–131
   'They set him down ... Like hell, he thought.'
   Franklin, hidden by a French family after an air-crash, is taken in a boat on a 'fishing trip' to avoid detection by the Germans at the farm. He is hidden under a tarpaulin, while the girl fishes, in full view of a soldier on the bridge.

2. ibid.
   (i) pp. 209–214 (Ch. 20) (ii) pp. 214–220

'He was within sight ... in fine cold drops together.'
Franklin, on the verge of freedom in Marseille, suddenly decides on a rash escape on a coal truck. He cannot climb on to the truck and is questioned by a gendarme. When he hears shooting he knocks the gendarme down and runs.

3. ibid.
   (i) pp. 243–246 (Ch. 23); (ii) pp. 249–252
   'In a few more moments ... where they had always been.'
   At the Spanish-French border station, Franklin's papers allow him an easy entry to Spain. The girl, however, is detained for questioning, and O'Connor, Franklin's fellow-crew-member, disappears, only to re-appear on the wrong side of the train, pursued by gendarmes and finally shooting one.

4. FRANK, Anne
   The Diary of Anne Frank
   pp. 22–29 (8.7.42–11.7.42)
   'Years seemed to have passed ... might hear us.'
   An SS call-up notice has come for Anne's sister, so to avoid this, the family goes into hiding with the help of Dutch friends. Having taken belongings to their hiding-place over a period of time, all they need to do is make a few final preparations and leave the next day.

5. SERRAILLIER, Ian
   The Silver Sword
   (i) pp. 41–45 (Ch. 6); (ii) pp. 33–36
   'That night ... hunger woke them.'
   The mother of Edek, Ruth and Bronia is taken away by the Nazis, and they are locked in their bedrooms. Edek gets out, releases his sisters and leads them away over the roof tops, just before their house is blown up.

6. ibid.
   (i) pp. 82–86 (Ch. 13); (ii) pp. 66–70
   'It was the hour ... go of it again.'
   In a train full of refugees, stories of escapes from Nazis are told. One boy hid underneath a goods train, only

managing to remain in position because water on his clothes froze him to the axle.
7. ibid.
(i) pp. 138–151 (Chs. 22, 23); (ii) pp. 117–128
'The farmer did not ... not even notice.'
The four Polish refugee children are threatened with deportation, when they have nearly reached Switzerland, their goal. The farmer with whom they have been staying furnishes them with canoes to escape from the village and reach the Danube. After various scares, they succeed.
8. SHOLOKHOV, Mikhail
Fierce and Gentle Warriors
pp. 69–73 ('The Fate of a Man', Ch. 4)
'Soon after that day ... in the fascist camps.'
It is Sokolov's job as a prisoner of war, to drive a German officer about. One day, he takes his chance, and storms through the German lines, and across no-man's land, with the officer recumbent behind him. He is joyfully received.

ESCAPE (from) SLAVERY

1. TWAIN, Mark
The Adventures of Huckleberry Finn
(i) pp. 288–293 (Ch. 40); (ii) pp. 344–348
'We were feeling pretty good ... bullet in the calf of his leg.'
Tom and Huck make off with Jim after many days of scheming, and seeking after effect. The escape is very nearly foiled at the last moment, but they reach the river, in spite of guns and dogs.

ESCAPE (from) SOLDIERS

1. FALKNER, J. Meade
Moonfleet
pp. 102–110 (Chs. 9, 10)

'But now a new thing ... the task he had performed.'
Elzevir and the wounded John Trenchard scale a narrow, vertiginous cliff-path, to evade a posse of soldiers. In spite of Elzevir's warning, John looks down and all but faints from dizziness and pain; but Elzevir manages to hold him, and bring them both to safety.

ESCAPE (from) THIEVES

1. BENTLEY, Phyllis
The Adventures of Tom Leigh
pp. 93–103 (Ch. 7)
'The wind was now howling ... I groaned and fainted.'
Tom breaks out of the workroom and discovers, as he had guessed, Jeremy and the pedlar, stealing a piece of cloth. He challenges them, there is a fight and Tom escapes within an inch of his life.
2. ibid.
see ARREST 2
3. HAUGAARD, Erich
The Little Fishes
pp. 129–134 (Ch. 13)
'The thief arranged for us to sleep ... and it is a good town.'
The children are made to sleep in a stable whose door is guarded by the thief. But the thief has drunk a good deal of wine, and he sleeps soundly. Guido discovers that by dislodging the slates above his head, he can make a hole big enough for them to crawl through.

ETIQUETTE

1. AUSTEN, Jane
Emma
pp. 275–281 (Ch. 32)
'The first subject ... into my mind.'
Mrs Elton, the vicar's new wife calls on Emma. Emma finds her 'absolutely insufferable', very full of herself, and very familiar.

2. CARY, Joyce
   The Horse's Mouth
   see SOCIAL CLASS 3
3. GASKELL, Mrs
   Cranford
   see PARTIES – TEAS 1
4. ibid.
   (i) pp. 105–111 (Ch. 8); (ii) pp. 115–120
   'Early the next morning ... obliged to decline.'
   The excitement in Cranford is great – Lady Glenmire is coming to stay. The genteel ladies are mortified when they are not invited to meet her, and then uncertain how to react when an invitation is issued after all.
5. GRIMBLE, Sir Arthur
   A Pattern of Islands
   pp. 21–23 (Ch. 2)
   'I worked hard ... his cold eyes.'
   A Gilbertese girl of seven teaches Arthur how to belch appreciation of good food, in the approved manner.
6. MARSHALL, James Vance
   Walkabout
   see EMBARRASSMENT 5
7. SPYRI, Johanna
   Heidi
   pp. 67–69 (Ch. 6)
   'You look just like ... Miss Rottenmeier's sitting-room.'
   At her first meal in Frankfurt, Heidi shows her total ignorance of 'manners'. She speaks in a familiar manner to the man-servant, puts a bread roll in her pocket, and finally falls asleep at table.
8. WELLS, H.G.
   Kipps
   pp. 5–6 (Bk. 1, Ch. 1, Sn. 1)
   'His Aunt and Uncle ... Sunday in the year.'
   Kipps lives with his Uncle and Aunt, whose eyes are always open to his misdemeanours, whose ears are attentive to his noises, and whose words more often than not, reprove him for his want of manners.
9. ibid.
   pp. 193–196 (Bk. 2, Ch. 3, Sn. 6)

'Among other projects ... Manners and Rules.'
Helen, his betrothed, gives Kipps a few hints as to how he might mend his accent, and his dress, so as to equip him for life in the society in which, as her husband, he will soon move.
10. ibid.
    pp. 272–276 (Bk. 2, Ch. 7, Sn. 6)
    'He found the dining-room ... entertained in the world.'
    Kipps dines at the Royal Grand Hotel. He tries to wear his wealth as if with practised ease, but he flouts every social convention in the book. He causes amusement among his fellow diners, and a resolve in his own mind to pretend to being a gentleman no more.
11. ibid.
    see MARRIAGE – QUARRELS 11

EVACUATION

see SECOND WORLD WAR – EVACUATION

EVANGELISM

see CHRISTIANITY – EVANGELISM

EVENING

1. ADAMS, Richard
   Watership Down
   pp. 129–130 (Ch. 18)
   'It was evening ... air that lay between.'
   Evening on Watership Down – golden light, humming insects, calling birds and a distant view of farms and fields.
2. CAMUS, Albert
   The Outsider
   see SUNDAY 1

EVICTION

1. GRICE, Frederick
   The Bonny Pit Laddie
   pp. 90–94 (Ch. 10)

'Branton possessed a railway ... aprons and wept.'

The colliery owner responds to the miners' strike by engaging a team of dockland roughnecks (or 'candymen') to turn the men, their families and all their belongings, out into the mud of the street.

2. ibid.
   see CHARITY 10

3. STEINBECK, John
   The Grapes of Wrath
   (i) pp. 25–28 (Ch. 5); (ii) pp. 30–33
   'The owners of the land ... perplexed and figuring.'

   The small farmers of Oklahoma and neighbouring states rent their land from banks – when the land does not produce enough, the banks farm it mechanically, evict the tenants, and bull-doze their houses and yards.

4. ibid.
   see HOME – LEAVING 8

EXAMINATIONS

see SCHOOL – EXAMINATIONS

EXCURSIONS

see also: HIKING;
HOLIDAYS

EXCURSIONS

1. BENNETT, Arnold
   Anna of the Five Towns
   pp. 139–143 (Ch. 9)
   'A carriage rolled by ... the special train.'

   The Sunday School Treat takes place in a field a train-ride away from Bursley. The children play while the teachers organize the teas. A downpour spoils the end of the day.

2. LEE, Laurie
   Cider with Rosie
   (i) pp. 143–145 (Ch. 11, 'Outings and Festivals'); (ii) pp. 187–190
   'Our village outings ... in the sky.'

   The Lees walk to Sheepscombe to visit relations – it is fine and hot, they sing hymns on the way, spend the afternoon playing with and fighting their cousins, and return sleepily through the dusk.

3. ibid.
   (i) pp. 145–150 (Ch. 11, 'Outings and Festivals'); (ii) pp. 190–196
   'The first Choir outing ... and hangmen.'

   The Choir Outing to Weston-super-Mare – a lively charabanc journey, a day on the muddy beach and patronising slot machines on the pier, followed by a long sleepy drive home.

4. 'MISS READ'
   Village School
   (i) pp. 209–213 (Bk. 3, Ch. 22); (ii) pp. 210–213
   'Barrisford, as everyone ... with respectful eyes.'

   Fairacre Sunday School and choir outing. The vicar gives the coach the freedom of the seaside until teatime. The country children approach the sea with caution.

5. THOMAS, Dylan
   A Prospect of the Sea
   pp. 127–136 ('A Story')
   'If you can call it ... to the flying moon.'

   The young Dylan goes for a charabanc outing with his uncle and his cronies, to Porthcawl; but the party has assembled for one reason only, and that not to paddle at Porthcawl. Dylan observes his elders making fools of themselves, the worse for drink.

6. THOMPSON, Flora
   Lark Rise to Candleford
   (i) pp. 333–337 ('Over to Candleford', Ch. 12); (ii) pp. 299–303
   'Very early ... two tall girls in white.'

   The day of the long-promised trip to Candleford to visit relations. A pony and cart have been hired, and the family leaves the hamlet at dawn to travel through unfamiliar countryside and villages to reach Candleford at lunch-time.

EXECUTION

1. BENTLEY, Phyllis
   The Adventures of Tom Leigh
   see TRIALS 2
2. CAMUS, Albert
   The Outsider
   pp. 107–113 (Part 2, Ch. 5)
   (Themes in Life and Literature, pp. 107–110)
   'I have just refused ... that anyhow, was something.'
   When he is not tantalising himself with thoughts of a reprieve, the young man is oppressed by the awful certainty of the guillotine. He lives from one dawn to the next, waiting and listening.
3. DOSTOYEVSKY, Fyodor
   The Idiot
   (i) pp. 60–62 (Part 1, Ch. 5); (ii) pp. 90–93
   (Impact Two, pp. 43–45)
   (Crime and Punishment pp. 60–61)
   ' "Just now I confess" began the prince ... paused, and looked around.'
   The prince describes the execution he has seen, to the Epanchin sisters. He recalls the face of the criminal as he mounted the scaffold, and imagines what his last tortured thoughts must have been. The prince impresses on his audience, his own wonderment at the relentlessness of death by guillotine.
4. HEMINGWAY, Ernest
   For Whom the Bell Tolls
   pp. 97–100 (Ch. 10)
   'It was early in the morning ... But none was shot.'
   The revolt begins in a small town. The barracks of the Guardia Civil is taken, and having got one of them to show him how his pistol works, Pablo shoots four 'civiles', one after the other in the back of the head.
5. ibid.
   pp. 101–109 (Ch. 10)
   'What was done?' ... enemies and should be killed.'
   Pilar tells of how her husband organ-

ized the killing of twenty fascists. He had them marched between two lines of peasants armed with flails and clubs, to be beaten to death, and then be thrown over a cliff into the river.

6. KOESTLER, Arthur
   Darkness at Noon
   (i) pp. 211–216 ('The Grammatical Fiction', Part 3); (ii) pp. 207–211
   'The drumming sounded ... shrug of eternity.'
   Rubashov has a last tapping conversation with the prisoner in the next cell, before he is taken out and hand-cuffed. He is led down to the cellars where the executions take place. The end is quick and unceremonious.
7. ORWELL, George
   Animal Farm
   see TRIALS 9

EXECUTION (by) FIRING SQUAD

1. GREENE, Graham
   The Power and the Glory
   (i) pp. 208–211 (Part 4); (ii) pp. 214–217
   'Mr Tench bent ... he felt deserted.'
   While Mr Tench, the dentist, is treating the Chief of Police, and is conscious of his own indigestion, the fugitive priest is shot by a firing squad in the yard below. Mr Tench recognizes him, and is sad.
2. SHOLOKHOV, Mikhail
   And Quiet Flows the Don
   see RUSSIAN REVOLUTION 3
3. ibid.
   pp. 604–610 (Part 4, Ch. 9)
   'The detachment of Tatarsk ... without a backward glance.'
   Dog eats dog; cossack turns against cossack. Those up eliminate those who are down, in the name of the Revolution all are a part of. A crowd of villagers has assembled to watch batches of Red Guards being shot. None enjoys the spectacle.
   see also: EXECUTION (by) HANGING 5

EXECUTION (by) GAROTTE

1. FORESTER, C.S.
   The Gun
   (i) pp. 119–123 (Ch. 13); (ii) pp. 101–105
   'O'Neill was too pre-occupied ... the man's neck.'
   Having entered the town of Leon, O'Neill, the guerrilla leader, orders a scaffold and municipal garotte to be erected. It is a necessary part of the public rejoicing and causes much excitement. The victims are collaborators with the French.

EXECUTION (by) GUILLOTINE

1. DICKENS, Charles
   A Tale of Two Cities
   see FRENCH REVOLUTION – GUILLOTINE 1

2. DOSTOYEVSKY, Fyodor
   The Idiot
   (i) pp. 18–20 (Part 1, Ch. 2); (ii) pp. 46–48
   (Impact Two, pp. 43–45)
   'H'm! yes – that's true ... treated so, no man, no man!'
   The prince describes to a servant an execution by guillotine that he has seen in France. Though they are both impressed by the fact that the guillotine eliminates pain, the prince is struck by the dreadful certainty of death it ensures.

EXECUTION (by) HANGING

1. DICKENS, Charles
   A Tale of Two Cities
   pp. 69–173 (Bk. 2, Ch. 15)
   'I am again at work ... the sky rests upon it.'
   A countryman tells six soldiers to bring a prisoner to their village – he is the man who killed their lord of the manor. He is kept in a cage for a number of days, and then hanged above the public fountain.

2. FORESTER, C.S.
   The Gun
   (i) pp. 23–27 (Ch. 3), (ii) 23–27
   ' "We have laid our hands ... were now ended.'
   A band of Spanish guerilleros have captured an informer against them, and mean to hang him. He tries to bargain but the noose is already on before he remembers a vital piece of information he has. He delivers it proudly, but has only gained 5 more minutes thereby.

3. JOHNSON, Dorothy M.
   The Hanging Tree
   see RESCUE (from) HANGING 1

4. ROBINSON, Rony
   A Walk to see the King
   pp. 74–77 (Ch. 31)
   'And then, from just outside ... chosen King Tyler.'
   A man is brought in who has been caught looting. Wat Tyler resolves to make an example of him. In spite of John Ball's protests, he has him hanged, then he has his hands cut off. Young Will falls asleep much troubled by these events.

5. SHOLOKHOV, Mikhail
   And Quiet Flows the Don
   pp. 610–612 (Pt. 4, Ch. 9)
   'By the time all ... spittle and tears.'
   When the Red Guards have been shot and hurriedly buried, it is the turn of their officers Kriroshlikov and Podtielkov, to be hanged. An unconscionable mess is made of the job. The latter is a big man, and his feet touch the ground. He slowly strangles.

EXPEDITIONS

see also: TRAVEL;
VOYAGES

EXPEDITIONS

1. BOMBARD, Alain
   The Bombard Story
   passim.
   A lone voyager hazards the Atlantic,

in a dinghy in order to prove that a castaway can survive at sea by eating and drinking fish.

2. HEYERDAHL, Thor
   The Kon-Tiki Expedition
   passim.
   An expedition by balsa-raft across the Pacific Ocean, in 1947.

3. ibid.
   see MOUNTAINS 1

4. MORROW, Honore
   The Splendid Journey
   see RIVERS - CROSSING 3

5. ibid.
   pp. 168–172 (Ch. 13)
   'The children took a long night's sleep ... leave behind us, Johnny?'
   John finds the Indian who was their lifeline to Dr Whitman, dead and scalped. This means that if they are to be saved, they must not rest. It is only when the children are united in resistance to him, that John faces them with this brutal truth.

EXPULSION

see SCHOOL – EXPULSION

EXTRA-SENSORY PERCEPTION

see SPIRITUALISM;
TELEPATHY

FACTORIES

see also: FIRE – FACTORY

FACTORIES

1. BENNETT, Arnold
   Anna of the Five Towns
   pp. 114–124 (Ch. 8)
   'Probably no-one ... till it is done.'
   Anna is shown by Henry Mynors over his pottery works. She sees the clay pass through all its processes, until it emerges into the warehouse as piles of pottery. She is amazed by all she sees.

2. GREENWOOD, Walter
   Love on the Dole

pp. 48–50 (Part 1, Ch. 6)
'The foundry! What ... But they *were* men.'
Marlowe's engineering foundry. The din, the reverberations of hammers, the shining molten metal, and the men, who *are* men.

3. SILLITOE, Alan
   Saturday Night and Sunday Morning
   pp. 23–24 (Part 1, Ch. 2)
   (Work and Leisure, pp. 89–91)
   'Arthur walked into a huge ... morning had lost its terror!'
   Monday morning at the lathe. Arthur is soon engulfed by all the noises and life of the bicycle factory, so that he quickly gets over the first shock of the new working week.

FAILURE

see FRUSTRATION

FAIRS (and) FÊTES

1. ALLEN, Eric
   The Latchkey Children
   pp. 20–22 (Ch. 2)
   'They stopped at the place ... 'There's upstairs and everything.' '
   Pursued by bigger boys, Froggy and Duke Ellington Binns take refuge in Battersea fun fair. But the House of Laughter seems to be fraught with more dangers than the world outside, so they leave in just as big a hurry.

2. KIRKUP, James
   The Only Child
   pp. 160–162 (Ch. 13)
   'An annual event ... next year!'
   'The Figure of Light' is a fearsome thing of struts and machinery. The views from the top are sickening, and the rapid descents are not made more enjoyable by the sight of half-rotten wood, and rusty bolts.

3. LAWRENCE, D.H.
   Sons and Lovers
   (i) pp. 3–5 (Ch. 1); (ii) pp. 9–12
   'William appeared at ... their white aprons.'

William goes with his mother to the wakes. He is full to the brim with excitement, and he wins two egg cups. But his mother's afternoon is spoilt because she is out of her natural element, and her husband is drinking his wage away in the pub.

4. LEE, Laurie
   Cider with Rosie
   (i) pp. 150–154 (Ch. 11, 'Outings and Festivals'); (ii) pp. 196–202
   'The Parochial Church tea ... finish the lot.'
   The Parochial Church tea – an opportunity for overeating, and a musical entertainment rounded off with a session of slap-stick.

5. MANSFIELD, Katherine
   The Garden Party
   see HOLIDAYS 2

6. NAUGHTON, Bill
   The Goalkeeper's Revenge
   (i) pp. 61–66 ('A good sixpenn'orth'); (ii) pp. 61–67
   'Three of us were on our way ... And I ran off home.'
   Three boys hump coal for two hours and earn sixpence each. They are determined to extract every bit of goodness from this pittance, at the fair. One buys black peas and potatoes, another wins a coconut, and the third feels cheated by an act involving a tamer with a whip, and a dispirited lion.

7. SILLITOE, Alan
   The Loneliness of the Long-distance Runner
   (i) pp. 39–43 ('Noah's Ark'); (ii) pp. 90–94
   'From the war memorial ... his cup back on the counter.'
   Colin and Bert eke out their few pennies at the Nottingham Goose Fair. They cheat and they scrounge where they can. They make a tidy sum, but it soon slips through their fingers in exchange for shrimps, candy-floss, and helter-skelter.

8. ibid.
   see ESCAPADES 10

9. SILLITOE, Alan
   Saturday Night and Sunday Morning
   pp. 152–154 (Part 1, Ch. 11)
   'He met Winnie and Brenda ... belly of its infernal noise.'
   The annual Goose Fair in Nottingham. Arthur takes his two married lady friends and treats them to paper hats, a roundabout, the Caterpillar, and the roll-a-penny stall. They throw respectability to the winds and enjoy themselves hugely.
   see also PRANKS 13

10. THOMPSON, Flora
    Lark Rise to Candleford
    see CELEBRATIONS – ROYAL JUBILEE 2

11. ibid.
    (i) pp. 505–509 (Ch. 33, 'Candleford Green'); (ii) pp. 444–447
    'The maypole had ... in the twilight.'
    Candleford Green holds its annual Feast, and the Green is covered with stalls, sideshows, merry-go-rounds and swingboats. A brass band plays for dancing.

12. WATERHOUSE, Keith
    There is a Happy Land
    pp. 70–76
    'I watched him go ... Betty I'd won it.'
    The boy visits the fair by himself; he rolls pennies and wins enough for a ride, on the helter-skelter, which is a disappointment. He is given a plate by a woman who takes pity on him.

FAITH

see also: RELIGION;
SPIRITUALISM;
SUPERSTITION

FAITH

1. CHURCH, Richard
   Over the Bridge
   pp. 180–181 (Ch. 15)
   'It is not easy to describe ... consuming my body.'
   A Damascene vision. The author, at his classroom desk, is illuminated by

the opening words of John's Gospel. A power sweeps through him, and a new confidence inspires him for good.

2. GALLICO, Paul
   The Snow Goose/The Small Miracle
   (i) pp. 43–47 ('The Small Miracle');
   (ii) pp. 63–69
   'Father Damico, who had a broad head ... but the answer is no.'
   Pepino believes that if he can take his sick donkey into the crypt where the tomb of St. Francis lies, she will be cured. But the lay Supervisor, and the Bishop, disapprove of such unconventional behaviour, in a profitable shrine.

3. ibid.
   (i) pp. 48–54 ('The Small Miracle');
   (ii) pp. 71–79
   'Never had any small boy ... fly back to his Violetta's side.'
   The orphan Pepino seeks an audience with the Pope, in the matter of his sick donkey. Pepino's ingenuous eyes, his nosegay, and his note, win his way past the Swiss guard and a host of prelates, to the great man himself – who grants his request.

4. GRIMBLE, Sir Arthur
   A Pattern of Islands
   pp. 130–133 (Ch. 12)
   'When a man is dying ... more and collapsed.'
   Fr. Choblet, a Roman Catholic priest, defies Island regulations, and a westerly gale, to paddle a canoe for twenty miles, and only half a canoe for a further eight, to give the last sacrament to a brother priest.

5. ibid.
   see SUPERSTITION 8

6. ibid.
   pp. 140–144 (Ch. 13)
   'A month later ... proud to accept.'
   Arthur is called to what would seem to be Fr. Choblet's death-bed. The priest is in great pain and is semi-delirious. Arthur gives him castor oil, and lies to him that he is administering healing medicine. The Father's faith is enough to see him through.

7. MARSHALL, James Vance
   Walkabout
   (i) pp. 43–45 (Chs 7, 8); 52–54 (Ch. 11); (ii) pp. 54–57; 67–68
   'White girl and black boy ... into the desert'; 'Physically the Australian ... come to claim him.'
   Mary and the bush boy stare at each other, the former because she is a girl and she fancies she sees desire in his eyes; and he believes he sees the spirit of Death in hers. From this moment, he is certain that Death, his greatest enemy, has set its seal on him, and this belief is in itself enough to kill him.

8. WRIGHT, Richard
   Black Boy
   pp. 43–45 (Ch. 2)
   'Uncle Hoskins had a horse ... barrier between us.'
   Uncle Hoskins takes Richard out in his horse and buggy. He makes believe that he is going to drive right out into the middle of the Mississippi. Richard is so frightened that he can never trust Uncle Hoskins again.

FALLING

see ACCIDENTS – FALLING

FAMILY

see also: BROTHERS; FATHERS; GRANDPARENTS; HOME; MOTHERS; PARENTS; RELATIVES

FAMILY

1. ALLEN, Walter
   All in a Lifetime
   pp. 64–66 (Ch. 7)
   'As we crossed the yard ... was the nonsense.'
   The Thompsons. They're a cut above families of Billy's acquaintance. Mr Thompson is a nice eater, the food is

ample, and the meal is conducted in simple good humour.

2. DICKENS, Charles
Great Expectations
(i) pp. 213–218 (Ch. 23); (ii) pp. 183–186
'It came to my knowledge ... the hopeless subject.'
The Pocket family at the dining table. The aristocratic Mrs Pocket mismanages the baby, and flies at her daughter when she comes to the rescue. Mr Pocket is amiable, ineffectual, and as a rule, perplexed.

3. ELIOT, George
The Mill on the Floss
pp. 332–334 (Ch. 1, Part 3)
'Certainly the religious ... with bitter herbs.'
The Dodson family stand together, consider themselves superior to all others and have a very strict code. Their ideas of duty and propriety are a mixture of Christian ethic and social custom.

4. FRANK, Anne
The Diary of Anne Frank
see PARENTS 2, 3

5. LAWRENCE, D.H.
Sons and Lovers
(i) pp. 63–65 (Ch. 4); (ii) pp. 82–84
'The only times ... closely in the warmth.'
Morel as family man. When he tells his children about life down the pit, and when he instructs them in a simple skill, he is almost the man his wife married.

6. ibid.
see MEALS – TEAS 1

7. LEE, Harper
To Kill a Mockingbird
(i) pp. 148–150 (Ch. 14); (ii) pp. 145–147
'I put on my pyjamas ... to run off to.'
Dill runs away from home, because there is no love there. He is deprived of being needed, so he makes for the Finch's where he has always been made welcome.

8. LEE, Laurie
Cider with Rosie
(i) pp. 41–43 (Ch. 4, 'The Kitchen'); (ii) pp. 61–63
'Meanwhile we lived ... no one quite understood.'
Laurie Lee describes his half-sisters and brothers.

9. ibid.
(i) pp. 48–53 (Ch. 4, 'The Kitchen'); (ii) pp. 70–77
(Here, Now and Beyond, pp. 47–50)
'The day was over ... that's all.'
An evening at home, the whole family in the kitchen – eating, homework, violin practice, keeping the fire alight, the arrival and gossip of the girls, drowsinesss.

10. NESBIT, E.
The Railway Children
see MISFORTUNE 5

11. SILLITOE, Alan
The Loneliness of the Long-distance Runner
(i) pp. 68–70 ('On Saturday Afternoon'); (ii) pp. 102–103
(Conflict 1, pp. 42–43)
'I've never known a family ... somebody's back gate.'
The writer's family is given to black looks. They infect each other with their peevishness, and are 'fed up' without quite knowing why. The 'old man' comes in and after a few blunt questions, sends his son to skulk outside.
see also: SUICIDE 14

12. SILLITOE, Alan
Saturday Night and Sunday Morning
pp. 67–70 (Part 1, Ch. 5)
'Sit down then, duck ... Favourites on Sunday morning.'
Aunt Ada's family: a hard-working, drinking, large-hearted lot, the products of two very different fathers. Ada has had a hard time of it, but she enjoys the attentions of a jealous husband, and several incomes.

13. TATE, Joan
Sam and Me
see HOME 9

FAMILY – FIGHTING

1. GORKY, Maxim
   Childhood
   (i) pp. 18–22 (Ch. 2); (ii) pp. 25–27
   'This was the beginning ... too glad
   to get out of that kitchen.'
   Gorky is initiated into the wild ways
   of the 'stupid tribe'. His uncles,
   Mikhail and Yakov, argue over their
   father's property. They come to
   blows, and draw blood before the
   whole household.
2. ibid.
   (i) pp. 109–113 (Ch. 5); (ii) pp.
   87–90
   'Sometimes grandmother would come
   in ... numbed by unbearable pain.'
   His Grandfather tells Gorky dark
   stories of the past. He reproaches
   himself on account of his wayward
   sons, beating himself frenziedly, as if
   doing penance. Grandmother tries to
   calm him. In his passion, he strikes
   her, and drives her from the room.
   Gorky, who has often tasted his
   violence, is stunned, by its infliction
   on his old grandmother.
3. ibid.
   (i) pp. 121–126 (Ch. 6); (ii) pp.
   96–99
   'I do not think that my grandfather. ... hauled me roughly to the
   attic.'
   The Kashirin household becomes a
   battleground when Uncle Mikhail's
   blood is up, and he has drunk too
   much. He comes rampaging, to intimidate his father into giving him the
   inheritance. In one of these threshold
   skirmishes, his mother's arm is broken.
4. ibid.
   see ASSAULT (by) BROTHERS 1
5. LEE, Laurie
   Cider with Rosie
   (i) pp. 175–177 (Ch. 13, 'Last Days');
   (ii) pp. 228–230
   'When the girls ... on the fireguard.'
   One of Laurie's half-sisters and her
   boyfriend confront the family with
   sudden marriage plans – a violent

argument ensues, ending in a fight in
which all participate.
6. MADDOCK, Reginald
   The Pit
   pp. 55–58 (Ch. 5)
   'When we go back to Massey's
   Farm ... and I wanted to get away.'
   The police have been to Butch's
   home, in his absence, and his father
   accepts the circumstantial evidence of
   theft, against his son. There is a
   violent argument: Mr Reece hits
   Butch; Jenny intervenes and is hit in
   her turn. This inflames Butch to
   righteous anger, and for the first
   time, he pays his father back for all
   the beatings he has received from
   him.

FAMILY – PARTIES

1. DICKENS, Charles
   Bleak House
   (i) pp. 612–615 (Ch. 49); (ii) pp
   612–615
   'It is the old girl's birthday ... this
   delightful entertainment.'
   It is Mrs Bagnett's birthday, and on
   this day all cooking and house-work is
   undertaken by her husband and
   children. The thought is kind, but she
   undergoes great trials watching their
   ineptitude.

FAMILY – QUARRELS

see also: MARRIAGE – QUARRELS;
QUARRELS – BROTHERS (and) SISTERS
QUARRELS – FATHERS (and) DAUGH-
TERS;
QUARRELS – MOTHERS (and) SONS

FAMILY – QUARRELS

1. BALDWIN, James
   Go Tell it on the Mountain
   pp. 43–48 (Ch. 1, 'The Seventh Day')
   'His father now turned ... to know
   that by now.'
   Roy has been stabbed by whites, and
   their father, feeling his prejudice to

be vindicated, points the moral home to Roy's brother John. Aunt Florence defends his family against his tirade; but her brother's blood is up. He slaps his wife's face, and then beats Roy when he speaks up for his mother. Florence has the last word.

2. CHURCH, Richard
   Over the Bridge
   see CYCLING 2

3. HINES, Barry
   A Kestrel for a Knave
   (i) pp. 43–48; (ii) pp. 35–39
   'What's tha want ... under the lines.'
   Billy has a routine argument – and punch-up – with his older brother, Jud, then his mother comes in to quell them. Mother, and Jud, exchange light-hearted insults, before both go out on the town, leaving Billy on his own, reading.

4. LAWRENCE, D.H.
   Sons and Lovers
   (i) pp.41–44 (Ch. 2), (ii) pp. 55–60
   'Sunday was the same ... she had loved him.'
   The Family turns against Morel. He filches sixpence from his wife's purse. Discovered, he makes as if to leave home; but he returns the same night humiliated by the failure of this histrionic ploy.
   see also: ASSAULT (by) HUSBANDS 1

5. ibid.
   (i) pp. 58–59 (Ch. 4), (ii) pp. 76–77
   'All the children ... to bed miserably.'
   William, roused by his father's bullying ways, challenges him to a fight on the hearth-rug. Like boxers, they dance, watchfully, until a word from Mrs Morel recalls them to their senses.
   see also: FATHERS 4

6. ibid.
   (i) pp. 213–215 (Ch. 8); (ii) pp. 262–264
   (Visions of Life 1, pp. 25–27)
   '"My Boy,' she said ... forget the scene.'
   Morel arrives home drunk, disturbing

a poignant mother-son scene. When he finds there is no supper for him, he destroys Paul's in his rage. Paul and his father very nearly come to blows. Only Mrs Morel's fainting brings them to their senses.

7. LAWRENCE, D.H.
   The Virgin and the Gipsy
   pp. 35–40 (Ch. 4)
   (Visions of Life 2, pp. 26–31)
   'Lucille at this time was ... intelligent, by the river.'
   Yvette and Lucille are dressmaking. The former is nettled by Aunt Cissie's preparations for tea, and by Granny's superstition about a mirror that is dropped. Tempers are lost, and hasty words are exchanged. Lucille is banished to her room, and Granny tells a lie.

8. TOWNSEND, John Rowe
   Gumble's Yard
   pp. 9–14 (Ch. 1)
   'Along the other side of the street ... mug of tea, I felt much better.'
   Sandra and Kevin are returning to their foster home for their Saturday lunch, when they see their uncle and his common-law wife, making off down the street, quarrelling. They fend for themselves, suspecting, but not knowing, that they have been abandoned.

9. WATERHOUSE, Keith
   Billy Liar
   pp. 78–82 (Ch. 6)
   'I reached Hillcrest ... I turned to go.'
   Billy arrives late for lunch – this misdemeanour releases a whole series of grievances from his parents, and Billy worsens the situation by being rude to his grandmother.

FAMILY – REUNIONS

1. GORKY, Maxim
   Childhood
   (i) pp. 14–17 (Ch. 1); (ii) pp. 22–24
   'I remember my grandmother's childlike ... magenta-oil of vitriol ...'

The steamboat reaches Nizhni, Grandmother's town, where Gorky and his mother are to live, in the Grandparental home. The whole ménage comes to meet the boat: there is considerable hugging and kissing. Gorky is on his guard.

2. THOMPSON, Flora
   Lark Rise to Candleford
   (i) pp. 340–346 ('Over to Candleford', Ch. 21); (ii) pp. 306–311
   'The inside of the house ... be getting on.'
   Laura's family visit their uncle and his family, who are well-to-do and live a very different kind of life. Laura is amazed by all she sees. The meeting ends on a bitter note when her father and Uncle quarrel over politics.

3. ibid.
   (i) pp. 348–351 ('Over to Candleford', Ch. 22); (ii) pp. 313–314
   'Laura had never known ... legs sticking up.'
   The second family they visit is a marked contrast to the first – here the atmosphere is easy-going and loving.

FARMING

1. DEFOE, Daniel
   Robinson Crusoe
   (i) pp. 85–87; (ii) pp. 116–118 (Ch. 11)
   'I was now, in the ... with corn and bread.'
   Man the farmer. Crusoe relearns by trial and error how to cultivate corn for his bread, and to regard all other animals as pests.

2. LAWRENCE, D.H.
   The White Peacock
   see RABBITS – CATCHING 1

3. LEE, Laurie
   Cider with Rosie
   (i) pp. 103–104 (Ch. 8, 'Winter and Summer'); (ii) pp. 139–140
   'So we went ... Walt Kerry.'
   The village boys go to help on Farmer Wells' farm on a very cold day, in order to get warm. They help in the cow-shed, Laurie feeding a calf.

4. LESSING, Doris
   The Grass is Singing
   pp. 106–112 (Ch. 6)
   'At lunch-time he did not speak ... about rabbits or turkeys.'
   One line after another suggests itself to Dick, as the way to make his farm pay. First it is bees, then it is pigs, and then turkeys. Each of these fads fails through bad luck and mismanagement, so that, when Dick suggests they breed rabbits, Mary tells him what she thinks of him as a farmer, and as a man.
   see also: AUTHORITY 5

5. MACKEN, Walter
   God made Sunday and Other Stories
   pp. 150–156 ('This was my day')
   'It was hard ... don't have much to do.'
   The farmer begins his day by shooting a fox. Subsequently, he avoids (barely) an enraged bull, and rescues a stray lamb, at no small risk to himself. He is not sure, at the end of the day, whether it has been a hard day or not.

6. MOORE, John
   Portrait of Elmbury
   pp. 64–68 (Part 3)
   'During that winter ... towards some distant brook.'
   There is a wide-spread epidemic of foot-and-mouth disease, which brings disaster to many farmers. Their entire herd must be slaughtered and burnt.

7. ibid.
   pp. 117–123 (Part 3)
   'Mr Jeff's farm had been sold ... with all my heart.'
   One of the large farms of the area is sold – the author takes part in the sale of the property, of the stock, and of the 'Tenant Right' (the work already completed for the following year). The whole sale gives a picture of a farmer's life.

8. STEINBECK, John
   The Grapes of Wrath
   see CAPITALISM 6

9. THOMPSON, Flora
Lark Rise to Candleford
(i) pp. 41–47 ('Lark Rise', Ch. 3); (ii) pp. 51–56
'When the men and boys ... as 'men's tales.' '
Men and boys in the fields of Oxfordshire, sowing broadcast, ploughing behind horses, and mowing with scythes. Field names and nicknames; respect (and muttered curses) paid to the bailiff; and a lunch of bread and cold bacon at the field edge.

FARMING – HARVEST

1. ACHEBE, Chinua
Things fall apart
(i) pp. 20–23 (Ch. 3); (ii) pp. 20–23
'After the wine had been drunk ... patience beyond words.'
Freak drought and heavy rains ruin Okonkwo's first crop of yams. He is having to support his parents, and prove himself, at a time when the world has gone mad – but he survives.

2. THOMPSON, Flora
Lark Rise to Candleford
(i) pp. 255–260 ('Lark Rise', Ch. 15); (ii) pp. 233–237
'Harvest time was a natural ... and the stripped fields.'
Very early in the morning, the village is astir for the harvest. In the 1880's the mechanical reaper is in the fields, but so, too, are the men with their scythes taking their pace from the 'King of the Mowers'. After three weeks of very long, busy days, the rickyard is full, and the fields are stripped.

FASHION

1. SEWELL, Anna
Black Beauty
pp. 52–56 (Ch. 10)
'I had often wondered ... what God has made.'
The horses discuss the cruelty to animals perpetrated in the name of

fashion – docking of tails, cutting dogs' ears and the wearing of blinkers.

2. THOMPSON, Flora
Lark Rise to Candleford
(i) pp. 101–103 ('Lark Rise', Ch. 6); (ii) pp. 102–104
'Delighted as the women ... anything, except food.'
The village is a year or two behind the fashion of the town, but it is none the less strictly adhered to. The cut of a dress is thought of as particularly important. The bustle is disparaged one day, and the next, it is 'all the go'.

FATHER CHRISTMAS

1. KIRKUP, James
The Only Child
see CHRISTMAS 7

FATHERS

see also: DEATH (of) FATHER;
FAMILY;
GRANDPARENTS

FATHERS

1. FOAKES, Grace
Between High Walls
pp. 5–6 (Ch. 3)
'I found my father ... you could do it.'
He is a forbidding man, Mr Foakes, and a hard taskmaster. He is the head of the household, to whom it is not easy for a young girl to relate.

2. GREENE, Graham
The Power and the Glory
(i) pp. 75–77 (Part 11, Ch. 1); (ii) pp. 80–83
'He walked across ... He turned his mule south.'
The fugitive priest confronts the daughter he fathered in a weak moment, but whom he does not know or understand. He wants to love her, he feels that attachment to her that a father should feel. But it is too late,

and he knows he can do nothing to help her, as a father should.

3. LAWRENCE, D.H.
Sons and Lovers
(i) pp. 58–59 (Ch. 4); (ii) pp. 76–77
'All the children ... to bed, miserably.
The Morel children are united in their fear and hatred of their violent, miner father. He feels that they are in league with their mother against him, and in his worst moments, returns their hatred.

4. ibid.
(i) pp. 59–62 (Ch. 4); (ii) pp. 77–81
'When William was growing ... too far to alter.'
A study in tension. The children loathe their father; they exclude him from all their conversation. Yet he is always there to be reckoned with in their thoughts, like a malignant cell.
see also: FAMILY 5

5. ibid.
see FAMILY – QUARRELS 6

6. LEE, Harper
To Kill a Mockingbird
(i) pp. 95–98 (Ch. 10); (ii) pp. 95–98
'Atticus was feeble ... touchdowns for the Baptists.'
Scout is ashamed of her father. It seems he can do none of the things a model father can do, like play football, and drink. She writes him off as too old at fifty.

7. ibid.
(i) pp. 98–105 (Ch. 10); (ii) pp. 98–104
'One Saturday, Jem ... just like me!'
Sequel to the above: Atticus Finch, without wanting to, without seeking to, proves himself in front of his children. He shoots a mad dog as if to the manner born.

8. STOLZ, Mary
Ready or Not
pp. 75–76 (Ch. 6)
'Verna and Morgan ... twice before they heard it.'
Morgan visits her friend Verna's house: the atmosphere is leaden with

the brooding temper of her father, who snaps rather than speaks. When he leaves the room, Mrs Herzog and the girls relax.

9. THOMAS, Leslie
This Time Next Week
see SAILORS 2

10. TWAIN, Mark
The Adventures of Huckleberry Finn
(i) pp. 20–24 (Ch. 5); (ii) pp. 69–72 (Conflict 1, pp. 44–47)
'I had shut the door ... make it warm for *him*.'
His father steals in upon Huck's newly settled life, and rages at the 'frills' his son is putting on, and at the 'airs' his education is giving him. He demands money for whisky.

11. WELLS, H.G.
Kipps
see BIRTH 10

12. WRIGHT, Richard
Black Boy
see HUNGER 12

FATHERS (and) DAUGHTERS

see also: QUARRELS – FATHERS (and) DAUGHTERS

FATHERS (and) DAUGHTERS

1. BANKS, Lynne Reid
The L-Shaped Room
pp. 33–36 (Ch. 2)
(*see also:* Conflict 2, pp. 22–24)
'That had been ... to seeing this.'
Having had her pregnancy confirmed, unmarried Jane goes to tell her father in his office. Annoyed by him, as usual, she tells him more brutally than she had wished, and only too late sees how she has hurt him.

2. JAMES, Henry
Washington Square
pp. 87–93 (Ch. 18)
'Catherine sat alone ... to see it out.'
Catherine is torn – she has no wish to offend her father, for whom she has a profound respect. He disapproves of her, however, and she determines to

defy him. The announcement of her intentions produces a difficult conversation, and attitudes on both sides are hardened.

3. LAWRENCE, D.H.
   The Rainbow
   see CHILDREN – TANTRUMS 3
4. ibid.
   pp. 118–120 (Ch. 4)
   'It was raining ... what was life to him.'
   Tom Brangwen sees his daughter, Anna, in the arms of his nephew, Will. He is proud and yet he is angry, because his rightful place in the affections of his daughter has been taken by a callow young man who would have Anna grow up too soon.
5. ibid.
   pp. 211–215 (Ch. 8)
   'From the first ... rose out of her sight.'
   Will Brangwen delights in his daughter. She runs to meet him from work, and joins with him in play. He talks to her of serious matters, and of fancies, dotingly.
6. ibid.
   pp. 221–223 (Ch. 8)
   (Young Impact 3, pp. 86–89)
   'The children were dressed ... he went his way.'
   Will asks his daughter to help him plant out some potatoes. She feels responsible helping him, but she does not do the job properly. Her father is insensitive to the effect his careless reproof has on her. It reinforces her own profound sense of failure.

FATHERS (and) SONS

1. LAWRENCE, D.H.
   Sons and Lovers
   see FAMILY – QUARRELS 5
2. THACKERAY, William
   Vanity Fair
   (i) pp. 224–227 (Ch. 24); (ii) pp. 279–281
   'There was a picture ... green leaves in Russell Square.'

Mr Osborne retires to his study on the news that his son has married the girl he had forbidden him. He looks over all the mementoes of his son, locks them away, burns his will and scratches George's name from the family bible.

FEAR

see also: COURAGE;
COWARDICE;
HORROR

FEAR

1. BALDWIN, Michael
   Grandad with Snails
   pp. 69–73 (Ch. 8)
   'Whose eye had I just ... coming back there again.'
   As he is finding his seat in the children's cinema, Michael steps on something he takes to be a boy's eye. He tries during two films to scrape the sticky mess off his foot, in fear of what the eyeless boy will do to him when the lights go on. An ice-cream wrapper found on his boot does not allay his fear.
2. DE JONG, Meindert
   The Wheel on the School
   see DAYDREAMS 2
3. ibid.
   (i) pp. 60–65 (Ch. 6); (ii) pp. 62–66
   'Eelka climbed heavily ... to have to stir again.'
   Eelka is trying to lower a heavy old wagon wheel from a hayloft by himself. He ties a rope to himself, and to the wheel, but he is not strong enough to hold it. Having been swept across the floor, he manages to save himself, half in, half out, till the rope breaks and the wheel falls.
   see also: FEAR (of) DOGS 1
4. DICKENS, Charles
   A Tale of Two Cities
   see ROBBERY – GRAVES 1

5. HOLBROOK, David
   Flesh Wounds
   see SECOND WORLD WAR – BOMBING 3
6. LESSING, Doris
   Nine African Stories
   pp. 26–29 ('The Old Chief Msh-langa')
   'Beyond our boundaries ... enclosing arm round the village.'
   A girl walking alone on the veld is suddenly seized by a very physical fear. She goes hot and cold, spins in panic, and sees her surroundings take on bizarre shapes. It is fear of the bigness and silence of the country, under the African sun.
7. MANNING, Olivia
   The Play Room
   pp. 171–174 (Sn. 2, Ch. 3)
   'The lowering sunlight ... down Rowantree Avenue.'
   Laura's friend Vicky and Vicky's boyfriend have left her in a remote lane while they go off to talk. Hours pass, it grows dark and cold, but they do not return. Laura has to walk long and frightening miles home.
8. TATE, Joan
   Whizz Kid
   pp. 11–15 (Clee Ch. 1)
   'I yawned ... scooped out melon. Empty.'
   Nibs has left Clee alone in the car in a lay-by at night for a few minutes – but he doesn't return. Clee is very scared and very confused about what to do.
9. WRIGHT, Richard
   Black Boy
   see FAITH 8

FEAR (of) ANIMALS

1. GRIMBLE, Sir Arthur
   A Pattern of Islands
   see OCTOPUS 3

FEAR (of) BULLYING

1. WRIGHT, Richard
   Black Boy
   see COURAGE 20

FEAR (of) DARKNESS

1. BAWDEN, Nina
   Carrie's War
   (i) pp. 48–51 (Ch. 4); (ii) pp. 42–45
   ' "There's nothing to mind" ... warmth and safety.'
   Carrie and Nick have been sent to collect a turkey for Christmas, but their way leads through a dark, eerie wood. They hear strange noises, see a queer gobbling creature and run blindly for the door of the house.

FEAR (of) DEATH

1. TWAIN, Mark
   The Adventures of Tom Sawyer
   see LOST (in) CAVES 1

FEAR (of) DOGS

1. DE JONG, Meindert
   The Wheel on the School
   (i) pp. 94–95 (Ch. 8); (ii) pp. 92–93
   'Lina took one step ... dry in the ebb tide.'
   Lina comes face to face with a growling dog, and is very scared. The first thing that comes into her mind is to sing to give herself courage. She sings long and loud, till she is out of reach.

FEAR (of) FIRE

1. SOUTHALL, Ivan
   Ash Road
   see FOREST – FIRES 3
2. ibid.
   pp. 142–147 (Ch. 11)
   'Stevie sat on the end ... she screamed "Come Down".'
   Stevie is alone in the house, and frightened. Then Pippa comes home and shouts him into frantic activity. They do all in their limited power to save the house from the fast approaching bush fire.

FEAR (of) FLYING

1. PEYTON, K.M.
   The Edge of the Cloud
   (i) pp. 39–42 (Ch. 4); (ii) pp. 51–54
   'The Fairman lurched towards them. ... said Sandy. 'You were fine.''
   Christina is persuaded to take the controls of a skeleton aeroplane. She panics, is comforted by Sandy, the sympathetic instructor, and is thoroughly ashamed of herself.
2. ibid.
   (i) pp. 105–109 (Ch. 10); (ii) pp. 130–135
   'She drove back to Elm Park ... Christina said no more.'
   There is such excitement at the flying prospects ahead, that Will browbeats Christina into looping the loop with him. She is terrified beyond words. At the last moment she leans out of the cockpit to stop Will from going through with the stunt.

FEAR (of) GHOSTS

1. LEE, Laurie
   Cider with Rosie
   (i) pp. 15–17 (Ch. 2, 'First Names');
   (i) pp. 29–31
   'But there was one ... in the pantry.'
   Sitting in the candle-light one evening the family hears the approach of a snorting, chain-clanking 'beast' – Jones's goat.
2. MANKOWITZ, Wolf
   Make me an Offer
   pp. 128–134 ('The Devil and the Cow')
   'Naturally my great grandmother ... my great grandmother cared.'
   Legend has it that the Devil inhabits the ruins on the hill – great-grandmother ignores this and goes to look for her cow. Igor, the carpenter, believes it, but goes to look for gold buried there. They frighten each other.

3. THOMPSON, Flora
   Lark Rise to Candleford
   (i) pp. 324–326 ('Over to Candleford', Ch. 20); (ii) pp. 292–293
   'When Laura said ... bear down on one.'
   Laura thinks she sees a ghost near a locked cupboard, and elaborates the story under questioning. No amount of explanation reassures her.

FEAR (of) HEIGHTS

1. ALLEN, Eric
   The Latchkey Children
   pp. 58–63 (Ch. 6)
   'Etty went over to the tree ... snatched it from him.'
   A kitten is stuck up in a tree. Etty and Billandben borrow a ladder, and the latter, against his better judgement, climbs up, to rescue it. He nearly manages, but nearly falls. Fear immobilises him, so that he has to be rescued in his turn.
2. FALKNER, J. Meade
   Moonfleet
   see ESCAPE (from) SOLDIERS 1

FEAR (of) INTRUDERS

1. DU MAURIER, Daphne
   Jamaica Inn
   pp. 174–175 (Ch. 12)
   'He threw back his head ... Harry the pedlar.'
   Mary, her aunt and her uncle, hiding in the inn after the final wrecking expedition hear someone outside.
2. FRANK, Anne
   The Diary of Anne Frank
   pp. 69–71 (25.3.43)
   'Yesterday, Mummy, Daddy, ... took us seriously.'
   In the evenings the Franks and Van Daans leave their hideout, to use the office space downstairs, as well. One evening they are disturbed by noises in the warehouse below, and retreat in great fear to the top of the house.

3. ibid.
    pp. 168–175 (11.4.44)
    'My head throbs ... courage and cheerfulness.'
    There is a break-in in the warehouse, and a real danger that the police will be called, and a search made. There follows a night of silent fear and discomfort until the truth is known.

FEAR (of) MONSTERS

1. GOLDING, William
    Lord of the Flies
    (i) pp. 46–48 (Ch. 2); 66–67 (Ch. 3); (ii) pp. 38–40; 56–58
    'He handed the conch ... the assembly was silent.'; ' "If it rains" ... "See? That's all." '
    The most fundamental of fears: the fear of the unknown. One of the 'littluns' says he has seen a 'beastie'. This fear infects the other small boys, and defies Ralph's efforts to reason with them.
2. WELLS, H.G.
    The War of the Worlds
    see MONSTERS 7
3. ibid.
    see PANIC 2, 3

FEAR (of) POLICE

1. GREENE, Graham
    The Power and the Glory
    (i) pp. 42–44 (Part 1, Ch. 4); (ii) pp. 47–49
    'Padre Jose went in ... unforgiveable sin, despair.'
    Padre Jose declines to satisfy a simple religious need – the need of parents for comfort at the young daughter's graveside – because religious expression has been banned by the authorities.

FEAR (of) PURSUERS

1. STEVENSON, R.L.
    Treasure Island
    see KILLING (in) SELF-DEFENCE 1

FEAR (of) SEA

1. SPERRY, Armstrong
    The Boy who was afraid
    pp. 2–4 (Ch. 1)
    'It was the sea ... under the assault.'
    Mafatu's fear of the sea is traced to its origins – at the age of three he and his mother were caught in a hurricane while out in a canoe. She managed to get him to a small island, but died almost immediately.

FEAR (of) STRANGERS

1. DICKENS, Charles
    Great Expectations
    (i) pp. 1–6; 12–18 (Chs. 1, 2, 3); (ii) pp. 1–5; 11–15
    (Loneliness and Parting, pp. 2–8)
    'Ours was the marsh ... home withou stopping.'; 'It was Christmas .. known where it was.'
    Young Pip is intimidated by a escaped convict into stealing a file and some food for him, from hi watchful sister. In mortal fear of the convict, and mindful of his threats Pip manages to steal away from the house, with the items demanded, t his rendezvous by the river.
2. TOWNSEND, John Rowe
    The Intruder
    pp. 4–10 (Ch. 2)
    'Colour was fading ... round his legs. Arnold Haithwaite, the Sand Pilot guides a mysterious stranger across the sands as the dangerous tide come in. At one point the stranger drag him into the water and they struggl – the stranger claims he fell and panicked. Arnold's mistrust and fea deepen when the man says he i Arnold Haithwaite.
3. ibid.
    see CRIME – DETECTION 3

FEAR (of) THIEVES

1. GASKELL, Mrs
    Cranford

(i) pp. 135–153 (Ch. 10); (ii) pp. 138–151
'I think a series ... in extrication.'
A number of curious events in Cranford arouse suspicions that a gang of thieves are at work. The ladies talk of nothing else, and take elaborate precautions against possible attack.

2. STEINBECK, John
The Pearl
pp. 35–38 (Ch. 3)
'The doctor shrugged ... with hope.'
Kino has found an enormous pearl, but in the midst of his elation, is afraid of thieves. In the middle of the night he hears an intruder whom he attacks and frightens away.

FEAR (of) TUNNELS

1. NESBIT, E.
The Railway Children
(i) pp. 175–177 (Ch. 11); (ii) pp. 188–191
'I'm going first ... in his natural voice.'
The children suspect that one runner in a Hare and Hounds Race has had an accident in a railway tunnel, so go in to investigate. They find it more frightening than they had expected, especially when a train thunders past them.

FEAR (of) WAR

1. CRANE, Stephen
The Red Badge of Courage
see WAR 3

FEAR (of) WITCHCRAFT

1. DE JONG, Meindert
The Tower by the Sea
see WITCHCRAFT 3

FÊTES

see FAIRS (and) FÊTES

FIGHTING

see also: ASSAULT; BOXING; BULLYING; FAMILY – FIGHTING; MARRIAGE – QUARRELS; REVENGE; WRESTLING

FIGHTING (by) ANIMALS

1. DURRELL, Gerald
My Family and Other Animals
pp. 204–208 (Part 3, Ch. 13)
'I was sitting in bed ... insects drifting about the lamp.'
A fight to the finish between an athletic lizard, and a pregnant mantis. They fight valiantly, and spectacularly, on the ceiling, and on Gerald's bed. Geronimo the lizard is victorious, after a fatal error on the part of Cicely the mantis.

2. LONDON, Jack
The Call of the Wild
pp. 36–38 (Ch. 3)
'Buck did not cry out ... and found it good.'
The long-delayed contest between Buck and Spitz is entered upon without warning, but both dogs know that this is it; that one of them will lead the pack, and the other will be torn limb from limb by it.

3. LONDON, Jack
White Fang
pp. 15–18 (Ch. 2)
'His was the luck ... He would go and see.'
The young cub, fresh in the world, happens on a nest full of ptarmigan chicks. The first he claps his jaws on tastes good, so he eats the lot. Then he has to reckon with their mother. He deals valiantly with her, but gives up under the rain of her pecks on his nose.

4. ibid.
see DOGS 8

97

FIGHTING (by) BOYS

1. BARSTOW, Stan
   Joby
   pp. 73–76 (Ch. 5)
   'Joby was alone ... up to Gus. It was enough.'
   Joby is annoyed at having been ejected from the cinema unjustly, so he is easily provoked into a fight with Gus, whose fault it was. It is a short-lived scuffle but honour is satisfied on both sides.

2. LESSING, Doris
   Nine African Stories
   see FRIENDS – BOYS 4

3. MADDOCK, Reginald
   The Pit
   pp. 43–47 (Ch. 4)
   'I found him with young Dawson ... before your mothers see you.'
   Butch Reece is determined to make Skiff Morrison confess to the crime of which he, himself, is accused. He takes him on, though Skiff is bigger than he is, and acquits himself well. They are both the bloodier for their scrap, but Butch warns Skiff that the fight has just begun.

4. SALINGER, J.D.
   The Catcher in the Rye
   pp. 47–49 (Ch. 6)
   'Ed Banky was the ... want to know the truth.'
   Holden accuses his room-mate of loose conduct. The next thing he knows, he's on his back on the floor. And the next thing after that, he has a bloody nose.

5. THOMAS, Dylan
   A Portrait of the Artist as a Young Dog
   pp. 39–40 ('The Fight')
   'I was standing ... show the blood-stains.'
   Dylan annoys Mr Samuels, and is annoyed in his turn, by a stranger who provokes him to fight. It is a hard fight, but a short one: Mr Samuel's shouts of encouragement unite the two boys as nothing else could have done.

6. THOMAS, Leslie
   This Time Next Week
   see INITIATION 5

7. TWAIN, Mark
   The Adventures of Tom Sawyer
   see RIVALS – BOYS 3

8. WATERHOUSE, Keith
   There is a Happy Land
   pp. 97–101 (Ch. 14); (Conflict 1, pp. 111–115); (Family and School, pp. 74–76)
   'It must have been ... shouting: "Laddy-lass".'
   The boy has been forced into a fight with a school mate, but thinks he will easily win. However, the spectators are against him and his opponent turns out to be very skilful. He is soundly beaten.

FIGHTING (by) BOYS (at) SCHOOL

1. DICKENS, Charles
   David Copperfield
   pp. 324–325 (Ch. 18)
   'The shade of a young butcher ... fought him.'
   Looking back on his school-days David Copperfield remembers a butcher whom he fought for no specific reason, and for whom he proved no match.

2. HINES, Barry
   A Kestrel for a Knave
   (i) pp. 90–95; (ii) pp. 73–77
   'At break Billy ... only two in sight.'
   Billy gets involved in a play-ground fight with the bully MacDowall. It begins as a slanging match, then, because Billy's family pride is hurt, he throws coke at his enemy. This leads to a very public fight on the coke-tip, and the intervention of the teacher on playground duty.
   see also: BULLYING (by) BOYS 3

3. HUGHES, Thomas
   Tom Brown's Schooldays
   pp. 223–229 (Part 2, Ch. 5)

'In another minute ... like running away.'

A first-class match between Tom and Slogger Williams, with seconds, sponges, and a referee. Half the school is out to watch, and even the Headmaster delays his intervention for as long as he decently can.

4. LLWELLYN, Richard
   How Green was my Valley
   pp. 168–170 (Ch. 17)
   'That first morning ... bag and can, and off.'
   Having suffered bullying on his first day at school, Huw is to learn to defend himself with his fists. At five in the morning he joins a group of other young men being trained by a prize-fighter up on the mountain.

5. ibid.
   pp. 171–173 (Ch. 18)
   'I had settled down ... round the corner.'
   Huw challenges Mervyn Phillips to a fight: although Mervyn is much bigger, Huw remembers all he has learnt from Dai Bando, the prize-fighter, and outwits him, laying him out.

6. WRIGHT, Richard
   Black Boy
   see INITIATION 11

7. ibid.
   pp. 106–108 (Ch. 5)
   'The first school day ... and was accepted.'
   Yet again, Richard is called upon to prove himself at another new school. This time, the two school bullies set upon him, and his defeat of them, in spite of his own injury, is well received by the other boys.

FIGHTING (by) GIRLS

1. LEE, Harper
   To Kill a Mockingbird
   (i) pp. 89–91 (Ch. 9); (ii) pp. 88–91
   'Francis grinned at me ... wouldn't let him.'
   Francis, Scout's tale-telling half-

cousin calls her father a nigger-lover. This provokes Scout to righteous fury, and a few telling blows, before she is grabbed and cooled.

FIGHTING (by) MEN

see also: RIVALS (in) LOVE

FIGHTING (by) MEN

1. AMIS, Kingsley
   Lucky Jim
   see RIVALS (in) LOVE 1

2. FIELDING, Henry
   Joseph Andrews
   see ASSAULT 2

3. SCHAEFER, Jack
   Shane
   pp. 95–102 (Ch. 9)
   'Morgan was in the lead ... and forward to the floor.'
   A saloon-bar fist-fight. Shane is set on by a gang of cowboys whose aim is to set him on the road out of town. He stands up for himself magnificently, but is the better for Joe's propitious entrance. Between them they cow the opposition in classic western style.

4. SILLITOE, Alan
   Saturday Night and Sunday Morning
   pp. 99–101 (Part 1, Ch. 7)
   'Four youths were amusing ... fastening his coat.'
   A dart stabs Arthur's leg as he sits drinking in the pub. The youth whose fault it is is churlish and unapologetic. Arthur, who has had enough to drink to tighten his fist, starts a classic pub brawl.

5. STEINBECK, John
   Of Mice and Men
   (i) pp. 65–68 (Ch. 3); (ii) pp. 53–56
   'The door opened. Slim ... avoided looking at Lennie.'
   Curly picks a fight with Lennie. He little realizes whom he is taking on. Lennie takes a lot of punishment, until his partner George encourages him to retaliate. Lennie squeezes

Curly's hand, and breaks all the bones in it.

6. WELLS, H.G.
   The History of Mr Polly
   see NEIGHBOURS 2

7. ibid.
   pp. 211–218 (Ch. 9, Part 8)
   'The private war ... an insecure victory.'
   Polly engages in breathless physical combat with Uncle Jim for possession of the Potwell Inn. He uses all his native cunning against a brute slowed down by beer.

8. ibid.
   pp. 219–226 (Ch. 9, Part 9)
   'The next day was ... a manner of means.'
   Uncle Jim disturbs a riverside picnic, and is set upon by the smart clients of the Potwell Inn. Polly is forward in the fray. The battle is inconclusive, but weight of numbers against him forces Jim to flee.

FIGHTING (by) MEN (with) GUNS

1. SCHAEFER, Jack
   Shane
   see KILLING (by) HIRED ASSASSIN 1

2. ibid.
   pp. 143-148 (Ch. 14)
   'Clumsy and tripping in my ... loose and falling with it.'
   A gun-fight. Shane guns down Wilson the hired killer, and Fletcher who has employed him, in order to make the country safe for the Starretts and their peace-loving kind. In the event, he is himself shot, but he weathers the wound like the superman that he is.

FIGHTING (by) MEN (with) KNIVES

1. FORESTER, C.S.
   The Gun
   (i) pp. 47–50 (Ch. 5); (ii) pp. 43–46
   'They felt better ... his wrist and fingers.'
   Two guerilla leaders argue over the use of the horse of one of them to drag the gun. El Bilbanito is confident he will win the ensuing knife fight, and makes a clever move to do so; by some chance or miscalculation, he suddenly finds himself sinking to the road, dying.

FIGHTING (by) MEN (with) STICKS

1. HUGHES, Thomas
   Tom Brown's Schooldays
   pp. 36–41 (Part 1, Ch. 2)
   'And now, while they ... Willis's crown for him.'
   One highlight of the village feast is the back-sword play between men armed with ash-sticks. The object of the 'game' is to break heads.

2. TREECE, Henry
   Hounds of the King
   pp. 77–82 (Part 2, Ch. 8)
   'It was the Monday after Easter Day ... push his way through bracken.'
   The London and Wallingford carles meet in combat with ash staves. What begins as a friendly contest, becomes a battle to the death. Beonorth and Fin survive the ordeal, at a price.

FIRE

see also: ESCAPE (from) FIRE;
FEAR (of) FIRES;
FOREST – FIRES;
RESCUE (from) FIRE

FIRE

1. DICKENS, Charles
   Great Expectations
   see HORROR 7

2. NESBIT, E.
   The Railway Children
   (i) pp. 119–129 (Ch. 8); (ii) pp. 133–143
   'So then they all went up ... would have done.'
   The children are fishing in the canal, when a barge ties up nearby. The bargee and his wife leave their baby

on board, while they go for a drink. Suddenly the children see smoke, realize there is a fire on the barge, and rush on board to save the baby. The parents are brought back and are duly grateful.

FIRE – FACTORY

1. GORKY, Maxim
   Childhood
   (i) pp. 80–86 (Ch. 4); (ii) pp. 67–71
   'Once when she was on her knees ... washstand in a dark corner.'
   The dyeworks is on fire. To the young Gorky, it is a brilliant spectacle. His grandmother organizes everybody to save the barn, and herself calms a frantic horse. The fire brigade arrives and quickly brings the drama to an end.

FIRE – FARM

1. HARDY, Thomas
   Far from the Madding Crowd
   (i) pp. 49–53 (Ch. 6); (ii) pp. 54–58
   'He turned to an opening ... like a windmill.'
   Gabriel happens on a serious farm fire. His presence of mind, and his quickness of action, prevent many wheat-ricks from being lost. The farm workers, his fellow fire-fighters, are duly appreciative.
2. PEYTON, K.M.
   Flambards in Summer
   (i) pp. 129–137 (Ch. 12); (ii) pp. 171–182
   'Christina slept, when sleep came ... 'I think I've had enough'.'
   Christina rides to the farm in search of Tizzy, only to find the building on fire, and Dick coaxing the horses out of the stables. Mark arrives, and helps Dick demolish the harness shed, so as to make a fire-lane between the cottage, and the newly build hay-ricks. The men are about to drop with exhaustion, when the local fire brigade arrives.

FIRE-FIGHTING

1. DURREL, Gerald
   My Family and Other Animals
   pp. 291–293 (Part 3, Ch. 18)
   'Theodore, meticulously buttering ... to ... er ... put out.'
   Theodore tells the story of the modernization of the Corfu Fire Service. The chief's intentions are admirable, but the results are pure slapstick. The firemen themselves are more difficult to modernize.
2. WELLS, H.G.
   The History of Mr Polly
   pp. 166–172 (Ch. 8, Part 3)
   'That was the beginning ... people on the roofs.'
   Fishbourne mobilises itself to put out the fire that Polly has started. The High Street is a confusion of fire-fighters, onlookers, and lengths of garden hose. Polly the while is on the roof.

FIRE – HOUSE

1. GODDEN, Rumer
   The Diddakoi
   pp. 124–127 (Ch. 6)
   'Make you some tea ... young Prudence Cuthbert.'
   Kizzy pours petrol on her little back-garden fire. The fire catches the thatch of the cottage, and spreads within minutes, threatening to engulf the room in which Kizzy's foster-mother is lying sick.
2. LEE, Harper
   To Kill a Mockingbird
   (i) pp. 74–77 (Ch. 8); (ii) pp. 74–77
   'Before I went to sleep ... fire in the kitchen stove.'
   The house across the street goes up in flames. The children are woken in the early hours, and told to stand in the street. Miss Maudie's house is gutted, but its neighbours are saved.
3. WELLS, H.G.
   The History of Mr Polly
   see FIRE – FIGHTING 2

RESCUE (from) FIRE 4
SUICIDE 16
4. WRIGHT, Richard
    Black Boy
    see BOREDOM 9

FIRE – LIGHTING

1. KING, Clive
    Stig of the Dump
    pp. 48–50 (Ch. 3)
    ' 'Come on, Stig, let's get ... a very
    precious thing indeed.'
    Stig tries to light the fire by swivelling
    a stick on a block of wood. Barney
    produces matches and Stig is amazed
    at the ease with which they produce
    fire. They soon have a good blaze.
2. MARSHALL, James Vance
    Walkabout
    (i) pp. 42–45 (Ch. 6); (ii) pp. 33–36
    (Young Impact 3, pp. 206–207)
    'The sun was setting ... wallaby
    baked gently.'
    The bush boy builds a fire just as his
    people have done for thousands of
    years; it is what sets him above the
    animals. Peter watches him, fas-
    cinated by an ancient novelty.
3. SPERRY, Armstrong
    The Boy who was afraid
    pp. 39–40 (Ch. 3)
    'At last Mafatu ... safer channels.'
    Mafatu makes fire with two pieces of
    wood, one of the first essentials on the
    island on which he has been ship-
    wrecked.

FIRE (at) SEA

1. CONRAD, Joseph
    Typhoon and Youth
    pp. 102–104; 105–107 ('Youth')
    'One Saturday evening ... splendour
    of sea and sky.'; 'Next day it was
    my ... to take the wheel himself.'
    The Judea's cargo catches fire. The
    crew become aware of noxious smoke
    seeping up from every crack in the

deck. Later it explodes, and the deck
is 'blown out of her.'
see also: SHIPWRECKS 4
2. FORESTER, C.S.
    The Ship
    see NAVY – DISCIPLINE 3

FIRE – STABLES

1. SEWELL, Anna
    Black Beauty
    pp. 73–77 (Ch. 16)
    'Later on in the evening ... well done
    by.'
    The horses are awoken in the inn
    stable by the smell of smoke, but
    many panic when the ostlers try to
    lead them out. Black Beauty's groom
    keeps him calm, and he and Ginger
    are rescued.

FIREWORKS

1. GROSSMITH, George and Weedon
    The Diary of a Nobody
    (i) p. 78 (Ch. 8); (ii) pp. 122–123
    'Lupin went with me ... time and
    money.'
    The Pooters go to a firework party.
    Mr Pooter burns himself, and inad-
    vertently dislodges a set piece. He
    concludes that fireworks are a waste
    of time and money.
2. WILDE, Oscar
    The Happy Prince and Other Stories
    see PRIDE 7

FIRST WORLD WAR

see also: ARMY – ENLISTMENT;
FLYING – 1914–18;
FLYING – ACCIDENTS – 1914–18

FIRST WORLD WAR

1. ALLEN, Walter
    All in a Lifetime
    pp. 160–162 (Ch. 13)
    'All that is what I forget ... game to
    the end.'
    The outbreak of the war comes as a

very considerable shock to men who have argued that the workers would not allow it. One worker sees his son espouse the national cause, like the good boy scout that he is, and he rejoices.

2. FORESTER, C.S.
The General
(i) pp. 204–209 (Ch. 21); (ii) pp. 200–204
'The Duke was worried about ... long-drawn agony of Arras.'
An insight into the reaction of the brass hats to the failure on the Somme. Their recipe is for more of everything. Even the news of a French mutiny only feeds their impatience for another big push.

3. PEYTON, K.M.
Flambards in Summer
see GRIEF 8

4. REMARQUE, Erich Maria
All Quiet on the Western Front
pp. 15–22 (Ch. 1)
'Kantorek had been our school-master ... we are old folk.'
Classmates have joined up together. Their old schoolteacher writes them patriotic letters. But already they are fewer in number than when they began. They visit a dying friend, and they age, as they seek meanings in his death.

5. ibid.
see WAR 4

6. ibid.
see STEALING (of) FOOD 5

7. SASSOON, Siegfried
Memoirs of a Fox-hunting Man
pp. 268–270 (Part 9, Sn. 4)
'Next day some new ... became clear to me.'
George meets, and befriends, a bro-ther officer, Dick Tiltwood. He shares with him his hunting memories, and his letters from an old hunting friend, Stephen Colwood, at the front. Then a telegram arrives reporting Stephen's death in action.

8. ibid.
pp. 300–304 (Part 10, Sn. 5)

'There was a continuous ... I knew Death then.'
George returns from his ten days leave, with smoked salmon for his friends. Dick has a headache, others mere heartache. Within a few hours of the salmon, Dick dies with a bullet in his throat.

FIRST WORLD WAR – BATTLES

see also: BATTLES – SOMME – 1916;
BATTLES – YPRES

FIRST WORLD WAR – BATTLES

1. REMARQUE, Erich Maria
All Quiet on the Western Front
pp. 101–105 (Ch. 6); (War pp. 55–57)
'It is nearly noon ... We pass them round.'
The French are driven back, and followed at spade-point, back to their trench. The author and his com-panions fight automatically, mind-lessly, killing so as not to be killed. They harvest as much French bread, corned beef, and cognac, as they can.

2. SASSOON, Siegfried
Memoirs of an Infantry Officer
pp. 54–56 (Part 4, Sn. 2)
'7.45. The barrage is now ... Feel a bit of a fraud.'
Extracts from Sherston's log of the attack at Mametz. Dispassionate details of the progress of the Man-chesters, of shells and casualties.

3. ibid.
see COURAGE 14

4. SHOLOKHOV, Mikhail
And Quiet Flows the Don
pp. 230–234 (Part 2, Ch. 2)
'The regiment had nearly ... his heavy foot into it.'
The fourth company rides into the attack, and on into an Austrian vil-lage, in hot pursuit of the enemy. Gregor plunges his lance through an Austrian, and finishes him off with

his sabre. It is his first kill, and it distracts him from all else.

5. ibid.
pp. 242–247 (Part 2, Ch. 3)
'Next morning Rvachev ... proud, smiling mouth.'
A group of cossacks engage a German patrol in a desperate skirmish of pursuit and counterpursuit. Most extricate themselves, but there are some nasty moments.

6. ibid.
pp. 260–272 (Part 2, Ch. 4)
'The following morning ... a black emptiness.'
The company is kept waiting in a wood for a long time, before they are finally ordered to attack. In the confusion of shots and bodies, Gregor lays about him with his sabre, until he himself is felled.

FIRST WORLD WAR – CONSCIENTIOUS OBJECTION

1. SASSOON, Siegfried
Memoirs of an Infantry Officer
pp. 217–218 (Part 10, Sn. 5); pp. 221–223 (Part 10, Sn. 6); pp. 235–236 (Part 10, Sn. 7)
'July was now a week old ... Colonel will think of it.'; 'I had to wait until ... with J.J. Rousseau'; 'It was obvious that ... finished with the war.'
Sherston sends a copy of his anti-war declaration to his colonel, whereupon he is called upon to present himself at the Depot. Fully expecting to be court-martialled, he is diagnosed as suffering from shell-shock, and committed to hospital to convalesce.

FIRST WORLD WAR – DESERTION

1. REMARQUE, Erich Maria
All Quiet on the Western Front
pp. 232–234 (Ch. 11)
'Every day and every hour ... more of Detering.'

One of Baumer's comrades-in-arms is reminded, by seeing cherry blossom, of his own farm. In a folly of homesickness, he deserts, is picked up by the military police, and is not heard of again.

FIRST WORLD WAR – GAS

1. GRAVES, Robert
Goodbye to all That
pp. 126–128 (Ch. 15)
'A grey, watery dawn ... the gas-company stampeded.'
Orders are given that gas is to be used in spite of the dead calm. But the orders to attack don't come; nor does the rum that should precede it. The gas proves to be a greater danger to those who discharge it than to the Germans.

2. REMARQUE, Erich Maria
All Quiet on the Western Front
pp. 60–65 (Ch. 4)
'We go back. It is time ... and extinguishes me.'
Heavy shelling that throws trees and coffins into the air, precedes the onset of gas. A friend warns Paul to put his gas mask on. Thus protected, they free and bind, a colleague's pinioned arm. The scene is one of confusion and horror.

FIRST WORLD WAR – HOME FRONT

1. FOAKES, Grace
Between High Walls
pp. 63–64 (Ch. 30)
'During the First ... another story.'
Wartime in the tenements means more of the same – hunger, and hardship. The air raids bring some excitement, but fortunately little damage. The local Germans, who are stoned, are among the hardest hit.

FIRST WORLD WAR – HOME LEAVE

1. REMARQUE, Erich Maria
   All Quiet on the Western Front
   pp. 157–160 (Ch. 7)
   'It is the last evening ... have come on leave.'
   The author's mother makes his last night on leave a trying one, by giving him advice about his conduct at the front. It is well-meaning, and ignorant, loving and pathetic.

FIRST WORLD WAR – HOSPITALS

1. REMARQUE, Erich Maria
   All Quiet on the Western Front
   pp. 218–223 (Ch. 10)
   'Sometimes there are red-cross ... known of such a thing.'
   Every day men die in the ward, and their beds are occupied by others. Peter is taken off to the 'Dying Room' and his friends despair of his life. They believe the worst of the surgeons, as of the whole hospital. But Peter comes back, like one who has risen from the dead.

FIRST WORLD WAR – INJURIES

1. GRAVES, Robert
   Goodby to All That
   pp. 180–183; 184–186 (Ch. 20);
   (Visions of Life 2, pp. 15–20)
   'The German batteries ... wounded and bound for home'; 'That evening, the R.A.M.C. ... by hospital ship.'
   Graves is given up for lost. He sustains a serious lung injury, and is placed on the casualty list. A letter of condolence is sent home to his mother. But Graves pulls through; he has always believed strongly in his chances of survival.

2. REMARQUE, Erich Maria
   All Quiet on the Western Front
   pp. 109–110 (Ch. 6)
   'The days go by ... nausea and retching.'
   Search parties fail to find a wounded soldier lying, moaning in no-man's land. He fills his listening comrades with impotent pity, and anger, until he, and his voice, dies.

3. ibid.
   pp. 204–208 (Ch. 10)
   'A few days later ... for the last time.'
   Paul and Albert are wounded in the legs as they march through an evacuated town. They are carted off to the dressing station, where, though he has to endure painful surgery, Paul refuses to be dosed with chloroform.

4. SASSOON, Siegfried
   Memoirs of an Infantry Officer
   pp. 110–113 (Part 6, Sn. 2)
   'After our first time ... do that sometimes, I'm told.'
   A brother officer describes in some detail, an attack in which he has been involved. It is a disorderly affair, indescribably noisy, and bloody. The speaker is shot in the throat.

5. ibid.
   pp. 162–168 (Part 8, Sn. 5)
   'Secret. The Bombing ... back in the tunnel.'
   After much waiting about for instructions, Sherston leads a bombing party. His own affected confidence heartens others, and the objective is reached easily enough. But a careless look about him, costs Sherston a bullet hole which puts a stop to his activities if not his fervour.

FIRST WORLD WAR – PACIFISM

1. GRAVES, Robert
   Goodbye to All That
   pp. 189–190 (Ch. 21)
   (War pp. 93–95)
   'To the Editor ... Yours, etc., A Little Mother.'
   The text of the celebrated open letter from 'A Little Mother' to Tommy Atkins, lambasting the pacifists, and

assuring the troops of the support of the women of England, in their sufferings.

FIRST WORLD WAR – PATROLS

1. GRAVES, Robert
pp. 110–112 (Ch. 14)
'My first night, Captain Thomas ... I had not stayed to watch.'
Graves is sent out with a Sergeant on night patrol, in No Man's Land. It is the first of many patrols at night that Graves undertakes, half out of a sense of personal honour, and half in hope of an arm or leg wound that will give him a holiday from the trenches.

2. ibid.
pp. 117–119 (Ch. 14)
'The colonel called for ... on the parquet floor.'
On a bright night, Graves and a Sergeant patrol in No Man's Land. They collect information that swells the German casualty list, at no small risk to themselves. An exchange of pleasantries with Fritz.

3. SASSOON, Siegfried
Memoirs of an Infantry Officer
pp. 23–29 (Part 2, Sn. 3)
'At ten o'clock ... or a railway accident.'
A party goes out at night to raid the enemy trench. Sherston would like to go with them, but is forbidden to do so by his C.O. But he makes himself useful bringing in the survivors, and exposes himself to danger in the recovery of a corpse.

4. ibid.
pp. 154–157 (Part 8, Sn. 4)
'When I had posted ... itself from the skull.'
In semi-darkness, Sherston goes out on a lone patrol in No Man's Land; he meets nobody. On the following morning he organizes an ammunition-carrying party. It is exhausting work, made the more dispiriting by the ubiquitous German dead.

FIRST WORLD WAR – RECRUITS

1. REMARQUE, Erich Maria
All Quiet on the Western Front
pp. 113–115 (Ch. 6)
'Suddenly the shelling ... haemorrhages and suffocation.'
The author, in mixed pity and contempt, reproaches the recruits for their blind stupidity and incompetence under stress, amounting to self-destruction.

FIRST WORLD WAR – SUPERSTITION

1. GRAVES, Robert
Goodby to All That
pp. 101–102 (Ch. 14)
'With the advance of ... Festubert in May.'
There is pessimism in the trenches, and superstitiousness. Graves, himself, has a 'feeling' that his life is charmed. He even sees the ghost of a man outside his billet, who he knows to have died a month or two before.

2. ibid.
pp. 159–163 (Ch. 18)
'In March I rejoined ... believe in superstition, but ...'
The officers' mess in the trenches. The adjutant rashly says how lucky officers have been to escape the casualty lists. His remark makes everybody superstitous and watchful; and indeed a spate of deaths does follow.

FIRST WORLD WAR – TRENCHES

1. GRAVES, Robert
Goodbye to All That
pp. 94–98 (Ch. 13)
'May 24th. Tomorow we return ... prize for still being here.'
Life in the trenches in the early months. The obsession of the men is to get themselves wounded so that they'll

be sent back to 'Blitey' away from the
hell of shells and killing.
2. ibid.
   see FIRST WORLD WAR – INJURIES 1
3. REMARQUE, Erich Maria
   All Quiet on the Western Front
   pp. 95–101 (Ch. 6)
   (War pp. 49–55)
   'The night is unbearable ... so much
   resistance.'
   Food-crazed rats and shell-crazed
   recruits. The French attack, following
   a noisy barrage. They are cut down
   by the German machine-guns. Both
   sides fight for their lives – like the
   rats.
   see also: FIRST WORLD WAR – BATTLES
   1
4. SASSOON, Siegfried
   Memoirs of a Fox-hunting Man
   pp. 312–313 (Part 10, Sn. 6)
   'My faithful servant ... for 'stand-
   to'.'
   Night-time in the trenches. George
   remembers that it is Easter Sunday.
   The memory is powerless to comfort
   him.

FISHING

see also SHARKS;
WHALES (and) WHALING

FISHING

1. BENNETT, Arnold
   Anna of the Five Towns
   pp. 161–164 (Ch. 10)
   'It was decided ... out of the Irish
   Sea.'
   The holiday-makers take a fishing
   trip from Port Erin in the Isle of
   Man. Anna finds sea-going in a small
   boat exhilharating and then terrifying, but is again delighted when she
   catches four mackerel.
2. CALDWELL, John
   Desperate Voyage
   pp. 57–59 (Ch. 8)
   'Noon had gone ... day's events in
   the log.'

A devilfish heaves into view and
presents an irresistible challenge to
the author. He hooks it, and makes
the line fast to the traveller. But, he
underestimates the strength of the
fish. It pulls the boat off course, and
threatens destruction to the port rail.
So he cuts the line and lets the brute
go.
3. ibid.
   see SHARKS 2
4. DURRELL, Gerald
   Birds, Beasts and Relatives
   pp. 63–66 (Part 2, 'The Bay of
   Olives')
   'Suddenly Taki stopped rowing ... an
   octopus *and* a scorpios.'
   Gerald, and his new friend Taki, go
   fishing by night. Taki uses his 8-foot
   trident to good effect, to spear a
   poisonous scorpios, and after a false
   start, a well-camouflaged octopus.
   This he kills, by digging his teeth into
   its fleshy head, so releasing himself
   from its tentacles.
5. ibid.
   pp. 111–113 (Part 3, 'Cuttlefish and
   Crabs')
   'It was Kokino who ... my story with
   raucous disbelief.'
   A peasant friend shows Gerald a
   patent way of fishing for male cuttlefish: he dangles a female cuttlefish,
   specially selected according to season,
   on a string attached to his toe. When
   he draws her up again, an amorous
   male is attached to her.
6. HEMINGWAY, Ernest
   The Old Man and the Sea
   pp. 38–43
   'The tuna, the fisherman ... nothing
   to be done.'
   The Old Man feels a big marlin
   nibbling at the sardine bait six hundred feet down. There are pulls on the
   line when the fish bites so the Old
   Man gives him more. This is the
   beginning of the long haul.
7. ibid.
   see DETERMINATION 3

8. ibid.
   see ANIMALS – SLAUGHTER 2
9. ibid.
   see DETERMINATION 4.
10. HUGHES, Thomas
    Tom Brown's Schooldays
    pp. 160–163 (Part 1, Ch. 9)
    'So one fine Thursday ... again by
    Velveteens.'
    A new keeper catches Tom fishing on
    his employer's side of the river. None
    of Tom's strategems will save him
    from a beating.
11. JEROME, Jerome K.
    Three Men in a Boat
    pp. 166–169 (Ch. 17)
    'We went into the parlour ... plaster
    of Paris.'
    There is a trout in a glass case moun-
    ted on the inn wall. George and J.
    expresss such interest in it, that every
    man who enters, including the publi-
    can regales them with a different
    story of how he caught it. An accident
    reveals the truth of the matter.
12. MACKEN, Walter
    God made Sunday and Other Stories
    pp. 84–89 ('The Big Fish')
    'The sun was warm ... clasped
    between his knees.'
    Joe is on holiday from school. He goes
    fishing with a bamboo rod. A pro-
    fessional fisherman asks Joe to
    accompany him in his boat. They
    catch an enormous trout together,
    crowning Joe's happiness.
13. ibid.
    pp. 89–92 ('The Big Fish')
    'They struck him late ... he rowed
    away.'
    Joe and the fisherman catch a twenty-
    five pound trout. It is the big fish of
    every fisherman's dreams; but to Joe's
    dismay and amazement, Mr Murphy
    the fisherman lets it go. He tries to
    explain himself to Joe, but without
    success.

FISHING (for) PEARLS

1. STEINBECK, John
   The Pearl
   pp. 15–20 (Ch. 2)
   'Now Kino and Juana ... pearl in the
   world.'
   Kino and Juana go pearl-fishing.
   Kino dives and gathers as many
   oysters as he can, the last one very
   large and ancient. In the boat he
   opens it, and discovers 'the greatest
   pearl in the world'.

FLOODS

see also: ESCAPE (from) FLOODS;
RESCUE (from) FLOODS

FLOODS

1. BERNA, Paul
   Flood Warning
   pp. 47–50 (Ch. 3)
   'Monsieur Sala returned to his ...
   between the tussocks of grass.'
   The school is threatened by rising
   flood-waters. What has been a mere
   inconvenience, is now a serious threat.
   Cut off, and without electricity, the
   school is at the uncertain mercy of the
   weather.
2. ibid.
   pp. 68–74 (Ch. 4)
   'Monsieur Bressay's face was pale ...
   caught them between the shoulder
   blades.'
   The flood waters go on rising. A
   permanent watch is kept on the sand-
   bag dam. M. Sala and Vignoles watch
   the water as it creeps up the outer
   wall, until the flood roars over the
   top, threatening to engulf them.
3. ibid.
   see ESCAPE (from) FLOODS 1
4. ibid.
   see RESCUE (from) FLOODS 1
5. BURTON, Hester
   The Great Gale
   pp. 33–38 (Chs. 4, 5)
   'Just after seven, they drifted ...

practical was wonderfully comforting.'

Alone in the house, Mary and Mark save as much that is movable from the downstairs rooms as they can from the water seeping in under the french windows. The telephone is out of order, and the lights go out.

6. ibid.
   pp. 70–71; 74–77 (Ch. 8)
   'When the sea broke ... was mopping the ugly cut.'; 'Suddenly another great wave ... home for them both.'
   Myrtle and her mother are in their back-parlour when sea-water invades their home. They clamber upstairs, then, as the water continues to rise, out on to the roof. They narrowly escape drowning when the house collapses.

7. ELIOT, George
   The Mill on the Floss
   pp. 634–639 (Ch. 5, Part 7)
   'At that moment ... towards the Mill?'
   In trying to rescue her landlord from their flooded house, Maggie is swept away in a boat by the current and floats through the submerged countryside.

8. FALKNER, J. Meade
   Moonfleet
   pp. 20–26 (Ch. 2)
   'On the third of November ... the truth is bad enough.'
   Strong winds and spring tides combine to flood Moonfleet village. During morning service in the church, rumblings are heard in the Mohune vault, to the evident consternation of the tiny congregation. The parson supposes that the coffins are awash, and bumping against each other.

9. LAWRENCE, D.H.
   The Rainbow
   pp. 245–250 (Ch. 9)
   'He started awake ... to Anna's house.'
   Tom Brangwen comes home drunk, one very wet night. He does not realise just how wet it is until a current of water throws him off his less than perfect balance, and he is a drowning man. His family wakes to find the house flooded with water from the canal.

10. LEE, Laurie
    Cider with Rosie
    (i) pp. 22–24 (Ch. 2, 'First Names');
    (ii) pp. 37–40
    'In the long ... looking for brooms.'
    After a long drought, it rains 'as it had never rained before' and Mrs Lee marshals her children with their brooms to repulse the flood. Sometimes it manages to enter the kitchen.

11. WYNDHAM, John
    The Kraken Wakes
    pp. 208–209; 213–215 (Phase Three)
    'It got across still more ... repairs against its next rise.'
    'In the weeks just before ... cascade on to the roadway.'
    The third phase of the invasion of our planet is the melting of the polar ice-caps and the consequent flooding of lowlands. Londoners watch familiar streets disappear under the swollen Thames. The authorities are reassuring, even as they move to higher floors.

12. ibid.
    see SURVIVAL 12

FLYING

see also: FEAR (of) FLYING

FLYING – 1900–14

1. PEYTON, K.M.
   The Edge of the Cloud
   (i) pp. 18–21 (Ch. 2); (ii) pp. 26–31
   'Now he was on his feet ... he said to the machine.'
   Eager for a job with aeroplanes, William offers to test a machine with a suspect engine. He is wonderfully happy to be in his element again, until, almost inevitably, the engine dies, and he has to manoeuvre the plane down under an electric wire.

2. ibid.
   see FEAR (of) FLYING 1
3. ibid.
   (i) pp. 74–83 (Ch. 8); (ii) pp. 92–103
   'It seemed to Christina ... Christina felt like a veteran.'
   Will has to deliver a Blériot aeroplane to a French client. Little suspecting her fear, he persuades Christina to fly with him, across the Channel. Her heart is in her mouth throughout the trip, listening to the variations in the engine noise. But when a bulb begins to leak oil, she is sure the end is near.
4. ibid.
   pp. 94–101 (Ch. 9); (ii) pp. 116–125
   'It was no day for regrets ... like the shoal of flashing minnows.'
   The picnic conversation turns to talk of looping the loop. Will is determined to prove that his aeroplane, and his nerve, will be equal to the strain. Christina wonders at her fiancé's sanity, and scarcely dares to watch his aerobatics.
5. ibid.
   see FEAR (of) FLYING 2
6. PEYTON, K.M.
   Flambards
   (i) pp. 131–134 (Ch. 10); (ii) pp. 162–166
   'We have a new engine ... deterioration of Dick's fortunes.'
   For the first time, Christina watches William take off in a home-made flying machine. She fears for him, and marvels at his coolness who is scared to ride a horse. The flight such as it is, is not altogether smooth.
   see also pp. 135–136
7. ibid.
   see HORSES – RACING 1

FLYING – 1939–45

1. BATES, H.E.
   The Purple Plain
   pp. 33–35 (Ch. 4)
   'In the early afternoon ... he could not see.'
   Forrester flies over the Burmese jungle with his new navigator, Carrington. He notices all the dry river beds, where he might land in case of trouble. They return safely to the airstrip, and the intense heat.

FLYING – ACCIDENTS

1. PEYTON, K.M.
   The Edge of the Cloud
   see FLYING – 1900–14 1
2. ibid.
   (i) pp. 141–145 (Ch. 13); (ii) pp. 174–181
   'She rarely watched the exhibitions ... who it was that had died.'
   Will and Sandy are giving a display of aerobatics at Hendon. Christina watches (and hides her eyes) in a judges' box. The performance is nearly over, and Christina has unsteeled herself, when one of the planes falls out of the sky. Christina cannot see which of the planes it is, and whether it is her friend or her fiancé who is dead.
3. PEYTON, K.M.
   Flambards
   see HORSES – RACING 1
4. TREVOR, Elleston
   The Flight of the Phoenix
   pp. 11–16 (Ch. 2)
   'In the unnatural hush ... and then the scream stopped.'
   A Skytruck is flying over the Libyan desert. Its radio aerial has been blown off, and its two engines have cut out in a blinding sandstorm. The pilot calls up all his skill to put her down; but it's a messy landing, and men die.
5. ibid.
   pp. 22–25 (Ch. 3)
   'By midnight the temperature ... signalling the empty sky.'
   Stock is taken after the crash. The chances of survival are discussed and reckoned good. But the wreckage of another aircraft is sighted, and the search for the overdue Skytruck is called off.

FLYING – ACCIDENTS – 1914–18

1. PEYTON, K.M.
   Flambards in Summer
   (i) pp. 83–87 (Ch. 8); (ii) pp. 114–119
   'Christina was frightened ... home not seeing any more.'
   The death of Christina's late husband is re-enacted before her eyes when a German plane crashes in her hay field. The pilot emerges, Christina is sickened by the sight of the young, dead, rear-gunner, and Dick rescues the third crew member just before the plane explodes into fragments of wood and metal.

FLYING – ACCIDENTS – 1939–45

1. BATES, H.E.
   Fair Stood the Wind for France
   (i) pp. 8–11 (Ch. 1); (ii) pp. 8–11
   'The mountains had already ... there was no remembering.'
   A bomber returning from Italy suddenly, and inexplicably loses one engine and has to make a forced landing in occupied France. The ground is too soft and the pilot is injured.
2. ibid.
   see INJURIES – ARM 1
3. BATES, H.E.
   The Purple Plain
   pp. 36–37 (Ch. 4)
   'But to his surprise ... wanted to die.'
   Forrester and Carrington, watch a Mosquito approach the air-strip too fast, and crash into a Dakota parked near the runway. With the cynicism of war-time they bemoan the loss of the planes, not the men.
4. ibid.
   pp. 105–108 (Ch. 12)
   'He was airborne ... awful power on his neck.'
   Forrester, with Blore and Carrington, is flying on a Second War mission in Burma, when an oil leak forces them to crash-land. The plane bursts into flames, and although they all get out, Carrington is badly burnt.

FLYING (at) NIGHT

1. SAINT-EXUPERY, Antoine de
   Night Flight
   pp. 9–14 (Ch. 1)
   'Already, beneath him ... immensity of the sea.'
   The pilot, Fabien, flies into the night above the sleeping villages of Argentina. He lands at one of them, for 10 minutes, before pressing on, his radio operator behind him, and his luminous dials in front.

FLYING (in) STORMS

1. SAINT-EXUPERY, Antoine de
   Night Flight
   pp. 57–61 (Ch. 12); 72–75 (Ch. 15); pp. 78–79 (Ch. 17); 85–87 (Ch. 20)
   'The Patagonia ... never could he rise.'; 'This slip of neatly ... began to climb.'; 'One of the radio ... hidden reef of land'; 'Comodoro Rivadavia ... what it will contain.'
   The night-mail from Patagonia flies into a storm. Fabien taps his instruments for all the information they can give him. Radio messages are uniformly storm-tidings; the plane drifts off course, and is lost beyond the reach of assistance; the radio operator manages to relay to base a report of their ignorance as to their position, and of the dwindling fuel supplies; Buenos Aires loses contact with the Patagonia mail and gives it up for lost.

FOG

1. BOMBARD, Alain
   The Bombard Story
   pp. 71–74 (Ch. 5)
   'The last day of May ... time have had to endure.'
   In a fog so thick the seafarers can't see the end of their own dinghy, first

a monstrous albino whale rises up out of the water, and then a siren and the noise of an engine break the silence, and test the nerve.

2. DICKENS, Charles
   Bleak House
   (i) pp. 1–2 (Ch. 1); (ii) pp. 1–2
   'London ... High Court of Chancery.'
   The opening of the book depicts a muddy, foggy London – a 'London particular'.

3. WOODS, James
   The Rain Islands
   see MANHUNT 6

FOOD (and) DRINK

see also: CHEESE; CHRISTMAS – DINNERS;
DRUNKENNESS; HOTELS (and) RESTAURANTS; MEALS;
PARTIES – DINNERS; PARTIES – TEAS;
SWEETS

FOOD (and) DRINK

1. ACHEBE, Chinua
   Things fall apart
   see LOCUSTS 1

2. BOMBARD, Alain
   The Bombard Story
   pp. 63–66 (Ch. 4)
   'We started to feel ... not been thrown upon it.'
   Hunger and thirst as experienced by seafarers without food or drink. They overcome their suspicion of sea-water, and their aversion to the raw flesh of a sea-perch.

3. ibid.
   see RAIN 1

4. GOLDING, William
   Pincher Martin
   see SURVIVAL 2

5. THOMPSON, Flora
   Lark Rise to Candleford
   (i) pp. 389–390 ('Over to Candleford', Ch. 25); (ii) pp. 346–347
   'All, excepting the poorest ... in a tea-kettle.'

In the 1880's food was cheap and plentiful in most households, and nobody worried about their figure. At her Aunt and Uncle's in Candleford Laura enjoys variety and abundance.

FOOTBALL

see also: RUGBY FOOTBALL

FOOTBALL

1. HINES, Barry
   A Kestrel for a Knave
   (i) pp. 113–127; (ii) pp. 92–103
   'The team broke ... or at Mr Sugden.'
   A games lesson: a period of purgatory for Billy Casper. Having no kit of his own, he is lent a pair of oversize shorts, and is put in goal, where he does not distinguish himself. His preoccupying thoughts are of keeping warm, and of getting home on the bell.

2. MADDOCK, Reginald
   Sell-out
   pp. 77–84 (Ch. 8)
   'I was at school at ten o'clock ... Paddy harder than any of us.'
   It is the morning of the Benton-Cronton football match. Danny has prayed hard that his best friend Joe, and he, might each score a goal. In spite of the strapping size of the opposition, his prayer is answered. He receives assistance from an unexpected quarter on the touchline.

FOREST

see also: JUNGLE

FOREST

1. MARSHALL, James Vance
   Walkabout
   (i) pp. 88–89 (Ch. 17); (ii) pp. 113–115
   'No less wonderful ... they saw the koala.'

The children penetrate the forest in the valley-of-waters-under-the-earth. Trees and creepers vie with each other for root space in the rich soil. For every plant that grows, another dies stretching for the light.

FOREST – FIRES

1. GOLDING, William
   Lord of the Flies
   (i) pp. 52–54; 56–60 (Ch. 2); (ii) pp. 44–46; 48–51
   'Ralph and Jack looked ... panting like dogs.'; ' "You said you wanted ... drum-roll continued.'
   The marooned boys light a fire on the mountain, to advertise themselves to passing ships. In their careless haste, they start a bigger fire than any of them had bargained for.

2. GUILLOT, René
   Kpo the Leopard
   see ESCAPE (from) FIRE 1

3. SOUTHALL, Ivan
   Ash Road
   pp. 11–15 (Ch. 1)
   'Wallace was half-awake ... all was a red glow.'
   Graham knocks over the methylated spirits, in the dark, and before he or Wallace can prevent it, a flame has grown into a raging fire. The boys panic, lose all control of the inferno, and run.

4. ibid.
   pp. 115–122 (Chs. 9, 10)
   'Gramps was stopped twice ... thirty-seven and drove away.'
   Gramps Fairhall is driving a sick man to the local hospital. He drives at speed through the forest on fire, until the car skids on molten tar and hits the banking. Despite this, Gramps remains remarkably cool.

5. ibid.
   see FEAR (of) FIRE 2

6. ibid.
   see RESCUE (from) FIRE 2, 3

FORGERY

1. BENTLEY, Phyllis
   Gold Pieces
   passim.
   Coiners at their illegal work, in a West Yorkshire Pennine valley, in the mid-eighteenth century.

2. MANKOWITZ, Wolf
   Make me an Offer
   pp. 137–143 ('A Life in Art')
   'What is the use ... in Constantin Guys.'
   Pelk can make superb copies of paintings – for personal satisfaction, he one day includes copies in a folder of originals in the gallery where he works. Unfortunately they are admired and bought, and he is firmly placed on the road to full-time forgery.

FORTUNE-TELLING

1. DICKENS, Charles
   David Copperfield
   see SUPERSTITION 2

2. GREENWOOD, Walter
   Love on the Dole
   pp. 100–102 (Part 2, Ch. 5)
   'Cards or tea-leaves?' ... reshuffled the cards.':
   Against her better judgement, Sal has let her mother take her to have her fortune told. But she feels she is cheapening her new friendship, so she leaves in contempt.

3. LAWRENCE, D.H.
   The Virgin and the Gipsy
   pp. 24–26 (Part 3)
   'The elderly woman ... 'With him-'.
   The gypsy's wife reads the palms of the eager girls, and satisfies their curiosity for secrets, with prophecies of interesting strangers, some of them identifiable.

FOXHUNTING

   see HUNTING – FOXES

113

FREEDOM

see also: BORSTAL;
ESCAPE;
PRISON;
RUNNING AWAY

FREEDOM

1. ORWELL, George
   1984
   (i) pp. 6–7; 9–11 (Ch. 1, Part 1); (ii)
   pp. 6; 8–10
   'Outside, even ... every moment
   scrutinized.'; 'For some reason ...
   April 4th 1984.'
   Winston rashly begins to write a diary
   of his thoughts – unheard of in the
   world of telescreens and Thought
   Police, prying into every movement,
   action and, if possible, thought.
2. ibid.
   see SPYING 1
3. ibid.
   (i) pp. 216–218 (Part 2, Ch. 9); (ii)
   pp. 168–170
   'A party member ... as doublethink.'
   The lack of freedom of a party member to think for himself is described.
4. ibid.
   see ARREST 12
5. ibid.
   see TORTURE 4
6. PATON, Alan
   Cry the beloved Country
   (i) pp. 29–31 (Bk. 1, Ch. 7); (ii) pp.
   33–36
   (i) 'He did not sit down ... you will
   see it one day.'
   (ii) 'He did not sit down ... That is
   kind of you.'
   John Kumalo tells his brother why he
   has not written about his new life in
   Johannesburg. He has made a complete break with the old tribal life,
   and with the church, so that he can be
   his own master. He finds much wrong
   with the black/white situation, but it
   gives him something to fight for.
7. SOUTHALL, Ivan
   Ash Road

pp. 4–6 (Ch. 1)
'The boys walked on along ... already
gone sour on them.'
Three boys are enjoying their first
real taste of freedom, in the Australian outback. They light up a fire
to cook coffee and sausages, and are
immediately rounded on by adults
whose concern is for freedom from
bush-fire.
8. THOMAS, Leslie
   This Time Next Week
   see also: ESCAPADES 11

FRENCH REVOLUTION

1. DICKENS, Charles
   A Tale of Two Cities
   passim.
   The growth of resentment and hatred
   against the ruling classes in the late
   1780's. The course of the revolution
   itself, showing the suffering on all
   sides.
2. ibid.
   pp. 220–224 (Bk. 2, Ch. 22)
   'Now from the other world ... in
   Saint Antoine's bosom.'
   A retired Minister, who had once told
   the people they could eat grass, is
   dragged back to Paris, paraded
   through the streets and brutally killed.
3. ibid.
   pp. 270–271 (Bk. 3, Ch. 4)
   'But, though the Doctor ... God's
   own Temple every day.'
   The Revolution follows its swift and
   terrible course, the horrors culmina-
   ting in the supreme dominance of the
   Guillotine.
4. ibid.
   pp. 275–276 (Bk. 3, Ch. 5)
   'These occupations brought her ... it
   had never been.'
   As Lucie watches her husband's window in the prison a crowd, five-hun-
   dred strong, sweeps past her dancing
   a grotesque and frightening dance,
   the Carmagnole.

FRENCH REVOLUTION – BASTILLE

1. DICKENS, Charles
   A Tale of Two Cities
   pp. 213–219 (Bk. 2, Ch. 21)
   'Saint Antoine had been ... "Thou didst it!" '
   The Bastille is stormed – the raging mob armed with guns, iron bars, knives, axes, and even paving stones surround the massive prison until a white flag appears, the drawbridge is lowered and they pour into the courtyard to kill and destroy.

FRENCH REVOLUTION – CAUSES

1. DICKENS, charles
   A Tale of Two Cities
   see POVERTY 8
2. ibid.
   see GOVERNMENT – ARISTOCRACY 1
3. ibid.
   see ACCIDENTS – ROAD 1

FRENCH REVOLUTION – GUILLOTINE

1. DICKENS, Charles
   A Tale of Two Cities
   pp. 362–365 (Bk. 3, Ch. 15)
   'Along the Paris streets ... count Two.'
   The tumbrils roll along the Paris streets, the crowds watch their grim passage, and the knitting women wait at the steps of the guillotine. As the heads fall, they count.

FRIENDS

see also: DEATH (of) FRIEND

FRIENDS

1. DE JONG, Meindert
   The Wheel on the School
   see OLD AGE 6

2. ibid.
   (i) pp. 48–57 (Ch. 5); (ii) pp. 51–58
   'Back in the fenced-in yard ... became a friend.'
   Pier and Dirk, in their quest for a wagon wheel, form a plan to look in the yard of Janus, the surliest man in the village. Once in the yard, they discover that Janus is not surly or fierce, but friendly and interested in what they are doing.
3. GORKY, Maxim
   Childhood
   see OUTSIDERS 3
4. WILDE, Oscar
   The Happy Prince and Other Stories
   (i) pp. 186–193 ('The Devoted Friend'); (ii) pp. 39–46
   'Good morning, little Hans ... for being generous.'
   In return for the promise of a delapidated wheelbarrow, the miller exploits the friendly gullible Hans. The miller talks about friendship, and Hans kills himself in its practice.

FRIENDS – BOYS

1. ELIOT, George
   The Mill on the Floss
   pp. 195–201 (Ch. 3, Part 2)
   'Mr Stelling wisely ... from a hunchback.'
   Tom Tulliver and Philip Wakem, soon to be schoolmates, meet for the first time – at first they are shy, then they boast, and end up being rather suspicious of each other as they are so very different.
2. GORKY, Maxim
   Childhood
   (i) pp. 186–192 (Ch. 9); (ii) pp., 139–144
   (Here, Now and Beyond, pp. 15–19)
   'Almost every day from noon ... Uncle Pyotr's cart in the yard.'
   Three boys play in a neighbouring yard. Gorky watches them, longing to play hide-and-seek. When the smallest hides in the well-bucket, and disappears as the rope pays out,

Gorky rushes over to help in the rescue. This is the beginning of friendship between Gorky and his neighbours.

3. KNOWLES, John
   A Separate Peace
   pp. 48–52 (Ch. 3)
   ' "Swimming in pools is screwy ... contains the truth.'
   Quite against the rules, Finny and Gene cycle to the coast. They swim there, eat hotdogs, and sleep out under the open New England sky. They are boys together, expressing themselves, in face of work schedules and schoolmasters.

4. LESSING, Doris
   Nine African Stories
   pp. 199–201 ('The Antheap')
   'At school it was not ... "See you tomorrow." '
   Tommy and Dirk, the pure-bred white, and the half-caste, meet in uneasy friendship in Tommy's school holidays. They exchange insults; then they fight, and feel better.

5. SALINGER, J.D.
   The Catcher in the Rye
   see ADOLESCENCE – BOYS 4

6. WELLS, H.G.
   Kipps
   pp. 7–9 (Bk. 1, Ch. 1, Sn. 1)
   'But it was through ... Kipps as he passed.'
   Kipps makes friends with Sid, the draper's son. They exchange second-hand abuse in passing, rise to a fight at the instance of the butcher's boy, and admire each other's bruises. Thus, they grow to be inseparable friends.

FRIENDS – CHILDREN

1. KIRKUP, James
   The Only Child
   pp. 98–103 (Ch. 8)
   'But when I reached ... of their own kind.'
   The four-year old Jim falls in with a dominant girl, older than himself, who takes him in hand. She is a madcap child, at once protective, and keen to show Jim life of a kind independent of parental constraints.

FRIENDS – GIRLS

1. AUSTEN, Jane
   Emma
   pp. 56–60 (Ch. 4)
   'Hariet Smith's intimacy ... friendly arrangement of her own.'
   Emma's new friend, Harriet Smith, is a simple passive girl, whom Emma hopes to 'improve'. An orphan with no station in life, she must be introduced to the ways of polite society, and protected from connections with a lower class.

2. O'BRIEN, Edna
   The Country Girls
   pp. 22–23 (Ch. 3)
   'I was wrapping myself up ... to have seen it.'
   Caithleen and Baba are friends, but it is a relationship of ruled and ruler. Baba is pretty, self-centred and affected. Caithleen is a follower, and, although more intelligent, allows herself to be treated quite harshly.

3. THOMPSON, Flora
   Lark Rise to Candleford
   (i) pp. 361–364 ('Over to Candleford', Ch. 23); (ii) pp. 323–325
   'But the girls ... alone with Polly.'
   Laura finds herself listening to the confidences of her school-friends on a wide variety of subjects: sweet-hearts, quarrels with other girls, and more depressing ones about problems at home.

FRIENDS – MEN

1. BATES, H.E.
   The Purple Plain
   pp. 127–134 (Ch. 14)
   'All the time Carrington ... never be broken.'
   Forrester has to carry his injured navigator as they try to reach civil-

isation after their plane has crashed in the Burmese jungle. All restraints are broken as they enter into light-hearted banter to keep their spirits up. Blore does not understand the joking.

2. SCHAEFER, Jack
   Shane
   see DETERMINATION 6

3. STEINBECK, John
   Of Mice and Men
   (i) pp. 8–17 (Ch. 1); (ii) pp. 12–19
   'In a moment Lennie ... a little night breeze.'
   The unfolding of the curious, but close, relationship between George and the simple giant Lennie. The former gives, and the latter takes. Between them, they weave an impossible dream, in which only Lennie implicitly believes.

4. WELLS, H.G.
   The History of Mr Polly
   pp. 17–22 (Ch. 1, Part 4)
   'Jolly days of companionship ... Mr Polly's memory.'
   Polly enjoys the frivolous company of Platt and Parsons, fellow apprentices 'in the drapery.' Their excursions on Sundays are the sole redeeming feature in an otherwise wholly tiresome week.

FROST

see also: ICE;
SNOW;
WINTER

FROST

1. LEE, Laurie
   Cider with Rosie
   (i) pp. 101–103 (Ch. 8, 'Winter and Summer'); (ii) pp. 136–139
   'Winter was no more ... awesome, welcome.'
   Everything is frozen hard – even the milkman's bucket of milk. The boys go out for the day and notice all the changes wrought by the frost.

2. WOOLF, Virginia
   Orlando
   pp. 23–25 (Ch. 1)
   'The Great Frost was ... the courtiers danced.'
   The writer, free from the constraints of strict fact, describes how the Great Frost of James 1st's reign turned people to stone where they stood; and how fashionable London society disported themselves on the frozen Thames.

3. ibid.
   pp. 43–44 (Ch. 1)
   'Some blind instinct ... number of cooking utensils.'
   After the Great Frost, the Great Thaw. Londoners of every rank, who had enjoyed the novelty of skating on the Thames are taken off guard by the sudden rush of water to the sea. This berg-bearing flood sweeps hundreds of people to their deaths.

FRUSTRATION

see also: LOVE – DISILLUSIONMENT;
MARRIAGE – DISILLUSIONMENT

FRUSTRATION

1. AMIS, Kingsley
   Lucky Jim
   see TRAVEL (by) BUS 1

2. CANAWAY, W.H.
   Sammy going South
   pp. 60–62 (Ch. 10)
   'Sammy saw the boy ... until the next day.'
   Sammy, trying to get to S. Africa from Egypt sees a bicycle, left by a boy who is fishing. He tries to ride it away, but he has not learnt to ride. He has to give up, scratched and bruised, in disgust.

3. GREENE, Graham
   The Power and the Glory
   see FATHERS 2

4. ibid.
   (i) pp. 98–110 (Part 2, Ch. 2); (ii) pp. 103–115

'The young men ... on to no end.'

The fugitive priest put his safety at risk in order to acquire some wine for the mass. He makes a dangerous and expensive deal, only to have the wine drunk before his eyes by the man whose job it is to arrest him.

5. JOYCE, James
   Dubliners
   see AMBITIONS – WRITING 1

6. LAWRENCE, D.H.
   The Rainbow
   see CHILDREN – TANTRUMS 3

7. WELLS, H.G.
   The History of Mr Polly
   pp. 1–4 (Ch. 1, Part 1)
   ' 'Hello', said Mr Polly ... an urgent hand.'

   Polly, a Fishbourne draper and a married man, complains to the sky about his cramping life. He is the pathetic victim of his narrow education, his conservatism, and his dyspepsia.

FUNERALS

see also: DEATH;
GRIEF

FUNERALS

1. ACHEBE, Chinua
   Things fall apart
   (i) pp. 109–112 (Ch. 13); (ii) pp. 109–112
   'Go-di-di-go-go ... few more steps and went away.'

   A great man, a warrior, and a man of wealth, has died. His death is publicly announced, and his funeral is attended by the whole clan. The ritual befits the death of a warrior, and of a man close to his ancestors.

2. CAMUS, Albert
   The Outsider
   pp. 22–27 (Part 1, Ch. 1)
   'The undertaker's men arrived ... twelve hours at a stretch.'

   The young man is attending his mother's funeral. He is unmoved by it, partly because he did not know his mother well, and partly because it is so hot. Everything and everyone merges in the heat-haze.

3. DICKENS, Charles
   Bleak House
   (i) pp. 138–139 (Ch. 12); (ii) pp. 138–139
   'Then the active and intelligent ... look here.'

   Nemo, the penniless law-writer, is buried without ceremony in a hideous graveyard, which is described in horrific detail.

4. DICKENS, Charles
   Great Expectations
   (i) pp. 313–316 (Ch. 35); (ii) pp. 268–271
   'At last, I came ... of clouds and trees.'

   Pip's sister has died. This does not occasion him great grief, but he attends the funeral, and submits himself by turns to the fussy attention of the village tailor, and his bibulous Uncle Pumblechook.

5. FORSTER, E.M.
   Howard's End
   see DEATH 5

6. GORKY, Maxim
   Childhood
   (i) pp. 5–6 (Ch. 1); (ii) pp. 15–16
   (Visions of Life 1 pp. 60–61)
   'My next vivid recollection ... so frequently and with such familiarity.'

   His father is buried, his grandmother weeps. It is raining and the ground is muddy. Gorky's prime concern is for two frogs who cannot jump out, before the grave is filled in.

7. LAWRENCE, D.H.
   Sons and Lovers
   (i) pp. 137–139 (Ch. 6); (ii) pp. 171–174
   (Impact Two, pp. 190–191)
   'On Saturday night ... themselves in the warmth.'

   Morel, and three sturdy neighbours bring William's coffin in, and lay it on chairs in the parlor. Mrs Morel is inconsolable; and her husband refrains from walking past the little hillside cemetery, in which William is buried.

8. LLWELLYN, Richard
How Green was my Valley
pp. 161–164 (Ch. 17)
'All the morning ... the tea, never stopping.'
A little girl has been murdered on the mountain, and the whole village turns out, for the funeral, making an impressive procession up to the graveyard. After the service, and the grief, tea for all those present.

9. SALINGER, J.D.
The Catcher in the Rye
pp. 161–162 (Ch. 20)
'Finally, I sat down ... feels like coming out.'
Late night drunken thoughts about death. Holden imagines all his relatives at his funeral, and his place in the cemetery. That's what riles him – being in a cemetery like his brother.

10. THOMPSON, Flora
Lark Rise to Candleford
(i) pp. 558–559 (Ch. 36, 'Candleford Green'); (ii) pp. 488–489
'The funerals ... before the fire.'
Candleford Green funerals were simple, and inexpensive. The meal provided afterwards is a necessity – little is eaten while the body is still in the house. It also serves to revive the bereaved and demonstrate that life has to go on.

11. WELLS, H.G.
The History of Mr Polly
pp. 55–70 (Ch. 4, Part 3)
(Impact 1, pp. 138–142)
'All the preparations ... than words could tell.'
Introductions and sherry precede the funeral of Polly's father; a fine meal of hot and cold meats, salad, cheese and ale, succeeds it. Polly enjoys himself, amusing his Larkins cousins, and Uncle Penstemon enjoys himself eating.

FUTURE

1. HUXLEY, Aldous
Brave New World
passim.
Huxley's future is very highly organized and controlled. Everybody has a place in the social and working pecking order. Satisfaction of the appetites is the highest good for which all strive.

2. ORWELL, George
1984
passim.
The future according to Orwell is no less regimented than Huxley's, (Brave New World) but the power in the land is the Thought Police rather than the Conditoning Centre. The individual is significant only as an atom of the state.

3. WELLS, H.G.
Kipps
pp. 258–262 (Bk. 2, Ch. 7, Sn. 4)
'Glad to see you ... What else can we expect?'
A friend of Sid's questions Kipps about his wealth and the effect this has had on his personal happiness. He goes on to aver that society is on a crash course; that there will be bloodshed and confusion, and no 'happiness' at all.

4. WELLS, H.G.
The Time Machine
pp. 29–32 (Ch. 5)
'In another moment ... strong silky material.'
The Time-Traveller has hurtled forward into the year 802,701. He finds the people very much feebler of body and intellect, but he admires their buildings, in spite of their decay.

5. ibid.
pp. 90–94 (Ch. 14)
'I have already told you ... sky was absolutely black.'
The end of the world is at hand. The Time-Traveller is astride his machine, on a crab-infested shore. The sun is large but affords little heat. Finally a

green slime is all that is left of life. The darkness, and silence, is absolute.

GALAPAGOS ISLANDS

1. CALDWELL, John
   Desperate Voyage
   see ISLANDS 1

GAMBLING

1. BARSTOW, Stan
   The Human Element
   pp. 30–35 ('Gamblers Never Win')
   'In the dusk ... run away from life itself.'
   Mr and Mrs Scurridge have a row about money. He blames her for not economising, and she blames him for wasting their money gambling. But she knows she is beaten, because his gambling has become compulsive.
2. ibid.
   pp. 48–49; 52–54 ('Gamblers Never Win')
   'He drank greedily ... his own heart-beats.'; 'Scurridge stared from ... that Rolls-Royce.'
   In the middle of a busy, crowded bar, Scurridge realises that his pools coupon, matched with the day's football results, has made him a rich man. He stands drinks to everyone present, before he reels home, in company with a dog and a bottle of rum.
3. GREENWOOD, Walter
   Love on the Dole
   pp. 111–115 (Part 2, Ch. 7)
   ' ...Aye, an' he's had ... y'cap, Harry, lad.'
   Incredibly, Harry wins twenty-two pounds for a threepenny bet. The paying-out attracts the entire neighbourhood.
4. HUGHES, Thomas
   Tom Brown's Schooldays
   see BULLYING (by) BOYS 5
5. JOHNSON, Dorothy M.
   The Hanging Tree
   pp. 79–81 ('The Hanging Tree')

'In Utah he met Harrigan ... never saw Harrigan again.'
When Doc Frail plays cards, he plays to win. He invests the money of a passing acquaintance in a card-game, and earns handsome interest, which they divide between them. But the game has unnerved Doc, and when the loser accuses him of cheating, he kills him.
6. LONDON, Jack
   The Call of the Wild
   pp. 77–82 (Ch. 6)
   'That winter, at Dawson ... enough to interrupt.'
   In an idle moment, Thornton bets that his dog can pull a sledge weighing a thousand pounds, and walk with it a hundred yards. The odds are put at two to one. The task appears to be impossible; but Buck is a formidable dog. In the event, Thornton is vindicated.
7. NAUGHTON, Bill
   Late Night on Watling Street
   pp. 26–29 ('A Skilled Man')
   'Here they are now ... drink, sometime, wait.'
   In a bowls match between Murphy, an unskilled labourer, and Smith, a skilled man, Edgar puts money that he can't afford on the latter. Smith leads, but Murphy catches up. The last end is a climax and a vindication.
8. SILLITOE, Alan
   Saturday Night and Sunday Morning
   pp. 73–74 (Part 1, Ch. 5)
   'Arthur went into the ... back into the pack.'
   Arthur plays cards with his cousins. He secretes two cards in his lap, and raises the odds. He wins handsomely, disguising his manoeuvre behind practised bluff.
9. THACKERAY, William
   Vanity Fair
   (i) pp. 362–364 (Ch. 36); (ii) pp. 429–431
   'The truth is ... present themselves very eagerly.'
   Mr and Mrs Rawdon Crawley have

no income, but he has an amazing skill at cards, and other games of chance. Young men are attracted to the Crawleys' parties by the charming wife, and then soundly defeated by the husband.

GAMES

see also: CHILDREN;
GANGS – CHILDREN;
KITE-FLYING;
PRANKS;
SONGS (and) RHYMES

GAMES

1. BALDWIN, Michael
   Grandad with Snails
   see PRANKS 1, 2, 4
2. CHURCH, Richard
   Over the Bridge
   pp. 130–132 (Ch. 12)
   'My nervous condition ... another as the driver.'
   Playground and street games. The author is appalled by the dangers of the 'living lassoo'; he finds the seasonal games more appealing: 'Cherry-ogg', conkers, hoops, and cotton-weaving.
3. HUGHES, Richard
   A High Wind in Jamaica
   (i) pp. 119–120 (Ch. 5); (ii) pp. 83–85
   'The children were ... dashed for the day.'
   The children use the wet deck of the listing schooner, as a toboggan slide. The Captain winces to see his pirate vessel used for a playground. He calls a halt to the game because he has no wish to mend the children's 'drawers'.
4. HUGHES, Thomas
   Tom Brown's Schooldays
   see FIGHTING (by) MEN (with) STICKS 1
5. LEE, Laurie
   Cider with Rosie
   see NIGHT 3

6. MANSFIELD, Katherine
   The Garden Party
   pp. 45–51 ('At the Bay', Part 1X)
   'A strange company assembled ... take the little boys home.'
   The children are playing a card game involving animal noises, in the wash-house. Lottie, the donkey, is slow to understand her responsibilities; she tires of the game as darkness falls, and all are distracted by talk of spiders and faces at the window.
7. 'MISS READ'
   Village School
   (i) pp. 16–18 (Part 1, Ch. 2); (ii) pp. 16–18
   'The school stands ... very happily together.'
   A village school playground and the ways in which the children adapt it – coke tips, and tree roots – to their own ends.
8. MOORE, John
   Portrait of Elmbury
   pp. 26–27 (Part 1)
   'If Alfie envied ... poetry to me still.'
   John and his sister watch the games of the children in the street from the isolation of their nursery window. The games all have their seasons, and a certain mystique in their accompanying rhymes.
9. NAUGHTON, Bill
   Late Night on Watling Street
   pp. 50–52 ('The Key of the Cabinet')
   ' "Now here you are" ... than can," he said.'
   It's 'strike-the-key' season. Boys attach a hollow key, stuffed with brimstone and potash, to one end of a piece of string, and a nail to the other end. They plug the nail into the key, and swing the string so that the head of the nail strikes a wall, and the 'bomb' explodes.
10. NAUGHTON, Bill
    One Small Boy
    see SEX – ENCOUNTERS 2
11. THOMPSON, Flora
    Lark Rise to Candleford

121

(i) pp. 149–157 ('Lark Rise', Ch. 9); (ii) pp. 143–150
'Of all the generations ... repeating a game.'
Stately, balletic country games played by the girls, to words as old as history.

12. ibid.
(i) pp. 157–159 ('Lark Rise', Ch. 9); (ii) pp. 150–152
'As well as the country ... longest row of pins.'
Girls' and boys' games that have been both more inter-regional, and more durable.

13. TWAIN, Mark
The Adventures of Huckleberry Finn
(i) pp. 13–16 (Ch. 3); (ii) pp. 61–64
'We played robbers now ... marks of a Sunday School.'
Tom Sawyer and his gang indulge in an elaborate pretence whereby a Sunday School party is transformed into a camel train of rich Arabs. The gang breaks up the party, and then, imagination flagging, it disbands.

14. TWAIN, Mark
The Adventures of Tom Sawyer
(i) pp. 63–66 (Ch. 8); (ii) pp. 63–65
'Just here the blast ... United States for ever.'
Tom and Joe Harper play at being Robin Hood. They take turns at being victor and vanquished, taking care the while to obey the spirit of the original.

15. WATERHOUSE, Keith
There is a Happy Land
pp. 2–6 (Ch. 1)
'It was in the middle ... over the handlebars.'
The boy and his friend play typical children's games – a secret language, punning book titles, pretend games, and tongue twisters.

GAMES – RACES

1. BERNA, Paul
A Hundred Million Francs
(i) pp. 9–14 (Ch. 1); (ii) pp. 7–12

'Gaby and the rest ... first time it's happened.'
The children of the Rue des Petits-Pauvres take turns to ride a headless, three-wheeled horse down a steep hill. When it comes to Tatave's turn, Old Zigon is pushing a pram full of bottles across his path. The collision is inevitable, the effects, shattering.

2. NAUGHTON, Bill
The Goalkeeper's Revenge
see COMPETITIONS – RACES 2

GAMES – ROMAN

1. SUTCLIFF, Rosemary
The Eagle of the Ninth
pp. 67–73 (Ch. 5)
'Whatever else of Rome ... right to witness it.'
The Saturnalia Games. First a bear is baited and killed by wolves; then a gladiator defends himself against a Fisher with a trident, and weighted net. Thumbs up save the former from certain death.

GANGS – BOYS

1. BALDWIN, Michael
Grandad with Snails
pp. 18–22 (Ch. 2)
'No sooner did I feel like this ... It nearly went on for ever.'
The author is inducted into his first gang, led by a borstal boy. Their speciality is harassing old ladies in the back alley, and holding their hats to ransom.

2. ibid.
pp. 22–27 (Ch. 2)
'One day as we marched in the alley ... so we smashed his glass-house.'
Two gangs come into conflict. Michael is worried about being involved in his first gang-fight, but Borstal, his leader, quickly puts the rival gang to rout with his air-rifle. The gang then turns its nefarious attentions on a neighbour's car.

3. LEE, Laurie
   Cider with Rosie
   (i) pp. 162–165 (Ch. 12, 'First Bite at
   the Apple'); (ii) pp. 211–215
   'A year or so ... Parish Church
   Council.'
   A group of adolescent village boys
   plan to rape mad Lizzy in the woods
   to combat their boredom and add to
   their knowledge. In the event they
   regret it before she even appears, and
   she fights back so they are glad to let
   her go.
4. NAUGHTON, Bill
   Late Night on Watling Street
   see PRANKS 12
5. TWAIN, Mark
   The Adventures of Huckleberry Finn
   (i) pp. 8–11 (Ch. 2); (ii) pp. 56–59
   'Now we'll start this band ... and I
   was dog-tired.'
   Tom and his friends meet by night in
   a cave and form themselves into a
   gang whose activities will be modelled
   on adventure books that Tom has
   read. They swear an oath of loyalty,
   and sign it with their own blood.
6. WRIGHT, Richard
   Black Boy
   see COURAGE 21

GANGS – CHILDREN

1. BERNA, Paul
   A Hundred Million Francs
   (i) pp. 79–81 (Ch. 4); (ii) pp. 77–79
   'Marion had discovered the spot ...
   gave him a terrific reception.'
   The children of the rue des Petits-
   Pauvres find a wooden shed, in a
   disused saw-mill, well-hidden from
   the eyes of grown-ups. Here they
   meet round a fire, to eat soup and
   baked potatoes, and exchange top-
   secret information.
2. HITCHMAN, Janet
   The King of the Barbareens
   see BULLYING (by) BOYS (and) GIRLS 1

GANGS – YOUTHS

see also: ASSAULT (by) GANGS –
YOUTHS;
KILLING (by) GANGS – YOUTHS

GANGS – YOUTHS

1. BARNES, Ron
   A Licence to Live
   pp. 40–45 (Ch. 5)
   'The best part of the lives ... and
   provide for them.'
   Ron falls in with a bunch of Teds.
   The Kingsland Road is their stamping
   ground, and the cinema is where they
   are most at home. They enjoy a joke,
   fish and chips, and big band music.
2. BARSTOW, Stan
   The Human Element
   see ASSAULT (by) GANGS – YOUTHS 1
3. ibid.
   see KILLING (by) GANGS – YOUTHS 1

GARDENS

1. BURNETT, Frances Hodgson
   The Secret Garden
   pp. 69–73 (Ch. 9)
   'It was the sweetest ... Martha was
   delighted.'
   Mary is in the Secret Garden at last.
   It hasn't been touched for ten years,
   and is very overgrown, but also very
   exciting. Mary is thrilled to find tiny,
   green shoots, and immediately begins
   to weed.

GHOSTS

see also: FEAR (of) GHOSTS;
SPIRITUALISM;
SUPERSTITION;
WITCHCRAFT

GHOSTS

1. DICKENS, Charles
   A Christmas Carol
   pp. 56–65 (Stave 1)

'After several turns ... bleak, dark night.'
The ghost of Jacob Marley, Scrooge's late partner, haunts him, to teach him the many errors of his ways.

2. DU MAURIER, Daphne
   Jamaica Inn
   pp. 111–115 (Ch. 8)
   'You're a good girl ... as though in prayer.'
   In a drunken dream, Joss Merlyn sees again the faces of people he has killed in shipwrecks, and describes them to Mary.

3. GOLDING, William
   Lord of the Flies
   (i) pp. 110–113 (Ch. 5); (ii) pp. 96–99
   'Argument started again ... the ship had gone.'
   The spectre of a Beast from the Sea is raised too late in the evening for reason to prevail. There is loose talk of ghosts; the idea is the product of collective fear.

4. THOMPSON, Flora
   Lark Rise to Candleford
   (i) pp. 59–60 ('Lark Rise' Ch. 4); (ii) pp. 66–67
   'But the children, listening ... wouldn't be let to.'
   The men of the village exchange ghost gossip in the 'Waggon and Horses'. But it is 'all entertainment'. They excite each other's curiosity, but do not believe their own stories.

GIFTS

see also: BIRTHDAYS – GIFTS;
CHARITY;
CHRISTMAS – GIFTS

GIFTS

1. ALCOTT, Lousia M.
   Little Women
   pp. 93–97 (Ch. 6)
   'Mother, I'm going to work ... coming to an end.'
   Beth works a pair of slippers for Mr

Laurence, to thank him for the use of his piano. In return, she receives a piano of her own.

2. BUTLER, Samuel
   The Way of all Flesh
   pp. 139–141 (Ch. 39)
   'Ernest had been out ... dozen messes – the more.'
   Ernest is fond of Ellen, who has been dismissed by his parents on account of her pregnancy; and he is ashamed of his parents' summary judgement. He runs after her carriage to give her his pocket money, his knife, and his watch.

3. LAWRENCE, D.H.
   The Rainbow
   pp. 312–315 (Ch. 11)
   'The barge lay ... weak little neck.'
   Ursula meets a large family. She is attracted to the baby, and the baby's father is attracted to Ursula, and to her name. He gives her name to his baby, and Ursula, in token of a strange bond, gives the baby her necklace.

4. MARSHALL, James Vance
   Walkabout
   see EMBARRASSMENT 5

5. STEINBECK, John
   The Red Pony
   pp. 8–12 (Ch. 1)
   'When the triangle sounded ... this afternoon' Jody said.'
   Jody gets up early because his father has a surprise for him. He thinks it may be an unpleasant one, but it turns out to be a red pony colt, and a morocco-leather saddle – a present beyond his dreams.

GIRLS

see also: ADOLESCENCE – GIRLS;
BULLYING (by) GIRLS;
FRIENDS – GIRLS

GIRLS

1. DE JONG, Meindert
   The Wheel on the School

(i) pp. 7–11 (Ch. 2); (ii) pp. 14–18
'Jella looked along ... staring at a house.'
The children of Shora have an hour off school, to wonder why the storks no longer nest there. The boys quickly tire of wondering, and go off to play. Lina, the only girl, is left to brood on the misfortunes of being a girl – and to find a solution to the problem.

2. FIELDING, Henry
   Joseph Andrews
   pp. 256–258 (Bk. 4, Ch. 7)
   'Habit, my good reader ... a dream betrayed it to her.'
   Fielding describes how, as a result of the way they are brought up to distrust the motives of all boys, girls fall in love rather despite their habitual leanings than because of them.

3. HITCHMAN, Janet
   The King of the Barbareens
   see SEX – ENCOUNTERS 1

4. ibid.
   see MENSTRUATION 1

5. LAWRENCE, D.H.
   The Rainbow
   see CHURCH – SERVICES 2

GOATS

1. THOMAS, Leslie
   This Time Next Week
   pp. 51–55 (Ch. 5)
   'Three of us he sent ... good and peaceful parting.'
   Three boys are sent to fetch a pair of goats for the gaffer. They do not come quietly: one does battle with a trolley-bus, and the other goes climbing. At the home, one dies by misadventure, in the kitchen, and the other survives to terrorise a neighbour.

GOD

see RELIGION

GOLD

1. PATON, Alan
   Cry, the Beloved Country
   see CAPITALISM 4

GOSSIP

1. AUSTEN, Jane
   Emma
   pp. 171–173 (Ch. 19)
   'Emma's politeness was at hand ... from his account of things.'
   Miss Bates talks almost non-stop to any visitor who calls. She recounts every detail of a story, but also jumps from one subject to another.

2. BARSTOW, Stan
   The Human Element
   see REVENGE 5

3. BRAITHWAITE, E.R.
   To Sir With Love
   pp. 5–6 (Ch. 1)
   'The crowded red double-decker ... bulwark of the adventurous.'
   The cheery urban peasants of London's East End joke freely about sex. On a crowded bus, they tell all, unashamedly, about their husbands.

4. THOMPSON, Flora
   Lark Rise to Candleford
   (i) pp. 104–106 ('Lark Rise', Ch. 6);
   (ii) pp. 105–107
   'One of the most dreaded ... she had her uses.'
   Mrs Mullins, a scandal-monger, is disliked and distrusted by the women of the hamlet, whilst Mrs Andrews often has something of real value to impart, and is no common scold.

GOVERNMENT

see also: AUTHORITY;
KINGS

GOVERNMENT

1. ALLEN, Eric
   The Latchkey Children
   pp. 83–85 (Ch. 8)

'There was a desk ... where the policeman was.'

Goggles sits in on a Commons debate. He is at once disillusioned by the bored uninvolvement of the Members, in the proceedings, and excited just by being there, where, he supposed, important things happened.

2. CARY, Joyce
   The Horse's Mouth
   pp. 270–272 (Ch. 32)
   'For the bus ... the spectre of Hell.'
   Gulley outlines his views on 'government', and demonstrates how a committee of committees cannot help being 'selfish, cruel, blind, deaf and dumb.'

GOVERNMENT – ARISTOCRACY

1. DICKENS, Charles
   A Tale of Two Cities
   pp. 109–114 (Bk. 2, Ch. 7)
   'Monseigneur one of the great ... on his way out.'
   Monseigneur is holding his fortnightly reception to which flock crowds of petitioners and hangers-on. The meaningless pomp, the arrogance, the greed and the selfishness are exposed in Dickens' satirical description.

2. ibid.
   see ACCIDENTS – ROAD

GOVERNMENT – DICTATORSHIP

1. ADAMS, Richard
   Watership Down
   pp. 240–244 (Ch. 27)
   'I don't think we need ... heard talking about it.'
   Holly describes life in Efrafa, where he was imprisoned for a few days. It is a large burrow, a rabbit police-state, where all the members obey very strict, but unnatural rules.

2. ORWELL, George
   Animal Farm
   (i) pp. 31–34 (Ch. 5); (ii) pp. 45–49
   'The whole farm was deeply ... there would be no more debates.'

The differences between the idealistic Snowball, and the dogmatic Napoleon, come to a head. When it looks as if Snowball (Trotsky) might win the day, Napoleon (Stalin) sets the dogs on him and has him run off the farm.

3. ibid.
   (i) pp. 47–48 (Ch. 7); (ii) pp. 66–67
   'In these days Napoleon ... to take them away.'
   Napoleon imposes his will on the hens, who refuse to allow their eggs to be taken for sale, by stopping their rations. Nine of the hens die, and the remainder capitulate.

4. ibid.
   see TRIALS 9

5. ORWELL, George
   1984
   (i) pp. 212–214 (Part 2, Ch. 9); (ii) pp. 166–167
   'But the problems ... part of the structure.'
   The problem of remaining in power, and how Oceania's party has solved it – 'by moulding the consciousness' of party members.

6. ibid.
   pp. 269–275 (Part 3, Ch. 3); (ii) pp. 211–216
   'Now I will tell ... is immortal.'
   O'Brien reveals that the object of the Party's power is power, nothing else, and that this can only be achieved by completely controlling men, mentally as well as physically.

GRANDPARENTS

see also: DEATH (of) GRANDPARENTS; OLD AGE

GRANDPARENTS

1. BALDWIN, Michael
   Grandad with Snails
   pp. 45–49 (Ch. 5)
   'I went down the wet street ... and I went sadly to bed.'
   Michael's seagoing Grandfather

comes home on leave. He brings tall, gruesome stories home with him, and a caseful of dirty washing.

2. GORKY, Maxim
   Childhood
   (i) pp. 10–14 (Ch. 1); (ii) pp. 19–22
   'When I woke up the steamer ... 'It'll do them good.' '
   Bewildered by all that is happening young Gorky attaches himself to his kindly old grandmother. She tells him secrets and tall stories. She is as soft and affectionate as a large cat.

3. ibid.
   see REVENGE 13

4. GRICE, Frederick
   The Bonny Pit Laddie
   pp. 66–67 (Ch. 8)
   'Old Mrs Ullathorne ... disturbed the silence.'
   In his grandmother's house, Dick can read, away from the noises of the village. Mrs Ullathorne is an offcomer, quite unlike the other pit-wives. Her strange ways are fascinating to her growing grandson.

5. THOMAS, Dylan
   Portrait of the Artist as a Young Dog
   pp. 23–28 ('A Visit to Grandpa's')
   'In the middle ... who has no doubt.'
   Dai Thomas indulges in childish fantasies during the night, and senile fancies during the day. He is, from top to bottom, a 'character.'

6. THOMPSON, Flora
   Lark Rise to Candleford
   (i) pp. 87–93 ('Lark Rise', ch. 5); (ii) pp. 90–96
   'The children's grandparents ... into thin air.'
   Laura's grandparents: their house and garden. Grandfather is religious and rheumatic, Grandmother has been beautiful in her time, and is still fastidious about her person, and her home.

GRIEF

see also: DEATH;
FUNERALS

GRIEF

1. BRONTË Charlotte
   Villette
   see LOVE – DISILLUSIONMENT 3

2. CANAWAY, W.H.
   Sammy going South
   p. 17 (Ch. 3)
   'He stood up ... for the time being.'
   Sammy has lost his parents in an air-raid in Cairo, and run away from the city. Alone on a beach he plays at bombing crabs, working the grief out of his system.

3. MACKEN, Walter
   God made Sunday and Other Stories
   pp. 12–17 ('God made Sunday')
   'I wound up my ... on a Monday.'
   A violent storm hits Colmain's village, and drowns her men at sea. Colmain loses two brothers and a father; his mother loses all but Colmain, and he, at fourteen, cannot console her. Grief ages her, and within three years kills her.

4. NAUGHTON, Bill
   One Small Boy
   pp. 274–281 (Bk. 3, Ch. 9)
   'He rested himself ... used to the din.'
   The whole house is full of mourning for the dead Willie, but Michael scarcely feels a part of it all. He sees his dead brother in his coffin, but cannot feel grief, until he overhears his uncle talk about him; then he has a good cry and feels better.

5. O'BRIEN, Edna
   The Country Girls
   pp. 48–53 (Ch. 5)
   'Outside in the porch ... the last day of childhood.'
   Caithleen is called out of a play at the Town Hall to be told that her mother has been drowned. She is surrounded by sympathetic friends, but feels desolate and hopeless.

6. PATON, Alan
   Cry, the Beloved Country
   (i) pp. 76–79 (Bk. 1, Ch. 15); (ii) pp. 94–98

'When the young man had gone ...
more that you ask.'

Rev. Kumalo's son is in prison, charged with the murder of a white man. Kumalo, in conversation with an English priest, allows his grief and bitterness to get the better of him, and is to some extent comforted.

7. ibid.

(i) pp. 93–98 (Bk. 2, ch. 1); (ii) pp. 114–118

'Jarvis turned these old thoughts ... crying and sobbing.'

Jarvis is surveying his S. African farm, and thinking of his only son, who has chosen a very different life, when he sees a police car approaching. The policemen break to him that his son has just been murdered by a 'native housebreaker.'

8. PEYTON, K.M.
Flambards in Summer
(i) pp. 83–90 (Ch. 80; (ii) pp. 114–123

'Christina was frightened ... too exhausted to cry any more.'

The death of Christina's late husband is re-enacted before her eyes, when a German plane crashes in her hayfield. The sight of the dead reargunner forces her to think about what she had tried to forget: she reads Will's, and others', letters, and ventilates too-long-repressed grief.

9. SHOLOKHOV, Mikhail
And Quiet Flows the Don
pp. 582–584; 585–588 (Part 4, Ch. 9)

'In the morning ... 'It sounds all right!' '; 'A platoon of Red Guards ... of human misery.'

The girl who had fought by his side, the girl who had nursed him back to life, the girl who bears his child, is shot by a Red Guard in a street skirmish. She dies in agony, and a good deal of Bunchuk dies watching her.

10. STEINBECK, John
The Red Pony
pp. 39–42 (Ch. 1)
(Loneliness and Parting pp. 9–11)

'Billy Buck stood up ... he'd feel about it?'

Jody's pony, Gabilan, wanders off in the night to die by himself. When Jody catches up with him, he finds buzzards about to make a meal of his pony. He catches one of them and beats it to death, to work out his grief.

11. THACKERAY, William
Vanity Fair
(i) pp. 349–352 (Ch. 35); (ii) pp. 415–418

'The news of the great fights ... pro patria mori.'

The effect of the lists of soldiers killed at Waterloo published by the Gazette, on those at home. Mr Osborne parted from his son on the worst possible terms, and news of his death fills him with gloom and remorse.

GUILLOTINE

see EXECUTION (by) GUILLOTINE;
FRENCH REVOLUTION – GUILLOTINE

GUNS

see FIGHTING (by) MEN (with) GUNS

GYPSIES

1. DURRELL, Gerald
Birds, Beasts and Relatives
see MAGIC 1

2. ELIOT, George
The Mill on the Floss
see RUNNING AWAY (from) HOME 2

3. GODDEN, Rumer
The Diddakoi
pp. 7–9; 18–20 (Ch. 1)

'Diddakoi/Tinker ... teased' said Mrs Blount.'; 'Mrs Cuthbert had opened ... have to go back.'

The children tease her at school in spite of what the teacher has said. Everything is unfamiliar to the half-gypsy, Kizzy, so she runs away from the teasing, back to the familiar.

4. ibid.
pp. 27–32 (Ch. 2)

'No child of ours ... away into the night.'

When her Gran dies, Kizzy is argued over. Relatives disown her, and burn her waggon. Before they can send her horse, Joe, to the knackers, she escapes with him, in the dark.

5. LAWRENCE, D.H.
The Virgin and the Gipsy
pp. 22–26 (Part 3)
(Themes in Life and Literature pp. 140–141)
'Ahead was a light cart ... 'With him—'

The car-excursion party happens on a small gypsy settlement. Yvette is struck by the proud, handsome, bearing of the man, and his loose-limbed wife. The girls have their fortunes told at a shilling a head.

6. THOMPSON, Flora
Lark Rise to Candleford
(i) pp. 23–24 ('Lark Rise', Ch. 2); 125–126 (Ch. 7); (ii) p. 36; 122–123
'In one little roadside ... was only a game.'; 'Gipys women with ... even more depressed.'

Gypsies as objects of childish fear and fascination; as craftsmen, salesmen, tellers of fortunes, and scroungers.

HALLOWE'EN

1. LEE, Harper
To Kill a Mockingbird
see ENTERTAINMENTS 2

HANGING

see EXECUTION (by) HANGING

HAPPINESS

1. ALCOTT, Louisa M.
Little Women
pp. 90–92 (Ch. 6)
'But Beth, though yearning ... state of beatitude.'

Beth is too shy to visit the Laurences next door, but when Mr Laurence invites her to play his grand piano, her shyness is forgotten. She plays and is blissfully happy.

2. DEFOE, Daniel
Robinson Crusoe
(i) pp. 94–96; (ii) pp. 128–130 (Ch. 12)
'In the middle of ... thankfulness for what we have.'

Crusoe learns contentment on his island; to be thankful for small mercies, and to desire nothing but what he could have.

3. MANSFIELD, Katherine
Bliss and Other Stories
pp. 95–100 ('Bliss')
'Although Bertha Young ... upstairs to dress.'

Bertha Young is in a childishly happy mood. She takes pleasure in her home, her husband, and her baby. She is in bliss to the point of hysteria.

4. MAUGHAM, W. Somerset
The Moon and Sixpence
see AMBITIONS 2

5. TATE, Joan
Sam and Me
see HOME 9

6. THOMAS, Leslie
This Time Next Week
pp. 92–93 (Ch. 8)
'There was one hour ... I was happy then.'

It is a winter afternoon. Leslie is temporarily free. He runs and feels good. He climbs a familiar tree to the top, and knows that this is happiness.

7. WELLS, H.G.
The History of Mr Polly
pp. 240–245 (Ch. 10, Part 3)
'Mr Polly sat beside ... sit here forever.'

Polly sits with the fat woman at the Potwell Inn, reflecting on the recent events. He 'wonders about life', and savours the sunset, and the stinging nettles by the hedge, that are the peace and satisfaction to which he has for so long looked forward.

HARVEST

see FARMING − HARVEST

HASTINGS, Battle

1. TREECE, Henry
    Hounds of the King
    see INVASIONS − NORMANS 1

HATRED

see also: CRUELTY;
RACISM

HATRED

1. BENTLEY, Phyllis
    The Adventures of Tom Leigh
    pp. 58−60 (Ch. 4)
    'But Jeremy's ill-will ... shrank from him.'
    The journeyman with whom Tom works is a mean, malicious man, who seeks to do him ill. On one occasion, he puts Tom's life in danger by hoisting him into the air on the end of a rope.
2. ORWELL, George
    1984
    (i) pp. 15−19 (Part 1, Ch. 1); (ii) pp. 11−16
    'It was nearly eleven ... IGNORANCE IS STRENGTH.'
    The workers of the Records Department gather together for the daily 'Two Minutes Hate', where they watch a programme of propaganda against the enemy and work off aggressive feelings.
3. STEINBECK, John
    The Grapes of Wrath
    see CAPITALISM 7
4. WRIGHT, Richard
    Black Boy
    see JEWS 1
5. ibid.
    see RACISM − AMERICA 8
6. ibid.
    pp. 157−160 (Ch. 9)

'My life now depended ... my hat and left.'
Richard sees and feels the extent of white hatred for the blacks. But he cannot get used to it, or learn to accept it. Nor can he disguise his feelings for the sake of expediency.

HEAT

1. BATES, H.E.
    The Purple Plain
    pp. 1−5 (Ch. 1)
    'Shy flocks ... or even ten years.'
    Forrester is stationed in Burma, and sharing a tent with Blore who seems not to suffer from the intense heat. It affects everything Forrester says and does, and his temper is very much the worse as a result of it.
2. CAMUS, Albert
    The Outsider
    pp. 24−27 (Part 1, Ch. 1)
    'The sky was already ... twelve hours at a stretch.'
    It is the morning of the funeral, and the young man has been up all night with the body of his mother. Nothing is quite real or memorable in the heat. The glare bleaches out the colours from everything and everyone.
3. ibid.
    see KILLING 2

HELL

1. JOYCE, James
    A Portrait of the Artist as a Young Man
    pp. 119−124 (Ch. 3)
    'The preacher's voice sank ... the devil and his angels.'
    At the festival of St Francis Xavier, the preacher describes in relentless, and imaginative detail, the torments of the damned in Hell.
2. ibid.
    see CONSCIENCE 7
3. ibid.
    pp. 131−133 (Ch. 3)

'– Last and crowning torture ... almighty and a just God.'

The preacher heaps upon all other pains that the damned will have to endure, the awfulness of eternity; the dread knowledge of the everlasting absence of God.

HERO-WORSHIP

1. BRONTË, Charlotte
   Villette
   pp. 18–20 (Ch. 2)
   'The pair seldom quarrelled ... to rise of her own accord.'
   The little girl, Paulina, has a 'crush' on Graham Bretton, comes alive only when he is there, waits on him hand and foot, and is extremely upset when he has friends to dine, and ignores her.
2. LAWRENCE, D.H.
   The Rainbow
   pp. 336–339 (Ch. 12)
   'Suddenly Ursula found ... now tacitly confessed.'
   A strong loving relationship develops between Ursula and her school-mistress, Miss Inger. Their passion is at once physical and emotional, and it is with difficulty that they constrain it within respectable bounds.
3. SASSOON, Siegfried
   Memoirs of a Foxhunting Man
   see HUNTING – FOXES 4

HIDING

1. HINES, Barry
   A Kestrel for a Knave
   (i) pp. 159–163; (ii) pp. 129–132
   'Chairs were scraped ... back of the shed.'
   Billy runs away from his big brother Jud who has come to school to pay Billy back for not laying his bet as instructed. He hides in the cloakroom, skulks along corridors, and finally resorts to the boiler room, where he sleeps a forgetful sleep.

2. PICARD, Barbara Leonie
   The Young Pretenders
   pp. 96–102 (Ch. 10)
   'On the Tuesday morning ... his hands over his face.'
   Francis is 'borrowing' shirts and a razor from his father's room for the Jacobite he and his sister are secretly sheltering. He is surprised by the valet and has to hide under the bed, while the valet searches for the missing shirts.
3. STEINBECK, John
   The Grapes of Wrath
   (i) pp. 48–50 (Ch. 6); (ii) pp. 53–56
   'Huh? No. I don't go ... old man's place.'
   Tom and two companions have just cooked supper on the farm from which his father has been evicted. They are disturbed by the present superintendent looking for trespassers, and lie low until he has gone.
4. TREASE, Geoffrey
   Cue for Treason
   pp. 29–38 (Chs. 3, 4)
   'Outside one of the big inns ... even if it ended in capture.'
   As a diversion from his problems, Peter pays to watch a play – and runs into his biggest problem, Sir Philip Morton. He is seen and chased. Peter hides in an old chest, and finds himself on stage as the coffinned king.

HIDING (from) ENEMY – 1939–45

1. BATES, H.E.
   Fair Stood the Wind for France
   (i) pp. 165–168 (Ch. 16); (ii) pp. 169–172
   'He stood still ... but wait again.'
   Franklin, hiding in an old mill, in occupied France, sees a stranger looking inquisitively round the farm during the absence of the family. He wonders whether he would shoot him if discovered.
2. FRANK, Anne
   The Diary of Anne Frank
   pp. 24–29 (9.7.42–11.7.42)

'So we walked … might hear us.'
Having received a call-up notice from the SS for Anne's sister, the Frank family have gone into hiding. Anne describes their new home, and the process of settling-in.

3. ibid.
p. 75 (1.5.43)
'If I just think … naughty little children.'
Anne reviews the situation in their hideout, and is amazed that the standard of living they had considered essential before the war can have dropped so.

4. ibid.
pp. 87–97 (4.8.43–23.8.43)
'Now that we have been … Breakfast!'
After a year in 'The Secret Annexe', Anne describes in great detail their daily routine, and the actions and reactions of all the participants.

5. ibid.
pp. 108–109 (24.12.43)
'I have previously … bring such relief.'
Anne allows herself a good grumble about their confinement, and its effect on the tempers of all concerned. Even now however, she realises she must be brave and grateful for being alive.

6. ibid.
pp. 147–149 (14.3.44)
Anne describes the poor food situation, and how it affects each member of the household.

HIGHWAYMEN

1. FIELDING, Henry
   Joseph Andrews
   see CHARITY 8
2. JOHNSON, Dorothy
   The Hanging Tree
   see ROBBERY 4
3. PICARD, Barbara Leonie
   The Young Pretenders
   pp. 188–192 (Ch. 18)
   'Seamus was still smiling … and this time, for good.'

Seamus tells Francis, his unwilling protector, how he came to be pursued by militiamen. He had robbed the Lord Lieutenant of Yorkshire, and then escaped again when he had been arrested.

HIKING

1. THOMAS, Dylan
   A Portrait of the Artist as a Young Dog
   pp. 84–88 ('Who do you wish was with us')
   'Birds in the Crescent … it's a record,' I said.'
   Dylan, and his older friend, Raymond Price, stride out with haversacks on their backs. They are elated to be within hearing of birdsong. They meet a band of cyclists with whom they exchange good-natured chaff, and whom they see again later, from the top deck of a bus.

HISTORY

1. JEROME, Jerome K.
   Three Men in a Boat
   see KINGS 1
2. ORWELL, George
   1984
   (i) pp. 41–55 (Ch. 4, Part 1); 47–51 (Ch. 4, Part 1); (ii) pp. 33–36; 38–42
   'With the deep … become uncertain.'; 'Three messages … or Julius Caesar.'
   Winston's work in the Ministry of Truth – as the political, economic or war situation changes, he and his colleagues have to change all records to conform with the state of affairs.
3. ibid.
   (i) p. 76 (Ch. 7, Part 1); (ii) pp. 61–62
   'In the old days … the kind, and …'
   An extract from a child's history book, showing how the facts have been manipulated to prove the Party's point.

4. ibid.
   (i) pp. 77–78 (Ch. 7, Part 1); (ii) pp.
   62–63
   (Themes in Life and Literature, pp.
   169–171)
   'How could you tell ... as a top hat.'
   Examples of statistics invented and
   published by the Party to paint a rosy,
   but false, picture of present conditions.
5. ibid.
   (i) pp. 78–85 (Ch. 7, Part 1); (ii) pp.
   63–68
   'The story really began ... all else
   follows.'
   Winston's proof that history is changed to suit the party – a photograph
   he sees destroying the Party's case
   against three traitors.
6. ibid.
   (i) pp. 218–220 (Ch. 9, Part 11); (ii)
   pp. 170–171
   'The alteration of the past ... the
   course of history.'
   The principle of the 'mutability of the
   past' analysed.
7. ROBINSON, Rony
   A Walk to see the King
   see PEASANTS' REVOLT 2

HOLIDAYS

   see also: EXCURSIONS;
   SEASIDE

HOLIDAYS

1. ALCOTT, Louisa M.
   Little Women
   see BOREDOM 1
2. MANSFIELD, Katherine
   The Garden Party
   pp. 231–236 ('Bank Holiday');
   (Impact 1, pp. 137–138)
   'A stout man with a pink face ...
   dazzling radiance to ... what?'
   A word-painting of a holiday crowd
   enjoying itself, responding to the
   overtures of salesmen and mounte-
   banks, listening to the music, basking
   in the sun, letting themselves go.

3. SPYRI, Johanna
   Heidi
   pp. 204–208 (Ch. 21)
   'As the sun rose ... she had ever
   known.'
   Invalid Clara is staying with Heidi
   and her grandfather on the mountain,
   and is enthralled by the life. She had
   never dreamed the mountains could
   be so wonderful and her health and
   appetite improve remarkably.
4. THOMAS, Dylan
   A Portrait of the Artist as a Young
   Dog
   pp. 52–61 ('Extraordinary Little
   Cough'); (Here, Now and Beyond,
   pp. 28–29)
   'One afternoon ... touching the
   flames.'
   Dylan goes on a camping holiday at
   Rhossilli, with three school friends.
   They travel on the roof of a lorry,
   having a high old time. They pitch
   camp in a field, romp on the sand,
   and pay court to three obliging girls.
5. THOMAS, Dylan
   Quite Early One Morning
   pp. 29–30; 32–33 ('Holiday Memory'); (Young Impact 3, pp. 92–93)
   'August Bank Holiday ... the sandy
   sandwiches'; 'There was cricket ...
   for ever and ever amen.'
   Dylan Thomas recaptures all the
   sand-tasting, sea-smelling impressions
   of an overcrowded beach. The modest
   undress, and the unassuming forget
   themselves.
6. THOMPSON, Flora
   Lark Rise to Candleford
   (i) pp. 381–384 ('Over to Candleford', Ch. 25); (ii) pp. 340–342
   'Candleford was but ... surprising
   household.'
   Although only a small town, Candleford seems very exciting to Laura.
   However their holiday has its country
   elements too – picnics, boating and a
   day's harvesting.

HOME

see also: ACCIDENTS – HOME;
EVICTION;
FAMILY; FATHERS;
HOMELESSNESS; MOTHERS;
RUNNING AWAY (from) HOME

HOME

1. BENNETT, Arnold
    Anna of the Five Towns
    pp. 105–107 (Ch. 7)
    'When, in a moment ... like a picture.'
    Anna's kitchen is a pleasant, homely, spotless room. The dresser, the pans, the fender all shine, and everything is in its place. Henry Mynors sees the reflection of Anna in the room.

2. DICKENS, Charles
    Bleak House
    see MOTHERS 3

3. ELIOT, George
    The Mill on the Floss
    pp. 323–325 (Ch. 9)
    'But the strongest influence ... changing your countryside.'
    After his bankruptcy Tulliver stays at the Mill, under a hated master, but he is almost content to do so because it has always been his home. He looks back over his life there.

4. FOAKES, Grace
    Between High Walls
    pp. 4–5 (Ch. 2)
    'When I was a little ... all that mattered.'
    The author's childhood bedroom, and the overcrowded kitchen, where everybody lives, and the author's mother works miracles in, on, and about the oven.

5. GORKY, Maxim
    Childhood
    (i) pp. 45–53 (Ch. 3); (ii) pp. 43–49; (Impact Two, pp. 62–65)
    'I have an especially vivid remembrance ... an elusive, inexplicable swiftness.'
    The extended family at play. When the beatings and quarrellings are over Uncle Yakov plays the guitar, and sings plaintive songs; and Tsiganok, and Grandmother dance, the one like an athlete, the other like a duchess. The vodka flows, and everybody is happy.

6. MANNING, Olivia
    The Play Room
    pp. 19–20 (Section 1, Ch. 1)
    ' 'Now' said Mrs Fletcher ... ever likely to know.'
    The Fletcher family's evening – argument over who is to wash up, no television until homework is done, father tinkering with a clock and Mother reading the paper.

7. SPYRI, Johanna
    Heidi
    pp. 20–23 (Ch. 2)
    'Heidi picked up ... I could get in it.'
    Heidi explores her grandfather's hut which is to be her home. She is delighted with everything, especially the bed she makes for herself in the hay-loft.

8. SUTCLIFF, Rosemary
    The Eagle of the Ninth
    pp. 163–165 (Ch. 13)
    'Guern's homestead ... by sharing his bowl.'
    The travellers are made welcome in the simple home of an apparently simple native hunter. It is a gloomy house, but it is warm with cooking and hospitality.

9. TATE, Joan
    Sam and Me
    pp. 7–14 (Ch. 1)
    'I remember the journey in the car ... Sam, or his mother and father.'
    A ten year old girl, from a children's home, is introduced to her new foster-parents and their son, Sam. She communicates little at first, and even when she is feeling more at home, she allows herself only a cautious happiness, for fear it might all be taken away.

10. THOMPSON, Flora
    Lark Rise to Candleford

(i) pp. 290–292 ('Over to Candleford', Ch. 17); (ii) pp. 263–265
'Laura's parents ... familiar mountains.'
The cottage where the children grew up is described in detail, as the setting for all their games and activities.

HOME – COMING

1. CARY, Joyce
   The Horse's Mouth
   pp. 8–11 (Ch. 2)
   'I could see my studio ... chased him out.'
   After a month in prison, Gulley Jimson returns to his studio, an old boat house on the Thames. In his absence it has been overrun by children with little respect for his property or his painting.

2. LAWRENCE, D.H.
   Sons and Lovers
   see CHRISTMAS 8

3. LLWELLYN, Richard
   How Green was my Valley
   pp. 64–71 (Ch. 7)
   'My father had made ... mixing for a start.'
   Huw's mother has been ill since the birth of Olwen, and his father has prepared a great celebration for her recovery. The house is painted and refurnished, and the whole village waits to welcome her back to their midst. There is singing and eating.

4. ibid.
   see SINGING 2

5. SHOLOKHOV, Mikhail
   And Quiet Flows the Don
   pp. 466–468 (Part 4, Ch. 1)
   'Yellow-white, billowing ... face out of the house.'
   Bunchuk arrives home from the war and the Revolution, for a brief interval with his old mother. Both have aged, but the old spark burns for a while, before Bunchuk has to be off again.

6. ibid.
   pp. 513–515 (Part 4, Ch. 3)

'As Piotra kissed his brother ... towards the stove.'
The rake-hero Gregor returns home after his exploits in the war, to a loyal wife, twins he has never seen, and a mother and a sister who can't fuss him enough.

7. THOMPSON, Flora
   Lark Rise to Candleford
   (i) pp. 583–587 ('Candleford Green', Ch. 38); (ii) pp. 510–513
   'Laura had been away ... God bless you!'
   After seven months away in her first job, Laura returns home for the weekend. At first she feels a little superior, but she soon settles back into home life, and is urged to come more often.

HOME – LEAVING

see also: EMIGRATION;
SECOND WORLD WAR – EVACUATION

HOME – LEAVING

1. BALDWIN, James
   Go Tell it on the Mountain
   pp. 77–82 (Part 2, 'Florence's Prayer') ('Breaking Away', pp. 4–7)
   'And it was this leave-taking ... wearing rags like yours.'
   Florence has made up her mind to leave. It is not easy: there are tears in her eyes; her mother is sick in bed; and her brother hectors her conscience as far as the gate. It is painful, but it is done.

2. BANKS, Lynne Reid
   The L-Shaped Room
   pp. 60–62 (Ch. 4)
   'He didn't know ... might tell everyone.'
   Jane has been turned out of the house because she's pregnant. She returns to collect her belongings (and a few of her father's) and finds the pull of home very strong.

135

3. CRANE, Stephen
The Red Badge of Courage
see ARMY – ENLISTMENT 1

4. DICKENS, Charles
Great Expectations
(i) pp. 178–180 (Ch. 19); (ii) pp. 152–154
'And now, those ... spread before me.'
Confident in his Great Expectations Pip leaves home in such a way as to preserve his self-importance. But the departure is not as easy as he had supposed it would be; his tears almost take him back.

5. HITCHMAN, Janet
The King of the Barbareens
see ORPHANS 5

6. LEE, Harper
To Kill a Mockingbird
see FAMILY 7

7. PATON, Alan
Cry, the Beloved Country
(ii) pp. 13–16 (Book 1, Ch. 3)
'The small toy train ... this world alone that was certain.'
Stephen Kumalo leaves home for Johannesburg, by train, to look for his sister. He is very apprehensive about the big city, but puts on an act of self-confidence in front of his fellow-travellers.

8. STEINBECK, John
The Grapes of Wrath
(i) pp. 73–76 (Ch. 9); (ii) pp. 79–82
'In the little houses ... cars had passed.'
Countless families are evicted from their farms by greedy landowners, and are forced to move west. They break up their homes, sell what they can, and pack most of the remainder, then depart quickly so that the pain is not prolonged.

9. THOMPSON, Flora
Lark Rise to Candleford
(i) pp. 171–172 ('Lark Rise', Ch. 10); (ii) pp. 162–163
'When the girls had been ... read her thoughts.'
A mother sees her daughter off at the station. She is leaving home for her first place in a distant household. The mother is at once proud, glad to have the daughter off her hands, and anxious.

10. ibid.
(i) pp. 439–443 ('Candleford Green', Ch. 30); (ii) pp. 389–392
'Laura sat up ... did her writing.'
Laura leaves Lark Rise by pony and cart with her father, to travel to her first job in the Post Office at Candleford Green. She looks back over the preparations for leaving, and anticipates the future with some trepidation.

11. TOWNSEND, Alan Rowe
Gumble's Yard
pp. 38–45 (Ch. 4)
'It was after midnight ... better when you've had some sleep.'
The children do a midnight flit. They move necessities on a hand-cart from what has been their home, to a den beyond the reach of the authorities. They narrowly escape a constable on patrol; young Harold goes back for the only present his father has ever given him.

12. WRIGHT, Richard
Black Boy
pp. 178–181 (Ch. 10)
'My chances forgetting ... what I can make of it.'
In order to save enough money to go north Richard steals from his employer. He engages in a crime hateful to him, only until he has reached his target; then he says goodbye to his mother, and to Jackson, Mississippi.

HOME – MAKING

1. ADAMS, Richard
Watership Down
pp. 68–72 (Ch. 12)
'To come to the end ... concerned with the work.'
After a difficult and dangerous journey, the rabbits reach a spot they feel

will be suitable to establish a new warren. They begin to dig.

HOME – REMOVAL

1. CHURCH, Richard
   Over the Bridge
   pp. 196–199 (Ch. 16)
   'Every week-end was now ... when the vans rolled up.'
   The Churches search for a house, beyond the reach of Battersea fogs. They find one that is very much à la mode in a Dulwich that is still very much a village. Richard is enchanted by it; so that when they leave the Battersea house, he doesn't once look back.
2. COOKSON, Catherine
   The Nipper
   pp. 17–21 (Ch. 2)
   'At four o'clock ... the biggest one.'
   Sandy and his mother have been forced to move to a near-derelict row of miners' cottages. They try to remain cheerful as they clean the place, but are horrified by their loud-mouthed neighbours.
3. NESBIT, E.
   The Railway Children
   (i) pp. 13–24 (Chs. 1, 2); (ii) pp. 19–30
   'Now, my pets ... we were up so early.'
   The children's mother announces that they are moving. All the dull, ugly things are packed to go with them, and they go by train to their new house. They arrive in the dark, have a long, muddy walk, and find no fire and no supper, although they had been ordered.
4. STOLZ, Mary
   Ready or Not
   pp. 19–25 (Ch. 2)
   'It was beginning to get ... sentiment would not be summoned.'
   For the umpteenth time the Connors are on the move – and it's generally down in the world. Everything is packed up and waiting to go, in rooms that seem bigger than usual. Breakfast is contrived before the removal men come, and the mood is changed.
5. TATE, Joan
   Clipper
   pp. 39–45 (Ch. 4)
   'It took us ages ... she did too.'
   Clee and Nibs move to London – they are moving to furnished accommodation, so stuff all their belongings in the car. They are greeted by the Friday evening rush-hour, and then a couple of very bare, grim rooms in a Victorian house off Tottenham Court Rd. Spirits sink.

HOMELESSNESS

1. CARY, Joyce
   The Horse's Mouth
   pp. 151–159 (Ch. 20)
   'The sixpenny doss ... why should you know?'
   Released from prison, without a home, Gulley goes to a doss-house. He meets an old friend, also homeless, and between fights for a frying-pan, with other residents, they discuss the harshness of life.
2. ibid.
   pp. 172–173 (Ch. 21)
   'Then I made for ... sixpence a night.'
   Gulley outwits other residents at the doss-house for a place at the fire to heat his supper.
3. PATON, Alan
   Cry, the Beloved Country
   (i) pp. 41–43 (Bk. 1, Ch. 9); (ii) pp. 48–55
   (i) 'This night, they are busy ... the rain and the winter.'
   (ii) 'All roads lead to ... the rain and the winter.'
   The weary and unsuccessful search of a black family for accommodation in Johannesburg. They leave the country, believing there to be work and money for all, and they end up living in awful conditions in Shantytown.

HOMESICKNESS

1. SPYRI, Johanna
   Heidi
   pp. 110–112 (Ch. 11)
   'Next evening Heidi ... Clara wanted her again.'
   Heidi grows more and more homesick in Frankfurt, and a book of stories about mountains which once made her happy, now brings tears to her eyes.

HOMOSEXUALITY

1. SALINGER, J.D.
   The Catcher in the Rye
   pp. 198–200 (Ch. 24)
   'Then something happened ... I can't stand it.'
   In the night, Mr Antolini caresses the sleeping Holden. Holden is awake immediately, and in no time he has dressed and made his excuses to leave the flat.

HONESTY

1. ALLEN, Walter
   All in a Lifetime
   pp. 122–123 (Ch. 11)
   'When the revelation came ... and for us all?'
   Tom has been expelled from college for cheating in his examinations. He has absolutely no regrets about his dishonesty, since, as he tells his father, he is not impressed by the fruits of honesty.

2. BRONTË, Charlotte
   Villette
   pp. 41–42 (Ch. 6)
   'This was an uncomfortable crisis ... and went below.'
   Lucy Snowe arrives at the wharf to be taken by watermen to her ship – it is the first time she has made such a journey, and she is first surrounded by competing watermen, then cheated by her eventual ferryman.

3. DICKENS, Charles
   Great Expectations
   (i) pp. 73–78 (Ch. 9); (ii) pp. 63–67
   'Boy! What like is ... do it no more.'
   Pip is called upon by his sister, and his uncle Pumblechook to give an account of his visit to Satis House. On an impulse, he improves on the facts, without scruple, but when he confesses to Joe, he is ashamed of himself and numbers himself among the damned.

4. MANKOWITZ, Wolf
   Make me an Offer
   see FORGERY 2

5. STEINBECK, John
   The Pearl
   pp. 28–35 (Ch. 3)
   'Standing in the doorway ... the brush house.'
   Earlier in the day, the doctor has refused to see Kino's son, bitten by a scorpion, because he thinks he will not be paid. When he hears that Kino has found an enormous pearl, he comes, administers suspicious remedies, and professes to be surprised to hear of the pearl.

6. WYNDHAM, John
   The Day of the Triffids
   see CONDITIONING 6

HORROR

see also: DREAMS;
FEAR;
MONSTERS

HORROR

1. BALDWIN, Michael
   Grandad with Snails
   pp. 63–68 (Ch. 7)
   'The bottom of the grave ... no-one loved me any more.'
   What began as a game, turns into a nightmare for Michael, its victim. He is all but interred in a half-dug grave. Just in time, desperation lends him strength, and he emerges dirty and

blooded. When he arrives home he is belted to compound his misery.

2. CHURCH, Richard
Over the Bridge
pp. 16–19 (Ch. 1)
'A boy hailed us; a big boy ... sick over the front step.'
The two brothers are carrying an acquarium home. They dread the attentions of the local rowdies; but these attentions are distracted by the pursuit of a drunken husband and his wife, her blouse gaping, and her eyeball hanging on her cheek.

3. COLLINS, Wilkie
The Moonstone
see SUICIDE 5

4. CRANE, Stephen
The Red Badge of Courage
pp. 58–60 (Ch. 7)
'A dull, animal-like ... guarding edifice.'
Fleming, on the run from the battleline, stumbles into a clearing where the corpse of a long-dead Union soldier, sitting upright against a tree, confronts him, almost accusingly.

5. ibid.
pp. 68–72 (Ch. 9)
'The tall soldier ... fierce wafer.'
Henry helps his friend, the tall soldier, in the procession of wounded from the battlefield. His friend suddenly breaks free, running, and refusing to be touched. Then he stops, and magnificently, dies, revealing the extent of his wound to amazed eyes.

6. DICKENS, Charles
Bleak House
(i) pp. 414–418 (Ch. 32); (ii) pp. 414–418
'It's eleven o'clock ... that can be died?'
Mr Guppy is waiting with his friend in the latter's room to collect some letters from the landlord. They are disturbed by a sooty greasy astmosphere, and finally go to search for the landlord. All they find is a heap of ashes.

7. DICKENS, Charles
Great Expectations
(i) pp. 450–453 (Ch. 49); (ii) pp. 387–388
'By the wilderness ... was still upon her.'
Pip imagines that he sees Miss Havisham hanging from a beam. The image is so strong that he goes back upstairs to assure himself that all is well, and witnesses her catching fire. She runs at him, shrieking, a column of flames, and he struggles to cover her with his coat.

8. DOSTOYEVSKY, Fyodor
The Idiot
see DREAMS 1

9. LESSING, Doris
The Grass is Singing
pp. 251–254 (Ch. 11)
'She was listening to the night ... darted down the plunging steel.'
There is an inevitability about her death at the hands of her one-time servant. Mary, demented by heat and disillusionment goes out to meet it. Inside, she is shut in; outside, in the storm she can see her tormentor, lover, saviour, killer – and have done with all miseries.

10. MANNING, Olivia
The Play Room
see FEAR 7

11. ibid.
see KILLING 7

12. PEYTON, K.M.
Flambards in Summer
see FLYING – ACCIDENTS – 1914–18 1

13. REMARQUE, Erich Maria
All Quiet on the Western Front
see FIRST WORLD WAR – GAS 2

14. STEVENSON, R.L.
Treasure Island
pp. 18–21 (Ch. 3)
'So things passed ... fresh in my heart.'
Jim's fear of the old pirate lodging at the 'Admiral Benbow' disappears in his fear of a menacing blind beggar who threatens them both. The shock kills the pirate.

15. ibid.
pp. 29–32 (Ch. 5)
'My curiosity, in a sense ... moved no more.'
Jim watches a group of pirates, led by the menacing blind man, searching his home where the pirate lodger had died. The blind man and the pirates quarrel, and he is deserted by them, left, staggering in the fog, where he is knocked down by a horse.

16. ibid.
see KILLING (in) SELF-DEFENCE 1

17. TOLKIEN, J.R.R.
The Hobbit
see COMPETITIONS 3

18. WELLS, H.G.
The Time Machine
pp. 61–65 (Ch. 9)
'I had to clamber down ... I was insensible.'
The Time-Traveller is determined to investigate the underworld, and the sub-human creatures that live and work there. He climbs down a shaft into the blackness of the Morlocks' chamber. It is only the light from his matches that enables him to free himself from their clutches.

19. WELLS, H.G.
The War of the Worlds
see MONSTERS 5

20. ibid.
(i) pp. 20–24 (Bk. 1, Ch. 5); (ii) pp. 27–31
'After the glimpse I had ... and strike me down.'
A crowd of spectators stand at some distance from the pit, awaiting developments. A deputation moves towards the Martians, holding a white flag. Smoke rises from the pit, and suddenly, a spray of fire leaps from a humped shape, and wipes out the deputation to a man.

21. WYNDHAM, John
The Kraken Wakes
see SEA – DIVING 2

22. ibid.
see MYSTERIES 11

23. ibid.
see MONSTERS 9

HORSES

1. PEYTON, K.M.
Flambards in Summer
(i) pp. 130–133 (Ch. 12); (ii) pp. 173–177
'Half way through the covert ... made off, Dick letting him go.'
The fire that has taken over the farm-house, threatens to envelop the stables. Dick tries to coax the fearful horses out. One, Punch, will not brave the screen of smoke, until Mark takes his horse to the doorway to tempt the panic-stricken animal out.
see also: FIRE – FARM 2

2. RAFTERY, Gerald
Snow Cloud, Stallion
pp. 19–21 (Ch. 2)
'The horse! ... as wild as a rabbit.'
Ken stalks a fine, wild stallion. The horse becomes aware of the boy's presence, rears, dashes at him, stalls, and gallops off.

3. ibid.
pp. 28–31 (Ch. 3)
'He was on the point ... responded to a human voice.'
Horse and boy meet again. They come close to the first stage of making friends, but the horse backs off nervously. That he looks back at Ken before galloping away, persuades the boy that the horse is not as wild as he had thought.

4. SASSOON, Siegfried
Memoirs of a Foxhunting Man
pp. 14–23 (Part 1, Sns. 2, 3); pp. 92–95 (Part 3, Sn. 4); pp. 151–154. (Part 5, Sn. 3)
'How vividly I ... females in the kitchen'; (On New Year's Day ... extra fifty pounds.'; 'Gazing at the nice ... change of ownership.'
Sassoon's mounts; each of his horses is a chapter in his progress, his prowess, as a riding and racing man.

5. SEWELL, Anna
   Black Beauty
   passim.
   Black Beauty's life from a happy youth on a farm, through periods as carriage horse, lady's mount, cab horse, and cart-horse back to a well-earned farm retirement.
6. ibid.
   see MARKETS 8

HORSES – BIRTH

1. STEINBECK, John
   The Red Pony
   pp. 88–92 (Ch. 3)
   'It seemed to Jody ... the air ahead of him.'
   Jody is wakened in the night to witness the birth of his colt. But things go wrong: Billy Buck has to kill the mare, and reach right inside for the white sac, before the life of the wet, black colt is assured.

HORSES – ILLNESS

1. STEINBECK, John
   The Red Pony
   pp. 33–42 (Ch. 1)
   'Jody was tired ... he'd feel about it.'
   Jody's pony, Gabilan, is sick. Billy Buck cuts a hole in his windpipe to facilitate breathing. Jody sleeps with Gabilan, but the pony makes off in the night. Jody follows his tracks in the dew, only to watch him die.

HORSES – MATING

1. STEINBECK, John
   The Red Pony
   pp. 71–74 (Ch. 3)
   'Jody took hold of ... most of the way home.'
   Jody is promised a colt that he might raise himself. He leads Nellie, the mare, to the neighbouring ranch, to be mated with Jess Taylor's stallion. Jody loses control and understanding, of subsequent events.

HORSES – RACING

1. PEYTON, K.M.
   Flambards
   (i) pp. 149–155 (Ch. 11); (ii) pp. 185–192
   'The starter had the ... started to graze.'
   It is the annual point-to-point. It is Mark's third on 'Treasure', and much money and self-respect has been staked on his winning. Just as he is fighting it out with a rival, on the home straight, William brings his flying-machine in to land, scattering horses and spectators.
2. SASSOON, Siegfried
   Memoirs of a Foxhunting Man
   (i) pp. 183–189 (Part 6, Sn. 4)
   'The first two races ... equivalent of Divinity.'
   George is very nervous before his first race, on his new horse Cockbird. He is daunted by the strength of the opposition, but Cockbird is not. He wins the race by a comfortable ten lengths, to win the Colonel's cup.

HORSES – RIDING

1. COOKSON, Catherine
   The Nipper
   pp. 134–137 (Ch. 10)
   'In the soft glow ... he gazed about him.'
   Sandy has to get to the Manor House as quickly as possible to warn the occupants of danger. He rides the Nipper, his pony, across country covering terrain and jumps he has never attempted before.
2. PEYTON, K.M.
   The Edge of the cloud
   (i) pp. 114–118 (Ch. 11); (ii) pp. 140–146
   'For once, on Wednesday afternoon ... never ride with him again.'
   For the first and last time, Christina goes horse-riding with William. His obvious distaste for it matches her joy in control of a powerful horse she can

understand. She takes a fence with all the old exhilaration and delight in her own horsemanship.

3. PEYTON, K.M.
   Flambards
   (i) pp. 43–50 (Ch. 3); (ii) pp. 57–66
   'Two days later Mark ... Dick said. 'I understand.''
   Mark puts Christina, a rider of only two months standing on a restless, temperamental horse, to test her. The horse runs away with her, and she is in real danger, until the groom intervenes. Fearful of his father, Mark swears the groom to secrecy about the incident.

HORSES – RIDING – ACCIDENTS

1. PEYTON, K.M.
   Flambards
   (i) pp. 1–5 (Ch. 1); (ii) pp. 11–16
   'The fox was running easily ... you old food horse?'
   A man hedging sees the beginning and end of a hunting accident. Young Will Russell, an inept unwilling huntsman, follows his thrusting brother through a gap; Will's horse is too strong for him, and too bold. Will is thrown off into a ditch, broken, semiconscious.

2. ibid. (i) pp. 79–83 (Ch. 6); (ii) pp. 103–108
   'Christina started to canter ... 'nag, nag, nag,' said Mark.'
   Determined to follow the pack, Mark leaps on Christina's fresh horse, leaving her without a mount. Worse, he puts the mare at a near-impossible fence; she somersaults, and throws Mark off. Mark's pride is dashed, the mare does not escape so lightly.

3. RAFTERY, Gerald
   Snow Cloud, Stallion
   pp. 47–51 (Ch. 5)
   'It was not much ... He actually looked sorry.'
   Boy and horse have become familiar enough with each other for Ken to groom him, even to ride him. Plainly,

Snow has been ridden before. Both enjoy the experience, until a pheasant startles the horse, and Ken is thrown off.

4. SEWELL, Anna
   Black Beauty
   see HUNTING – HARES 1

5. ibid.
   (i) pp. 132–136 (Ch. 25); (ii) pp. 113–115
   'We left the carriage ... at Farmer Grey's.'
   Black Beauty's groom had had too much to drink, and does not notice a loose nail in his shoe. He drives the horse on, until the pain is so bad he stumbles and the rider is thrown.

6. ibid.
   see HORSES – RUNAWAYS 3

HORSES – RUNAWAYS

1. KIRKUP, James
   The Only Child
   pp. 107–108 (Ch. 8)
   'In those days ... the world of pain.'
   The children are nearly run down by a runaway horse, foaming at the mouth, and dragging a cart haplessly after it. It slithers on cobbles, its legs break, and it has to be shot.

2. PEYTON, K.M.
   Flambards
   see HORSES – RIDING 3

3. SEWELL, Anna
   Black Beauty
   (i) pp. 124–127 (Ch. 24); (ii) pp. 107–109
   'Oh! do not hurry ... wildly round him for help.'
   Lady Anne's horse is startled and bolts – Black Beauty and his rider try to catch up with them. They lose her, catch sight again and finally find she has been thrown, at a ditch.

HORSES – TRAINING

1. RAFTERY, Gerald
   Snow Cloud, Stallion
   pp. 40–43 (Ch. 4)

'Then Snow walked calmly ... sorrow on his face.'

Ken tempts the stallion with sugar. Snow takes it. Then Ken gets him to follow him, to earn more lumps. Ken pats him, then commands Snow to leave him, until the next lesson.

see also: HORSES – RIDING – ACCIDENTS 3

2. SEWELL, Anna
   Black Beauty
   (i) pp. 13–17 (Ch. 3); (ii) pp. 26–31
   'I was now beginning ... that is the way.'
   Black Beauty is fortunate in her master, who breaks him in gently and kindly. First he has to get used to bit and bridle then saddle, shoes and harness. He is even taught not to fear trains.

3. ibid.
   pp. 31–35 (Ch. 7); (ii) pp. 39–43
   'One day when Ginger ... a good feed.'
   Ginger tells of the cruelty with which she was trained. She was forced rather than persuaded, to wear the bit and bridle, and worked until she was ready to drop. One day she threw her rider in a desperate temper.

4. STEINBECK, John
   The Red Pony
   pp. 18–23 (Ch. 1)
   'Billy Buck kept his word ... had forced through.'
   Jody begins the training of his new pony; first the halter-breaking, then the saddle and bridle. He looks ahead with some apprehension to when he will ride for the first time.

see also: HORSES – ILLNESS 1

HOSPITALITY

1. ADAMS, Richard
   Watership Down
   pp. 83–85 (Ch. 13)
   'No human beings ... silent for a time.'
   The wandering rabbits are received by the rabbits of a large and pros-

perous burrow. The welcome, however, is not as warm as they expected.

2. SERRAILLIER, Ian
   The Silver Sword
   see CHARITY 12

3. SHUTE, Nevil
   A Town like Alice
   see CHARITY 13

4. SUTCLIFF, Rosemary
   see HOME 8

HOSPITALS

see also: FIRST WORLD WAR – HOSPITALS;
ILLNESS;
INJURIES

HOSPITALS

1. BARSTOW, Stan
   Joby
   pp. 83–87 (Ch. 5)
   'Ten minutes later ... deserted road and ran into the town.'
   On impulse, Joby visits the hospital where his mother is a patient. He is overawed by the heavy quiet in the hospital. His curiosity is strong, but it is overcome by his fear. He runs off on a second impulse.

2. BARSTOW, Stan
   A Kind of Loving
   see ACCIDENTS (at) HOME 1

3. GRAVES, Robert
   Goodbye to all That
   see SOCIAL – CLASS 6

4. HITCHMAN, Janet
   The King of the Barbareens
   pp. 13–16 (Ch. 1); (That Once Was Me, p. 43)
   'Once when Aunt Alice ... clothes – and boots.'
   The artist as a young mischief maker goes down first with a mastoid, then with rheumatic fever. The hospital and the patient make enemies of each other, and both are glad when she is discharged.

5. LAWRENCE, D.H.
Sons and Lovers
see INJURIES − LEG 1
6. REMARQUE, Erich Maria
All Quiet on the Western Front
see FIRST WORLD WAR − HOSPITALS 1

HOTELS (and) RESTAURANTS

1. HILDICK, E.W.
Birdy in Amsterdam
see MEALS − BREAKFASTS 2
2. LAWRENCE, D.H.
Sons and Lovers
(i) pp. 96−97 (Ch. 5); (ii) pp.
122−123; (Work and Leisure, pp.
13−14)
'Where should we go ... thankful to
be clear.'
Paul and his mother go to a
Nottingham restaurant for dinner.
They are conscious of eating beyond
their means, and for Paul at any rate,
the offhandedness of the waitress further wounds his pride.
3. STOLZ, Mary
Ready or Not
see WORK 9
4. STOREY, David
This Sporting Life
pp. 84−87 (Part 1, Ch. 4)
'Howton Hall's an old ... with the
sunset.'
With more money in his pocket than
he's ever had before, Arthur feels up
to taking Mrs Hammond and the kids
to a posh restaurant. He is utterly
unabashed by the snooty waiter, to
the point of questioning the bill.
5. WELLS, H.G.
Kipps
see ETIQUETTE 10

HOUSES

1. AUSTEN, Jane
Pride and Prejudice
(i) pp. 218−220 (Ch. 43); (ii) pp.
204−205 (Vol. 3, Ch. 1)
'Elizabeth, as they drove ... the
furniture of Rosings.'

Visiting a 'stately-home' at the beginning of the nineteenth century.
Elizabeth with her aunt and uncle on
a tour of Derbyshire visit Pemberley
to admire the house and grounds.
2. DEFOE, Daniel
Robinson Crusoe
see CASTAWAYS 5

HOUSEWORK

1. ALCOTT, Louisa M.
Little Women
see MEALS − DINNERS 1
2. JEROME, Jerome K.
Three Men in a Boat
pp. 23−26 (Ch. 3)
'So, on the following evening ... to do
a little thing like that!'
Uncle Podger hangs a picture. He
involves every member of the family
in a job that is punctuated with
accidents and curses; and that in the
end, is indifferently done.
3. KIRKUP, James
The Only Child
pp. 74−77 (Ch. 5)
'Each day of the week ... a satisfying
moment.'
The week is divided into chores. Monday is washing day, Tuesday, ironing
day, Wednesday, baking day, Thursday, mending day, Friday, cleaning
day, and Saturday, shopping day.
Only Sunday stands apart from the
bustle, for a quick breather.

HUMILIATION

see also: EMBARRASSMENT;
SHAME

HUMILIATION

1. BARSTOW, Stan
The Human Element
pp. 133−135 ('The Desperadoes');
(Crime and Punishment, pp. 62−66)
'They made a circuit ... to get away
with.'
Vince is having a kiss and a cuddle

with his new girl-friend when the dance bouncer catches them in the glare of his torch. Vince is angry but impotent; his girl is humiliated.

2. DICKENS, Charles
   Great Expectations
   see SOCIAL CLASS – SNOBBERY 4

3. DOSTOYEVSKY, Fyodor
   The Idiot
   (i) pp. 103–107 (Part 1, Ch. 9); (ii) pp. 136–140
   'Ferdishenko led the general up ... His eyes shone with a blaze of hatred.'
   The garrulous General humiliates his son Gania, when he tells a tall story to the company. Gania's loved one, Nastasia, listens, rapt, until the end, when she recalls that she has read the selfsame story in a newspaper. The General is covered with confusion.

4. ELIOT, George
   The Mill on the Floss
   pp. 74–80 (Ch. 7, Part 1); ('Growing Up', pp. 28–34)
   'Tom followed Maggie ... mute resignation.'
   Maggie, tired of comments about her unruly hair, chops off a large amount. Unfortunately she chooses the day her very particular aunts are visiting, and she is scolded and teased unmercifully.

5. FIELDING, Henry
   Joseph Andrews
   pp. 285–289 (Bk. 4, Ch. 14)
   'About an hour after ... Christian could deny it.'
   A chapter of accidents in which Parson Adams is both victim and priest. He disturbs Beau Didapper in bed with Mrs Slipslop, but in the dark, he falls upon the latter. Thus discovered, he beats a hasty retreat, covered only by his confusion. He compounds the comedy of errors by mistaking the chaste Fanny's bed for his own.

6. FORSTER, E.M.
   A Passage to India
   pp. 17–19 (Part 1, Ch. 2)

'Old Callendar wants to see me ... into a mosque to rest.'
A summons from his superior arrives for Dr Aziz while he is dining with friends. He affects indifference to the whims of his masters, but he complies. When he finds out that Callendar is not at home, and there is no message for him, Aziz feels he has been snubbed.

7. GOLDING, William
   Lord of the Flies
   (i) pp. 154–158 (Ch. 8); (ii) pp. 137–141
   'Piggy looked up ... Ralph watched him.'
   Jack calls a meeting to tempt the boys away from Ralph and his rule-based authority. He appeals to their fighting spirit. But the boys do not flock to Jack's banner. He goes off by himself, humiliated.

8. GREENWOOD, Walter
   Love on the Dole
   see INITIATION 1

9. GROSSMITH, George and Weedon
   The Diary of a Nobody
   (i) pp. 31–33 (Ch. 3); (ii) pp. 53–56
   'Cummings called ... back of my neck.'
   Mr Pooter and his wife take friends from out of town, to the theatre for the evening. They discover that their tickets are out of date. In addition, Mr Pooter loses his press-on bow-tie.

10. ibid.
    (i) pp. 137–141 (Ch. 18); (ii) pp. 219–225
    'The night of the East ... had to endure.'
    The Pooters attend the East Acton Volunteer Ball. Charles, and companions, eat and drink on the assumption that refreshments are all included. He is shocked and humiliated when presented with the bill. He has money enough for this, but not for the cab home. Further humiliation.

11. HARDY, Thomas
    Far from the Madding Crowd

145

(i) pp. 129–132 (Ch. 16); (ii) pp. 131–133
'On a week-day ... walked rapidly away.'

Frank, a young cavalry sergeant, is kept waiting a half an hour at the altar-rail, by his young bride. He stands stock still, enduring the sniggering of curious women, until his resolve breaks, and he leaves the church, to meet his intended in the street outside.

12. LAWRENCE, D.H.
Sons and Lovers
see FAMILY – QUARRELS 4

13. ibid.
(i) pp. 69–71 (Ch. 4); (ii) pp. 89–92
'Mrs Morel's intimacy, ... on these occasions.'

Paul is sent to collect his father's weekly wage. He is small, and overawed by being among so many rough and mocking grown men. He almost misses his turn, and in his nervousness, he gives a poor account of his learning at the 'stoppages' counter.

14. NAUGHTON, Bill
One Small Boy
pp. 130–132 (Bk. 2, Ch. 2)
'The first two days ... thought of Robert Emmet.'

Required to recite a verse in front of the class, Michael trips over a word which, mocked by Miss Skegham, he is unable to correct. He refuses to be humiliated further, and is caned for his pains.

15. THOMAS, Leslie
This Time Next Week
see COURTSHIP – DATING 5

16. TROLLOPE, Anthony
Barchester Towers
see COURTSHIP – PROPOSALS (of) MARRIAGE 15

17. ibid.
see REVENGE 24

18. WELLS, H.G.
Kipps
see ETIQUETTE 9

19. WRIGHT, Richard
Black Boy
see SHYNESS 4

HUNGER

1. CALDWELL, John
Desperate Voyage
pp. 101–103; 105–109 (Ch. 12)
'I remembered that it is ... and swam merrily away'; 'I caught the same fish ... I was at peace.'

In the extremes of his hunger, the author polishes off the last of his food. He is now dependent on what he can catch. And when nothing bites, he eats the bait, his tooth powder, a chamois leather, and an incautious bird.

2. CANAWAY, W.H.
Sammy going South
pp. 57–59 (Ch. 10)
'Sammy had slept ... Sammy walked on.'

Making his way alone through the Sudan, Sammy is hungry, thirsty and lonely. Some native fishermen give him some melon which he quickly eats.

3. CHAPLIN, Sid
The Leaping Lad and Other Stories
see STEALING (of) FOOD 2

4. GREENE, Graham
The Power and the Glory
(i) pp. 138–141 (Part 2, Ch. 4); (ii) pp. 144–146
'He shut the door ... and left the kitchen.'

The priest, at the bottom of his fortunes, vies with a broken-backed mongrel bitch for a meaty bone. Animal cunning and desperation arm him against the pathetic bitch.

5. HAUGAARD, Erich
The Little Fishes
see CHARITY 11

6. ibid.
pp. 26–34 (Ch. 3)
'My father died in Africa ... as soon as I saw her.'

Begging for bread in wartime Naples.

Young Guido has learnt most of the dodges. Stealing comes less easily to him, but hunger drives him to steal a loaf from an unguarded bakery; and it keeps him from sharing his prize with a friend.

7. ORWELL, George
1984
see POVERTY 14

8. ibid.
(i) pp. 277–278 (Part 3, Ch. 3); (ii) p. 218
'He had stopped ... some malignant disease.'
Winston sees his starving body for the first time after weeks of torture.

9. SERRAILLIER, Ian
The Silver Sword
(i) pp. 75–77 (Ch. 12); (ii) pp. 61–63
'The village of Kolina ... the smallest person there.'
Three children, refugees from Warsaw at the end of the war, reach a village where a Russian field kitchen is being set up. The food queues are orderly until one boy drops his bowl – there is an incredible scramble to fight for the remains.

10. STEINBECK, John
The Grapes of Wrath
(i) pp. 219–225 (Ch. 20); (ii) pp. 231–238
'Ma knelt beside ... the stack of tin dishes.'
The Joad family have just settled in a camp of immigrants to California by themselves. The talk is of unemployment, and lack of money – Ma is surrounded by hungry children as she cooks supper, and feels obliged to give them some, thus incurring their parents' displeasure.

11. WILLIAMSON, Henry
Tarka the Otter
(i) pp. 110–113 (Ch. 10); (ii) pp. 113–116
'While the pallor of the day ... opened and closed.'
So hungry are the otters, that they attack a wild swan, also weakened by hunger. They drag it to the shore, where they kill it, before they have eaten much, a fox and then a badger take over from them.

12. WRIGHT, Richard
Black Boy
pp. 11–13 (Ch. 1)
'Hunger stole upon me ... too young to know.'
Hunger, the physical craving for food, becomes Richard's preoccupation. He learns a simple fact of life: that food is got by working, and that his father who worked for their food, has left them.

HUNTING

see also: ANIMALS – CATCHING; ANIMALS – TRAPPING

HUNTING

1. GOLDING, William
Lord of the Flies
(i) pp. 165–168 (Ch. 8); (ii) pp. 146–149
(Themes in Life and Literature, pp. 197–200)
'Far off along the beach ... the centre of the clearing.'
Jack and his gang hunt and kill a nursing sow. This is the act which guarantees his authority over those boys who have deserted Ralph. As hunters, his boys are united in a primitive lust for blood.
see also: RELIGION – PRIMITIVE 1

2. LESSING, Doris
Nine African Stories
see ANTS 1

3. LONDON, Jack
The Call of the Wild
pp. 35–36 (Ch. 3)
'At the mouth of the Tahkeena ... hell's chorus of delight.'
The dog team chases a rabbit, in full cry, Buck in the lead. Old hunting instincts break through the veneer of his domestication. But it is Spitz who drives in to the kill.
see also: FIGHTING (by) ANIMALS 2

4. SPERRY, Armstrong
    The Boy who was Afraid
    see KILLING − ANIMALS 2

HUNTING − BIG GAME

1. CANAWAY, W.H.
    Sammy going South
    pp. 125−127 (Ch. 21)
    'Sammy was frightened ... no movement.'
    Sammy is taught to shoot by a poaching big-game hunter, and soon uses his new skill to kill a leopard and save their lives.
2. GUILLOT, René
    Kpo the Leopard
    pp. 105−116 (Ch. 10)
    'Look. Not that way ... To horse!'
    A Tuareg chief's son sees cheetahs hunting and determines to capture one. After a chase, and a fight, seen also from the animals' viewpoint, he finally succeeds − and discovers it is a leopard, not a cheetah, that he has netted.
3. ibid.
    see INITIATION 3

HUNTING − DEER

1. CHURCH, Richard
    The White Doe
    pp. 172−175 (Ch. 22)
    'Tom's voice was hushed ... over the broken soil.'
    Tom and Billy see the doe and her white fawn. The magic of the scene is shattered by Harold Sims with his dog and his gun, intoxicated by the excitement of the chase.

HUNTING − FOXES

1. MOORE, John
    Portrait of Elmbury
    pp. 150−152 (Part 4)
    'I enjoyed my hunting ... ride away down the road.'
    The author looks back over his hunting days. Although he enjoyed it, he

admits that it is an anarchic pastime, ignoring all rights of property.

2. PEYTON, K.M.
    Flambards
    see HORSES − RIDING − ACCIDENTS 1
3. ibid.
    (i) pp. 77−78 (Ch. 6); (ii) pp. 100−102
    'Mr Lucas's hounds ... splintering past her face.'
    Proud of herself in a new riding habit, and exhilarated by her own newly acquired skills, Christina enjoys her hunting. She is especially pleased with herself when she jumps a difficult fence.
4. SASSOON, Siegfried
    Memoirs of a Foxhunting Man
    pp. 45−49 (Part 1, Sn. 7)
    'Emboldened by the fact ... even know my name.'
    George rides to hounds with his groom, for the second time. He is overshadowed by the young and immaculate Denis Milden; but his real undoing is in his loud expressed hope that the pack will not see the fox.
5. ibid.
    pp. 145−153 (Part 5, Sn. 2)
    'At nine o'clock next ... jumped in your boots.'
    Some of the magic of riding to hounds with like-minded country gentlemen: rituals and rivalries.
6. THACKERAY, William
    Vanity Fair
    (i) pp. 455−457 (Ch. 45); (ii) pp. 531−532
    'But the greatest day ... wondering and happy.'
    Young Rawdon is very impressed by the meet of the hunt at Queen's Crawley − the huntsman and his hounds, the smart, young gentlemen on their hacks, which they exchange for hunters, and the Master, Sir Huddlestone.
7. THOMPSON, Flora
    Lark Rise to Candleford

(i) pp. 475–478 ('Candleford Green', Ch. 32); (ii) pp. 419–422
'The road past ... hungry at night.'
The Hunt meets on Candleford Green, and is the focus of attention of the whole village. Laura sees many new faces, and envies the riders. Some of the men follow the hunt all day on foot.

HUNTING – GAZELLES

1. GUILLOT, René
   Kpo the Leopard
   pp. 127–134 (Ch. 11)
   'You'll never be able ... beat in her breast.'
   Amastan has tamed a leopard, and the two are inseparable. He takes Kpo hunting, to see if she will obey, and not escape – she hunts well, but is disappointed when her master slits the gazelle's throat, to give her the blood from his own hands. She is deprived of the pleasure of tearing the animal to pieces.

HUNTING – HARES

1. SEWELL, Anna
   Black Beauty
   pp. 23–26 (Ch. 2)
   'Before I was two ... for one little hare.'
   Black Beauty sees his first hunt – the horses and the hounds are chasing a hare, and the dogs corner it in the next field. A rider is thrown, and killed, and the horse has to be destroyed. Black Beauty is mystified by it all.

HUNTING – OTTERS

1. WILLIAMSON, Henry
   Tarka the Otter
   (i) pp. 164–172 (Ch. 15); (ii) pp. 170–178
   'He was awakened ... vanished in a wave.'
   Tarka is awakened by hounds at the

entrance to his holt. He escapes them, but is pursued through the water and over land until he reaches the sea.

2. ibid.
   (i) pp. 220–222 (Ch. 19); (ii) pp. 224–227
   'Hands held ... jaws were smashed.'
   Tarquol, Tarka's cub, is cornered with him in tree roots. Forced to leave this security, Tarquol runs over a field to a farmyard, where he is easily, and brutally, caught, by the hounds.

3. ibid.
   (i) pp. 227–229 (Ch. 20); (ii) pp. 231–233
   'The water of the pool ... quiet meadow beyond.'
   Tarka sees the hounds and the huntsmen from under the water. Although he is tiring, he still manages to escape them.

4. ibid.
   (i) pp. 231–233 (Ch. 20); (ii) pp. 235–237
   'At the beginning ... and nothing more.'
   After nine hours, Tarka is exhausted, and leaves the water. He is immediately caught by the hounds, but even now he fights back, and slips into the water, pursued by his enemy Deadlock. They both die in the final struggle.

HUNTING – WOLVES

1. SHOLOKHOV, Mikhail
   And Quiet Flows the Don
   pp. 168–171 (Part 1, Ch. 11)
   'Gregor led the saddled ... the flask off his back.'
   Gregor accompanies the Listnitskys on a hunting expedition. There's hard riding, and a keen wind that brings tears to the eyes. Old Listnitsky rises to the excitement of the chase, but it's Gregor who has to put paid to the wolf.

HURRICANES

1. CALDWELL, John
   Desperate Voyage
   pp. 71–75 (Ch. 9)
   'Cat's-paws dappled ... was a well-found boat.'
   The area north of the Cook Islands is notorious for its hurricanes. The squalls begin on cue, and clouds race past just above the mast. The author makes all the necessary preparations, goes below, and lashes himself on to his bunk.

2. ibid.
   pp. 75–79 (Ch. 9)
   'Along about two in the morning ... lashings over me.'
   The hurricane rises and 'Pagan' pitches horribly. The author has to see to a broken shroud, but the wind and the sea threaten to sweep him overboard. They succeed in doing just this, and it is only by immense good luck, that he is swept in the same way, back into his cabin.
   see also: SURVIVAL (at) SEA 3

3. HUGHES, Richard
   A High Wind in Jamaica
   (i) pp. 30–39 (Ch. 1, Part 4); (ii) pp. 24–30
   'It was the custom that ... empire of nightmare.'
   Thunder and lightning herald a tropical storm of such proportions that if it had occurred to Emily, she would have had to call it a hurricane. It kills, it destroys, and it scares the Thorntons into sending the children to England.

HUSBANDS

   see ASSAULT (by) HUSBANDS;
   FATHERS;
   MARRIAGE

ICE

   see also: FROST;
   SNOW;
   WINTER

ICE

1. GORKY, Maxim
   Childhood
   see ASSAULT (by) BROTHERS 1

2. NAUGHTON, Bill
   Late Night on Watling Street
   see PRANKS 12

ICE – SKATING

1. LEE, Laurie
   Cider with Rosie
   (i) pp. 104–105 (Ch. 8, 'Winter and Summer'); (ii) pp. 140–141
   'Wan' a know summat? ... played too long.'
   Jones's pond is frozen, and the village turns out to enjoy it; some can skate properly, others merely slide and sit down frequently.

2. 'MISS READ'
   Village School
   (i) pp. 111–112 (Part 2, Ch. 12); (ii) pp. 110–111
   'For three days ... their pond again.'
   The whole village takes to Mr Roberts's duck pond. The older generation show the younger a turn or two on the ice, and Mrs Roberts shows farming hospitality to all-comers in her warm kitchen.

ICE – SKATING – ACCIDENTS

1. ALCOTT, Louisa M.
   Little Women
   pp. 113–117 (Ch. 8)
   'Everybody is so hateful ... come upon her.'
   Jo is angry with Amy, and does not warn her of the thin ice. Amy falls in, but is quickly rescued. Jo is full of remorse.

2. THOMPSON, Flora
   Lark Rise to Candleford
   (i) pp. 364–365 ('Over to Candleford', Ch. 23); (ii) p. 326

'Sliding on the ice ... a green bay-tree.'

The hamlet children enjoy sliding on the ice, but one day Laura falls through, and her friends run away in panic. She manages to climb out, but receives smacks as well as sympathy on her return home.

ILLNESS

see also: DOCTORS; HORSES – ILLNESS; HOSPITALS; INJURIES; MEDICINE – PRIMITIVE; SURGERY

ILLNESS

1. AUSTEN, Jane
   Emma
   pp. 123–129 (Ch. 12)
   'While they were thus ... any renewal of it.'
   Mr Woodhouse and his daughter, Isabella, share an interest in illnesses and remedies for them. They exchange the opinions of their physicians, but disagree as to the best course to be taken.

2. BURNETT, Frances Hodgson
   The Secret Garden
   see CHILDREN – TANTRUMS 1

3. FOAKES, Grace
   Between High Walls
   pp. 67–68 (Ch. 33)
   'Every year about ... not happen today.'
   Disease is a frequent visitor to the tenements at the beginning of the century. Scarlet fever, diphtheria, and whooping cough are all more or less deadly enemies.

4. LAWRENCE, D.H.
   Sons and Lovers
   see DEATH (of) BROTHER 2

5. LEE, Laurie
   Cider with Rosie
   (i) pp. 117–118 (Ch. 9, 'Sick Boy');
   (ii) pp. 156–157
   'But secretly, silently ... saved me.'
   While Mrs Lee is in bed after the

birth of Laurie's younger brother, he falls ill, and is supposed by the housekeeper to have died. Mrs Lee finds him, being laid out, just in time.

6. STEINBECK, John
   The Pearl
   see SCORPIONS 3

7. TWAIN, Mark
   Tom Sawyer
   see TEETH 1

ILLNESS – DYSENTERY

1. MORROW, Honoré
   The Splendid Journey
   pp. 41–46 (Chs. 3, 4)
   'So all that day the Sagers ... aged thirty-eight years.'
   Captain Shaw's company of migrants is low on food, and morale. Henry Sager bags a couple of buffalo, but the chase costs him precious strength. His illness worsens, and his resolve weakens, until he dies, right beside his unsuspecting daughter.

ILLNESS – FEVER

1. LEE, Laurie
   Cider with Rosie
   (i) pp. 118–125 (Ch. 9, 'Sick Boy');
   (ii) pp. 157–167
   'It was soon ... forever ill.'
   As a child Lee suffered many fevers, when he had vivid hallucinations. During one bout he is shocked to hear talk of fetching the Vicar and his father, but he soon recovers.

2. SHOLOKHOV, Mikhail
   And Quiet Flows the Don
   pp. 528–531 (Part 4, Ch. 4)
   'The first sight ... dry, yellow brow.'
   Bunchuk wakes after three weeks of delirium to the loving ministrations of Anna, his loyal would-be wife. He is still weak and racked by fever-pains – but he is alive.

ILLNESS – GOUT

1. DICKENS, Charles
   Bleak House
   (i) pp. 200–201 (Ch. 16); (ii) pp. 200–201
   'Sir Leicester receives ... an inch with him.'
   Sir Leicester Dedlock is suffering from the gout, but he accepts it without question, as it is the family disease, and his forefathers all suffered stoically before him. It is part of his heritage.

ILLNESS – MALARIA

1. CANAWAY, W.H.
   Sammy going South
   pp. 30–31 (Ch. 6)
   'Sammy pushed on ... the statue's feet.'
   Sammy, making his way alone through the Egyptian desert, catches malaria. He becomes delirious, and is even more confused by an avenue of sphinxes he comes upon.

ILLNESS – NERVOUS

1. BRONTË, Charlotte
   Villette
   p. 143 (Ch. 15)
   'Indeed there was no way ... Most true was it.'
   Lucy Snowe, left alone in the school for the long holiday, suffers a nervous illness, insomnia followed by nightmare-torn sleep.

ILLNESS – SCARLET FEVER

1. ALCOTT, Louisa M.
   Little Women
   pp. 245–247 (Ch. 18)
   'Beth did have the fever ... better be sent for." '
   Beth has scarlet fever, and at times is delirious. She is lovingly nursed by her sisters, but all miss the steadying

influence of their mother, absent in Washington.

ILLNESS – SMALLPOX

1. DICKENS, Charles
   Bleak House
   (i) pp. 446–448 (Ch. 35); (ii) pp. 446–448
   'I lay ill ... I should see again.'
   Esther has caught smallpox, and remembers her delirium, and the delusions it brings.

ILLNESS – WHOOPING COUGH

1. HITCHMAN, Janet
   The King of the Barbareens
   pp. 33–36 (Ch. 2)
   'At five and a half ... restrained with difficulty.'
   The writer catches whooping-cough and sets her education back by years. She survives, to everybody's surprise (and chagrin). One doctor undresses her and another vaccinates her, before she is committed, much against her will, to a sanatorium.

INDIA

   see BRITISH EMPIRE – INDIA;
   RACISM – INDIA

INDIANS – NORTH AMERICA

1. MORROW, Honoré
   The Splendid Journey
   pp. 101–108 (Ch. 8)
   'A warm wind rose ... 'They've robbed us!' he shouted.'
   The children encounter a group of Indians camped beside the Snake River. They do not appear to be really hostile, though they do insist that the children remain with them. John keeps watch, planning escape, but he falls asleep, and in the night, the Indians rob them, and make off.

INDOCTRINATION

see also: CONDITIONING

INDOCTRINATION

1. ORWELL, George
   1984
   see HATRED 2
2. ibid.
   (i) pp. 157–159 (Part 2, Ch. 5); (ii)
   pp. 124–126
   'She was used ... all the time, aren't
   they?'
   Julie conforms outwardly to the Party
   image, while inwardly rebelling. She
   does not however question its
   existence, or even many of its claims.

INGENUITY

1. ADAMS, Richard
   Watership Down
   pp. 174–186 (Ch. 22)
   ' 'Now one evening ... grandfather
   always said.'
   The Prince Rabbit, El-Ahrairah, outwits the human prince Rainbow. He
   steals a field full of carrots, and
   manages to make Prince Rainbow's
   spy look very foolish.
2. DE JONG, Meindert
   The Wheel on the School
   (i) pp. 58–67 (Ch. 6); (ii) pp. 60–68
   'Eelka had been given ... to get it to
   the school.'
   A farmer offers Eelka an old waggon
   wheel if he can get it down from the
   hayloft. He decides he needs no help,
   and gets to work with a rope over a
   beam. The rope is too short, and not
   strong enough; the wheel breaks as it
   drops to the ground. Eelka is still
   determined and puts it roughly
   together again.
3. ELIOT, George
   The Mill on the Floss
   see PEDLARS 2
4. FORESTER, C.S.
   The Gun
   (i) pp. 32–36 (Ch. 4); (ii) pp. 31–34

'El Bilbanito examined it ... trial
should be made.'
The guerillero band find the fine
eighteen-pound cannon hidden by a
retreating army – the barrel intact,
but the rest has to be renewed. Skill
and materials are scarce, but a very
presentable job is made.

5. ibid.
   (i) pp. 41–44 (Ch. 5); (ii) pp. 38–41
   'Far and wide ... the aid of the gun.'
   Having repaired the gun, the guerilleros have to drag it over mountain
   paths, to the edge of the plain. With a
   strangely assorted team of animals,
   and painfully slowly, they finally
   reach their destination.
6. GASKELL, Mrs
   Cranford
   (i) pp. 119–120 (Ch. 8); (ii) pp.
   125–126
   ' 'Yes,' said that lady ... in pussy's
   inside.'
   Mrs Forrester recounts the tale of her
   best lace collar. One day while she
   was soaking it in milk, her cat swal-
   lowed it. She treasured it so much
   that she gave the cat some tartar
   emetic, and was overjoyed when the
   collar 'returned to sight.'
7. KING, Clive
   Stig of the Dump
   pp. 32–38 (Ch. 2)
   'These are jam-jars ... he'd finished a
   job.'
   Barney takes a load of old tins and
   jam jars to his caveman friend. They
   quickly find a use for them – the tins,
   without tops and bottoms make a
   chimney, the jars a window.
8. MANKOWITZ, Wolf
   Make me an Offer
   see MARKETS 5
9. ibid.
   see ESCAPE (from) POLICE 1
10. NAUGHTON, Bill
    The Goalkeeper's revenge
    see STEALING (of) FOOD 4
11. NESBIT, E.
    The Railway Children
    see ESCAPADES 7

12. ibid.
(i) pp. 46–53 (Ch. 3); (ii) pp. 56–62
'It was the very next day ... a little girl.'
The children's mother is ill, but they cannot afford all the things the doctor recommends. They therefore contact an old gentleman who waves to them from the 9.15 train every morning, and he helps.

INITIATION

1. GREENWOOD, Walter
   Love on the Dole
   pp. 50–53 (Part 1, Ch. 6); (Conflict 2, pp. 26–30)
   'And such as would take ... his face following.'
   Harry is subjected to the indignities, petty and deeply humiliating, of the greenhorn foundry worker – and thus becomes one of the boys.

2. GUILLOT, René
   Kpo the Leopard
   pp. 58–60 (Ch. 6)
   'Kpo would always remember ... round the wood.'
   Kpo the leopard watches young cheetahs being tested by their elders. Each animal has to catch a guinea-fowl as it flies out of the bushes, beaten out by the older cheetahs. Only one fails.

3. ibid.
   pp. 139–146 (Ch. 12)
   'Amastan. Taitok came in ... Emir's son unhindered.'
   The Emir's son is put to the test – he must kill the first lion of the hunt. He falters, and is attacked, but his faithful leopard springs to the rescue. The boy is badly wounded, but the lion is killed.

4. SUTCLIFF, Rosemary
   The Eagle of the Ninth
   see RELIGION – PRIMITIVE 5

5. THOMAS, Leslie
   This Time Next Week
   pp. 39–41 (Ch. 4)

'Porky, Chesty, Ear'ole ... Good old monkey!'
As a new arrival at the orphanage, Leslie is called upon to prove himself. He is nicknamed Monkey, he bests the boy who names him in a bloody dormitory skirmish – and is still called Monkey notwithstanding his victory.

6. TREECE, Henry
   Hounds of the King
   pp. 48–53 (Part 1, Ch. 5)
   'Beonorth looked down the long table ... warriors of his loyal to him.'
   Before he can join the Housecarles, Beonorth has to submit himself to tests that measure his thresholds of pain and fear. He fights with staves, carries a hot spit in his bare hands, and guards a corpse in a dark vault by night.

7. ibid.
   pp. 54–57 (Part 1, Ch. 5)
   'The night of his initiation ... that way, the feasting began.'
   It is the night of the oath-taking, and Beonorth is inducted into the Housecarles with due ceremony. He has fasted, shaved, and stood for hours, so that it is with difficulty that he answers the formula questions. Afterwards there is feasting and sumptuous gifts.

8. WILLIAMSON, Henry
   Tarka the Otter
   (i) pp. 29–31 (Ch. 2); (ii) pp. 28–31
   'While the moon was full ... dropped them into the river.'
   Tarka and his sister otter cubs are introduced to new food – fish, frogs and eels. As they gain strength, their mother introduces them to water – she coaxes Tarka in, with a reward of fish. He is afraid, but soon begins to enjoy it.

9. ibid.
   (i) pp. 34–36 (Ch. 2); (ii) pp. 35–36
   'Fish were brought alive ... drink your blood.'
   The cubs are taught to fish, and Tarka quickly learns how to chase his

prey. He is very proud of his first catch – a tadpole.

10. WRIGHT, Richard
   Black Boy
   see COURAGE 20

11. ibid.
   pp. 78–80 (Ch. 3)
   'After breakfast, Uncle Clark ... I had been accepted.'
   A new school forces on Richard the need to prove himself all over again. A gang of boys taunts him, and he has to defend himself. He acquits himself well enough to win ungrudging respect.

12. ibid.
   see FIGHTING (by) BOYS (at) SCHOOL 7

INJURIES

   see also: ACCIDENTS; FIRST WORLD WAR – INJURIES;
   ILLNESS;
   SCORPIONS; SNAKES;
   WAR – INJURIES

INJURIES – ARM

1. BATES, H.E.
   Fair Stood the Wind for France
   (i) pp. 12–13 (Ch. 2); (ii) pp. 12–14
   'More and more the pain ... with terrifying force.'
   Following an air crash in wartime, Franklin suffers from a severe injury to his left arm. It bleeds profusely, and the flow has to be stopped by a tourniquet.

2. ibid.
   (i) pp. 59–60 (Ch. 6); (ii) pp. 60–61
   'Suddenly without warning ... a nurse came in.'
   The doctor removes the bandage from the wound for the first time, and its extent and seriousness become evident. The removal is a sickening experience.

3. ibid.
   (i) pp. 110–112 (Ch. 11); (ii) pp. 113–114

'Franklin reached up ... he had no left arm.'
Franklin comes round after the amputation of his arm. It is difficult to regain consciousness, and when he does, he discovers the loss of his arm.

INJURIES – EYE

1. BALDWIN, Michael
   Grandad with Snails
   pp. 36–38 (Ch. 4)
   'Brownskin went to Borstal ... so I stowed them.'
   Michael's eye is prodded with a clothes peg, in a fight. The eye is supposedly undamaged, but a serious defect is brought to light which means that Michael has to wear spectacles with an occluder.

INJURIES – HEAD

1. TATE, John
   Whizz Kid
   see ASSAULT 6

INJURIES – LEG

1. LAWRENCE, D.H.
   Sons and Lovers
   (i) pp. 83–87 (Ch. 5); (ii) pp. 106–111
   'About a year after ... proceeded to live happily.'
   Morel smashes his leg at the colliery, and he has to be taken to hospital. He is badly hurt, and feverish, and he squirms under hospital regulations; but the main burden of his injury falls on Mrs Morel who has to visit him and suffer his self-pity.

INJURIES – WRIST

1. WELLS, H.G.
   Kipps
   pp. 60–64 (Bk. 1, Ch. 2, Sn. 3)
   'There came a time when ... going to break like that?'
   In a chivalrous, and over-forceful

attempt to open a window for a lady, Kipps breaks the glass and cuts his wrist rather badly. He plays his injury down in manly fashion but enjoys the anxious attentions he is paid.

INSANITY

INSECTS

INSECTS

'This doll's house garden ... young when I last saw him.'
Young Gerald is a close observer of the insects in his family's new garden. He is particularly fascinated by lacewing flies that lay eggs on stilts, and by an earwig – whose activities he guards jealously from intruders – hatching out a fine brood of baby earwigs.

INTERROGATION

'I didn't give a thought ... I went looking for Skiff Morrison.'
The biscuit Skiff Morrison has given Butch, becomes a piece of police evidence. Butch is accused, by implication, of having broken into the school tuckshop, and stolen biscuits and money. Butch realises that it was

Skiff who was the thief, but honour forbids him to speak the truth.
'Kathleen Fawcett, Barbara ... started twittering.'
The mother of one of the girls calls all the children into her house to interrogate them, about a suspected incident in the rhubarb fields. She gets little information and deals out many meaningless warnings.
'It was a real interrogation room ... heaved the door shut again.'
In a big house, somewhere in the Austrian Alps, Giles is having classified information prised out of him by uniformed 'heavies'. He has lost account of time, and of his part in what he is convinced is a worthless cause.

INTERVIEWS

INTERVIEWS

'The interview took place ... out of it in the end.'
A friend arranged for Dick to be interviewed for a job as a journeyman apprentice in a chemist's shop. He is tested, in a number of ways, and is not found wanting. The job is a pass out of the pit, into a 'new world'.

'Question. What did Louie look like? ... and so the tests began.'

Jim Shaw, and other hopefuls, apply at the New Day Dairy for a job with Louie. The boys line up to have their hands inspected, and to answer one or two questions. The elimination begins.

4. HINES, Barry
    A Kestrel for a Knave
    (i) pp. 168–172; (ii) pp. 137–140
    'Billy sat back and ... all the way home.'
    Billy has an interview with the Youth Employment Officer at school. He is preoccupied, and returns answers that do not do him justice. He has no idea what he wants to do; his idée fixe is that he will not go down the pit like his brother Jud.

5. LAWRENCE, D.H.
    Sons and Lovers
    (i) pp. 94–96 (Ch. 5); (ii) pp. 119–122
    (Work and Leisure, pp. 10–13)
    'Can I see Mr Jordan? ... But they don't.'
    Paul goes with his mother for an interview for a job as spiral clerk, with Thomas Jordan and Son – Surgical Appliances. Mr Jordan is an irascible man who finds fault with Paul. Paul is confused into embarrassment; but he gets the job.

6. 'MISS READ'
    Village School
    see TEACHING – INTERVIEWS 2

7. THOMPSON, Flora
    Lark Rise to Candleford
    (i) pp. 166–170 ('Lark Rise', Ch. 10); (ii) pp. 158–161
    'Of course there were ... four large helpings.'
    Laura accompanies a friend when she goes four miles across the country to be interviewed for a place in a grey-stone mansion. The 'Missis' informs the interviewee of the nature of the work and of the terms of employment, and then she feeds her young visitors. Laura's friend is twelve years old.
    see also: SERVANTS 7

INTRUDERS

see FEAR (of) INTRUDERS;
RESCUE (from) INTRUDERS

INVASIONS

1. FRANK, Anne
    The Diary of Anne Frank
    see SECOND WORLD WAR – D-DAY 1

INVASIONS – MARTIANS

1. WELLS, H.G.
    The War of the Worlds
    see MYSTERIES 6
2. ibid.
    see HORROR 19

INVASIONS – NORSEMEN

1. TREECE, Henry
    Hounds of the King
    pp. 118–123 (Part 3, Ch. 15)
    'Later in the day a big man ... this was the end of the world.'
    Beonorth and Finn free themselves from their shackles, then see, through a hole in the cell wall the invading ships, of Hardrada the Norwegian, and of the rebel Tostig, flying the Wessex Dragon. They drag themselves from their captivity, to alert Harold to the danger afoot.

INVASIONS – NORMANS

1. TREECE, Henry
    Hounds of the King
    pp. 143–150 (Part 3, Ch. 17)
    'On the slope beneath him were set up ... the dew that was already falling.'
    The 'Battle of Hastings'. Beonorth witnesses its early stages from a clump of bushes, then, when he sees the reverses suffered by the English, he rushes through the Norman lines to do his duty by his king.

157

INVASIONS – RUSSIANS

1. SERRAILLIER, Ian
   The Silver Sword
   see ARMY 3

INVENTIONS

1. BALCHIN, Nigel
   The Small Back Room
   pp. 23–26 (Ch. 2)
   'Come on,' I said ... 'That's the idea.'
   The research team analyses weird and
   wonderful suggestions by inventors,
   crack and crackpot, for weapons that
   will bring the enemy to his knees.
2. WELLS, H.G.
   The Time Machine
   pp. 13–14 (Ch. 2)
   'The Thing the Time ... said he was
   damned.'
   The Time Traveller demonstrates to
   his close, but sceptical, friends, a
   model of his Time Machine. He pulls
   a lever, and the model flies off into
   the future, to the amazement of all
   present.

ISLANDS

   see also: CASTAWAYS;
   RESCUE (from) ISLANDS;
   SURVIVAL (on) ISLANDS

ISLANDS

1. CALDWELL, John
   Desperate Voyage
   pp. 44–47 (Ch. 6)
   'Though I wasn't on a ... sea room to
   the South.'
   The author anchors in an attractive
   cove. He climbs a rock face meaning
   to leave his mark prominently among
   others, but he is scared off by a
   monster, half lizard, half dragon. He
   leaves in a hurry; the cove has lost
   much of its attractiveness for him.

JEALOUSY

1. BARSTOW, Stan
   The Human Element
   see REVENGE 5
2. ELIOT, George
   The Mill on the Floss
   see REVENGE 10
3. HARDY, Thomas
   Far from the Madding Crowd
   see KILLING (by) RIVALS (in) LOVE 1
4. HARDY, Thomas
   Under the Greenwood Tree
   pp. 133–138 (Part 3, Ch. 3)
   'It was a morning ... come courting
   me!'
   Fancy inquires about a girl with
   whom her betrothed had been seen to
   dance. She is so jealous that she
   pretends to him, later, that his rival
   has proposed to her; but Dick sees
   through her ploy, and her jealousy is
   exposed for what it is.
5. LAWRENCE, D.H.
   The Rainbow
   pp. 66–67 (Ch. 2)
   (Young Impact 3, pp. 84–86)
   (Come Down and Startle, pp. 41–44)
   'The first morning ... be no altering
   it.'
   Lydia Lensky marries again. Her
   daughter, Anna, wakes up in the
   morning, and is dismayed to find
   Brangwen, her new father, in bed
   with Lydia. She protests and resists
   Brangwen's attempts to accommodate
   her in the big bed. She wants to be
   alone with her mother.
6. ibid.
   see FATHERS (and) DAUGHTERS 4
7. ibid.
   pp. 125–126 (Ch. 4)
   'He spoke to his uncle ... would have
   agreed.'
   Will Brangwen asks his aunt and
   uncle if he can be married to Anna.
   He loves her, but he has not considered how he is to keep her. Tom is
   angry because he is jealous. He is not
   ready yet, to let Anna go.

8. LAWRENCE, D.H.
Sons and Lovers
(i) pp. 211–213 (Ch. 8); (ii) pp. 259–262
(Impact Two, pp. 178–182)
(Visions of Life 4, pp. 22–25)
'Paul sat pretending ... take her, my boy.'
Mrs Morel is jealous of Paul. She feels Miriam, whom he sees so frequently, is seducing him away from her. Paul is like a young husband to her, and she cannot bear the thought of sharing him with a young woman whose demands on him are as pressing as her own.

9. ibid.
see FAMILY – QUARRELS 6

10. MANNING, Olivia
The Play Room
pp. 37–40 (Section 1, Ch. 2)
'Tom said, 'We'll be home ... Perhaps I invented it.'
On holiday, Laura contemplates returning home to her despised mother, and remembers her jealousy of the little brother who took her place in her mother's affections.

11. SHOLOKHOV, Mikhail
And Quiet Flows the Don
pp. 284–286 (Part 2, Ch. 6)
'On the Sunday ... before her own eyes.'
Natalia visits her husband's lover, hopefully, hopelessly; and is cruelly rebuffed. There is nothing Natalia can do to plead her cause with the termagant Aksinia.

12. TWAIN, Mark
The Adventures of Tom Sawyer
see CHILDREN (in) LOVE 3

JEWS

1. FRANK, Anne
The Diary of Anne Frank
pp. 15–16 (20.6.42)
'My father was 36 ... I into the first.'
At the beginning of her diary, Anne describes her family and background. Having emigrated to Holland to escape Hitler's anti-Jewish laws, they then find themselves in 1940 subject to these same laws, after the invasion.

2. ibid.
pp. 42–44 (9.10.42)
'I've only got ... enemies in the world.'
Anne describes the fate of many of their Jewish friends not in hiding.

3. ibid.
pp. 174–175 (11.4.44)
'Now there are debates ... reached my goal.'
After a night of danger of being discovered, Anne reviews the situation of the Jews, and looks optimistically to better days.

4. ibid.
pp. 197–199 (22.5.44)
'On 20th May Daddy lost ... hope it will.'
As the war drags on, and the Dutch suffer more, their attitude to the Jews has hardened. Anne regrets this deeply, and fears for their situation after the war.

5. WRIGHT, Richard
Black Boy
pp. 51–53 (Ch. 2)
'My mother and Aunt Maggie ... cultural heritage.'
Black children taunt local Jews because the Jews killed Christ. They are brought up to hate them, and bait them by singing cruel, abusive songs.

JUBILEES

see CELEBRATIONS – ROYAL JUBILEE

JUMBLE SALES

1. 'MISS READ'
Village School
(i) pp. 124–126 (Part 2, Ch. 14); (ii) pp. 124–126
'Mrs Pringle and the ... to look, either.'
The vicar's wife makes an uncharacteristic faux pas. Setting things out for a jumble sale, with Mrs Pringle,

the school cleaner, she passes a depre-
cating remark about a carved table. It
turns out to have belonged to Mrs
Pringle's mother-in-law. Mrs Pringle
takes umbrage.

2. ibid.
(i) pp. 126–128 (Part 2, ch. 14); (ii)
pp. 126–128
'At seven o'clock ... with a face like
thunder.'
The ladies of the village tumble over
themselves to root out a bargain. A
formidable local gypsy tries to beat
down the price on a pair of trousers,
but she is put to rout.

JUNGLE

see also: FOREST;
LOST (in) JUNGLE;
SURVIVAL (in) JUNGLE

JUNGLE

1. BOULLE, Pierre
The Bridge on the River Kwai
(i) pp. 87–89 (Part 3, Ch. 2); (ii) pp.
99–101
'I saw it through my glasses ... his
sores were alive with them.'
Joyce, the would-be saboteur,
describes to his C.O., the difficulties
he has encountered in the Siamese
jungle: the darkness, the narrow
paths, the leeches, and the ants.

2. HEYERDAHL, Thor
The Kon-tiki Expedition
pp. 53–55 (Ch. 3)
'When we cut our moorings ... heaps
of green bananas.'
Heyerdahl, a companion, and two
South American Indians float the
balsa logs down the jungle river. At
the edge of the solid wall of jungle on
either side, they see brightly coloured birds and iguanas, as well as
suspicious natives.

JUSTICE

see also: EXECUTION;
PROTEST;
PUNISHMENT;
TRIALS

JUSTICE

1. ACHEBE, Chinua
Things fall apart
pp. 9–12 (Ch. 2)
'Okonkwo had just blown ... lived in
Okonkwo's household.'
A woman from Okonkwo's village is
murdered while at the market of a
neighbouring village. At a public
meeting, an ultimatum is despatched:
there must be compensation or war.
The offending village duly surrenders
a young man and a virgin.

2. ibid.
pp. 51–55 (Ch. 7)
'Okonkwo sat in his Obi ... afraid of
being thought weak.'
The elders of the village decide that
the young man, the murder-price,
should be killed. Okonkwo, who has
grown fond of the boy, is unhappy,
but he lends his hand in the killing
when the time comes.

3. ibid.
see TRIALS 1

4. ibid.
see MISSIONARIES 1

5. ibid.
see BRITISH EMPIRE – NIGERIA 5

6. DICKENS, Charles
Bleak House
(i) pp. 2–3 (Ch. 1); (ii) pp. 2–3
'On such an afternoon ... rather than
come here!'
The Court of Chancery is described,
with all its muddle and its resultant
tragedies.

7. ibid.
(i) pp. 503–504 (Ch. 39); (ii) pp.
503–504
'The one great principle ... eminently
respectable legion, Vholes.'
"The one great principle of the

English Law is to make business for itself." The whole 'system' is justified on the grounds that without it many people would be unemployed.

8. DICKENS, Charles
A Tale of Two Cities
see PUNISHMENT 6

9. KAFKA, Franz
The Trial
pp. 234–237 (Ch. 9)
'Won't you come down here?' ... I am now going to shut it.'
The priest who has revealed himself as belonging to the court, explains in a parable to K, how a plaintiff can be deluded by the court. The parable is about a poor man's access (or lack of it) to the inner workings of the law.

10. PATON, Alan
Cry, the Beloved Country
(i) pp. 107–108 (Bk. 2, Ch. 5); (ii) pp. 136–137
'At the head of the court ... are in the house.'
A black boy is about to be tried for the murder of a white man. The role of the judge, and the quality of the justice are examined by the narrator.

KIDNAPPING

see also: ESCAPE (from) KIDNAPPERS

KIDNAPPING

1. WYNDHAM, John
Chocky
pp. 127–135 (Ch. 5)
'I rang the police the next ... let herself cry.'
Matthew is the victim of a most mysterious kidnapping. His father is not called upon to pay a ransom, and, though they pretend to Matthew that he is in hospital with a broken leg, his kidnappers treat him kindly.

KILLING

see also: ANIMALS – SLAUGHTER;
EXECUTION

KILLING

1. BOULLE, Pierre
The Bridge on the River Kwai
see WAR 1

2. CAMUS, Albert
The Outsider
pp. 58–64 (Part 1, Ch. 6)
'The light was almost vertical ... door of my undoing.'
Almost by chance, the young man is confronted on the beach by his friend's antagonist. The young man, by chance, is armed. It is unbearably hot; it is as if the heat pulls the trigger, and kills the Arab, a near-stranger to his killer.

3. DICKENS, Charles
Bleak House
(i) pp. 609–611 (Ch. 48); (ii) pp. 609–611
'A very quiet night ... shot through the heart.'
Mr Tulkinghorn returns, unsuspecting, to his chambers through a peaceful London night. A shot is heard, the peace outside is disturbed but the body is not discovered until the following day, by cleaners.

4. DU MAURIER, Daphne
Jamaica Inn
see SHIPWRECKS 8

5. HUGHES, Richard
A High Wind in Jamaica
(i) pp. 173–178 (Ch. 7, Part 2); (ii) pp. 120–123
'It was very unfortunate ... meaningless stare.'
Emily knifes the bound Dutch captain she has been commisioned to guard. In a fit of tears, she slashes at him with the knife he has been stretching out to grab. He dies, and Emily's 'innocence' dies with him.

6. MANNING, Olivia
The Play Room
pp. 171–174 (Sn. 2, Ch. 3)
see FEAR 7

7. ibid.
pp. 179–183 (Sn. 2, Ch. 3)

'No-one spoke ... looks like murder all right.'

Laura leads the police to the place where she knows her friend Vicky and boyfriend spent some of the evening. In showing them the door to a derelict hangar, she discovers Vicky's dead body.

8. SCHAEFER, Jack
    Shane
    see FIGHTING (by) MEN (with) GUNS 2

9. SHOLOKHOV, Mikhail
    And Quiet Flows the Don
    pp. 254–255 (Part 2, Ch. 4)
    'During August the twelfth ... an obstinate silence.'

    Gregor falls in with Uriupin. The latter notices Gregor's woeful unwarlikeness, and so takes him in hand. He shows him how, with a single sabre thrust, he can cleave a man in two, and suffer no complicating remorse.

10. ibid.
    pp. 547–549 (Part 4, Ch. 6)
    'After a week of this ... out into the yard.'

    It is Bunchuk's job to execute counter-revolutionaries. One half of him relishes the work for the good of the Revolution, and the other half of him is revolted by it. Anna wants him to leave it, but he sets his teeth.

11. STEINBECK, John
    Of Mice and Men
    (i) pp. 91–97 (Ch. 5); (ii) pp. 72–77
    'Curly's wife came around ... last manger and disappeared.'

    Lennie, the simple giant, strokes a woman's hair because it is soft, and he likes soft things. But he is far from gentle; Curly's wife shouts out, Lennie panics, tightens his unknowing grip on her mouth and breaks her neck.

12. STEINBECK, John
    The Pearl
    pp. 78–84 (Ch. 6)
    'The trackers were long ... cry of death.'

    Kino resolves to kill the men who are pursuing him. When they make camp, he creeps up stealthily and attacks at the moment that one of them fires in the direction of the cave where his son is crying. Kino succeeds in killing his enemies, but the gunman succeeds in killing the baby.

13. TWAIN, Mark
    The Adventures of Huckleberry Finn
    (i) pp. 152–154 (Ch. 21); (ii) pp. 203–206
    (Visions of Life 1, pp. 53–56)
    'The nearer it got to noon ... his heels and walked off.'

    The drunken Boggs provokes the aristocratic Sherburn into threatening to kill him. Boggs continues to abuse Sherburn about the town, in spite of his friends' efforts to stop him, until he is stopped in his tracks by a bullet.

KILLING (of) ANIMALS

1. ADAMS, Richard
    Watership Down
    pp. 160–165 (Ch. 21)
    'Yes, I know three ... he was dead.'

    Holly describes how he escaped when the man came and pumped gas into the warren, and killed all but three rabbits.

2. SPERRY, Armstrong
    The Boy who was Afraid
    see COURAGE 17

3. STEINBECK, John
    The Red Pony
    see GRIEF 10

4. ibid.
    see BOREDOM 7

5. TREVOR, Elleston
    The Flight of the Phoenix
    see SURVIVAL (in) DESERTS 2

6. WRIGHT, Richard
    Black Boy
    see CRUELTY (to) ANIMALS 7

KILLING (by) BOYS

1. GOLDING, William
    Lord of the Flies
    (i) pp. 221–223 (Ch. 11); (ii) pp. 199–200

'Piggy's voice penetrated ... no sound came.'

Piggy's appeal to reason fails. It evokes only vicious hatred. Roger leans on the lever that upsets the rock that knocks Piggy down forty feet on to rock, and his death.

KILLING (by) GANGS – YOUTHS

1. BARSTOW, Stan
   The Human Element
   pp. 140–144 ('The Desperadoes')
   (Crime and Punishment, pp. 72–77)
   'Finch came up beside him ... He was alone.'
   The gang waits for Mr Jackson on the edge of the common. Vince plans to rough him up a little to avenge a private wrong; but Vince has a knife, and in the heat of the fight Jackson gets it in the stomach.

2. LEE, Laurie
   Cider with Rosie
   (i) pp. 68–71 (Ch. 6, 'Public Death, Private Murder'); (ii) 95–98
   'Soon after the First ... dead now anyway.'
   A man returns to the village from the Colonies, boasting of his success there and annoying all by his manner. On his way home he is ambushed by a group of young men, who beat him to death. The Police never discover the truth.

KILLING (by) HIRED ASSASSIN

1. SCHAEFER, Jack
   Shane
   pp. 114–116 (Ch. 11)
   'It took Frank Torrey ... he sagged to the floor.'
   Fletcher's hired gunman provokes Ernie Wright, an inoffensive, but impulsive farmer into drawing his gun. Ernie is killed as a lesson to his kind, to fall in with Fletcher's plans.

KILLING (by) PARTNERS (in) CRIME

1. TWAIN, Mark
   The Adventures of Tom Sawyer
   (i) pp. 68–73 (Ch. 9); (ii) pp. 67–71
   (Visions of Life 1, pp. 13–19)
   'This was a damper ... was complete again, too.'
   There is a fight in the graveyard: Injun Joe kills Dr Robinson, in payment of an old score, and blames fellow body-snatcher Muff Potter. But Tom and Huck have witnessed the fight, and know better.

KILLING (by) RIVALS (in) LOVE

1. HARDY, Thomas
   Far From the Madding Crowd
   (i) pp. 444–447 (Ch. 53); (ii) pp. 416–419
   'There was no music ... of preventing him.'
   It is Christmas Eve, and Boldwood has held Bathsheba to her reluctant promise to marry him; but Troy, presumed dead, returns to claim her. She resists him, screaming, and Boldwood shoots him down, out of jealous, thwarted love.

2. HARDY, Thomas
   Tess of the D'Urbervilles
   (i) pp. 493–497 (Ch. 56); (ii) pp. 425–429
   'Mrs Brooks, the lady ... watering-place.'
   Tess is staying with her first lover, when her lover returns from abroad to claim her. The landlady sees what effect his visit has on Tess, but she does not interfere until blood seeps through the floor above, and she fears murder has been done.

KILLING (in) SELF-DEFENCE

1. STEVENSON, R.L.
   Treasure Island
   pp. 158–166 (Ch. 26)

'The wind, serving us ... into the water.'

Jim in the company of one wounded pirate, is trying to bring the Hispaniola, to land. The pirate tricks him, and tries to attack him, but Jim escapes up the rigging. As a dagger pierces his shoulder, he fires his pistols and kills his pursuer.

KINGS

1. JEROME, Jerome K.
    Three Men in a Boat
    pp. 104–108 (Ch. 11)
    'The sun had got more powerful ... know, been firmly laid.'
    An evocation of the scene at Runnymede in 1215. There's colour, noise, and a lively anticipation of the coming of King John. The Barons have the King in their power. The day is heady with a sense of history.

2. ROBINSON, Rony
    A Walk to see the King
    pp. 25–26 (Ch. 9)
    'At the Tower ... could not change that.'
    Richard 11, a boy of 14, muses on the fate of his predecessors, and on the judgements of history. He is playing with toy soldiers with the Treasurer's daughter. She is bored by the game, and Richard's powers to command her attention are limited.

3. ibid.
    pp. 72–77 (Ch. 31)
    'After more drinks ... chosen King Tyler.'
    The would-be rebels play-act the England of the future. John Ball is King, and all men are equal. Wat Tyler is contemptuous of this milk-and-water utopia. His vision is of an England cleansed by the sword. He practises what he preaches by having one of his own men summarily hanged for looting.

4. ibid.
    see PEASANTS' REVOLT 2

5. TREECE, Henry
    Hounds of the King
    pp. 86–91 (Part 2, Ch. 10)
    'They rode on towards Oxford ... will do well to look out.'
    The enfeebled King Edward confronts the rebel earls Edwin and Morcar. They challenge him to reinstate the hated Tostig, brother of Harold Godwinson, who himself has designs on the throne. Edward virtually gives the northern earls a free hand in their domains. Harold is enraged ... the more because he is impotent to intervene.

6. TWAIN, Mark
    The Adventures of Huckleberry Finn
    (i) pp. 164–166 (Ch. 23); (ii) pp. 216–218
    (Rogues and Vagabonds, pp. 53–55)
    'By and by, when they was asleep ... tell them from the real kind.'
    The behaviour of their passenger, a royal pretender, surprises Jim. He had supposed that Kings behaved in a dignified manner. Huck, who knows a little about history, and in particular, Henry VIII, has never had any illusions about Kings.

KITE-FLYING

1. NAUGHTON, Bill
    One Small Boy
    pp. 247–249; 251–252 (Bk. 3, Ch. 6)
    (Here, Now and Beyond, pp. 191–195)
    'The soft and distant ... back in five minutes''; 'How's she been ... Goodnight, Herbert.''
    Michael meets his friend Herbert letting out a magnificent kite on its string. He lets it out so far that the kite disappears out of sight of the naked eye. Herbert pays out every foot of the string, only to let go of it, and lose his kite.

LANDSCAPE

see also: SOUTH AFRICA – LANDSCAPE;
TOWNS (and) CITIES

LANDSCAPE

1. BENNETT, Arnold
   Anna of the Five Towns
   pp. 155–157 (Ch. 10)
   'They walked straight ... the Mourne
   Mountains of Ireland.'
   Anna and Henry take an evening
   walk above Port Erin in the Isle of
   Man. As they climb Bradda, the
   whole coastline, and that of Ireland
   are gradually revealed to them.
2. FORSTER, E.M.
   Howard's End
   pp. 156–157 (Ch. 19)
   'If one wanted ... encircles England.'
   Forster describes the view from the
   Purbeck Hills over a large rolling
   section of the South Coast and its
   hinterland.

LANGUAGE

see also: SCHOOL – SUBJECTS – LATIN

LANGUAGE

1. FORESTER, C.S.
   The Gun
   (i) pp. 63–69 (Ch. 8); (ii) pp. 56–61
   ' "El Capitan? " ... hoist the cutter
   in.'
   A Spanish guerilla leader comes
   aboard an English frigate, during the
   Peninsular War, to ask for ammu-
   nition. Neither Captain speaks the
   other's language, so they resort to all
   manner of signs and sketches to convey their meaning – with success.
2. GRIMBLE, Sir Arthur
   A Pattern of Islands
   see EMBARRASSMENT 1
3. LEWIS, C.S.
   Out of the Silent Planet
   pp. 54–57 (Ch. 9)

(Come Down and Startle, pp.
143–145)
'Then something happened ... In the
end, he did so.'
A curious animal comes up out of the
water. Ransom and the animal
exchange gestures of attack, defence,
and friendship. And then the animal
uses language and attempts to make
itself understood. Ransom, the
philologist, is fascinated.
4. MOORE, John
   Portrait of Elmbury
   pp. 62–63 (Part 3)
   'The duties of an articled clerk ...
   always rosy-fingered.'
   In the family auctioneering firm, the
   author learns a whole new vocabulary,
   or set of vocabularies, for each trade
   and profession for whom the firm
   acts.
5. ORWELL, George
   1984
   (i) pp. 54–57 (Part 1, Ch. 5); (ii) pp.
   44–46
   'How is the dictionary ... is uncon-
   sciousness.'
   Syme, of the Research Department,
   explains the evolution of Newspeak,
   whose main aim is to limit thought to
   the politically acceptable by drasti-
   cally reducing vocabulary.
6. TWAIN, Mark
   The Adventures of Huckleberry Finn
   (i) pp. 85–86 (Ch. 14); (ii) pp.
   134–136
   'I never see such a nigger ... argue.
   So I quit.'
   Huck tries to impresss upon Jim that
   Frenchmen speak in a way he would
   not understand. He takes the different
   languages of the animals as an
   analogy. Jim cannot understand how,
   if a Frenchman is a man, he can't
   'talk like a man'.
7. WELLS, H.G.
   Kipps
   pp. 212–214 (Bk. 2, Ch. 5, Sn. 2)
   'All that declining summer ... 'Oo I
   will,' said Kipps.'
   As part of his campaign to better

himself socially, Kipps comes up against the problem of aitches. He wrestles with the difference between 'as' and 'has'; and he loses.

LAW

see JUSTICE;
RULES

LEADERS

see AUTHORITY

LEARNING

see also: CONDITIONING;
EDUCATION;
INDOCTRINATION;
SWIMMING – LEARNING

LEARNING

1. ALCOTT, Louisa M.
   Little Women
   see WORK 1
2. LONDON, Jack
   The Call of the Wild
   see DOGS – TRAINING 1
3. LONDON, Jack
   White Fang
   pp. 1–5 (Ch. 1)
   'The grey cub's eyes ... his mental make-up.'
   White Fang learns how to live with his mother, his brothers and sisters, his own rage, his father's disappearances and his mother's reproofs.
4. ibid.
   pp. 11–15 (Ch. 2)
   'A great fear came upon him ... between objects and himself.'
   The cub passes beyond the lip of the cave, into a troubling, risky, exciting world of hurts and surprises. He falls, encounters other animals, and learns how a wolf moves.
5. ibid.
   see FIGHTING (by) ANIMALS 3
6. THOMPSON, Flora
   Lark Rise to Candleford

(i) pp. 4–6 (Ch. 1); 31–33 (Ch. 2, 'Lark Rise'); (ii) pp. 20–21; 42–44 'Looking at the hamlet ... their sharp ears'; 'When Laura approached ... the store of others.'
Laura and Edmund learn by asking questions (and they learn whom not to ask). Their schooling is not of the best, but they are avid readers; they pick up scraps and they piece them together.

7. WRIGHT, Richard
   Black Boy
   pp. 18–21 (Ch. 1)
   'In the immediate neighbourhood ... I kept them to myself.'
   Richard's curiosity is awakened. He is eager for knowledge. He learns to count from the coalman and obscenities from his school friends. He learns something of what it means to be black, and he learns to use his new knowledge with a finer discrimination.
8. ibid.
   see RACISM – AMERICA 7
9. WYNDHAM, John
   The Day of the Triffids
   see SURVIVAL 11

LEAVETAKING

see also: HOME – LEAVING;
SCHOOL – LEAVING

LEAVETAKING

1. ALLEN, Walter
   All in a Lifetime
   see EMIGRATION 1
2. BUTLER, Samuel
   The Way of All Flesh
   see PARENTS 1
3. CHURCH, Richard
   Over the Bridge
   pp. 163–165 (Ch. 14)
   'Mother and Father took ... leading me to abrupt tumbles.'
   Holborn Viaduct Station on an Autumn afternoon. Richard is off to the coast for the winter to convalesce.

It is his first parting from his parents. It is a painful and poignant occasion.

4. DICKENS, Charles
Bleak House
(i) pp. 25–26 (Ch. 3); (ii) pp. 25–26
'The letter gave me ... to watch for London.'
Esther Summerson, an orphan, has spent six years teaching in a private school, and is leaving to become a companion to a young lady in London. Everyone is very kind, and she is very sad, but strives hard to cheer up and stifle her sobs.

5. GRICE, Frederick
The Bonny Pit Laddie
see EMIGRATION 3

6. HOLBROOK, David
Flesh Wounds
pp. 64–66 (Ch. 1)
'The RAC OCTU ... the coloured signals! '
Paul and Lucy have spent an unsatisfactory leave together. Paul is restless with the imminence of action. Lucy is a distracting softness to the maturing soldier. They part tearfully on a station platform.

7. HUGHES, Thomas
Tom Brown's Schooldays
pp. 64–67 (Part 1, Ch. 4)
'Tom and his father ... of sight and hearing.'
On the eve of his departure for Rugby School, Tom is given carefully-considered advice by his father. The words still ring in his ears in the darkness of the next morning; but he takes the leavetaking like a man.

8. LAWRENCE, D.H.
The Rainbow
pp. 422–424 (Ch. 14)
'Ursula left school ... God, were over.'
Ursula leaves the board school where she has taught, and fought, with mixed feelings. She is moved by the farewells, and the good will of her pupils, but she is glad that what has, at times, been an ordeal, is over.

9. MANSFIELD, Katherine
The Garden Party
pp. 171–174 ('The Voyage')
'The Picton boat was due ... patches of them, on the dark hills.'
Fenella is going with her grandmother on the Picton packet boat. Her father is on board saying his farewells. He presses a shilling into Fenella's hand, then rushes down the gangplank just before the mooring rope is thrown on to the wharf, and the boat steams out into the night.
see also: VOYAGES 9

10. PATON, Alan
Cry, the Beloved Country
(i) pp. 140–142 (Bk. 2, Ch. 12); (ii) pp. 174–178
(Making Contact, pp. 32–35)
'They passed again ... speak of it further.'
Absalom Kumalo has been sentenced to death for murder. His father visits him for the last time in prison.

11. REMARQUE, Erich Maria
All Quiet on the Western Front
see FIRST WORLD WAR – HOME LEAVE 1

12. THACKERAY, William
(i) pp. 287–292 (Ch. 30); (ii) pp. 347–353
'Now the Major ... aide-de-camp's wife.'
The contrast between two army wives as their husbands leave for the Battle of Waterloo – the normally self-centred Mrs O'Dowd works hard to send the Major off well-prepared, whereas Becky and Rawdon spend their last hours together discussing their ailing finances, and when he has gone her first thoughts are for these.

LECTURING

1. AMIS, Kingsley
Lucky Jim
pp. 221–227 (Ch. 22)
'Welch uttered the preludial ... roar of wordless voices.'
It is the evening of Dixon's public

lecture about 'Merrie England'. He has had too much to drink, with the unwitting result that he imitates his superiors, declaims, loses his place and all contact with his astonished audience.

LEISURE

see also BOREDOM;
CINEMA;
CONCERTS;
ENTERTAINMENTS;
FAIRS (and) FETES
see also: Under particular sports and pastimes.

LEISURE

1. CHURCH, Richard
   Over the Bridge
   pp. 92–93 (Ch. 9)
   'One such failure ... rolling-stock and engines.'
   Jack is a passionate railway modeller. He has made a large locomotive from plans in a boys' comic. It's a beautiful piece of work, but it defies his efforts to start it. When it does start, its career is dramatic, and its end explosive.
2. GORKY, Maxim
   Childhood
   see HOME 5
3. LEE, Laurie
   Cider with Rosie
   see FAMILY 9

LEISURE – FUTURE

1. HUXLEY, Aldous
   Brave New World
   pp. 76–77 (Ch. 6)
   'Odd, odd, odd ... quiet!' he shouted.'
   Bernard Marx, who questions the accepted values of the Brave New World, is impatient with the highly organized, mass leisure activities laid on for normal alphas.

LEOPARDS

1. GUILLOT, René
   Kpo the Leopard
   pp. 2–8 (Ch. 1)
   'Abga was hunting ... cat-fish for his cub.'
   A leopard's day – after a night of hunting, the day is a time for rest, and return to the lair, where the female guards the cub. The male, uneasy in the daylight, digs up a catfish for his cub.
2. ibid.
   pp. 9–14 (Ch. 2)
   'These early days ... opening her eyes.'
   A leopard cub's day – a cosy, lazy day, in the protective security of her parents, amused by the birds, the butterflies, the tricks of the light in the trees, and yet beginning to learn the ways of the forest.

LIFE

1. ALLEN, Walter
   All in a Lifetime
   pp. 220–221 (Ch. 15)
   'I see now that ... him under its foot.'
   What is this life if full of the routines of existence. Billy, now an old man contemplates the absurdity of it all.
2. WELLS, H.G.
   The History of Mr Polly
   see FRUSTRATION 7

LOCUSTS

1. ACHEBE, Chinua
   Things fall apart
   (i) pp. 49–51 (Ch. 7); (ii) pp. 49–51
   'In this way the moons ... eaten with solid palm-oil.'
   A skyful of locusts descend on Okonkwo's village, and settle for a night. But this is no plague. During the night, the villagers collect the sleeping locusts in baskets, roast them, and eat them.

LONDON

1. CARY, Joyce
   The Horse's Mouth
   pp. 66–67 (Ch. 12)
   'On the Surrey side ... Sno hurry.'
   Twilight on the Thames through the eye of a painter – the colours, the cloud-shapes, the water, the boats and the boatmen.
2. CHURCH, Richard
   Over the Bridge
   see TOWNS (and) CITIES 3
3. DICKENS, Charles
   Bleak House
   see FOG 2
4. ibid.
   see POVERTY 7
5. FOAKES, Grace
   Between High Walls
   passim.
   Childhood in an East London tenement at the beginning of the century.
6. FORSTER, E.M.
   Howard's End
   pp. 102–103 (Ch. 13)
   'To speak against London ... up in the sky.'
   London grows, changes, and is polluted by the motor car. Forster muses on the character of London.
7. WELLS, H.G.
   The War of the Worlds
   see MONSTERS 8
8. WOOLF, Virginia
   Orlando
   see FROST 2, 3
9. ibid.
   pp. 157–159 (Ch. 4)
   'At length she came home ... century had begun.'
   The London of 1800 is favourably compared with that of Elizabeth; it is more orderly, more comprehensively planned. The street cries and the lawlessness have given way to the carriage and the nightwatchmen.
10. WYNDHAM, John
    The Day of the Triffids
    pp. 151–153 (Ch. 9)
    'It was the memory ... and then slunk off.'
    London, deserted except for the occasional blind vagrant. The streets are empty, and the shop-fronts stove in by desperate survivors of the day of the Triffids.
11. ibid.
    pp. 230–232 (Ch. 15)
    'For safety's sake ... about them on foot.'
    By the time Bill Mason returns to London, the weeds are taking over, the cats and dogs are wilder, and the buildings are growing daily more precarious.
12. WYNDHAM, John
    The Kraken Wakes
    see FLOODS 11, 12

LONELINESS

1. BRONTË, Charlotte
   Villette
   pp. 241–243 (Ch. 24)
   'Following that evening ... Otherwise I was not ill.'
   Lucy Snowe suddenly receives no more letters from her friend Graham Bretton, and feels intensely lonely. The Post-hour is one of dreadful suspense.
2. BURNETT, Frances Hodgson
   The Secret Garden
   pp. 36–40 (Ch. 4)
   'To her surprise ... other things to do.'
   Orphaned Mary has been taken to a large unfriendly mansion in Yorkshire, and has no friends. With the help of a robin, she admits her loneliness to a surly old gardener, and they find some common ground.
3. DE JONG, Meindert
   The Wheel on the School
   see GIRLS 1
4. ELIOT, George
   Silas Marner
   pp. 16–17 (Ch. 2)
   'His first movement ... the gathering gloom.'

Silas, wrongly accused of a robbery and expelled from his community, sets up as a weaver in a new village. He tries to overcome his loneliness by working long hours, until gradually the gold he is amassing becomes a substitute for the human affection he lacks.

5. STEINBECK, John
The Grapes of Wrath
(i) pp. 42–44 (Ch. 6); (ii) pp. 47–49
'Muley said over the fire ... d'graveyard ghos'.'
Muley has stayed on his old farm when the rest of the family have been driven west by their evicting landlords. He tells of his loneliness, revisiting old haunts and feeling very bitter.

LOST

1. ALAIN-FOURNIER
Le Grand Meaulnes
pp. 39–41 (Part 1, Ch. 8)
'At half past one ... the least meaning to ...'
In a borrowed carriole, in unfamiliar country, Le Grand Meaulnes gets himself hopelessly lost. The horse gets a stone in its hoof, he bangs his knee ... night falls. Meaulnes passes from desperation to a queer exhilaration.

2. CANAWAY, W.H.
Sammy going South
pp. 87–92 (Ch. 14)
'Somewhere not far off ... of the Land Rover.'
Sammy has smashed the Land Rover engine, and deserted his despised companion, who panics and wanders in erratic circles, finally losing all sense of direction. He is found by the Game Warden, the following day.

3. PATON, Alan
Cry, the Beloved Country
(i) pp. 38–49 (Bk. 1, Ch. 8); (ii) pp. 43–45
'A woman opened the door ... Stay well, Mrs Mkize.'

(i) pp. 43–48 (Bk. 1, Ch. 10); (ii) pp. 57–64
(i) 'And this ... you comfort me.'
(ii) 'And this is Shanty Town ... many things in mind.'
(i) pp. 49–53 (Bk. 1, Ch. 11); (ii) pp. 64–67
'I have been thinking ... about the world.'
(i) pp. 54–57 (Bk. 1, Ch. 12); (ii) pp. 72–77
(i) 'Mr Msimangu ... there in the taxi.'
(ii) 'Mr Msimangu ... make you warm again.'
(i) pp. 64–65 (Bk. 1, Ch. 14); (ii) pp. 83–84
'When the last thing ... know what he said.'
Rev. Kumalo has come to Johannesburg to find his son who has not written for some time. He is soon on his trail, but every enquiry proves fruitless, as his son is always one step ahead. Each stage suggests further trouble, and the news of the murder of a white man arouses great fear in Kumalo.

LOST (in) CAVES

1. TWAIN, Mark
The Adventures of Tom Sawyer
(i) pp. 209–216 (Ch. 32); (ii) pp. 191–197
(Visions of Life, pp. 38–44)
'Now to return to Tom ... utter darkness reigned.'
Tom and Becky realise that they are lost in McDougal's cave. It is a long time since they have heard the other children's voices, and they cannot remember how they came in. Despair sets in when their last candle gutters, and dies.

LOST (in) DESERTS

1. MARSHALL, James Vance
Walkabout
(i) pp. 14–18 (Ch. 3); (ii) pp. 17–21

'Sturt Plain, where ... hungry any more.'
Mary and Peter, sole survivors of an air-crash in the Northern Territory of Australia, are lost and helpless. Without food, and with no knowledge of the country, their plight seems desperate.

2. TREVOR, Elleston
    The Flight of the Phoenix
    see DESERTS 4

LOST (in) JUNGLE

1. BATES, H.E.
    The Purple Plain
    pp. 138–141 (Ch. 15)
    'He made Carrington comfortable ... Blore began to scream.'
    Forrester, Carrington and Blore are trying to reach civilisation from the Burmese jungle where their plane has crashed. Blore, however, goes off by himself with all the equipment, and Forrester has to go after him. His anger mounts as he searches in the moonlight.

LOST (in) MAZE

1. JEROME, Jerome K.
    Three Men in a Boat
    pp. 56–58 (Ch. 6)
    'Harris asked me ... on our way back.'
    A reminiscence of Hampton Court Maze. Harris armed with a ground-plan, and an infallible method of getting out, attracts to himself a crowd of desperate trippers anxious for the exit. But the plan is a fraud, and the method fails. The crowd loses confidence in Harris.

LOST (on) MOORS

1. BENTLEY, Phyllis
    Gold Pieces
    pp. 7–15 (Ch. 1)
    'It is very easy ... I ran towards it.'
    Dick Wade decides to explore Erring-den Moor, because it is new territory and his parents don't seem too keen. He goes bilberrying, but forgets the time, and it is already dusk when he hears a dog howling for help. By the time he has found it, it is dark and he is completely lost.

2. DU MAURIER, Daphne
    Jamaica Inn
    see MOORS 2

LOST (in) MOUNTAINS

1. LLWELLYN, Richard
    How Green was my Valley
    pp. 51–54 (Ch. 6)
    'The snow was falling faster ... "O Huw".'
    Huw is leading his mother down from the mountain when they get lost in a snow storm. As they fall in drifts, it becomes more and more difficult to move, until his mother suddenly collapses. He gets her to the road, but has to stand in the river to stop her falling in.

2. MORROW, Honoré
    The Splendid Journey
    pp. 160–164 (Ch. 13)
    'John roused the children ... on the fire and went to bed.'
    Matilda strays out of the Sager camp in the night. John rouses the other children, and they search for her until they drop. John is worried about wolves, and as if to confirm his fears, he finds the pony half-eaten in the meadow. But he also finds Matilda, asleep with the cow.

LOVE

see also: ADOLESCENCE – BOYS (in) LOVE;
ADOLESCENCE – GIRLS (in) LOVE;
ASSAULT – RIVALS (in) LOVE;
CHILDREN (in) LOVE;
COURTSHIP; FAMILY;
JEALOUSY; RIVALS (in) LOVE;
SEX

LOVE

1. DICKENS, Charles
   Great Expectations
   (i) pp. 140–145 (Ch. 17); (ii) pp. 121–124
   'Biddy, said I ... or go home?'
   Pip is in courtly love with Estella, and confides to Biddy that he wishes to be a gentleman on her account. Biddy is so understanding and sincere, that Pip wonders that he can prefer the distant Estella.

2. DU MAURIER, Daphne
   Jamaica Inn
   pp. 118–119 (Ch. 9)
   'There remained ... to see him again.'
   Mary Yellan thinks about her attraction to Jem Merlyn, and realises that there is neither reason nor romance in love. Men and women are like animals.

3. ibid.
   pp. 134–135 (Ch. 9)
   'She leant back ... Christmas Day tomorrow.'
   Mary realises that once she has really fallen for Jem, this makes her weaker, and she is no longer entirely in control of herself.

4. ELIOT, George
   Middlemarch
   pp. 163–165 (Bk. 2, Ch. 16)
   'This last thought ... been conscious of.'
   Rosamond's feelings for Lydgate are analysed – she is in love rather with what he is, than with himself. She assumes that her feeling is returned.

5. ELIOT, George
   The Mill on the Floss
   pp. 494–499 (Ch. 6, Part 6)
   'Maggie was seated ... burst into tears.'
   Stephen, almost engaged to Lucy, comes to see Maggie, almost engaged to Philip, when she is alone one evening, because he is obsessed with her. They talk embarrassedly, walk in silence and both feel the attraction, which unsettles them so.

6. FIELDING, Henry
   Joseph Andrews
   see GIRLS 2

7. HARDY, Thomas
   Under the Greenwood Tree
   see PRIDE 3

8. LAWRENCE, D.H.
   Sons and Lovers
   (i) pp. 158–160 (Ch. 7); (ii) pp. 196–199
   (Impact Two, p. 112)
   'One evening in the summer ... delirium in his veins.'
   Miriam shows Paul a wild-rose bush in the hope that in responding to nature, he will quicken to her too. But she is too intense for him, like the scent of roses, and he feels imprisoned.

9. ibid.
   (i) pp. 167–170 (Ch. 7); (ii) pp. 206–210
   'On the Easter Monday ... was fulfilled in her.'
   Miriam and Paul, among others, go on an excursion to Wingfield Manor. They share and Miriam treasures, lovers' trivia. They dream. Paul arrives home tired. Miriam is fulfilled.

10. ibid.
    (i) pp. 304–306 (Ch. 12); (ii) pp. 370–374
    'He was in a delirium ... moodily beside him.'
    Paul is nervous, in the aftermath of his affair with Miriam, in his new relationship, with the more mature, challenging Clara. He is intoxicated by her nearness to him, as hyperconscious of her every movement, as any lover.

11. LAWRENCE, D.H.
    The Virgin and the Gipsy
    pp. 65–67 (Part 7)
    'I think life's awfully difficult ... Charles smoked for some moments.'
    Ever since the gypsy first looked at her in his penetrating way, Yvette has felt different – and confused. She asks her liberated friends, the East-

woods, if they would call this feeling love. They are not at all sure.

12. MANSFIELD, Katherine
Bliss and Other Stories·
pp. 173–179 ('Feuille D'Album')
'He really was ... handed her an egg.'
The timid young artist, whom women of the world have tried to seduce, falls incapably in love with a girl who lives across the street. With difficulty, he breaks out of his self-imposed régime, to make a lover's overtures.

13. MANSFIELD, Katherine
The Garden Party
see COURTSHIP – PROPOSALS (of) MARRIAGE 12

14. ibid.
pp. 203–212 ('The Singing Lesson')
'With despair – cold, sharp despair ... glowing with expression.'
Miss Meadows has received a letter from her betrothed which dashes her hopes of matrimony. She conducts a class of girls in the singing of a dirge. Then she receives a telegram countermanding the letter, and her conducting is con brio.

15. O'BRIEN, Edna
The Country Girls
pp. 61–65 (Ch. 7)
'I was standing outside ... deathless song.'
Mr Gentleman, a middle-aged neighbour of Caithleen's, gives her a lift and later takes her out to lunch. She is lonely and inexperienced and accepts his attentions eagerly, arriving home in a state of bliss.

16. TATE, Joan
Sam and Me
pp. 21–26 (Ch. 2)
'It was the summer holidays ... 'No I'm not. I know.' '
On the moors, in summer, Sam disturbs Jo's simple trust in him. She has regarded him as any ordinary brother, whose relationship with her is uncomplicated. But he reminds her that she is not his sister, when, for the first time, he kisses her.

17. TATE, Joan
Whizz Kid
pp. 87–95 (Ch. 1, Nibs)
'She was the funniest-looking ... know her name.'
Nibs explains, or rather finds it difficult to explain, how he was attracted to Clee. Small and quiet, she was very different from previous girl-friends, and his reaction was a new one for him too.

18. THACKERAY, William
Vanity Fair
(i) pp. 108–110 (Ch. 12); (ii) pp. 151–154
'We have talked ... every schoolmaster perish miserably.'
Amelia Sedley is in love. Unlike so many young ladies of the time she is not marrying for wealth or position – hers is a true, humble, devoted, romantic love.

LOVE – DESIRE

1. LAWRENCE, D.H.
Sons and Lovers
(i) pp. 178–179 (Ch. 7); (ii) pp. 219–221
'One evening he and she ... of humiliation.'
Paul badly wants to express his love for Miriam, in a kiss, a caress; and she waits for him. But he cannot, because his relationship has never been of that free and easy kind. She exudes a kind of spirituality, and he can't kiss that.

2. ibid.
pp. 289–291 (Ch. 11); (ii) pp. 353–355
'They lingered a little ... in what he felt.'
Paul and Miriam consummate their awkward, highly-strung love, and they destroy it. The act is too self-conscious. Miriam gives herself almost dutifully, like a sacrifice. They talk about marriage again, but they know the idea to be vain.

3. ibid.
(i) pp. 336–339 (Ch. 12); (ii) pp. 409–413
'At last Mrs Radford roused ... immediately he fell asleep.'
Secretly, though not silently, Paul and Clara meet to exchange kisses and caresses, while Clara's mother is asleep upstairs. They enjoy each other, but incompletely. Clara refuses to let Paul take her to bed with him.

LOVE – DISILLUSIONMENT

1. BARSTOW, Stan
   A Kind of Loving
   pp. 128–131 (Part 1, Ch. 7, Sn. 1)
   'Was that right?' she says ... so's we can beat it.'
   The joy has gone out of Vic's feeling for Ingrid. She all but surrenders herself to him on demand, out of simple, unsuspecting love for him; and he, who felt so tenderly for her when she walked at a distance, wants only to be away from her, to think, and plot a way of handing in his notice to her.
2. ibid.
   pp. 195–198 (Part 2, Ch. 4, Sn. 5)
   'Let's get it straight, then ... laid eyes on her.'
   Vic is trapped. Ingrid tells him that she is almost certainly pregnant. Vic is bitter and graceless in the extreme. Ingrid sobs but is far from blaming Vic for the mess they are in. He who once loved her curses his misfortune for having met her.
3. BRONTË, Charlotte
   Villette
   pp. 268–270 (Ch. 26)
   'What should I do ... beside a newly-sodded grave.'
   Lucy Snowe realises that Graham is in love with Paulina, and determines to dispose of his letters, which she has treasured. She very methodically finds a container and a hiding-place – a hollow tree. She feels she is "burying a grief".

4. LAWRENCE, D.H.
   Sons and Lovers
   (i) pp. 217–222 (Ch. 9); (ii) pp. 266–272
   'He took no notice ... to cycle with Edgar.'
   Paul is cruel to Miriam: he criticises her for her intensity and hunger for love. He cannot find the words to tell her that he cannot give her what she wants. The accord between them is taut with misunderstanding; then he cuts it, because his mother has the more tenacious hold on him.
5. ibid.
   (i) pp. 224–225 (Ch. 9); (ii) pp. 274–277
   'After tea she stood ... they went indoors.'
   Paul comes within an ace of proposing marriage to Miriam. They both know it is a forlorn idea: Paul only floats it because of pressure from his family to decide. Miriam would like to be married to Paul, but she knows, in her head, that they are unsuited to each other.

LOVE (at) FIRST SIGHT

1. ALAIN-FOURNIER
   Le Grand Meaulnes
   pp. 61–66 (Part 1, Ch. 15)
   'Next morning Meaulnes ... would have liked to say?'
   Meaulnes wanders in the grounds of the château, and passes by a striking young woman, to whom he feels immediately drawn. They go on an excursion by pleasure-boat, in company, and later, they exchange promising compliments.
2. BALDWIN, James
   Go Tell it on the Mountain
   pp. 174–177 (Part 2, 'Elizabeth's Prayer')
   'On a bright, summer day ... you was mighty pretty.'
   Elizabeth has been sent to buy some lemons. She is eighteen. Richard is sitting on the counter reading. He is

twenty-two. They exchange light conversation, and christian names, and an unspoken promise to meet again.

3. DICKENS, Charles
David Copperfield
pp. 450–452; 453–458 (Ch. 26)
'We turned into ... with Dora.'; 'All I know ... for I got none.'
David Copperfield meets the daughter of his employer, and falls instantly in love with her, without even having heard her speak. He can think of nothing else, and wanders round London in the hope of seeing her.

4. ELIOT, George
Middlemarch
pp. 116–118 (Bk. 1, Ch. 12)
'Mr Lydgate was rather late ... opposing to the actual.'
Rosamond Vincy has always imagined a 'lover and bridegroom who was not a Middlemarcher'. She therefore expects to fall in love with the new doctor, Lydgate, and is not surprised to find what a charming man he is.

5. HARDY, Thomas
Under the Greenwood Tree
see CHRISTMAS – CAROLS 2

6. JAMES, Henry
Washington Square
pp. 18–21 (Ch. 4)
'Mrs Penniman, with more buckles ... would be expected of her.'
Catherine is a stolid young lady, with few social graces. When she is introduced to a very handsome, self-confident young man at a party, she is as silent as usual, but more than usually impressed by his looks and manner.

7. MACKEN, Walter
God made Sunday and Other Stories
pp. 29–33 ('God made Sunday')
'I had a young bull ... the world. That's all.'
Colmain takes a young bull-calf to market to sell it, but the bull runs off. Colmain chases it and makes a pretty fool of himself in the process. A pretty girl captures the calf, and captivates Colmain. In no time, he is as dreamy as a poet.

LUDDITES

1. BRONTË, Charlotte
Shirley
(i) pp. 29–33 (Ch. 2); (ii) pp. 63–66
'The night was still ... and the rescue party set out.'
The new frames destined for Hollow's Mill have been smashed by Luddites on Stilbro' Moor. The mill owner rallies his friends to ride out and recover them.

2. ibid.
(i) pp. 341–345 (Ch. 19); (ii) pp. 334–337
'I wonder if there are ... had not occupied an hour.'
Hollow's Mill is under siege, but it is well defended. Windows are broken, but little other damage is done. The attackers get more than they bargained for.

MADNESS

1. DICKENS, Charles
David Copperfield
(i) pp. 201–205 (Ch. 14); (ii) pp. 257–261
'I wish you'd go ... than anybody else.'
Mr Dick is absorbed in the writing of a 'Memorial', but is continually confused by the entry of Charles I into it. He fails to keep him out, and never gets any further. David's aunt ridicules the idea that he might be a little mad.

2. HITCHMAN, Janet
The King of the Barbareens
pp. 87–91 (Ch. 4)
'The only person who, ... I have ever seen cried.'
Elsie has a certain rapport with a mentally deficient old lady, Miss Pankhurst. She is the least 'normal' individual of all the oddities in the institution, but she seems to be contented in her own, autistic fashion.

3. LEE, Laurie
   Cider with Rosie
   see SUICIDE 7
4. LLWELLYN, Richard
   How Green was my Valley
   pp. 132–135 (Ch. 15)
   'Gwilym's house was the end ...
   humming to the fire.'
   Marged mistakes Huw for his brother, Owen, who rejected her love,
   and threatens to kill him. After a wild
   chase up the mountain she collapses.
   He builds a fire to keep her warm,
   but somehow after he has left her, the
   fire envelopes her.
5. THOMPSON, Flora
   Lark Rise To Candleford
   (i) pp. 484–486 ('Candleford Green',
   Ch. 32); (ii) pp. 426–428
   'For Candleford Green ... to help
   him.'
   Candleford Green has its village idiot,
   mostly harmless and even gentle, but
   sometimes potentially violent if provoked, as he is by the village children.

MAGIC

see also: SUPERSTITION

MAGIC

1. DURRELL, Gerald
   Birds, Beasts and Relatives
   pp. 199–201 (Sn. 4, 'The Talking
   Head')
   'Do you want to see the Head?' ...
   see how it was possible.'
   The gypsy shows Gerald the disem-
   bodied head of which he has boasted.
   Gerald is amazed to hear it talk, and
   move, seemingly alive, without any
   lower parts to sustain it. With permission, Gerald examines the head in
   its box, very closely, but he cannot see
   how it is done, and the gypsy will only
   say that it is magic.
2. GRIMBLE, Sir Arthur
   A Pattern of Islands
   see SUPERSTITION 5
3. ibid.
   pp. 91–95 (Ch. 8)

'No further word ... the Gilbert
Islands.'
Arthur witnesses the calling of the
porpoises. Several of those 'friends
from the west' respond to a caller's
dream. They swim into the lagoon
straight into the waiting arms of the
babbling, clapping villagers. Feasting
and dancing follow.
4. ibid.
   see SUPERSTITION 6
5. WELLS, H.G.
   The Time Machine
   see INVENTIONS 2

MAGNA CARTA

1. JEROME, Jerome K.
   Three Men in a Boat
   see KINGS 1

MALARIA

see ILLNESS – MALARIA

MANHUNT

see also: ESCAPE;
HIDING

MANHUNT

1. DICKENS, Charles
   Great Expectations
   (i) pp. 1–6 (Ch. 1); 16–21 (Ch. 3);
   35–43 (Ch. 5); (ii) pp. 1–5; 14–18;
   30–37
   'Ours was the ... without stopping.'; 'It was a rimy ... was still
   going.'; 'At last, Joe's job ... over
   with him.'
   Pip gives assistance to an escaped
   convict, by stealing food for him.
   Later, he is in on the hunt for him
   with no taste for his being caught.
   But he is caught, and the look that he
   gives Pip is one that the boy finds it
   difficult to understand; and impossible to forget.
2. GREENE, Graham
   The Power and the Glory

(i) pp. 66–72 (Part 2, Ch. 1); (ii) pp. 71–78

'The Consecration was in ... bring him along.'

The soldiers enter the village where the fugitive priest has just said mass. His wife covers up for him, and despite the lieutenant's suspicions, and the taking of an innocent hostage, the priest is passed over. The soldiers leave the village and so, soon after, does the priest.

3. LONDON, Jack
White Fang
see RESCUE (from) INTRUDERS 1

4. PATON, Alan
Cry, the Beloved Country
see LOST 3

5. STEINBECK, John
The Pearl
pp. 69–78 (Ch. 6)
'What is the matter ... over the land.'
Kino, his wife and child are escaping from their town, where he has killed a man. They soon realise they are being followed, and have to go through increasingly difficult terrain to try to shake off their pursuers.

6. WOOD, James
The Rain Islands
pp. 175–195 (Chs. 9, 10)
'Linda had already ... she said quietly.'
In thick fog, Major Scott and his companions tail the boat of some communist spies. They finally meet on the shore of a small Icelandic island, where Scott's boat is rammed, but the spies are all killed. One of Scott's companions is also killed.

MANNERS

see ETIQUETTE

MARKETS

see also: SHOPS

MARKETS

1. BERNA, Paul
A Hundred Million Francs
(i) pp. 18–20 (Ch. 1); (ii) pp. 16–18
'The Gang had reached ... revolting mixture at the other.'
In the Square de la Libération, market traders are setting up their stalls for the Thursday evening market. Among them is Roublot, the cheap-jack who sells mincers. The children do not like him, but they stay to listen to his patter, and to mock.

2. FOAKES, Grace
Between High Walls
p. 15 (Ch. 7)
'Watney Street was a narrow ... due to arrive.'
The author accompanies her mother to the Saturday market in Watney Street. Quantities and prices of the meat and vegetables for the Sunday dinner, as well as of the second-hand clothes, are engraved on her memory, as an index of their poverty.

3. GRICE, Frederick
The Bonny Pit Laddie
pp. 15–16 (Ch. 2)
'To come upon ... the last trip home.'
The Ullathorne family is in Durham, shopping. They stop to listen to the patter of the salesmen in the market-place. The pot-man, in particular, commands attention.

4. MANKOWITZ, Wolf
A Kid for Two Farthings
pp. 26–29 (Ch. 2)
'Joe ran quickly through ... handed over the rabbit.'
Joe walks between stalls selling singing-birds, day-old chicks, and white rabbits. He resists all these, because he is in search of a unicorn.

5. MANKOWITZ, Wolf
Make me an Offer
pp. 22–24 ('Make me an Offer')
'About twenty years ... start to laugh.'
The narrator tells how his father became a successful stall-holder on a

London market by specialising in one article each week. He follows his father, and succeeds himself.

6. MOORE, John
   Portrait of Elmbury
   pp. 37–39 (Part 1)
   'There was one day ... good will among men.'
   The Christmas Market day in Elmbury is almost as great a festival as Christmas itself. The streets are packed with men and animals; money and drink flow.

7. ibid.
   pp. 75–79 (Part 3)
   'In the early spring ... and millionaires too.'
   The articled clerks in the auctioneering firm have their work cut out on market day, when they have complicated accounts to keep and irate farmers to placate.

8. SEWELL, Anna
   Black Beauty
   pp. 141–145 (Ch. 32)
   'No doubt a horse fair ... beautiful mash ready for me.'
   Black Beauty experiences his first horse fair. He is horrified by the broken-down old horses he sees, and the rough buyers, but is relieved when he is bought by a clean, kind man.

MARRIAGE

see also: COURTSHIP – PROPOSALS (of) MARRIAGE;
DIVORCE; WEDDINGS

MARRIAGE

1. AUSTEN, Jane
   Pride and Prejudice
   (i) pp. 1–3 (Ch. 1); (ii) pp. 5–7 (Vol. 1, Ch. 1)
   'It is a truth ... visiting and news.'
   Mrs Bennett is anxious that her husband should visit their new neighbour, an eligible bachelor, as she has five marriageable daughters. He, by con-

trast, is less than keen to make such an obvious overture.

2. BRONTË, Charlotte
   Shirley
   (i) pp. 377–380 (Ch. 21); (ii) pp. 365–368
   ' 'My dear, 'ere long again began ... they may change for the worse.'
   Having tried to dissuade Caroline from seeking a place as a governess, Mrs Pryor gives her the example of her own unhappy circumstances, as a basis from which to discourage her from getting married.

3. ibid.
   (i) pp. 465–467 (Ch. 27); (ii) pp. 443–445
   'Miss Keeldar and her uncle ... further trouble on the subject.'
   Mr Sympson decides that it is time his niece was married. He makes suggestions regarding suitable husbands, and is rather surprised that Miss Keeldar has her own views on the subject.

4. DEFOE, Daniel
   Moll Flanders
   see COURTSHIP 4

5. GORKY, Maxim
   Childhood
   (i) pp. 247–254 (Ch. 11); (ii) pp. 181–185
   'My father's mother died when he was ... curds like so much gravel ...'
   Grandmother tells young Gorky the story of his parents' turbulent courtship and marriage: of how she connived at their secret marriage, preventing her husband and sons by vital minutes from intervening; and of how she visits them after the wedding, with food and comfort.

6. GREENWOOD, Walter
   Love on the Dole
   see PAWNBROKERS 3

7. TROLLOPE, Anthony
   Barchester Towers
   see WOMEN – RIGHTS 2

MARRIAGE – ARRANGED

1. ACHEBE, Chinua
   Things fall apart
   pp. 63–66 (Ch. 8)
   'There were seven men ... brought in a pot of palm-wine.'
   The fathers of Akueke and Ibe, her suitor, meet to discuss the bride-price. They bargain and come to an agreement. The match is then celebrated with food and wine.

2. ibid.
   see WEDDINGS 1

3. SHOLOKHOV, Mikhail
   And Quiet Flows the Don
   pp. 69–72 (Part 1, Ch. 5)
   'Gregor spared neither whip ... pretending he had not heard.'
   The heads of the Melekhov and Korshunov households discuss a marriage that will be of advantage to both sides. Both sell the merits respectively of son and daughter, but agreement is deferred.

MARRIAGE – DISILLUSIONMENT

1. LAWRENCE, D.H.
   The Rainbow
   pp. 175–179 (Ch. 6)
   'Directly, it occurred ... 'I do,' she said.'
   Anna knows she is pregnant, but she cannot tell Will, because of the hardness between them. She tells her parents and they comfort her. When she tells her husband he feels still more cut off from her, as if he was no longer necessary to her.

2. LAWRENCE, D.H.
   Sons and Lovers
   (i) pp. 11–14 (Ch. 1); (ii) pp. 19–24
   'The next Christmas ... would not have done.'
   The love between Walter and Gertrude does not last long: he deceives her, and she begins to lose all confidence in him. He seeks the company

of his workmates and she turns for comfort to her new baby.

3. LESSING, Doris
   The Grass is Singing
   pp. 61–67 (Ch. 3)
   'It was a long way ... whom she had wounded.'
   Dick drives his new wife, Mary, out to his remote farm. She has a townswoman's romantic vision of life on the veld, but she is unready for the poverty of the house she is being invited to make her home. She makes her distaste obvious. Dick's bedtime gropings are unreproved, and undesired.
   see also: RUNNING AWAY 5

4. TATE, Joan
   Sam and Me
   pp. 77–84 (Ch. 6)
   'We had both wanted children ... I lay there all night, without sleeping.'
   No baby arrives to fulfil Sam's and Jo's joint ambition. Jo is a good housewife, and is tireless in her search for ways to please her husband. But she does not satisfy him. She effaces herself to such an extent, that there is too little of herself to give.

MARRIAGE – QUARRELS

1. BARSTOW, Stan
   A Kind of Loving
   pp. 223–225; 225–227 (Part 2, Ch. 6, Sn. 2); (Impact Two, pp. 71–74)
   'I've been there about six ... getting rid of it'; 'One day the phone ... years of it to come.'
   Vic has mother-in-law trouble. She comes between him and his wife, making up Ingrid's mind for her, and judging Vic as if he was her schoolboy son. Ingrid sides with her mother against him, until he feels bound to admit, in a heated moment, that he wishes he hadn't married her.

2. BUTLER, Samuel
   The Way of all Flesh
   pp. 46–50 (Ch. 13)

'A due number of old shoes ... inn at Newmarket.'
Theobald and Christina, after thirty minutes of wedded bliss, argue about whose responsibility it is to order their first dinner. Christina, who has lately promised to obey, humbly accedes.

3. ELIOT, George
Middlemarch
pp. 575–580 (Bk. 6, Ch. 58)
'Dear Rosy, lay ... way of living.'
As a result of a too-hasty marriage and extravagant living and entertaining, Rosamond and Lydgate are deeply in debt. Their relationship does not help them in this crisis, and there is bitterness and argument.

4. FIELDING, Henry
Joseph Andrews
pp. 102–105 (Bk. 2, Ch. 5)
'As soon as the passengers ... held in her left hand.'
The host belabours his wife for paying attention to a footman (the wounded Joseph), Parson Adams intervenes to check the surly host, and blows are exchanged in a cause whose origins are obscured by its effects: spilt puddings, bloody noses, and a handful of hair.

5. LAWRENCE, D.H.
Sons and Lovers
(i) pp. 21–26 (Ch. 1); (ii) pp. 31–37
'The next day was a work-day ... his drunkenness.'
Morel comes home drunk. Mrs Morel reproaches him for his extravagance. They shout at each other, call each other a liar, and almost come to blows. Morel shuts his wife out of the house. She paces the garden, and he sleeps with his head on the kitchen table, until, exhausted, she raps on the window to be let in.

6. ibid.
see DRUNKENNESS 8

7. SILLITOE, Alan
The Loneliness of the Long-distance Runner
pp. 111–119 ('The Match')

'Bristol City had played ... left him for the last time.'
It is a foggy Saturday afternoon, and Notts. have played badly. Lennox is irritable, and flies off the handle at home, at the least excuse. He provokes his wife to home-truths, and silences her with blows.

8. THOMPSON, Flora
Lark Rise to Candleford
(i) pp. 548–551 ('Candleford Green', Ch. 36); (ii) pp. 480–482
'But over the case ... for Sammy's comfort.'
Most unusually, Sammy beats Susan, and she, without telling him or anyone else takes out a summons against him. He serves a month's imprisonment and she goes with her children to the workhouse to shame him further. On his release they are happily re-united and live at peace.

9. TROLLOPE, Anthony
Barchester Towers
pp. 133–137 (Ch. 17)
'All this time ... his domestic chaplain.'
The Bishop of Barchester determines to escape from his wife's dictatorship, and chooses the naming of the warden of a Hospital as his battleground. From the moment he enters his wife's room, however, his strength and courage fail him.

10. ibid.
pp. 214–219 (Ch. 26)
'It was hardly an hour ... to my Lord alone?" '
Mrs Proudie attempts to reaffirm her dominance over her husband, the Bishop, but he, strengthened by the presence of his chaplain, stands his ground. Mrs Proudie *appears* to be defeated.

11. WELLS, H.G.
Kipps
pp. 349–353 (Bk. 3, Ch. 2, Sn. 3)
'He was too astonished ... generously buttered toast.'
The Kippses have words. Mrs Kipps has disgraced herself in front of cal-

lers. Kipps, who is convincing himself, that he has married beneath himself, and that polite society means to shun him, is utterly unforgiving.

MARRIAGE – RECONCILIATION

1. LAWRENCE, D.H.
   Sons and Lovers
   (i) pp. 406–409 (Ch. 14); (ii) pp. 493–497
   'Clara took off her ... he murmured, broken.'
   Now that Paul's mother has died, he can no longer relish Clara's company; and she realises that he has lost his manliness somehow. He is suddenly mean in her eyes, and less than Dawes. Paul leaves the two of them alone together, to be reconciled; remarried.

MASSACRES

1. ACHEBE, Chinua
   Things fall apart
   see MISSIONARIES 1

MATERIALISM

see also: MISERS;
WEALTH

MATERIALISM

1. BRAINE, John
   Room at the Top
   pp. 27–29 (Ch. 3)
   'I took a seat ... to myself not others.'
   From a café table, Joe Lampton sees a smart young man of means, the owner of an Aston Martin, and a girl with a Riviera tan. He resolves to enjoy such luxuries himself, one day.
2. BRONTË, Charlotte
   Shirley
   see SELFISHNESS 1
3. O'BRIEN, Robert C.
   Mrs Frisby and the Rats of NIMH
   pp. 145–152 (Thorn Valley)

'So we built ourselves ... there's a drought.'
The super-intelligent rats build up a luxurious life for themselves, with electricity, running water and air-conditioning. They are however discontented, and resolve to set up a simpler existence.

4. STOREY, David
   This Sporting Life
   pp. 108–112 (Part 1, Ch. 4)
   'One Sunday morning ... and with life-fatigue.'
   The rising rugby star looks in on his parents. They criticise the company he keeps, and the crude ambitions he evinces. He is after money, and he's not concerned where it comes from.

MATING

see HORSES – MATING;
SNAKES – MATING;
TORTOISES – MATING

MEALS

see also: CHRISTMAS – DINNERS;
PARTIES;
PICNICS

MEALS – BREAKFASTS

1. BRONTË, Charlotte
   Jane Eyre
   see SCHOOLS – BOARDING – FIRST DAY
   2
2. HILDICK, E.W.
   Birdy in Amsterdam
   pp. 57–58 (Ch. 7)
   'The breakfast ... while I'm at it.'
   Birdy and Fixer are staying, free, at an Amsterdam hotel, and are determined to make the most of what is provided. Therefore they eat an enormous breakfast, trying everything that is offered.
3. HUGHES, Thomas
   Tom Brown's Schooldays
   see TRAVEL (by) STAGE-COACH 3

MEALS – DINNERS

1. ALCOTT, Louisa M.
   Little Women
   pp. 158–162 (Ch. 11)
   'Leaving the others ... olives and fun.'
   Mrs March leaves her daughters in charge of the house one Saturday, and Jo confidently promises to cook lunch. Naturally nothing goes right and an unexpected visitor receives an inedible meal.

2. DICKENS, Charles
   David Copperfield
   pp. 471–475 (Ch. 28)
   'On the occasion ... a greater success.'
   David Copperfield entertains his old friends Mr and Mrs Micawber and Traddles, in his lodgings. His landlady is neither the best nor the most dependable of cooks, however, and they end up cooking slices of the undercooked leg of mutton over the fire.

3. DURRELL, Gerald
   Birds, Beasts and Relatives
   pp. 156–160 (Sn. 3, 'Owls and Aristocracy')
   'I, filled with champagne and brandy ... and flamboyantly sick.'
   A bloated countess entertains Gerald to dinner. Course follows course, delicacy succeeds delicacy, until, in spite of some minutes respite after the roast boar, all Gerald's trouser buttons are undone to allow for expansion.

4. GRIMBLE, Sir Arthur
   A Pattern of Islands
   pp. 52–57 (Ch. 4)
   'It all began ... and Olivia wept.'
   Arthur and his wife throw a tropical dinner-party for the Old Man, Arthur's venerable superior. The food is out of tins, but this, in their remote situation, is a real luxury. The dinner is a catastrophe, from the soup to the plum pudding.

5. LAWRENCE, D.H.
   Sons and Lovers
   see HOTELS (and) RESTAURANTS 2

MEALS – TEAS

1. LAWRENCE, D.H.
   Sons and Lovers
   (i) pp. 320–322 (Ch. 12); (ii) pp. 390–393
   'The Morels lived in ... at the bottom of her.'
   Paul brings Clara home to meet his parents. She is nervous, but everyone is on his best behaviour – even Morel's gallantry is impressive – and the visit is judged a success.

2. THOMAS, Dylan
   A Portrait of the Artist as a Young Dog
   pp. 14–17 ('The Peaches')
   'It was to be a special ... grew softer and died.'
   Wealthy Mrs Williams brings her spoilt son Jack to tea at Gorsehill Farm. She is in a hurry to leave; but she would not have appreciated in any case the 'best room', Sunday clothes, and a can of peaches as symbols of unusual luxury, accorded in her honour.

MEDICINE

see also: DOCTORS;
HOSPITALS;
ILLNESS;
INJURIES;
SURGERY

MEDICINE

1. GRIMBLE, Sir Arthur
   A Pattern of Islands
   see FAITH 4

MEDICINE – PRIMITIVE

1. HARDY, Thomas
   The Return of the Native
   see SNAKES 2

2. LESSING, Doris
   Nine African Stories
   pp. 11–14 ('No Witchcraft for Sale')
   'The Farquars had been ... God is
   very good.'
   The white boy grows up to lord it over
   the black servant, but when a snake
   spits poison in young Teddy's eyes, it
   is Gideon who, using native herbs and
   knowhow, saves Teddy from going
   blind.

3. TWAIN, Mark
   The Adventures of Tom Sawyer
   (i) pp. 45–48 (Ch. 6); (ii) pp. 46–49
   'What's that you got? ... – but don't
   you tell.'
   Tom and Huck exchange remedies.
   They debate the merits of one method
   after another, of getting rid of warts.
   Huck favours a method using a dead
   cat because he heard it from a
   reputed witch.

MEMORIES

1. SHOLOKHOV, Mikhail
   And Quiet Flows the Don
   see WAR – MEMORIES 1

MEMORIES (of) BABYHOOD

1. HITCHMAN, Janet
   The King of the Barbareens
   pp. 8–10 (Ch. 1)
   'How far back ... two and a bit.'
   Improbably, the writer remembers
   that she remembered being born. She
   recalls two sisters who stepped in and
   out of her life within twenty-four
   hours, and the end of the First World
   War.

2. KIRKUP, James
   The Only Child
   pp. 13–15 (Ch. 1)
   'Early photographs ... mother and
   father.'
   Babyhood remembered in the sound
   and smell of the pram, in a near-
   accident, and in two young baby-
   snatchers put firmly in their place.

MEMORIES (of) CHILDHOOD

1. BAWDEN, Nina
   Carrie's War
   (i) pp. 9–18 (Ch. 1); (ii) pp. 7–15
   'Carrie had often dreamed ... when
   he was young.'
   Carrie revisits with her children the
   Welsh mining town to which she and
   her brother were evacuated as children. It looks somewhat different, but
   she quickly recaptures something of
   her childhood experience in a wood
   outside the town, as her children
   realise from her strange behaviour.

2. CHAPLIN, Sid
   The Leaping Lad and Other Stories
   pp. 64–69 ('The Bridge')
   'One night, when ... was built again.'
   The writer remembers his early
   closeness to his parents, and the
   distance at which he was set by
   brothers and sisters. The gap is only
   bridged when he learns how his
   parents have suffered for their children; in particular, in childbirth.

3. CHURCH, Richard
   Over the Bridge
   pp. 28–31 (Ch. 3)
   'Neither my brother nor I ... tied
   under their chins.'
   The author and his mother sit in the
   sun in the park. He collects things,
   and discovers their touch and smell.
   Two ladies stop and talk to him, and
   he registers their soft voices, and their
   bloomers.

4. DICKENS, Charles
   David Copperfield
   pp. 61–65 (Ch. 2)
   'The first objects ... what I saw.'
   David looks back to the first objects,
   scenes and people he remembers – his
   mother, Peggotty their servant, the
   house and its layout, the neighbouring
   churchyard, and the pew in church.

5. GORKY, Maxim
   Childhood
   (i) pp. 1–6 (Ch. 1) (ii) pp. 13–16
   'On the floor beneath ... so frequently and with such familiarity.'

Death, birth, and attendant emotions crowd in early upon Gorky. He is bewildered, though apparently unaffected by his father's death, and funeral. His strongest impression is of his grandmother come from Nizhni Novgorod with enfolding love and sympathy.

6. LAWRENCE, D.H.
   The Rainbow
   see FATHERS (and) DAUGHTERS 6

7. LEE, Laurie
   Cider with Rosie
   (i) pp. 1–3 (Ch. 1, 'First Light'); (ii) pp. 9–13
   'I was set down ... for twenty years.'
   At the age of three, Laurie Lee arrives at his new home in Slad village, fears he is lost, and enjoys the chaos and the garden.

8. ibid.
   (i) pp. 3–5 (Ch. 1, 'First Light'); (ii) pp. 13–15
   'Now I measured ... or destroy.'
   Once established in the new house Laurie Lee begins to widen his horizons by exploring the different rooms, and the garden. In the kitchen he makes the acquaintance of water.
   see also: WATER 2

9. TATE, Joan
   Clipper
   pp. 72–76 (Ch. 7)
   'I've always thought ... stuck around my room.'
   Justifying her use of the word 'darkies' Clee remembers a song she learnt as a child about 'the darkies Sunday School'.

10. THOMAS, Dylan
    Quite Early one Morning
    pp. 8–10; 12–14 ('Reminiscences of Early Childhood' – 2nd version)
    (Impact 1, pp. 83–84; p. 107)
    'I like very much ... to swallowing tadpoles.'; 'And that park grew ... order, and no end.'
    Dylan swims in a Swansea sea of images: the park where secret societies played their pretend games, the beach, the fish-and-chip smelling streets, and the fantasies of schoolboys.

11. ibid.
    see CHRISTMAS 12

12. ibid.
    see SCHOOL – REPORT 1

MENSTRUATION

1. HITCHMAN, Janet
   The King of the Barbareens
   pp. 123–125 (Ch. 6)
   'Most women can ... They don't.'
   Elsie is quite unprepared for her first menstrual period. She imagines she is suffering from a wasting disease. She accepts that it will happen every month, because she is told it will; but she doesn't know why.

METHODISTS

1. THOMPSON, Flora
   Lark Rise to Candleford
   (i) pp. 233–236 ('Lark Rise', Ch. 14); (ii) pp. 215–218
   'The Methodists were ... fascinating thought.'
   Laura attends a Methodist service in one of the Hamlet cottages. She is fascinated by the impassioned, impromptu, confessions, and testimonies, and by the familiar mode of addressing God.

2. WRIGHT, Richard
   Black Boy
   pp. 132–136 (Ch. 6)
   'My mother began ... hooky from church.'
   There is an evangelical revival at the local black Methodist Church. Richard is among a hard core of youths who resist the call, until his mother's tears persuade him to be baptised in spite of his principles.

MINING

1. CHAPLIN, Sid
   The Leaping Lad and Other Stories
   see CONSCIENCE 2

2. COOKSON, Catherine
The Nipper
pp. 48–54 (Ch. 5)
'Sandy had seen ... go along out and eat it.'
Sandy goes down the mine for the first time, and is horrified by the cage, the child labour, the cruelty of the men, the size of the passages and the face, and finally the back-breaking work he has to do.

3. GRICE, Frederick
The Bonny Pit Laddie
see STRIKES 2

4. ibid.
pp. 118–122 (Ch. 14)
'It was a bright cold morning ... seen for a year.'
Dick starts work as a miner alongside his brother. His job is to open and shut the gallery door for passing traffic. It is a lonely job and the hours of waiting pass slowly.

5. LLEWELLYN, Richard
How Green was my Valley
pp. 281–284 (Ch. 20)
'Ivor came off ... as your own skin.'
Huw goes down the mine for the first time – from the moment the cage drops to coming up at night he is afraid, but he enjoys the feeling of being a man, and he appreciates the freedom outside.

MINING – ACCIDENTS

1. CHAPLIN, Sid
The Leaping Lad and Other Stories
pp. 32–35 ('Hands')
'Father and son stripped ... hands of his father.'
Father and son are trapped at the coal-face, when the latter moves a vital prop, and causes a rock-fall. Rescuers succeed in getting the younger man out, but all that is visible of his father are his hands.

2. ibid.
pp. 143–149 ('The Cage')
'Four men stood ... rope sang to him.'

Two cages collide in the shaft, and four miners are trapped. They crawl out and are hauled by bucket to the surface. Carr, more accident-hardened than his mates, volunteers to be the last to go up.

3. GRICE, Frederick
The Bonny Pit Laddie
pp. 134–138 (Ch. 16)
'Branton was in many ... men to emerge.'
Mr Sleath, the colliery manager, has not complied with the law, and provided a second shaft, for safety's sake. Thus, when the pithead gear collapses down the single shaft, the twenty miners down below are effectively entombed.

4. ibid.
pp. 138–141 (Ch. 16)
'By this time ... closed their eyes.'
The miners, trapped by the collapse of the winding-gear, and the shaft-walls, sit and wait for the expected rescuers. There is conversation, prayer, speculation and despair.

5. LAWRENCE, D.H.
Sons and Lovers
see INJURIES – LEG 1

MISCARRIAGE

1. BARSTOW, Stan
A Kind of Loving
see ACCIDENTS (at) HOME 1

MISERS

1. DICKENS, Charles
A Christmas Carol
pp. 46–52 (Stave 1) and *passim*
'Oh! But he was ... was usual with him.'
Scrooge refuses to exchange the season's greetings with his nephew, and to be charitable. He is sparing in his use of fuel, and in the wage he pays to his ill-used clerk.

2. ibid.
pp. 53–56 (Stave 1)

'Scrooge took his melancholy ... to take his gruel.'
He lives the life of a recluse in a dingy quarter. He broods over a low fire, satisfied that he has nothing to learn about economy.

3. ibid.
pp. 128–134 (Stave 5)
'Running to the window ... Every One!'
The other side of the Scrooge-hoarded coin. Having learnt his hard lesson from the three spirits, Scrooge is generous, happy, big-hearted, indulgent – in fact, quite unrecognizable.

4. ELIOT, George
Silas Marner
see LONELINESS 4

5. ibid.
pp. 19–23 (Ch. 2)
'Gradually the guineas ... in the barren sand.'
Silas, deprived of all human affection, centres his life on the gold he is amassing, and finds his only pleasure and solace in counting it. He becomes a typical miser figure.

6. ibid.
pp. 46–49 (Ch. 5)
'Anyone who had looked ... close to the Rainbow.'
Silas returns from an errand to count his beloved gold – but the hiding-place is empty. He is unwilling to believe this, but finally the dreaded truth is unmistakably clear, and he rushes out to find help.

7. ibid.
pp. 87–88 (Ch. 10)
'But while poor Silas's loss ... seeks to be heard.'
Silas feels 'the withering desolation' of his bereavement ... the loss of his gold, and finds no comfort. He continues to work, but with no enthusiasm, and moaning from time to time.

MISFORTUNE

see also: ACCIDENTS;
DEATH;
GRIEF

MISFORTUNE

1. ACHEBE, Chinua
Things fall apart
see FARMING – HARVEST 1

2. GROSSMITH, George and Weedon
The Diary of a Nobody
see HUMILIATION 9

3. HARDY, Thomas
Far from the Madding Crowd
(i) pp. 39–42 (Ch. 5) (ii) pp. 44–48
'One night, when Farmer Oak ... and nothing more.'
Gabriel's younger, over-zealous sheep dog exceeds his duties. He herds two hundred ewes to their deaths, in a chalk-pit. With them, go Gabriel's hopes of prosperity, as a property-owning sheep-farmer.

4. HEMINGWAY, Ernest
The Old Man and the Sea
see SHARKS 7

5. NESBIT, E.
The Railway Children
(i) pp. 1–12 (Ch. 1); (ii) pp. 9–19
'They were not railway ... Ruth was sent away.'
Roberta, Peter and Phyllis have a happy home life until one evening their father is called away. Their whole life changes – servants are sent away, Mother is absent often, and begs them to be good and helpful.

6. WELLS, H.G.
Kipps
pp. 355–358 (Bk. 3, Ch. 3, Sn. 1)
'Next morning came a remarkable ... in the chiffonier.'
A telegram arrives which heralds financial ruin for the Kippses. Their solicitor has speculated with their inheritance, and lost the lot. Kipps is frantic and disposed to act violently.

MISSIONARIES

1. ACHEBE, Chinua
   Things fall apart
   (i) pp. 124–127 (Ch. 15); (ii) pp. 124–127
   'Have you heard?' asked Obierika ... where everybody is like them?'
   A white man comes to the village of Abame in Nigeria. The oracle has told the villagers that the white man will do them harm, so they kill him. Some weeks later, white men come again, and slaughter the villagers while they are at market. Few survive the massacre.

2. ibid.
   (i) pp. 131–134 (Ch. 16); (ii) pp. 131–134
   'The arrival of the missionaries ... mind was greatly puzzled.'
   The white man brings his curious and paradoxical religion to the Ibo tribesmen of Nigeria. The missionaries and their interpreters are mocked by most, but there are those to whom the poetry of this creed appeals.

3. ibid.
   (i) pp. 135–138 (Ch. 17); (ii) pp. 135–138
   'The missionaries spent their first ... It was a good riddance.'
   The elders of the village of Mbanta are tolerant of the white man and his new religion, in the belief that their own gods will teach him a lesson. But the church remains unmolested and makes its first converts.

4. ibid.
   see BRITISH EMPIRE – NIGERIA 2

5. ibid.
   (i) pp. 166–172 (Ch. 22); (ii) pp. 166–172
   'Mr Brown's successor ... spirit of the clan was pacified.'
   Mr Smith is a zealous, uncompromising missionary. One of his likeminded followers provokes a clash with the spirits and leaders of Umuofia. Mr Smith stands his ground with courage, but he cannot prevent his church being burnt down.

MONARCHY

see KINGS

MONDAY

1. SILLITOE, Alan
   Saturday Night and Sunday Morning
   see FACTORIES 3

2. TWAIN, Mark
   The Adventures of Tom Sawyer
   see TEETH 1

MONSTERS

see also: DRAGONS;
FEAR (of) MONSTERS;
RUNNING AWAY (from) MONSTERS

MONSTERS

1. CALDWELL, John
   Desperate Voyage
   see ISLANDS 1

2. HUGHES, Ted
   The Iron Man
   pp. 19–22 (Ch. 2)
   'One evening a farmer's son ... back into the sea.'
   The Iron Man climbs up out of the sea. Hogarth tells his father, and his father tells all the other farmers in the area. For most of them, the first real evidence to support Hogarth's story, is that their farm machinery has been eaten.
   see also: MYSTERIES 5

3. ibid.
   pp. 38–43 (Ch. 4)
   'One day there came ... the size of Italy.'
   A vast and terrifying monster flies out of an invading star, and lands on Australia. The world has watched it coming, and now it watches and waits, in fear and trembling.
   see also: CHALLENGES 6

4. WELLS, H.G.
   The Time Machine
   see HORROR 18
5. WELLS, H.G.
   The War of the Worlds
   (i) pp. 16–19 (Bk. 1, Ch. 4); (ii) pp. 23–26
   'When I returned to the Common ... pawing the ground.'
   A metal disc on the grounded cylinder unscrews, and a grey writhing creature emerges, having large staring eyes, and many tentacles. The crowd around the pit recoils; all but one man, who falls into the pit, and is lost.
6. ibid.
   see HORROR 19
7. ibid.
   (i) pp. 59–62 (Bk. 1, Ch. 12); (ii) pp. 66–69
   'We remained at Weybridge ... into the river out of my sight.'
   The Martians are spotted, advancing towards Chertsey. They bring the heat-ray into action with deadly effect. There is panic by the Thames, among the boats. The author jumps into the river to be safe from the flames, but he can't resist a jump of jubilation when the gun batteries fell one of the giants.
8. ibid.
   (i) pp. 166–170 (Bk. 2, Ch. 8); (ii) pp. 176–180
   'It was already past noon ... summit of Primrose Hill.'
   London is a dead city, and the writer is the only mortal alive in it – or so he supposes. He hears the wailing of a Martian, but he is past fear. He approaches it, and is prepared to surrender himself to the monster; but he sees that the power of the Martians is at an end; they have fallen to bacteria.
9. WYNDHAM, John
   The Kraken Wakes
   pp. 134–143 (Phase Two)
   'Down by the waterfront ... my feelings on it quite a bit.'
   The monsters come up from the sea and wreak havoc in the village square, until they are dive-bombed. Their movements are closely observed and recorded. Phyllis is saved by her husband from certain death.

MOORS

see also: LOST (on) MOORS

MOORS

1. DU MAURIER, Daphne
   Jamaica Inn
   pp. 33–35 (Ch. 4)
   'The Moors were even wilder ... there was silence.'
   Mary Yellan explores the moors for the first time, and finds them bleak and mysterious.
2. ibid.
   pp. 78–82 (Ch. 6)
   'The two women ... hopelessly lost.'
   In trying to follow Joss Merlyn, Mary gets completely lost – the ground is difficult and marshy, and she is caught in the mist. She is found by Francis Davey, Vicar of Altarnum.
3. MADDOCK, Reginald
   The Pit
   pp. 16–20 (Ch. 2)
   'I made for the Moors ... sadder sheep than that one.'
   On the run from school, Butch Reece makes for the moors, where he climbs his favourite hill and thinks. He takes up a personal challenge by wading from tussock to squelching tussock, across a dangerous bog. He then frees a ewe from entwining gorse, and finds her lamb in still worse case.

MORNING

see also: DAWN;
MEALS – BREAKFASTS

MORNING

1. ADAMS, Richard
   Watership Down

pp. 92–96 (Ch. 14)

'When Hazel woke ... with his front paws.'

The rabbits wake in their new warren, and are taken out by their hosts to feed on rubbish dumped by the farmer. It is a beautiful morning, and they are glad to feed in peace at last.

2. HUGHES, Thomas
   Tom Brown's Schooldays
   see TRAVEL (by) STAGE-COACH 3

3. O'BRIEN, Edna
   The Country Girls
   pp. 5–8 (Ch. 1)
   'I wakened quickly ... The tea was cold.'
   Caithleen wakes up early, and during her morning routine we learn a lot about her family and their circumstances. She dresses, doesn't wash and goes down to breakfast of boiled egg from their own hens.

4. SOUTHALL, Ivan
   Josh
   pp. 15–18 (Ch. 4)
   'A jug with blue flowers on it ... You poor old thing.'
   Josh wakes up on the first morning of his holiday with Aunt Clara. The room is unfamiliar, he can't find the bathroom, and Clara tantalises him with a huge cup of tea. He rushes out to a toilet across the yard, and falls over the cat.

5. WATERHOUSE, Keith
   Billy Liar
   pp. 6–11 (Ch. 1)
   'It was a day for big decisions ... live somewhere else.'
   Billy Fisher's morning routine never varies, even to the deep-breathing, the toe exercising and the inane conversation he has with his parents and grandmother when he goes down late to breakfast.

MOTHERS

see also: DEATH (of) MOTHER; FAMILY

MOTHERS

1. BARSTOW, Stan
   Joby
   see HOSPITALS 1

2. CARY, Joyce
   The Horse's Mouth
   pp. 196–200 (Ch. 24)
   'Neat little terrace house ... That's safe.'
   Nosy Barbon's mother does not approve of her son's ambition to be an artist, and she does not hide her contempt for Gulley Jimson, his painter friend.

3. DICKENS, Charles
   Bleak House
   (i) pp. 33–35 (Ch. 4), (ii) pp. 33–35
   'Mrs Jellyby ... on Africa again.'
   Esther and Ada are introduced into the Jellyby household, where they find Mrs Jellyby so preoccupied with African affairs that she has no time for her children, not even with heads through railings or falling downstairs.

4. ibid.
   (i) pp. 93–97 (Ch. 8); (ii) pp. 93–97
   'These young ladies ... compliment of being natural.'
   Mrs Pardiggle introduces her children to Esther and Ada – each has been forced to contribute to the 'good causes' she supports, and their resentment is clearly seen, both in her presence and out of it.

5. GASKELL, Mrs
   Cranford
   see RUNNING AWAY (from) HOME 3

6. HINES, Barry
   A Kestrel for a Knave
   (i) pp. 22–25, (ii) pp. 18–20
   'The estate was teeming ... wait 'til tonight.'
   Billy comes home after his paper round to find his mother dressing after her night with Reg. She is off hand with Billy until he refuses to run an errand for her on the ground that he will be late for school; then she domineers.

7. LAWRENCE, D.H.
Sons and Lovers
see BABIES 1

8. ibid.
see JEALOUSY 8

9. ibid.
see DEATH (of) MOTHER 4

10. LEACH, Christopher
Answering Miss Roberts
see ADOPTION 3

11. LEE, Laurie
Cider with Rosie
(i) pp. 93–94 (Ch. 7 'Mother'); (ii)
pp. 126–127
(Impact Two, pp. 182–183)
'Our Mother ... her jaunty spirit.'
Lee describes his extravagant romantic mother, and how she brought them
up to have a sense of beauty.

12. WRIGHT, Richard
Black Boy
pp. 72–74 (Ch. 3)
'My mother became too ill ... I could
not answer.'
Richard's mother suffers a stroke.
Richard has been working for a while,
to help support the family, but now
for the first time, he looks ahead to
the insecurity of life without his
mother.

MOTHERS (and) DAUGHTERS

1. FRANK, Anne
The Diary of Anne Frank
pp. 73–74 (2.4.43)
'Oh, dear ... when they do hear it.'
Anne has offended her mother by
refusing her offer of saying her
prayers with her, but she defends her
refusal. By her criticisms of her
daughter, her mother has, in Anne's
eyes, repudiated her, and the love
between them has gone.

2. ibid.
see PARENTS 2

3. ibid.
pp. 109–110 (24.12.43)
'In spite of all ... make her unhappy.'
Anne is feeling depressed by their
confinement in 'The Secret Annexe' –

she is lonely, and regrets that she
cannot turn to her mother for help
and comfort.

4. ibid.
pp. 111–114 (2.1.44–5.1.44)
'This morning ... in her heart.'
Looking back over her diary entries,
Anne is shocked to see how bitter she
was about her mother in the early
days. She has since matured, and
realises that the fault is as much on
her side. She accepts and tries to
adapt to the present situation, understanding both herself and her mother
better.

5. ibid.
pp. 119–120 (12.1.44)
'Everyone here is reading ... all
about it.'
Anne looks again at her disappointment in her mother, and regrets
her mother's lack of response to her
overtures.

MOTHERS (and) SONS

see also: QUARRELS – MOTHERS (and)
SONS

MOTHERS (and) SONS

1. BALDWIN, James
Go Tell it on the Mountain
pp. 26–28 (Part 1, 'The Seventh
Day')
'Then his mother called him ... Your
daddy gets home.'
An affecting scene between Johnny
and his mother. He helps her about
the house, and she pays him in
birthday money, and implicit love. He
wants to please her, so he expresses
love for the Lord, because he knows
that this of all things will please her
most.

2. LAWRENCE, D.H.
Sons and Lovers
see JEALOUSY 8

MOTORING

see TRAVEL (by) CAR

MOUNTAINS

see also: LOST (in) MOUNTAINS

MOUNTAINS

1. HEYERDAHL, Thor
   The Kon-Tiki Expedition
   pp. 47–50 (Ch. 3)
   'It was good going ... the embrace of welcome.'
   Heyerdahl, and one of his companions have to cross the Andes in search of balsa wood. They pass through Indian villages, cross deserts of sand and cactus, reach freezing heights, and finally drop down into the jungle. Here they have to cross a river with their jeep on a balsa raft.
2. SPYRI, Johanna
   Heidi
   pp. 29–32 (Ch. 3)
   'It was very beautiful ... over the grey peaks.'
   Heidi goes up the mountain with Peter and his goats, to their pasture. She is thrilled with all she sees – the bright flowers, the craggy slopes and peaks, and the enormous hawk circling overhead.

MURDER

see KILLING

MUSIC

see also: CHRISTMAS – CAROLS;
ORGAN;
PIANO;
SINGING;
SONGS (and) RHYMES

MUSIC

1. FORSTER, E.M.
   Howard's End
   pp. 31–33 (Ch. 5)
   'For the Andante had begun ... he says other things.'
   A concert of Beethoven's Fifth Symphony – Helen Schlegel sees a complete fantasy world of heroes and goblins as she listens.

MUSIC – JAZZ

1. HILDICK, E.W.
   Birdy in Amsterdam
   pp. 83–91 (Ch. 9)
   'The Inferno was what ... impressed' he said.'
   Birdy and Fixer visit a club in Amsterdam. They are amazed at the noise, the variety of dress of the audience, and the skill of the main attraction of the evening – a group of Jazz musicians.

MUSIC – POP

1. MANKOWITZ, Wolf
   Make me an Offer
   pp. 74–78 ('Expresso Bongo')
   'I knew Bongo ... I love those words.'
   The narrator is promoting a teenage pop-star, starting him off in a coffee bar. A record company talent-spotter admits to hating the sound but seeing money in it.

MUTINY

1. FORESTER, C.S.
   The Gun
   see REVOLT 1
2. STEVENSON, R.L.
   Treasure Island
   pp. 66–72 (Ch. 11)
   ' 'No, not I,' ... shouted 'Land-ho!' '
   Jim overhears a conversation between Silver and two of the sailors during which he learns that many of them are pirates, after Flint's treasure for themselves, and planning mutiny to get it.
3. ibid.
   see SIEGES 4

MYSTERIES

1. BOMBARD, Alain
   The Bombard Story
   see FOG 1
2. FALKNER, J. Meade
   Moonfleet
   see FLOODS 8
3. GRIMBLE, Sir Arthur
   A Pattern of Islands
   see SUPERSTITION 6
4. ibid.
   see MAGIC 3
5. HUGHES, Ted
   The Iron Man
   pp. 31–33 (Ch. 3)
   'So the Spring came ... They did not
   look back.'
   The Iron Man is buried under the hill,
   and no more is heard of him until a
   family picnicking on the hill, lose
   their lunch down a widening crack.
   When an iron hand reaches from this
   crack, the family runs for its car.
6. WELLS, H.G.
   The War of the Worlds
   (i) pp. 8–11 (Bk. 1, Ch. 2); (ii) pp.
   16–19
   'Then came the night ... Ottershaw
   bridge to the sand-pits.'
   A large metal cylinder drops out of
   the sky, into a sand-pit, on Horsell
   Common. Ogilvy connects it with
   recent activity on Mars, and supposes
   that sounds that he hears from inside,
   are the death-yells of Martians roast-
   ing slowly.
7. WYNDHAM, John
   The Day of the Triffids.
   see PLANTS 1, 2
8. WYNDHAM, John
   The Kraken Wakes
   pp. 11–13 (Phase One)
   'I'm a reliable witness ... placid,
   empty, unperturbed.'
   A radio script-writer and his wife
   watch five mysterious fire-balls dive
   into the Atlantic in a hiss of steam.
   The crew is put at action stations, but
   the fireballs disappear without trace,
   and the danger passes.

9. ibid.
   pp. 17–18 (Phase One)
   'I kept that appointment ... they are
   highly vulnerable.'
   A R.A.F. Flight-Lieutenant sees a
   number of U.F.O.'s similar to the
   fireballs seen by the Watsons. He
   signals to them but receives no
   response. He shoots at them and
   destroys one, at some risk to himself.
10. ibid.
    see DIVING 2
11. ibid.
    pp. 94–98 (Phase Two)
    'The meritorious it will be recalled ...
    down there in the Deeps.'
    A number of ships are reported to
    have foundered unaccountably in
    mid-Ocean. Some say the Russians
    are responsible, others blame a mon-
    ster living in the Deeps. The latter
    theory gains ground when an Ameri-
    can flotilla is put to flight.

NAPOLEONIC WARS

see PENINSULAR WAR

NATIVITY PLAYS

see CHRISTMAS – NATIVITY PLAYS

NAVIGATION

see SAILING – NAVIGATION

NAVY

1. FORESTER, C.S.
   The Ship
   pp. 10–15 (Ch. 1)
   'In the galley, the Paymaster ... had
   played their part.'
   The ship's six-hundred-man crew is
   fully fed in half an hour. The Paymaster Commander's carefully-laid
   plans work to perfection, from the
   opening of the tins, to the collection
   of the mess-traps.

NAVY – DISCIPLINE

1. FORESTER, C.S.
   The Ship
   see SECOND WORLD WAR – SEA
   BATTLES 3
2. ibid.
   pp. 79–84 (Ch. 14)
   'On the bridge ... to a close approxi-
   mation.'
   H.M.S. Artemis fires a salvo into the
   Italian battleship and then beats a
   retreat into the smoke-screen. There,
   she almost collides with her sister-ship
   HMS Hera. The captain recalls a
   similar calculated risk taken years
   before, in defiance of strict naval
   discipline.
3. ibid.
   pp. 140–145 (Ch. 22)
   'When that six-inch shell ... filling
   the whole magazine.'
   X-turret is enveloped in flames. The
   gunners evacuate, but the officer in
   charge has to stay to give the order to
   flood the magazine. Ordinary Seaman
   Triggs, his hands burning, turns the
   wheels which let in the sea.

NAVY – SECOND WORLD WAR

see SECOND WORLD WAR – SEA
BATTLES

NEIGHBOURS

1. SILLITOE, Alan
   Saturday Night and Sunday Morning
   pp. 116–121 (Part 1, Ch. 8)
   'House-roofs were flushed ... do his
   fifteen days.'
   An unseemly brawl in the yard. The
   Bulls have accused Arthur of taking
   pot-shots at them with his air-rifle.
   Fred holds them off, but Arthur
   brazens it out. There is slanging,
   scuffling and much opening and shut-
   ting of doors.
2. WELLS, H.G.
   The History of Mr Polly
   pp. 151–156 (Ch. 7, Part 6)

'Then one day Mr Polly ... (Kik)'
said Mr Rusper.'
An argument with another neighbour,
Rusper, follows hard on the heels of a
collision between Polly on his bicycle,
and Rusper's pavement display. Blows
are exchanged. They are bound over
to keep the peace. The entire affair is
undignifying in the extreme.

NEW YEAR

see CELEBRATIONS – NEW YEAR

NEW YORK

1. ALLEN, Walter
   All in a Lifetime
   see TOWNS (and) CITIES 1

NEWSPAPERS

1. BRAITHWAITE, E.R.
   To Sir with Love
   pp. 159–161 (Ch. 20)
   'Later that week ... very distressed
   about the whole thing.'
   Greenslade School is the subject of a
   newspaper report. The school co-
   operates with the reporter and two
   cameramen, in the belief that its
   reputation can only be enhanced by
   publicity. But when the report appears
   it is so edited as to confirm all the
   prejudices of its detractors.
2. TROLLOPE, Anthony
   The Warden
   pp. 130–133 (Ch. 14)
   'Who has not heard ... thunderbolts
   from Mount Olympus.'
   Trollope's satirical view of the power
   of the press, in which he casts the
   newspaper, 'The Jupiter', in the role
   of the god on Mount Olympus. He
   demonstrates how the paper alone
   knows all secrets, and also recognises
   right from wrong.
3. ibid.
   pp. 145–147 (Ch. 15)
   'The fire has gone too far ... the
   paper required it.'

John Bold asks the Editor of The Jupiter to abandon a cause he had previously championed. the editor refuses such 'interference' regardless of the rights or wrongs of the case, thus demonstrating the 'purity' of his motives.

4. WAUGH, Evelyn
    Scoop
    pp. 28–40 (Bk. 1, Ch. 3, Part 2)
    'The bells of St Bride's ... for the evening edition.'
    William Boot, is given his first assignment as a Fleet Street journalist, in error. He is sent to cover the predicament of a cabinet minister's wife, stuck in a public convenience, in her car.

5. ibid.
    pp. 40–42 (Bk. 1, Ch. 3, Part 3)
    'Twenty minutes later ... the middle of July.'
    William is ushered into the formidable presence of Lord Copper of 'The Beast' newspaper. He receives his marching orders, and a concise definition of what the readership will want to read – news that conforms to the paper's policy.

6. ibid.
    pp. 66–67 (Bk. 1, Ch. 5, Part 1)
    'Corder looked at him ... power of the press for you.'
    A seasoned journalist explains to William how a newspaper scoop is the product of ingenuity, rather than of luck. He describes how an eminent American columnist gives rise to a revolution, just by using his imagination.

NIGHT

see also: DAWN;
EVENING

NIGHT

1. GORKY, Maxim
    Childhood

194

(i) pp. 279–282 (Ch. 12); (ii) pp. 201–203
'Except for rainy days, I spent ... harmony with all living things.'
On summer nights, Gorky and his Grandmother sleep out under the stars. His grandmother tells him stories, which heighten all his own impressions of the noise, and the feel of the night. He finds this nighttime closeness to nature, immensely refreshing.

2. GRICE, Frederick
    The Bonny Pit Laddie
    pp. 106–107 (Ch. 13)
    'At the top of the field ... stillness seemed to deepen.'
    Dick is out at night. He listens to all the sounds of the night, and feels its stillness to be almost palpable.

3. LEE, Laurie
    Cider with Rosie
    (i) pp. 114–115 (Ch. 8 'Winter and Summer'); (ii) pp. 153–154
    'When darkness fell ... there even yet.'
    On a hot summer's night the village boys get up to play Fox and Hounds through the moonlit countryside.

4. SAINT-EXUPERY, Antoine de
    Night Flight
    see FLYING (at) NIGHT 1

5. THOMAS, Dylan
    Portrait of the Artist as a Young Dog
    pp. 7–11 ('The Peaches')
    'The grass-green cart ... until I slept.'
    Young Dylan waits for his Uncle Jim to drink his fill at the pub, then rides on the cart with him to his Uncle's farmhouse. His aunt makes him feel warm and welcome, he enjoys a midnight supper, and goes to bed in 'hollow fear' of the dark, benighted house.

6. ibid.
    pp. 62–64 ('Just like little dogs')
    'Standing alone under ... the cherry night.'
    Dylan stands out of the wind, under a railway arch, with two young men who smoke in silence. He makes a

mental catalogue of the sounds he can hear, and of the last things to be seen in the lowering night.

NIGERIA

1. ACHEBE, Chinua
   Things Fall Apart
   passim.
   A Nigerian's eye-view of colonial Nigeria at the end of the nineteenth century: of native life, and of the coming of the missionaries.

NOISE

1. LESSING, Doris
   Nine African Stories
   pp. 187–188 ('The Antheap')
   'It was to this silence ... that real silence had been.'
   Young Tommy grows up in a silent household, beside a noisy mine. One day, the machinery stops and he hears real silence for the first time. He is terrified. All subsequent noises are measured against this silence.

NORMANS

1. TREECE, Henry
   Hounds of the King
   see INVASIONS – NORMANS 1

NOTTINGHAM

1. LAWRENCE, D.H.
   Sons and Lovers
   see TOWNS (and) CITIES 7
2. SILLITOE, Alan
   The Loneliness of the Long Distance Runner
   see FAIRS (and) FETES 7, 8
3. SILLITOE, Alan
   Saturday Night and Sunday Morning
   see FAIRS (and) FETES 9

NUCLEAR WAR

see WAR – NUCLEAR

NURSING

1. BRONTË, Charlotte
   Shirley
   (i) pp. 559–561 (Ch. 32); (ii) pp. 525–527
   'Mr MacTurk, the surgeon ... remembers to obey *me*.'
   Moore undergoes surgery at the hands of Mr MacTurk, then nursing at the hands of Mrs Horsfall. Neither is very gentle, or tender, to their patient, but both mean to cure him.

OCTOPUS

1. DURRELL, Gerald
   Birds, Beasts, and Relatives
   see FISHING 4
2. GRIMBLE, Sir Arthur
   A Pattern of Islands
   pp. 69–70 (Ch. 6)
   'I certainly should ... himself adrift.'
   Arthur's fear of Octopus is heightened by his first-hand view of what a tentacle can do to a man.
3. ibid.
   pp. 74–79 (Ch. 6)
   'But that very quality ... and was sick.'
   He has the opportunity to watch two experienced divers killing octopus: one acts as the bait, the other does the killing. The young men then ask Arthur if he would like to be the bait. He finds it impossible to refuse, his honour being at stake.
4. HEYERDAHL, Thor
   The Kon-Tiki Expedition
   (i) pp. 117–119 (Ch. 5); (ii) pp. 115–118
   'The marine creature ... the zoologists we have met.'
   Heyerdahl and his companions make the acquaintance of squids when they begin to find them on board in the morning. They are puzzled about how they could get there, until they see a shoal of them shoot up out of the water.

5. SPERRY, Armstrong
The Boy who was afraid
see SEA – DIVING 1

OLD AGE

see also: DEATH (in) OLD AGE;
GRANDPARENTS

OLD AGE

1. ALLEN, Walter
All in a Lifetime
pp. 13–16 (Ch. 3)
'Father!' Will said ... I'd committed myself.'
His son and daughter-in-law come to fetch Dad, in the belief that he is too old to cope by himself. Mr Ashted bows to the inevitable, and goes with them, though he knows it is a mistake.
2. ibid.
SEE DEATH 1
3. BARSTOW, Stan
The Human Element
pp. 11–16 ('The End of an Old Song'); (Young Impact 3, pp. 75–82)
'He was already ... she was defeated.'
An old man lies near to death. It is Christmas, and he sets his heart on hearing carols played by the band of which he was once a member. The band comes to play especially for him, so that he dies with a smile on his face.
4. BAWDEN, Nina
Carrie's War
(i) pp. 77–81 (Ch. 7); (ii) pp. 68–73
'April – and Carrie met ... not ordinary.'
Carrie is taken to have tea with an old lady, Mrs Gotobed. She is rather afraid of her, her questions and her strange habit of dressing up in the best clothes of her youth.
5. CARY, Joyce
The Horse's Mouth
pp. 32–38 (Ch. 9)
'But when we came ... and the old Eve.'

Gully Jimson, and a bar-maid friend, visit one of the women of his youth, to enquire after some of his paintings. She is old and haggard, and yet he keeps recognising the old Sara, in looks and behaviour.
6. DE JONG, Meindert
The Wheel on the School
(i) pp. 11–19 (Ch. 2); (ii) pp. 18–24
'Once more Lina ... why yes!'
Grandmother Sibble befriends Lina, who has been left to her own devices by the rest of her friends. Lina is surprised at how understanding she is, and at all she can tell her of the past.
7. DICKENS, Charles
Bleak House
see ECCENTRICS 2
8. DURRELL, Gerald
My Family and Other Animals
pp. 223–227 (Part 3, Ch. 14)
'Mother dear,' Kralefsky called ... whispering court of flowers.'
Gerald is introduced to his tutor's mother. She is a once-beautiful old lady with very long auburn hair. If she is a little eccentric (enjoying as she does, a close personal relationship with flowers), she radiates contentment and dignity.
9. HEMINGWAY, Ernest
The Old Man and the Sea
pp. 5–6, 14–16, 90–93
'He was an old ... Haven't we?';
'When the boy came ... What are we eating'; 'On this circle ... in the water.'
The whole (short) novel is about an old man. The selected passages say something about his character and appearance. The whole story tells of his courage and resoluteness.
10. LEE, Harper
To Kill a Mockingbird
(i) pp. 105–106, 112–114 (Ch. 11);
(ii) pp. 105–106, 111–114
'When we were small ... man who ever lived.'; 'The following Monday ... the day was ours.'
Mrs Henry Lafayette Dubose, a vicious and cantankerous old woman

who appears to take pleasure in abuse: Jem is engaged to read to her, in her sick bed – a job he does not enjoy.

11. LEE, Laurie
    Cider with Rosie
    (i) pp. 58–61 (Ch. 5, 'Grannies in the Wainscot'); (ii) pp. 83–87
    'You going bald ... went to the woods.'
    Laurie Lee describes one of his neighbours, Granny Trill, who seems ancient, keeps eccentric hours, spends time doing her hair and reading an almanac, and tells her life story to the children.

12. ibid.
    (i) pp. 76–78 (Ch. 6, 'Public Death, Private Murder'); (ii) pp. 106–108
    'Winter, of course ... silk handkerchief.'
    The Lees visit Mr and Mrs Davies – Mr Davies is ill, and when they visit again later he is in bed and sinking.

13. ibid.
    (i) pp. 99–100 (Ch. 7, 'Mother'); (ii) pp. 134–135
    'As time went on ... four-year old daughter.'
    Mrs Lee grows old and more eccentric; she loses her sense of time, and lives just as she wants with no family to make demands of her. Her absent husband's death finally unhinges her reason.

14. SASSOON, Siegfried
    Memoirs of a Foxhunting Man
    (i) pp. 57–58 (Part 2, Sn. 3); (ii) pp. 69–71
    'The Tea Tent was ... Flower Show Match.'
    Miss Maskall, born in the year of Waterloo, is stone-deaf and cantankerous. The scourge of Roman Catholics, she is hugely delighted to hear about cheating in the prize vegetable competition.

15. STEINBECK, John
    The Red Pony
    pp. 50–55 (Ch. 2)

'It's an old man outside ... grew on the side-hills.'
An old man, Gitano, comes to the ranch, where he says he was born, and where he says he will die. Carl Tiflin says he must move on. He has no time for sentiment: he judges a man according to his usefulness, in the same way as he judges a horse.

16. THOMPSON, Flora
    Lark Rise to Candleford
    (i) pp. 70–76 ('Lark Rise', Ch. 5); (ii) pp. 76–81
    'The old people who were ... into the eighties.'
    The declining splendour of a couple of country characters: Old Sally and Dick. Their long, low, thatched cottage is full of wild scents and old world hardware; and their garden is full of heavy-scented flowers. Their present is a pot-pourri of their bucolic past.

17. ibid.
    (i) pp. 76–84 ('Lark Rise', ch. 5); (ii) pp. 81–88
    'Sally and Dick were ... tobacco is to a smoker.'
    The domestic economy of Queenie and Twister is more spartan than the above, but it is no less interesting to a young girl. Queenie keeps bees, and a less than hard-working husband. She teaches him a lesson one day, that is never forgotten.

18. ibid.
    (i) pp. 84–87 ('Lark Rise', Ch. 5); (ii) pp. 88–90
    'There had been, when Laura ... that graceful action.'
    The Major is a kind old gentleman. In return for help given to him by their mother, he gives the children little presents. But as he grows old, so his health worsens, and he is consigned to the work-house. He does not go willingly, and in protest at being forced, he dies.

19. SHOLOKHOV, Mikhail
    And Quiet Flows the Don
    see WAR – MEMORIES 1

OMDURMAN, BATTLE

1. CHURCHILL, W.S.
My Early Life
see BATTLES – OMDURMAN – 1898 1

ORGAN

1. THOMAS, Leslie
This Time Next Week
see ACCIDENTS 4

ORPHANS

see also: ADOPTION;
RUNNING AWAY (from) ORPHANAGE

ORPHANS

1. BENTLEY, Phyllis
The Adventures of Tom Leigh
pp. 16–20 (Ch. 2)
'When I came to myself ... and cry like a girl.'
Tom wakes up from a two-week coma. He discovers that he is in a poorhouse, that his father died when he fell on rocks in the dark, and that he has been taken for a vagrant.

2. BRONTË, Charlotte
Jane Eyre
(i) pp. 1–15 (Chs. 1, 2); (ii) pp. 9–20
'There was no possibility ... closed the scene.'
Jane Eyre has been taken in by a very unwilling aunt, and feels herself to be a misfit and a burden on everyone. She tries to please, but is continually tormented and reprimanded. A tussle with her bullying cousin lands her in the red room, as punishment, a room shut up since her uncle's death there.

3. BURNETT, Frances Hodgson
The Secret Garden
pp. 9–12 (Ch. 1)
'At that very moment ... the little rustling snake.'
Cholera breaks out – Mary is frightened by the wailing when her Indian Ayah dies, and shuts herself in her room. Here she is forgotten, in the panic, until she is found two days later when parents and servants have died.

4. GODDEN, Rumer
The Diddakoi
see GYPSIES 4

5. ibid.
pp. 67–70 (Ch. 4)
'Mr Blount fetched Kizzy ... nuns,' said Mrs Cuthbert.'
The court is in session to decide the future of Kizzy, an orphaned half-gypsy. Kizzy demonstrates her contempt for the court, and the court demonstrates its powerlessness over her.

6. HITCHMAN, Janet
The King of the Barbareens
pp. 19–21 (Ch. 1)
'I was becoming too much ... any of its people.'
Gran and Granpa are too old to manage their wayward orphan granddaughter. Despite her promise to the child's mother, and her own good will, Gran surrenders Elsie to officialdom, in the person of Miss Browne.

7. ibid.
pp. 103–105 (Ch. 5)
'I was so used to moving ... morbid fancies.'
Once again, Elsie is on the move, being shunted from one well-meaning foster-mother to the next, and being told to be grateful at every stage. She tries to be likeable, but the deprivation of love she has suffered, will out.

8. MACKEN, Walter
God made Sunday and Other Stories
pp. 65–72 ('God made Sunday')
'One day I found ... and he is still here.'
An orphan boy, in the nominal charge of his wayfaring grandfather, enjoys fishing with Colmain; he is even a positive help to the childless fisherman. Finally, the grandfather shrugs off the boy, and leaves Colmain to pick up the pieces.

9. THOMAS, Leslie
This Time Next Week
pp. 10–14 (Ch. 1)
'I am not going ... a home – once anyway.'
The author is introduced to Dr. Barnardo's. It is an unprepossessing, Victorian building, and the first inmate he meets pronounces life there to be 'bloody 'orrible'.

OTTERS

1. WILLIAMSON, Henry
   Tarka the Otter
   (i) pp. 17–21 (Ch. 1); (ii) pp. 16–19
   'Her dark form ... away from the water.'
   Having hidden from hounds all day the otter is hungry, and leaves her shelter to catch a fish. She is joined by her mate, and they swim together. She eats the sea-trout he catches but doesn't want.
2. ibid.
   (i) pp. 23–28 (Ch. 1); (ii) pp. 22–27
   'The eldest and biggest ... remembering Tarka.'
   Tarka, and his two sisters, spend their first weeks in the security of the holt. When their eyes open after a month, they begin to move, explore and play. Tarka's curiosity soon lands him in trouble.
3. ibid.
   see INITIATION 8, 9
4. ibid.
   (i) pp. 79–80 (Ch. 6); (ii) pp. 81–83
   'Some days after ... a cub called Tarka.'
   The life of the otter family, the games and the hunting together, comes to an end when the bitch leaves the cubs, for a new mate. They cannot understand her behaviour, and Tarka even fights the intruder.

OTTERS – COURTSHIP

1. WILLIAMSON, Henry
   Tarka the Otter

(i) pp. 83–87 (Ch. 7); (ii) pp. 86–90
'He had been travelling ... for her mate.'
Tarka meets a companion of his cubhood, White-tip, and begins an elaborate series of courtship games. Before long, however, an older, more experienced otter takes her away, and Tarka is left to be consoled by White-tip's foster mother.

OUTSIDERS

see also: ECCENTRICS;
INITIATION

OUTSIDERS

1. GODDEN, Rumer
   The Diddakoi
   see GYPSIES 3
2. ibid.
   see BULLYING (by) GIRLS 1
3. GORKY, Maxim
   Childhood
   (i) pp. 150–154; 164–173 (Ch. 8); (ii) pp. 115–118; 125–131
   'Two draymen and a tall glum Tartar ... I retorted and went into the garden.'; 'We had become friends ... who represent its finest sons.'
   'That's Fine' is a boarder in the Kashirin household. Curiosity draws Gorky to him, because he dabbles in chemistry, and has a knack of reading Gorky's mind. But the boy is warned off 'That's Fine', because he is unconventional and might 'teach' Gorky things beyond a Kashirin's understanding.
4. HITCHMAN, Janet
   The King of the Barbareens
   see BULLYING (by) BOYS (and) GIRLS 1
5. LONDON, Jack
   White Fang
   pp. 56–62 (Ch. 6)
   'Lip-Lip continued ... he found himself.'
   Part wolf, part dog, White Fang is shunned by the other dogs of the

Indian camp as an alien. He has to develop a tougher exterior, and a fierce independence in order to survive. It is kill or be killed.

6. SPERRY, Armstrong
   The Boy who was afraid
   pp. 3–10 (Ch. 1)
   'Sometimes now ... who was afraid.'
   Despite his name which means Stout Heart, Mafatu is afraid of the sea, as the result of an accident in his childhood. In a tribe which worships courage, he is considered unworthy by both the adults and by his contemporaries, and given menial tasks to do.

7. THOMPSON, Flora
   Lark Rise to Candleford
   see MADNESS 5

PACIFISM

see FIRST WORLD WAR – PACIFISM

PAINTING

1. CARY, Joyce
   The Horse's Mouth
   pp. 22–25 (Ch. 6)
   ' 'B-but, Mr Jimson ... life isn't worth living.'
   Nosy wants to be an artist, and hangs around Gulley Jimson's studio. Gulley is depressed about his painting, and tries to discourage the boy with the story of his father who lost favour with the R.A.

2. ibid.
   pp. 69–75 (Ch. 13)
   'If while I am dictating ... this rackety life.'
   Gulley Jimson traces his development as a painter, explaining that he 'never meant to be an artist'. His career progressed almost by mistake, as he tried to find his true style.

3. ibid.
   pp. 242–243 (Ch. 30)
   'But afterwards, when I took ... the crickets are right.'
   Gulley Jimson, always on the look-out for somewhere to paint, finds 'a gem'

of a wall. An idea for a raising of Lazarus comes to him, and in no time the outlines are sketched in.

4. LAWRENCE, D.H.
   Sons and Lovers
   see PRIDE 4

5. ibid.
   see COMPETITIONS 2

6. MAUGHAM, W. Somerset
   The Moon and Sixpence
   pp. 46–49 (Ch. 12)
   'He was perfectly cool ... go and have dinner.'
   A painful interview with the errant Strickland. It has been supposed that he left his wife for another woman; but he affirms that he has left her to paint. He is without remorse; his mind is made up.

PANIC

see also: FEAR

PANIC

1. BATES, H.E.
   The Purple Plain
   pp. 63–69 (Ch. 7)
   'She suddenly pointed across ... at last she sat down.'
   A Burmese village has been bombed. The grief-stricken wailing turns to the sounds of protest and panic. Forrester, an R.A.F. officer fears for his jeep, and going to move it gets caught up in the stream of fleeing, panicking villagers.

2. WELLS, H.G.
   The War of the Worlds
   (i) pp. 78–81 (Bk. 1, Ch. 14); (ii) pp. 86–90
   'At that time there was ... again into the streets.'
   London is fired by the news of the approach of the Martians. Rumours and hard facts vie with each other in the popular imagination. Everywhere there is the noise and excitement of mass evacuation.

3. ibid.
(i) pp. 90–91; 95–102 (Bk. 1, Ch. 16); (ii) pp. 99–100; 104–111
'So you understand ... the road to St. Albans'; 'My brother noticed ... my brother had come.'
The roads northwards out of London are crowded with fugitives from the Martians, on foot and in every imaginable conveyance. It is almost impossible to cross this torrent without being carried away by it.

PARENTS

see also: FATHERS;
MOTHERS

PARENTS

1. BUTLER, Samuel
The Way of all Flesh
pp. 253–256 (Ch. 69)
'In coming to the conclusion ... in front of him.'
Ernest's parents meet him at the prison on the day of his release. His sentence has convinced him that his parents' influence on him has not been benign; therefore, he tells them that they must never try to see him again.

2. FRANK, Anne
The Diary of Anne Frank
pp. 47–49 (7.11.42)
(Conflict I, pp. 50–52)
'Mummy is frightfully irritable ... reach bursting point.'
Anne feels somewhat persecuted by her parents, especially as she seems to be told off more than her older sister. She examines her relationship with her parents, and her preference for her father.

3. ibid.
pp. 151–152 (17.3.44)
'A sigh of relief ... good-looking boy.'
Both Anne and Margot resent the fact that they are treated as children by their parents. They have both matured a great deal during their period in hiding, and feel misunderstood.

4. LEACH, Christopher
Answering Miss Roberts
see ADOPTION 2

5. MADDOCK, Reginald
Sell-out
pp. 54–60 (Ch. 6)
'My mother and Walter Higgins ... and I sat in my Dad's chair.'
It comes as quite a shock to Danny to learn from his step-sister, that his mother and Walter Higgins have got married. He is as confused by her obvious bitterness and apprehension, as he is by his own. He truants from school to see if she has told him the truth.

6. STOREY, David
This Sporting Life
see MATERIALISM 4

PARTIES

see also: BIRTHDAYS;
CHRISTMAS;
FAMILY – PARTIES;
FUNERALS;
WEDDINGS

PARTIES

1. ALAIN-FOURNIER
Le Grand Meaulnes
pp. 56–60 (Part 1, Ch. 14)
'It was the sort of meal ... next room was his wife.'
Le Grand Meaulnes, dreaming wakefully, happens on a wedding party in a country château. All is 'en fête', eating, dancing, playing at theatricals. He drifts into a dining-room, where children are looking at albums, and a beautiful girl is playing the piano.
see also: LOVE (at) FIRST SIGHT 1

2. ALCOTT, Louisa M.
Little Women
pp. 46–49 (Ch. 3)
' "Such fun, only see ... be elegant or die.'

Meg and Jo are invited to a New Year's Eve party. They spend much time and trouble on smartening up their worn clothes in order to appear elegant.

3. FITZGERALD, F. Scott
    The Great Gatsby
    pp. 45–47 (Ch. 3)
    (Impact I, p. 29)
    'There was music ... party has begun.'
    A wealthy, but mysterious neighbour of the narrator's holds extravagant parties – marquees, lights, quantities of food, bands, and hordes of uninvited guests.

4. GROSSMITH, George and Weedon
    The Diary of a Nobody
    (i) pp. 84–87 (Ch. 9); (ii) pp. 133–137
    'A red-letter day ... spooney old thing.'
    The Pooters give a party in honour of their son's engagement. There is some 'skylarking' and some anxiety about the adequacy of food and drink. Mr Pooter's employer turns up – he is not amused.

5. ibid.
    see HUMILIATION 10

6. KING, Clive
    Stig of the Dump
    pp. 110–113 (Ch. 7)
    'They came out at last ... each other to be quiet.'
    Barney, as a caveman, and Lou, as a leopard, go to a fancy dress party. There is dancing, a variety of games, and then the lights fuse, and Lou organises a 'leopard-hunt'.

7. MANSFIELD, Katherine
    Bliss and Other Stories
    see CHILDREN 2

8. STOLZ, Mary
    Ready or Not
    pp. 142–145 (Ch. 10)
    'Verna and her mother ... to pile a plate for himself.'
    A noisy teenage party. It is Verna's really, but it has to be held at Betty's because of Verna's disapproving father. It takes a long time to get

going, and when it does, and everyone is dancing, there are hammerings of protest from downstairs.

9. TOLKIEN, J.R.R.
    The Hobbit
    (i) pp. 6–11 (Ch. 1); (ii) pp. 6–11
    'The next day he had ... set out everything afresh.'
    The Hobbit expects (or rather, has forgotten about) a visitor for tea. But he opens the door – repeatedly – to a multitude of visitors, who make free with the contents of his larder.

10. TROLLOPE, Anthony
    Barchester Towers
    pp. 313–315 (Ch. 36)
    'The trouble in civilised life ... Mrs Clantantram was announced.'
    Despite all the apparent difficulties in doing so, Miss Thorne of Ullathorne attempts to 'entertain' the hundreds of guests at her party. She provides countless amusements for them.

11. TROLLOPE, Anthony
    The Warden
    pp. 61–64 (Ch. 6)
    'The party went off ... three and thirty points.'
    The Warden gives a small party. At first there is little mixing, but music for dancing brings the shy young men and women together. The older ones play cards.

12. ZINDEL, Paul
    The Pigman
    pp. 101–109 (Ch. 13)
    'I really did think ... That's when I passed out.'
    With a free hand to treat Mr Pignati's house in his absence, as if it was theirs, John and Lorraine throw a party for their high school friends. By any standards, it is a wild party, and it is reaching a peak of chaos when Mr Pignati returns.

PARTIES – DINNERS

1. COLLINS, Wilkie
    The Moonstone
    pp. 77–80 (1st period, Ch. 10)

'Looking back at the birthday ... over their wine.'

Rachel's birthday dinner is not a success – the company seems ill-assorted, and all manage to make a faux-pas of some sort. Conversation finally dies altogether.

2. FITZGERALD, F. Scott
   The Great Gatsby
   pp. 14–20 (Ch. 1)
   'We walked through ... street at dusk.'
   Nick goes to dinner with his rich and beautiful cousin, Daisy, her husband and a friend, Miss Baker. Conversation is gay, witty and superficial, but there is an under-current of dissatisfaction.

3. GRIMBLE, Sir Arthur
   A Pattern of Islands
   see MEALS – DINNERS 4

PARTIES – TEAS

1. GASKELL, Mrs
   Cranford
   (i) pp. 98–104 (Ch. 7); (ii) pp. 110–114
   'The spring evenings ... much more pressing.'
   Miss Barker invites the genteel ladies of Cranford to tea – she is on the fringes of this circle, and the party is not quite of the type usually given, especially in the matter of food. However, cards are played and there is polite conversation.

2. LEE, Harper
   To Kill a Mockingbird
   (i) pp. 234–237 (Ch. 24); (ii) pp. 231–235
   'Calpurnia wore her ... sin and squalor.' 'Yes, Ma'am.' '
   Scout has to sit in with her Aunt's missionary circle so that she will learn to be a lady. She is taxed about her 'vocation', and is told about the sin and squalor prevailing among the unchristian Mrunas.

PARTING

see LEAVETAKING

PAWNBROKERS

1. ALLEN, Walter
   All in a Lifetime
   pp. 40–42 (Ch. 6)
   'We did not live ... of ritual value only.'
   Every Monday, the Ashteds take their Sunday clothes to the pawnbroker's, and every Saturday they redeem them again, in order to observe the decencies.

2. BAWDEN, Nina
   On the Run
   pp. 112–115 (Ch. 12)
   'The pawn shop ... without looking back.'
   Ben needs money to help a friend, and tries to pawn a prized jade horse. The pawn-broker, seeing its value, refuses to lend money on it, but buys it at a ridiculously low price.

3. GREENWOOD, Walter
   Love on the Dole
   pp. 30–32 (Part 1, Ch. 4)
   'He glanced at the ... in this perplexing world.'
   It is Monday morning and the housewives of Salford come to the pawnshop to pawn what little finery there is in their lives, for the week's groceries.

PEACE

see CELEBRATIONS – PEACE;
FIRST WORLD WAR – PACIFISM

PEARL-FISHING

see FISHING (for) PEARLS

PEASANTS' REVOLT

1. ROBINSON, Rony
   A Walk to see the King
   see KINGS 3

2. ibid.
pp. 96–99 (Ch. 43)
'The King called for tea ... the young king had been.'
Richard commands history to be written in his own image. He recounts his version of how the Peasants' Revolt came to nothing, when Wat Tyler drew his sword in the King's presence, and was killed by the King's loyal servants. Richard is confident of history's approval.

PEDLARS

see also: SALESMEN

PEDLARS

1. DURRELL, Gerald
   My Family and Other Animals
   pp. 46–50 (Part 1, Ch. 3)
   (Young Impact 1, pp. 15–16)
   'Perhaps one of the most weird ... to and fro, dimly and heavily.'
   The rose-beetle man wears a motley collection of clothing, and carries on his back, in his pockets, and on his hat, a fascinating menagerie: including birds, beetles, and tortoises. The pedlar is dumb, but not uncommunicative.
2. ELIOT, George
   The Mill on the Floss
   pp. 384–394 (Part 5, Ch. 2)
   'You needn't stay ... a shameful price.'
   Bob Jakin, a packman, sees that Mrs Clegg, for all her superior ways, will be prey to a litle flattery. Without her realising what is happening, he bargains with her over some cloth, and ends up somewhat the richer.

PENINSULAR WAR

1. BRONTË, Charlotte
   Shirley
   see SELFISHNESS 1
2. FORESTER, C.S.

204

The Gun
see SIEGES 2

PENINSULAR WAR – BATTLES

1. FORESTER, C.S.
   The Gun
   (i) pp. 76–97 (Ch. 10); (ii) pp. 66–87
   'There was something ... the foot of the wall.'
   A small French garrison guarding a bridge is attacked by a band of guerilleros. The French commander is confident, until he sees and experiences the massive gun they have. He refuses to surrender – the building is virtually destroyed, and the attack is swift and merciless, leaving no Frenchman alive.
2. ibid.
   (i) pp. 178–187 (Ch. 19); (ii) pp. 150–158
   'Jorge left the gun ... would not close.'
   The guerilleros, with their massive gun, ambush a famous and confident French regiment, which is powerless against the gun. Wholesale slaughter follows.

PENINSULAR WAR – RETREAT

1. FORESTER, C.S.
   The Gun
   (i) pp. 1–6 (Ch. 1); (ii) pp. 5–9
   'A defeated army ... plains to Madrid.'
   The defeated, ragged, wounded Bourbon army is retreating through the mountains of Galicia, from the French. It is winter, and progress is exceptionally slow and difficult. An enormous gun has to be abandoned when it overturns.

PERSEVERANCE

see DETERMINATION

PETS

1. DURRELL, Gerald
   My Family and Other Animals
   see TORTOISES 1
2. ibid.
   see SCORPIONS 2
3. ibid.
   see TOADS 1
4. ibid.
   see DOGS 3
5. HINES, Barry
   A Kestrel for a Knave
   (i) pp. 142–147; (ii) pp. 116–119
   'Mr Farthing followed ... out of the shed.'
   Billy shows off his kestrel to Mr Farthing, his teacher. Billy is proud of his pet, and he and Mr Farthing grope for words to express the differentness of the bird from other pets.
6. HUGHES, Richard
   A High Wind in Jamaica
   (i) pp. 237–239 (Ch. 9, Part 3); (ii) pp. 161–163
   'For a few moments ... utterly untamable.'
   Harold, a young acquaintance of Emily's keeps a year-old alligator. Emily borrows the alligator for a night – she lets it crawl into her night-gown – so that she can say, 'There was once a girl called Emily, who slept with an alligator ...'
7. LESSING, Doris
   Nine African Stories
   see DEATH (of) ANIMALS 2

PIANO-PLAYING

1. CHURCH, Richard
   Over the Bridge
   pp. 93–97 (Ch. 9)
   'After this glorious defeat ... to which he agreed.'
   For some time, Jack has extracted self-taught sounds out of the old Broadwood White Piano. Then a piano-tuner comes and puts magic into the Beethoven Sonata with which Jack has been wrestling for so long.
2. ibid.
   pp. 109–112 (Ch. 10)
   'Then, one day toward Christmas ... The new piano come?'
   Jack's persistence is rewarded. His parents have acquired a Lingmann piano – a pianist's instrument. Jack seats himself at it with proper gravity, and is inspired.
3. THOMAS, Leslie
   This Time Next Week
   pp. 126–130 (Ch. 12)
   'In the summer the mudpatch ... more either. It's possible.'
   Leslie learns to appreciate music, in spite of himself. He treks miles to concerts, and even shells out a large part of his pocket money to take piano-lessons. But the old dear, his teacher, has neither a very grand piano, nor a very wide repertoire.

PICKPOCKETS

1. DEFOE, Daniel
   Moll Flanders
   see STEALING 1
2. ibid.
   (i) pp. 181–182; (ii) pp. 201–202
   'The next thing of moment ... is to be transported.'
   Confirmed in her life of crime by repeated success, Moll is ever on the watch for a prize. A lady obliges with a gold one, in a crowd thick enough to obscure the theft. A young fellow is suspected and dealt street justice.
   see also: SHOPLIFTING 4
3. ibid.
   (i) pp. 192–194; (ii) pp. 212–214
   'It was now a merry time ... and his purse of gold.'
   A gentleman of good breeding, but of weak head, befriends Moll at Bartholomew Fair. Befuddled with drink, he is nevertheless chivalrous, and when he brings Moll to bed, it is with her consent. But she relieves him of

his portable assets, as he sleeps, for
services rendered.
4. ibid.
(i) pp. 221–223; (ii) pp. 242–243
'The next day I dressed ... visit my
Lady Betty.'
Moll tricks the footman of a young
girl of means, into giving her information about her. Then she tricks the
girl into believing she is a friend of
the family, getting close enough to
her in the crowd, to steal her gold
watch.

PICNICS

1. JEROME, Jerome K.
   Three Men in a Boat
   pp. 115–117 (Ch. 12)
   'To return to our present trip ... we
   reached Maidenhead.'
   The party eats cold beef. It is a pity
   there is no mustard – but the craving
   passes. But when there is no tin-
   opener to open the pineapples, the
   party waxes frenzied. But not even
   frenzy will open the tin, so it's consigned to the river.

PIGS

1. LAWRENCE, D.H.
   The White Peacock
   pp. 229–230 (Part 2, Ch. 6)
   'During Leslie's illness ... as she
   rolled past.'
   Cyril watches George feeding the
   pigs. Ten piglets leave no room for the
   eleventh. George gives them their
   head for a while, then he kicks them
   aside to allow the shrieking runt to
   sate himself.

PIRATES

1. STEVENSON, R.L.
   Treasure Island
   pp. 1–7 (Ch. 1)
   'I remember him ... many evenings
   to come.'
   A frightening old sailor comes to

lodge at the inn of Jim's father. He
tells terrifying tales of pirates, he
drinks and rages at other customers,
and he enlists Jim's help in looking
out for a 'sea-faring man with one
leg'.
2. ibid.
   see MUTINY 2

PLANTS

1. WYNDHAM, John
   The Day of the Triffids
   pp. 37–41 (Ch. 2)
   'My introduction to a triffid ... the
   remains on a bonfire.'
   The triffids begin to excite attention.
   They walk, and more seriously, they
   pack a poisonous punch which the
   young Bill Mason is lucky to survive.
2. ibid.
   pp. 46–48 (Ch. 2)
   'The sun was close ... I'd put my
   money on.'
   In addition to their other accom-
   plishments, the triffids are suspected
   of being able to talk to each other,
   and of being intelligent.
3. ibid.
   see DISASTERS 2

PLATYPUS

1. MARSHALL, James Vance
   Walkabout
   (i) pp. 76–77 (Ch. 15); (ii) pp. 98–99
   'When the children ... gently rising
   valley.'
   The children watch three platypuses
   playing in a shallow muddy pool.
   They are the strangest creatures they
   have ever seen. Peter steps on a twig,
   and frightens them back into the deep
   safety of their burrows.

POACHING

1. BALDWIN, Michael
   Grandad with Snails
   pp. 102–106 (Ch. 12)

'The sun came leaping ... tomorrow in the hedge.'
Silky takes Michael shooting with him. They are supposed to be after rabbits, so Michael is surprised when Silky shoots two cock-pheasants. Michael hides the pheasants, and Silky hides the gun.

2. HUGHES, Thomas
   Tom Brown's Schooldays
   see FISHING 10

3. LAWRENCE, D.H.
   The White Peacock
   pp. 78–80 (Part 1, Ch. 6)
   'We set off at a swinging pace ... 'Good night.' '
   The gamekeeper surprises George and Cyril in the dark of the evening. He has a rabbit and one of George's snares. George demands these, but the gamekeeper refuses to deliver them up, and to clinch the argument he fells first George, then Cyril.

4. WILLIAMSON, Henry
   Tarka the Otter
   (i) pp. 67–68 (Ch. 5); (ii) pp. 70–72
   (i) 'The ominous sound ... dogs be about.' (ii) 'A low sound ... dogs be about.'
   On a cloudy night, the otters see some men spearing fish by torch-light with a pitchfork. The attempt is unsuccessful – one man is speared by the pitchfork, and a boy drops the fish when he is bitten by an otter.

POETRY

see also: WRITING (and) WRITERS

POETRY

1. FORESTER, C.S.
   The Ship
   pp. 86–89; 91–92 (Ch. 15)
   'How're you getting on ... as used by Keats in 'St Agnes' '; 'Up to the present moment ... seek out her enemies once more.'
   The captain's secretary discovers a poet. He is a curly pompom gunner,

and a genius. He writes Shakespearean sonnets to a Gravesend barmaid. In the wake of an encounter with Italian bombers, he feels a sonnet-cycle coming on.

2. JOYCE, James
   Dubliners
   see AMBITIONS – WRITING 1

3. WOOLF, Virginia
   Orlando
   pp. 61–63 (Ch. 2)
   'But it was not until the Malmsey ... another glass of wine.'
   Orlando discusses with the poet Nick Greene, work of contemporary poets – great Elizabethans all. Greene is scathing.

4. ibid.
   pp. 71–73 (Ch. 2)
   'Another metaphor, by Jupiter! ... nothing whatever.'
   In search of truth, Orlando dabbles with images. He is out for fame as a poet, but nothing works – until he realises he has been writing to please everyone else but himself.

POLICE

see also: ARREST;
ESCAPE (from) POLICE;
FEAR (of) POLICE

POLICE

1. LEACH, Christopher
   Answering Miss Roberts
   see PROTEST 5

2. MANKOWITZ, Wolf
   Make me an Offer
   see ESCAPE (from) POLICE 1

3. NAUGHTON, Bill
   Late Night on Watling Street
   see ACCIDENTS – ROAD 4

4. ORWELL, George
   Animal Farm
   see GOVERNMENT – DICTATORSHIP 2

5. ORWELL, George
   1984
   see FREEDOM 3

6. ibid.
   see ARREST 12
7. STEINBECK, John
   The Grapes of Wrath
   (i) pp. 204–205 (Ch. 19); (ii) pp. 215–217
   'There's thirty thousan' ... nothin' that'll stop 'em.'
   The unemployed, hungry migrants to California covet any uncultivated piece of land, and some even dare to plant vegetables. They are soon dissuaded by the police who ruin the crops, and chase off the trespassers.
8. ibid.
   (i) pp. 228–233 (Ch. 20); (ii) pp. 240–245
   'A new Chevrolet coupe ... look of conquest.'
   An employer comes to the migrants' camp looking for labourers, but when some of the men press their claims too hard he calls his companion from the car – the deputy sheriff. Trouble breaks out and the deputy sheriff is knocked out.
9. TATE, Joan
   Sam and Me
   see STEALING (of) BABIES 1

POLITICS

see also: AUTHORITY;
CAPITALISM;
COMMUNISM;
GOVERNMENT;
SOCIALISM

POLITICS

1. ALLEN, Walter
   All in a Lifetime
   pp. 136–138 (Ch. 12)
   'When the Independent Labour ... as they always do!'
   The newly-formed Independent Labour Party has a hard job establishing itself; and Billy has a hard job holding an audience, as a pavement speaker. He has none of the

fire of his colleague, George Thompson.
2. BALCHIN, Nigel
   The Small Back Room
   pp. 36–38 (Ch. 3)
   'The Old Man ... introduced us to him.'
   The Minister comes to look round the offices of the research team. Careful preparations precede his visit, but it is evident that the Minister is quite out of his depth.

POLITICS – ELECTIONS

1. ALLEN, Walter
   All in a Lifetime
   pp. 177–180 (Ch. 14)
   'At the General Election ... that defiantly enough.'
   A safe Tory seat falls to the Labour candidate. It is 1924, and the Labour Party is a new force. It is one with which the 'safe Tory' has not reckoned.

POP MUSIC

see MUSIC – POP

POPE

1. GALLICO, Paul
   The Snow Goose/The Small Miracle
   see FAITH 3

POTTERY

1. DEFOE, Daniel
   Robinson Crusoe
   (i) pp. 89–90; (ii) pp. 120–122 (Ch. 11)
   ' 'It would make the reader ... have had it been.'
   Man the potter. Crusoe badly needs vessels of some kind for cooking and storage; so by dint of much unsuccessful experiment he fashions crude pots for his use.

POVERTY

see also: HOMELESSNESS;
HUNGER;
TRAMPS

POVERTY

1. ALLEN, Walter
    All in a Lifetime
    see PAWNBROKERS 1
2. BENTLEY, Phyllis
    The Adventures of Tom Leigh
    see ORPHANS 1
3. BRONTË, Charlotte
    Shirley
    (i) pp. 138–141 (Ch. 8); (ii) pp. 158–160
    'Farren, as he went home ... my friends!' they separated.'
    Farren has been made redundant at the mill. His home is clean, but bare. It is a house in which the Rev. Hall sees want and coming misery. Mr Hall knows Farren to be a good man, therefore he lends him money.
    see also: PRIDE 1
4. DEFOE, Daniel
    Moll Flanders
    see SHOPLIFTING 3
5. DICKENS, Charles
    Bleak House
    (i) pp. 125–126 (Ch. 10); (ii) pp. 125–126
    'The air of the room ... down upon the bed.'
    Mr. Tulkinghorn, the lawyer visits the room of Nemo, a law-writer. It is dark, dirty and almost bare. Nemo accords well with the appearance of his room.
6. ibid.
    (i) pp. 202–204 (Ch. 16); (ii) pp. 202–204
    'Jo sweeps his crossing ... beginning to close in.'
    Jo, the crossing-sweeper's life and surroundings are described – he lives in a decaying slum, Tom-all-Alone's, he is totally ignorant except of his own job, and he is pushed around by the rest of the world.
7. ibid.
    (i) pp. 285–286 (Ch. 22); (ii) pp. 285–286
    'When they come ... by way of table.'
    Mr Bucket and Mr Snagsby walk through Tom-all-Alone's, a decaying slum in London, where they see filth and ruins, pass a fever case and look for Jo, the crossing-sweeper.
8. DICKENS, Charles
    A Tale of Two Cities
    pp. 36–39 (Book 1, Ch. 5)
    'A large cask of wine ... took no warning.'
    A cask of wine falls from a cart and spills its contents in the street. The starving joyless inhabitants of St. Antoine in Paris make merry with what they can save, but it does little to ease the misery of their situation.
9. FOAKES, Grace
    Between High Walls
    pp. 49–52 (Ch. 25)
    'I believe it was ... pleasures and were happy.'
    Hard times in East London before the First World War. The author's father is forward in a strike at the docks and he loses his job. The children eat at the Soup Kitchens and the East End Mission. There is pilfering and a widespread drowning of sorrows.
10. FORSTER, E.M.
    Howard's End
    pp. 179–180 (Ch. 22)
    'A word of advice ... are in pain.'
    Mr Wilcox puts forward his views on helping the poor – one must not be sentimental, it is destined that there shall be rich people and poor people in the world.
11. GORKY, Maxim
    Childhood
    (i) pp. 304–310 (Ch. 13); (ii) pp. 218–222
    'Once more I was living ... five or ten copecks apiece.'
    The Kashirin household is at its

lowest ebb. Grandfather and grandmother divide what few spoils there
are left to be divided. Much is sold.
Gorky earns a few copecks by collecting rubbish and selling it to scrap-
merchants. What he doesn't earn, he
steals, as almost everyone in his part
of the town accounts it no sin to do.

12. HAUGAARD, Erich
    The Little Fishes
    see HUNGER 6

13. LEE, Harper
    To Kill a Mockingbird
    (i) pp. 176–177 (Ch. 17); (ii) pp.
    173–175
    'Every town the size ... his skin was
    white.'
    The Ewell family: 'poor white trash'
    of colour-conscious Alabama. They
    live in a shack by the refuse heap; but
    they are white, therefore are not alto-
    gether outcast.

14. ORWELL, George
    1984
    (i) pp. 165–168 (Ch. 7, Part 2); (ii)
    pp. 131-133
    'His father had disappeared ... or
    other to die.'
    Winston remembers his childhood
    when he fought his mother and sister
    to get more food.

15. SEWELL, Anna
    Black Beauty
    pp. 173–176 (Ch. 39)
    'One day, a shabby ... a warning for
    us.'
    A cabman tells of his hard life in
    London in the 1870's. He defends his
    shabby overworked horse, and his
    apparent cruelty by showing how hard
    he has to work to make any profit at
    all.

16. STEINBECK, John
    The Grapes of Wrath
    see SELFISHNESS 10

POWER

see AUTHORITY

PRANKS

see also: ESCAPADES;
TEASING

PRANKS

1. BALDWIN, Michael
   Grandad with Snails
   pp. 28–35 (Ch. 5)
   'We did not smash ... policeman had
   gone for hours.'
   Michael's gang torments a neighbour,
   by poking out the panes of his
   glasshouse, through a hole in the
   fence. They tire of single panes, after
   a while, and break the lot. Trouble
   ensues, but sweet-as-pie Michael
   keeps out of his way.

2. ibid.
   pp. 38–44 (Ch. 4)
   (Family and School, pp. 43–46)
   'We started to play a new sort ... The
   strap was their only revenge.'
   Michael and his gang are the terrors
   of the street: they tie door knockers
   together (with hilarious results), per-
   secute the milkmen (as well as his
   customers), and hide workmen's ladders, while they are still up them.

3. ibid.
   see HORROR 1

4. ibid.
   pp. 158–163 (Ch. 19)
   'The corpse hung against ... front
   door to my mother.'
   Tony and Michael hang a dummy
   corpse from a pine-tree, one moonlit
   night. Then they sit back to await
   developments. But these threaten to
   be complicated; so they cut the
   dummy down, and run home with it.

5. BENTLEY, Phyllis
   Gold Pieces
   see ADOLESCENCE – BOYS 2

6. GASKELL, Mrs
   Cranford
   (i) pp. 75–79 (Ch. 6); (ii) pp. 93–96
   'Poor Peter's career ... flogged Peter.'
   Peter does not live up to the expec-
   tations of his family – instead of

studying seriously he spends much time on practical jokes. His sister recounts two of these, the second resulting in a very severe punishment.

7. GORKY, Maxim
Childhood
(i) pp. 257–259 (Ch. 11); (ii) pp. 187–188
'Well, so they moved into the wing ... him as much as you liked.'
Maxim enjoys playing practical jokes. He puts glass jars in the window, so that the wind whistles among them, and alarms the superstitious Kashirins. When wolves enter the town because of the cold, Maxim stuffs the heads of dead ones, and scares neighbours out of their wits.

8. HILDICK, E.W.
Louie's Lot
pp. 108–117 (Chs. 20, 21)
'It was on the third morning ... his quick efficient service.'
Jim is doing well on the milk-round until customers start complaining that their orders have not been complied with. Jim collects the notes next morning and it is discovered that they have all been forged by someone with a grudge against Jim.

9. HITCHMAN, Janet
The King of the Barbareens
pp. 53; 63–64 (Ch. 3)
'On the other side ... round the house.'; 'Looking back now ... rabbits after that.'
The village boys smoke an old man out of his house; and the game-keeper lodger plays practical jokes on 'Mum' and Elsie. He goes too far when he pretends that the rabbit they have eaten was a tom cat.

10. HUGHES, Thomas
Tom Brown's Schooldays
pp. 72–73 (Part 1, Ch. 4)
'It pays uncommon ... he might join them.'
Tom hears tales out of school about the behaviour of Rugby boys on the end-of-term stage-coach. They arm themselves with pea-shooters and risk the consequences of firing at Irish navvies.

11. LEE, Harper
To Kill a Mockingbird
(i) pp. 257–258 (Ch. 27); (ii) pp. 255–256
'Maycomb was itself ... hounds were returned.'
Children move all the furniture from the living room to the cellar by night, at the house of two deaf old ladies. they do it as a hallowe'en joke – and in large measure, it achieves its object.

12. NAUGHTON, Bill
Late Night on Watling Street
pp. 43–49 ('Taddy the Lamplighter')
'Through the dense narrow ... did over old Taddy.'
A gang of boys prepare an icy patch, disguised with snow, for Taddy the Lamplighter, and 'knocker-up', to slip on. He does, and his right hand is put out of action. Ashamed, the boys help Taddy to perform his duties, and give him the last laugh.

13. SILLITOE, Alan
Saturday Night and Sunday Morning
pp. 154–156 (Part 1, Ch. 11)
'Winnie clamoured for the Ghost ... the next roundabout.'
Arthur and his lady-friends go on the ghost-train. Arthur, in a high mood, runs ahead of the car and adds to the thrills with roaming hands. But he jumps back into the wrong car, frightens a staid matron, and gets caught up in ghostly drapes.

14. SPYRI, Johanna
Heidi
pp. 81–82 (Ch. 8)
'Hurry, Miss ... the kittens were safe.'
Heidi arrives late for the evening meal having been out without permission. When she is being told off, the kittens which she has smuggled in begin to miaou. Miss Rottenmeier is furious, thinking it is Heidi, and then terrified when she sees the kittens themselves.

15. ZINDEL, Paul
   The Pigman
   pp. 18–20 (Ch. 3)
   'I suppose it all started ... Not murdered him.'
   Four adolescents amuse themselves by phoning strangers and contriving to keep them on the line for as long as possible. The record for one of these conversations is two hours and twenty-six minutes.

PRAYER

1. GORKY, Maxim
   Childhood
   see RELIGION 6
2. HUGHES, Thomas
   Tom Brown's Schooldays
   pp. 175–177 (Part 2, Ch. 1)
   'I have already described ... fourteen years old.'
   The new boy does an unheard-of thing. He says his prayers before going to bed. The other boys in the dormitory ridicule him, but Tom is touched.
3. NAUGHTON, Bill
   One Small Boy
   pp. 160–162 (Bk. 2, Ch. 5)
   'He was relieved ... on our side.'
   Miss Skegham pours public scorn on the purse that Michael has made. In their prayers, Michael and his friend Charlie wish her unholy ill. They scheme revenge and pray for its success.
   see also: REVENGE 20
4. STEINBECK, John
   The Grapes of Wrath
   see RELIGION – RITES 3

PRESS

see NEWSPAPERS

PRIDE

see also: SHOWING – OFF

PRIDE

1. BRONTË, Charlotte
   Shirley
   (i) pp. 321–324 (Ch. 18); (ii) pp. 317–319
   'Good evening, William ... I see a great deal of distress.'
   William Farren, who had confessed poverty to the Rev. Hall, now asserts his rough workman's pride in his self-sufficiency. It is, as he says, a clean, Yorkshire pride.
2. HARDY, Thomas
   Far from the Madding Crowd
   (i) pp. 156–163 (Ch. 21); (ii) pp. 155–161
   'Gabriel Oak had ceased ... smiled on him again.'
   Bathsheba's sheep stray into young clover, and get 'blasted'. There is only one man who can cure them, and that is Gabriel Oak; but Bathsheba will not recall her dismissed shepherd – until the sheep dying about her, overcome her pride. Then she sends a peremptory message to Oak, which is another mistake.
3. HARDY, Thomas
   Under the Greenwood Tree
   pp. 143–147 (Part 4, Ch. 1)
   'Dick, dressed in his ... and go by himself.'
   Dick calls for Fancy on his half-holiday, to go nutting with him. He finds her making some alterations to a dress. He waits, at her request, expecting she will soon finish. But she is in no hurry, so with most of the afternoon wasted, Dick goes off nutting by himslef.
4. LAWRENCE, D.H.
   Sons and Lovers
   (i) pp. 183–184 (Ch. 8); (ii) pp. 226–227
   'To console his mother ... All his work was hers.'
   Paul and his mother go to Nottingham Castle to see his two prize paintings. Mrs Morel goes by herself, more than

once, to gloat, and to muse on her son's bright future.
see also: COMPETITIONS 2
5. MACKEN, Walter
God made Sunday and Other Stories
see SAILING 6
6. THOMPSON, Flora
Lark Rise to Candleford
(i) pp. 263–266 ('Lark Rise', Ch. 15) (ii) pp. 240–242
'Then there were rumours ... Queen's jubilee present.'
Miss Ellison makes a collection of pennies from every woman in the Hamlet towards a Jubilee gift for Queen Victoria. Mrs Parker is left out, until Laura pleads with Miss Ellison not to make an exception of one whose pride is easily bruised.
7. WILDE, Oscar
The Happy Prince and Other Stories
(i) pp. 202–203; 205–208 ('The Remarkable Rocket'); (ii) pp. 58–59; 61–65
'Then the moon rose ... fell into the mud.'; 'After some time ... and he went out.'
There is nothing quite so remarkable in the world, to the rocket, as himself. He is convinced of his importance, even when he is rejected and explodes unremarked.

PRIMITIVE PEOPLES

see also: CANNIBALS;
MEDICINE – PRIMITIVE;
RELIGION – PRIMITIVE

PRIMITIVE PEOPLES

1. ACHEBE, Chinua
Things fall apart
see CELEBRATION – NEW YEAR 1
2. ibid.
see MARRIAGE – ARRANGED 1
3. ibid. *see* TRIALS 1
4. ibid.
see WEDDINGS 1
5. ibid.
see FUNERALS 1

6. GRIMBLE, Sir Arthur
A Pattern of Islands
see SUPERSTITION 7
7. HUGHES, Richard
A High Wind in Jamaica
(i) pp. 13–14 (Ch. 1, Part 2); (ii) pp. 12–13
'She pushed on ... and still inhabited.'
Emily comes upon a village of descendants of negro slaves. They are as scared of her – a white – as she is fascinated by them. She enjoys her uniqueness among them, and is ecstatic when they present her with flowers.
8. HUXLEY, Aldous
Brave New World
pp. 91–93 (Ch. 7)
'When they were half-way up ... close, of the drums.'
Bernard and Lenina visit a savage reservation. Lenina is appalled by the filth and disease, the unfordly family life of the savages. Bernard, on the other hand, affects respect for the unconditioned simplicity of life outside the Brave New World.
9. MARSHALL, James Vance
Walkabout
(i) pp. 20–26 (Ch. 5); (ii) pp. 25–32
'The girl's first ... was out of sight.'
Two American children lost in the North Australian Desert, meet an Aborigine boy. They look each other up and down. It is a long time before the ice is broken. Mary feels an instinctive superiority over the bush boy, in spite of the fact that he has the means to survive, and they have not.
10. ibid.
see FIRE – LIGHTING 2
11. ibid.
see EMBARRASSMENT 5
12. ibid.
see FAITH 7

PRISON

see also: BORSTAL;
EXECUTION;

213

PRISON

1. CAMUS, Albert
   The Outsider
   pp. 75–84 (Part 2, Ch. 2)
   'There are some things ... are like in prison.'
   The young man has killed an Arab. He is visited in prison, by his mistress. She comes only once. Thereafter, he adapts himself to loneliness, to deprivation and to long hours of remembering. He sleeps most of the time, and muses away the rest.
   see also: EXECUTION 2

2. DEFOE, Daniel
   Moll Flanders
   (i) pp. 235–238; (ii) pp. 255–259
   'It was but three days ... who have experienced it, as I have.'
   Moll is apprehended by two 'open-mouthed' wenches as she is about to make off with a haul of brocaded silk. She pleads the innocence of her intention, but is committed to Newgate. There, with the gallows ahead, she broods on her past, and on the 'dreadful place' to which she has been brought.
   see also: TRIALS 4

3. DICKENS, Charles
   A Tale of Two Cities
   pp. 253–256 (Bk. 3, Ch. 1)
   'The Prison of La Force ... rose above them.'
   Darnay is taken to La Force, where he briefly meets other aristocratic prisoners before being taken into solitary confinement. Here all he can think of is his father-in-law who had been in the Bastille.

4. GREENE, Graham
   The Power and the Glory
   (i) pp. 117–123 (Part 2, Ch. 3); (ii) pp. 122–128
   'A voice near his foot ... black cotton glove.'
   The fugitive priest is in prison for being in possession of spirits. He confesses to the other inmates of his crowded cell, that he is a priest. He is resigned to being discovered now, and shot, like a real martyr, though he knows well enough that he is no better than any of his fellow prisoners, and deserves no distinction.

5. KOESTLER, Arthur
   Darkness at Noon
   (i) pp. 16–19 ('The First Hearing', Part 7); (ii) pp. 21–24
   'The procession had ... revolver-case attached to it.'
   Rubashov's first morning in prison. He is quite familiar with the routine, but he almost misses his breakfast, having reported sick so as to be left in bed. He hammers on the door for it, and so it comes – grudgingly.

6. ibid.
   (i) pp. 108–115 ('The Second Hearing' Part 6); (ii) pp. 110–116, (Visions of Life 4, pp. 41–47)
   'The day before ... WRETCHED OF THE EARTH.'
   There is an atmosphere of anticipation in the prison. Political executions are imminent. A prisoner is dragged along the corridor, whimpering. Rubashov recognizes him as his old comrade, Bogrov.

7. STEINBECK, John
   The Grapes of Wrath
   (i) p. 21 (Ch. 4); (ii) pp. 25–26
   'I'd do what I done ... the bell to go off.'
   Tom Joad recounts his prison experience to an acquaintance. He didn't have a hard time, and would not be deterred from committing the same crime again.

8. ibid.
   (i) pp. 44–46 (Ch. 6); (ii) pp. 50–52
   'For a long time ... work the gover'-ments.'
   Tom tells another acquaintance about his crime and prison sentence, and puzzles about the reasons for punishment.

PRISON – RUSSIA

1. SOLZHENITSYN, Alexander
   One Day in the Life of Ivan Den-isovich
   pp. 23–26
   'Just at that blissful moment … see more clearly while counting.'
   The prisoners are frisked to make sure they are not wearing any extra clothing, or to prevent them taking anything outside the gates, or just to keep them guessing. Buinovsky is found to be wearing a waistcoat. He insults the guard who takes it from him, and is sentenced to ten days in the cells for his pains.

2. ibid.
   see SECOND WORLD WAR – RUSSIA 2

3. ibid.
   pp. 90–93
   'There lay the camp, just as … it would have been out of place.'
   The 104th work-team has arrived at the gates of the prison camp after a day's building. They are searched. Shukhov remembers only just in time that he has a hacksaw blade in his pocket. The guard misses it by a moment.

4. ibid.
   pp. 113–115
   'The two hundred voices in Shuk-hov's … praise the Lord and sit tight.'
   A guard enters Shukhov's hut. He has come for Buinovsky who has been sentenced to ten days 'hard' in the cells for talking out of turn. The others know what appalling cold and privation he will suffer and they are grateful they have been spared.

PRISON (of) WAR

see also: ESCAPE (from) PRISON (of) WAR

PRISON (of) WAR

1. BOULLE, Pierre
   The Bridge on the River Kwai
   see ARMY – DISCIPLINE 2

2. SHOLOKHOV, Mikhail
   Fierce and Gentle Warriors
   pp. 64–69 ('The Fate of a Man', Ch. 3)
   'At the beginning of September … out of that, either.'
   The prisoners are worked extremely hard, and punished likewise. Sokolov is overheard making a complaint, and is whisked off to the commandant to answer for himself. Only his refusal to be brow-beaten and his soldierly dignity, save him from summary execution.

3. SHUTE, Nevil
   A Town like Alice
   see SECOND WORLD WAR – MALAYA 1

PROPAGANDA

see also: INDOCTRINATION

PROPAGANDA

1. ORWELL, George
   1984
   see HISTORY 2–6

PROPERTY

see MATERIALISM;
WEALTH

PROPERTY – DEVELOPING

see AMBITIONS – PROPERTY DEVELOPING

PROPOSALS (of) MARRIAGE

see COURTSHIP – PROPOSALS (of) MARRIAGE

PROTEST

1. ALLEN, Eric
   The Latchkey Children
   pp. 24–27 (Ch. 3)
   'Goggles was the first ... 'Ah. Yes, I see.' '
   Workmen are marking out the ground around an old tree in the children's playground. They are going to build a concrete railway engine in its place. Goggles is indignant that the children have not been asked. He decides to call a protest meeting.

2. ELIOT, George
   Middlemarch
   pp. 534–539 (Bk. 6, Ch. 56)
   'The submarine railway ... taken care of there.'
   The railway comes to Middlemarch; a group of rustics, ignorant of what it means, but aroused by gossip, attack the surveyors of the Railway Company.

3. GREENWOOD, Walter
   Love on the Dole
   pp. 201–205 (Part 3, Ch. 10)
   'He gazed down the long ... the surging masses.'
   The Means Test and the cutting of the dole have enflamed the working men of Salford. They march to the town hall and engage in running battles with the police.

4. HITCHMAN, Janet
   The King of the Barbareens
   pp. 164–166 (Ch. 7)
   'With approaching Spring ... her hat. Remember?'
   Summer hats are distributed at Barnado's. Elsie doesn't like the one she is given, and she is outspoken enough to say so. Her independence of mind is rewarded. Miss Thomas is shocked more by the novelty of the protest, than by Elsie's reasoning.

5. LEACH, Christopher
   Answering Miss Roberts
   pp. 99–103 (Ch. 8)
   'Leading it were a group ... to be placed in the van.'

Walking in London, alone, in the evening, Katie comes upon a political protest march, and joins it for want of anything else to do. She finds herself in the front row, as the marchers charge a line of police at the end of Downing St. She is arrested.
see also: ARREST 11

6. MANKOWITZ, Wolf
   Make me an Offer
   see REVOLT 4

7. PATON, Alan
   Cry, the Beloved Country
   (i) pp. 34–47; 40–41 (Bk. 1, Ch. 8); (ii) pp. 39–41; 46–47
   'The next morning ... something to marvel me.' (i) 'He called Kumalo ... light was green.'; (ii) 'He called Kumalo ... he beats me, Msimangu said.'
   The blacks of Johannesburg boycott the buses because the fares are far too high for their wages. Many have to walk, some travel by bicycle, and others are helped by white people who sympathise and give lifts even though it is illegal.

8. ibid.
   (ii) pp. 157–160 (Bk. 2, Ch. 9)
   'The great bull voice ... difficult to hear.'
   Gold has been found – the white men will make fortunes – and John Kumalo addressing a crowd of black people, forcibly suggests that they should see some of the profits too.

9. STEINBECK, John
   The Grapes of Wrath
   (i) pp. 336–340 (Ch. 26); (ii) pp 351–355
   'The wizened man ... stung and burned.'
   Outside the well-guarded camp where they are working, Tom meets some men who are picketing the camp because of the ridiculously low wages. Their protest won't work, but they feel they must protest. The group is broken up by guards and Tom kills one of them.

PUBLIC HOUSES

see also: DRUNKENNESS

PUBLIC HOUSES

1. WATERHOUSE, Keith
   Billy Liar
   see ENTERTAINMENTS 5

PUNISHMENT

see also: BORSTAL;
EXECUTION;
PRISON;
REVENGE;
SCHOOL – EXPULSION

PUNISHMENT

1. ALCOTT, Louisa M.
   Little Women
   pp. 98–103 (Ch. 7)
   ' "In debt, Amy ... pathetic figure before them.'
   Amy takes a bag of forbidden limes to school, and revels in the attention they earn her from her friends. However, she is betrayed to the teacher, and severely punished.

2. ALMEDINGEN, E.M.
   Little Katia
   see TEMPTATION 1

3. ibid.
   pp. 49–51 (Ch. 5)
   'Ah, a letter from ... and nobody came.'
   Katia has chosen to forgo something pleasant in the future in preference to immediate punishment for stealing plums. She finds she is excluded from a very exciting day out.

4. BARSTOW, Stan
   Joby
   pp. 58–65 (Ch. 4)
   'The cinema was perhaps ... you hadn't done. That hurt.'
   There is trouble before the film starts at the Tuppeny Rush. One of Gus Wilson's pellets hits the elderly attendant, who vents his anger, and injured

pride, on Joby. He is given his money back, and thrown out.

5. DICKENS, Charles
   David Copperfield
   pp. 129–131; 135–136 (Chs. 5, 6)
   'I gazed upon ... that placard.'
   'It was no other ... ever afterwards.'
   David is sent to a very strict school, after biting his stepfather's hand, and is forced to wear a placard bearing the words 'Take care of him, he bites.' He suffers agonies before the arrival of the other boys, in anticipation of their reactions, but on the whole they are not cruel.

6. DICKENS, Charles
   A Tale of Two Cities
   pp. 68–69 (Ch. 2, Book 2)
   'They hanged at Tyburn ... afraid of that.'
   'The Old Bailey in the late eighteenth century attracted large crowds to watch the condemned leaving for Tyburn, the pillory and the whipping post. A treason case, with the consequent 'quartering' was a special draw.

7. FRANK, Anne
   The Diary of Anne Frank
   pp. 17–18 (21.6.42)
   'Our whole class ... always jokes about it.'
   Anne works well at school, but annoys one teacher by her constant chattering. He sets her essay after essay as punishment until with the help of a friend she produces a poem in which she gets her own back – luckily the teacher takes it as a joke.

8. GASKELL, Mrs
   Cranford
   see PRANKS 6
   GORKY, Maxim
   Childhood
   (i) pp. 212–215 (Ch. 10); (ii) pp. 158–160
   'Soon mother energetically undertook ... lowering her head, 'Go away.' '
   His mother, determined to take Gorky's education in hand, has him

217

learn poetry by heart. His maverick imagination substitutes wrong words, to his mother's annoyance, and his own confusion. He is made to stand in the corner – and this novel punishment further bewilders him.

10. HITCHMAN, Janet
    The King of the Barbareens
    see STEALING 6

11. LAWRENCE, D.H.
    Sons and Lovers
    (i) pp. 48–51 (Ch. 3); (ii) pp. 64–68
    'Suddenly one morning ... he sat down.'
    Mrs Morel's neighbour complains to her about William's misbehaviour. Mrs Morel listens to William's side of the story and lets him off with a caution. But the neighbour also complains to her husband, who is less forgiving. Only Mrs Morel's intervention saves William from a thrashing.

12. LEE, Laurie
    Cider with Rosie
    (i) p. 29 (Ch. 3 'Village School'); (ii) pp. 45–47
    (Conflict I, pp. 110–111)
    'Vera was another ... one has forgotten.'
    Laurie Lee first meets punishment, and is bewildered by it, when he hits Vera on the head beacuse her curly hair is springy.

13. ibid.
    (i) pp. 156–158 (Ch. 12, 'First bite at the apple'); (ii) pp. 205–206
    'This advantage ... to the parish.'
    The young lads of the village run as wild as any city gang but are dealt with by the villagers, not by the police and the courts.

14. STEINBECK, John
    The Grapes of Wrath
    (i) pp. 277–278 (Ch. 22), (ii) pp. 291–292
    'When the committee ... wept miserably.'
    Ruthie trying to lord it over other children in their new camp, tries to break in on a game. The other children leave her the equipment and let her play alone.

PUNISHMENT – CAPITAL

see EXECUTION

PUNISHMENT – CONFINEMENT

1. ALMEDINGEN, E.M.
   Little Katia
   pp. 27–30 (Ch. 3)
   'One day, the morning lessons ... I felt grateful.'
   Katia's geography lesson prevents her joining her cousins in a game. She is so cross, she gets all the answers wrong, and is shut in the school-room while the rest of the family has dinner.

2. BRONTË, Charlotte
   Jane Eyre
   (i) pp. 7–15 (Ch. 2); (ii) pp. 14–20
   'I resisted all the way ... closed the scene.'
   Jane has finally given way to her dislike of her tormentor, her cousin John Reed, and fought back when attacked. As punishment she is shut in the red room, unused since her uncle's death there. She broods on her miserable life, is afraid of the growing dark, and finally believes a sudden ray of light to be the herald of her uncle's ghost.

3. ELIOT, George
   Silas Marner
   pp. 149–153 (Ch. 14)
   'It was an influence ... frowns and denials.'
   Silas has adopted an orphan girl upon whom he lavishes all the affection previously destined for his gold. She becomes mischievous, and Silas is forced to punish her—however, the punishment is unsuccessful, and Eppie finds that being shut in the coal hole is a game.

PUNISHMENT – CORPORAL

1. BUTLER, Samuel
   The Way of all Flesh
   pp. 80–81 (Ch. 22)
   (Conflict I, pp. 12–13)
   'I was there on a Sunday ... red-handed as he was.'
   Young Ernest is reproved for saying 'Tum' instead of 'Come'. His father insists that he say 'Come' like everybody else. Ernest cannot, so is beaten, for being 'self-willed and naughty.'

2. DICKENS, Charles
   David Copperfield
   pp. 102–105; 106–110 (Ch. 4)
   'Shall I ever forget ... contaminated one another.'; 'One morning ... on my remembrance.'
   David is given lessons at home, and has to recite them before his mother, step-father and step-aunt. He is afraid of the last two and continually stumbles and dries up. Finally he is beaten by his step-father, bites the cane-holding hand and is locked in his room for five days.
   see also: PUNISHMENT 5

3. GORKY, Maxim
   Childhood
   (i) pp. 23–32 (Ch. 2); (ii) pp. 28–34
   (Conflict I, pp. 31–35)
   'One day my grandfather asked me ... 'Don't, Father! Let him go!' '
   It is a part of the savagery of the Nizhni ménage, that childhood crimes are punished by severe beatings. Gorky who has never been 'thrashed' himself, is obliged to watch the ritual played out on one of the Sashas, before having to bend, on his own account, to his grandfather's implacable birch.

4. ibid.
   (i) pp. 37–39 (Ch. 2); (ii) pp. 38–39
   'My grandfather's visit ... Ivanushka the Fool.'
   Some tips from an old hand on how to lessen the pain of corporal punishment.

5. GRICE, Frederick
   The Bonny Pit Laddie
   see SCHOOL – EXPULSION 1

6. MACKEN, Walter
   God Made Sunday and Other Stories
   see TRUANCY 6

7. PEYTON, K.M.
   Flambards
   see DISMISSAL 6

PUNISHMENT – CORPORAL – SCHOOL

1. HINES, Barry
   Kestrel for a Knave
   (i) pp. 65–71; (ii) pp. 53–58
   'The three smokers ... second made him sick.'
   Mr Gryce has three smokers, MacDowall alleged to have coughed in assembly, Billy for falling asleep, and a messenger, in his office. He lectures them for the unoriginality of their crimes, then spends his impatience in the strokes of a stick on their palms.

2. JOYCE, James
   A Portrait of the artist as a Young Man
   pp. 48–51 (Ch. 1)
   (Conflict I, pp. 131–133)
   (Visions of Life 2, pp. 36–39)
   'The door opened quietly and closed ... The door closed behind him.'
   The Prefect of Studies sees that Stephen is not working. He jumps to conclusions, pays no attention to Stephen's innocent protests, and hits him on the open palms, with a pandy bat, in front of the class. Pain, shame, and rage combine in tears.

3. LAWRENCE, D.H.
   The Rainbow
   see TEACHING – DISCIPLINE 4

4. LLWELLYN, Richard
   How Green was my Valley
   pp. 173–175 (Ch. 8)
   'And there he was ... geography, I sat.'
   Mr Jonas finds Huw fighting, and

canes him for it. In front of the class he has him bend over another boy's back, and hits till the stick breaks.

5. NAUGHTON, Bill
One Small Boy
see HUMILIATION 14

6. ibid.
pp. 167–169 (Bk. 2, Ch. 6)
'As they marched ... one you," she said.'
The entire class is caned, one by one, with the object of punishing among the innocents, those guilty of having cut the oranges off Miss Skegham's miniature orange tree.

7. ibid.
pp. 192–198 (Bk. 2, Ch. 9)
(That Once was Me, pp. 68–71)
'At Catechism that morning ... massacre!" whispered Sheed.'
Miss Skegham has inadvertently poked her cane in Charlie's eye, and it swells up enormously. He fetches his mother from the mill, and she swings into action against the teacher, in high indignation.

8. WRIGHT, Richard
Black Boy
pp. 90–92 (Ch. 4)
'The religious school ... quit the school.'
Addie is insecure in her role as Richard's Aunt and schoolteacher. She provokes a confrontation between them, so that by beating him she will subject him to her rule. Richard takes his punishment, resentfully, protesting his innocence.

QUARRELS

see also: FAMILY – QUARRELS;
MARRIAGE – QUARRELS

QUARRELS

1. FRANK, Anne
The Diary of Anne Frank
pp. 38–40 (28.9.42)
'I had to stop ... their true characters.'

In the confined space of the hideout there is much bickering between the adults, often directed at Anne. She describes one quarrel ('discussion') which took place between Mrs Frank and Mrs Van Daan, resulting in the latter's revealing a hitherto unseen coarseness.

2. NAUGHTON, Bill
Late Night on Watling Street
pp. 11–12 ('Late Night on Watling Street')
'Just then the juke-box ... with the last dart.'
Willie puts his money in the juke-box. Jackson, who has already made it clear that he wants quiet, approaches him, spoiling for a fight; but Walter, Willie's driver, intervenes. There are moments of tense deadlock until the record stops.

3. TOWNSEND, John Rowe
The Intruder
pp. 130–135 (Ch. 22)
'The rain stopped ... the main street.'
The stranger who has come to live at Arnold's house has completely taken charge. He erects a sign 'Bay View Private Hotel' although the house has been called Cottontree House for two centuries, then proposes to chop down the historic cotton tree. Arnold is furious, they quarrel, and even scuffle.

4. WATERHOUSE, Keith
There is a Happy Land
pp. 8–10 (Ch. 1)
('Growing Up', pp. 43–45)
'After a bit he dropped ... because I couldn't move.'
A wrestling game between the boy and Ted ends in a real fight when the boy bites Ted's leg. They both say more than they mean and end up swearing at each other. The boy is very upset.

5. WELLS, H.G.
The History of Mr Polly
pp. 142–145 (Ch. 7, Part 4)
'Rumbold, the china-dealer ... obtusely as ever.'
Polly, out of boredom, engages his

neighbour Rumbold, in trivial, uncivil argument. Polly resists a temptation to kick his neighbour's ample rear.

6. ibid.
    see NEIGHBOURS 2

QUARRELS – BROTHERS (and) SISTERS

1. ELIOT, George
    The Mill on the Floss
    pp. 37–43 (Ch. 5, Part 2)
    'O don't bother Maggie ... what was downstairs.'
    Maggie has forgotten to feed Tom's rabbits and they have died. He is very angry, and she is very miserable. She hides in the attic and refuses to come down until Tom is friends with her again.
2. NESBIT, E.
    The Railway Children
    see ACCIDENTS (at) HOME 2

QUARRELS – CHILDREN

1. ALMEDINGEN, E.M.
    Little Katia
    pp. 83–87 (Ch. 9)
    'Alas, as days grew ... My fault ...'
    Katia finds her beloved cousin growing away from her, and seeking the company of a third cousin, Nadia. Katia and Nadia have two serious insult-throwing quarrels.

QUARRELS – FATHERS (and) DAUGHTERS

1. GORKY, Maxim
    Childhood
    (i) pp. 229–234 (Ch. 10); (ii) pp. 169–172
    'There were two or three such evenings ... a scratch is a decoration.'
    A suitor comes to the Kashirin household to propose marriage to Gorky's widowed mother. She refuses to see him, and even takes her clothes off, so as to prevent her father from dragging her to him against her will.

Gorky hears evidence of a noisy struggle, and is confused.

QUARRELS – LOVERS

1. BANKS, Lynne Reid
    The L-Shaped Room
    pp. 180–183 (Ch. 15)
    'We were late ... and touched him.'
    Depressed by her unmarried pregnancy, Jane gets annoyed first by her expanding figure, then by her long hair, as she is preparing for a party. She vents her anger on Toby, and despite all his efforts to be reasonable with her, they quarrel.

QUARRELS – MOTHERS (and) SONS

1. MANKOWITZ, Wolf
    Make me an Offer
    pp. 79–80 ('Expresso Bongo')
    'I looked him over ... smoking behind him.'
    Bongo has just been 'spotted' by Mr Mayer of a record company, and he has a regular session in a West End coffee bar. His mother feels she should be receiving more money from him and a bitter argument ensues.

RABBITS

1. ADAMS, Richard
    Watership Down
    passim.
    A small group of rabbits desert their ancient warren when one predicts its imminent destruction. They set out on a long, difficult and dangerous search for a new home.
2. ibid.
    pp. 132–135 (Ch. 18)
    'Since each one ... made it for us.'
    The difficulties for a rabbit of climbing a steep slope are very different from those experienced by a man. Hazel and two others climb to the top of the Down unable to see where they are going.

RABBITS – CATCHING

1. LAWRENCE, D.H.
   The White Peacock
   pp. 63–66 (Part 1, Ch. 5)
   'We moved across to the standing ... soon all was finished.'
   The young people visit the Saxtons' farm. George is mowing with rhythmic, beautiful sweeps of the scythe. As the corn is laid low, rabbits are discovered and chased. Cyril cannot bring himself to kill them, though they are pests.

2. SOUTHALL, Ivan
   Josh
   see ANIMALS – TRAPPING 2

RACE

   see RACISM

RACES

   see COMPETITIONS – RACES;
   GAMES – RACES

RACISM

   see also: JEWS

RACISM – AMERICA

1. BALDWIN, James
   Go Tell it on the Mountain
   pp. 185–192 (Part 2, 'Elizabeth's Prayer')
   (Impact Two, pp. 154–160)
   'She lived quite a long way ... dead among the scarlet sheets.'
   When Richard doesn't turn up for a date, Elizabeth fears the worst. Then policemen come and question her. Richard is in gaol, falsely accused of robbing a store. His experience of racial hatred has embittered him, and, though he is acquitted, he kills himself.

2. LEE, Harper
   To Kill a Mockingbird
   passim.
   Two children learn through wit-
   nessing the trial of a negro youth, defended by their own lawyer father, the extent of colour prejudice in their town.

3. ibid.
   (i) pp. 124–125 (Ch. 12); (ii) pp. 122–123
   'When they saw ... to have you all.'
   Scout and Jem go to the Negro church with Calpurnia their cook, and experience racial prejudice against whites. Lula, a trouble-maker, challenges Calpurnia, and demands to know why she is bringing white children to church.

4. ibid.
   (i) pp. 203–204 (Ch. 19); (ii) pp. 200–202
   'Robinson, you're pretty good ... I didn't go to be.'
   Tom Robinson, a negro accused of raping a white girl, is cross-examined by the prosecuting counsel, who clearly demonstrates his prejudice in his scornful treatment of Tom.

5. ibid.
   (i) pp. 209–212 (Ch. 20); (ii) pp. 207–209
   'Gentlemen,' he was saying ... are created equal.'
   Atticus gives his final speech to the jury in the Tom Robinson trial. He clearly points out its racial character, and reminds the jury that in court all men are equal.

6. WRIGHT, Richard
   Black Boy
   passim.
   Richard grows up into a hostile environment. His consciousness of the odds against him, grow as misfortune accumulates, and escape to a 'free' north becomes an abiding passion.

7. ibid.
   pp. 39–42 (Ch. 2)
   'At last we were ... kill the first.'
   The important matter of Richard's skin-colour comes to the fore in a conversation with his mother. She is guarded, and irritated by his questions, but Richard learns enough

to know that as a black he will have problems.

8. ibid.
   pp. 63–64 (Ch. 2)
   'A dread of white people … thousand lynchings.'
   A hatred of white people is slowly bred into Richard with every new story that he is told about them, and with every new rumour that he hears.

9. ibid.
   see HATRED 6

10. ibid.
    pp. 166–169 (Ch. 9)
    'The climax came … like a blind man.'
    His immediate superiors at work intimidate Richard into leaving his job, because he is not the sort of humble nigger they have expected. There is nothing Richard can do despite his employer's kindness, because he knows he would be putting his life at risk.

RACISM – BRITAIN

1. BRAITHWAITE, E.R.
   To Sir with Love
   pp. 34–36 (Ch. 4)
   'Shortly after our return … and was violently sick.'
   His qualifications and experience fit the author for a job as a communications engineer; but the colour of his skin disbars him. He attends for interview, but plainly the event is a (courteous) formality. When it is over, he is sick with disillusionment and bitterness.

RACISM – CENTRAL AMERICA

1. STEINBECK, John
   The Pearl
   pp. 7–12 (Ch. 1)
   (Young Impact 2, pp. 106–110)
   'The doctor,' she said … between his fingers.'
   Kino's and Juana's baby has been bitten by a scorpion. Knowing the French doctor will not visit a native village, they go to him, but the doctor refuses even to see them.

RACISM – INDIA

1. FORSTER, E.M.
   A Passage to India
   pp. 26–30 (Part 1, Ch. 3)
   'Meanwhile the performance ended … his trap to be brought round.'
   Adela and Mrs Moore are at the club, among the Masters of India. They are curious to see 'the real India.' This amuses the hardened Anglo-Indians, whose advice to the new comers is to stick to their own sort, and keep the natives at a distance.

2. ibid.
   pp. 158–163 (Part 2, Chs. 16, 17)
   'So the cavalcade ended … for this, you shall squeal.'
   Dr Aziz is arrested at the station on a charge of assault. He goes to pieces, but his friend Fielding takes charge, and assures Mr Turton, the Collector, that there has been a mistake. But Turton has already made up his mind: an English girl has been assaulted, and must be avenged.

RACISM – RHODESIA

1. LESSING, Doris
   The Grass is Singing
   see AUTHORITY 5

2. ibid.
   pp. 138–141 (Ch. 7)
   'At the week's end … waiting for her to finish.'
   The natives come up to the house for their pay. She deducts a sizeable sum (as she had threatened to do) from the wages of those who had reported late for work. There is much murmuring, but she hates them so much that she finds it easy to be resolute.

3. ibid.
   see AUTHORITY 6

RACISM – SOUTH AFRICA

1. LESSING, Doris
   Nine African Stories
   see MEDICINE – PRIMITIVE 2
2. PATON, Alan
   Cry, the Beloved Country
   passim.
   Through the search for his son in
   Johannesburg, and the son's subsequent trial for the murder of a
   white man, the Rev. Kumalo discovers the extent of racial ill-feeling
   in S. Africa.
3. ibid.
   (i) pp. 33–34 (Bk. 1, Ch. 7); (ii) pp.
   37–38
   (i) 'He is a big man ... work for it.'
   (ii) 'He is a big man ... grave and
   sombre words.'
   Msimangu analyses the black's position in S. Africa – he sees it as a
   desire for power but it is a corrupt
   desire. What is needed is a corporate
   effort by both black and white for the
   good of the country.
4. ibid.
   (ii) pp. 67–72 (Bk. 1, Ch. 12)
   'Have no doubt ... he gives too
   much.'
   A white man has been murdered –
   the reactions of the whites are various,
   some demanding stronger police,
   some reform of the system. No-one
   knows the answer to the problem, and
   little can be done while the root
   cause, fear, is so strong.
5. ibid.
   (ii) pp. 126–127 (Bk. 2, Ch. 3); (i)
   pp. 105–106 (Bk. 2, Ch. 4); (ii) p.
   134
   'The other papers ... read them
   again.'; 'The truth is ... me a minute.'
   Arthur Jarvis, a champion of the
   rights of the blacks, analyses the
   racial situation in S. Africa, and condemns the exploitation of blacks by
   whites.
6. ibid.
   pp. 130–131 (Bk. 2, Ch. 4)

'We've been agitating ... get a
republic.'
A middle-aged white S. African
defends the position of his people, and
sweeps aside black Trade Unions, and
demands for more money in the
mines.

7. ibid.
   (i) pp. 120–122 (Bk. 2, Ch. 7); (ii)
   pp. 150–151
   'It is hard to be born ... course that is
   right.'
   Jarvis reads some papers written by
   his son, recently murdered by a black
   boy. His son examines the identity of
   a white S. African, and his own
   solution to the problems posed by it.
8. ibid.
   see PROTEST 8

RAILWAYS

1. CHURCH, Richard
   Over the Bridge
   see LEISURE 1
2. ELIOT, George
   Middlemarch
   see PROTEST 2
3. NESBIT, E.
   The Railway Children
   see COURAGE 12
4. WAUGH, Evelyn
   Scoop
   pp. 196–200 (Bk. 3, Ch. 2, Part 2)
   'That evening, some time ... walk to
   the house.'
   The city-bred Mr Salter is not
   amused by his train-journey, nor by
   his inconclusive interview with a
   grinning rustic at Boot Magna Halt.
   Having no confidence in the latter's
   qualifications to drive, he decides to
   cover the rest of his journey on foot.
   see also: EMBARRASSMENT 10

RAIN

   see also: FLOODS;
   STORMS

RAIN

1. BOMBARD, Alain
   The Bombard Story
   pp. 167–168 (Ch. 12)
   'Land! Land!' ... always came in time.'
   At last it rains. After three weeks of drinking salt water and fish-juice, Alain savours the water that he manages to collect in the rubber tent sheet.
2. DICKENS, Charles
   Bleak House
   (i) pp. 75–76 (Ch. 7); (ii) pp. 75–76
   'While Esther sleeps ... shadow on the ground.'
   It is raining steadily in Lincolnshire. Can anyone, especially the animals, imagine it ever being fine again?
3. LEE, Laurie
   Cider with Rosie
   see FLOODS 10
4. STEINBECK, John
   The Grapes of Wrath
   see DROUGHT 4

RAPE

1. FIELDING, Henry
   Joseph Andrews
   see ASSAULT 2
2. SHOLOKHOV, Mikhail
   And Quiet Flows the Don
   pp. 211–213 (Part 1, Ch. 13)
   'The dreary, monotonous ... he felt like crying.'
   A mob of soldiers, billeted, bored, rape the only girl on the estate, one after another. Gregor comes upon the unlovely scene in the stables, and does his best to break it up – but he is silenced.

RATS

1. O'BRIEN, Robert C.
   Mrs Frisby and the Rats of NIMH
   see RATS – CATCHING 1
   see also: CONDITIONING 4, 5

2. ORWELL, George
   1984
   see TORTURE 5

RATS – CATCHING

1. O'BRIEN, Robert C.
   Mrs Frisby and the Rats of NIMH
   pp. 89–95 ('The Market Place', 'In the Cage')
   'One evening in early autumn ... wheeled into the building.'
   When the rats return to the vegetable market at dusk, they are surprised by men with lights and nets. Those who do not escape are taken in a lorry to a large building where they are locked in cages.

READING

1. CHURCH, Richard
   Over the Bridge
   see SCHOOL – SUBJECTS 1
2. DICKENS, Charles
   Great Expectations
   see EDUCATION 1
3. GORKY, Maxim
   Childhood
   (i) pp. 96–100 (Ch. 5); (ii) pp. 78–81
   'I remember one quiet evening ... I'll give you five copecks.'
   To distract his own selfish attention from his illness, his grandfather teaches Gorky his letters. Gorky learns fast; his grandfather's enthusiasm is infectious, and soon they are both shouting at each other in their shared excitement.
4. NAUGHTON, Bill
   The Goalkeeper's Revenge
   (i) pp. 112–119 ('Maggie's First Reader'); (ii) pp. 112–119
   'The best housewife ... well worth waiting for.'
   Maggie Gregory is the model housewife, until the priest discovers she can't read. He persuades young Timothy to teach his mother, which he does. So intoxicated by her new skill does Maggie become, that she

forgets her duty to her family, and reads the day through.

5. SPYRI, Johanna
   Heidi
   pp. 183–189 (Ch. 19)
   'Next day Peter went ... He could read.'
   Heidi persuades Peter to learn to read, so that he can read hymns to his blind grandmother. He is afraid of the school he might otherwise have to go to, and she is very patient with him, so that in a short time he can do what the local schoolmaster has tried for years to teach him.

6. THOMPSON, Flora
   Lark Rise to Candleford
   (i) pp. 31–33 ('Lark Rise', Ch. 2); (ii) pp. 42–44
   'When Laura approached ... magnet drew steel.'
   Their father teaches Laura and Edmund to read. When the symbols acquire meaning for Laura, and she can make sense of enough words to understand the whole, her joy is boundless. She reads anything she can get her hands on, in spite of the admonitions of neighbours.

7. WRIGHT, Richard
   Black Boy
   pp. 217–221 (Ch. 13)
   'That night in my ... about with me each day.'
   By borrowing a white friend's library card, Richard is initiated into a new world of thinking and feeling. His reading of 'white' novels gives him a fresh insight into the whites with whom he lives and works.

REBELS

see also: PROTEST;
REVOLT

REBELS

1. ROBINSON, Rony
   A Walk to see the King
   pp. 66–71 (Ch. 31)

'Wat Tyler was having ... wink back – not at a priest.'
The men of Kent, at the instigation of John Ball, the mad priest, act out the meeting that they are to have on the following morning with the young King Richard. Wat Tyler pulls a knife on the pretend king, and is felled for it.

2. ibid.
   see PEASANTS' REVOLT 2

3. SILLITOE, Alan
   The Loneliness of the Long-distance Runner
   see BORSTAL 1

4. ibid.
   see RUNNING 1

5. SILLITOE, Alan
   Saturday Night and Sunday Morning
   pp. 196–197 (Part 2, Ch. 15)
   'Once a rebel ... to do the same to me.'
   Arthur takes a jaundiced view of the world of employers, politicians and union leaders. He looks forward to the day when he and his like will cry 'enough!', man the machine-guns, and make an end of government.

REBELS (at) SCHOOL

1. BALDWIN, Michael
   Grandad with Snails
   pp.147–157 (Ch. 18)
   Conflict I, pp. 124–130)
   'Up at the Village Hall ... something very important.'
   Miss Rose has the upper hand until the unkempt, unruly Piper comes back to school. He charms the girls, and teaches the boys bravado. He is more submissive in Mr Noake's class, until Mr Noake canes him. Then, he gives as good as he gets.

2. CHURCH, Richard
   Over the Bridge
   see TEACHERS 1

3. GORKY, Maxim
   Childhood
   see SCHOOL 1

REFUGEES

see also: ESCAPE;
RUNNING AWAY

REFUGEES

1. BATES, H.E.
   The Purple Plain
   see PANIC 1
2. SERRAILLIER, Ian
   The Silver Sword
   (i) pp. 70–74 (Ch. 11), (ii) pp. 57–60
   'Spring was bursting ... who refuse
   it.'
   Two sisters and their friend set out
   from Warsaw at the end of the war,
   first to find their brother in a transit
   camp, then their parents in Switzerland. They join many other refugees
   on the road.
3. ibid.
   see HUNGER 9
4. ibid.
   see CHARITY 12
5. WELLS, H.G.
   The War of the Worlds
   see PANIC 2

RELATIVES

see also: AUNTS; COUSINS; DEATH;
FAMILY; GRANDPARENTS;
UNCLES

RELATIVES

1. KIRKUP, James
   The Only Child
   pp. 23–26 (Ch. 2)
   'When I think of my ... his devilish
   wink.'
   Granny Johnson is an imperious, but
   kindly lady, Uncle Bob, a veteran of
   the Somme, shaves himself in a
   fascinating way, Aunt Lyallie speaks
   with a Scottish accent, and her youngest son brushes his teeth with soot.
2. WELLS, H.G.
   The History of Mr Polly
   see WEDDINGS 16

RELIGION

see also: BAPTISM; CHRISTIANITY;
CHURCH; CONSCIENCE;
HELL; METHODISTS;
MISSIONARIES; PRAYER;
ROMAN CATHOLICS

RELIGION

1. CALDWELL, John
   Desperate Voyage
   pp. 136–137 (Ch. 14)
   'For the next two days ... hypothesis
   of a creator.'
   He has been an atheist for a good
   many years, but alone, and lost, on
   the Pacific Ocean, the author finds
   comfort in the Bible, and in the belief
   in a Good Captain piloting his boat.
2. DEFOE, Daniel
   Robinson Crusoe
   (i) pp. 157–159; (ii) pp. 213–215
   (Ch. 20)
   'From these things I began ... means
   of salvation.'
   Having taught him much else, it
   remains for Crusoe to teach Friday
   about God. He does his sincere best,
   but is confused by the pertinent
   questions of his pupil regarding
   predestination.
3. ELIOT, George
   The Mill on the Floss
   pp. 355–359 (Part 4, Ch. 3)
   'In writing the history ... antiquated
   times.'
   The poor need some sort of faith to
   keep them going – Maggie, suffering
   her father's bankruptcy, and worsening family relationships, turns to a
   strict creed of self-denial, almost of
   martyrdom.
4. GALLICO, Paul
   The Snow Goose/The Small Miracle
   see FAITH 2, 3
5. GORKY, Maxim
   Childhood
   (i) pp. 69–78 (Ch. 4); (ii) pp, 60–66
   'I lay on a wide bed ... it was
   impossible not to believe her.'

227

His Grandmother's prayers reveal her childlike faith in a Fatherly God, to the young, listening Gorky. She tells him about God, and his angels; and about the mischief-making demons, that crowd the attic of her mind like cockroaches.

6. ibid.
pp. 127–132 (Ch. 7); (ii) pp. 100–103
'At a very early date ... even dearer and more comprehensible to me.'
The young Gorky listens to his Grandmother at her fervent prayers. He understands her God better, one day, when he avenges an insult paid her by a neighbour. His Grandmother takes him to task for presuming to do God's work.

7. ibid.
(i) pp. 132–138 (Ch. 7); (ii) pp. 103–107
'At my lessons my grandfather ... burned at the stake and skinned alive.'
Gorky understands that men create God in their own image. His Grandfather's hard, vengeful despot is very different from his Grandmother's kindly and forgiving Father. Gorky finds it hard to believe that the former is other than a terrible extension of his Grandfather.

8. GREENE, Graham
the Power and the Glory
see PRISON 4

9. GRIMBLE, Sir Arthur
A Pattern of Islands
see FAITH 4, 6

10. MORROW, Honoré
The Splendid Journey
see AUTHORITY 7

11. THOMAS, Dylan
A Prospect of the Sea
see EASTER 4

RELIGION – PRIMITIVE

1. GOLDING, William
Lord of the Flies
(i) pp. 169–170 (Ch. 8); (ii) pp. 150–151

(Themes in Life and Literature, pp. 201–202)
' "How can we make ... the open beach.'
Jack reserves the head of the sow killed by him and his gang, for the 'Beast' on the mountain. The 'Beast' is the symbol of all that is unknown and frightening to these boys, and as such, it has to be appeased with sacrifices.

2. GRIMBLE, Sir Arthur
A Pattern of Islands
see SUPERSTITION 7

3. MARSHALL, James Vance
Walkabout
see FAITH 7

4. SPERRY, Armstrong
The Boy who was Afraid
see COURAGE 15

5. SUTCLIFF, Rosemary
The Eagle of the Ninth
pp. 188–195 (Ch. 14)
'Next day began ... darkened cave of Mithra.'
It is the feast of New Spears in the Highland clan, when boys are initiated as warriors. Priests emerge from a sacred barrow dressed only in animal-skins. They dance weirdly by torch-light.

RELIGION – PURITAN

1. STEINBECK, John
The Grapes of Wrath
(i) pp. 269–271 (Ch. 22); (ii) pp. 283–285
'Gonna stay? ... shone with virtue.'
A self-righteous 'religious' woman regales the pregnant and ingenuous, Rosasharn with gruesome tales of what will happen to her baby if she joins in with the dancing and acting in the camp.

RELIGION – RITES

see also: BAPTISM;
CHURCH – FESTIVALS;
CHURCH – SERVICES; FUNERALS;

ROMAN CATHOLICS – COMMUNION;
ROMAN CATHOLICS – CONFESSION;
WEDDINGS

RELIGION – RITES

1. GREENE, Graham
    The Power and the Glory
    see FEAR (of) POLICE 1
2. SHUTE, Nevil
    A Town like Alice
    (i) pp. 130–132 (Ch. 5); (ii) pp.
    124–125
    'In Kuantan ... to the hospital.'
    A Japanese Captain has had an
    Australian crucified for stealing his
    prize chickens. When he discovers the
    man is not dead, he attempts to fulfil
    the man's last wishes. Unable to do
    so, he has to follow his religious
    beliefs and allow the man to live.
3. STEINBECK, John
    The Grapes of Wrath
    (i) pp. 182–184 (Ch. 18); (ii) pp.
    193–194
    'A large woman ... a food dish.'
    Granma Joad is ill, and a group of
    Jehovah's Witnesses offer to pray
    over her. Ma refuses, but they return
    to their own tent and hold a very
    noisy prayer meeting there.

RELIGION – SCEPTICISM

1. HITCHMAN, Janet
    The King of the Barbareens
    pp. 101–102 (Ch. 4)
    'It was no doubt ... I should under-
    stand.'
    Elsie is a sceptic. She takes a child's
    common-sense view of problems posed
    by religious belief. She doubts, she
    shocks; she is untroubled by the
    prayers that are said for her soul.

REMORSE

see CONSCIENCE

RESCUE

1. CHURCH, Richard
    The White Doe
    see COURAGE 3

RESCUE (of) ANIMALS

1. ALLEN, Eric
    The Latchkey Children
    see FEAR (of) HEIGHTS 1

RESCUE (from) ANIMALS

2. FIELDING, Henry
    Joseph Andrews
    pp. 201–206 (Bk. 3, Ch. 6)
    'Joseph, who whilst he was ... instead
    of sticking to a hare.'
    Parson Adams gets caught up in a
    hunt. The hare is torn to pieces a few
    feet from him, so that the hounds
    worry his cassock at the same time.
    He takes flight, but the huntsman
    urges his hounds to harry the Parson,
    until Joseph flies to his rescue with a
    flailing cudgel.
3. HARDY, Thomas
    The Mayor of Casterbridge
    see BULLS 1

RESCUE (of) ANIMALS

4. MACKEN, Walter
    God made Sunday and Other Stories
    see FARMING 5
5. ibid.
    pp. 177–181 ('No Medal for Matt')
    'It was some while ... of the lobster
    boat.'
    The truant Matt sees a rabbit below
    him on a cliff ledge. He climbs down
    to it, afraid but determined, and
    carries it to safety. He does not know
    that his father has been watching his
    climb, from a boat.
6. PEYTON, K.M.
    Flambards in Summer
    see HORSES 1

RESCUE (from) ASSAULT

1. COOKSON, Catherine
   The Nipper
   pp. 25–28 (Ch. 2)
   'He told himself ... and ran for home.'
   While out rabbiting, Sandy hears a cry for help. He discovers two boys stoning an old one-legged man, and scares them off. Later he is rewarded with a big fat hare.
2. FIELDING, Henry
   Joseph Andrews
   see ASSAULT 2

RESCUE (from) CANNIBALS

1. DEFOE, Daniel
   Robinson Crusoe
   (i) pp. 146–149; (ii) pp. 197–201 (Ch. 18)
   'About a year and a half ... and went to sleep.'
   A dream comes true. Crusoe's thought that he might rescue one of the victims of the cannibals is realized in the rescue of man Friday from a fate worse than death.

RESCUE (from) DROWNING

1. DE JONG, Meindert
   The Wheel on the School
   see COURAGE 7
2. ibid.
   (i) pp. 130–138 (Ch. 10); (ii) pp. 124–132
   'Janus looked away ... above the thundering sea.'
   Old Douwa and Little Lina are stranded by the incoming tide, on top of an upturned boat. They are rescued, together with the wheel they have found, by a horse and cart which are floated out to them.
3. ibid.
   (i) pp. 204–209 (Ch. 15); (ii) pp. 192–197
   'In the dinghy ... was on the dike.'
   The longed-for storks are stranded on a sand-bank, too exhausted to reach the shore. Janus, the teacher and some of the children row out to them, against the tide, and rescue them from drowning.

RESCUE (from) FIRE

1. NESBIT, E.
   The Railway Children
   see FIRE 2
2. SOUTHALL, Ivan
   Ash Road
   pp. 148–151 (Ch. 12)
   'The end was coming ... some things were not.'
   Grandpa Tanner lowers two infants in his charge down a well. The forest fire is approaching fast. He looks at his homestead – all that he has – and wishes that he had the strength to fight the fire for it.
3. ibid.
   pp. 163–164; 165–167 (Ch. 14)
   'Peter ran hard ... But not Gran Fairhall.'; 'Peter ran on as if ... and crawled, even snakes.'
   Peter, a weak, at times mean-spirited boy, grows up when he determines to save his defeated Grandmother from the forest fire. He drives her by main force and will-power, to the comparative safety of water.
4. WELLS, H.G.
   The History of Mr Polly
   pp. 172–177 (Ch. 4, Part 4)
   'Her eyes had not ... embrace of Miriam.'
   Polly rescues his elderly neighbour, Rumbold's deaf mother-in-law. He leads her, protesting and bewildered, across the roof to a waiting ladder and the embraces of the crowd below. Polly, the arsonist, is everybody's hero.

RESCUE (from) FLOODS

1. BERNA, Paul
   Flood Warning
   pp. 130–134 (Ch. 7)

'Five minutes had hardly elapsed ...
Vignoles smiled and nodded.'
The fog clears, and makes a way for a whirligig of rescue helicopters. It is some time before the three survivors are spotted; then a helicopter homes in on the tower, and a nylon ladder is lowered for one evacuee at a time, to climb.

2. BURTON, Hester
   The Great Gale
   pp. 42–47 (Ch. 5)
   'Out of the shelter of the house ...
   'Where shall we go?' '
   The children row against wind, and flood-tide, across the broad, to the Foulgers' house. By the time they get there, the water is almost up to the eaves and old Jim is cutting his way through the thatch.

RESCUE (from) HANGING

1. JOHNSON, Dorothy M.
   The Hanging Tree
   pp. 171–176 ('The Hanging Tree')
   'The rabble. The rabble ... her eyes were shining.'
   Doc Frail is to be hanged for murder, by the revengeful rabble of Skull Creek. Elizabeth, whom he has courted, and protected, throws all her gold, nugget by nugget, towards the rabble to buy them off. Greed overcomes them, and Doc Frail is freed.

RESCUE (from) INTRUDERS

1. LONDON, Jack
   White Fang
   pp. 204–210 (Ch. 20)
   'It was about this time ... significantly at each other.'
   A dangerous man, whom Judge Scott consigned to prison for fifty years, escapes, and makes for the Judge's house to have his revenge. But he reckons without the wolfdog, White Fang, who guards the household.

RESCUE (from) ISLANDS

1. GOLDING, William
   Lord of the Flies
   (i) pp. 246–248 (Ch. 12); (ii) pp. 221–223
   'He staggered to his ... cruiser in the distance.'
   Ralph is saved from certain death at the hands of Jack's savages – and they are saved from themselves – by the arrival of a British naval officer and ratings. The boys are taken off the burning island.

2. WOOD, James
   The Rain Islands
   pp. 132–138 (Ch. 7)
   'I hustled him ... seen her before.'
   Major Scott has taken prisoner the man sent to capture him, but they are now both stranded on an uninhabited, Icelandic island. Scott lights a fire in order to attract attention, and is rewarded by the appearance of a fishing boat.

RESCUE (from) MUD

1. DURRELL, Gerald
   My Family and Other Animals
   see SHOOTING 1

2. MADDOCK, Reginald
   The Pit
   pp. 97–105 (Ch. 10)
   'Bob and I set off ... nothing more than dinner.'
   A young boy is being sucked into the mud of the infamous Pit. He is already up to his armpits when Butch arrives. The police, and several adults, including the boy's father, are there, but nobody seems to be doing anything. Butch defies warnings, and jumps from tussock, to tussock, to the island in the middle. From there, he is near enough to pull the boy out on the end of a rope.

RESCUE (from) SEA

1. HARDY, Thomas
    Far from the Madding Crowd
    see SWIMMING 2
2. HEYERDAHL, Thor
    The Kon-Tiki Expedition
    pp. 158–160 (Ch. 6)
    'On 21 July ... He had let it go.'
    Trying to prevent a sleeping-bag
    falling overboard, Herman does so
    himself. Although he swims des-
    perately hard, the raft is blown along
    even faster. After a number of unsuc-
    cessful attempts Knut reaches him
    with the lifebelt.
3. WOOD, James
    The Rain Islands
    pp. 65–70 (Ch. 4)
    'It was dark ... you are Kopur.'
    Major Scott has been attacked on an
    apparently uninhabited island, and
    left in a leaking boat, to float out to
    sea. He is picked up by an Icelandic
    whale-boat, while clinging to a piece
    of wreckage from the boat.

RESCUE (from) SHARKS

1. GRIMBLE, Sir Arthur
    A Pattern of Islands
    pp. 61–64 (Ch. 5)
    'That kind of single ... policeman of
    him.'
    Teriakai, a Gilbertese prisoner, over-
    comes tiger-sharks, a storm, a maze
    of reeds, and miles of running, to
    enlist help in the rescue of two British
    sailors, stranded eight miles out in the
    lagoon. He is awarded the bronze
    medal of the Royal Humane Society
    for his very considerable pains.

RESCUE (from) WELL

1. GORKY, Maxim
    Childhood
    see FRIENDS – BOYS 2

RESOURCES

1. O'BRIEN, Robert C.
    Mrs Frisby and the Rats of NIMH
    see MATERIALISM 3
2. WYNDHAM, John
    Chocky
    pp. 142–144 (Ch. 11)
    'Yes. You have not done badly ... So
    is XXXXX.'
    A being from another planet, criti-
    cises Earthmen for their prodigality
    with limited fossil fuels. She advises
    the use of the fuels only in the har-
    nessing of cosmic radiation whose
    supply is limitless.

RESPECT

1. DOSTOYEVSKY, Fyodor
    The Idiot
    see TEMPTATION 2
2. LEE, Harper
    To Kill a Mockingbird
    see FATHERS 6, 7
3. STEINBECK, John
    Of Mice and Men
    see AUTHORITY 9
4. WRIGHT, Richard
    Black Boy
    see COURAGE 21
5. ibid.
    see INITIATION 11

RESTAURANTS

see HOTELS (and) RESTAURANTS

RETREAT

see PENINSULAR WAR – RETREAT

REUNIONS

see FAMILY – REUNIONS

REVENGE

1. ACHEBE, Chinua
    Things fall apart
    see JUSTICE 1

2. ibid.
   see JUSTICE 2
3. ibid.
   see MISSIONARIES 1
4. ibid.
   see BRITISH EMPIRE – NIGERIA 4
5. BARSTOW, Stan
   The Human Element
   pp. 86–92 ('The Fury')
   'There were times ... in their hutches.'
   Mr Fletcher keeps rabbits and dotes on them. His wife is made jealous by the attention he pays to them, as well as to another woman. She kills his rabbits before he has a chance to explain his innocence of what a neighbour's gossip had charged him with.
6. ibid.
   see KILLING (by) GANGS – YOUTHS 1
7. CANAWAY, W.H.
   Sammy going South
   pp. 77–79 (Ch. 13)
   'Sammy's first flush ... smiling sweetly.'
   Sammy's lone journey is broken when he is found by an Italian reporter. He soon tires of his new companion, and is finally disillusioned when he is taken to a doctor for fourteen injections. He retaliates by ripping up all the fabric in his room.
8. ibid.
   p. 85 (Ch. 14)
   'Abu Lubaba was the nicest man ... his friend, his rescuer?'
   Sammy despises his 'rescuer' the Italian journalist, and while he is away from the Land Rover in which they are going south, Sammy smashes as much of the engine as possible and runs away.
9. DICKENS, Charles
   A Tale of Two Cities
   see FRENCH REVOLUTION 2
10. ELIOT, George
    The Mill on the Floss
    pp. 119–123 (Part 1, Ch. 10)
    'All the disagreeable recollections ... what they'll come to.'
    Maggie has quarrelled with her

brother, Tom, and is jealous when he goes for a walk with their cousin Lucy. When he tells her to leave them alone, she is so cross she pushes Lucy in some mud.

11. ibid.
    pp. 434–436 (Part 5, Ch. 7) 'Simmering in this way ... even I' the world.'
    Tulliver, earlier ruined by Wakem, has managed to pay off all his debts. He meets Wakem on his way home from a meeting of creditors and first speaks his mind to him, then, enraged, beats him.
12. FALKNER, J. Meade
    Moonfleet
    pp. 95–103 (Ch. 9)
    'I made as if I ... panting, but safe.'
    Block has bound his old enemy, Maskew, and prepares to shoot him in cold blood, to avenge his own son's death at Maskew's hands. He intimidates Maskew by hanging his life on a pin, in a candle. Before the pin falls he reduces his enemy to tears.
13. GORKY, Maxim
    Childhood
    (i) pp. 219–225 (Ch. 1); (ii) pp. 162–166
    (Visions of Life I, pp. 64–68)
    'That was in the evening ... grandfather could be heard in the passage.'
    Grandfather flies into a tantrum and knocks Grandmother about. Gorky, determined to pay him out, cuts up his favourite calendar with figures of all the saints on it. He is caught in the act, and only the intervention of his mother saves him from an immediate beating.
14. GRICE, Frederick
    The Bonny Pit Laddie
    pp. 39–43 (Ch. 6)
    'Mr Sleath, who ... or wonderfully brave.'
    The pit overman is thrown into the colliery pond by miners whom he has wronged. Kit and Dick watch the act of revenge, and wonder that their own father could be a party to it.

15. HARDY, Thomas
    The Mayor of Casterbridge
    see ASSAULT (by) RIVALS (in) LOVE 1
16. HINES, Barry
    Kestrel for a Knave
    see BULLYING (by) TEACHERS 2
17. ibid.
    (i) pp. 180–186; (ii) pp. 147–152
    'Their living-room light ... milk on
    the cloth.'
    Billy failed to place a bet for his
    brother Jud, as instructed. In revenge
    Jud has killed Billy's pet kestrel.
    There is nothing Billy can do to even
    the score. He asks his mother to hit
    Jud, but she will not.
18. NAUGHTON, Bill
    Late Night on Watling Street
    see ACCIDENTS – ROAD 4
19. NAUGHTON, Bill
    One Small Boy
    see PRAYER 3
20. ibid.
    pp. 163–167 (Bk. 2, Ch. 6)
    'The next morning ... crowded and
    lively.'
    Michael and Charlie get their own
    back on their teacher by cutting all
    the oranges off the miniature orange
    tree that she prizes so highly.
    see also: PUNISHMENT – CORPORAL –
    SCHOOL 6
21. REMARQUE, Erich Maria
    All Quiet on the Western Front
    pp. 45–48 (Ch. 3)
    'Tjaden has a special grudge ... as
    "young heroes".'
    The four friends have their revenge on
    the martinet Corporal Himmelstoss.
    They waylay him in the dark, cover
    his head, punch him, de-bag him, and
    whip him, till they are satisfied that
    they have taught him a lesson.
22. SPYRI, Johanna
    Heidi
    pp. 212–215 (Ch. 22)
    'Uncle Alp was out ... and settled her
    there.'
    Peter is jealous of Clara, who he
    thinks has stolen Heidi from him. On
    the day that the girls are to accom-

pany him to the higher pastures he
pushes her wheelchair over a cliff,
hoping to prevent the outing.
23. STEINBECK, John
    The Red Pony
    see GRIEF 10
24. TROLLOPE, Anthony
    Barchester Towers
    pp. 413–416 (Ch. 46)
    'The Signora was ready ... chose to
    be revenged.'
    Signora Neroni is tired of the unwel-
    come advances of Mr Slope, and tor-
    ments him in public as a result. She
    manages to touch on two very sore
    spots.

REVOLT

see also: FRENCH REVOLUTION;
PEASANTS' REVOLT;
REBELS;
RUSSIAN REVOLUTION

REVOLT

1. FORESTER, C.S.
   The Gun
   (i) pp. 144–151 (Ch. 15); (ii) pp.
   122–128
   'At midnight ... a dead despot deser-
   ved.'
   O'Neill is unpopular both with the
   men and with the officers – he is
   arrogant and cruel. At a midnight
   counsel of war the officers stand up
   against him, and are then at a loss to
   know what to do with him. He solves
   the problem by trying to escape, and
   starting a fight in which he is killed.
2. HEMINGWAY, Ernest
   For Whom the Bell Tolls
   see EXECUTION 4
3. HUGHES, Thomas
   Tom Brown's Schooldays
   pp. 135–137 (Part 1, Ch. 8)
   'While matters were in ... turned the
   corner.'
   Tom leads a fags' revolt against
   Flashman and his fellow fifth-form
   bullies. They bar themselves in their

study and refuse to do the bullies' bidding.

4. MANKOWITZ, Wolf
   Make me an Offer
   pp. 99–102 ('The Day Aunt Chaya was buried')
   'The revolutionary party ... who could forgive?'
   Chaya makes up for her lack of height by her revolutionary zeal, and is chosen to throw a bomb at a clerk in the army recruitment office. Unfortunately she misses and destroys the town's prized bronze horse.

5. ORWELL, George
   Animal Farm
   (i) pp. 3–5 (Ch. 1); (ii) pp. 7–10
   'All the animals were now ... until it is victorious.'
   Three days before his death, Old Major the boar, fires the blood of all his fellow farm animals, with a desire for rebellion. The spirit of this parody of the Russian Revolution of 1917 is born.

6. ibid.
   (i) pp. 11–13 (Ch. 2); (ii) pp. 18–21
   'Now, as it turned out ... that it was all their own.'
   The old régime of Farmer Jones is so decadent with drink and idleness that the animals take possession of the farm much more easily than they have expected. They are ecstatic in their new-found freedom.

7. ibid.
   (i) pp. 24–27 (Ch. 4); (ii) pp. 36–40
   'Early in October, when ... on the dead sheep.'
   Farmer Jones with a number of colleagues, attempts to repossess his farm; but the animals have expected this counter-revolutionary move, and so under Snowball's heroic leadership, the men are beaten back, and put to ignominious flight.

8. ROBINSON, Rony
   A Walk to see the King
   see KINGS 3

9. ibid.
   see PEASANTS' REVOLT 2

REVOLT (at) SCHOOL

1. BRAITHWAITE, E.R.
   To Sir with Love
   pp. 147–152 (Ch. 19)
   'Just about this time a new supply ... the staffroom in search of Bell.'
   The class is goaded into revolt against Mr Bell, their P.T. teacher. Bell obliges Fatty Buckley to vault a horse, in spite of the boy's obvious fear. Almost inevitably, Buckley injures himself. Potter is barely restrained from going for Bell with the broken leg of the horse.

2. LEE, Laurie
   Cider with Rosie
   (i) pp. 30–33 (Ch. 3, 'Village School'); (ii) pp. 48–51
   (Impact Two, pp. 143–144)
   'My first days ... and weeping.'
   The teacher in the Big Room lives up to her nickname, Crabby, but her repressiveness leads finally to rebellion. Spadge Hopkins stands up to her and deposits her on top of a cupboard before leaving.

RIDDLES

1. TOLKIEN, J.R.R.
   The Hobbit
   (i) pp. 66–74 (Ch. 5); (ii) pp. 66–74
   'Deep down here by the ... 'A promise is a promise.'
   Bilbo exchanges riddles with the hungry Gollum in a grim bid to cheat him of his dinner.
   see also: COMPETITIONS 3

RIDING

see HORSES – RIDING

RIOTS

1. DICKENS, Charles
   A Tale of Two Cities
   pp. 158–160 (Bk. 2, Ch. 14)
   'His son obeyed ... progress of a mob.'

The mob following the funeral procession of a spy runs wild – to show their disrespect they take over the hearse and drive to the churchyard with great rejoicing. The high spirits finally lead to vandalism.

2. GREENWOOD, Walter
   Love on the Dole
   see PROTEST 3

RIVALS – BOYS

1. BARSTOW, Stan
   Joby
   pp. 34–41 (Ch. 2)
   'Below the cricket field ... was going to be all right.'
   Joby and Snap meet up with Gus Wilson and his gang. There is much baiting, and playing for advantage. Gus plays a trick on Joby, but neither is in fighting mood. Joby is occupied by the thought of his mother's impending operation; and this is not a matter for the ears of Gus Wilson.

2. GOLDING, William
   Lord of the Flies
   (i) pp. 64–65 (Ch. 3); (ii) pp. 54–56
   'Ralph turned to ... play with the grass.'
   A clash of priorities. Ralph believes shelter is the first priority; Jack believes it is meat. Neither can convert the other to his point of view. They look at each other, 'baffled in love and hate.'

3. TWAIN, Mark
   The Adventures of Tom Sawyer
   (i) pp. 6–9 (Ch. 1); (ii) pp. 11–14
   'The summer evenings ... adamantine in its firmness.'
   Tom meets a stranger, a boy of his own age, dressed neatly in spite of its not being Sunday. They square up to each other like fighting cocks and exchange insults before blows. The victory is Tom's for what it is worth.

RIVALS – CHURCHES

1. BRONTË, Charlotte
   Shirley
   see CHURCH – FESTIVALS 1

RIVALS (in) LOVE

see also: ASSAULT (by) RIVALS (in) LOVE;
KILLING (by) RIVALS (in) LOVE

RIVALS (in) LOVE

1. AMIS, Kingsley
   Lucky Jim
   pp. 204–210 (Ch. 20)
   'What, finally, is the ... who went out in silence.'
   Bertrand storms into Dixon's room and warns him to stay away from Christine. Dixon, in pleasurable anticipation of bringing things to a head, provokes Bertrand to an exchange of blows.

2. BRAINE, John
   Room at the Top
   pp. 38–42 (Ch. 4)
   'When we were putting ... 'How pretty' I said.'
   Joe is smitten by a young actress in the local Thespians. He meets her backstage and is encouraged to think there might be a chance for him. Then he meets her beau, the suave Jack Wales, and the fight is on.

3. ibid.
   see SOCIAL CLASS – CLIMBING 1

4. BRONTË, Emily
   Wuthering Heights
   (i) pp. 96–100 (Ch. 11); (ii) pp. 106–110
   'He descended ... you leave me!'
   Edgar Linton attempts to turn Heathcliff out of the house, for his unwelcome attention to Mrs Linton. Heathcliff refuses to leave quietly, especially when Edgar is provoked into dealing him a blow. But Edgar has the advantage of numbers. Heathcliff leaves, and Edgar and Mrs

Linton argue until the latter throws a fit.

5. DICKENS, Charles
   Great Expectations
   (i) pp. 397–401 (Ch. 43); (ii) pp. 341–344
   'Having thus cleared ... obliged to give way.'
   Pip, on his way to Estella, runs into Bentley Drummle, of whose attentions to Estella, he is painfully aware. The two snarl at each other and jockey for advantage. Drummle plays a trump when he announces that he is to dine with Estella.

6. HARDY, Thomas
   The Mayor of Casterbridge
   see ASSAULT (by) RIVALS (in) LOVE 1

7. LAWRENCE, D.H.
   Sons and Lovers
   (i) pp. 341–344 (Ch. 13); (ii) pp. 415–419
   'Soon after Paul ... that's what he wants.'
   Paul comes into conflict with Clara's ex-husband, Baxter Dawes. Dawes makes fun of Paul in front of his friends, and goads him into throwing beer into his face. A fight is averted, however, when the 'chucker-out' eases Baxter Dawes into the street. Paul is much shaken by this encounter.
   see also: ASSAULT (by) RIVALS (in) LOVE 2

8. PEYTON, K.M.
   Flambards
   see COURTSHIP – PROPOSALS (of) MARRIAGE 13

9. SHOLOKHOV, Mikhail
   And Quiet Flows the Don
   see JEALOUSY 11

RIVERS

see also: TRAVEL (by) BOAT

RIVERS

1. CANAWAY, W.H.
   Sammy going South
   see TRAVEL (by) BOAT 1

2. WILLIAMSON, Henry
   Tarka the Otter
   (i) pp. 63–64 (Ch. 5); (ii) pp. 66–67
   'Early one morning ... immense roar of the fall.'
   The otter family follows the river downstream, with the help of rushing flood-water. Enjoying the different speeds of the water they reach a weir.

RIVERS – CROSSING

1. HEYERDAHL, Thor
   Kon-Tiki Expedition
   pp. 49–50 (Ch. 3)
   'Not till the road ... the embrace of welcome.'
   Heyerdahl, and a companion, are in the Ecuadorian jungle in search of balsa to build the Kon-Tiki. When their way is barred by a river, they find themselves, and their jeep, on a balsa raft.

2. KIRKUP, James
   The Only Child
   see TRAVEL (by) BOAT 3

3. MORROW, Honoré
   The Splendid Journey
   pp. 91–96 (Ch. 7)
   'The next day dawned clear ... dough the size of a walnut.'
   The trail stops on the banks of the rushing Snake river. The children make a raft of their wagon, and hitch it behind the long-suffering oxen. Their raft rides well up in the water, but the oxen are all but carried off by the current. Betsy the cow saves the day.

4. RAFTERY, Gerald
   Snow Cloud, Stallion
   pp. 127–130 (Ch. 13)
   'Underneath the spar ... waded ashore behind him.'
   The stream is swollen by the rain, and the bridge is blocked by a broken-down truck. So Ken and Snow have to swim across. Snow is unwilling, but it is his strength which saves Ken from being dragged under by a sunken bough.

ROADS

1. ADAMS, Richard
   Watership Down
   pp. 58–60 (Ch. 10)
   "There's a good road there ... as soon as I can."
   The wandering rabbits come to a road, the first most have ever seen. Bigwig tries to explain what it is, but they are all very wary.

ROADS – ACCIDENTS

see ACCIDENTS – ROAD

ROBBERY

see also: PICKPOCKETS;
SHOPLIFTING;
STEALING

ROBBERY

1. DEFOE, Daniel
   Moll Flanders
   (i) pp. 166–167; (ii) pp. 185–187
   'I went out now by daylight ... necessity drove me to.'
   Temptation has struck once. It is not long before another prize offers itself in the shape of a lost child, and a gold necklace. Moll jusitifies the separation of the two, by looking upon the theft as a lesson to the child's neglectful parents.
   see also: STEALING 1

2. FIELDING, Henry
   Joseph Andrews
   see CHARITY 8

3. HAUGAARD, Erich
   The Litle Fishes
   pp. 117–122 (Ch. 12)
   'It is not true that ... gallop down the sideroad.'
   A stranger tricks his way on to a farmer's cart. He makes polite conversation until the farmer's guard is down, then he pulls out a knife and demands the farmer's purse. The

latter is so taken unawares that he offers no resistance.

4. JOHNSON, Dorothy M.
   The Hanging Tree
   pp. 88–92 ('The Hanging Tree')
   'Elizabeth Armistead ... lay dead beside the road.'
   The stage-coach carrying Mr Armistead and his daughter Elizabeth (among others) to a new life in Skull Creek, is held up, miles from anywhere. The driver and Mr Armistead are shot dead for minor indiscretions, and Elizabeth is carried off, screaming, in the runaway coach.

5. PATON, Alan
   Cry, the Beloved Country
   (ii) pp. 18–20 (Bk. 1, Ch. 4)
   'A young man came ... much sympathy and much advice.'
   Stephen Kumalo is confused and frightened when he arrives in Johannesburg for the first time. A young man helps him to find his bus, but then disappears with a pound, supposedly to buy Kumalo's bus ticket. He does not return.

6. TREASE, Geoffrey
   Cue for Treason
   pp. 209–216 (Ch. 22)
   'We slept soundly that night ... The miracle had happened.'
   On the wild fells, rough miners rob Peter and Kit of their money and their mounts. They then march them to within yards of a hole from which they would never again emerge, when other horses are heard. The robbers make off leaving Peter and Kit with nothing but their lives.

ROBBERY – GRAVES

1. DICKENS, Charles
   A Tale of Two Cities
   pp. 162–164 (Bk 2, Ch. 14)
   'Thus the evening ... he fell asleep.'
   Jerry is anxious to find out what his father does when he goes 'fishing' so often, and so mysteriously, at night. He follows him to a graveyard, and is

horrified to see him digging up a coffin.

2. TWAIN, Mark
The Adventures of Tom Sawyer
see KILLING (by) PARTNERS (in) CRIME 1

ROMAN CATHOLICS

see also: HELL;
POPE

ROMAN CATHOLICS

1. GALLICO, Paul
The Snow Goose/The Small Miracle
see FAITH 2, 3

ROMAN CATHOLICS – COMMUNION

1. NAUGHTON, Bill
One Small Boy
pp. 78–82 (Bk. 1, Ch. 11)
'Through the grey ... clemmed with hunger.'
It is Michael's first communion. He follows all the ritual of the catholic order with the eye of a novice, and with some irreverence.

ROMAN CATHOLICS – CONFESSION

1. JOYCE, James
A Portrait of the Artist as a Young Man
pp. 140–147 (Ch. 3)
'He cowered in the shadow ... The ciborium had come to him.'
Having been made conscious of his state of sin, and having sweated under the eye of a fervent hell-fire preacher, Stephen makes his confession in fear and trembling. After the event, he is absurdly happy.

2. NAUGHTON, Bill
One Small Boy
pp. 66–69 (Bk. 1, Ch. 9)
'Shortly before noon ... on his back.'
The whole class is taken into church

to confess their sins, before their first communion. The first boy, Ernest Keating, speaks very audibly, to the vast amusement and edification of his friends. Michael has difficulty repressing bad thoughts.

ROMAN EMPIRE

1. SUTCLIFF, Rosemary
The Eagle of the Ninth
pp. 97–99 (Ch. 7)
'Marcus leaned back ... it ceased to matter.'
Marcus asks his slave, once a freeman of the Brigantes, why his people resent the coming of the Romans. Esca explains that Roman ways are not the ways of the British. They are as East is to West.
see also: GAMES – ROMAN 1

ROYAL JUBILEES

see CELEBRATIONS – ROYAL JUBILEE

ROYALTY

see KINGS

RUGBY – FOOTBALL

1. HUGHES, Thomas
Tom Brown's Schooldays
pp. 83–84 (Part 1, Ch. 5)
'Oh, but do show me ... and play-up well.'
The game as played at Rugby School. One of its exponents reveals its mysteries to a new boy.

2. LLEWELLYN, Richard
How Green was my Valley
pp. 236–237 (Ch. 24)
'The other team ... five points, to the good.'
Huw watches a Rugby match between his village and another, one of his brothers as referee and another, Davy, playing. Davy demonstrates his skill very early in the match.

3. STOREY, David
This Sporting Life
pp. 21–23 (Part 1, Ch. 2)
'I jumped up and down ... chatter of communal relief.'
A minor game in the reserves. Arthur pulls his weight because this is all the style he has. He is aware of the crowd, and hates them for making him suffer.

4. ibid.
pp. 37–41 (Part 1, Ch. 2)
(Work and Leisure, pp. 93–98)
'At Thursday night training ... damn thing to tire me.'
Arthur is being watched with an eye to his being promoted. He senses he is being deprived of the ball, by his own hooker, so he punches him in the scrum. Arthur's game picks up after this.

5. ibid.
pp. 210–211 (Part 2, Ch. 3)
(Conflict 2, pp. 67–69)
'Frank Miles made me ... professional signature.'
Arthur plays a brutal game. He relishes his strong-man rôle, cultivates it to please the crowd.

6. ibid.
pp. 246–249 (Part 2, Ch. 6)
'I followed Frank ... Maurice was telling me.'
A game full of fast action, scrums, sudden bursts for the line, tackles. It's glorious and agonizing and inconclusive.

RULES

1. GOLDING, William
Lord of the Flies
(i) pp. 43–44; 54–55 (Ch. 2); (ii) pp. 36; 46–47
'He lifted the shell on ... Bong! Doink!'; 'I got the conch! ... the right things.'
The marooned schoolboys realise the need for rules. They draw on their English public school breeding for inspiration. They accept the discipline of speaking in turn, and of keeping a fire going.

2. (i) pp. 98–101 (Ch. 5); (ii) pp. 86–89
' "The thing is" ... "do what I say." '
Ralph has to call an assembly to remind the boys of the rules, and to record his impression that things were 'breaking up'.

3. ibid.
see AUTHORITY 2

4. ORWELL, George
Animal Farm
(i) pp. 14–15 (Ch. 2); (ii) pp. 22–23
'The pigs now revealed ... Commandments by heart.'
The pigs hand down seven commandments, and have them inscribed on the barn wall. These enshrine the essential principles of animalism by which the free animals are to live.
see also: SOCIAL CLASS – PRIVILEGE 1

5. ibid.
(i) pp. 83–85 (Ch. 10)
'One day in early summer ... to wear on Sundays.'
The seven commandments are now one. It is that there is one law for the rich, and one for the poor. The pigs have betrayed the Revolution by aping the men whom they had expelled.

6. STEINBECK, John
The Grapes of Wrath
(i) pp. 167–173 (Ch. 17); (ii) pp. 177–184
'The cars of the migrant ... stretched ahead.'
The countless families migrating to California, gather together in different camps each night, and as the journey progresses rules, customs and procedures evolve, so that the camp is a self-contained community even if its members change.

RUNNING

1. SILLITOE, Alan
The Loneliness of the Long-distance Runner

pp. 37–40 ('The Loneliness of the Long-distance Runner', Part 3)
'I went once around the field ... not in the way they tell me.'
Smith is running in the Borstal Long Distance Cross Country Running Race (All England), determined not to win it; this, despite his effortless ability to do so. He enjoys his running, only when he is running for himself.

RUNNING AWAY

see also: ESCAPE;
HOME – LEAVING;
PANIC;
REFUGEES

RUNNING AWAY

1. DICKENS, Charles
David Copperfield
pp. 235–244 (Ch. 13)
'For anything I know ... helpless and dispirited.'
David runs away from his miserable life and job in London, but has his money stolen at the start of his journey to his aunt in Dover. He sells some clothes, and walks all the way, falling in with rough company.

2. ELIOT, George
The Mill on the Floss
pp. 572–578 (Part 6, Ch. 13)
'O have we passed ... land of the west.'
As a result of unforeseen circumstances Maggie and Stephen, although they have renounced all hope of marriage, go rowing alone together. They row too far, again by chance, but Stephen persuades Maggie that Fate is pushing them towards elopement. They continue on their journey down-river on a cargo boat.

3. GODDEN, Rumer
The Diddakoi
see GYPSIES 4

4. LAWRENCE, D.H.

Sons and Lovers
see ARMY – ENLISTMENT 3

5. LESSING, Doris
The Grass is Singing
pp. 118–125 (Ch. 6)
'In the afternoons, these days ... the tones of their voices changed.'
In the depths of her depression, Mary thinks of the days before she was married, when she lived and worked in town, and had money and friends. The idea of running away grows in her mind; but when she makes the break, and applies for her old job back, she is not wanted. When her husband chases after her, she resigns herself to continued misery with him.

6. MAUGHAM, W. Somerset
The Moon and Sixpence
see PAINTING 6

7. MORROW, Honoré
The Splendid Journey
pp. 15–24 (Ch. 2)
'No matter how hurried ... handed John his water-bottle.'
Burning with resentment under the strong hand of his father's discipline, John Sager slips away from the family wagon, and makes for the hills. He is robbed of his clothes by a passing Indian. Realising the plight he is in, John throws himself on the mercy of the Scout Kit Carson, who insists that he return to his family.

8. TREASE, Geoffrey
Cue for Treason
pp. 19–23 (Ch. 2)
'We had our swim ... to get it with a vengeance.'
The law is after young Peter Brownrigg for his part in destroying Sir Philip's new enclosure and shying a rock at the gentleman himself. In view of Sir Philip's standing with the magistrates, his father advises Peter to lie low for a while.

9. WELLS, H.G.
The History of Mr Polly
pp. 184–186 (Ch. 9, Part 1)
'But when a man ... and primroses.'
After the Great Fishbourne Fire,

Polly feels purged. He resolves to 'clear out', to leave Miriam provided for, and to strike out on an entirely new road, with twenty pounds in his pocket.

RUNNING AWAY (from) HOME

see also: HOME – LEAVING

RUNNING AWAY (from) HOME

1. BAWDEN, Nina
   On the Run
   pp. 123–130 (Ch. 14)
   'Lil started being useful ... wings to their feet.'
   Lil, Thomas, and Ben are running away from home, and intend to stow away in a furniture van. Lil distracts the driver, and they all hide inside. It is a long and uncomfortable journey, and it is only with difficulty, and luck, that they get out at the other end.

2. ELIOT, George
   The Mill on the Floss
   pp. 126–139 (Part 1, Ch. 11)
   'Maggie's intentions ... O father, father!'
   Maggie, having pushed her cousin into some mud, fears punishment and runs away to the gypsies, who she hopes will make her their Queen. The reality is less enchanting, and she is glad to be returned to her father.

3. GASKELL, Mrs
   Cranford
   (i) pp. 80–88 (Ch. 6); (ii) pp. 96–102
   'My dear, that boy's trick ... lie on her breast.'
   Miss Matty tells how her brother ran away from home after a flogging from his father, the result of a practical joke he had played on his sister. His disappearance seriously affects his parents, and his mother slowly fades away to her death.

4. HAUGAARD, Erich
   The Little Fishes
   pp. 45–48 (Ch. 4)

'My mother died in the Spring ... in Naples, I threw it away.'
At the age of eleven, Guido runs away from the village where he lives with his aunt. He takes the 25 lire that his mother left him when she died, and catches a train for Naples. He tricks the ticket-seller into believing that he is to be met by his uncle, and that his journey is aboveboard.

5. LEE, Harper
   To Kill a Mockingbird
   see FAMILY 7

RUNNING AWAY (from) MONSTERS

1. WELLS, H.G.
   The War of the Worlds
   see PANIC 2, 3

RUNNING AWAY (from) ORPHANAGE

1. WRIGHT, Richard
   Black Boy
   pp. 24–27 (Ch. 1)
   'The orphan home ... watched closely after that.'
   Hard times oblige Richard's mother to commit him to an orphanage. He is always hungry there, and is afraid of Miss Simon, the lady in charge. He awaits an opportunity to run away, but he is returned to the home by the police.

RUSSIA

see PRISON – RUSSIA;
RUSSIAN CIVIL WAR;
RUSSIAN REVOLUTION

RUSSIAN CIVIL WAR

1. SHOLOKHOV, Mikhail
   And Quiet Flows the Don
   see KILLING 10

2. ibid.
   see GRIEF 9

3. ibid.
   see EXECUTION (by) FIRING SQUAD 3
4. ibid.
   see EXECUTION (by) HANGING 5

RUSSIAN REVOLUTION

1. ORWELL, George
   Animal Farm
   see REVOLT 5, 6
2. SHOLOKHOV, Mikhail
   And Quiet Flows the Don
   see COMMUNISM 4
3. ibid.
   pp. 429–435 (Part 3, Ch. 5)
   'He did not drop off ... came from her lips.'
   Bunchuk, onetime deserter, rejoins his comrades to encourage them to flout the orders of their officers. But they are indecisive and only quick action by Bunchuk prevents Kalmikov, the company commander, from gaining the advantage. Bunchuk has him executed on the 'us or them' principle.
   see also: RUSSIIAN CIVIL WAR 1–4
4. SHOLOKHOV, Mikhail
   Fierce and Gentle Warriors
   pp. 23–26 ('The Rascal', Ch. 2)
   'The grandfather took the side ... pressed them down with his hands.'
   Mishka's father tells him how he was put down by the landowners, how he was inspired by the Bolsheviks, and met Lenin himself. Young Mishka is inspired in his turn.
5. ibid.
   see COMMUNISM 5

SAILING

   see also: BOATS (and) BOATING

SAILING

1. CALDWELL, John
   Desperate Voyage
   pp. 12–15 (Ch. 2)
   'There is one great hazard ... the jib the hard way.'
   The author takes in the jib in a high

wind. A miscalculation finds him wallowing in the sea astern. He clings to his lifeline, but cannot regain the boat without losing his grip on the jib. But by a miracle, the sail is caught on the hook at the end of the line, so it is saved.
2. ibid.
   see HURRICANES 1
3. ibid.
   see SURVIVAL (at) SEA 3
4. HEYERDAHL, Thor
   The Kon-Tiki Expedition
   see SEA 3
5. JEROME, Jerome K.
   Three Men in a Boat
   pp. 155–157 (Ch. 15)
   'Sailing is a thing that wants ... cheap at any price.'
   J. and a friend go sailing for the first time. They make a mess of hoisting the sail, but once it's up they go at a cracking pace, until they run into a mud bank. The expedition is costly but educational.
6. MACKEN, Walter
   God made Sunday and Other Stories
   pp. 25–28 ('God Made Sunday')
   'This was my boat ... on a Tuesday.'
   Proud of his new boat, and of himself, Colmain defies the warnings of his friends, and puts to sea. Within a short time he realises that the wind is stronger than he thought, and his new sail is in rags. But the boat, and the humbled Colmain in it, is lifted on to sand with little other damage done.

SAILING – NAVIGATION

1. CALDWELL, John
   Desperate Voyage
   pp. 16–18 (Ch. 3)
   'Those first nine days ... to go round the world.'
   Navigation techniques are simply learnt, and the necessary instruments are cheaply bought. The author describes his excitement when he masters the basics.

SAILORS

1. BALDWIN, Michael
   Grandad with Snails
   see GRANDPARENTS 1
2. THOMAS, Leslie
   This Time Next Week
   pp. 16–20 (Ch. 2)
   'Every now and then ... one of his fractured ribs.'
   Leslie's father is a sailor. When he is at home, he is by turns a warm-hearted father, and a reckless buffoon. Leslie's mother might often have wished him dead, but she rejoices when he survives a bomb-blast in Barcelona harbour.

SALESMEN

see also: BUYING (and) SELLING (by)
DEALERS;
MARKETS;
PAWNBROKERS;
PEDLARS;
SHOPS

SALESMEN

1. FOAKES, Grace
   Between High Walls
   pp. 34–35 (Ch. 17)
   'On Sunday afternoons ... had my sympathy.'
   The Muffin man, Swannee the smoked haddock seller, the Italian icecream makers, the paper men, and the beggars – callers who bring a touch of the exotic into the streets.
2. KIRKUP, James
   The Only Child
   pp. 80–85 (Ch. 5)
   'The cry of the coalman ... buy rhubarb!'
   Salesmen and women pass down the Back Lane on their appointed days selling coal, fish, fruit, tea, muffins, and newspapers. All have their idiosyncrasies, cries, and positions in an informal pecking order.

3. THOMPSON, Flora
   Lark Rise to Candleford
   (i) pp. 120–123 ('Lark Rise', Ch. 7);
   (ii) pp. 118–121
   'Callers made a pleasant ... larger, smoother tomato.'
   Jerry Parish brings a cartload of bloaters – all with soft roes – and small, sour oranges; but few of the hamlet women have pence enough for luxuries such as these.
4. ibid.
   (i) pp. 128–131 ('Lark Rise', Ch. 7);
   (ii) pp. 125–128
   'There was no tallyman ... of beer on tap.'
   Gullible housewives buy wooden washstands, zinc baths, and barrels of beer on the instalment plan.The salesman of the first commodities collects as much of his dues as he thinks will be forthcoming, the brewer takes the debtors to court.
5. ibid.
   (i) pp. 133–137 ('Lark Rise', Ch. 7);
   (ii) pp. 130–133
   'The greatest thrill of all ... cheap-jack came.'
   A cheap-jack tries to tempt the villagers to buy his crockery and glassware; but he does very modest trade.

SATURDAY

1. GREENWOOD, Walter
   Love on the Dole
   pp. 53–55 (Part 1, Ch. 7)
   'Ten bob a week ... Saturday Pay Day.'
   The workers at Marlowe's pour out of the factory at the noon siren, with money jingling in their pockets, and football, winnings, and beer, uppermost in their minds.

SAVAGES

see CANNIBALS;
CHILDREN (as) SAVAGES;
PRIMITIVE PEOPLES

SCHOOL

see also: EDUCATION;
FIGHTING (by) BOYS (at) SCHOOL;
PUNISHMENT – CORPORAL – SCHOOL;
REBELS (at) SCHOOL;
REVOLT (at) SCHOOL;
SCHOOLS;
SUNDAY – SCHOOL;
TEACHING;
TRUANCY

SCHOOL

1. GORKY, Maxim
   Childhood
   (i) pp. 291–297 (Ch. 12); (ii) pp. 209–213
   'Much time flowed emptily by ... sit quiet! Yes, quiet!'
   Gorky is a mischief at school. He finds the lessons boring, and the teachers, objects of fun. It is not until a kindly bishop comes to the school, and speaks sympathetically to him, that Gorky decides to behave himself.

SCHOOL – ASSEMBLY

1. HINES, Barry
   A Kestrel for a Knave
   (i) pp. 56–59; (ii) pp. 46–48
   'Hymn number one ... which are in heaven.'
   Mr Gryce, the Headmaster, presides at morning assembly. A boy coughing excites his anger, and vindictiveness, so that any religious atmosphere there might have been is quite dissipated.
2. POINTON, Barry
   Break – in
   pp. 53–56 (Ch. 4)
   'School Assembly. No sign ... and girls were dismissed.'
   The invariable routine of sitting, praying, singing and listening. Among the school notices is the announcement of a table-tennis fixture with the local grammar school. The members of the team are bidden to show themselves, and be applauded.

3. ibid.
   pp. 93–97 (Ch. 8)
   'Friday was year assembly ... and assembly was over.'
   The year tutor announces that an English teacher is leaving the school. The teacher is applauded. Then the victorious table-tennis team is paraded to further applause and congratulation. Denton is unmoved by it all.

SCHOOL – DISCIPLINE

see PUNISHMENT – CORPORAL – SCHOOL;
REBELS (at) SCHOOL;
REVOLT (at) SCHOOL;
TEACHING – DISCIPLINE

SCHOOL – EXAMINATIONS

1. CHURCHILL, W.S.
   My Early Life
   pp. 23–24 (Ch. 2)
   'I had scarcely ... some other cause.'
   Churchill passes into Harrow as fate saw fit. He is required to sit an entrance examination; but the Headmaster takes this ritual no more seriously than Churchill does.
2. HUGHES, Thomas
   Tom Brown's Schooldays
   pp. 130–132 (Part 1, Ch. 8)
   'Tom, as has been said ... before second lesson.'
   Dr Arnold interrupts Tom's classroom mischief with his regular visit to test the boys' Latin. It is not an edifying occasion.

SCHOOL – EXPULSION

1. GRICE, Frederick
   The Bonny Pit Laddie
   pp. 61–63 (Ch. 8)
   'All these activities ... taken on at the colliery.'
   Kit plays truant. On his return, the Headmaster punishes him more severely than ever before, then expels him. Kit wins a moral victory.

2. O'BRIEN, Edna
   The Country Girls
   pp. 110–115 (Ch. 12)
   (Crime and Punishment pp. 9–16)
   'But all the time ... tomorrow,' she
   told us.'
   Baba is determined to leave the convent she and Caithleen hate so much.
   When Caithleen is already in trouble,
   she carries out a plan to get them
   expelled – they write an obscene
   messsage on a holy picture, and the
   expulsion is not long in following its
   discovery.

SCHOOL – INSPECTION

1. 'MISS READ'
   Village School
   (i) pp. 62–65 (Part 1, Ch. 8); (ii) pp.
   63–65
   'There were several bunches ... to
   know!' I thought.'
   A lady in beige arrives unexpectedly
   and announces herself as the needle-
   work inspector. She scorns the fine
   pieces of work she is shown: they are
   all out of date and excessively fussy.
2. THOMPSON, Flora
   Lark Rise to Candleford
   (i) pp. 202–205 ('Lark Rise', Ch. 12);
   (ii) pp. 188–191
   'Her Majesty's Inspector ... of sight
   and hearing.'
   The school inspector comes, and
   everyone, including the teacher, is on
   his best behaviour. He cows all
   comers and puts them firmly in their
   appointed place.

SCHOOL – LEAVING

1. DICKENS, Charles
   Bleak House
   see LEAVETAKING 4
2. LAWRENCE, D.H.
   The Rainbow
   see LEAVETAKING 8
3. NAUGHTON, Bill
   One Small Boy
   pp. 260–263 (Bk. 3, Ch. 7)

'This is the last ... he had it in him.'
It is Michael's last day at St.
Stephen's. He avoids having to confess to the class that he does not know
what he is going to do. He is suitably
sad during the last assembly in the
hall, but slips away before it is finished, to collect his school leaving
papers.
4. STOLZ, Mary
   Ready or Not
   pp. 167–171 (Ch. 11)
   'They yawned, first Morgan ... they
   didn't hear her.'
   The girls have only one more day of
   school left. Morgan, alone, appears to
   harbour some regrets. Betty announces grandly that she'll go to college,
   and Verna, less grandly, that she has
   got a job in a cafeteria. Morgan has
   no plans – only wistful regrets.

SCHOOL – REGISTRATION

1. HINES, Barry
   A Kestrel for a Knave
   (i) pp. 54–56; (ii) pp. 48–50
   'Billy had been standing ... the whole
   grid.'
   The register is taken in Billy's class.
   He jokes absent-mindedly, confusing
   Mr Crosley into marking an absentee
   present.
2. 'MISS READ'
   Village School
   (i) pp. 22–26 (Part 1, Ch. 3); (ii) pp.
   22–26
   'My desk was being ... we were all
   present.'
   New pupils are introduced, an informal 'assembly' is conducted, dinner
   money is taken, and somehow, amid
   all the business, the register is taken.

SCHOOL – REPORT

1. THOMAS, Dylan
   Quite Early one Morning
   pp. 83–84 ('Return Journey')
   'Oh yes, I remember ... the school
   magazine.'

His schoolmaster remembers Dylan as one who got up to the normal, the expected kinds of mischief. On the credit side is the fact that he edited the school magazine.

SCHOOL – SUBJECTS

1. CHURCH, Richard
   Over the Bridge
   pp. 67–68 (Ch. 6)
   'Long after I started ... been woven of horsehair.'
   The traumas of learning to read and reckon. The author reproaches himself for a besetting idleness of mind. Letters and numbers are major hurdles, physical and moral.
2. HINES, Barry
   A Kestrel for a Knave
   see FOOTBALL 1

SCHOOL – SUBJECTS – ARITHMETIC

1. GRICE, Frederick
   The Bonny Pit Laddie
   pp. 3–4 (Ch. 1)
   'Every school-day ... teachers took over.'
   Every day at the pit-village school starts in the same way: with tables chanted by the whole school, watched over by Mr Allcroft, the Headmaster.

SCHOOL – SUBJECTS – ART

1. 'MISS READ'
   Village School
   see CHILDREN 5
2. NAUGHTON, Bill
   One Small Boy
   pp. 127–129 (Bk. 2, Ch. 2)
   'He went off to find ... mind was a cabbage.'
   In Miss Skegham's class, pupils are permitted to draw only tulips. They graduate to roses and hyacinths when they are considered capable. Michael nearly brings Miss Skegham down

upon his head, by drawing the profile of a man.
3. THOMAS, Dylan
   A Portrait of the Artist as a Young Dog
   p. 41 ('The Fight')
   (Conflict 1, p. 135)
   'In Mr Trotter's ... except Mr Trotter.'
   In the drawing class, the boys of 4A draw naked girls, surreptitiously, and inaccurately. They gossip, and they speculate. The boys enjoy the drawing class, but the teacher does not.

SCHOOL – SUBJECTS – GEOGRAPHY

1. 'MISS READ'
   Village School
   (i) pp. 107–108 (Part 2, Ch. 12); (ii) pp. 106–107
   'Playtime over ... out pretty good!'
   Miss Read impresses upon her mixed bunch of all-age village children, the wonders of the world, with the aid of a sturdy globe. She twirls it and explains about night and day. One boy, at least, is impressed.

SCHOOL – SUBJECTS – LATIN

1. CHURCHILL, W.S.
   My Early Life
   pp. 18–19 (Ch. 1)
   'When the last sound ... solace and profit.'
   Churchill, on his first day at prep. school, comes face to face with the First Declension. He is suitably mystified.
2. ELIOT, George
   The Mill on the Floss
   pp. 179–181 (Ch. 1, Part 2)
   'Now then Maggie ... Let me go on.'
   Maggie is testing Tom on his Latin homework. He doesn't understand it, he hasn't learnt it properly, but he still tries to appear superior to his little sister. She is fascinated.

3. HUGHES, Thomas
   Tom Brown's Schooldays
   see SCHOOL – EXAMINATIONS 2

SCHOOLS – BOARDING

1. GRAVES, Robert
   Goodbye to All That
   pp. 37–39 (Ch. 6)
   'From my first moment ... by cynicism and foulness.'
   As a new inmate at Charterhouse, Graves is lonely and 'different'. The school is boorishly attached to games and decidedly agin book-learning. The bookish, sensitive Graves comes near to breakdown.
2. ibid.
   pp. 40–44 (Ch. 7)
   'Half-way through ... answer the letter.'
   Graves takes up boxing to protect himself against the hearties, who rule the roost at Charterhouse. The Vth form asserts its privileges in the face of First Eleven muscle-power, and makes life easier for the likes of Graves, the poet.
3. HUGHES, Thomas
   Tom Brown's Schooldays
   pp. 57–59 (Part 1, Ch. 3)
   'Now the theory ... good deal of his new life.'
   Young Tom is at a private boarding school under the superintendence of two bored ushers. Things get off to a bad start when his first letter home miscarries.
4. ibid.
   see REVOLT 3
5. ibid.
   see SERVANTS 2
6. JOYCE, James
   A Portrait of the Artist as a Young Man
   pp. 8–15 (Ch. 1)
   (Come Down and Startle, pp. 60–62)
   'The wide playgrounds ... the earth moved round always.'
   Young Stephen is a long way from home. He reflects on his recent

experiences of noisy, aggressive, and curious boys, and counts the days to Christmas.

SCHOOLS – BOARDING – FIRST DAY

1. ALMEDINGEN, E.M.
   Litte Katia
   pp. 170–174 (Ch. 17)
   'One golden October ... to echo her.'
   Katia goes as a boarder to Madame Guinter's, the best girls' school in Tver. She is discouraged by her first view of it, but soon finds a friend. After a bad start, she gives a good account of herself in the first lesson, but is horrified by the food.
2. BRONTË, Charlotte
   Jane Eyre
   (i) pp. 47–57 (Ch. 5); (ii) pp. 47–54
   'The night passed rapidly ... first day at Lowood.'
   Jane Eyre's first day at school begins with burnt porridge, and a feeling of comfortless loneliness. After a morning's lessons the superintendent, from her own generosity, provides bread and cheese to supplement the spoilt breakfast; the rest of the day's meals are dreary enough. Jane makes friends with a fellow pupil.
3. CHURCHILL, W.S.
   My Early Life
   pp. 17–19 (Ch. 1)
   'The school my parents ... solace and profit.'
   Young Churchill attends prep. school. His mother leaves him with the Headmaster, and the Headmaster leaves him with the First Declension. He makes very little of it.
4. HUGHES, Thomas
   Tom Brown's Schooldays
   pp. 107–110 (Part 1, Ch. 6)
   'I say, were you ever tossed ... to meditate upon.'
   Tom and a friend are tossed in a blanket as tradition requires. It's a dangerous game, but because they do not resist, they suffer no harm.

5. O'BRIEN, Edna
The Country Girls
pp. 73–79 (Ch. 8)
'The convent was a grey ... deathly, unhappy silence.'
Caithleen and Baba arrive at the convent where they are to be boarders. They have tea, and go to chapel before going up to their dormitory. 'Everyone seemed to be eating or crying for their mothers.'

6. ibid.
pp. 80–86 (Ch. 9)
'We were wakened ... It was almost dusk.'
The first full day at the convent – drill in the open yard, a head inspection, Latin, English and Maths, a nauseating Lunch, more lessons and a walk.

SCHOOLS – ELEMENTARY

1. DICKENS, Charles
Great Expectations
(i) pp. 79–81 (Ch. 10); (ii) pp. 68–69
'The felicitous idea ... these circumstances.'
In an effort, to grow uncommon, and book-learned like Estella, Pip is enrolled at the local Dame School. When the boys are not fighting and being cuffed, they read aloud from tattered Testaments. The circumstances are not propitious for education.

2. THOMPSON, Flora
Lark Rise to Candleford
(i) pp. 190–193 ('Lark Rise', Ch. 11); (ii) pp. 178–180
'The schoolmistress in charge ... she was pages ahead.'
The unimaginative grind at the Fordlow National School: the four r's (the usual three, and a liberal dash of established religion), copying copperplate maxims, and laboured reading aloud.
see also: SCHOOL – INSPECTION 2

3. WELLS, H.G.
The History of Mr Polly
pp. 7–11 (Ch. 1, Part 2)

'I remember seeing ... something for a living.'
Polly's education does little or nothing for him. It stunts his 'curiosities and willingness'. He attends a National School where economy is all and a good memory for Gradgrind facts is the most lauded asset.

SCHOOLS – ELEMENTARY – FIRST DAY

1. BALDWIN, Michael
Grandad with Snails
pp. 140–146 (Ch. 17)
'So this was the New School ... the long rows of wet cabbages.'
A hotchpotch of arithmetic and religion greets Michael and his mother, at the new school. Mr Noake is handy with a cane, and the light-fingered Sheild is handy with the school soap. Michael is led, unprotesting to Miss Rose's class.

2. LEE, Laurie
Cider with Rosie
(i) pp. 26–28 (Ch. 3, 'Village School');
(ii) pp. 42–44
(Conflict 1, p. 100)
'The village school ... our wandering fingers.'
Laurie Lee's first day at the village school, where he is an unwilling and disappointed pupil. After a week he feels like a veteran.

SCHOOLS – INFANTS

1. KIRKUP, James
The Only Child
pp. 123–130 (Ch. 10)
'Day followed day ... and charity.'
Jim settles in at school; but there is a soullessness about it, and a want of imagination. Jim's fancies are scoffed at, and his loneliness is exploited by bullies, who stuff him into a rubbish bin, and leave him there.

SCHOOLS – INFANTS – FIRST DAY

1. KIRKUP, James
   The Only Child
   pp. 121–123 (Ch. 10)
   (Impact Two, pp. 141–142)
   'But when I started ... not be mended.'
   Jim makes an unencouraging start. The teacher frightens him, and he wets the floor. Sent back to school after dinner, much against his will, he makes a paperchain. But at the school gate, an older girl, destroys it – and a little of Jim's innocence.

SCHOOLS – PRIMARY

1. 'MISS READ'
   Village School
   (i) pp. 227–230 (Part 3, Ch. 24); (ii) pp. 228–230
   'It was the last day ... young lady's humiliation.'
   All the children are given jobs to do. Miss Read inquires into pupil numbers for the next school year, and 'Constantinople' is raided for words.

SCHOOLS – PRIMARY – FIRST DAY

1. LEE, Harper
   To Kill a Mockingbird
   (i) pp. 21–28 (Ch. 2); (ii) pp. 21–28
   'Jem condescended ... a pretty little thing.'
   Scout gets into trouble on her first morning, for being able to read ahead of everybody else; and then for trying to teach her teacher. To her mystification, she has to stand in the corner.
2. ibid.
   see TEACHING – FIRST DAY 6
3. 'MISS READ'
   Village School
   see SCHOOL – REGISTRATION 2

SCHOOLS – SECONDARY

1. ALLEN, Walter
   All in a Lifetime
   pp. 46–47; 48–49 (Ch. 6)
   'After that, my education ... I was proud of it'; 'Yet it was a wonderful ... then 'Dismiss!' '
   Billy goes to the High School, a Victorian Gothic marvel. He is not there for long, and he is aware of his social inferiority, but the headmaster alone is an experience to be savoured.
2. POINTON, Barry
   Break-in
   pp. 5–10 (Ch. 1)
   'Right, Mr Foster ... waited for time to pass.'
   Having been interviewed by his year tutor, for wearing red socks, Denton joins his friend in the form-room. They commiserate with each other about school uniform, routine, examinations and lectures from teachers from across the generation gap. They wait for the afternoon to pass.
3. WELLS, H.G.
   Kipps
   pp. 9–13 (Bk. 1, Ch. 1, Sn. 2)
   'Cavendish Academy, the school ... severities, for an hour.'
   The Cavendish Academy, under the capricious Mr Woodrow. Education is a window-dressing for parents; what takes place in the classroom is more often mere containment. The young Kipps learns to pass the time.

SCHOOL – SECONDARY – FIRST DAY

1. LLWELLYN, Richard
   How Green was my Valley
   pp. 141–148 (Ch. 16)
   'I started off to school ... your conduct acordingly.'
   Huw proves his intellectual worth, but is scorned by both pupils and teacher on his first day. The pupils ruin his

books, and pencil box, and he ends up in a fight.

SCORPIONS

1. DURRELL, Gerald
    My Family and other Animals
    pp. 70–72 (Part 1, Ch. 5)
    'He sighed deeply but ... a scorpion bottle with me.'
    An old peasant recommends to Gerald a remedy against scorpion-stings. He shows him a phial containing a dead scorpion, and olive oil that has absorbed its poison; and he tells him about a shepherd friend who died of the sting, unremedied.
2. ibid.
    pp. 128–132 (Part 2, Ch. 9)
    'But the shyest and most ... before seeing them again.'
    Gerald flouts a rule of the household when he brings a matchbox full of scorpions (a mother and her babies) into the house. Larry opens the box thinking to find a match, and all hell is let loose over the dinner table.
3. STEINBECK, John
    The Pearl
    pp. 4–7 (Ch. 1)
    (Young Impact 2, pp. 104–106)
    'The sun was warming ... turned to moans.'
    Kino's baby, Coyotito, is stung by a scorpion, which he has been unable to catch in time. His wife Juana immediately tries to suck out the poison.

SCULPTURE

1. CARY, Joyce
    The Horse's Mouth
    pp. 250–256 (Ch. 31)
    'There was the usual ... see out of his eyes.'
    Abel is stuck with his war memorial, and Gulley tries to help. Lolie, Abel's wife and model is worried about her husband but continues to pose in odd positions until inspiration returns.

SEA

see also: FEAR (of) SEA;
RESCUE (from) SEA;
SHIPWRECKS;
SURVIVAL (at) SEA;
VOYAGES

SEA

1. GOLDING, William
    Pincher Martin
    see SHIPWRECKS 10
2. HEMINGWAY, Ernest
    The Old Man and the Sea
    pp. 24–27
    'The old man drank ... big one with them.'
    The old man rows out into the Gulf, very early in the morning. In the darkness, he hears the plashing of other oars. He reflects upon the fishes and birds, and upon the sea, his wife, his trouble and strife.
3. HEYERDAHL, Thor
    The Kon-Tiki Expedition
    pp. 78–81 (Ch. 4)
    'As the troughs ... in a sardine tin.'
    The first three days and nights of the expedition prove to be the hardest, in the wind and heavy seas of the Humboldt current. In two-hour shifts, the men spend the whole time steadying the steering oar, and trying to keep the raft stern to the sea and wind.
4. ibid.
    pp. 119–121 (Ch. 5)
    'Then Erik had the idea ... truer one than ours.'
    Erik makes a diving basket to protect them when going below the raft to make repairs. It also provides a new form of entertainment as there is so much to see under the water.
5. MACKEN, Walter
    God made Sunday and Other Stories
    see SWIMMING – LEARNING 1

SEA – BATTLES – 1939–45

see SECOND WORLD WAR – SEA
BATTLES

SEA – DIVING

1. SPERRY, Armstrong
   The Boy who was afraid
   pp. 58–61 (Ch. 4)
   'How fantastic ... an eternity.'
   Mafatu drops his knife in the sea, and
   conquering his fear, dives to retrieve
   it. He is attacked by an octopus but
   manages to kill it.
2. WYNDHAM, John
   The Kraken Wakes
   pp. 28–33 (Phase One)
   'Soon after sunrise we were ... volleys
   were fired over the spot.'
   Two naval technicians go down twelve
   hundred fathoms, in the Caribbean,
   in a bathyscope. Their mission is to
   find a reported marine intelligence.
   They see it and report, until com-
   munication with the surface is interrupted ...

SEA – TIDES

1. BAWDEN, Nina
   On the Run
   pp. 153–158 (Ch. 17)
   'When Ben woke, ... a marvellous,
   dramatic sight.'
   Lil, Ben and Thomas are hiding in a
   cave in the cliffs. They wake in the
   night to find the tide fast approaching
   – and notice the high tide mark high
   on the walls. Thomas and Lil manage
   to climb a chimney to a higher cave,
   but Ben, spurred on by terror, has to
   climb the cliff face.
2. TOWNSEND, John Rowe
   The Intruder
   pp. 153–157 (Ch. 25)
   'Not that place ... scared, scared!'
   Jane persuades Jeremy to drive out to
   the ruined church, accessible only by
   a causeway at high tide, despite the
   coming storm. She is exhilarated by
   the weather, and refuses to go back

when he leaves – when sudden fear
changes her mind, and it is too late
and she is cut off.
3. ibid.
   pp. 162–166 (Ch. 26)
   'Once on the beach ... to the stranger.'
   Arnold is pursued by the mysterious
   stranger who has come to live in their
   house. He runs on to the sands as the
   tide is rising, backed by a strong
   wind, knowing that he can escape but
   the stranger probably cannot.
4. ibid.
   pp. 167–175 (Ch. 27)
   'She was salty ... He must be.'
   Arnold escaping from his pursuer,
   reaches the ruined church where Jane
   is cut off by the tide. The water is still
   rising and they have to break down
   part of a wall in order to climb the
   tower and save themselves.

SEASIDE

1. KIRKUP, James
   The Only Child
   pp. 175–181 (Ch. 14)
   (Come Down and Startle, pp. 90–93)
   'A little farther along ... sixth birthday.'
   Jim paddles in the company of forth-
   right, high-spirited women, and
   overdressed men. He has his tea on
   the beach with his parents, and
   watches a sand-sculptor build a
   music-hall complete with sea-shell
   footlights.
2. KNOWLES, John
   A Separate Peace
   see FRIENDS – BOYS 3
3. LEE, Laurie
   Cider with Rosie
   see EXCURSIONS 3
4. 'MISS READ'
   Village School
   see EXCURSIONS 4
5. STEINBECK, John
   The Pearl
   pp. 13–14 (Ch. 2)
   'The town lay ... this area.'

A hot, hazy morning on the beach —
the buildings, the boats, the sea, and
the mirage-laden air.

6. THOMAS, Dylan
   *A Portrait of the Artist as a Young
   Dog*
   pp. 108–110 ('One Warm Saturday')
   'The young man ... tents of towels.'
   Dylan takes in the sights and sounds
   of Porthcawl beach on a warm Saturday evening. For a moment or two he
   is part of it; but he knows he is as
   apart from what he sees, as Mr
   Matthews, the hellfire beach preacher.

7. THOMAS, Dylan
   A Prospect of the Sea
   see EXCURSIONS 5

8. THOMAS, Dylan
   Quite Early one Morning
   see HOLIDAYS 5

SECOND WORLD WAR

see also: ARMY; ESCAPE – SECOND
WORLD WAR;
FLYING – 1939–45;
FLYING – ACCIDENTS – 1939–45;
HIDING (from) ENEMY – 1939–45;
JEWS – SECOND WORLD WAR;
PRISON (of) WAR; TANKS

SECOND WORLD WAR

1. FRANK, Anne
   The Diary of Anne Frank
   pp. 62–63 (13.1.43)
   'Everything has upset me ... wait for
   death.'
   The state of the war, the suffering of
   millions especially Jews and Dutch
   people, as seen from the Frank
   Family's hideout at the beginning of
   1943.

2. HOLBROOK, David
   Flesh Wounds
   pp. 189–191 (Ch. 6)
   ' "Spread out," ... huge human
   agonies.'
   The tanks are in action. Shelling is
   heavy, knocking men over with their

screaming blasts. The noise is fright-
ful, and the fear disabling.

3. ibid.
   see SECOND WORLD WAR – BOMBING 3

4. ibid.
   see WAR – INJURIES 1

5. ibid.
   see ARMY – DEMOBILIZATION 1

SECOND WORLD WAR – AMERICA

1. KNOWLES, John
   A Separate Peace
   pp. 42–44 (Ch. 3)
   'Everyone has a moment ... being
   unpatriotic.'
   pp. 108–109 (Ch. 7)
   'I turned and trudged ... among
   heroic men.'
   pp. 158–159 (Ch. 10)
   'That night I made ... saved our
   lives.'
   The war seems an awful long way
   away from the sheltered concerns of
   the Devon School. It is the time when
   Gene grows up and feels like an
   American; when he does his bit with
   school friends, shovelling snow from a
   railway line, and when he turns out to
   be surplus to the war's requirements.

2. ibid.
   see ARMY – ENLISTMENT 2

SECOND WORLD WAR – BOMBING

1. ALLEN, Walter
   All in a Lifetime
   pp. 18–20 (Ch. 3)
   'Lens-grinding was ... twenty years I
   should think.'
   Billy is persuaded to shelter under the
   stairs during heavy bombing. He is
   sure the bombs are directed at him.
   One bonus is the glass lying about
   afterwards, that he can use for his
   lens-grinding.

2. HAUGAARD, Erich
   The Little Fishes
   pp. 80–85 (Ch. 8)

'It was the smell of dust ... filled me with shame.'

Bombs have been dropped on Guido's part of town. He picks his way through the rubble, to an old woman who has lost her cat. Then he walks to the ruin of a friend's house, and imagines her body, dead, and buried under the crumbled walls.

3. HOLBROOK, David
   Flesh Wounds
   pp. 195–197 (Ch. 7)
   'As Paul and his crews ... bottles in their hands.'
   A pilotless bomber is hit, and breaks away from its Squadron, to create terror among British tank crews, at which it dives with its cargo of bombs.

4. THOMAS, Leslie
   This Time Next Week
   pp. 62–65 (Ch. 6)
   'In the empty hours ... young criminal under his care.'
   The orphanage is in the thick of the bombing. When the alarm is raised, all the boys are shepherded into shelters in the grounds. From here they can hear the dreaded doodle-bugs, and watch the Gaffer running about accounting for all his charges.

SECOND WORLD WAR – BURMA

1. BATES, H.E.
   The Purple Plain
   pp. 55–60 (Chs. 6, 7)
   'And then suddenly, he was not ... weak and quivering.'
   A Burmese village is bombed during the Second World War. Forrester and a Burmese girl shelter together, then help with the wounded when the raid is over. Forrester is angered by all the futile suffering.
   see also: PANIC 1

SECOND WORLD WAR – D-DAY

1. FRANK, Anne
   The Diary of Anne Frank

pp. 203–204 (6.6.44)
' "This is D-day ... in September or October.'
D-Day as seen from the Secret Annexe – Anne feels that at last friends are approaching.

2. HOLBROOK, David
   Flesh Wounds
   pp. 100–104 (Ch. 3)
   'And there he saw France ... watching tankmen's souls.'
   The French coast is sighted. There is an incredible number of boats about. Suddenly a salvo of enemy shells, and corpses in a boat, rob the scene of its magnificence.

3. ibid.
   pp. 106–107 (Ch. 3)
   'Had he looked at ... into the French beach.'
   Paul's turn comes. It's time for his waterborne tank to take to the ferry that will take it ashore.

4. ibid.
   pp. 110–112 (Ch. 3)
   'After so many years ... through the turret hole.'
   The Sherman tank and her crew. The shelling of a tank is the death of a monster. It's a dramatic and unnerving sight.

SECOND WORLD WAR – DUNKIRK

1. GALLICO, Paul
   The Snow Goose/The Small Miracle
   (i) pp. 23–26; 26–30 ('The Snow Goose'); (ii) pp. 31–35; 36–41
   'Frith saw the yellow light ... back to the empty lighthouse.'; 'Now the story becomes ... big goose. Whatcher know?'
   Frith finds Philip making ready to sail to Dunkirk, to add his boat to the fleet evacuating the stranded troops. A cockney soldier describes later how brave and untiring Philip has been, and how the snow goose has been a talisman of good fortune.

SECOND WORLD WAR – EVACUATION

1. BARNES, Ron
   A Licence to Live
   pp. 2–3 (Ch. 1)
   'Well we finally made it ... cup of tea' said my father.'
   The Barnes family is billeted in a big old house in the country. Ron's father dismantles a barn at the back for firewood, since there is nothing else to burn. The billeting officer is very annoyed, but on his next visit, he brings coal.

2. BAWDEN, Nina
   Carrie's War
   (i) pp. 19–25 (Ch. 2); (ii) pp. 16–21
   'He threw up ... the pretty one, really.'
   Carrie and Nick are evacuated during the Second World War, to a Welsh mining-town. Their mother had been brave at the parting, but they feel lonely and isolated on arrival especially when the children are being chosen by the townspeople. They are left almost to the last, and taken only reluctantly.

3. ibid.
   (i) pp. 25–30 (Ch. 2); (ii) pp. 21–26
   'Miss Evans walked ... real-life OGRE.'
   The children go with Miss Evans to their new home. They are amazed by the rules about keeping the house clean, made by Mr Evans, and are glad to be out of his way when he comes home.

4. SHUTE, Nevil
   A Town like Alice
   (i) pp. 35–41 (Ch. 2); (ii) pp. 37–42
   'Soon the married women ... all his endeavour.'
   As the Japanese make their way south through Malaya, the Europeans are evacuated. Jean Paget and her friends, the Hollands, start out on their journey, and encounter difficulties right from the beginning.

SECOND WORLD WAR – MALAYA

1. SHUTE, Nevil
   A Town like Alice
   (i) pp. 41–49 (Ch. 2); (ii) pp. 42–49
   'The Japanese came ... and went away.'
   The Japanese occupy Panong, where a group of Europeans are awaiting evacuation. The men are taken away, and the women and children are kept prisoner in an office. They are not ill-treated, but are neglected, and then told to begin a long march to a camp.

2. ibid.
   (i) pp. 49–57 (Ch. 2); (ii) pp. 49–56
   'For the remainder of the day ... ever saw of him.'
   The group of English women and children begin their long march to a prison camp. It is hot and wearying, and the older women suffer especially. One woman dies, and the group insists on resting for a day.

SECOND WORLD WAR – POLAND

1. SERRAILLIER, Ian
   The Silver Sword
   see ARMY 3

SECOND WORLD WAR – RATIONING

1. BARNES, Ron
   A Licence to Live
   pp. 10–12 (Ch. 1)
   'Almost every commodity ... the rat race began.'
   Acute shortages in the East End, making do and mending, sweet coupons, and the black market.

SECOND WORLD WAR – RUSSIA

1. SHOLOKHOV, Mikhail
   Fierce and Gentle Warriors

pp. 56–62 ('The Fate of a Man', Ch. 2)
'But I didn't get in even … drove us on farther.'
A Russian ex-combatant tells of how he narrowly escaped death, only to be captured by the Germans. He tells of how his fellow countrymen bore him up in his wounded state, of how a doctor helped him, and of how the Germans shot those they supposed were Jews.
see also: PRISON (of) WAR 2

2. SOLZHENITSYN, Alexander
    One Day in the Life of Ivan Denisovich
    pp. 48–50
    'They'd given Kilgas twenty-five years ˋ… the forest again next morning.'
    Shukhov is near the end of his prison term. He was sentenced on a trumped up charge of collaborating with the Germans, though in reality he was an escaped P.O.W. He reflects, with others, on his eight years in Russian labour-camps.

SECOND WORLD WAR – SEA-BATTLES

1. FORESTER, C.S.
    The Ship
    see SHIPS – GUNS 1
2. ibid.
    pp. 52–56 (Ch. 9)
    'The Italian fleet was up … to the send of the sea.'
    HMS Artemis is one of five light cruisers accompanying the Malta convoy. She is about to close with the Italian fleet. The crew is told 'the situation'. All is eager expectation.
3. ibid.
    pp. 64–69 (Ch. 11)
    'Artemis was flying … a horde of Calibans.'
    The five British cruisers lay a thick smoke screen to cover their approach to within range of the Italian fleet. The captain gives orders that ensure

the ship's readiness to fire, on emergence from the smoke.
4. ibid.
    see NAVY – DISCIPLINE 2
5. ibid.
    pp. 100–103 (Ch. 17)
    'The enemy's salvoes were creeping … in the gloom of the smoke-screen.'
    An Italian shell scores a hit. It wipes out the crew of a pompom gun, and bursts just beneath the upper deck, wreaking particular havoc in the officers' wardroom. A huge, jagged hole is torn in the ship's side, but the ship's efficiency is unimpaired.

SECOND WORLD WAR – SIAM – SURRENDER

1. BOULLE, Pierre
    The Bridge on the River Kwai
    see ARMY – DISCIPLINE 1

SELF-SACRIFICE

1. FALKNER, J. Meade
    Moonfleet
    see SHIPWRECKS 9
2. JOHNSON, Dorothy M.
    The Hanging Tree
    see RESCUE (from) HANGING 1
3. WILDE, Oscar
    The Happy Prince and Other Stories
    (i) pp. 161–166 ('The Happy Prince'); (ii) pp. 15–21
    'Who are you? … at the Prince's feet.'
    The Prince sacrifices his jewels on behalf of the poor of his city, and the swallow sacrifices his winter-warmth in Egypt, to do the Prince's bidding.
4. ibid.
    see FRIENDS 4

SELFISHNESS

see also: MATERIALISM;
MISERS

SELFISHNESS

1. BRONTË, Charlotte
   Shirley
   (i) pp. 166–167 (Ch. 10); (ii) pp. 183–184
   'Time wore on ... a nation of shopkeepers!'
   The author criticises the British 'mercantile classes', at the time of the Peninsular War, for their single-minded concern for trade. The war distresses them, only because it touches their purses.
2. CHAPLIN, Sid
   The Leaping Lad and Other Stories
   see CONSCIENCE 2
3. DICKENS, Charles
   Bleak House
   (i) pp. 68–71 (Ch. 6); (ii) pp. 68–71
   'Are you arrested ... Good night.'
   Mr Skimpole is arrested for debt and appeals to Esther and Richard for help, on the grounds that he does not understand money, and therefore should be allowed to enjoy his life without such worries.
4. ibid.
   (i) p. 478 (Ch. 37); (ii) p. 478
   'I certainly did not see ... it may be so.'
   Mr Skimpole explains how he believes some people are made to suffer in order that he may count his blessings by comparison.
5. FIELDING, Henry
   Joseph Andrews
   see CHARITY 8
6. HARDY, Thomas
   Under the Greenwood Tree
   see PRIDE 3
7. HAUGAARD, Erich
   The Little Fishes
   see HUNGER 6
8. O'BRIEN, Edna
   The Country Girls
   pp. 30–32 (Ch. 3)
   'Have you nits ... I was clumsy.'
   Baba visits her friend Caithleen's house, while her mother is away. She acts as if she owns both Caithleen and the house.
9. SHOLOKHOV, Mikhail
   Fierce and Gentle Warriors
   see COMMUNISM 5
10. STEINBECK, John
    The Grapes of Wrath
    (i) pp. 30–32 (Ch. 5); (ii) pp. 35–37
    'At noon the tractor driver ... after the tractor.'
    The driver of the tractor who is bulldozing the houses and lands of evicted farmers turns out to be a local boy. He is not ashamed, and describes how he needs the money.
11. WILDE, Oscar
    The Happy Prince and Other Stories
    (i) pp. 177–179 ('The Selfish Giant');
    (ii) pp. 27–30
    'Every afternoon ... what he has done.'
    The giant builds a high wall round his garden and forbids the children to play in it. As a result the Spring does not come to his garden – until the day the children find a hole in the wall.
12. ibid.
    see FRIENDS 4

SELLING

see BUYING (and) SELLING (by)
DEALERS;
MARKETS;
PEDLARS;
SALESMEN

SERVANTS

1. GASKELL, Mrs
   Cranford
   (i) pp. 36–37 (Ch. 3); (ii) pp. 64–65
   'This subject of servants ... prayers at ten.'
   Miss Matty's servant-maid is forbidden to have followers, but the narrator suspects that she does not obey this rule.
2. HUGHES, Thomas
   Tom Brown's Schooldays
   pp. 154–155 (Part 1, Ch. 9)

'So East and Tom ... I couldn't sit in it.'

The sixth form praepostors complain about their fags, their workshyness and independence, in just the same way as they might have heard their parents talk of the servants.

3. LEE, Laurie
   Cider with Rosie
   (i) pp. 83–87 (Ch. 7, 'Mother'); (ii) pp. 114–119
   'When her brothers ... so exciting.'
   Mrs Lee reminisces about her days in service – the grand meals, the entertaining, the long hard days, the fun 'below-stairs' and two encounters with the Gentry.

4. LESSING, Doris
   The Grass is Singing
   see AUTHORITY 5

5. PEYTON, K.M.
   Flambards
   (i) pp. 70–72 (Ch. 5); (ii) pp. 90–93
   'Soon the horses were ... not be born into them.'
   As Christina grows older, and more proficient as a horesewoman, she senses the social gap between herself and Dick the groom, looming larger. She talks to Will about it, and he shocks her by suggesting that social distinctions should be based on merit.

6. THOMPSON, Flora
   Lark Rise to Candleford
   see INTERVIEWS 7

7. ibid.
   pp. 172–174 ('Lark Rise', Ch. 10); (ii) pp. 163–165
   'The girls who 'went into ... children on Saturday.'
   The duties, the fare, the social lives, and the pitiable wages of girls in service in the Oxfordshire of the 'eighties.

SEX

see also: LOVE – DESIRE

258

SEX

1. BRAITHWAITE, E.R.
   To Sir with Love
   see GOSSIP 3

2. HUXLEY, Aldous
   Brave New World
   pp. 35–37 (Ch. 3)
   'Outside in the garden ... Mustapha Mond.'
   The Director of the Central London Hatchery and Conditioning Centre watches with approval young children engaging in simple love-play. He tells his students of how, in the past, such instincts had to be repressed, with dire results.

3. LAWRENCE, D.H.
   The Virgin and the Gipsy
   pp. 62–64 (Part 7)
   'What is it, Lucille ... 'Quite!' said Yvette.'
   The two sisters exchange views about sex. Lucille is frankly disgusted by the thought of it, and can't believe it has much to do with love. Yvette, is not so sure: she believes that she might fall in love, even that she might be in it. But she is confused by the sex part of it.
   see also: LOVE 11

4. TATE, Joan
   Sam and Me
   pp. 38–43 (Ch. 3)
   'There must have been twenty ... dullness of passed-on information.'
   Shirley, one of Jo's workmates, introduces her into a new world of dating, and pre-marital sex. Jo longs to ask Shirley to explain such things to her, but Shirley takes it all so much for granted, that she can't begin to fathom Jo's ignorance.

SEX – EDUCATION

1. BARSTOW, Stan
   Joby
   pp. 67–72 (Ch. 4)
   'Joby had never been alone ... about it,' Joby said.'

Molly McCleod goes spying on her big sister, and Joby goes with her. They see her with a boy, making abandoned love. Joby's sex-awareness is found wanting, so Molly takes it upon herself to educate him.

2. LEE, Harper
   To Kill a Mockingbird
   (i) pp. 148–150 (Ch. 14); (ii) pp. 145–147
   'I must have slept ... to run off to.'
   Dill gets into bed with Scout to tell her his troubles, and why he ran away from them. He suggests to her that they might have a baby, but neither has much idea as to the technicalities.

3. LEE, Laurie
   Cider with Rosie
   (i) pp. 155–156 (Ch. 12, 'First Bite at the Apple'); (ii) pp. 203–205
   'So quiet ... the separate trees.'
   Laurie, at the age of eleven or twelve, has his first encounter with the opposite sex – Jo, a quiet and mysterious girl, allows him to explore, but in a very detached way.

4. ibid.
   (i) pp. 159–162 (Ch. 12, 'First Bite at the Apple'); (ii) pp. 207–211
   'The day Rosie Burdock ... she came again.'
   During hay-making Laurie drinks 'Cider with Rosie' and they lie down together under a hay-wagon. He experiences a new bliss and walks home in a dream.
   see also: GANGS – BOYS 3

5. THOMPSON, Flora
   Lark Rise to Candleford
   see BIRTH 9

SEX – ENCOUNTERS

1. HITCHMAN, Janet
   The King of the Barbareens
   pp. 106–108 (Ch. 5)
   'One such afternoon ... made no sense at all.'
   On the heath, one afternoon, Elsie is accosted by a man; improper suggestions are made to her, before she

runs off to tell her foster-parents. Their unsympathetic inquiries do nothing to mitigate her growing fears.

2. NAUGHTON, Bill
   One Small Boy
   pp. 118–122 (Bk. 2, Ch. 1)
   'A few yards away ... cosy bed?' he thought.'
   Michael falls in with three girls and some younger children, playing at hospitals. Michael is prevailed upon to play the part of a wounded officer. When one of the girls has him to herself, she explores his private parts with all the authority of a trained nurse.

3. O'BRIEN, Edna
   The Country Girls
   pp. 154–155 (Ch. 16); pp. 158–166 (Ch. 17); (*see also:* Growing Up, pp. 79–81)
   'Two rich men ... got anything new.'
   'The foyer of the hotel ... life was just beginning.'
   Caithleen and Baba have a date with two rich, middle-aged men. They go out for a meal, and then to the home of one of them. Baba enjoys playing 'woman of the world' but Caithleen is uncomfortable and unhappy. She is angered by Harry's advances, and is relieved when they finally get away.

4. ZINDEL, Paul
   The Pigman
   pp. 91–94 (Ch. 11)
   'The sun was shining, and the ice ... and she was lovely.'
   John and Lorraine are alone in Mr Pignati's house preparing for dinner. John dresses in Mr Pignati's clothes, and Lorraine in his wife's. This touch of fantasy is enough to excite John to careless romantic raptures.

SHAME

see also: EMBARRASSMENT; HUMILIATION

SHAME

1. DICKENS, Charles
   Great Expectations
   see SOCIAL CLASS – SNOBBERY 4
2. GORKY, Maxim
   Childhood
   see SUICIDE 6
3. MANKOWITZ, Wolf
   Make me an Offer
   pp. 115–127 ('The Portrait')
   'Not very many strangers ... should be in pawn.'
   An old Orthodox Jewish Man has his portrait painted, by an artist who likes his face. The picture later turns up, a hundred fold, on Ikons on a market stall. The old man has to buy the lot, to save himself the shame.
4. PATON, Alan
   Cry, the Beloved Country
   (i) pp. 123–129 (Bk. 2, Ch. 8); (ii) pp. 152–157
   'One of the favourite nieces ... for lunch, she said.'
   Rev. Kumalo is making enquiries in Johannesburg about someone from his village. At the house of a white family he is horrified to come face to face with the father of the man murdered by his own son – at first he is overcome, then haltingly explains who he is. His admission is received with sympathy.

SHARKS

1. CALDWELL, John
   Desperate Voyage
   pp. 6–11 (Ch. 1)
   'At 10 a.m. I found a new ... don't haul sharks aboard!'
   It is the author's ambition to have a shark's jawbone to show his wife. He does battle with a blunt-faced monster and he subdues it after prodigious work with an axe. But the cost to his boat is much more than he should have paid.
2. ibid.
   pp. 137–143 (Ch. 14)

'Near the bow, and on ... afternoon and all night.'
A shark that could solve all the author's food problems swims lazily near the boat. It waits while he fashions a spear, and presents itself conveniently to be killed. But the author is not to have his prize. Other sharks finish him off under the author's eyes.

3. GRIMBLE, Sir Arthur
   A Pattern of Islands
   pp. 58–60 (Ch. 5)
   'Thirty-five years ... hundred yards off.'
   Shark-fishing in the Gilbert and Ellice Islands in the days of the ironwood hook. A Tarawa friend engages a tiger shark in single combat, knifing it as it lunges at him, as if unpeeling a banana.
4. ibid.
   see RESCUE (from) SHARKS 1
5. ibid.
   pp. 66–68 (Ch. 5)
   'I gave up fishing ... consolation prize.'
   Arthur asks to be allowed to 'bag' a tiger shark of his own. He does not realize what he is asking. Inexperienced as he is, he is unprepared for the dance the dying shark leads him, and for the 'innocent fun' he gives the watching villagers.
6. ibid.
   see SUPERSTITION 8
7. HEMINGWAY, Ernest
   The Old Man and the Sea
   pp. 99–103; 107–110; 113–115; 118–120
   'They sailed well ... down very slowly'; 'He had sailed ... on to her course.'; 'The next shark ... down from the fish.'; 'He was stiff ... weight beside her.'
   The sharks mutilate the marlin that the old man has spent so much time and effort in catching. The old man does his exhausted best to beat them off, but he cannot prevent his marlin being torn apart.

8. HEYERDAHL, Thor
The Kon-Tiki Expedition
pp. 91–93 (Ch. 4)
'Knut had been squatting ... of the whale shark.'
Knut looks up from washing in the sea, and finds himself staring into the face of a 'sea-monster.' The whale shark follows, and circles the raft for an hour, to the delight and amazement of all on board – none has ever seen any creature so long.

9. ibid.
pp. 111–113 (Ch. 5)
'We became acquainted ... the only vulnerable points.'
The men are fascinated by sharks, and determined to catch one. Using a dolphin as bait they finally manage it, and the shark puts up only a token resistance.

10. SPERRY, Armstrong
The Boy who was Afraid
pp. 47–51 (Ch. 4)
'Fishing with a line ... his master's cheek.'
A shark has been robbing Mafatu's traps – he appears one day as the boy is inspecting the traps, and nearly catches Mafatu's dog. Furious, Mafatu leaps into the water and stabs the shark.

SHEEP

1. BALDWIN, Michael
Grandad with Snails
pp. 119–125 (Ch. 14)
'Next morning, it was raining ... I noticed Silky was crying.'
A malevolent ram is to be sold; but first it has to be manoeuvred up a ramp, and into a lorry. Michael scares it into position, very deftly, but the ram shows something of its fighting spirit before it is driven away.

2. HARDY, Thomas
Far from the Madding Crowd
see PRIDE 2

3. SCHAEFER, Jack
Old Ramon

pp. 22–28 (Ch. 3)
'And now we must cross ... dog, cringing and ashamed.'
The boy and the old man are herding sheep. They have to cross a river. The sheep have to be persuaded across by being given an example by the leaders of the flock. The boy's dog panics the stragglers, the line bunches, and two sheep have to be rescued from the current.

SHIPS

see also: BOATS (and) BOATING;
FIRE (at) SEA;
NAVY;
SHIPWRECKS;
VOYAGES

SHIPS – GUNS

1. FORESTER, C.S.
The Ship
pp. 39–41 (Ch. 7)
'All down the line ... 'Range two-nine-ho.'
Leading Seaman Alfred Lightfoot keeps a line of Italian cruisers in his rangefinder, and he keeps his cool under fire ... until the Italians turn tail. Then his cockney exuberance gets the better of him.

2. ibid.
pp. 95–97 (Ch. 16)
'The ship passed out of the smoke ... hands and keen eyes.'
Gunners and gun are a sequence of smooth, mechanical movements, directed to the firing of a shell every ten seconds. The writing, like the action, is precise.

3. ibid.
see SECOND WORLD WAR – SEA
BATTLES 5

SHIPWRECKS

see also: CASTAWAYS;
STORMS (at) SEA

SHIPWRECKS

1. BOMBARD, Alain
   The Bombard Story
   pp. 19–20 (Ch. 2)
   'Shipwrecks fall into ... the risk of one life.'
   The lot of the shipwrecked mariner, and his chances of survival. Bombard stakes his life on a theory that might be the saving of several thousand.

2. ibid.
   pp. 209–212 (Ch. 14)
   'Barbados is one of the ... of a surfeit of food.'
   After so long at sea, the landing is as hazardous as any other part of the voyage. 'L'Hérétique' beaches on Barbados, and Alain is received rapturously and confusedly.

3. CALDWELL, John
   Desperate Voyage
   pp. 152–156 (Ch. 15)
   'I hauled southward ... warmth and fell asleep.'
   'Pagan' ends its voyage, and its days on a coral reef, within yards of landfall. The author clambers off it, falls asleep on the reef, is wakened by the tide, and floats to the beach on the mast of the now broken boat.

4. CONRAD, Joseph
   Typhoon and Youth
   pp. 114–116 ('Youth')
   'It was bright as day ... her creed and her name.'
   The crew of the Judea enjoy a last meal, lit by the flames of its cargo, before taking to the boats. Before sailing away, they watch the Judea go down in a cloud of steam.

5. DEFOE, Daniel
   Robinson Crusoe
   (i) pp. 10–12 (ii) pp. 14–18 (Ch. 1)
   'The sixth day of ... what was yet before me.'
   A terrible storm blows up, and the crew have to abandon ship, when it is plain that pumping will not save her. Crusoe is terribly frightened throughout.

6. ibid.
   (i) pp. 32–37; (ii) pp. 46–51 (Ch. 5)
   'In this distress ... on such an occasion.'
   The ship founders on a sand bank. The storm threatens to break her up, so the men launch the ship's boat. But when this overturns, they are thrown into the sea, and only Crusoe makes it to the shore.

7. DICKENS, Charles
   David Copperfield
   see STORMS 4

8. DU MAURIER, Daphne
   Jamaica Inn
   pp. 159–166 (Ch. 11)
   'After a while ... by the tide.'
   Mary Yellan has been forced by her uncle to accompany him and his friends on a wrecking expedition. She watches the ship founder, the crew die, and the gang steal what they can before dawn surprises them.

9. FALKNER, J. Meade
   Moonfleet
   pp. 208–221 (Ch. 18)
   'The ship that was to carry us ... then I caught the rope.'
   The slave-ship carrying Elzevir and John to oriental plantations, makes heavy weather in the Channel. The slaves are set at liberty to shift for themselves, when the sails go, and the crew abandons ship. John and Elzevir make it to the beach, but the latter is caught in the under-tow and loses his own life, saving John's.

10. GOLDING, William
    Pincher Martin
    pp. 11–18; 20–23 (Ch. 1)
    'He got the rubber tube ... smoke and green welter.'; 'Help! Help! Survivor! ... He lay still.'
    A survivor bobs helplessly on the swell; he inflates his life-belt, swims fitfully, and calls out into the mist. He is washed up on to a barren rock, the butt of forces he barely understands.

11. HEYERDAHL, Thor
    The Kon-Tiki Expedition

pp. 188–194 (Ch. 7)
'A few minutes later ... to work around us.'
The only way to land is to drift straight for a treacherous coral reef. The raft is lifted high into the air, and thrown down on to the reef by the sea, and the men have to cling on desperately for some time before she is washed far enough in to be able to jump to safety.

SHOOTING

1. DURRELL, Gerald
   My Family and Other Animals
   pp. 180–186 (Part 2, Ch. 12)
   'Leslie had returned from a trip ... attempts on my life for one day.'
   A comic episode in which Larry, stung into defending his claim that he can shoot as well as Leslie, blasts off at a pair of snipe from the insecurity of a narrow plank-bridge. He falls in and is rescued, protesting, by the rest of the family heaving on the gun.

2. LEE, Harper
   To Kill a Mockingbird
   see FATHERS 7

3. SCHAEFER, Jack
   Shane
   pp. 58–62 (Ch. 5)
   (Young Impact 1, pp. 67–69)
   'It was plain that ... down from the mountains.'
   Bob is practising with his old gun, pretending to shoot Indians. Shane, despite himself, shows him how to wear his holster, and draw, at lightning speed. He has evidently had painful practice.

SHOPLIFTING

1. BARSTOW, Stan
   Joby
   pp. 105–107 (Ch. 7)
   'Gus knew all the orchards ... somewhere an' look where we've got.'
   In a chemist's shop, Joby is introduced to a new and exciting game:

while the shopkeeper is in his back room, his mates help themselves to what they fancy. Joby is so scared he has to leave, empty-handed.

2. ibid.
   pp. 118–123 (Ch. 8)
   (That Once Was Me, pp. 78–83)
   'Joby threw the ball ... good talking to, didn't he?'
   Joby and his friends are caught shoplifting. Successes have made them over-confident. The shopkeeper takes the boys into the back room and has them empty their pockets. Then he lets them off with an inspired caution.

3. DEFOE, Daniel
   Moll Flanders
   (i) pp. 162–165; (ii) pp. 181–185
   'We lived in an uninterrupted course ... for three or four days.'
   Moll's husband dies. She knows abject poverty for two years, before she yields to the temptation to make her living dishonestly. She steals a bundle of linen, and some silver. The act weighs on her conscience, for a while.
   see also: PRISON 2;
   ROBBERY 1

4. ibid.
   (i) pp. 184–189; (ii) pp. 204–208
   'I was soon informed that some ... I had heard in a great while.'
   Moll dons a man's clothes, and accompanies a young fellow on shoplifting expeditions, without making herself known to him. Thus, when the latter is caught, all Moll has to do is to resume her customary dress and let the young man take the rap.

5. ibid.
   see PICKPOCKETS 3, 4

6. HINES, Barry
   A Kestrel for a Knave
   (i) pp. 13–16; (ii) pp. 10–12
   'A bell tinkled ... deliver on time.'
   Mr Porter, the newsagent, berates Billy for arriving late on his newspaper round, for having no bicycle, and for giving cheek. Billy justifies

himself, and steals some chocolate for his breakfast.

7. ibid.
(i) pp. 42–43; (ii) p. 34
'He looked in at ... into the arcade.'
Wanting a book about falconry, and being balked at the public library, Billy browses in the local bookshop, and makes off with the book of his choice, concealed inside his jacket.

SHOPS

see also: MARKETS;
PAWN-BROKERS;
PEDLARS;
STREET-TRADERS

SHOPS

1. WELLS, H.G.
The History of Mr Polly
see DISMISSAL 7
2. WELLS, H.G.
Kipps
see WORK – APPRENTICESHIP 2

SHOWING OFF

1. BARSTOW, Stan
The Human Element
pp. 21–24 ('One of the Virtues')
'The holidays came ... my young life.'
Will inherits his Grandfather's gold watch. Anxious to impress his friends, he takes it to school. But on the way to school, he comes off his bicycle, and the gold watch is smashed beyond repair.
2. ELIOT, George
The Mill on the Floss
pp. 218–221 (Ch. 5, Part 2)
'I say Maggie ... his being alive.'
Tom has a surprise for Maggie – he has borrowed a sword to show off his skill, but she is more afraid than amused. As he is cavorting about he slips and hurts his foot.
3. HARDY, Thomas
Far from the Madding Crowd

(i) pp. 212–218 (Ch. 28); (ii) pp. 205–210
'The hill opposite ... He had kissed her.'
Sergeant Troy gives Bathsheba a stunning exhibition of swordplay. She is vastly impressed by his dexterity, but only realises that it is a mating ritual, when the jaunty sergeant kisses her.
4. HARDY, Thomas
Tess of the D'Urbervilles
(i) pp. 64–67 (Ch. 8), (ii) pp. 63–66
'Having mounted beside ... said the young man.'
Alec D'Urberville, with Tess beside him in the gig, urges the horse to a frightening speed downhill. By so doing he intimidates Tess into letting him kiss her.
5. LAWRENCE, D.H.
Sons and Lovers
(i) pp. 149–151 (Ch. 7); (ii) pp. 186–188
'Miriam came later ... in the middle air.'
Paul Morel meets Miriam at the Willey Farm. She shows him her swing in the barn, because she wants to share something precious with him. While he enjoys himself, showing off, she is infected by his enthusiasm and vigour.
6. POINTON, Barry
Break-in
see WEALTH 2
7. WATERHOUSE, Keith
There is a Happy Land
pp. 12–14 (Ch. 2)
'Get down as far ... 'Might as well,' she said.'
Having quarrelled with Ted, the boy meets a new girl to their street and tries to impress her – by pretending he has a broken arm, and airing his knowledge of the district.

SHYNESS

1. ALCOTT, Louisa M.
Little Women
see HAPPINESS 1

2. ibid.
   see GIFTS 1
3. BERNA, Paul
   Flood Warning
   see TEACHING – DISCIPLINE 1
4. WRIGHT, Richard
   Black Boy
   pp. 64–65 (Ch. 2)
   (Family and School, pp. 64–65)
   'I lived in West Helena ... emotion surged through me.'
   First day at a new school, and Richard is called upon to write his name and address on the blackboard. He is so paralysed by all the strange faces, that, though he can write, and hates himself for his shyness, he doesn't write a word.

SIEGES

1. BRONTË, Charlotte
   Shirley
   see LUDDITES 2
2. FORESTER, C.S.
   The Gun
   (i) pp. 127–130 (Ch. 13); (ii) pp. 108–111
   'His heart almost ... had its effect.'
   Having entered the town of Leon, the guerrilleros with their gun, set about taking the citadel where the French are hiding. Their bombardment causes no retaliation, a fact which puzzles them, until they discover the French are dying inside the citadel from the arsenic the Spanish have mixed with the flour.
3. HEMINGWAY, Ernest
   For Whom the Bell Tolls
   see SPANISH CIVIL WAR 2
4. STEVENSON, R.L.
   Treasure Island
   pp. 109–113 (Ch. 18)
   'We made our best speed ... over the stockade.'
   The captain and loyal crew-members make for the stockade, where they are to protect themselves from the mutineers. They are attacked by rifle-fire, lose one man, and then suffer a bombardment from the ship's cannon.
5. ibid.
   pp. 129–133 (Ch. 21)
   '"If you please sir ... as bad to bear.'
   The mutineers attack the stockade once again, and this time reach the log-house, forcing a hand-to-hand fight. They are eventually beaten back.
6. SUTCLIFF, Rosemary
   The Eagle of the Ninth
   pp. 40–43 (Ch. 3)
   'It was a full daylight ... every man of the garrison.'
   The Exeter garrison is under siege by British warriors fired by a fanatical Druid. At first, the mist prevents the signal-smoke rising, but as the mist finally lifts, the signal is given, and is answered.
   see also: BATTLES 4
7. TREASE, Geoffrey
   Cue for Treason
   pp. 180–187 (Ch. 19)
   'Just as I passed through ... bracken like adders.'
   Sir Philip comes looking for Peter Brownrigg. His father refuses entry to Sir Philip's men, bars the door, and makes it hot for at least one of the besiegers. Peter and Kit escape through a back window, to alert near neighbours.

SIGHT

see also: BLINDNESS

SIGHT

1. CHURCH, Richard
   Over the Bridge
   pp. 72–76 (Ch. 7)
   'A medical examination at school ... in me, and to correct.'
   A pair of spectacles opens up a whole new world to a boy – a world of which he had no idea he was deprived. The fulness of the new experience is quite shattering.

SIN

1. BALDWIN, James
   Go Tell it on the Mountain
   pp. 9–11 (Part 1, 'The Seventh Day')
   'There was sin among them ... closer
   day by day.'
   The preacher reproaches young Elisha
   and Ella Mae, before the congregation, not of any palpable impro-
   priety in their relationship, but of
   giving the Devil an occasion to strike.
   Everyone is made aware of the nature
   of sin.

SINGING

1. AMIS, Kingsley
   Lucky Jim
   pp. 36–38 (Ch. 4)
   'Of course, this sort ... I didn't seem
   to hear ...'
   A musical get-together at the Pro-
   fessor's. Dixon has been dragooned
   into singing tenor – or pretending to.
   His silence is not noted until the
   tenors divide, and Dixon's part goes
   missing.
2. LLEWELLYN, Richard
   How Green was my Valley
   pp. 232–233 (Ch. 24)
   'So Wyn went ... His dearest
   pleasure.'
   The Morgans are celebrating the
   return of their sons, and as the party
   grows, it moves out into the street.
   Here, to the music of Wyn's harp,
   they sing, "filling the valley with
   song".
3. 'MISS READ'
   Village School
   (i) pp. 45–52 (Part 1, Ch. 6); (ii) pp.
   45–52
   'The heavy church door ... on the
   flinty road.'
   A hyperactive choir master, and a
   village choir set in its ways, make for
   a stormy, unmelodious session. There
   are words, and excess of feeling, but
   there is not much music.

SISTERS

see FAMILY;
QUARRELS – BROTHERS (and) SISTERS

SKATING

see ICE – SKATING

SLAUGHTER

see ANIMALS – SLAUGHTER

SLAVERY

1. TWAIN, Mark
   The Adventures of Huckleberry Finn
   (i) pp. 94–99 (Ch. 16); (ii) pp.
   144–149
   (Visions of Life 2, pp. 70–77)
   'There warn't nothing to do ... come
   handiest at the time.'
   Freedom for Jim, the runaway slave,
   is almost in sight. Because he has
   abetted Jim in his escape, Huck's
   conscience begins to plague him, such
   is his belief that a slave is mere
   property. But when the opportunity
   offers itself, to surrender him, Huck's
   loyalty to his friend triumphs over his
   conditioning.
   see also: ESCAPE (from) SLAVERY 1

SMELLS

1. KIRKUP, James
   The Only Child
   pp. 55–57 (Ch. 3)
   (Impact Two, pp. 59–60)
   'I can still remember ... essence of
   misery.'
   Granny Kirkup's house has a whole
   range of smells of its own, (quite
   different from Granny Johnson's
   snuff and Woodbines), from its plant-
   laden front porch, to its cooking
   smells inside.

SMOKING

1. TWAIN, Mark
    The Adventures of Tom Sawyer
    (i) pp. 118–120 (Ch. 16); (ii) pp.
    110–112
    'The lads came gaily back ...
    disagreed with them.'
    Tom and Joe get Huck to teach them
    how to smoke a pipe. They are
    marvellously proud of this new
    accomplishment, until sickness over-
    takes them, and they are exhausted
    with retching.

SMUGGLING

1. DU MAURIER, Daphne
    Jamaica Inn
    pp. 41–42 (Ch. 4)
    'She got out of bed ... a door slam-
    med.'
    The scene in the inn yard as goods are
    loaded and unloaded at night.
2. FALKNER, J. Meade
    Moonfleet
    pp. 41–45 (Chs. 3, 4); pp. 49–51 (Ch.
    4)
    'Then, having settled these impor-
    tant ... will reckon with him.'; 'The
    carrying was over ... the treasure of
    life.'
    Young John Trenchard is disturbed
    while treasure-seeking in the Mohune
    vault, by smugglers using the vault to
    hide contraband liquor. He conceals
    himself, and overhears the smugglers'
    conversation, their singing, and their
    solemn toasts to Blackbeard who
    watches over the casks.
    see also: TREASURE – SEEKING 1

SNAKES

1. CANAWAY, W.H.
    Sammy going South
    pp. 29–30 (Ch. 5)
    'They were crossing ... curling up to
    sleep.'
    Sammy's guide, blinded when a rock
    exploded in his face, and delirious,

doesn't see the snake which slides
towards him and strikes him. He dies
soon after.

2. HARDY, Thomas
    The Return of the Native
    (i) pp. 345–350 (Bk. 4, Ch. 7); (ii)
    pp. 312–316
    'Yeobright walked on ... and anoin-
    ted the wound.'
    On his way to her house, Yeobright
    comes upon his mother, lying insen-
    sible on the heath. He carries her to a
    shelter, but it becomes plain that she
    is suffering from an adder-bite.
    According to local folklore, the wound
    is anointed with the oil of three dead
    adders fried over a fire.
3. SCHAEFER, Jack
    Old Ramon
    pp. 46–48 (Ch. 6)
    'The Flock plodded steadily ... on the
    palm of his hand.'
    The sheep stare, bemused, at a
    rattlesnake in their midst. One of the
    young, headstrong dogs goes for the
    snake, but Old Ramon is there first.
    He knocks the dog away with his
    stick, breaks the neck of the snake
    with the same stick, and stamps on its
    head.

SNAKES – CATCHING

1. DURRELL, Gerald
    My Family and Other Animals
    pp. 263–266 (Part 3, Ch. 17)
    'Cutting across the first ... mixture
    of interest and amusement.'
    The dogs light upon a pair of courting
    water-snakes. Gerald has been wan-
    ting one of these for his collection, for
    a long time. One is easily caught, but
    Gerald has to go wading, and
    thrashing about in muddy water, for
    the other.

SNAKES – MATING

1. DURRELL, Gerald
    Birds, Beasts and Relatives

pp. 187–188 (Sn. 4, 'The Talking Head')
'Roger and I were sitting ... from the field of love?'
Gerald witnesses the mating of two snakes. They stare at each other a while, then the male twines himself round the female. Unfortunately, the dog interrupts the act.

SNOBBERY

see SOCIAL CLASS-SNOBBERY

SNOW

see also: CHRISTMAS;
FROST;
ICE;
WINTER

SNOW

1. CHAPLIN, Sid
   The Leaping Lad and Other Stories
   pp. 70–73 ('Quite a Journey')
   'Jos lay in bed ... hard, tiring work.'
   In spite of deep drifts, and snow still falling, Jos sets out on his bike for the back-shift at the pit. He has to carry the bike most of the way, and he falls in ditches up to his chin – but he goes.
2. LEE, Harper
   To Kill a Mockingbird
   (i) pp. 70–73 (Ch. 8); (ii) pp. 70–73
   'Next morning I awoke ... always have an idea.'
   Jem and Scout see snow for the first time. It is a pitiably light fall, but they manage, by dint of building a mud core, to make a quite convincing snowman.
3. LEE, Laurie
   Cider with Rosie
   see CHRISTMAS – CAROLS 3
4. THOMAS, Dylan
   A Prospect of the Sea
   see CHRISTMAS 11

SNOW – STORMS

1. LLWELLYN, Richard
   How Green was my Valley
   see LOST (in) MOUNTAINS 1

SOCIAL CLASS

see also: AMBITIONS – SOCIAL
CLIMBING

SOCIAL CLASS

1. ALLEN, Walter
   All in a Lifetime
   pp. 44–45 (Ch. 6)
   'Throughout my life ... It was exactly like that.'
   The Ashteds are on a Bank Holiday walk, in their Sunday best. A gentleman and his sons, on horseback stop to watch them pass. Young Billy is conscious of their disdain.
2. BRONTË, Charlotte
   Shirley
   (i) pp. 374–377 (Ch. 21), (ii) pp. 363–365
   'You told me before ... a little if you please.'
   Mrs Pryor recalls her experience as a governess in an aristocratic family. Though she was made to know her place, she is without any bitterness in her respect for the 'higher classes of society.'
3. CARY, Joyce
   The Horse's Mouth
   pp. 182–188 (Ch. 22)
   'Just then the Beeders ... I had wine.'
   Sir William and Lady Beeder have invited Gulley Jimson to their flat, as they are interested in his painting. He is so impressed with their aristocratic politeness that he allows himself to be extremely rude, knowing they will ignore it.
4. CHURCH, Richard
   Over the Bridge
   see AMBITIONS 1
5. DICKENS, Charles

Hard Times
see DIVORCE 1

6. GRAVES, Robert
    Goodbye to all That
    pp. 19–20 (Ch. 2)
    'Though I have asked ... Church of England.'
    The young Graves learns his place, when, at the age of 4, he is hospitalized with scarlet fever. He takes his superiority to the lower classes very much for granted.

7. HUXLEY, Aldous
    Brave New World
    see CONDITIONING 2

8. LAWRENCE, D.H.
    Sons and Lovers
    (i) pp. 255–256 (Ch. 10); (ii) pp. 311–314
    'Mother, I want an ... to marry a lady.'
    Paul begins to mix with the middle-classes. He wears William's evening dress-suit when he goes out to dinner in the evenings. His mother is delighted, hoping he will grow into a gentleman, and marry a lady. Paul scorns such ambitions; he professes to want to remain among 'the common people.'

9. LEE, Laurie
    Cider with Rosie
    see SERVANTS 3

10. ORWELL, George
    1984
    (i) pp. 73–76 (Part 1, Ch. 7); (ii) pp. 59–61
    'If there was hope ... animals are free.'
    The life of the proletariat (proles), politically unconscious, over-worked and poor.

11. ibid.
    (i) pp. 206–212 (Part 2, Ch. 9); (ii) pp. 162–166
    'Chapter 1 ... made permanent.'
    The inevitability of any society dividing into High, Middle and Low; how the high have always been overthrown but replaced by a new high; how the High of Oceania have con-solidated their position and eliminated possibility of equality.

12. PEYTON, K.M.
    Flambards
    see SERVANTS 5

13. PICARD, Barbara Leonie
    The Young Pretenders
    pp. 68–72 (Ch. 7)
    'On Sunday morning ... by her ladyship's kindness.'
    Sir John and Lady Rimpole, their children and their household attend church every Sunday morning. The ordering of the procession and the behaviour of all concerned never varies, as all know their place.

14. THOMPSON, Flora
    Lark Rise to Candleford
    (i) pp. 209–211 ('Lark Rise', Ch. 12); (ii) pp. 194–196
    'Squire at the Manor ... or with conviction.'
    The poor gentry of Lark Rise, the Squire and his mother, Mrs Bracewell, the 'Lady of the Manor'. That they occupy the 'big house' is their only excuse for lordly hauteur. Of other qualifications they have none.

15. ibid.
    (i) pp. 321–324 ('Over to Candleford', Ch. 19); (ii) pp. 289–292
    'Apart from politics ... the poor lady.'
    The attitude of the hamlet people to the upper-classes – true respect for their titled gentry, and landowners and J.P.'s, horrified admiration for the wild lives of some, but little respect for the 'nouveau riche'. There is little or no desire to see change in the social order.

16. ibid.
    (i) pp. 413–415 ('Over to Candleford' Ch. 27); (ii) pp. 366–368
    'It was still ... six o'clock in the morning.'
    At the forge at Candleford Green there is a definite hierarchy – the mistress, the foreman, the maid and the workmen. Their positions are

demonstrated by where they sit at the table.

17. ibid.
(i) pp. 481–483 ('Candleford Green' Ch. 32); (ii) pp. 424–425
'At the time ... as the Church tower.'
The Vicar and his wife hold an important position in the village: he preaches the preservation of the existing social order, and she does good work among the parishioners.

18. TROLLOPE, Anthony
Barchester Towers
pp. 306–307 (Ch. 35)
'No-one who has not had ... the rest of the tenantry.'
Miss Thorne encounters difficulties in arranging her enormous party for gentry and tenantry. How is she to draw the line between the two?

19. WOOLF, Virginia
Orlando
pp. 135–138 (Ch. 4)
'To give a truthful account ... it was not enough.'
Orlando moves confidently in the high society of Queen Anne's reign. It has been important to her to see and be seen, but increasingly, the mannered wit palls and she appreciates more the society of her dog.

SOCIAL CLASS – CLIMBING

1. BRAINE, John
Room at the Top
pp. 161–164 (Ch. 20)
(Conflict 2, pp. 100–102)
'She and Jack were part ... compelled to hate him.'
It is the night of the Warley Civic Ball. The rising star from working-class Dufton sees and hears what he is up against in his attempt on Susan Brown. His rival, the name-dropping, ex-officer, Jack Wales has all the strong cards, and he plays them.

2. THACKERAY, William
Vanity Fair
(i) pp. 553–561 (Ch. 48); (ii) pp. 476–483

'At last Becky's kindness ... the Peerage all right.'
Becky has schemed all her adult life to be accepted by the high society of London. The culmination of all her ambitious manoeuverings is her presentation at Court.

3. TROLLOPE, Anthony
Barchester Towers
pp. 315–317 (Ch. 36)
'The next comer ... the bottom of the dining-room table.'
Mrs Lookaloft and her daughters hoist themselves up a rung of the social ladder, when they unexpectedly join the party in Ullathorne House, rather than the tenantry in the grounds as had been intended.

4. ibid.
pp. 344–348 (Ch. 39)
' "I do tell 'ee plainly ... in the world at large.'
The farmers' wives, in their rightful place in marquees in the grounds, are scandalised by Mrs Lookaloft's effrontery in taking her daughters to the party in the House.

5. WELLS, H.G.
Kipps
see ETIQUETTE 9

6. ibid.
see LANGUAGE 7

7. ibid.
see ETIQUETTE 10.

SOCIAL CLASS – PRIVILEGE

1. ORWELL, George
Animal Farm
(i) pp. 21–22 (Ch. 3); 42–43 (Ch. 6)
(ii) pp. 32–33; 59–61
'The mystery of where ... for the pigs alone.'; 'It was about this time ...about that either.'
In one insidious way after another, the pigs reserve privileges to themselves – milk, windfall apples, beds in the farmhouse and shorter working hours – and justify them to the other animals on the grounds of their

responsibilities and arduous brain-work.

2. ibid.
   (i) pp. 70–72 (Ch. 9); (ii) pp. 95–97
   'Meanwhile life was hard ... Derby soup tureen.'
   The food rations of the common brawn-workers, are cut. But the pigs continue to enjoy an immunity from worsening conditions.

SOCIAL CLASS – SNOBBERY

1. AUSTEN, Jane
   Pride and Prejudice
   (i) pp. 59–61 (Ch. 14); (ii) pp. 58–60 (Vol. 1, Ch. 14)
   'During dinner ... no partner in his pleasure.'
   Mr Collins reveals the full extent of his fawning admiration for his bene-factress, and makes himself ridiculous in his snobbish view of the world.

2. ibid.
   (i) pp. 146–152 (Ch. 29); (ii) pp. 138–143 (Vol. 2, Ch. 6)
   'As the weather was fine ... into his own hands.'
   Mr and Mrs Collins and their guests dine with Lady Catherine de Bourgh, Mr Collins' benefactress. Elizabeth is confirmed in her suspicion that this lady is an autocratic snob.

3. DICKENS, Charles
   Bleak House
   (i) pp. 175–178 (Ch. 14); (ii) pp. 175–178
   'He was a fat old ... a sex you are.'
   Esther meets Mr Turveydrop, father of the dancing master, and 'a model of Deportment'. Every gesture and every word is calculated to impress, and he has no time to consider other people's feelings, not even his late wife's or his son's. He lives on the memory of one encounter with the Prince Regent.

4. DICKENS, Charles
   Great Expectations
   (i) pp. 65–68 (Ch. 8); (ii) pp. 56–58

'Miss Havisham beckoned ... on it and cried.'
Estella's mockery makes Pip ashamed of his coarse hands, and thick working boots. For the first time in his life, he is conscious of being 'common'. He sees himself through Estella's contemptuous eyes, and he is ashamed.

5. FORESTER, C.S.
   The General
   (i) pp. 15–20 (Ch. 2); (ii) pp. 15–20
   'On the same leave Curzon ... of a matter of course.'
   Newly honoured, Curzon visits relatives of his in Brixton. He is painfully aware of their social inferiority, but as he leaves them, he reflects upon how different things might have been.

6. ibid.
   (i) pp. 75–79 (Ch. 9); (ii) pp. 74–77
   ' 'Damn it all, Maud ... C.B., D.S.O., Twenty-second Lancers.'
   The marriage is (virtually) arranged between General Curzon and Lady Emily. The Duchess is mortified that her daughter should be marrying beneath her, to a man of little means, and less blood.

7. GASKELL, Mrs.
   Cranford
   (i) pp. 95–98 (Ch. 7); (ii) pp. 108–110
   'Now Mrs Fitz-Adam ... Mrs Fitz-Adam persevered.'
   The genteel society of Cranford con-siders whether Mrs Fitz-Adam is to be 'called-upon' or not. Her parents were farmers, and although her brother is the doctor, their name is Hoggins, which is considered coarse. She is however accepted, by all except one.

8. THOMAS, Leslie
   This Time Next Week
   see COURTSHIP – DATING 5

SOCIAL REFORM

1. TROLLOPE, Anthony
   The Warden

271

pp. 147–150 (Ch. 15)
'In former times ... the last half century.'
Trollope claims, tongue in cheek, that all great social reforms are affected by the novelist, who exposes the evils of mid-nineteenth century society. John Bold reads the first episode of a novel criticising the income of the church.

SOCIALISM

1. ALLEN, Walter
    All in a Lifetime
    see POLITICS 1
2. GREENWOOD, Walter
    Love on the Dole
    pp. 180–184 (Part 3, Ch. 7)
    'Outside Marlowe's ... howl of the hooter.'
    An argument about capital and labour outside the engineering works. Larry's eloquence on behalf of the working man falls on dull ears.
3. WELLS, H.G.
    Kipps
    pp. 200–205 (Bk. 2, Ch. 4, Sn. 2)
    'His steps led him out ... exemplary suggestions.'
    Kipps meets his old neighbour Sid Pornick. Sid is proud of himself for being a self-made man. When he hears of Kipps's good fortune, he takes refuge from envy by calling himself a socialist, and implacable opponent of wealth.
4. ibid.
    pp. 263–266 (Bk. 2, Ch. 7, Sn. 4)
    'Kipps was moved to speak ... Mrs Sid, a little severely.'
    Masterman expounds socialism to Kipps. He does it with vigour, and bitterness, as one who has been ill-used. His pessimism is profound, and affecting.

SOMME, BATTLE

see BATTLES – SOMME – 1916

SONGS (and) RHYMES

1. KIRKUP, James
    The Only Child
    pp. 39–41 (Ch. 2)
    'Perhaps I had been ... and far away.' '
    The writer recalls street games and their accompanying chants: ball-bouncing games, with just a dash of scandal to them.
2. ibid.
    pp. 91–96 (Ch. 7)
    'I always took ... his boat comes in.'
    Dancing rhymes of the street are contrasted with the altogether more proper, if at times mystifying, rhymes said and sung by parents, last thing at night.
3. ibid.
    pp. 137–143 (Ch. 11)
    'It was not just ... Baby's on the floor.'
    An anthology of songs and snatches danced, counted, undressed, and skipped to, on Tyneside in the Twenties.
4. THOMPSON, Flora
    see GAMES 11, 12

SOUTH AFRICA

1. PATON, Alan
    Cry, the Beloved Country
    passim.
    see RACISM – SOUTH AFRICA 2–8
2. ibid.
    (i) pp. 7–8 (Bk. 1, Ch. 1); (ii) pp. 7–8
    'There is a lovely road ... keep them any more.'
    The valley of the Umzimkulu. The surrounding hills are green and well-tended; the valley and lower slopes are bare and overworked.
3. ibid.
    see CAPITALISM 4

SPACE – TRAVEL

1. LEWIS, C.S.
    Out of the Silent Planet
    pp. 38–45 (Ch. 7)

' "Having a doze?" ... forest of the huge plants.'
The space-travellers land, and without ceremony, step out on to the planet. Work awaits them, but Ransom snatches some vivid impressions of his surroundings, before a band of sorns interrupts their lunch, and he is able to escape.

2. ibid.
pp. 45–49 (Ch. 8)
'A month of inactivity ... not now. Presently.'
Ransom is in flight from his kidnappers in a new world. He notices everything acutely, but hunger and weariness overtake him. He spends the night beside a warm stream.

3. ibid.
pp. 157–162 (Ch. 21)
'It was well for him ... bitter, please," said Ransom.'
The space-travellers are on the way back to Earth, with limited supplies of oxygen, and water. The position of the Moon threatens to throw them right off course. It is exceedingly hot. But they make it, and Ransom awakes to rain.

SPANISH CIVIL WAR

1. HEMINGWAY, Ernest
For Whom the Bell Tolls
see EXECUTION 4, 5

2. ibid.
pp. 296–305 (Ch. 27)
'Dying was nothing and he had ... orders being carried out.'
The fascists have a band of republican guerillas pinned down on a bare hilltop. The fascist first officer believing the guerillas are dead, exposes himself and shouts insults at them. The guerillas shoot him before they are themselves bombed.

3. ibid.
pp. 404–409 (Ch. 43)
(War, pp. 29–34)
'Robert Jordan lay behind ... kill them and we kill them.'

Jordan watches the bridge from his vantage point. He has the sentry in his sights, and his life at the press of his finger. He takes that life, and so begins the attack on the bridge.

4. ibid.
pp. 416–420 (Ch. 43)
'He listened to the noise ... he hated everyone he saw.'
A bridge is blown that will frustrate the fascist advance. Jordan, the 'Inglés', lays the fuses, and gives the order when the first truck is heard. The old man, Anselmo, is killed by flying metal. This and the tension leaves Jordan emotionally empty.

SPIRITUALISM

see also: GHOSTS;
SUPERSTITION;
TELEPATHY

SPIRITUALISM

1. DURRELL, Gerald
Birds, Beasts and Relatives
pp. 29–32 (Part 1, 'A Brush with Spirits')
'At Margo's insistence ... Mrs Haddock and her several disciples.'
Margo is receiving 'treatment' for her spots, via Mrs Haddock, a medium. Mrs Durrell, and the still more sceptical Cousin Prue insist on accompanying her. Mrs Haddock goes into a trance. Prue screams when a cat jumps on to her lap, and the séance breaks up in confusion, with Mrs Durrell calling the whole thing 'nonsense.'

2. GREENWOOD, Walter
Love on the Dole
pp. 98–99 (Part 2, Ch. 5)
'As Mrs Hardcastle ... to be too familiar.'
Mrs Jike communes with the 'spirets' and answers her neighbours' questions by banging her knee under the table twice for 'no', three times for 'yes'.

273

3. GRIMBLE, Sir Arthur
A Pattern of Islands
pp. 125–129 (Ch. 11)
'Arorae lies ... left at Arorae.'
An aged witch calls up the spirit of 'the Ancestor' to answer one of Arthur's irreverent, incredulous questions.

4. GROSSMITH, George and Weedon
The Diary of a Nobody
(i) pp. 164–171 (Ch. 22); (ii) pp. 263–273
'I don't know why ... enter the house again.'
One of Carrie's friends arranges a series of séances at the Pooter's home. Charles is sceptical – even condemning – but allows himself to become involved when events take an interesting turn. He takes offence at a personal question and brings the séances to an inconclusive end.

SPORT

see also: BOWLS; BOXING; CRICKET; FOOTBALL; RUGBY FOOTBALL; RUNNING; SWIMMING; WRESTLING

SPORT

1. STOREY, David
This Sporting Life
see RUGBY FOOTBALL 4, 5

2. SUTCLIFF, Rosemary
The Eagle of the Ninth
see GAMES – ROMAN 1

SPRING

1. BURNETT, Frances Hodgson
The Secret Garden
see GARDENS 1

2. ibid.
pp. 200–202 (Ch. 23)
' "It's magic," said Mary ... and think over.'
Ten-year-old Colin is in a garden for the first time in his life, and thrilled by it. He watches the spring awakening of plants, animals and insects.

3. MANKOWITZ, Wolf
A Kid for Two Farthings
pp. 68–70 (Ch. 7)
'The morning the Spring ... hurry as well.'
Spring comes to the East End. It comes in a goat gambolling, and a fillip in the hat trade.

4. 'MISS READ'
Village School
see EASTER 2

SPYING

1. ORWELL, George
1984
(i) pp. 26–27 (Part 1, Ch. 2); 66–67 (Part 1, Ch. 5); (ii) pp. 22–23; 52–54
'Up with your hands! ... to the Thought Police.'; 'At this moment, he was dragged ... right idea, eh?'
Parson's children, members of the Spies, taunt Winston with accusations of thought crime. He is on the guard all the time against those who might find fault in a careless expression. Parsons compounds his confusion by praising his children for their zeal.
see also: SPYING 3

2. ibid.
(i) pp. 176–178 (Part II, Ch. 8); (ii) pp. 140–141
'Then there is ... that is settled.'
Winston and Julia visit O'Brien whom they believe to be part of the Brotherhood – he asks them to what lengths they would be prepared to go as spies, and enumerates horrific possibilities.

3. ibid.
(i) pp. 238–239 (Part 3, Ch. 1); (ii) p. 187
'What are you ... right spirit anyway.'
Parsons' daughter denounces him.

4. WOOD, James
The Rain Islands
pp. 60–65 (Ch. 4)

' "If Sauckel's on his way ... and into space.'

Major Scott is interested in the activities of a yacht-owner, whom he suspects of some crime. He lands on an uninhabited island, visited by this man, in order to search for clues. He discovers to his cost that it is not uninhabited.

STEALING

see also: PICKPOCKETS;
ROBBERY;
SHOPLIFTING;
TEMPTATION

STEALING

1. DEFOE, Daniel
   Moll Flanders
   (i) pp. 170–173; (ii) pp. 190–193
   'However, at last I got some quilting ... never thought possible in me.'
   Moll wins a silver mint mug in a careless tavern. She confides in her governess, who pawns it for her, and sets her firmly on the road to crime.

2. DE JONG, Meindert
   The Wheel on the School
   (i) pp. 36–42 (Ch. 4); (ii) pp. 40–45
   'It was four o'clock ... if you're tempted.'
   The children of Shora are looking for wagon wheels for storks to nest on. Jella is the first to return to school, led by the ear by an irate farmer. Jella had 'borrowed' the farmer's wheel.

3. DICKENS, Charles
   Great Expectations
   see FEAR (of) STRANGERS 1

4. GORKY, Maxim
   Childhood
   see POVERTY 11

5. HINES, Barry
   A Kestrel for a Knave
   (i) pp. 17–18; (ii) pp. 13–14
   'A milk dray whined ... on up the hill.'
   Billy steals a bottle of orange and a carton of eggs from a milk dray, while the milkman's back is turned. It is a neat manoeuvre, capped by his scrupulous return of the empty bottle.

6. HITCHMAN, Janet
   The King of the Barbareens
   pp. 66–70 (Ch. 3)
   'Sometimes I earned ... was for my good.'
   Elsie is blackmailed by a schoolfriend into stealing from her 'Mum'. When she takes ten shillings and buys sweets, adults make enquiries, and the game is up. She is punished by being deprived of the food she likes.

7. MADDOCK, Reginald
   The Pit
   see INTERROGATION 2

8. NESBIT, E.
   The Railway Children
   see ESCAPADES 7

9. PICARD, Barbara Leonie
   The Young Pretenders
   pp. 196–198 (Ch. 19)
   'Seamus looked amused ... that never understands.'
   Francis condemns village children for stealing raspberries from their estate. Seamus defends them, and explains how some people steal from a real need in a very unequal society.

10. SILLITOE, Alan
    The Loneliness of the Long-distance Runner
    pp. 21–26 ('The Loneliness of the Long-distance Runner', Part 2)
    'My pal Mike got let off ... was diced out between us.'
    Smith and his pal Mike are patrolling the foggy backstreets of the town looking for openings, when they spy an unattended baker's shop. In no time they are in and out again with the cash-box, over-confident of their success.

11. STEINBECK, John
    The Pearl
    see FEAR (of) THIEVES 2

12. WRIGHT, Richard
    Black Boy
    see HOME – LEAVING 12

13. WYNDHAM, John
   The Day of the Triffids
   see CONDITIONING 6

STEALING (of) BABIES

1. TATE, Joan
   Sam and Me
   pp. 71–77 (Ch. 6)
   'I was out of the house ... let out into the yard to play.'
   Jo surrenders herself, and the baby she has stolen, to the police. She is relieved that the truth is out, and that the days of anxious, pretended motherhood are over. She is treated sympathetically. Her husband comes to fetch her, and he too, is all understanding.

STEALING (of) FOOD

1. BAWDEN, Nina
   Carrie's War
   (i) pp. 30–31 (Ch. 3); (ii) pp. 34–36
   'Carrie wasn't really ... round his trousers.'
   Carrie and Nick have been evacuated to the house of a very strict Welsh shop-keeper. They help in the shop, until Nick steals some biscuits. He is only saved from a beating by his threat to tell his teacher he is not getting enough to eat.

2. CHAPLIN, Sid
   The Leaping Lad and Other Stories
   pp. 91–93 ('Grace before meat')
   'In the year of 'twenty-six ... fullness thereof, Amen.'
   A man, his wife, and child walk through fields standing thick with ripe crops. It is 1926. The man steals out in the night, to gather food for his family. His conscience is uneasy, but his need is great.

3. HAUGAARD, Erich
   The Little Fishes
   see HUNGER 6

4. NAUGHTON, Bill
   The Goalkeeper's Revenge

(i) pp. 15–19 ('Seventeen Oranges');
(ii) pp. 15–19
'I used to be so fond ... inside something shocking.'
A light-fingered carter is caught by a policeman patrolling the docks, with seventeen oranges hidden about his person. While the policeman is away looking for a witness for the prosecution, the carter eats the oranges, and so destroys the evidence.

5. REMARQUE, Erich Maria
   All Quiet on the Western Front
   pp. 82–87 (Ch. 5)
   'When we break ... dark, deep sleep.'
   Two hungry soldiers steal a goose (in spite of high walls and a guard dog). They roast it, and baste it, and eat like kings. They share it with friends, and it becomes a powerful token of their friendship.

STORMS

see also: FLYING (in) STORMS;
HURRICANES;
SNOW – STORMS

STORMS

1. BAWDEN, Nina
   On the Run
   see SEA – TIDES 1

2. BERNA, Paul
   Flood Warning
   pp. 36–40 (Ch. 2)
   'Monsieur Sala was ... at the other end of the room.'
   A storm breaks over the sleeping school, Mr Sala is woken in mid-dream by a window shattering. Glass and other debris is blown everywhere. Masters meet, the window is boarded up, beds are remade, and a watch is set.

3. DE JONG, Meindert
   The Tower by the Sea
   see WITCHCRAFT 2

4. DICKENS, Charles
   David Copperfield
   pp. 857–865 (Ch. 55)

'It was a murky confusion ... stilled for ever.'

David Copperfield goes to Yarmouth to visit his old friend, Ham. He arrives in the middle of a terrible storm. On the second day, a schooner is wrecked not far from the beach. Ham, whom David has not seen till now, goes to rescue a lone survivor, but they are both drowned.

5. DU MAURIER, Daphne
Jamaica Inn
see TRAVEL (by) STAGE-COACH 2

6. HARDY, Thomas
Far from the Madding Crowd
(i) pp. 291–295 (Ch. 37); (ii) pp. 277–281
'A light flapped ... now, at any rate.'

While the heavens crash and rage above his head, and lightning flashes illuminate the farm, with a horrible intensity, Gabriel Oak and Bathsheba labour in the night to cover the corn-stacks before they are ruined by the rain.

7. KIRKUP, James
The Only Child
see TRAVEL (by) BOAT 3

8. MACKEN, Walter
God made Sunday and Other Stories
pp. 12–15 ('God made Sunday')
'I wound up my ... the sea-wrack.'

A sudden, violent storm hits the writer's island. He and his mother fear for their men at sea in flimsy boats. The boy keeps vigil all night, until the sky stops its roaring. But the boats don't come back.
see also: GRIEF 3

9. SERRAILLIER, Ian
The Silver Sword
(i) pp. 170–177 (Ch. 27); (ii) pp. 144–150
'It was the morning ... heart of the storm.'

The Polish refugee children are about to leave for Switzerland to be reunited with their parents. However they go for a walk on the lake shore before their boat leaves, and are caught in a freak storm. One boy is swept into the

lake in an old boat, and the others follow, to try to save him.

10. SEWELL, Anna
Black Beauty
pp. 60–63 (Ch. 12)
'One day late in the autumn ... for I was tired.'

Black Beauty with his master and groom are caught in a fierce storm – the roads are partly under water, a tree is blown down in the path, and the bridge they have to cross is sub-merged, thus hiding a break in the middle.

11. TOWNSEND, John Rowe
The Intruder
pp. 80–81 (Ch. 13)
'Next afternoon ... the open fire.'

Arnold, and his friends Peter and Jane go for a walk along the exposed Westmorland coast in a squally wind, feel exhilarated and get very wet.

12. TWAIN, Mark
The Adventures of Tom Sawyer
(i) pp. 121–123 (Ch. 17); (ii) pp. 112–115
'About midnight, Joe ... sleep on anywhere around.'

In the middle of the night, the boys are roused from their open-air sleep by the gathering of a spectacular storm. They crouch in their tent until that is blown away, and spend the rest of the night wet, but thankful that the lightning has spared them.

STORMS (at) SEA

see also: SHIPWRECKS

STORMS (at) SEA

1. BOMBARD, Alain
The Bombard Story
pp. 134–135 (Ch. 11)
'Monday had brought ... and you will win.'

Not far from the Canaries, L'Héréti-que' runs into a squall. Alain bales out for two hours with his hands and a hat. He is cold and exhausted, but victorious.

2. CONRAD, Joseph
    Typhoon and Youth
    pp. 22–23 ('Typhoon', Part 2)
    'All the Chinamen ... a typhoon coming on.'
    The mate writes up the ship's log. The record is of a growing swell, of still, hot air, and a falling barometer. In short, what the captain calls 'dirty weather.'

3. ibid.
    pp. 30–32 ('Typhoon', Part 2)
    'Captain MacWhirr opened his eyes ... stars had disappeared.'
    The captain wakes to rushing noises, and lively agitation of the ship. He struggles into his seaboots, and oilskin coat, and, fighting the wind pace by pace, he gains the bridge, and grasps intelligence of the situation.

4. ibid.
    pp. 34–36 ('Typhoon', Part 3)
    (Making Contact, pp. 13–16)
    'It unveiled for a sinister ... judge things coolly.'
    There are not images enough to express the full force of the gale that is unleashed upon the ship. Jukes gives himself up for lost, until the captain grapples with him in the sea that has flooded the bridge. It is impossible to stand and take stock.

5. ibid.
    pp. 60–62 ('Typhoon', Part 5)
    (Visions of Life 2, pp. 13–15)
    'He waited. Before his ... from STOP to FULL.'
    The Nan-Shan barely rides a monstrous wave. The sea sweeps her from end to end, before she falls never-endingly into the waiting trough. Down in the engine-room, they are sure the upper deck must have gone.

6. ibid.
    pp. 95–98 ('Youth')
    'It was January ... is an inhuman thing.'
    The barque Judea runs into a frightful gale: the men are hard put to it

pumping out the sea, the deck-house is washed away – indeed everything movable is lost – and the mulatto steward loses his mind.

7. FALKNER, J. Meade
    Moonfleet
    see SHIPWRECKS 9

8. SPERRY, Armstrong
    The Boy who was afraid
    see FEAR (of) SEA 1

9. ibid.
    pp. 14–19 (Ch. 2)
    'It was an ominous ... came and passed.'
    Mafatu has left his island in a canoe, to prove that he is not afraid of the sea. He is caught in a fierce storm, but remains afloat.

10. WOOD, James
    The Rain Islands
    pp. 139–142 (Ch. 7)
    'We were midway ... we had arrived.'
    Rescued from an uninhabited Icelandic island by a fishing boat, Major Scott finds himself in the middle of a tremendous storm, as they cross to the mainland.

STRIKES

see also: TRADE UNIONS; UNEMPLOYMENT

STRIKES

1. FOAKES Grace
    Between High Walls
    see POVERTY 9

2. GRICE, Frederick
    The Bonny Pit Laddie
    pp. 71–77 (Ch. 9)
    'One day when Dick ... the stoppage was complete.'
    Mr Sleath, the colliery owner, passes a new and very unpopular regulation. The men meet and resolve to strike in defence of their own, less exacting, methods of working.

3. ibid.
    pp. 78–80 (Ch. 10)

'For the first few days ... whist or rummy.'

The striking miners amuse themselves for a few days, but they are not used to idling; so they keep themselves in trim, and eke out their supplies of household coal, by picking on the slag heap.

see also: CHARITY 10

4. LLEWELLYN, Richard
   How Green was my Valley
   pp. 188–191 (Ch. 20)
   'We are out, now ... killing the police.'

   The miners are on strike, and conditions in the village get steadily worse. Food is short, and Huw shares his lunch with a school friend Shani. The men are idle, then form a choir, then disband again when they have no strength to walk to practices. People begin to die.

SUFFRAGETTES

1. ALLEN, Walter
   All in a Lifetime
   pp. 139–140 (Ch. 12)
   'Fanny took to the attendant ... these great truths.'

   Fanny is a great fighter for causes. Her zeal for female suffrage goes hand-in-hand with her passionate socialism, and vegetarianism. She is even caught indoctrinating baby Will.

SUICIDE

1. ACHEBE, Chinua
   Things Fall Apart
   see BRITISH EMPIRE – NIGERIA 4

2. BALDWIN, James
   Go Tell it on the Mountain
   see RACISM – AMERICA 1

3. BARSTOW, Stan
   Joby
   pp. 97–100 (Ch. 6)
   'Joby left the house as ... 'No but most of 'em.'

   Snap's uncle, has hung himself. Joby and his mates discuss the best way of

committing suicide. They reject one method after another as being too painful or too slow. They debate whether suicide is courageous or cowardly.

4. BATES, H.E.
   The Purple Plain
   pp. 158–162 (Ch. 15)
   'All the time he fought ... in the white sand.'

   The possibility of Forrester, Carrington, and Blore reaching civilisation from the Burmese jungle where their plane has crashed is growing more remote. Forrester and Blore come to blows as a result of the tension and Blore is hurt. While Forrester goes to fetch him some water, he shoots himself.

5. COLLINS, Wilkie
   The Moonstone
   pp. 167–170 (1st Period, Ch. 19)
   'As I got near the shore ... slope of the beach.'

   Sergeant Cuff and Betteredge are following the foot prints of a servant girl who is missing. They lead to the quick-sand, and gradually the men realise the girl's fate.

6. GORKY, Maxim
   Childhood
   (i) pp. 196–201 (Ch. 9); (ii) pp. 146–150
   'His mute nephew had gone ... short and fat and ugly.'

   A policeman comes to arrest Uncle Pyotr. It is clear to Gorky from the gloom that descends upon the household, that the drayman has been involved in a crime disgraceful beyond words. Then a neighbour rushes in and leads the family to Pyotr's body. He has slit his throat, having been discovered robbing churches.

7. LEE, Laurie
   Cider with Rosie
   (i) pp. 71–75 (Ch. 6, 'Public Death, Private Murder'); (ii) pp. 98–104
   'Grief of madness ... into that pond.'

   Miss Flynn, beautiful and strange, is found drowned in Jones's pond, causing much talk among gossipping women and curious children.

8. ibid.
(i) pp. 136–138 (Ch. 10, 'The Uncles'); (ii) pp. 180–183
'When he married ... long time,' he said.'
Uncle Sid gets into trouble with his employers, the Bus Co., for drinking. Each time he is suspended he 'attempts suicide'. The last time, he is really sacked, and Laurie and his brother find him 'hanging' from a tree, waiting for them.

9. LESSING, Doris
The Grass is Singing
see HORROR 9

10. SHOLOKHOV, Mikhail
And Quiet Flows the Don
pp. 175–180 (Part 1, Ch. 11)
'Pelagea fretted whilst ... to the sea of Azov.'
She is unable to bear the humiliation of her husband's neglect, and worse, the tongues of neighbours, and vicious rumour – Natalia tries to kill herself, messily, with a scythe.

11. SHUTE, Nevil
On the Beach
pp. 134–138 (Ch. 5)
'About this radiation sickness ... face up to things,' he said.'
Peter tries to explain to Mary that they will all get radiation sickness, and that it will be better to kill themselves before they are too ill. Mary does not wish to accept the truth and is angry.

12. ibid.
pp. 159–162; 170–172 (Ch. 6)
'The Chief of the Boat ... at this radiation level.'; 'At twenty minutes past ten ... on course, ten knots.'
Yeoman Swain escapes from his submarine into the radio-active atmosphere of his home town. He is determined to spend his last days at home, although everyone there has already been dead a year.

13. ibid.
pp. 255–260 (Ch. 9)

'He got back to his little flat ... and drank.
Peter has made a temporary recovery from radiation sickness, but he hides it from Mary, as she and the baby are so ill. They decide that they wish to end their lives together.

14. SILLITOE, Alan
The Loneliness of the Long-distance Runner
(i) pp. 68–76 ('On Saturday Afternoon'); (ii) pp. 102–110
'I once saw a bloke ... I want to stay where I am.'
The writer happens on a man who is about to hang himself. He gives assistance and offers advice. It is not taken, and the attempt fails. A policeman arrives and takes the man away, promising him five years for his 'crime'.

15. WELLS, H.G.
The History of Mr Polly
pp. 160–163 (Ch. 8, Part 1)
'Mr Polly designed ... he said at last.'
Polly resolves to make an end to things. His wife, his job, his indigestion combine to persuade him to make his house his funeral pyre.

16. ibid.
pp. 162–166 (Ch. 8, Part 2)
'For twenty minutes ... he repeated, 'Fire!'
Polly sets the scene for his suicide attempt. He pours paraffin everywhere and yet improvises the appearance of an accident. He sits on the stairs, razor in hand and watches the flames mount. At the last minute, he gets hot legs, and cold feet.
see also: FIRE – FIGHTING 2

SUMMER

1. ALAIN-FOURNIER
Le Grand Meaulnes
pp. 128–130 (Part 2, Ch. 1)
'The donkey really belonged ... a banal little outing.'
A bathing party by the Cher. The sights and sounds of an August

afternoon, with school examinations over, and thirst on everyone's mind.

2. LEE, Laurie
   Cider with Rosie
   (i) pp. 110–114 (Ch. 8 'Winter and summer'); (ii) pp. 148–153
   (Come Down and Startle, pp. 84–85)
   'Summer, June summer ... go to bed.'
   Summer seen in the early morning as the reflection of the lake on the bedroom ceiling, later in the dust and grass of the roadside, then in games by the river, finally in a rush of memories.

SUNDAY

1. CAMUS, Albert
   The Outsider
   pp. 29–32 (Part 1, Ch. 2)
   'After lunch I felt ... my life had changed.'
   The young man spends almost all his Sunday afternoon and evening on the balcony. He watches people doing Sunday things: he watches the trams and the clouds, he smokes and eats chocolate, alive to atmosphere.

2. FOAKES, Grace
   Between High Walls
   pp. 30–33 (Ch. 15)
   'Try, if you will ... vividly to my mind.'
   An East London Sunday: Sunday quiet, Sunday best, and Sunday-school. The author goes to evening service with her parents, but she can't attend to the preacher for watching the down-and-outs itching and scratching in the gallery.

3. LAWRENCE, D.H.
   The Rainbow
   pp. 270–273 (Ch. 10)
   'She was happy at home ... in dreams, unassailed.'
   Ursula is going through a religious phase. Sunday is a special day for her, as a result. But it is a special day in the life of the whole family, with an atmosphere all its own.

SUNDAY – SCHOOL

1. TWAIN, Mark
   The Adventures of Tom Sawyer
   (i) pp. 26–34 (Ch. 4); (ii) pp. 29–36
   'Sabbath school hours ... the rest of the scene.'
   Tom loathes going to Sunday School. There is one aspect of it, though, that he can exploit to his greater glory. He trades treasure for tickets, and is awarded a Bible on the strength of his supposed learning of Scripture verses. But his glory is short-lived.

SUPERSTITION

see also: FAITH;
FORTUNE – TELLING;
MEDICINE – PRIMITIVE;
WITCHCRAFT

SUPERSTITION

1. BAWDEN, Nina
   Carrie's War
   (i) pp. 59–61 (Ch. 5); (ii) pp. 52–54
   ' "Oh, it's a foolish tale ... that way from home!" '
   Hepzibah, housekeeper at Mrs Goto-bed's, tells the children the legend of a skull, kept in the library. It was supposed to bring disaster if it was removed from the house.

2. DICKENS, Charles
   David Copperfield
   pp. 49–50 (Ch. 1)
   'Whether I shall turn ... no meandering.'
   David Copperfield was born on a Friday at midnight, and women of the neighbourhood prophesy his future on the strength of day and time. The caul with which he was born is offered for sale, as protection against drowning.

3. GOLDING, William
   Lord of the Flies
   see FEAR (of) MONSTERS 1

4. GRAVES, Robert
   Goodbye to All That

5. GOLDING, William
   Lord of the Flies
   see RIVALS – BOYS 2
6. ibid.
   see HUNTING 1
7. JOHNSON, Dorothy M.
   The Hanging Tree
   pp. 42–47 ('Journal of Adventure')
   'He had found adventure ... but he had not died.'
   Edward Morgan, in flight from Indians, is thrown when his horse stumbles in a creek. Both he and his horse suffer broken legs. He holes up under an upturned tree. He makes out for some days, unhopeful of surviving the winter, until a Crow squaw happens past.
8. LONDON, Jack
   White Fang
   see OUTSIDERS 5
9. SERRAILLIER, Ian
   The Silver Sword
   (i) pp. 46–50 (Ch. 7); (ii) pp. 37–40
   'They made their new home ... on the black market.'
   Edek, Ruth and Bronia, whose parents are both in the hands of the Nazis, learn to fend for themselves, first in the cellar of a bombed house, then in a shelter in the woods outside the city.
10. WELLS, H.G.
    The War of the Worlds
    (i) pp. 152–159 (Bk. 2, Ch. 7); (ii) pp. 163–169
    'This isn't a war' ... has come back to his own.'
    An artillery man describes to the writer, the way in which he intends to survive the invasion of the Earth by Martians. He will go underground, he says, and be one of the scavengers in the sewers of London, eating the crumbs from the Martians' table. It is the only way, he says.
11. WYNDHAM, John
    The Day of the Triffids
    pp. 202–204 (Ch. 12)
    'Curiously I realised ... Do you agree with that?'
    The group realises that they are going

to have to learn self-sufficiency. Coker instructs them in how they will have to make use of the world's accumulated knowledge, and go on learning.

12. WYNDHAM, John
    The Kraken Wakes
    pp. 215–217; pp. 220–222 (Phase Three)
    'But though it was bad here ... the police and the military.'; I don't propose to deal ... gulls stood instead.'
    The waters continue to rise in London and elsewhere. Armed gangs prowl the city, looting. Those with property on higher ground, fence themselves in with their food supplies, in hopes of the survival of the fattest.

SURVIVAL (in) DESERTS

1. TREVOR, Elleston
   The Flight of the Phoenix
   see DESERTS 5
2. ibid.
   pp. 146–149 (Ch. 18)
   'The birds came sailing in ... for them, as they had asked.'
   Vultures make for the corpse of the camel before Crow and Bellamy. Crow fires at the birds, killing two of them. Bellamy drains their blood into a jerrican, then flings them away to distract the other birds, while he and Crow tap the camel of what moisture remains in it, in their own desperate bid for survival.

SURVIVAL (on) ISLANDS

1. GOLDING, William
   Pincher Martin
   see SHIPWRECKS 10
2. ibid.
   pp. 56–60; 60–65; 65–67 (Ch. 4)
   'He lay with the pains ... He watched dully.'; 'Presently he began ... beyond the backwash.'; 'He climbed down the rock ... settled down again.'
   As day dawns, so the survivor sees beyond his aches and pains, the

desperateness of his position, and the necessity of food and water to his survival. He busies himself with thoughts of rescue, and schools himself to keep a clear head, so as not to be beaten by common fear.

see also: CASTAWAYS 9

3. SPERRY, Armstrong
The Boy who was Afraid
pp. 43–48 (Ch. 4)
'The very next morning ... see it flash.'
Mafatu settles down to life on the island on which he has been shipwrecked: he keeps his fire alight, he begins to make a canoe, and a raft, he makes clothes and a house, and he fashions his own tools.

SURVIVAL (in) JUNGLE

1. BATES, H.E.
The Purple Plain
pp. 108–115 (Ch. 12)
''Blore!' he said ... he had ever known.'
Forrester, Blore, and Carrington have crashed on a dry river-bed in Burma. Carrington is badly burnt. Blore turns out to have a wonderful assortment of things in the pack he has rescued from the plane, and they make Carrington and then themselves as comfortable as they can, before thinking about their future.

2. ibid.
pp. 121–124 (Ch. 13)
'The heat kept ... dominant nurses are.'
Forrester begins to plan – he sees their only hope as walking along the river bed, which should lead to a river and thence a road. He quashes all Blore's and Carrington's fairly reasonable objections with a blind optimism.

see DETERMINATION 2

SURVIVAL (at) SEA

1. BOMBARD, Alain
The Bombard Story
see EXPEDITIONS 1
2. CALDWELL, John
Desperate Voyage
see HURRICANES 2
3. ibid.
pp. 86–89 (Ch. 10)
'The mast had snapped ... on the opposite horizon.'
'Pagan' is dismasted. The hurricane has done its worst. What is more, the cabin is dangerously full of water. The author sets to bailing out with a bucket. In his anxiety and exhaustion, a good many vital things go overboard, but the hurricane has spent itself.
4. ibid.
pp. 96–99 (Ch. 11)
'Pangs of uneasiness ... rolled in for the night.'
The author is lost, near foodless and waterless, and exhausted. He works out his position very roughly and rations his few provisions. The situation is grim but not yet desperate.
5. ibid.
see HUNGER 1
6. HEYERDAHL, Thor
The Kon-Tiki Expedition
pp. 98–103 (Ch. 5)
'Whatever these sun-worshippers' plans ... one world to the other.'
Heyerdahl gives an account of the food he and his companions ate on board the raft, and compares it with what the original Kon-Tiki might have eaten.
7. SPERRY, Armstrong
The Boy who was Afraid
pp. 19–21 (Ch. 2)
'there was no morning ... broke from him.'
After a violent storm, Mafatu drifts for days in an open canoe. Most of his stores have been lost overboard, and he is scorched by the sun. At last he sees land.

SWEETS

1. KIRKUP, James
   The Only Child
   pp. 109–111 (Ch. 9)
   'The occasions ... "wigga-wagga" toffee.'
   The adult James relives the touch and taste of the liquorice, sherbet, and toffee confections that tickled the palate of the infant Jim.

2. SILLITOE, Alan
   Saturday Night and Sunday Morning
   see TEASING 6

SWIMMING

   see also: DROWNING

SWIMMING

1. CHURCHILL, W.S.
   My Early Life
   pp. 44–45 (Ch. 3)
   'My brother and I ... will remember it too.'
   Churchill comes very near to drowning, with his brother, in the lake of Lausanne.

2. HARDY, Thomas
   Far from the Madding Crowd
   (i) pp. 378–381 (Ch. 47); (ii) pp. 358–360
   'Troy wandered along ... they were bound.'
   Troy seeks to drown his problems in a restful swim, and all but drowns himself. He is carried out to sea by a fast current; but while making for a spit, he is picked up by crew-members in a rowing boat.

3. HUGHES, Richard
   A High Wind in Jamaica
   (i) pp. 9–10 (Ch. 1, Part 1); (ii) pp. 10–11
   'The best fun ... terrible rheumatics.'
   The Thornton children and their bathing-pool. A question of decency. A negro bathes there after a hearty meal, and is drowned.

4. KNOWLES, John
   A Separate Peace
   pp. 44–47 (Ch. 3)
   'One day he broke ... somewhat expressionless voice.'
   Finny breaks the school 100 yds. free style record. He is confident that he can break the record-holder's time, so he does it. Gene times him, and tries to persuade him to do it again, officially, but Finny swears Gene to secrecy about the feat. His impulse has been satisfied.

SWIMMING – LEARNING

1. MACKEN, Walter
   God made Sunday and Other Stories
   pp. 18–20 ('God made Sunday')
   'But I wasn't afraid ... how to swim.'
   Colmain has lost his father and brothers at sea. He hates the sea. He knows he must master it so he jumps in at the end of a rope, and flails about learning to swim. Soon, he is at home in the sea, pleased that he has proved it to be no more than water.

2. NAUGHTON, Bill
   One Small Boy
   pp. 172–173 (Bk. 2, Ch. 7)
   'After tea he had ... you and God alone.'
   Michael goes to the local baths after school, to learn to swim. Having washed himself in the plunge bath, he makes his first essay from the side. A boy gives him some advice. He takes it, and swims.

TANKS

1. HOLBROOK, David
   Flesh Wounds
   pp. 79–82 (Ch. 2)
   'Paul's regiment was due ... objectives he was given.'
   Paul is in a tank regiment. They will land on the Normandy beaches in waterproofed American Shermans. Each is a tightly-organized realisation of months of hard training.

285

2. ibid.
   see SECOND WORLD WAR – D-DAY 3, 4
3. ibid.
   pp. 159–161 (Ch. 4)
   'When they returned ... bare earth of the field.'
   Rumours of an invulnerable German tank spread among the British tank crews. When a tank looms out of the smoke, the latter let all hell loose against it, only to discover that it's a British Churchill.

TEACHERS

see also: BULLYING (by) TEACHERS;
TEACHING

TEACHERS

1. CHURCH, Richard
   Over the Bridge
   pp. 133–136 (Ch. 12)
   'I was given cards ... whole and fatal significance.'
   Mr Burgess is an awesome headmaster. Boys wet their pants and otherwise break under the strain, just waiting for the judgement of cane. His sense of theatre is unfailingly gratified, and is unchecked even by dramatic rebellion.
2. MOORE, John
   Portrait of Elmbury
   pp. 45–48 (Part 2)
   'One evening in the summer ... lie on either side.'
   Three boys discover one of their masters shares their enthusiasm for caterpillars and moths. He invites them to his cottage, where they are impressed by his collection of moths and books, and his record as a cricketer.

TEACHING

see also: CONDITIONING;
DOGS – TRAINING;
HORSES – TRAINING;

INDOCTRINATION;
LECTURING

TEACHING

1. BRAITHWAITE, E.R.
   To Sir with Love
   see CRIME – JUVENILE 1
2. LAWRENCE, D.H.
   The Rainbow
   see LEAVETAKING 8
3. STOLZ, Mary
   Ready or Not
   pp. 39–40 (Ch. 3)
   'Mrs Reinholt stood now ... what to have for dinner.'
   A classroom vignette, through the eyes of Mrs Reinholt, a disillusioned, but still caring English teacher. She sets the class a routine 'theme' and reflects on her own inadequacies.

TEACHING – DISCIPLINE

1. BERNA, Paul
   Flood Warning
   pp. 20–22; pp. 23–26 (Ch. 1)
   'Monsieur Sala sipped his tea ... imprisoned in his own shyness.';
   'Monsieur Sala was among the last ... did not stop again.'
   A shy and studious teacher, M. Sala, is dismissed from his post because of his lack of class control. Then, on his last tour of duty, a freak weather condition abets a decisiveness in him which surprises everyone.
2. BRAITHWAITE, E.R.
   To Sir with Love
   pp. 64–69 (Ch. 8)
   'Thereafter, I tried very hard ... of bringing the fact home to them.'
   The atmosphere in Braithwaite's class is strained, and at times hostile. He despairs of ever understanding such unamenable pupils. It takes a piece of crude misbehaviour on the part of the girls to anger him into demanding a certain standard of conduct; and into enforcing it.

see also: CHALLENGES 2;
CRIME – JUVENILE 1

3. BRONTË, Charlotte
   Villette
   pp. 69–70 (Ch. 8)
   ' "Will you," she said ... "Ça va." '
   Lucy Snowe, engaged as governess to the headmistress's children, is suddenly asked to teach English to a full class of Labassecouriennes. There is incipient trouble, but despite language difficulties, she keeps control.

4. LAWRENCE, D.H.
   The Rainbow
   pp. 397–400 (Ch. 13)
   'Go back and do ... some beaten sat.'
   Ursula screws herself to the striking point. She is confronted by Williams, the class clown. Seeing his challenge as a test of her authority, she beats him to the ground. The class is quiet, but only at the expense of Ursula's finer feeling.

5. THOMPSON, Flora
   Lark Rise to Candleford
   (i) pp. 195–196 ('Lark Rise', Ch. 11);
   (ii) pp. 182–183
   'As Miss Holmes went ... to see governess.'
   Miss Holmes at the Fordlow National School uses the cane on the older boys, the eleven year olds, on the point of leaving. As a pioneer in state education, she is 'breaking the ground' ready for a better seed.

6. ibid.
   (i) pp. 198–202 ('Lark Rise', Ch. 11);
   (ii) pp. 185–188
   'That mistress was not ... their outlook on life.'
   The effective and respected Miss Holmes is replaced – for a time – by a young lady of good intent, but uninspiring mien, Miss Higgs. She is superseded in her turn.

TEACHING – FIRST DAY

1. BRAITHWAITE, E.R.
   To Sir with Love
   pp. 13–14; 17–18 (Ch. 2)
   'From the Headmaster's office ... different around here.'; 'I looked around the room ... shown to their fellows.'
   Braithwaite's first impressions of the East End school to which he has been appointed. He looks in on a class of frighteningly mature adolescents, before wandering about the building on his own. He is depressed by the atmosphere, and abashed by the crowd noise.

2. ibid.
   pp. 50–57 (Ch. 6)
   'In the classroom, I stood in front ... until the bell rang.'
   Braithwaite's first brush with his class of rangy teenagers. The art mistress advises him to assume firm control from the start. At the risk of being unfriendly, he sets out to do just this.
   see also: TEACHING – DISCIPLINE 2

3. LAWRENCE, D.H.
   The Rainbow
   pp. 367–369 (Ch. 13)
   'On Friday her father ... return of tramping feet.'
   Ursula is full of passionate ideals. She will be God's gift to the teaching profession. As she travels to her first appointment, on the first day, her heart sinks with apprehension and suspense.

4. ibid.
   pp. 374–377 (Ch. 13)
   (Impact Two, pp. 149–151)
   'In the porch where ... alone that mattered.'
   An urban board school. From the first, Ursula is out of her element. The building is confining, and the children would have her confining, too. Her teaching is fear-bound; her hold on her class, precarious.

5. LEE, Harper
   To Kill a Mockingbird
   see SCHOOLS – PRIMARY – FIRST DAY 1

6. ibid.
   (i) pp. 31–34 (Ch. 3); (ii) pp. 31–34

'I returned to school ... lived in a hall.'

Miss Caroline, the new, young, sensitive teacher of the first grade, is much put out by the insanitariness of one of her pupils. She asks him to withdraw; he does so, and he never returns.

TEACHING – INTERVIEWS

1. BRAITHWAITE, E.R.
   To Sir with Love
   see RACISM – BRITAIN 1
2. 'MISS READ'
   Village School
   (i) pp. 90–96 (Part 2, Ch. 11); (ii) pp. 90–96
   'There were only three ... in a cup of tea.'
   Three candidates present themselves to a panel of local worthies, for the post of Assistant Mistress at the small village school. The first candidate withdraws her application, the second is a bundle of nerves, and the third is just the job.

TEAS

see MEALS – TEAS;
PARTIES – TEAS

TEASING

see also: CHALLENGES;
PRANKS

TEASING

1. BALDWIN, Michael
   Grandad with Snails
   pp. 94–100 (Ch. 11)
   'Silky was a young man ... Ingrowing whiskers – that's it.'
   Michael is evacuated to a farm. The farmer tricks him into filling his shoes with sheep's dung. He is persuaded that this will help whiskers to grow on his nine-year old cheeks, so as to qualify him for rabbit-shooting.

2. BAWDEN, Nina
   On the Run
   pp. 86–88 (Ch. 9)
   'The stiff, defiant look ... softness the next.'
   Ben has cut his knee badly on some glass, and Lil examines it. She spins a gruesome tale of glass travelling round inside the body, till it pierces the heart; and is believed. When she relents, she does in fact clean the wound very efficiently.

3. GODDEN, Rumer
   The Diddakoi
   see GYPSIES 3

4. GORKY, Maxim
   Childhood
   (i) pp. 27–29 (Ch. 2); (ii) pp. 31–32
   'By Saturday I too had managed ... as she led me into the house.'
   His grandfather's business is dyeing. Gorky supposes that his apprenticeship might as well begin sooner rather than later; Sasha puts him up to starting on the white tablecloth. In all innocence, Gorky dips it in the indigo. Retribution, when it comes, is swift and terrible.
   see also: PUNISHMENT – CORPORAL 3

5. KING, Clive
   Stig of the dump
   pp. 68–73 (Ch. 5)
   'As he came near ... my friend,' said Barney.'
   Barney throws lumps of earth down on three boys in the chalk pit he considers to be his own. They cannot see him, but trick him by going away, and then sneaking up on him when he is in their den.

6. SILLITOE, Alan
   Saturday Night and Sunday Morning
   pp. 58–60 (Part 1, Ch. 4)
   'Arthur took a five-pound ... back to the house.'
   When Arthur dangles a fiver (too) near to his nephew, young William grabs it to realise its worth in dolly-mixtures at the corner shop. Arthur runs after him, rescues the fiver, and

quietens William with a penn'orth of caramels.

7. TWAIN, Mark
The Adventures of Huckleberry Finn
(i) pp. 5–7 (Ch. 2); (ii) pp. 53–55
'We went tiptoeing ... been rode by witches.'
Tom and Huck steal out of the house by night. In doing so, they wake Jim, who comes out and listens. But Jim falls asleep on watch, and while he sleeps, Tom leaves signs of his passing, which Jim later attributes to witches.

TEETH

1. TWAIN, Mark
The Adventures of Tom Sawyer
(i) pp. 40–43 (Ch. 6); (ii) pp. 42–45 (Family and School, pp. 57–60)
'Monday morning found ... the bedpost, now.'
It's Monday morning. Tom thinks he'll avoid school by feigning illness. But he miscalculates when he draws attention to his loose tooth. Before he can protest, it is clean out, at the end of a silk thread.

TELEPATHY

1. THOMPSON, Flora
Lark Rise to Candleford
(i) pp. 560–562 ('Candleford Green' Ch. 36); (ii) pp. 490–491
'Laura's mother ... loaded with fruit.'
Laura's mother is unexpectedly called to visit a dying cousin, who does not know she is coming. No-one meets her on the way, and yet the cousin tells her nurse that she can see them, and describes what she is carrying long before her arrival.

TEMPTATION

1. ALMEDINGEN, E.M.
Little Katia
pp. 43–46 (Ch. 5)
'It so happened ... with my choice.'

A marvellous selection of fruit stands on the dining-table, ready for a dinner party. Katia cannot resist the plums, and steals three, when no-one is about. Her adopted mother finds her out, and is calm but very angry.

2. DOSTOYEVSKY, Fyodor
The Idiot
(i) pp. 164–167 (Part 1, Ch. 16); (ii) pp. 204–207
'Nastasia Philipovna seized the packet ... laughing and shouting and whistling.'
Nastasia tests her rejected suitor. She throws a hundred thousand roubles on the fire, and declares that they are his if he will salvage them. But Gania, accused of being mercenary, stands his ground and watches the flames lick the packet. When he faints, Nastasia rescues the money and tells the amazed onlookers, that Gania is to have the money, because he has earned her respect.

3. NAUGHTON, Bill
pp. 212–213 (Bk. 3, Ch. 2)
'He went softly ... I've seen no pears.'
There is a pear in the baking tin. Michael is tempted. He reasons that it will do him good, so he eats it privately in the closet. He enjoys it. There is another pear in the tin, and he eats that too – but he does not enjoy it.

TERROR

see FEAR; HORROR;
PANIC

THIEVES

see ESCAPE (from) THIEVES;
FEAR (of) THIEVES;
ROBBERY;
STEALING

THUNDER

see HURRICANES;
STORMS

TOADS

1. DURRELL, Gerald
   My Family and Other Animals
   pp. 209–213 (Part 3, Ch. 13)
   'To the left of the villa ... beard with his thumb.'
   Gerald finds two unusually large common toads in the garden. Spiro is sick at the sight of them, and Theodore, delighted by them, makes them a gift of an earthworm. Gerald keeps them under his bed, where they grin lugubriously, and eat insects he knocks off the light for them.

TORTOISES

see also: TURTLES

TORTOISES

1. DURRELL, Gerald
   My Family and Other Animals
   pp. 50–52 (Part 1, Ch. 3)
   'The new arrival was duly ... throughout the burial service.'
   Gerald buys a sprightly little tortoise, that the family christens Achilles. He forces attention to himself in many aggravating ways but when he goes missing, all the family search for him, baiting him with his beloved strawberries.

TORTOISES – MATING

1. DURRELL, Gerald
   My Family and Other Animals
   pp. 114–117 (Part 2, Ch. 8)
   'This must have been ... the nearest Clover Patch.'
   The tortoises emerge from their winter hibernation, and proceed with the important business of courtship (often involving jousts with rival

suitors), and mating. The coupling of tortoises is more comic than awesome.

TORTURE

1. KOESTLER, Arthur
   Darkness at Noon
   (i) pp. 82–86 ('The Second Hearing' Part 2); (ii) pp. 84–88
   'The day after the first ... their game of chess.'
   Two examining magistrates discuss the methods to be used to extract a confession from Rubashov. The one believes that only some form of physical or mental torture will be effective; the other holds to the etiquette of persuasion.
2. ibid.
   (i) pp. 169–172 ('The Third Hearing'; Parts 3 and 4); 184–189; 191–193 ('The Third Hearing', Part 6); (ii) pp. 169–172; 184–188; 190–192
   'The next thing he could ... 'Die in silence.'; 'After five or six ... his aching skull.'; 'Comrade Rubashov, I hope ... matter of constitution.'
   Under considerable pressure, of light, constant questioning, and sleeplessness, Rubashov confesses to having enacted in the counter-revolutionary interest, what has only passed through his mind. The difference between truth and fancy is blurred; his signature is the price he pays for the long sleep he needs.
3. ORWELL, George
   1984
   (i) pp. 245–248 (Part 3, Ch. 2); (ii) pp. 192–195
   'He was lying ... and the dead.
   Winston is repeatedly beaten when he first arrives at the Ministry of Truth – sometimes he confesses uncommitted crimes immediately, sometimes he endures it much longer. Later interrogations are accompanied by infliction of smaller pains.
4. ibid.
   (i) pp. 250–251; 255–257 (Part 3, Ch. 2); (ii) pp. 196–197; 200–202

'Without any warning ... said Winston.'; 'Do you remember ... I don't know.'

Winston is given (presumably) electric shock treatment of varying intensity, with the desired final result – capitulation on the question 2 plus 2 equals five.

5. ibid.
(i) pp. 289–293 (Part 3, Ch. 5); (ii) pp. 227–230
'You asked me ... and not open.'
In room 101 Winston is brought face to face with his greatest fear – rats, which will gnaw his face if he does not give in.

TOWNS (and) CITIES

1. ALLEN, Walter
All in a Lifetime
pp. 102–105 (Ch. 10)
'I look back to my months ... was no place for me.'
Billy's first impressions of New York are of its immense size, its mixture of smells and life-styles, and its extremes of wealth and poverty.

2. BENNETT, Arnold
Anna of the Five Towns
pp. 23–26 (Ch. 1)
'As they approached ... never suspended.'
The new park in Bursley is opened and crowds flock to see it. It is a brave attempt to create a natural landscape in the midst of the grimness of the surrounding industry; but it cannot compensate for the ugliness and pollution.

3. CHURCH, Richard
Over the Bridge
pp. 55–57 (Ch. 5)
'The Battersea that I explored ... captivity for another week.'
Battersea life. The street, the whitewash, the ebbing and flowing Thames, and the pigeons flying on Sunday afternoons.

4. FITZGERALD, F. Scott
The Great Gatsby

p. 29 (Ch. 2)
'About half-way ... dumping ground.'
On a train journey to New York, one sees a strange desolate spot, apparently all grey, and dominated by a gigantic advertisement hoarding, a pair of bespectacled eyes.

5. LAWRENCE, D.H.
The Rainbow
pp. 11–13 (Ch. 1)
'About 1840 ... going on beyond them.'
First a canal is cut across the Brangwen farm, and then a railway traverses it; and all the time the collieries approach, with their attendant redbrick house-rows.

6. ibid.
pp. 345–346 (Ch. 12)
'He lived in a large ... mood become concrete.'
Uncle Tom lives at Wiggiston, a new development of red-brick houses built, like those who live in them, to serve the Colliery. To the sensitive Ursula, it is all unutterably sterile.

7. LAWRENCE, D.H.
Sons and Lovers
(i) pp. 270–271 (Ch. 10); (ii) pp. 330–332
'They went together ... across the country.'
Paul and Clara gaze out over Nottingham from the Castle, and express loathing of merely expedient urban development. Paul is more optimistic; he expects that, 'the town will come right.'

8. LESSING, Doris
Nine African Stories
pp. 82–85 ('A Home for the Highland Cattle')
'The city, seen from the air ... It is a city of gardens.' '
Salisbury(?), Rhodesia, a sprawling, ugly, beautiful, modern city, with a history. There are suburbs, and slums, chimneys and concrete towers; but the trees redeem.

9. PATON, Alan
Cry the Beloved Country

pp. 17–21 (Bk. 1, Ch. 4)
'And now the buildings ... to feel welcome and secure.'
Stephen Kumalo arrives in Johannesburg for the first time. He has lived all his life in the country, and is confused and frightened by the noise, the size of the buildings, the traffic and the crowds. He is robbed by a man who pretends to help him.

10. SEWELL, Anna
    Black Beauty
    pp. 156–158 (Ch. 35)
    'It is always difficult ... eight minutes to twelve o'clock.'
    London suffered its traffic jams even in the days of horses and carriages. Black Beauty is a cab horse, and sometimes gets stuck, sometimes weaves a way through.

TRADE

see BUYING (and) SELLING (by)
DEALERS;
MARKETS; PEDLARS;
SALESMEN; SHOPS

TRADE UNIONS

see also: STRIKES;
WORK

TRADE UNIONS

1. ALLEN, Eric
   The Latchkey Children
   pp. 135–139 (Ch. 13)
   'Duke Ellington Binn's father didn't ... this day's business is over.'
   One of the workers who is supposed to be chopping up the tree in the playground, has a conscientious objection to the job. He appeals to his union's rules, and he and his colleague outface the angry foreman.

2. DICKENS, Charles
   Hard Times
   (i) pp. 134–141 (Book 2, Ch. 4); (ii) pp. 144–152

'Oh my friends ... the giant Bounderby.'
One Slackbridge exhorts his co-workers of Coketown to join the United Aggregate Tribunal. He berates poor Stephen Blackpool for his conscientious objection to joining.

3. ibid.
   see DISMISSAL 3

TRAMPS

1. CARY, Joyce
   The Horse's Mouth
   see HOMELESSNESS 1, 2

2. GRAVES, Robert
   Goodbye to All That
   pp. 257–258 (Ch. 29)
   'Ex-service men ... asking us for money.'
   Mr and Mrs Graves 'adopt' a thirteen year old girl on the road with her ex-serviceman father. The country is full of such men, the 'heroes' for whom there are no homes (though there are as many rogues among them, as unfortunates).

3. THOMPSON, Flora
   Lark Rise to Candleford
   (i) pp. 126–128 ('Lark Rise', Ch. 7); (ii) pp. 123–125
   'There must have been ... the brotherhood of man.'
   Ingenious tricksters and 'plain beggars'. They roam in large numbers in the Oxfordshire country-side of the 1880's, boiling up their tea-cans, selling rubbish and trading on the pity of gullible cottagers.

TRAPPING

see ANIMALS – TRAPPING

TRAVEL

see also: ACCIDENTS – ROAD;
CYCLING;
RAILWAYS;
VOYAGES

TRAVEL

1. BENNETT, Arnold
   Anna of the Five Towns
   pp. 148–153 (Ch. 10)
   'It was an incredible day ... It was all unspeakable.'
   Anna departs for the Isle of Man with the Suttons, the first time she has left home. She is enthralled by everything – the train ride, Liverpool, the ship and the glittering expanse of sea.

TRAVEL (by) BOAT

see also: VOYAGES

TRAVEL (by) BOAT

1. CANAWAY, W.H.
   Sammy going South
   pp. 67–69 (Ch. 11)
   'The paddle-steamer ... suddenly clean and good.'
   Sammy is travelling south by paddle-steamer through the Sudan, in the company of some pilgrims returning from Mecca. They pass for days through areas of tall grass, and suffer the smell of a dead hippo.
2. ELIOT, George
   The Mill on the Floss
   see RUNNING AWAY 2
3. KIRKUP, James
   The Only Child
   pp. 147–149 (Ch. 12)
   'Right from the start ... to Cockburn Street.'
   Crossing the Tyne by ferry boat is always an exciting experience, but once, when the family misses the last ferry, and has to engage a flyboatman at night (in a thunderstorm), young Jim suffers a surfeit of excitement.
4. SERRAILLIER, Ian
   The Silver Sword
   (i) pp. 148–150 (Ch. 23); (ii) pp. 126–127
   'They turned the canoe ... hauled it ashore.'
   Ruth and her sister Bronia are escaping by canoe. The canoe is old, and they are not skilled, but they manage to negotiate rapids safely, only to fall asleep later and run on to a rock.

TRAVEL (by) BUS

1. AMIS, Kingsley
   Lucky Jim
   pp. 239–246 (Ch. 24)
   'Dixon ran out into ... 'Sorry, George.'
   Dixon must meet a girl at the station. A bus will get him there before she entrains for London. He runs for it, but once he is on it, the bus crawls, and by the time it arrives, the train has gone.

TRAVEL (by) CAR

1. FORSTER, E.M.
   Howard's End
   pp. 184–185 (Ch. 23)
   'A motor-drive ... they had arrived.'
   Margaret is driven through Hertfordshire, and thereby gets a very fleeting imprecise impression of that county.
2. LEE, Laurie
   Cider with Rosie
   see COUNTRY – LIFE 4
3. PEYTON, K.M.
   Flambards
   (i) pp. 107–109 (Ch. 7); (ii) pp. 136–138
   'There was a honking noise ... off the engine regretfully.'
   It is 1910, as William says, and cars have been around for fifteen years; but Christina is more used to hacking along these Essex lanes. She is sceptical about motor cars, but finds the experience nonetheless exhilarating.

TRAVEL (by) CHARABANC

1. LEE, Laurie
   Cider with Rosie
   see EXCURSIONS 3

TRAVEL (by) STAGE-COACH

1. DICKENS, Charles
   A Tale of Two Cities
   pp. 15–18 (Book 1, Ch. 2)
   'It was the Dover Road ... quickened by expectation.'
   Travel by the Dover Mail in the 1780's is a cold, uncomfortable and dangerous business. On a certain November night, this journey is no exception, and the sound of a galloping horse behind sets all hearts beating.

2. DU MAURIER, Daphne
   Jamaica Inn
   pp. 1–3; 10–12 (Ch. 1)
   'The coach rumbled away ... in a cloud.'
   Mary Yellan travels by coach to her new home at Jamaica Inn, through a fierce storm, which grows worse as they cross the bare moors.

3. HUGHES, Thomas
   Tom Brown's Schooldays
   pp. 67–71 (Part 1, Ch. 4)
   'I sometimes think that ... clock strikes eight.'
   A very early morning ride from Islington to Rugby, with a stop for a hot, and very substantial breakfast, to combat the cold.

4. ibid.
   see PRANKS 10

TRAVEL (by) TRAIN

1. WAUGH, Evelyn
   Scoop
   see RAILWAYS 4

TRAVEL (by) TRAM

1. KIRKUP, James
   The Only Child
   pp. 52–55 (Ch. 3)
   (Impact 1, p. 14)
   'The river lay ... home by his wife.'
   All the magic of tram-travel, (especially by night), is recalled lovingly: the varnished wood, the brass railings, the lurching at corners, and the flashing of the wires.

TREASURE-SEEKING

1. FALKNER, J. Meade
   Moonfleet
   pp. 37–44 (Ch. 3); 50–61 (Ch. 4)
   'Eagerness would not let ... if they see me with a spade.'; 'So the meeting broke up ... senseless to the ground.'
   John Trenchard climbs down into the Mohune vault, in search of Blackbeard's treasure. He hears voices, so hides behind a coffin. It happens that the voices belong to smugglers. They do not discover him, but they seal the vault after them, when they leave.
   see also: SMUGGLING 2

2. ibid.
   pp. 167–177 (Ch. 15)
   'The bucket was large ... I gave him the 'jewel.' '
   Blackbeard's diamond is thought to be embedded in the wall of a well in the castle courtyard, at Carisbrooke. John is let down in the bucket, and he finds the diamond. The Turnkey, who has been made privy to the search, claims a half-share in the prize. A fight ensues, and the Turnkey is pitched, by mistake, down the well.

3. TOLKIEN, J.R.R.
   The Hobbit
   see DRAGONS 1

TREES – FELLING

1. CHURCH, Richard
   The White Doe
   pp. 44–46 (Ch. 5)
   'Father and son worked ... the winter branches.'
   The woodman and his son, Tom, fell an oak. They secure the tree with ropes and then both take an end of the two-handed saw. The oak falls exactly as planned.

2. ibid.
   pp. 89–94 (Ch. 11)

'Margaret carried the sacks ... something was wrong.'
The woodman takes his son and two friends to help him fell an oak on a very snowy day. One of the pegs slips from the icy ground and the tree falls the wrong way, on to the woodman.

3. KING, Clive
Stig of the Dump
pp. 43–47 (Ch. 3)
'Barney ran off ... what a lot of firewood!'
Barney and his caveman friend, Stig, fell a tree for firewood. With his grandfather's axe and cross-cut saw, and very little knowledge they finally manage to bring down a sizeable ash tree.

TRIALS

see also: CHALLENGES;
INITIATION;
JUSTICE

TRIALS

1. ACHEBE, Chinua
Things Fall Apart
pp. 79–85 (Ch. 10)
'Large crowds began to gather ... great land case began.'
A wife-beating case is heard by the Spirits of the Departed of Umuofia. The prosecution and defence cases are heard, then, with due pomp, a decision is arrived at. It is an awesome ceremony.

2. BENTLEY, Phyllis
The Adventures of Tom Leigh
pp. 152–156 (Ch. 10)
'There was a pause now ... "It is the law." '
The judge sums up the case against the three accused. It is a damning one. He leaves the jury in no doubt as to Tom's credibility. The jury accordingly find the accused guilty, and the judge sentences them to be hanged by the neck.

3. BRAITHWAITE, E.R.
To Sir with Love
see CRIME – JUVENILE 1

4. DEFOE, Daniel
Moll Flanders
(i) pp. 245–247; (ii) pp. 266–267
'Well, there was no remedy ... either to God or man.'
The charge is breaking and entering with intent to commit a felony. Moll pleads movingly in mitigation of her offence, and the court is visibly affected. But the judges pass a sentence of death on her, all the same.

5. DICKENS, Charles
A Tale of Two Cities
pp. 278–282 (Bk. 3, Ch. 6)
'The Dread Tribunal ... over the streets.'
Darnay appears before the Tribunal who every day condemn scores of people to death. His case, however, is carefully and cleverly presented, the crowd is swayed, and the jury finally pronounces him innocent amid scenes of rejoicing.

6. DOSTOYEVSKY, Fyodor
The Idiot
see TEMPTATION 2

7. FORSTER, E.M.
A Passage to India
pp. 212–219; 221–224 (Part 2, Ch. 24)
'The court was crowded ... he was powerless.'; 'So peace was restored ... of descending dust.'
Anglo-India is on trial. The British phalanx is all but united in its contempt for the natives, and the latter in its loathing of the oppressors. Aziz is charged with assaulting Miss Quested. In a clear-sighted moment, Adela withdraws the charge, and all hell breaks loose.

8. KAFKA, Franz
The Trial
pp. 45–48 (Ch. 2)
'K felt as though he were entering ... black bushes above his eyes.'
An Alice-in-Wonderland of a trial. Strange men in strange clothes stand

ready in a packed hall to judge Joseph K. K. is bewildered, but encouraged by what he takes to be a positive attitude towards him, on the part of one section of the audience.

9. ORWELL, George
Animal Farm
(i) pp. 48–49; 51–53 (Ch. 7); (ii) pp. 67–69; 72–74
'All this while no more ... showed their side teeth.'; 'Four days later, in the ... the expulsion of Jones.'
Snowball is used as the scapegoat for all that goes wrong on the farm. Napoleon purges the animal ranks of 'secret agents' of Snowball, by setting the dogs on all who confess to assorted misdemeanours. Thus Orwell satirized the Moscow Show Trials of the 1930's.

10. PATON, Alan
Cry, the Beloved Country
(i) pp. 108–117 (Bk. 2, Ch. 5); 134–140 (Bk. 2, Ch. 11); (ii) pp. 137–144; 168–174
'They call for silence ... according to the custom.'; 'The people stand ...not lightly done.'
Absalom Kumalo is tried for the murder of a white man. His story is simple, and he has no other defence than his fear of the white man who discovered him stealing. His two companions deny their complicity, but he is sentenced to death.

TRIALS – INQUEST

1. WOOD, James
The Rain Islands
pp. 10–27 (Chs. 1, 2)
'I found myself ... and myself.'
Major Scott serves on the Jury at the inquest into the death of a seaman, lost overboard. The captain and his crew are questioned, and although it is obvious that there is something peculiar in the case, the verdict is 'Accidental Death.'

TRUANCY

1. GORKY, Maxim
Childhood
(i) pp. 238–241 (Ch. 11); (ii) pp. 175–177
'After the Christmas holidays ... And so it was settled.'
As a result of an embarrassing incident in class, Sasha truants from school. When he and Gorky are questioned, Sasha tries to lie his way out of a beating – but he makes a poor job of it. Gorky is also beaten for being an accessory.

2. GRICE, Frederick
The Bonny Pit Laddie
pp. 4–7 (Ch. 1)
(Family and School, pp. 112–113)
'The Headmaster looked at him ... Mr Allcroft to take him back.'
Dick's brother is truanting from School. The Headmaster asks a lot of questions which Dick cannot answer, and threatens his brother with dire punishment on his return.

3. ibid.
see SCHOOL – EXPULSION 1

4. JOYCE, James
Dubliners
pp. 18–22 ('An Encounter')
'The summer holidays were near ... crumbs of our provisions.'
Three school friends plan a summer's day away from lessons, to cross the Liffey by ferryboat. One fails to turn up at the appointed place, so the other two walk out to the docks by themselves, eat biscuits and chocolate for lunch, and lie in the grass of a sloping bank.

5. KNOWLES, John
A Separate Peace
see FRIENDS – BOYS 3

6. MACKEN, Walter
God made Sunday and Other Stories
pp. 176–177 ('No Medal for Matt')
(That Once Was Me, pp. 72–73)
'Matt was filled ... a chain on it.'
Matt has been punished unjustly at school. He expects his father to right

the wrong, and when he doesn't Matt's sense of injustice is increased. For the first time in his life, he truants.
see also: RESCUE (of) ANIMALS 5

7. THOMAS, Leslie
    This Time Next Week
    see ESCAPADES 11

TURTLES

1. STEINBECK, John
    The Grapes of Wrath
    (i) pp. 11–13 (Ch. 3); (ii) pp. 16–17
    'The sun lay ... a fraction in the dust.'
    The progress of a land-turtle from the roadside verge, over the edge of the road and across it, is described in minute detail. Its efforts are rewarded by a knock from a truck, but it continues uninjured.

UNCLES

see also: FAMILY;
RELATIVES

UNCLES

1. BARNES, Ron
    A Licence to Live
    pp. 24–26 (Ch. 2)
    'My Uncle George ... would call broke.'
    Uncle George is a character: he takes the family for outings in his horse and cart; he sleeps off a drunken stupor in the street; and has a row with the neighbour about a nanny goat.
2. LEE, Laurie
    Cider with Rosie
    (i) pp. 131–134 (Ch. 10, 'The Uncles'); (ii) pp. 174–178
    'My first encounter ... so we believe.'
    Uncle Ray's visit to the Lees is like a prolonged holiday – he flirts with the girls, amuses the boys, and goes off on long drinking bouts, arriving home grinning or blood-stained after a bicycle crash.

UNEMPLOYMENT

see also: STRIKES;
TRADE UNIONS;
WORK – SEEKING

UNEMPLOYMENT

1. FOAKES, Grace
    Between High Walls
    see POVERTY 9
2. GREENWOOD, Walter
    Love on the Dole
    pp. 154–157 (Part 3, Ch. 4)
    'The day was Monday ... head but did not speak.'
    At the end of his apprenticeship, Harry, a fully-fledged engineer, is on the dole. He queues up at the Labour Exchange to sign on.
3. ibid.
    pp. 158–161 (Part 3, Ch. 4)
    'At this hour there ... when Ah do?'
    Harry goes the rounds of the factories and warehouses in search of work. Always, the answer is the same: No hands wanted.
4. ibid.
    pp. 169–172 (Part 3, Ch. 6)
    'It got you slowly ... and drifted away.'
    The slow and insidious moral and physical deterioration of a man years out of work.
5. ibid.
    see PROTEST 3
6. HARDY, Thomas
    Far from the Madding Crowd
    (i) pp. 43–45 (Ch. 6); (ii) pp. 49–51
    'Two months passed away ... to a destitute man.'
    The destitute Gabriel seeks employment at Casterbridge hiring-fair. He offers himself as a bailiff in vain. He then tries as a shepherd, but farmers are suspicious of him because he has owned his own flock, and lost it.
7. HITCHMAN, Janet
    The King of the Barbareens
    pp. 193–195 (Ch. 9)

'I was well known ... shred of human dignity.'

The writer recalls the not-so-good old days of unemployment in the 1930's. She remembers a naive plan she conceived for putting men to work on planting oases, and she remembers the bitterness of long hours in the Labour Exchange queues.

8. TREASE, Geoffrey
   Cue for Treason
   pp. 60–64 (Ch. 7)
   'It is a hard profession ... die of cold in a ditch.'
   Desmond's acting troupe hits hard times. Peter reflects on the hardships that await him: to be unemployed during an Elizabethan winter, and to be on the run in severe times, is daunting; but he resolves not to beg.

9. WELLS, H.G.
   The History of Mr Polly
   see WORK – SEEKING 4

VANDALISM

1. MADDOCK, Reginald
   Sell-out
   pp. 7–15 (Ch. 1)
   'So that night ... as I turned in at our gate.'
   His mother tells Danny that she is going to marry again. For Danny, to whom the memory of his father is still dear, this sounds like a betrayal. He vents his bitterness on gaslamps in a nearby street. The police are called, but Danny is hidden by two classmates.

2. NAUGHTON, Bill
   One Small Boy
   see REVENGE 20

VIKINGS

see INVASIONS – NORSEMEN

VIOLENCE

see ASSAULT; BULLYING;

298

FAMILY-FIGHTING; FIGHTING; KILLING; VANDALISM

VOYAGES

1. ALLEN, Walter
   All in a Lifetime
   pp. 92–94 (Ch. 9)
   'All my possessions ... I realised that I had lost it.'
   The stench, the noise, and the overcrowding in the steerage accommodation, on a ship of European emigrants to America.

2. BENNETT, Arnold
   Anna of the Five Towns
   see TRAVEL 1

3. BOMBARD, Alain
   The Bombard Story
   passim.
   see EXPEDITIONS 1

4. ibid.
   pp. 143–145 (Ch. 11)
   'At dawn I collected ... after the evening meal.'
   The day's routine: a catalogue of fishing, inspection of dinghy and of self, and taking bearings. Alain both keeps himself occupied, and afloat.

5. ibid.
   see CASTAWAYS 1

6. CALDWELL, John
   Desperate Voyage
   passim.
   A lone voyage across the Pacific by a love-sick yachtsman who learns how to sail as he goes along, in a boat that looks less and less like a yacht with every storm.

7. GRIMBLE, Sir Arthur
   A Pattern of Islands
   pp. 5–8 (Ch. 1)
   'We reached Australia ... tranced with watching.'
   Arthur and his bride, Olivier, sail from Australia to Ocean Island, in a 33-year-old Pacific tramp. It is neither a comfortable voyage, nor an auspicious beginning for a career in the Colonial Administrative Service.

8. HILDICK, E.W.
Birdy in Amsterdam
pp. 29–32 (Ch. 3)
'Fixer – I think I'm gonna ... let well alone.'
Birdy, the Pop Whistler, and Fixer, his manager, both teenagers, make their first journey abroad – Harwich to the Hook. Birdy is seasick, and all Fixer's efforts to keep his mind off his suffering are in vain.

9. MANSFIELD, Katherine
The Garden Party
pp. 171–182 ('The Voyage')
'The Picton boat was due ... slowly it turned on the beach.'
Fenella travels with her grandmother through the night. They share a cabin – to Fenella's confusion and wonderment – and arrive at their home port in the grey of the next morning.

WALKING

see HIKING

WAR

see also: AMERICAN CIVIL WAR; ARMY;
BATTLES; BOER WAR;
CRUELTY (in) WAR; FIRST WORLD WAR;
FRIENDS – MEN (in) WAR;
INVASIONS; NAVY;
PENINSULAR WAR;
SECOND WORLD WAR; SIEGES

WAR

1. BOULLE, Pierre
The Bridge on the River Kwai
(i) pp. 144–147 (Part 4, Ch. 5); (ii) pp. 161–165
'The time passed desperately ... fatigue in every muscle.'
As he waits for the time to blow up the bridge, Joyce rehearses in his mind, how he will kill a Jap who discovers the fuse-wire, in the silent, efficient way he has been taught. He tortures himself with wondering whether he will be capable of it.

2. CHURCHILL, Winston S.
My Early Life
pp. 72–73 (Ch. 5)
'However, within measure ... a gentleman's game.'
Churchill's youthful philosophy of war; his love of pageantry; his loathing of mere 'brutish mutual extermination'.

3. CRANE, Stephen
The Red Badge of Courage
pp. 32–36 (Ch. 3)
'Absurd ideas ... and turned away.'
The youth is assailed by doubts as to how he will conduct himself in battle. He resolves upon haranguing his comrades on the absurdity of war, on dying in order to escape, and then on living until he has seen action with his own eyes.

4. REMARQUE, Erich Maria
All Quiet on the Western Front
pp. 172–178 (Ch. 9)
'There's a great deal ... merely for the inspection.'
A front-line inspection by the Kaiser prompts searching questions in the ranks, about the cause of the war, its purpose, and about the benefits, if any, that accrue from it. The questions remain unanswered.

5. SHOLOKHOV, Mikhail
And Quiet Flows the Don
see KILLING 9

WAR – BOMBING

1. CANAWAY, W.H.
Sammy going South
pp. 3–5 (Ch. 1)
'He did not hear the planes ... the boy's sobbing.'
Sammy is playing by the Suez Canal when the planes bomb Cairo. He is shocked, but quickly recovers while helping a stall-holder stacking his wares. When he returns home he discovers the street destroyed and his parents dead.

WAR – FUTURE

1. ORWELL, George
   1984
   (i) pp. 191–193 (Part 2, Ch. 9); (ii)
   pp. 151–153
   'To understand the nature ... essentially different.'
   The reasons for a continuous war in 1984 – mostly concerned with the internal situation in the countries of the three great powers, and little to do with territorial or idealogical aims. It is a low-key war.
2. ibid.
   (i) pp. 199–200 (Part 2, Ch. 9); (ii)
   pp. 156–157
   'There are therefore ... never been repeated.'
   A look at the future of the 1984 war – more sophisticated weapons but no innovations.

WAR – INJURIES

1. HOLBROOK, David
   Flesh Wounds
   pp. 204–207 (Ch. 7)
   'Paul helped with some ... the same public house.'
   Paul is sheltering in a house under fire. He sustains a shoulder wound which at first he makes light of. But he turns out to be an emergency case.

WAR – MEMORIES

1. SHOLOKHOV, Mikhail
   And Quiet Flows the Don
   pp. 99–101 (Part 1, Ch. 6)
   'He embraced the bony ... snoring comfortably.'
   Two old contemptibles reminisce about their war experiences. Both get carried away by their narratives, and neither pays any attention to the other. Grishaka has the last word, but only because his neighbour has fallen asleep.

WAR – NUCLEAR

1. SHUTE, NEVIL
   On the Beach
   pp. 14–16 (Ch. 1)
   'He glanced at the younger man ... they were there still.'
   USS Scorpion is at sea when nuclear war breaks out in the Northern Hemisphere. The Captain can make no contact with the States, and cannot even surface, due to the high level of radioactivity, until he reaches Australia.
2. ibid.
   pp. 37–40 (Ch. 1)
   ' 'But Port Moresby's out ... another drink, Dwight.'
   Dwight and Moira consider the approach of radioactivity from the Northern Hemisphere. Dwight is calm and reasonable, Moira is angry.
3. ibid.
   pp. 73–78 (Ch. 3)
   'I'd settle for the things ... they'd gone too far.'
   Officers of the last remaining operational submarine in the world attempt to trace the progress of the nuclear war which devastated the Northern Hemisphere.
4. ibid.
   pp. 165–169 (Ch. 6)
   'Dwight went forward ... humid stuffiness of the submarine.'
   Lieutenant Sunderstrom investigates the radioactive transmitting station at Seattle, from which signals have been received. He finds no-one alive, and a window-frame blowing against the transmitting key.

WATER

see also: FLOODS;
RAIN;
RIVERS;
SEA

WATER

1. HINES, Barry
    A Kestrel for a Knave
    pp. 105–106
    (Young Impact 2, pp. 49–51)
    'The toilets were empty ... at a lathered palm.'
    Billy is alone in the school toilets, listening to, and watching, water. He makes bubbles with liquid soap, and enjoys their colours.

2. LEE, Laurie
    Cider with Rosie
    (i) pp. 5–6 (Ch. 1, 'First Light'); (ii) pp. 15–16
    'The scullery was a mine ... with me to this day.'
    Laurie Lee first makes the acquaintance of water at the age of three, and rejoices in all its possibilities.

3. ibid.
    see FLOODS 10

WATERLOO, BATTLE

see BATTLES – WATERLOO – 1815

WEALTH

see also: AMBITIONS – WEALTH;
MATERIALISM;
MISFORTUNE;
SOCIALISM

WEALTH

1. BENNETT, Arnold
    Anna of the Five Towns
    pp. 109–111 (Ch. 8)
    'Anna began to receive ... and thou'rt bound.'
    Anna is disturbed and bewildered by the arrival of the first interest on her newly inherited fortune. Furthermore, she does not feel able to spend any of her money.

2. POINTON, Barry
    Break in
    pp. 111–117 (Ch. 9)

'My wife likes visitors' ... he walked down the drive.'
Denton is invited into a house on the moneyed side of town. He is introduced to a lame boy of his own age who lacks nothing in the way of material possessions. His room is chockful of expensive playthings. All that is lacking is someone with whom he can share them.

3. SILLITOE, Alan
    The Loneliness of the Long-distance Runner
    pp. 18–21 ('The Loneliness of the Long-distance Runner', Part 2)
    'I don't say to myself ... we got so clever at it.'
    The Smiths enjoy spending the insurance and benefits accruing to them from the death of the family's breadwinner. They buy new clothes, and a 21-inch television, which introduces them to still undreamt-of luxuries.

4. STEINBECK, John
    The Pearl
    passim.
    The tragic results of the pursuit of wealth – Kino is the victim of unscrupulous traders, thieves, and his own anger, which leads him to kill to protect his pearl.

5. ibid.
    pp. 21–25 (Ch. 3)
    'A town is a thing ... I myself saw it.'
    Kino has found an enormous pearl, and immediately the whole town is interested in him. He plans what he will do with his wealth.

6. ibid.
    pp. 55–64 (Ch. 5)
    'The late moon ... thou also with God.'
    Kino's enormous pearl brings him serious trouble – he fights with his wife who tries to throw it away, he kills a man who tries to steal it, he finds his canoe ruined when he tries to escape, and his house ransacked and burnt. He and his wife and child have to escape on foot.

7. WELLS, H.G.
Kipps
pp. 125–129 (Bk. 1, Ch. 6, Sn. 5)
'Ullo, Uncle, didn't see ... all come about.'
Kipps arrives home with news of his good fortune. His uncle and aunt refuse to believe that their nephew is not drunk, or that he is not the victim of a practical joke, until evidence is forthcoming. Then, their amazement is truly gratifying.

8. ibid.
pp. 131–133 (Bk. 1, Ch. 6, Sn. 6)
'It was about everything ... beginning the new life.'
Kipps dreams about how he will spend his legacy. His dreams turn into a nightmare distortion of the past. He wakes with a shriek, and re-adjusts himself, slowly, to the scarcely credible present.

9. WOOLF, Virginia
Orlando
pp. 103–107 (Ch. 3)
'Slowly she began to feel ... England the very next day.'
Abroad among gypsies to whom property is theft, Orlando longs for England, where her property and lineage are respected. Her lush estate appears to her in a vision that clinches her decision to return.

WEATHER

see also: FROST; HEAT
HURRICANES; RAIN;
SNOW;
SPRING; SUMMER;
STORMS; WINTER

WEATHER

1. JEROME, Jerome K.
Three Men in a Boat
pp. 42–45 (Ch. 5)
'George got hold of the paper ... had something to do with it.'
J muses on the folly of giving credit to weather-forecasts. He remembers

cruel days of disillusionment, and arguments with barometers.

WEDDINGS

1. ACHEBE, Chinua
Things Fall Apart
pp. 105–108 (Ch. 12)
'Early in the afternoon ... present of two cocks to them.'
Akueke is married to Ibe. There is much exchanging of gifts, feasting and dancing. The two families swear friendship to each other, before the bride is taken to her suitor's home, with ribald songs and gaiety.

2. BARSTOW, Stan
A Kind of Loving
pp. 7–12; 16–18 (Part 1, Ch. 1, Sns. 1, 2)
'The wedding was about ... the wedding's under way.'
'Well once they begin ... the Old Man says.'
The family gets itself dressed and ready for the wedding of Victor's sister. Vic's father is not looking forward to it all. He is especially put out by all the expense involved in having the reception at the premier hotel in Cressley, and he tells his wife so in the car.

3. ibid.
pp. 215–217 (Part 2, Ch. 6, Sn. 1)
'But this is no fairy-tale ... muster one at all.'
A registry-office wedding; a quiet family affair whose object is to have the decent thing done by an 18 year-old, three months pregnant. But the send-off, is not without its ration of smiles.

4. BRONTË, Charlotte
Jane Eyre
(i) pp. 346–353 (Ch. 26); (ii) pp. 285–290
'Sophie came at seven ... we found the carriage.'
Jane and Mr Rochester are to be married quietly, early one morning. There are no guests, but Jane sees two

men lurking in the shadows at the back of the church. When the clergyman asks if there is any 'impediment', one of these men comes forward declaring Mr Rochester is already married. The service is stopped and the truth told.

5. DICKENS, Charles
David Copperfield
(i) pp. 144–147 (Ch. 10); (ii) pp. 198–202
'At length ... its homely procession.'
Peggotty and Mr Barkis take David and little Emily out for the day in the horse and cart. It is not until the former return from a visit to a church that the latter learn they have just been married. The day passes in simple celebration.

6. DURRELL, Gerald
Birds, Beasts and Relatives
pp. 46–49 (Part 2, 'The Christening')
'When you were invited to a wedding ... the hands on a clock face.'
The Durrells are invited to a village wedding, conducted in the traditional Greek manner. The engagement, and housewarming parties, precede the ceremony itself a long and quiet ritual, punctuated by the exchange of garlands. And then it's all jollification again.

7. FORSTER, E.M.
Howard's End
pp. 204–208 (Ch. 26)
'Gathering that the wedding-dress ... agreed with her.'
Evie Wilcox's wedding – bustling preparations, view of the wedding-dress, followed by a comparatively quick and insignificant ceremony and reception.

8. HARDY, Thomas
Far from the Madding Crowd
see HUMILIATION 11

9. LAWRENCE, D.H.
The Rainbow
pp. 133–134; 136–137 (Ch. 5)
'It was a beautiful ... absurd he

was!'; 'When they were out ... himself go at last.'
Anna and her cousin Will are married. Anna enjoys parading herself in front of her relations; Tom Brangwen is less enthusiastic about giving her away.

10. LAWRENCE, D.H.
Sons and Lovers
(i) pp. 243–244 (Ch. 9); (ii) pp. 297–299
'Annie, too, was getting ... it was all over.'
Annie is married to Leonard. It is a sudden brisk affair. Annie is sad on leaving home and all the Morels are somewhat critical of her; but Mrs Morel knows Leonard to be genuine in his affection for Annie, therefore she finds it in her head to be philosophical about losing her.

11. LESSING, Doris
Nine African Stories
pp. 138–140 ('A Home for the Highland Cattle')
'In a mood of grim despair ... arranged the thing. What now?'
Charlie, the black servant brings the bride-price, a picture of Scottish cattle, to Theresa's father. He, who remembers a time of greater dignity and self-respect, is contemptuous of the token. But the marriage is sealed after a fashion.

12. LLEWELLYN, Richard
How Green was my Valley
pp. 12–15 (Ch. 2)
'Ivor got married ... my sisters behind us.'
Ivor and Bronwen's wedding in the new chapel, and reception in a marquee, is an occasion enjoyed by the whole village: enormous quantities of food, races for the children, and singing in the evening.

13. SHOLOKHOV, Mikhail
And Quiet Flows the Don
pp. 91–94 (Part 1, Ch. 6)
'Four gaily-painted ... mutters curses to himself.'
The Melekhov family travels to the home of the in-laws to be, in a pro-

cession of wagonettes. Ritual bargains are struck. A meal is eaten from which the bride and groom have to abstain, and Gregor takes a long hard look at Natalia.

14. ibid.
pp. 94–95 (Part 1, Ch. 6)
'On its return ... on the restive horses.'
The church service follows the meal at the Korshunovs. By the time it is done, Gregor is thoroughly disenchanted with the event, and with his bride.

15. WELLS, H.G.
The History of Mr Polly
pp. 111–117 (Ch. 6, Part 4)
(Good Time, pp. 95–96)
(Growing Up, pp. 93–96)
'Mr Polly's marriage ... his principal tooth.'
Polly is married to his cousin Miriam. The deed is done hurriedly, yet inexorably. Polly is yoked despite himself.

16. ibid.
pp. 122–129 (Ch. 6, Parts 6, 7)
'They're coming,' he said ... got to tackle 'em.'
The reception of the wedded couple is noisy and convivial. Much of bottles, uncles, and pie.

WHALES

1. BOMBARD, Alain
The Bombard Story
see FOG 1

WHALES (and) WHALING

1. WOOD, James
The Rain Islands
pp. 76–80 (Ch. 4)
'We must have tailed ... the open sea.'
Major Scott is aboard a whale-boat when whales are sighted. Having driven them into a fiord, the whalers go out in small boats to kill them,

with lances and knives. It is a scene of primitive frenzy, and blood.

WINEMAKING

1. LEE, Laurie
Cider with Rosie
(i) pp. 55–56 (Ch. 5, 'Grannies in the Wainscot'); (ii) pp. 79–82
'Granny Wallon's wines ... in the window.'
Granny Wallon, the Lees' neighbour, devotes much time and attention to making wine – much of her year is spent thus, and the Lees sample the products.

2. THOMPSON, Flora
Lark Rise to Candleford
(i) pp. 116–120 ('Lark Rise', Ch. 6); (ii) pp. 115–118
'Almost every garden ... we've got our pride.'
Country recipes for camomile tea, 'yarb beer', wines and mead. Laura recalls a time when she was rude to her Uncle Reuben when she was the worse for this last liquor.

WINTER

see also: CHRISTMAS;
FROST;
ICE;
SNOW

WINTER

1. ALMEDINGEN, E.M.
Little Katia
pp. 53–54 (Ch. 6)
'And then winter ... caught a cold.'
The delights of a Russian winter – sleigh-rides, snowmen, and games in the snow.

2. DURRELL, Gerald
My Family and Other Animals
pp. 176–178 (Part 2, Ch. 12)
'Winter came to the island ... and leaped upon the shore.'
The coming of winter to Corfu. First the wind, then the calm. Then the

wind again, and a pall of grey over the foam-flecked sea.

3. THOMPSON, Flora
   Lark Rise to Candleford
   see ICE – SKATING – ACCIDENTS 2

4. WILLIAMSON, Henry
   Tarka the Otter
   (i) pp. 104–107 (Ch. 9); (ii) pp. 106–110
   'Old Nog the heron ... alone at the slide.'
   The cold winter is hard for the otters, when the pools and streams are frozen. Greymuzzle and Tarka have a cub to feed: they make a fishing hole in the ice, and go down to the estuary for other food. Birds and other otters are in difficulties too.

5. ibid.
   see HUNGER 11

WITCHCRAFT

see also: GHOSTS;
SUPERSTITION

WITCHCRAFT

1. DE JONG, Meindert
   The Tower by the Sea
   pp. 26–34
   'Anyone in the ancient churchyard ... just one thing – WITCHERY.'
   A child alerts the old crones of the village to the 'conversation' between the white, blue-eyed cat, and the magpie, in the churchyard. They attribute this unusual state of affairs to witchcraft.

2. ibid.
   pp. 65–69
   'The storm lashed over the dunes ... we've got to do something.'
   A storm is raging over Katverloren, the children of the village lie sick of a fever, and otherwise unaccountable events, are all put down to witchcraft. The frightened villagers toy with the idea of destroying a putative witch.

3. ibid.
   pp. 75–79; 83–85; 90–92

'It was perhaps two hours later ... and save our children.'; 'In the square under ... would be all she'd need.'; 'In Katverloren the rain had stopped ... she was led away.'
All the fear and tension in the village is concentrated in the enigmatic figure of the wise old woman. An insensate mob of villagers tears down her house, and prepares to burn her – and all their problems – at the stake.

4. HARDY, Thomas
   The Return of the Native
   (i) pp. 420–423 (Bk. Fifth, Ch. 7); (ii) pp. 372–374
   'The distant light which ... red as it lay.'
   The mother of a sick son makes a wax effigy of Eustacia Wildeve, in the belief that she is a witch who has worked a spell. Having made a passable likeness of Eustacia she sticks it full of pins, and holds it over the fire. Eustacia is drowned soon after.

5. MADDOCK, Reginald
   The Pit
   pp. 52–55 (Ch. 5)
   'She was on the road past Massey's farm ... but that doesn't make her a witch.'
   Butch and his friends watch Widow Baxter cross the moor. Many believe, because she keeps cats, and is a recluse, that she is a witch. The belief seems to be confirmed when she walks across a bog; but Butch is not so sure.

6. SHOLOKHOV, Mikhail
   And Quiet Flows the Don
   pp. 13–16 (Part 1, Ch. 1)
   'The Melekhov farm ... in a sheepskin.'
   Prokoffey returns from the Turkish war, with a mystery of a wife. The superstitious villagers take her for a witch. When the cattle go down with disease the villagers hail Prokoffey's wife out of her hut, and trample her underfoot.

WOLVES

see also: HUNTING – WOLVES

WOLVES

1. DEFOE, Daniel
   Robinson Crusoe
   (i) pp. 217–219; (ii) pp. 291–305
   (Ch. 26)
   'This gave us leisure ... storm once a week.'
   All Crusoe's adventures hardly prepare him for a fight to the finish with ravenous wolves in the foothills of the Pyrenees. It is a desperate contest.
2. LONDON, Jack
   White Fang
   see LEARNING 3, 4
3. ibid.
   see FIGHTING (by) ANIMALS 3
4. MORROW, Honoré
   The Splendid Journey
   see LOST (in) MOUNTAINS 2

WOMEN

1. BRONTË, Charlotte
   Shirley
   (i) pp. 325–330 (Ch. 18); (ii) pp. 320–324
   'Joe Scott had sauntered forth ... Mrs Gill's store-room.'
   Conversation falls to politics. Shirley is no ignoramus, but Joe Scott refuses to take her seriously, because she is a woman. He takes his text from the Bible, for his opinion of woman's low estate.
2. SILLITOE, Alan
   Saturday Night and Sunday Morning
   pp. 38–39 (Part 1, Ch. 2)
   'But, all said and done ... worth their weight in gold.'
   Arthur weighs up what a woman means to him. He regards them as a very mixed blessing. But he is prepared to risk the wrath of their husbands for the chance of a night with them.

WOMEN – RIGHTS

1. DEFOE, Daniel
   Moll Flanders
   (i) pp. 57–62; (ii) pp. 74–79
   'This knowledge I soon ... herself on her undoer, man.'
   The marriage market favours the men in eighteenth century London. Moll conspires with her neighbour to blackguard an amorous, and promiscuous sailor who has wronged the latter, to such effect that the sailor is shamed into fidelity.
2. TROLLOPE, Anthony
   Barchester Towers
   pp. 435–436 (Ch. 49)
   'And now it remained ... a trusting and loving wife.'
   A Victorian view of women and marriage. A woman needs a husband to realise her full potential, and she can do nothing by herself.

WORK

see also: ACCIDENTS (at) WORK;
DISMISSAL;
FACTORIES; HOUSEWORK;
INTERVIEWS; STRIKES;
TRADE UNIONS; UNEMPLOYMENT
see also: under partic. kinds of work:
e.g. MINING, TEACHING etc.

WORK

1. ALCOTT, Louisa M.
   Little Women
   pp. 163–165 (Ch. 11)
   'What a dreadful day ... and they did.'
   After a week of idleness, Mrs March leaves her daughters in charge of the housework. Neither the idleness nor the unaccustomed work suits them, and Mrs March draws a lesson from this.
2. BARNES, Ron
   A Licence to Live
   pp. 27–32 (Ch. 3)
   'I wanted to be ... Result: the sack.'

Against his mother's wishes, Ron gets a job as a learner sign-writer. His early excitement becomes disillusionment, at the hands of the hard-swearing, bullying Irish foreman. Ron can't do a thing right. He has to leave in the end out of sheer nervousness.

3. CHURCH, Richard
   The White Doe
   see TREES – FELLING 1

4. GREENWOOD, Walter
   Love on the Dole
   see FACTORIES 2

5. ibid.
   see INITIATION 1

6. MOORE, John
   Portrait of Elmbury
   pp. 15–18 (Part 1)
   'But for their obstinacy ... tyrants great and small.'
   Elmbury's unemployed are often without a regular job through choice. They prefer to take odd-jobs, when they want and of a type they enjoy.

7. SILLITOE, Alan
   Saturday Night and Sunday Morning
   see FACTORIES 3

8. STEINBECK, John
   The Grapes of Wrath
   (i) pp. 7–9 (Ch. 2); (ii) pp. 12–13
   'The driver chewed ... to drive trucks.'
   A long-distance lorry driver picks up a hitch-hiker, although it is against the rules. He describes the hardships of a truck driver's life.

9. STOLZ, Mary
   Ready or Not
   pp. 185–187 (Ch. 13)
   'Chatham's was a large ... the plate before her.'
   Morgan spends hot summer days serving steaming food in an insalubrious cafeteria. Mr Krebble, the manager, is not a happy man, the fans curl in the hot air, and the customers appear to eat without enjoyment. It is unedifying work.

10. TATE, Joan
    Whizz Kid
    pp. 39–41 (Clee, Ch. 3)

'But my careers ... the sack for me.'
Clee has had a number of jobs, but has been successful in none – she couldn't make wreaths in the flower shop, she was bored by pricking out plants in greenhouses and was made redundant as a dry-cleaners' delivery girl.

11. THOMPSON, Flora
    Lark Rise to Candleford
    (i) pp. 457–460 ('Candleford Green', Ch. 31); (ii) pp. 404–406
    'For the first few ... could bring her.'
    Laura begins work in Candleford Green Post Office, and finds it somewhat confusing. However, she soon settles down and enjoys the contact with the villagers.

12. TWAIN, Mark
    The Adventures of Tom Sawyer
    (i) pp. 9–15 (Ch. 2); (ii) pp. 14–20 (Visions of Life 1, pp. 47–52)
    'Saturday morning was come ... then they would resign.'
    Tom is given a Saturday job to do. He envies all his friends their weekend freedom; but by making the job he is doing seem attractive, quite unlike work, he persuades his friends to part with their treasures for a share in it.

13. WATERHOUSE, Keith
    Billy Liar
    pp. 24–29 (Ch. 2)
    'Off Market St ... said: 'Who?' '
    Billy Fisher arrives for work at Shadrack and Duxbury's Undertakers. The office is gloomy, there is little to do, and the three young clerks spend their time exchanging jokes and music-hall banter.

14. WRIGHT, Richard
    Black Boy
    see RACISM – AMERICA 10

WORK – APPRENTICESHIP

1. BENTLEY, Phyllis
   The Adventures of Tom Leigh
   pp. 27–33 (Ch. 2)
   'I entered soberly ... new life as an apprentice.'

The overseer of the poor makes an application to the magistrate to have Tom Leigh bound apprentice to a clothier. A Mr Firth accepts Tom for seven years, the terms are (reluctantly) agreed upon, and the indentures are signed.

2. WELLS, H.G.
Kipps
pp. 35–38 (Bk. 1, Ch. 2, Sn. 2)
(Work and Leisure, pp. 38–42)
'The indentures that bound ... always Carshot nagged.'
The lot of the draper's apprentice. For seven years, Kipps is bound hand and foot. He learns very little, and is put upon very much.

WORK – DISMISSAL

see DISMISSAL

WORK – FIRST DAY

1. CHURCH, Richard
Over the Bridge
pp. 236–239 (Ch. 18)
'On the morning of the 21st ... adventure of commencing author.'
With reluctance and misgiving, Richard presents himself at the Land Registry in Lincoln's Inn Fields, to start work as a boy clerk in the Civil Service. He befriends another new boy, and in their lunch hour they rejoice over mutual interests.

2. HILDICK, E.W.
Louie's Lot
pp. 92–95 (Ch. 17)
'Never in his life ... 'Good afternoon' said Louie.'
It is Jim's first morning, as a milk roundsman. He has slept on beyond the bell of the alarm. He has ten minutes in which to wash, dress, grab some breakfast, and rush to the milk-float, where the sour-faced Louie is waiting for him.

3. ibid.
pp. 96–106 (Chs. 18, 19)

'For three-fifths of a second ... didn't think much of you, either.'
Jim's first morning on the milk-round. He thinks he is doing well, though his employer is unforthcoming. Louie is too busy satisfying the unusual orders of his customers to exchange pleasantries with his assistants.

4. LAWRENCE, D.H.
Sons and Lovers
(i) pp. 101–109 (Ch. 5); (ii) pp. 128–137
(Work and Leisure, pp. 19–28)
'At eight o'clock ... It's ever so nice.'
Paul's first day at Jordan's, Surgical Appliances. He meets Mr Poppleworth, 'spiral boss', and the girl machinists. He copies, checks, invoices, and parcels; and is scolded at every false move by the amiable Poppleworth.

5. TATE, Joan
Sam and Me
pp. 33–38 (Ch. 3)
'The woman in the employment agency ... room full of bored girls.'
Jo gives a poor account of herself at the employment agency. She lands a clerical job at the Health Office, about which she has no illusions. Her first impressions of the work and of the office atmosphere are confusing, and unhopeful. Her duties, quickly learnt, quickly pall.

WORK – PAYDAY

1. GREENWOOD, Walter
Love on the Dole
see SATURDAY 1

2. LAWRENCE, D.H.
Sons and Lovers
see HUMILIATION 12

3. LESSING, Doris
The Grass is Singing
see RACISM – RHODESIA 2

4. LLEWELLYN, Richard
How Green was my Valley
pp. 6–9 (Ch. 1)
'All the women ... behind your tongue.'

Saturday is pay-day in the Welsh mining-village, and the women are waiting at their doors as the men come from the midday shift. Saturday dinner is a special meal, and afterwards pocket money is given out from the money-box.

5. THOMPSON, Flora
Lark Rise to Candleford
(i) pp. 52–54 ('Lark Rise', Ch. 3); (ii) pp. 60–62
'On Friday evening ... made of elastic.'
The patrician, but not unkindly, farmer pays his labourers. He gives credit, or a mild rebuke, when he feels it to be due. The men give their half-sovereign to their wives, keeping back a shilling for themselves.

WORK – SEEKING

1. GREENWOOD, Walter
Love on the Dole
see UNEMPLOYMENT 3

2. MANSFIELD, Katherine
Bliss and Other Stories
pp. 130–135 ('Pictures')
'Ten minutes later, a stout lady ... It cheered her wonderfully.'
The forlorn Miss Moss traipses from one film studio to another in search of a crowd part so that she might pay her rent. She is disappointed in each of them, so she sits in the square and has a good cry.

3. NAUGHTON, Bill
The Goalkeeper's Revenge
(i) pp. 102–111 ('A Real Good Smile'); (ii) pp. 102–111
'At the time I'm talking of ... lose one if you overdid it.'
Fresh out of school, young Billy is groomed for a job in the locosheds. He is advised by a neighbour to stand erect, to speak out, and to smile, when he asks Mr Bidwell, the boss, for a job. Everything goes wrong, but Billy gets the job, anyway, for what Mr Bidwell calls his honesty.

4. WELLS, H.G.
The History of Mr Polly
pp. 35–39 (Ch. 3, Part 1)
'Port Burdock was never ... the prospective employer.'
Polly, unemployed, seeks a situation. He does not take to joining the pushing young men of his day in the search for a job that he has every expectation of disliking.

WORSHIP

see CHURCH – SERVICES;
METHODISTS;
RELIGION;
ROMAN CATHOLICS

WRESTLING

1. ACHEBE, Chinua
Things Fall Apart
see CELEBRATIONS – NEW YEAR 1

2. DURRELL, Gerald
My Family and Other Animals
pp. 240–243 (Part 3, Ch. 15)
'I became so used ... 'He died,' said Larry.'
His tutor, indulging in wild daydreams, tells Gerald about his one time prowess as a wrestler. Gerald corners him into demonstrating a throw. His tutor is gentle with Gerald; Gerald is less gentle with his tutor.

3. MANKOWITZ, Wolf
A Kid for Two Farthings
pp. 103–111 (Ch. 10)
'The M.C. introduced ... was out cold.'
The local boy is drawn against the ungentlemanly Python. Young Shmule concedes a good deal to his opponent, but he fights cleanly, and his youth wins out.

4. NAUGHTON, Bill
Late Night on Watling Street
pp. 128–130 ('The Half-Nelson Touch')
'At the time there ... night in the week.'

Three professional wrestlers have a trick that never fails to stir an audience, and that assures them of a lucrative return bout. One of them, from the audience, takes on an unpopular winner, and beats him convincingly; and quite harmlessly.

WRITING (and) WRITERS

see also: AMBITIONS – WRITING;
POETRY

WRITING (and) WRITERS

1. FRANK, Anne
    The Diary of Anne Frank
    pp. 13--16 (14.6.42–20.6.42)
    'On Friday 12th June … to the present day.'
    Anne has received a diary for her thirteenth birthday. After describing her birthday itself, she explains why she is going to write a diary, what she hopes to put in it, and what she hopes to gain from it.
2. GRAVES, Robert
    Goodbye to All That
    pp. 249–251 (Ch. 28)
    'We took tea in the drawing-room … what happened to them.'
    Mr and Mrs Graves visit Thomas Hardy near Dorchester. Hardy discusses his poetry writing method, and expresses his impatience with critics, and autograph-hunters.
3. TROLLOPE, Anthony
    The Warden
    see SOCIAL REFORM 1
4. WRIGHT, Richard
    Black Boy
    pp. 144–148 (Ch. 7)
    'The eighth grade days … my being alive.'
    Out of sheer boredom, Richard writes a story. It is accepted for publication by the local black newspaper. He yearns to write, in face of as much discouragement as was ever offered to a budding author.

YOUTHS

see ADOLESENCE;
ASSAULT (by) GANGS – YOUTHS;
GANGS – YOUTHS;
KILLING (by) GANGS – YOUTHS

YPRES, BATTLE

see BATTLES – YPRES

ZOOS

1. ZINDEL, Paul
    The Pigman
    pp. 43–48 (Ch. 6)
    'John and I arrived … statements five and six are true.'
    In spite of herself, Lorraine goes to the zoo, with John and Mr Pignati. She is abused by the peanut lady, and attacked by a peacock. John and Lorraine leave Mr Pignati to ride on the touring car, and all three make fools of themselves in the Monkey house.

Author Index

Introduction

The following author-entries are listed alphabetically. Where there is more than one book by the same author, the books are ordered alphabetically by title. The date at which the book was first published is given, together with (in most cases) the name of its first publisher. The standard or school edition (or editions) to which page-references are made throughout the subject-index, are given next, with the hardback preceding the paper-back edition where both are included. In each case, the publisher's name is followed, in brackets, by the name of the series (e.g. Puffin, New Windmill Series &c.) where this applies.

The period, and the place, in which the story is set follows upon these publishing details. Both are as exact, or as approximate, as information given in, or inferred from the text allows. The passages selected from the book are then listed in alphabetical order, by subject-name and number, as they appear in the subject-index. Cross-references, as opposed to main entries, are given in brackets.

Abbreviations used:
F.P. = First published
H.E.B. = Heinemann Educational Books
O.U.P. = Oxford University Press
P = Place
T = Time

ACHEBE, Chinua

Things Fall Apart
F.P. Wm. Heinemann Ltd. 1958
(i) HEB (New Windmill Series)
(ii) HEB (African Writers Series)
T.: the end of the 19th century
P.: Nigeria

British Empire – Nigeria 1–4;
Celebrations – New Year 1; (Courtship –
    Proposals (of) Marriage) 1;
(Determination) 1; (Drought) 1;
Farming – Harvest 1; (Food (&) Drink)
    1; Funerals 1;
Justice 1–5;
Locusts 1;
Marriage – Arranged 1, 2; (Massacres) 1;
    (Misfortune) 1; Missionaries 1–5;
Nigeria 1;
(Primitive Peoples) 1–5;
(Revenge) 1–4;
(Suicide) 1;
Trials 1;
Weddings 1; (Wrestling) 1;

ADAMS, Richard

Watership Down
F.P. Rex Collings 1972
Penguin Books (Puffin)
T.: the present
P.: Berkshire Downs

Animals – Trapping 1;
Creation1;
Escape 1, 2; Evening 1;
Government – Dictatorship 1;
Home-making 1; Hospitality 1;
Ingenuity 1;
Killing (of) Animals 1;
Morning 1;
Rabbits 1, 2; Roads 1;

ALAIN-FOURNIER

Le Grand Meaulnes
F.P. in France 1913
Penguin Books (trans. by Frank Davison)
T.: the turn of the 20th century
P.: Cher, Central France

Birth 1;
(Death (in) Childbirth) 1;
Lost 1; Love (at) First Sight 1;
Parties 1;
Summer 1;

ALCOTT, Louisa M.

Little Women
F.P. 1868 in America
Penguin Books (Puffin)
T.: 1860's
P.: America

(Acting) 1;
Boredom 1;
(Charity) 1; Christmas 1; (Conscience) 1;
Death (of) Baby 1;
Entertainments 1;
Gifts 1;
Happiness 1; (Holidays) 1; (Housework)
    1;
Ice-Skating – Accidents 1; Illness – Scar-
    let Fever 1;
(Learning) 1;
Meals – Dinners 1;
Parties 2; Punishment 1;
(Shyness 1, 2);
Work 1;

ALLEN, Eric

The Latchkey Children
F.P. O.U.P. 1963
O.U.P. (Oxford Children's Library)
T.: the 1960's
P.: Chelsea and other riverside parts of
    West London

(Dismissal) 1;
Fairs (&) Fêtes 1; Fear (of) Heights 1;
Government 1;
Protest 1;
(Rescue (of) Animals) 1;
Trade Unions 1;

ALLEN, Walter

All in a Lifetime
F.P. Michael Joseph 1959
Longmans (Heritage of Literature Series)

T.: a lifetime, between the late 19th century, until the mid-1950's
P.: Birmingham

Boxing 1;
(Challenges) 1; Crime 1;
Death 1, 2;
Emigration 1, 2;
Family 1; First World War 1;
Honesty 1;
(Leavetaking) 1; Life 1;
(New York) 1;
Old Age 1, 2;
Pawnbrokers 1; Politics 1; Politics – Elections 1; (Poverty) 1;
Schools – Secondary 1; Second World War – Bombing 1; Social Class 1; (Socialism) 1; Suffragettes 1;
Towns (&) Cities 1;
Voyages 1;

ALMEDINGEN, E.M.

Little Katia
F.P. O.U.P. 1966
O.U.P. (Paperback)
T.: second quarter 19th century
P.: Tsarist Russia

Boredom 2;
Christmas 2;
Death (of) Aunt 1;
Punishment 2, 3; Punishment – Confinement 1;
Quarrels – Children 1;
Schools – Boarding – First day 1;
Temptation 1;
Winter 1;

AMIS, Kingsley

Lucky Jim
F.P. Gollancz 1954
Penguin Books
T.: the 1950's
P.: a provincial university

(Fighting (by) Men) 1; (Frustration) 1;
Lecturing 1;
Rivals (in) Love 1;

Singing 1;
Travel (by) Bus 1;

AUSTEN, Jane

Emma
F.P. 1816
Penguin Books
T.: early 19th century
P.: Surrey

Courtship – Proposals (of) Marriage 2;
Dances 1;
Etiquette 1;
Friends – Girls 1;
Gossip 1;
Illness 1;

AUSTEN, Jane

Pride and Prejudice
F.P. 1813
(i) HEB (Guide Novel Series)
(ii) New American Library (Signet Classic)
T.: early 19th century
P.: Hertfordshire, London, and Kent

Courtship 1; Courtship – Proposals (of) Marriage 3;
Houses 1;
Marriage 1;
Social Class – Snobbery 1, 2;

BALCHIN, Nigel

The Small Back Room
F.P. Colls 1943
Hutchinson Educational Ltd. (Unicorn Books) (slightly abridged)
T.: the early 1940's
P.: London and elsewhere.

Alcoholism 1;
Bombs 1; Bombs – Disposal 1;
Inventions 1;
Politics 2;

313

BALDWIN, James

Go Tell it on the Mountain
F.P. Michael Joseph 1954
Longmans (Heritage of Literature Series)
T.: the last third of the 19th century, the first third of the 20th century
P.: Harlem, N.Y.

(Arrest) 1;
Baptism 1;
Church – Services 1;
Family – Quarrels 1;
Home – Leaving 1;
Love (at) First Sight 2;
Mothers (&) Sons 1;
Racism – America 1;
Sin 1; (Suicide) 2;

BALDWIN, Michael

Grandad with Snails
F.P. Routledge & Kegan Paul 1960
Hutchinson Educational (Unicorn Books)
T.: the late 1930's
P.: unspecified town and country

Adolescence – Boys 1;
Celebrations – Royal Jubilee 1; (Cinema) 1;
Fear 1;
(Games) 1; Gangs – Boys 1, 2; Grandparents 1;
Horror 1;
Injuries – Eye 1;
Poaching 1; Pranks 1–4;
Rebels (at) School 1;
(Sailors) 1; Schools – Elementary – First Day 1; Sheep 1;
Teasing 1;

BANKS, Lynne Reid

The L-Shaped Room
F.P. Chatto and Windus 1960
Penguin Books
T.: late 1950's
P.: London

Birth 2;
Fathers (&) Daughters 1;

314

Home – Leaving 2;
Quarrels – Lovers 1;

BARNES, Ron

A Licence to Live
F.P. Hackney WEA and distributed by Centreprise Publishing Project 1974
T.: 1939–1973
P.: Hackney, E, London.

Christiantiy – Conversion 1;
Gangs – Youths 1;
Second World War – Evacuation 1; Second World War – Rationing 1;
Uncles 1;
Work 2;

BARSTOW, Stan

The Human Element
F.P. (as 'The Desperadoes') Michael Joseph 1961
Longmans (Longman Imprint Books)
T.: the 1950's
P.: the West Riding of Yorkshire

Assault (by) Gangs – Youths 1, 2;
(Christmas – Carols) 1; (Courtship) 2;
Dances 2; (Death (in) Old Age) 1;
Gambling 1, 2; (Gangs – Youths 2, 3) (Gossip) 2;
Humiliation 1;
(Jealousy) 1:
Killing (by) Gangs – Youths 1;
Old Age 3;
Revenge 5, 6;
Showing-Off 1;

BARSTOW, Stan

Joby
F.P. Michael Joseph 1964
HEB (New Windmill Series)
T.: August 1939
P.: the West Riding of Yorkshire

(Boys) 2;
(Cinema) 2;
Daydreams 1;
Fighting (by) Boys 1;

Hospitals 1;
(Mothers) 1;
Punishment 4;
Rivals – Boys 1;
Sex – Education 1; Shoplifting 1, 2;
  Suicide 3;

BARSTOW, Stan

A Kind of Loving
F.P. Michael Joseph 1960
Penguin Books
T.: the late 1950's
P.: Cressley, an imaginary town in the
  industrial West Riding of Yorkshire

Accidents (at) Home 1; Accidents – Road
  – Drunkenness 1;
Courtship – Dating 1; Courtship –
  Engagement 1;
(Hospitals) 2;
Love – Disillusionment 1, 2;
Marriage – Quarrels 1; (Miscarriage) 1;
Weddings 2, 3;

BATES, H.E.

Fair Stood the Wind for France
F.P. Michael Joseph 1944
(i) Longmans (Modern Reading)
(ii) Penguin Books
T.: The Second World War
P.: France

Escape – Second World War 1–3;
Flying – Accidents – 1939–45, 1, 2;
Hiding (from) Enemy – 1939–45 1;
Injuries – Arm 1–3;
(Surgery) 1;

BATES, H.E.

The Purple Plain
F.P. Michael Joseph 1948
Nelson (Reading Today)
T.: Second World War
P.: Burma

Courage 1, 2;
Determination 2;

Flying – 1939–45 1; Flying – Accidents –
  1939–45 3, 4; Friends – Men 1;
Heat 1;
Lost (in) Jungle 1;
Panic 1;
(Refugees) 1;
Second World War – Burma 1; Suicide 4;
  Survival (in) Jungle 1, 2;

BAWDEN, Nina

Carrie's War
F.P. Victor Gollancz 1973
(i) HEB (New Windmill Series)
(ii) Penguin Books (Puffin)
T.: Second World War
P.: a small Welsh mining town

Fear (of) Darkness 1;
Memories (of) Childhood 1;
Old Age 4;
Second World War – Evacuation 2, 3;
  Stealing (of) Food 1; Superstition 1;

BAWDEN, Nina

On the Run
F.P. Victor Gollancz 1964
HEB (New Windmill Series)
T.: 1960's
P.: London and Henstable, a seaside town

Boredom 3;
Escape (from) Kidnappers 1;
Pawnbrokers 2;
Running Away (from) Home 1;
Sea – Tides 1; (Storms) 1;
Teasing 2;

BENNETT, Arnold

Anna of the Five Towns
F.P. Methuen 1902
Penguin Books
T.: end of the 19th century
P.: the Potteries

Birthdays 1;
Christianity – Evangelism 1;
Excursions 1;
Factories 1; Fishing 1;

Home 1;
Landscape 1;
Towns (&) Cities 2; Travel 1;
(Voyages) 2;
Wealth 1;

BENTLEY, Phyllis

The Adventures of Tom Leigh
F.P. Macdonald and Co. (Publishers) Ltd.
  1964
HEB (New Windmill Series)
T.: 1722
P.: the Halifax area of the West Riding of
  Yorkshire

Arrest 2;
Escape (from) Thieves 1, 2; (Execution)
  1;
Hatred 1;
Orphans 1;
(Poverty) 2;
Trials 2;
Work – Apprenticeship 1;

BENTLEY, Phyllis

Gold Pieces
F.P. Macdonald and Co. (Publishers) Ltd.
  1968
Penguin Books (Puffin)
T.: 1769
P.: Cragg Vale and Halifax, Yorks.

Adolescence – Boy 2; Arrest 3;
Forgery 1;
Lost (on) Moors 1;
(Pranks) 5;

BERNA, Paul

Flood Warning
F.P. in France 1960
F.P. The Bodley Head Ltd. 1962
HEB (New Windmill Series) (trans. John
  Buchanan-Brown)
T.: the present (December)
P.: a boarding-school near to the Rivers
  Authion and Loire, Anjou, France

316

Escape (from) Floods 1, 2;
Floods 1–4;
Rescue (from) Floods 1;
(Shyness) 3; Storms 2; (Survival) 1, 2;
Teaching – Discipline 1;

BERNA, Paul

A Hundred Million Francs
F.P. in France 1955
F.P. The Bodley Head 1957
(i) Longmans (Pleasure in Reading)
(ii) Penguin Books (Puffin)
T.: 1950's
P.: Louvigny-Triage, an outlying district
  of Paris

(Accidents) 1;
Games – Races 1; Gangs – Children 1;
Markets 1;

BOMBARD, Alain

The Bombard Story
F.P. Editions de Paris 1953
Penguin Books (trans. by Brian Connell)
T.: 1952
P.: the Mediterranean, and the Atlantic
  from Casablanca to Barbados

Castaways 1, 2;
Expeditions 1;
Fog 1; Food (&) Drink 2, 3;
(Mysteries) 1;
Rain 1;
Shipwrecks 1, 2; Storms (at) Sea 1; (Sur-
  vival (at) Sea) 1;
Voyages 3–5;
Whales 1;

BOULLE, Pierre

The Bridge on the River Kwai
F.P. in France 1952
F.P. Secker and Warburg 1954
(i) HEB (New Windmill Series) (trans.
  by Xian Fielding)
(ii) Collins (Fontana Books)
T.: 1942
P.: Siam (Thailand)

Army – Discipline 1, 2;
Jungle 1;
(Killing) 1;
(Prison (of) War) 1;
(Scond World War – Siam – Surrender)
   1;
War 1;

BRAINE, John

Room at the Top
F.P. Eyre and Spottiswoode 1957
Penguin Books
T.: the 1950's
P.: Warley, an imaginary, well-to-do Lancashire wool-town

Accidents – Road – Drunkenness 2;
   (Ambitions – Wealth) 1;
(Capitalism) 1; Courtship – Dating 2;
Materialism 1;
Rivals (in) Love 2, 3;
Social Class – Climbing 1;

BRAITHWAITE, E.R.

To Sir with Love
F.P. The Bodley Head 1959
HEB (New Windmill Series)
T.: the 1950's
P.: a secondary school in the East End of London

(Boxing) 2; (Bullying (by) Teachers) 1;
Challenges 2; Crime – Juvenile 1;
Gossip 3;
(Interviews) 1;
Newspapers 1;
Racism – Britain 1; Revolt (at) School 1;
(Sex) 1;
(Teaching) 1; Teaching – Discipline 2;
   Teaching – First Day 1, 2; (Teaching-
   Interviews) 1; (Trials) 3;

BRONTË, Charlotte

Jane Eyre
F.P. 1847
(i) Longmans (Heritage of Literature)
(ii) Penguin Books

T.: first half of the 19th century
P.: mainly at Thornfield Hall, Yorks.

Bullying (by) Boys 1;
Courtship – Proposals (of) Marriage 4;
Death (of) Friend 1;
Orphans 2;
Punishment – Confinement 2;
Schools – Boarding – First Day 2;
Weddings 4;

BRONTË, Charlotte

Shirley
F.P. 1849
(i) O.U.P. (World's Classics)
(ii) Penguin Books (Penguin English
   Library)
T.: 1811–12
P.: a mill village in the W. Riding of
   Yorkshire

(Celebrations) 1; Charity 2–4; Church-
   Festivals 1;
(Encounters) 1;
Luddites 1, 2;
Marriage 2, 3; (Materialism) 2;
Nursing 1;
(Peninsular War) 1; Poverty 3; Pride 1;
(Rivals – Churches) 1;
Selfishness 1; (Sieges) 1; Social Class 2;
   (Surgery) 2;
Women 1;

BRONTË, Charlotte

Villette
F.P. 1853
J.M. Dent and Sons Ltd. (Everyman
   Paperback)
T.: the 1840's
P.: a fictionalised Brussels, Belgium

Art 1;
Celebrations 2;
(Grief) 1;
Hero-worship 1; Honesty 2;
Illness – Nervous 1;
Loneliness 1; Love – Disillusionment 3;
Teaching – Discipline 3;

BRONTË, Emily

Wuthering Heights
F.P. 1847
(i) HEB (Guide Novel Series)
(ii) Penguin Books
T.: mid-19th century
P.: The West Riding of Yorkshire

Death (in) Childbirth 2; Death (in) Old Age 2;
Rivals (in) Love 4;

BURNETT, Frances Hodgson

The Secret Garden
F.P. 1911
Penguin Books (Puffin)
T.: early 1900's
P.: India and Yorkshire

Birds – Nesting 1;
Children – Tantrums 1;
Gardens 1;
(Illness) 2;
Loneliness 2;
Orphans 3;
Spring 1, 2;

BURTON, Hester

The Great Gale
F.P. O.U.P. 1960
O.U.P. (Oxford Children's Library)
T.: January 1953
P.: a coastal village in Norfolk

Floods 5, 6;
Rescue (from) Floods 2;

BUTLER, Samuel

The Way of all Flesh
F.P. 1903
Longmans (Heritage of Literature Series)
T.: the 19th century
P.: London and rural parishes

Christianity – Evangelism 2; Courtship – Proposals (of) Marriage 5;
Dismissal 2;

318

Gifts 2;
(Leavetaking) 2;
Marriage – Quarrels 2;
Parents 1; Punishment – Corporal 1;

CALDWELL, John

Desperate Voyage
F.P. Gollancz 1950
HEB (New Windmill Series)
T.: 1946
P.: the Pacific

(Castaways) 3;
Fishing 2, 3;
(Galapagos Islands) 1;
Hunger 1; Hurricanes 1, 2;
Islands 1;
(Monsters) 1;
Religion 1;
Sailing 1–3; Sailing – Navigation 1; Sharks 1, 2; Shipwrecks 3; Survival (at) Sea 2–5;
Voyages 6;

CAMUS, Albert

The Outsider
F.P. in France 1942
Penguin Books (Penguin Modern Classics) (trans. Stuart Gilbert)
T.: the 1940's
P.: French-occupied Algeria

(Evening) 2; Execution 2;
Funerals 2;
Heat 2, 3;
Killing 2;
Prison 1;
Sunday 1;

CANAWAY, W.H.
Sammy going South
F.P. Hutchinson and Co. Ltd. 1961
Nelson (Reading Today)
T.: 1956
P.: Egypt, Sudan, Uganda, S. Africa

(Accidents) 2;
Blindness 1;

(Death (in) War) 1;
Escape 3;
Frustration 2;
Grief 2;
Hunger 2; Hunting – Big Game 1;
Illness – Malaria 1;
Lost 2;
Revenge 7, 8; (Rivers) 1;
Snakes 1; (Survival) 3;
Travel (by) Boat 1;
War – Bombing 1;

CARY, Joyce

The Horse's Mouth
F.P. Michael Joseph 1944
Penguin Books (Penguin Modern Classics)
T.: 1938–39
P.: London

(Ambitions – Painting) 1;
Buying (and) Selling (by) Dealers 1;
(Etiquette) 2;
Government 2;
Home – Coming 1; Homelessness 1, 2;
London 1;
Mothers 2;
Old Age 5;
Painting 1–3;
Sculpture 1; Social Class 3;
(Tramps) 1;

CHAPLIN, Sid

The Leaping Lad
F.P. 1946
Longman Group Ltd. (Longman Imprint Books)
T.: the 1920's and 1930's
P.: the Durham Coalfield

(Birth) 3;
Conscience 2;
(Hunger) 3;
Memories (of) Childhood 2; (Mining) 1;
Mining – Accidents 1, 2;
(Selfishness) 2; Snow 1; Stealing (of) Food 2;

CHURCH, Richard

Over the Bridge
F.P. Wm. Heinemann 1955
HEB (New Windmill Series)
T.: 1900–1913
P.: Battersea and Dulwich Village

Ambitions 1;
Boats (&) Boating 1;
Christmas – Dinners 1; (Civil Service) 1;
    Cycling 1, 2;
Faith 1; (Family – Quarrels) 2;
Games 2;
Home – Removal 1; Horror 2;
Leavetaking 3; Leisure 1; (London) 2;
Memories (of) Childhood 3;
Piano-playing 1, 2;
(Railways) 1; (Reading) 1; (Rebels (at)
    School) 2;
School – Subjects 1; Sight 1; (Social
    Class) 4;
Teachers 1; Towns (&) Cities 3;
Work – First Day 1;

CHURCH, Richard

The White Doe
F.P. Wm. Heinemann 1968
Puffin Books
T.: 1910
P.: an English country estate

(Accidents) 3;
(Climbing) 1; Courage 3;
Deer 1;
(Rescue) 1;
Trees – Felling 1, 2;
(Work) 3;

CHURCHILL, W.S.

My Early Life
F.P. 1930
Collins (Fontana Books)
T.: 1874–1908
P.: England, India, The Sudan, S. Africa

Battles 1; Battles – Omdurman – 1898 1;
    (Boer War) 1; (British Empire – India)
    1;

(Cavalry Charges) 1;
Escape (from) Prison (of) War 1-3;
(Omdurman - Battle) 1;
School - Examinations 1; School - Subjects - Latin 1; Schools - Boarding - First Day 3; Swimming 1;
War 2

COLLINS, Wilkie

The Moonstone
F.P. 1868
Collins (Fontana Books)
T.: 1848-9
P.: Yorkshire and London

Boredom 4;
Christianity - Evangelism 3;
(Horror) 3;
Parties - Dinners 1;
Suicide 5;

CONRAD, Joseph

Typhoon and Youth
Typhoon F.P. 1903
Youth F.P. 1902
Heinemann (Guide Novels)
T.: the turn of the 19th century
P.: the Far Eastern high seas

Fire (at) Sea 1;
Shipwrecks 4; Storms (at) Sea 2-6;

COOKSON, Catherine

The Nipper
F.P. Macdonald 1970
Penguin Books (Puffin)
T.: early 1800's
P.: mining area of Northumberland

Caves 1; Courage 4, 5;
Home - Removal 2; Horses - Riding 1;
Mining 2;
Rescue (from) Assault 1;

CRANE, Stephen

The Red Badge of Courage
F.P. 1895

Hutchinson Educational Ltd. (Unicorn Books)
T.: the American Civil War (1861-1865)
P.: various Union Camps, and battlefields in the region of Washington

American Civil War 1; American Civil War - Battles 1-3; Army - Enlistment 1;
Cowardice 1;
(Death (in) War) 2; (Desertion) 1, 2;
(Fear (of) War) 1;
(Home-Leaving) 3; Horror 4, 5;
War 3

DEFOE, Daniel

Moll Flanders
F.P. 1772
(i) J.M. Dent and Sons (Everyman's Library)
(ii) Pan Books Ltd. (Pan Classics)
T.: early 18th century
P.: Colchester, London, Virginia et al.

(Arrest) 4;
Courtship 3, 4; (Crime) 2-4;
(Drunkenness) 1;
(Marriage) 4;
Pickpockets 1-4; (Poverty) 4; Prison 2;
Robbery 1;
Shoplifting 3-5; Stealing 1;
Trials 4;
Women - Rights 1;

DEFOE, Daniel

Robinson Crusoe
F.P. 1719
(i) J.M. Dent and Sons Ltd. (Everyman's Library)
(ii) New American Library (Signet Classics)
T.: the second half of the 17th century
P.: an island off the north coast of Venezuela

Cannibals 1; Castaways 4, 5;
Farming 1;
Happiness 2; (Houses) 2;
Pottery 1;

Religion 2; Rescue (from) Cannibals 1;
Shipwrecks 5, 6;
Wolves 1;

DE JONG, Meindert

The Tower by the Sea
F.P. 1950
Hutchinson Educational (Unicorn Books)
T.: an indeterminate time in the super-
stitious past
P.: Katverloren, a Dutch dune village

Cats) 1; Conditioning 1;
Fear (of) Witchcraft) 1;
Storms) 3;
Witchcraft 1–3;

DE JONG, Meindert

The Wheel on the School
F.P. Harper and Brothers New York 1954
i) HEB (New Windmill Series)
ii) Penguin Books (Puffin)
T.: early 20th century
P.: Shora, Friesland

Courage 6, 7;
Daydreams 2; (Dogs) 1;
Fear 2, 3; Fear (of) Dogs 1; Friends 1, 2;
Girls 1;
Ingenuity 2;
Loneliness) 3;
Old Age 6;
Rescue (from) Drowning) 1–3;
Stealing 2; Survival 4;

DICKENS, Charles

Bleak House
F.P. 1852–3
i) J.M. Dent and Sons Ltd. (Everyman's
Library)
ii) Everyman paperback
T.: early years of Victoria's reign
P.: London and Lincolnshire

Arrest 5;
Birthdays) 2; Blackmail 1;
Charity 5–7; Christianity – Evangelism 4;

Courtship – Proposals (of) Marriage 6,
7;
Death (of) Child 1;
Eccentrics 1, 2;
Family – Parties 1; Fog 2; Funerals 3;
(Home) 2; Horror 6;
Illness – Gout 1; Illness – smallpox 1;
Justice 6, 7;
Killing 3;
Leavetaking 4; (London) 3, 4;
Mothers 3, 4;
(Old Age) 7;
Poverty 5–7;
Rain 2;
(School – Leaving) 1; Selfishness 3, 4;
Social Class – Snobbery 3;

DICKENS, Charles

A Christmas Carol
F.P. 1843
Penguin Books ('The Christmas Books
Vol. 1' – 'A Christmas Carol' and 'The
Chimes')
T.: Christmas, early in Victoria's reign
P.: the City of London

Christmas 3–5; Christmas – Dinners 2;
Death 3;
Ghosts 1;
Misers 1–3;

DICKENS, Charles

David Copperfield
F.P. 1850
Penguin Books
T.: second quarter of the 19th century
P.: London and Yarmouth

Courtships – Proposals (of) Marriage 8;
Death (of) Mother 1, 2; Death (of) Wife
1;
Drunkenness 2;
Fighting (by) Boys (at) School 1; (For-
tune-Telling) 1;
Love (at) First Sight 3;
Madness 1; Meals – Dinners 2; Memories
(of) Childhood 4;
Punishment 5; Punishment – Corporal 2;
Running Away 1;

(Shipwrecks) 7; Storms 4; Superstition 2;
Weddings 5;

DICKENS, Charles

Great Expectations
F.P. 1861
(i) Longmans (Heritage of Literature Series)
(ii) Longmans (Great Writing in English)
T.: mid 19th century
P.: a village in the marsh-country near to the Thames estuary; and London

Challenges 3; Crime 5;
Eccentrics 3, 4; Education 1;
Family 2; Fear (of) Strangers 1; (Fire) 1; Funerals 4;
Home – Leaving 4; Honesty 3; Horror 7; (Humiliation) 2;
Love 1;
Manhunt 1;
(Reading) 2; Rivals (in) Love 5;
Schools – Elementary 1; (Shame) 1; Social Class – Snobbery 4; (Stealing) 3;

DICKENS, Charles

Hard Times
F.P. 1854
(i) Thomas Nelson and Sons Ltd.
(ii) Panther Books
T.: mid 19th century
P.: Coketown – a fictional northern industrial town

Dismissal 3; Divorce 1;
Education 2;
(Social Class) 5;
Trade Unions 2, 3;

DICKENS, Charles

A Tale of Two Cities
F.P. 1859
New American Library (Signet Classics)
T.: 1780's and 1790's
P.: London and Paris

Accidents – Road 1;
Death 4;
(Execution (by) Guillotine) 1; Execution (by) Hanging 1;
(Fear) 4; French Revolution 1–4; French Revolution – Bastille 1; French Revolution – Causes 1–3; French Revolution – Guillotine 1;
Government – Aristocracy 1, 2;
(Justice) 8;
Poverty 8; Prison 3; Punishment 6;
(Revenge) 9; Riots 1; Robbery – Grave 1;
Travel (by) Coach 1; Trials 5;

DOSTOYEVSKY, Fyodor

The Idiot
F.P. 1868
(i) Dent (Everyman's Library)
(ii) Penguin (trans. by David Magarshack)
T.: mid-19th century
P.: St. Petersburg and Pavlovsk, Russia

(Challenges) 4; Dreams 1;
Executions 3; Execution (by) Guillotine 2
(Horror) 8; Humiliation 3;
(Respect) 1;
Temptation 2; (Trials) 6;

DU MAURIER, Daphne

Jamaica Inn
F.P. Victor Gollancz Ltd. 1936
Nelson (Reading Today)
T.: beginning of the 19th century
P.: Bodmin Moor, Cornwall

(Conscience) 3;
Drunkenness 3;
Fear (of) Intruders 1;
Ghosts 2;
(Killing) 4;
(Lost (on) Moors) 2; Love 2, 3;
Moors 1, 2;
Shipwrecks 8; Smuggling 1; (Storms) 5;
Travel (by) Stage Coach 2;

DURRELL, Gerald

Birds, Beasts and Relatives
F.P. Wm. Collins 1969
Collins (Fontana)
T.: 1934–1939
P.: Corfu, Greece

Birth 4;
Crabs 1;
Dogs 2;
Fishing 4, 5;
(Gypsies) 1;
Magic 1; Meals – Dinners 3;
(Octopus) 1;
Snakes – Mating 1; Spiritualism 1;
Weddings 6;

DURRELL, Gerald

My Family and other Animals
F.P. Rupert-Hart Davies 1956
Penguin Books
T.: 1934–39
P.: Corfu

Birds – Nesting 2;
Courtship 5;
Dogs 3;
Eccentrics 5;
Fighting (by) Animals 1; Fire – Fighting
    1;
Insects 1;
Old Age 8;
Pedlars 1; (Pets) 1–4;
Rescue (from) Mud) 1;
Scorpions 1, 2; Shooting 1; Snakes –
    Catching 1;
Toads 1; Tortoises 1; Tortoises – Mating
    1;
Winter 2; Wrestling 2;

ELIOT, George

Middlemarch
F.P. 1872
New American Library (Signet Classic)
T.: about 1830
P.: a midlands town, and surrounding
    villages

Art 2;
Love 4; Love (at) First Sight 4;
Marriage – Quarrels 3;
Protest 2;
(Railways) 2;

ELIOT, George

The Mill on the Floss
F.P. 1860
Longmans (Heritage of Literature Series)
T.: 1830's–40's
P.: Lincolnshire

Brothers 1;
Children – Tantrums 2;
(Elopement) 1;
Family 3; Floods 7; Friends – Boys 1;
(Gypsies) 2;
Home 3; Humiliation 4;
(Ingenuity) 3;
(Jealousy) 2;
Love 5;
Pedlars 2;
Quarrels – Brothers (&) Sisters 1;
Religion 3; Revenge 10, 11; Running
    Away 2; Running Away (from) Home
    2;
School – Subjects – Latin 2; Showing-off
    2;
(Travel (by) Boat) 2;

ELIOT, George

Silas Marner
F.P. 1861
Longmans (Heritage of Literature Series)
T.: early years of the 19th century
P.: Warwickshire, although not by that
    name

Crime – Detection 1;
Loneliness 4;
Misers 4–7
Punishment – Confinement 3;

FALKNER, J. Meade

Moonfleet
F.P. 1898
Edward Arnold Ltd.

T.: middle to late 18th century
P.: a fishing village behind Chesil Bank on the Dorset Coast

Assault 1; Auctions 1;
Escape (from) Soldiers 1;
(Fear (of) Heights) 2; Floods 8;
(Mysteries) 2;
Revenge 1, 2;
(Self-Sacrifice) 1; Shipwrecks 9; Smugglers 2; (Storms (at) Sea) 7;
Treasure – Seeking 1, 2;

FIELDING, Henry

Joseph Andrews
F.P. 1742
New American Library (Signet Classic)
T.: mid 18th century
P.: London and the English countryside

Assault 2;
Charity 8;
(Fighting (by) Men) 2;
Girls 2;
(Highwaymen) 1; Humiliation 5;
(Love) 6;
Marriage – Quarrels 4;
(Rape) 1; Rescue (from) Animals 2; (Rescue (from) Assault) 2; (Robbery) 2;
(Selfishness) 5;

FITZGERALD, F. Scott

The Great Gatsby
F.P. in America 1926
Penguin Books (Penguin Modern Classics)
T.: 1920's
P.: Long Island, New York

Accidents – Road – Drunkenness 3; Ambitions – Wealth 2;
Parties 3; Parties – Dinners 2;
Towns (&) Cities 4;

FOAKES, Grace

Between High Walls
F.P. Shepheard-Walwyn Ltd. 1972

Pergamon Press (Athena Books)
T.: the last years of the 19th century and the first 20 odd years of the 20th century
P.: Wapping, East London

Cats 2; Celebrations 3; Christmas 6;
Fathers 1; First World War – Home Front 1;
Home 4;
Illness 3;
London 5;
Markets 2;
Poverty 9;
Salesmen 1; (Strikes) 1; Sunday 2;
(Unemployment) 1;

FORESTER, C.S.

The General
F.P. Michael Joseph 1936
(i) HEB (New Windmill Series)
(ii) Penguin Books
T.: 1899–1917
P.: South Africa, and the Western and Home Fronts 1914–18

Battles – Somme – 1916 1; Battles – Ypres 1; Boer War 2;
(Cavalry Charges) 2; (Courtship) 6;
First World War 2;
Social Class – Snobbery 5, 6;

FORESTER, C.S.

The Gun
F.P. The Bodley Head Ltd. 1933
(i) Longmans (Heritage of Literature Series)
(ii) Pan Books
T.: 1810–11 Peninsular War
P.: Northern Spain

Battles 2;
Cruelty (in) War 1;
(Desertion) 3;
Execution (by) Garrotte 1; Execution (by) Hanging 2;
Fighting (by) Men (with) Knives 1;
Ingenuity 4, 5;
Language 1;

(Mutiny) 1;
(Peninsular War) 2; Peninsular War –
   Battles 1, 2; Peninsular War – Retreat
   1;
Revolt 1;
Sieges 2;

FORESTER, C.S.

The Ship
F.P. Michael Joseph 1943
Penguin Books
T.: 1942
P.: the Mediterranean

(Fire (at) Sea) 2;
Navy 1; Navy – Discipline 1–3;
Poetry 1;
Second World War – Sea Battles 1–5;
   Ships – Guns 1–3;

FORSTER, E.M.

Howards End
F.P. 1910
Penguin Books (Penguin Modern Clas-
   sics)
T.: Edwardian period
P.: London and country seats in Hert-
   fordshire and Shropshire

Charity 9; Christmas – Shopping 1;
   (Concerts) 1;
Death 5;
(Funerals) 5;
Landscape 2; London 6;
Music 1;
Poverty 10;
Travel (by) Car 1;
Weddings 7;

FORSTER, E.M.

A Passage to India
F.P. Edward Arnold 1924
Penguin Books (Penguin Modern Clas-
   sics)
T.: the early 20th century
P.: Chandrapore on the River Ganges,
   and elsewhere in India

(Arrest) 6;
(British Empire – India) 2;
Humiliation 6;
Racism – India 1, 2;
Trials 7;

FRANK, Anne

The Diary of Anne Frank
F.P. in Holland 1947
Pan Books (trans. B.M. Mooyaart-
   Doubleday)
T.: 1942–4
P.: Amsterdam

Adolescence – Girls 1–5; Adolescence –
   Girls (in) Love 1, 2;
Escape – Second World War 4;
(Family) 4; Fear (of) Intruders 2, 3;
Hiding (from) Enemy – 1939–45 2–6;
(Invasions) 1;
Jews 1–4;
Mothers (&) Daughters 1–5;
Parents 2, 3; Punishment 7;
Quarrels 1;
Second World War 1; Second World War
   – D-day 1;
Writing (&) Writers 1;

GALLICO, Paul

The Snow Goose/The Small Miracle
F.P. Michael Joseph 1941 and 1951
(i) Longmans (Pleasure in Reading)
(ii) Penguin Books
The Snow Goose –
   T.: the 1930's & 1940's
   P.: the Essex Marshes & the
      English Channel
The Small Miracle –
   T.: the recent past
   P.: Assisi and Rome, Italy

Birds 1;
Faith 2, 3;
(Pope) 1;
(Religion) 4; (Roman Catholics) 1;
Second World War – Dunkirk 1;

GASKELL, Mrs

Cranford
F.P. 1851
(i) J.M. Dent and Sons Ltd. (Everyman's Library)
(ii) Penguin Books (Penguin English Library – 'Cranford' and 'Cousin Phillis')
T.: 1830's, 40's
P.: Cranford (Knutsford, Ches.)

Death (of) Father (&) Sister 1;
Etiquette 3, 4;
Fear (of) Thieves 1;
Ingenuity 6;
(Mothers) 5;
Parties – Teas 1; Pranks 6; (Punishment) 8;
Running – Away (from) Home 3;
Servants 1; Social Class – Snobbery 7;

GODDEN, Rumer

The Diddakoi
F.P. Macmillan 1972
Penguin Books (Puffin)
T.: the present
P.: a village near Rye, Sussex

Bullying (by) Girls 1;
Fire – House 1;
Gypsies 3, 4;
Orphans 4, 5; (Outsiders) 1, 2;
(Running Away) 3;
(Teasing) 3;

GOLDING, William

Lord of the Flies
F.P. Faber and Faber 1954
(i) Faber and Faber (Educational Edition)
(ii) Faber (Paper Covered Edition)
T.: the Present
P.: an uninhabited tropical island

(Animals – Slaughter) 1; Authority 1–4;
Castaways 6; Challenges 5; Children (as) Savages 1–4; Conscience 4;
(Democracy) 1;

326

Fear (of) Monsters 1; Forest – Fires 1; Ghosts 3;
Humiliation 7; Hunting 1;
Killing (by) Boys 1;
Religion – Primitive 1; Rescue (from) Islands 1;
Rivals – Boys 2; Rules 1–3;
(Superstition) 3; (Survival) 5, 6;

GOLDING, William

Pincher Martin
F.P. Faber and Faber 1956
Faber Paper Covered Edition
T.: the Second World War
P.: a rock in mid-Atlantic

Birds 2;
Castaways 7–10;
Drunkenness 4;
(Food (&) Drink) 4;
(Sea) 1; Shipwrecks 10; Survival (on) Islands 1, 2;

GORKY, Maxim

Childhood
F.P. in Russia 1913
(i) O.U.P. (The World's Classics) (trans. by Margaret Wettlin, revised by Jessie Coulson)
(ii) Penguin Books (Penguin Classics) (trans. by Ronald Wilks)
T.: the 1870's and 1880's
P.: Nizhni Novgorod, Russia

Accidents (at) Work 1; Assault (by) Brothers 1;
Death (of) Mother 3; (Drunkenness) 5, 6;
Family – Fighting 1–4; Family – Reunions 1; Fire – Factory 1; (Friends) 3; Friends – Boys 2; Funerals 6;
Grandparents 2, 3;
Home 5;
(Ice) 1;
(Leisure) 2;
Marriage 5; Memories (of) Childhood 5;
Night 1;
Outsiders 3;
Poverty 11; Pranks 7; (Prayer) 1; Punishment 9; Punishment – Corporal 3, 4;

Quarrels – Fathers (&) Daughters 1;
Reading 3; (Rebels (at) School) 3; Religion 5–7; (Rescue (from) Well) 1; Revenge 13;
School 1; (Shame) 2; (Stealing) 4; Suicide 6;
Teasing 4; Truancy 1;

GRAVES, Robert

Goodbye to All That
F.P. Jonathan Cape 1929
Penguin Books (Penguin Modern Classics)
T.: before, during and after the First World War
P.: chiefly in Northern France and Oxford

Climbing 2;
First World War:
 – Gas 1;
 – Injuries 1;
 – Pacifism 1;
 – Patrols 1, 2;
 – Superstition 1, 2;
 – Trenches 1, 2;
(Hospitals) 3;
Schools – Boarding 1, 2; Social Class 6; (Superstition) 4;
Tramps 2;
Writing (&) Writers 2;

GREENE, Graham

The Power and the Glory
F.P. Wm. Heinemann Ltd. 1940
(i) HEB (Modern Novel Series)
(ii) Penguin Books
T.: the late 1930's
P.: Mexico

Arrest 7;
Execution (by) Firing-Squad 1;
Fathers 2; Fear (of) Police 1; Frustration 3, 4;
Hunger 4;
Manhunt 2;
Prison 4;
(Religion) 8; (Religion – Rites) 1;

GREENWOOD, Walter

Love on the Dole
F.P. Jonathan Cape 1933
Penguin Books (Penguin Modern Classics)
T.: the late 1920's and early 1930's
P.: Salford, Lancs.

(Capitalism) 3;
Dawn 1;
Factories 2; Fortune – Telling 2;
Gambling 3;
(Humiliation) 8;
Initiation 1;
(Marriage) 6;
Pawnbrokers 3; Protest 3;
(Riots) 2;
Saturday 1; Socialism 2; Spiritualism 2;
Unemployment 2–5;
(Work) 4, 5; (Work – Payday) 1; (Work-Seeking) 1;

GRICE, Frederick

The Bonny Pit Laddie
F.P. O.U.P. 1960
O.U.P. (Oxford Children's Library)
T.: the turn of the present century
P.: a Durham pit-village

Charity 10;
Emigration 3; Escapades 1; Eviction 1, 2;
Grandparents 4;
Interviews 2;
(Leavetaking) 5;
Markets 3; Mining 3, 4; Mining – Accidents 3, 4;
Night 2;
(Punishment – Corporal) 5;
Revenge 14;
School – Expulsion 1; School – Subjects – Arithmetic 1; Strikes 2, 3;
Truancy 2, 3;

GRIMBLE, Sir Arthur

A Pattern of Islands
F.P. John Murray 1952
John Murray (Junior Edition)

T.: 1913–1919
P.: the Gilbert and Ellice Islands

Arrest 8;
Cricket 1;
Embarrassment 1; Etiquette 5;
Faith 4–6; (Fear (of) Animals) 1;
(Language) 2;
Magic 2–4; Meals – Dinners 4; (Medicine) 1; (Mysteries) 3, 4;
Octopus 2, 3;
(Parties – Dinners) 3; (Primitive Peoples) 6;
(Religion) 9; (Religion – Primitive) 2; Rescue (from) Sharks 1;
Sharks 3–6; Spiritualism 3; Superstition 5–7; Surgery 3;
Voyages 7;

GROSSMITH, George and Weedon

The Diary of a Nobody
F.P. 1892
(i) HEB (New Windmill Series)
(ii) J.M. Dent and Sons Ltd. (Everyman Paperback)
T.: the late Victorian period (c. 1891)
P.: Holloway – a middle-class London suburb

Children 1;
Dances 3; Dreams 2;
Fireworks 1;
Humiliation 9, 10;
(Misfortune) 2;
Parties 4, 5;
Spiritualism 4;

GUILLOT, René

Kpo, the Leopard
F.P. O.U.P. 1955
HEB (New Windmill Series) (trans. Gwen Marsh)
T.: the present
P.: West Africa

Deserts 1;
Escape (from) Fire 1;
(Forest – Fires) 2;

328

Hunting – Big Game 2, 3; Hunting – Gazelles 1;
Initiation 2, 3;
Leopards 1, 2;

HARDY, Thomas

Far from the Madding Crowd
F.P. 1874
(i) Macmillan and Co. Ltd. (The Scholar's Library)
(ii) Macmillan and Co. Ltd. (Papermac)
T.: middle to late Victorian period
P.: Weatherbury, near Casterbridge; otherwise Puddletown near Dorchester, Dorset

Country – Life 1; (Courtship) 7; Courtship – Proposals (of) Marriage 9;
(Embarrassment) 2; Encounters 2;
Fire – Farm 1;
Humiliation 11;
(Jealousy) 3;
Killing (by) Rivals (in) Love 1;
Misfortune 3;
Pride 2;
(Rescue (from) Sea) 1;
(Sheep) 2; Showing – Off 3; Storms 6;
Swimming 2
Unemployment 6;
(Weddings) 8;

HARDY, Thomas

The Mayor of Casterbridge
F.P. 1886
(i) Macmillan and Co. Ltd. (The Scholar's Library)
(ii) Macmillan and Co. Ltd. (The New Wessex Library)
T.: the late Victorian period
P.: the Market Town of Casterbridge otherwise Dorchester, Dorset

Assault (by) Rivals (in) Love 1;
Bulls 1;
Divorce 2;
(Rescue (from) Animals) 3; (Revenge) 15; (Rivals (in) Love) 6;

HARDY, Thomas

The Return of the Native
F.P. 1878
i) Macmillan and Co. Ltd. (The Scholar's
Library)
ii) Macmillan and Co. Ltd. (New
Wessex Edition)
T.: the middle of the 19th century
P.: Egdon Heath, otherwise the moorland,
N.E. of Dorchester, Dorset

Drowning 1;
Medicine – Primitive) 1;
Snakes 2; (Superstition) 8;
Witchcraft 4;

HARDY, Thomas

Tess of the D'Urbervilles
F.P. 1891
i) Macmillan and Co. Ltd. (The Scholar's
Library)
ii) Macmillan and Co. Ltd. (Papermac)
T.: the late Victorian period
P.: Blackmore Vale and elsewhere in rural
Dorset

Accidents – Road 2;
Baptism 2;
Killing (by) Rivals (in) Love 2;
Showing – Off 4;

HARDY, Thomas

Under the Greenwood Tree
F.P. 1872
Macmillan and Co. Ltd. (Papermac)
T.: middle to late 19th century
P.: Mellstock, a Dorsetshire farming vil-
lage

Christmas – Carols 2; Country – Life 2;
Courtship 8;
Jealousy 4;
Love) 7; (Love (at) First Sight) 5;
Pride 3;
Selfishness) 6;

HAUGAARD, Erich

The Little Fishes
F.P. Victor Gollancz Ltd. 1967
HEB (New Windmill Series)
T.: 1943
P.: Naples, and the road to Cassino, S.
Italy

Charity 11;
Escape (from) Thieves 3;
Hunger 5, 6;
(Poverty) 12;
Robbery 3; Running Away (from) Home
4;
Second World War – Bombing 2; (Sel-
fishness) 7; (Stealing (of) Food) 3;

HEMINGWAY, Ernest

For Whom the Bell Tolls
F.P. Jonathan Cape 1941
Penguin Books
T.: 1938
P.: Spain

Bull-fighting 1, 2;
Execution 4, 5;
(Revolt) 2;
(Sieges) 3; Spanish Civil War 1–4;

HEMINGWAY, Ernest

The Old Man and the Sea
F.P. Jonathan Cape 1952
Jonathan Cape
T.: the recent past
P.: the Gulf Stream off the coast of
Havana, Cuba

Animals – Slaughter 2–4;
(Dawn) 2; Determination 3, 4;
Fishing 6–9;
(Misfortune) 4;
Old Age 9;
Sea 2; Sharks 7;

HEYERDAHL, Thor

The Kon-Tiki Expedition
F.P. George Allen and Unwin 1950

Penguin Books
T.: 1947
P.: USA, Ecuador, the Pacific Ocean

Expeditions 2, 3;
Jungle 2;
Mountains 1;
Octopus 4;
Rescue (from) Sea 2; Rivers – Crossing 1;
(Sailing) 4; Sea 3, 4; Sharks 8, 9; Shipwrecks 11; Survival (at) Sea 6;

HILDICK, E.W.

Birdy in Amsterdam
F.P. Macmillan Education Ltd. 1970
Macmillan Education Ltd. (Topliner)
T.: 1970
P.: Harwich – Hook ferry, and Amsterdam

Art – Modern 1;
Hotels (&) Restaurants 1;
Meals – Breakfasts 1; Music – Jazz 1;
Voyages 8;

HILDICK, E.W.

Louie's Lot
F.P. Macmillan Education Ltd. 1965
Macmillan Education Ltd. (Topliner)
T.: the Present
P.: an urban dairy and milk-round

Competitions – Races 1;
(Dawn) 3;
Interviews 3;
Pranks 8;
Work – First Day 2, 3;

HINES, Barry

Kestrel for a Knave
F.P. Michael Joseph Ltd. 1968
(i) Pergamon Press (Athena Books)
(ii) Penguin Books ('Kes')
T.: the present
P.: Barnsley, the West Riding of Yorkshire

Birds – Catching 1; Brothers 2, 3; Bullying (by) Boys 2, 3; Bullying (by) Teachers 2;
Dawn 4;
Family – Quarrels 3; Fighting (by) Boys (at) School 2; Football 1;
Hiding 1;
Interviews 4;
Mothers 6;
Pets 5; Punishment – Corporal – School 1;
Revenge 16, 17;
School – Assembly 1; School – Registration 1; (School – Subjects) 2
Shoplifting 6, 7; Stealing 5;
Water 1;

HITCHMAN, Janet

The King of the Barbareens
F.P. Putnam 1960
Penguin Books (Peacock)
T.: the period between the two World Wars
P.: Norfolk

(Adolescence – Girls) 6; Ambitions – Acting 1;
Bullying (by) Boys (and) Girls 1;
(Gangs – Children) 2; (Girls) 3, 4;
(Home – Leaving) 5; Hospitals 4;
Illness – Whooping-cough 1;
Madness 2; Memories (of) Babyhood 1 Menstruation 1;
Orphans 6, 7; (Outsiders) 1;
Pranks 9; Protest 4; (Punishment) 10;
Religion – Scepticism 1;
Sex – Encounters 1; Stealing 6;
Unemployment 7;

HOLBROOK, David

Flesh Wounds
F.P. Methuen and Co. 1966
Longmans (Longman Imprint Books)
T.: 1942–45
P.: Cambridge and Normandy

Army 1, 2; Army – Demobilisation 1 Army – Inspection 1;
(Fear) 5;

Leavetaking 6;
Second World War 2–5; Second World War – Bombing 3; Second World War – D-Day 2–4;
Tanks 1–3;
War – Injuries 1;

HUGHES, Richard

A High Wind in Jamaica
F.P. Chatto and Windus 1929
(i) Chatto and Windus (Queen's Classics)
(ii) Penguin Books
T.: one of the first 25 years or so, of the present century
P.: Jamaica and the high seas

Adolescence – Girls 7;
Earthquakes 1;
Games 3;
Hurricanes 3;
Killing 5;
Pets 6; Primitive Peoples 7;
Swimming 3;

HUGHES, Ted

The Iron Man
F.P. Faber and Faber 1968
Faber (Paper Covered Edition)
T.: the Present
P.: undefined

Challenges 6;
Monsters 2, 3; Mysteries 5;

HUGHES, Thomas

Tom Brown's Schooldays
F.P. Macmillan 1856
Penguin Books (Puffin)
T.: the 1830's
P.: Uffington, Berks. and Rugby School

Bullying (by) Boys 4, 5;
Competitions) 1; (Conscience) 5;
Fighting (by) Boys (at) School 3; Fighting (by) Men (with) Sticks 1; Fishing 10;
(Gambling) 4; (Games) 4;
Leavetaking 7;
Meals – Breakfasts) 2; (Morning) 2;

(Poaching) 2; Pranks 10; Prayer 2;
Revolt 3; Rugby – Football 1;
School – Examinations 2; (School – Subjects – Latin) 3; Schools – Boarding 3–5; Schools – Boarding – First Day 4; Servants 2;
Travel (by) Stage-Coach 3, 4;

HUXLEY, Aldous

Brave New World
F.P. Chatto and Windus 1932
Penguin Books
T.: the future
P.: London, New Mexico and elsewhere

Cinema – Future 1; Conditioning 2, 3; Courtship 9;
Death 6;
Education – Future 1;
Future 1;
Leisure – Future 1;
Primitive Peoples 8;
Sex 2; (Social Class) 7;

JAMES, Henry

Washington Square
F.P. in America 1880
Penguin Books (Penguin Modern Classics)
T.: second quarter of the 19th century
P.: New York

Courtship 10;
(Determination) 5; Doctors 1;
Fathers (&) Daughters 2;
Love (at) First Sight 6;

JEROME, Jerome K.

Three Men in a Boat
F.P. 1889
Penguin Books
T.: the 1880's
P.: the Thames

(Antiques) 1; Art 3;
(Beauty) 1; Boats (&) Boating 2, 3;
Camping 1; Cheese 1;
Fishing 11;

331

(History) 1; Housework 2;
Kings 1;
Lost (in) Maze 1; (Magna Carta) 1;
Picnics 1;
Sailing 5;
Weather 1;

JOHNSON, Dorothy M.

The Hanging Tree
F.P. André Deutsch 1959
Hutchinson Educational Ltd. (Unicorn
Books)
T.: second half of the 19th century
P.: the Wild West

(Execution (by) Hanging) 3;
Gambling 5;
(Highwaymen) 2;
Rescue (from) Hanging 1; Robbery 4;
(Self-sacrifice) 2; Survival 7;

JOYCE, James

Dubliners
F.P. Jonathan Cape 1914
Penguin Books (Penguin Modern Clas-
sics)
T.: the beginning of the 20th century
P.: in and about Dublin

Ambitions – Writing 1;
Children (in) Love 1; Christmas – Din-
ners 3;
Death 7; Death (of) Brother 1;
(Frustration) 5;
Poetry 2;
Truancy 4;

JOYCE, James

A Portrait of the Artist as a Young Man
F.P. in America 1916
Penguin Books (Penguin Modern Clas-
sics)
T.: the end of the 19th century
P.: Sallins, County Kildare and Dublin,
Ireland

Conscience 6–8;
Hell 1–3;

332

Punishment – Corporal – School 2;
Roman Catholics – Confession 1;
Schools – Boarding 6;

KAFKA, Franz

The Trial
F.P. in Germany 1925
Penguin Books (Penguin Modern Clas-
sics) (trans. by Willan and Edwin
Muir)
T.: undefined
P.: undefined

Arrest 9;
Justice 9;
Trials 8;

KING, Clive

Stig of the Dump
F.P. Penguin Books (Puffin) 1963
Penguin Books (Puffin)
T.: the present
P.: Kent

Accidents – Falling 1;
(Caves) 2;
Fire – Lighting 1;
Ingenuity 7;
Parties 6;
Teasing 5; Trees – Felling 3;

KIRKUP, James

The Only Child
F.P. Collins 1957
Pergamon Press (Athena Books)
T.: the Twenties
P.: South Shields

(Bullying (by) Boys) 6;
(Celebrations) 4; Christmas 7;
Easter 1; Embarrassment 3;
Fairs (&) Fêtes 2; (Father Christmas) 1
Friends – Children 1;
Horses – Runaways 1; Housework 3;
Memories (of) Babyhood 2;
Relatives 1; (Rivers – Crossing) 2;
Salesmen 2; Schools – Infants 1; School
– Infants – First Day 1; Seaside 1

Smells 1; Songs (&) Rhymes 1-3; (Storms) 7; Sweets 1; Travel (by) Boat 3; Travel (by) Tram 1;

KNOWLES, John

A Separate Peace
F.P. Martin Secker and Warburg 1959
HEB (New Windmill Series)
T.: 1942-1943
P.: a Boys' Boarding School in New Hampshire, USA

(Accidents – Falling) 2; Army – Enlistment 2;
Daring 1, 2; Death (of) Friend 2;
Friends – Boys 3;
(Seaside) 2; Second World War – America 1, 2; Swimming 4;
(Truancy) 5;

KOESTLER, Arthur

Darkness at Noon
F.P. Jonathan Cape 1940
(i) Longmans (Heritage of Literature Series)
(ii) Penguin Books (Penguin Modern Classics) (trans. by Daphne Hardy)
T.: the late 1930's. The Moscow Show Trials
P.: Soviet Russia

Arrest 10;
(Communism) 1;
Execution 6;
(Interrogation) 1;
Prison 5, 6;
Torture 1, 2;

LAWRENCE, D.H.

The Rainbow
F.P. Methuen 1915
Penguin Books
T.: three generations spanning the second half of the 19th century and the early years of the 20th century
P.: the Erewash valley on the Notts-Derbyshire border

(Adolescence – Girls) 8;
(Birth) 5;
Children – Tantrums 3; Church – Services 2; (Courtship – Proposals (of) Marriage) 10;
(Drowning) 2; (Drunkenness) 7;
(Embarrassment) 4;
Fathers (&) Daughters 3-6; Floods 9; (Frustration) 6;
Gifts 3; (Girls) 5;
Hero-Worship 2;
Jealousy 5-7;
Leavetaking 8;
Marriage – Disillusionment 1; Memories (of) Childhood 6;
(Punishment – Corporal – School) 3;
(School – Leaving) 2; Sunday 3;
(Teaching) 2; Teaching – Discipline 4; Teaching – First Day 3, 4; Towns (&) Cities 5, 6;
Weddings 9;

LAWRENCE, D.H.

Sons and Lovers
F.P. 1913
(i) HEB (Modern Novel Series)
(ii) Penguin Books
T.: the last years of the 19th, and the first of the twentieth centuries
P.: Eastwood, ('Bestwood') Notts.

Army – Enlistment 3; (Assault (by) Husbands) 1; Assault (by) Rivals (in) Love 2;
Babies 1; Birthdays – Gifts 1; (Boys) 1;
Christmas 8; Competitions 2; Courtship 11, 12; Courtship – Engagement 2;
Death (of) Brother 2, 3; Death (of) Mother 4; Dismissal 4; Drunkenness 8-10;
Fairs (&) Fêtes 3; Family 5, 6; Family – Quarrels 4-6; Fathers 3-5; (Fathers (&) Sons) 1; Funerals 7;
(Home-Coming) 2; (Hospitals) 5; Hotels (&) Restaurants 2; Humiliation 12;
(Illness) 4; Injuries – Leg 1; Interviews 5;
Jealousy 8, 9;
Love 8-10; Love – Desire 1-3; Love – Disillusionment 4, 5;
Marriage – Disillusionment 2; Marriage –

Quarrels 5, 6; Marriage – Reconciliation 1; (Meals – Dinners) 5; Meals – Teas 1; (Mining – Accidents) 5; (Mothers) 7–9; (Mothers (&) Sons) 2; (Nottingham) 1;
(Painting) 4, 5; Pride 4; Punishment 11; Rivals (in) Love 7; (Running Away) 4; Showing – Off 5; Social Class 8; Towns (&) Cities 7;
Weddings 10; Work – First Day 4; (Work – Pay Day) 2;

LAWRENCE, D.H.

The Virgin and the Gipsy
F.P. Wm. Heinemann 1930
Penguin Books
T.: the 1920's
P.: Derbyshire

Courtship – Proposals (of) Marriage 11; Family – Quarrels 7; Fortune – Telling 3; Gypsies 5;
Love 11;
Sex 3;

LAWRENCE, D.H.

The White Peacock
F.P. Wm. Heinemann 1911
Penguin Books
T.: the end of the 19th century
P.: a rural valley in Nottinghamshire

(Assault) 3;
Death (of) Father 1;
(Farming) 2;
Pigs 1; Poaching 3;
Rabbits – Catching 1;

LEACH, Christopher

Answering Miss Roberts
F.P. Macmillan Education Ltd. 1968
Macmillan Education Ltd. (Topliner)
T.: the recent past
P.: London and elsewhere

Adoption 1–3; Arrest 11;
(Mothers) 10;
(Parents) 4; (Police) 1; Protest 5;

LEE, Harper

To Kill a Mocking Bird
F.P. Wm. Heinemann 1960
(i) HEB (New Windmill Series)
(ii) Penguin Books
T.: the 1930's
P.: Maycomb County, Alabama, USA

Aunts 1;
(Babies) 2;
Church – Services 3;
(Dogs) 4;
Entertainments 2; Escapades 2, 3;
Family 7; Fathers 6, 7; Fighting (by) Girls 1; Fire – House 2;
(Hallowe'en) 1; (Home – Leaving) 6;
Old Age 10;
Parties – Teas 2; Poverty 13; Pranks 11;
Racism – America 2–5; (Respect) 2; (Running Away (from) Home) 5;
Schools – Primary – First Day 1, 2; Sex – Education 2; (Shooting) 2; Snow 2;
Teaching – First Day 5, 6;

LEE, Laurie

Cider with Rosie
F.P. The Hogarth Press 1959
(i) Chatto and Windus (Queen's Classics)
(ii) Penguin Books
T.: period between the two World Wars
P.: Slad village, near Stroud, Glos.

(Assault (by) Gangs – Youths) 3;
(Beauty) 2;
Celebrations – Peace 1, 2; Christmas – Carols 3; Collecting 1; Country – Life 3, 4; Courtship 13; Cricket 2; (Crime – Juvenile) 2;
(Drowning) 3;
Excursions 2, 3;
Fairs (&) Fêtes 4; Family 8, 9; Family – Fighting 5; Farming 3; Fear (of) Ghosts 1; Floods 10; Frost 1;
(Games) 5; Gangs – Boys 3;
Ice – Skating 1; Illness 5; Illness – Fever 1;
Killing (by) Gangs – Youths 2;
(Leisure) 3;

(Madness) 3; Memories (of) Childhood 7, 8; Mothers 11;
Night 3;
Old Age 11–13;
Punishment 12, 13;
(Rain) 3; Revolt (at) School 2;
School – Elementary – First Day 2; (Seaside) 3; Servants 3; Sex – Education 3, 4; (Snow) 3; (Social Class) 9; Suicide 7, 8; Summer 2;
(Travel (by) Car) 2; (Travel (by) Charabanc) 1;
Uncles 2;
Water 2, 3; Winemaking 1;

LESSING, Doris

The Grass is Singing
F.P. Michael Joseph 1950
HEB (New Windmill Series)
T.: the 1940's
P.: Rhodesia

Authority 5, 6;
Dawn 4;
Farming 4;
Horror 9;
Marriage – Disillusionment 3;
Racism – Rhodesia 1–3; Running Away 5; (Servants) 4; (Suicide) 9;
(Work – Payday) 3;

LESSING, Doris

Nine African Stories
F.P. in 'African Stories' Michael Joseph 1964
Longmans (Longman Imprint Books)
T.: the early 1950's
P.: South Africa and Rhodesia

Ants 1;
(Blindness) 2;
Death (of) Animals 1, 2;
Fear 6; (Fighting (by) Boys) 2; Friends – Boys 4;
(Hunting) 2;
Medicine – Primitive 2;
Noise 1;
(Pets) 7;
(Racism – South Africa) 1;

Towns (&) Cities 8;
Weddings 11;

LEWIS, C.S.

Out of the Silent Planet
F.P. The Bodley Head 1938
Longmans (Heritage of Literature Series)
T.: the present
P.: England, space, and Malacandra (Mars)

(Encounters) 3;
Language 3;
Space – Travel 1–3;

LLEWELLYN, Richard

How Green was my Valley
F.P. Michael Joseph 1939
New English Library
T.: late 19th, early 20th century
P.: a mining village in S. Wales

Boxing 3;
Church – Services 4; (Courage) 8;
Escapades 4, 5;
Fighting (by) Boys (at) School 4, 5; Funerals 8;
Home – Coming 3, 4;
Lost (in) Mountains 1;
Madness 4; Mining 5;
Punishment – Corporal – School 4;
Rugby Football 2;
Schools – Secondary – First Day 1; Singing 2; (Snowstorms) 1; Strikes 4;
Weddings 12; Work – Pay Day 4;

LONDON, Jack

The Call of the Wild
F.P. 1903
Longmans (Heritage of Literature Series)
T.: late 1890's
P.: the Klondike and elsewhere in Yukon Territory, Canada

(Challenges) 7; Cruelty (to) Animals 1, 2;
Dogs 5–7; Dogs – Training 1;
Fighting (by) Animals 2;
Gambling 6;

335

Hunting 3;
(Learning) 2;

LONDON, Jack

White Fang
F.P. 1905
HEB (New Windmill Series)
T.: the 1890's
P.: the Yukon, Canada, and California

(Animals (of) prey) 1;
Dogs 8; Dogs – Loyalty 1, 2;
(Escape (from) Prison) 1;
Fighting (by) Animals 3, 4;
Learning 3–5;
(Manhunt) 3;
Outsiders 5;
Rescue (from) Intruders 1;
(Survival) 8;
(Wolves) 2, 3;

MACKEN, Walter

God Made Sunday and Other Stories
F.P. Macmillan and Co. Ltd. 1962
Pan Books
T.: the present
P.: Galway, W. Ireland

Beauty 3; Birth 6; Bulls 2;
(Circus) 1; (Climbing) 3; (Courage) 9,
10; Cruelty (to) Animals 3;
Dogs 9;
Farming 5; Fishing 12, 13;
Grief 3;
Love (at) First Sight 7;
Orphans 8;
(Pride) 5; (Punishment – Corporal) 6;
Rescue (of) Animals 4, 5;
Sailing 6; (Sea) 5; Storms 8; Superstition
9; Swimming – Learning 1;
Truancy 6;

MADDOCK, Reginald

The Pit
F.P. Collins 1966
Macmillan Education Ltd. (Topliner)
T.: the present

P.: A small town on the edge of the moors
in the North of England

(Challenges) 8;
Family – Fighting 6; Fighting (by) Boys
3;
Interrogation 2;
Moors 3;
Rescue (from) Mud 2;
(Stealing) 7;
Witchcraft 5;

MADDOCK, Reginald

Sell-Out
F.P. Collins 1969
Macmillan Education Ltd. (Topliner)
T.: the present
P.: a run-down Northern Industrial town

Football 2;
Parents 5;
Vandalism 1;

MANKOWITZ, Wolf

A Kid for Two Farthings
F.P. André Deutsch Ltd. 1953
HEB (New Windmill Series)
T.: c. 1950
P.: Aldgate, in the East End of London

Baths 1;
Markets 4;
Spring 3;
Wrestling 3;

MANKOWITZ, Wolf

*Make me an Offer, Expresso Bongo and
other Stories*
'Make me an Offer' F.P. André Deutsch
1952
'Expresso Bongo' F.P. in book form by
Ace Books 1960
Short Stories from 'The Mendelman Fire'
first collected in book form by André
Deutsch 1957
Hutchinson Educational Ltd. (Unicorn
Books)

T.: 1950's; late 19th century, early 20th century
P.: London; Russia

(Antiques) 2;
Buying (&) Selling (by) Dealers 2;
Escape (from) Police 1;
Fear (of) Ghosts 2; Forgery 2;
(Honesty) 4;
(Ingenuity) 8, 9;
Markets 5; Music – Pop 1;
(Police) 2; (Protest) 6;
Quarrels – Mothers (&) Sons 1;
Revolt 4;
Shame 3;

MANNING, Olivia

The Play Room
F.P. Wm. Heinemann 1969
HEB (New Windmill Series)
T.: Late 1960's
P.: suburbs of Portsmouth

Dances 4;
Fear 7;
Home 6; (Horror) 10, 11;
Jealousy 10;
Killing 6, 7;

MANSFIELD, Katherine

Bliss and Other Stories
F.P. Constable 1920
Penguin Books (Penguin Modern Classics)
T.: the beginning of the 20th century
P.: variously in Europe

(Ambitions – Acting) 2; Animals – Slaughter 5;
Children 2;
Happiness 3;
Love 12;
(Parties) 7;
Work – Seeking 2;

MANSFIELD, Katherine

The Garden Party
F.P. 1922

Penguin Books (Penguin Modern Classics)
T.: the first quarter of the 20th century
P.: England

Children 3, 4; Courtship – Proposals (of) Marriage 12;
Dances 5; Death 8, 9;
(Fairs (&) Fêtes) 5;
Games 6;
Holidays 2;
Leavetaking 9; Love 13, 14;
Voyages 9;

MARSHALL, James Vance

Walkabout
F.P. (as 'The Children') Michael Joseph 1959
(i) HEB (New Windmill Series)
(ii) Penguin Books (Peacock)
T.: the present
P.: the desert, the Northern Territory of Australia

Australia 1;
Birds – Australia 1, 2;
(Death) 10;
Embarrassment 5; (Etiquette) 6;
Faith 7; Fire – Lighting 2; Forest 1;
(Gifts) 4;
Lost (in) Deserts 1;
Platypus 1; Primitive Peoples 9–12;
(Religion – Primitive) 3;

MAUGHAM, W. Somerset

The Moon and Sixpence
F.P. Wm. Heinemann 1919
Penguin Books
T.: the end of the 19th century and the beginning of the 20th century
P.: London, Paris, and Tahiti

Ambitions 2; (Ambitions – Painting) 2; Art 4;
(Happiness) 4;
Painting 6;
(Running Away) 6;

'MISS READ'

Village School
F.P. Michael Joseph 1955
(i) Longmans (Modern Reading Series)
(ii) Penguin Books
T.: the early 1950's
P.: Fairacre, a country village in the South

Children 5; Christianity – Conversion 2; Country Life 5;
Doctors 2; (Drunkenness) 11;
Easter 2; (Embarrassment) 6; Excursions 4;
Games 7;
Ice – Skating 2; Interviews 6;
Jumble Sales 1, 2;
School – Inspection 1; School – Registration 2; (School – Subjects – Art) 1; School – Subjects – Geography 1; Schools – Primary 1; Schools – Primary – First Day 3; (Seaside) 4; Singing 3; (Spring) 4;
Teaching – Interviews 2;

MOORE, John

Portrait of Elmbury
F.P. Collins 1946
Pan Books
T.: 1913–1945
P.: Elmbury (Tewkesbury)

Buying (&) Selling (by) Dealers 3;
(Christmas) 9;
Farming 6, 7;
Games 8;
Hunting – Foxes 1;
Language 4;
Markets 6, 7;
Teachers 2;
Work 6;

MORROW, Honoré

The Splendid Journey
F.P. (as 'On to Oregon') 1928
HEB (New Windmill Series)
T.: the 1840's
P.: the Oregon Trail

Authority 7;
(Courage) 11;
(Death (of) Father) 2;
Expeditions 4, 5;
Illness – Dysentery 1; Indians – North America 1;
Lost (in) Mountains 2;
(Religion) 10; Rivers – Crossing 3; Running Away 7;
(Wolves) 4;

NAUGHTON, Bill

The Goalkeeper's Revenge
F.P. George G. Harrap 1961
(i) HEB (New Windmill Series)
(ii) Penguin Books (Puffin)
T.: the inter-war years
P.: the back-streets of industrial Lancashire

(Accidents – Road) 3;
Christmas – Gifts 1; Competitions – Races 2;
(Death (of) Child) 2;
Fairs (&) Fêtes 6;
(Games – Races) 2;
(Ingenuity) 10;
Reading 4;
Stealing (of) Food 4;
Work – Seeking 3;

NAUGHTON, Bill

Late Night on Watling St.
F.P. McGibbon and Kee 1959
Longmans (Longman Imprint Books)
T.: the years between the two World Wars
P.: Bolton, Lancs., and elsewhere

Accidents – Road 4;
(Bowls) 1;
Daydreams 3; (Dismissal) 5; Drunkenness 12;
Escapades 6;
Gambling 7; Games 9; (Gangs – Boys) 4;
(Ice) 2;
(Police) 3; Pranks 12;
Quarrels 2;

(Revenge) 18;
Wrestling 4;

NAUGHTON, Bill

One Small Boy
F.P. McGibbon and Kee 1957
Longmans (Longman Imprint Books)
T.: the 1920's
P.: Towlton (Bolton), Lancs.

Accidents (at) Work 2; (Assault) 4;
Baptism 3;
Cinema 3;
(Games) 10; Grief 4;
Humiliation 14;
Kite – Flying 1;
Prayer 3; Punishment – Corporal –
   School 5–7;
Revenge 19, 20; Roman Catholics –
   Communion 1; Roman Catholics –
   Confession 2;
School – Leaving 3; School – Subjects –
   Art 2; Sex – Encounters 2; Swimming
   – Learning 2;
Temptation 3;
(Vandalism) 2;

NESBIT, E.

The Railway Children
F.P. 1906
(i) HEB (New Windmill Series)
(ii) Penguin Books (Puffin)
T.: early 1900's
P.: a London suburb, and an unspecified
   village

Accidents (at) Home 2;
Birthdays 3; Birthdays – Gifts 2;
(Conscience) 9; Courage 12, 13;
Escapades 7, 8;
(Family) 10; Fear (of) Tunnels 1; Fire 2;
Home – Removal 3;
Ingenuity 11, 12;
Misfortune 5;
(Quarrels – Brothers (&) Sisters) 2;
(Railways) 3; (Rescue (from) Fire) 1;
(Stealing) 8;

O'BRIEN, Edna

The Country Girls
F.P. Hutchinson 1960
Penguin Books
T.: 1950's
P.: Irish Republic – a village, a convent
   school and Dublin

(Death (of) Mother) 5;
Entertainments 3;
Friends – Girls 2;
Grief 5;
Love 15;
Morning 3;
School – Expulsion 2; Schools – Boarding
   – First Day 5; Selfishness 8; Sex –
   Encounters 3;

O'BRIEN, Robert C.

Mrs Frisby and the Rats of NIMH
F.P. in GB Victor Gollancz 1972
Penguin Books (Puffin)
T.: the present
P.: USA

(Animals – Experiments) 1;
Conditioning 4, 5;
Materialism 3;
(Rats) 1; Rats – Catching 1; (Resources)
   1;

ORWELL, George

Animal Farm
F.P. Secker and Warburg 1945
(i) HEB (New Windmill Series)
(ii) Penguin Books (Penguin Modern
   Classics)
T.: undefined (before and after 1917)
P.: a farm in England (Soviet Russia)

Communism 2;
Execution 7;
Government – Dictatorship 2–4;
(Police) 4;
Revolt 5–7; Rules 4–5; (Russian
   Revolution) 1;
Social Class – Privilege 1, 2;
Trials 9;

ORWELL, George

1984
F.P. Martin Secker and Warburg 1947
(i) HEB (Modern Novel Series)
(ii) Penguin Books (Penguin Modern Classics)
T.: 1984
P.: London

Arrest 12; (Automation) 1;
Capitalism 2;
Freedom 1–5; Future 2;
Government – Dictatorship 5, 6;
Hatred 2; History 2–6; Hunger 7, 8;
Indoctrination 1, 2;
Language 5;
(Police) 5, 6; Poverty 14; (Propaganda) 1;
(Rats) 2;
Social Class 10, 11; Spying 1–3;
Torture 3–5;
War – Future 1, 2;

PATON, Alan

Cry, the beloved country
F.P. Jonathan Cape 1944
(i) Longmans (Abridged Edition)
(ii) Penguin Books
T.: 1940's
P.: S. Africa: Ndotsheni and Johannesburg

Capitalism 4;
Drought 2, 3;
Freedom 6;
(Gold) 1; Grief 6, 7;
Home – Leaving 7; Homelessness 3;
Justice 10;
Leavetaking 10; Lost 3;
(Manhunt) 4;
Protest 7, 8;
Racism – South Africa 2–8; Robbery 5;
Shame 4; South Africa 1–3;
Towns (&) Cities 9; Trials 10;

PEYTON, K.M.

The Edge of the Cloud
F.P. O.U.P. 1969
(i) O.U.P. (Paperback)
(ii) Penguin Books (Puffin)

340

T.: 1912–1914
P.: Kingston, Surrey, and Hendon, Middlesex

Fear (of) Flying 1, 2; Flying – 1900–14
1–5; Flying – Accidents 1, 2;
Horses – Riding 2;

PEYTON, K.M.

Flambards
F.P. O.U.P. 1967
(i) O.U.P. (Paperback)
(ii) Penguin Books (Puffin)
T.: 1908–1912
P.: hunting country in Essex 40 miles out of London

Courtship – Proposals of Marriage 13;
Dismissal 6;
Flying – 1900–14 6, 7; (Flying – Accidents) 3;
Horses – Racing 1; Horses – Riding 3;
Horses – Riding – Accidents 1, 2;
(Horses – Runaways) 2; Hunting – Foxes 2, 3;
(Punishment – Corporal) 7;
(Rivals (in) Love) 8;
Servants 5; (Social Class) 12;
Travels (by) Car 3;

PEYTON, K.M.

Flambards in Summer
F.P. O.U.P. 1969
(i) O.U.P. (Paperback)
(ii) Penguin Books (Puffin)
T.: the last years of the First World War
P.: a country house and farm in Essex, 40 miles from London

Birth 7;
Fire – Farm 2; (First World War) 3;
Flying – Accidents 1914–18 1;
Grief 8;
(Horror) 12; Horses 1;
(Rescue (of) Animals) 6;

PICARD, Barbara Leonie

The Young Pretenders
F.P. Edmund Ward Ltd. 1966
Penguin Books (Puffin)
T.: 1746
P.: North Yorkshire

Escapades 9; Escape (from) Pursuers 1;
Hiding 2; Highwaymen 3;
Social Class 13; Stealing 9;

POINTON, Barry

Break – in
F.P. Macmillan and Co. Ltd. 1974
Macmillan Education Ltd. (Topliner)
T.: the present
P.: Eccleshall – a town with a comprehensive school and housing estates

(Boredom) 5;
School – Assembly 2, 3; Schools – Secondary 2; (Showing Off) 6;
Wealth 2;

RAFTERY, Gerald

Snow Cloud, Stallion
F.P. The Bodley Head Ltd. 1953
Longmans (Pleasure in Reading Series)
T.: the present
P.: Vermont, USA

Horses 2, 3; Horses – Riding – Accidents
3; Horses – Training 1;
Rivers – Crossing 4;

REMARQUE, Erich Maria

All Quiet on the Western Front
F.P. in Germany in 1929
HEB (New Windmill Series) (trans. A.W. Wheen)
T.: the First World War
P.: the Western Front

Army – Discipline 3, 4; Army – Enlistment 4; (Assault) 5;
(Desertion) 4;
First World War 4–6; F.W.W. – Battles
1; F.W.W. – Desertion 1; F.W.W. – Gas 2; F.W.W. – Home Leave 1;
F.W.W. – Hospitals 1; F.W.W. – Injuries 2, 3; F.W.W. – Recruits 1;
F.W.W. – Trenches 3;
(Horror) 13; (Hospitals) 6;
(Leavetaking) 11;
Revenge 21;
Stealing (of) Food 5; (Surgery) 4;
War 4;

ROBINSON, Rony

A Walk to see the King
F.P. Thomas Nelson 1974
Thomas Nelson (Getaway Books)
T.: 1381
P.: Kent and London

(Democracy) 2;
Execution (by) Hanging 4;
(History) 7;
Kings 2–4;
Peasants' Revolt 1, 2;
Rebels 1, 2; (Revolt) 8, 9;

SAINT-EXUPERY, Antoine de

Night Flight
F.P. in France 1931
HEB (New Windmill Series) (trans. by Curtis Cate)
T.: c. 1930
P.: Buenos Aires and the night sky to the South

Authority 8;
Flying (at) Night 1; Flying (in) Storms 1;
(Night) 4;

SALINGER, J.D.

The Catcher in the Rye
F.P. in G.B. Hamish Hamilton 1951
Penguin Books
T.: c. 1950
P.: New York

Adolescence – Boys 3–5;
Courtship 14; Cowardice 2;

Fighting (by) Boys 4; (Friends – Boys) 5;
    Funerals 9;
Homosexuality 1;

SASSOON, Siegfried

Memoirs of a Fox-Hunting Man
F.P. Faber and Faber 1928
Faber (Paper Covered Edition)
T.: the Edwardian peace, and the years up
    to and including the first years of the
    Great War
P.: the fox-hunting country of Kent

Army – Enlistment 5;
Church – Services 5; Cricket 3;
(Easter) 3; Embarrassment 7, 8;
First World War 7, 8; First World War –
    Trenches 4;
(Hero-Worship) 3; Horses 4; Horses –
    Racing 2; Hunting – Foxes 4, 5;
Old Age 14;

SASSOON, Siegfried

Memoirs of an Infantry Officer
F.P. Faber and Faber 1930
Faber (Paper Covered Edition)
T.: the First World War
P.: the Western Front, Kent (et al.)

Courage 14;
Drunkenness 13;
First World War – Battles 2, 3; F.W.W.
    – Conscientious Objection 1; F.W.W. –
    Injuries 4, 5; F.W.W. – Patrols 3, 4;

SCHAEFER, Jack

Old Ramon
F.P. André Deutsch 1962
HEB (New Windmill Series)
T.: the recent past and present
P.: New Mexico, USA

(Bears) 1;
Deserts 2; Dogs 10;
Sheep 3; Snakes 3;

SCHAEFER, Jack

Shane
F.P. André Deutsch
HEB (New Windmill Series)
T.: the summer and autumn of 1889
P.: a valley in Wyoming, USA

Determination 6;
Fighting (by) Men 3; Fighting (by) Men
    (with) Guns 1, 2; (Friends – Men) 2;
(Killing) 8; Killing (by) Hired Assassin 1;
Shooting 3;

SERRAILLIER, Ian

The Silver Sword
F.P. Jonathan Cape 1956
(i) HEB (New Windmill Series)
(ii) Penguin Books (Puffin)
T.: 1940–1945
P.: Warsaw, and the road through Ger-
    many to Switzerland

Army 3;
(Canoeing) 1; Charity 12; Chimpanzees
    1;
Escape (from) Prison (of) War 4; Escape
    – Second World War 5–7;
(Hospitality) 2; Hunger 9;
(Invasions – Russians) 1;
Refugees 2–4;
(Second World War – Poland) 1; Storms
    9; Survival 9;
Travel (by) Boat 4;

SEWELL, Anna

Black Beauty
F.P. 1877
Penguin Books (Puffin)
T.: 1870's
P.: London and Home Counties

Battles 3;
Cruelty to Animals 4, 5;
(Drunkenness) 14;
Fashion 1; Fire – Stables 1;
Horses 5, 6; Horses – Riding – Accidents
    4–6; Horses – Runaways 3; Horses
    –Training 2, 3; Hunting – Hares 1;

Markets 8;
Poverty 15;
Storms 10;
Towns (&) Cities 10;

SHOLOKHOV, Mikhail

And Quiet Flows the Don
F.P. in USSR in 1929
Penguin Books (trans. by Stephen Garry)
T.: before, during and after the First
World War
P.: the Don Region and elsewhere in
Russia

Birth 8; Brothers 4;
(Cavalry charges) 3; Communism 3, 4;
Execution (by) Firing Squad 2, 3; Exe-
cution (by) Hanging 5;
First World War – Battles 4–6;
Grief 9;
Home – Coming 5, 6; Hunting – Wolves
1;
Illness – Fever 2;
Jealousy 11;
Killing 9, 10;
Marriage – Arranged 3; (Memories) 1;
(Old Age) 19;
Rape 2; (Rivals (in) Love) 9; (Russian
Civil War) 1–4; Russian Revolution 2,
3;
Suicide 10;
(War) 5; War – Memories 1; Weddings
13, 14; Witchcraft 6;

SHOLOKHOV, Mikhail

Fierce and Gentle Warriors
F.P. Doubleday 1967
HEB (New Windmill Series) (trans. by
Miriam Norton)
'The Rascal' –
T.: The early 1920's
P.: The Don Region of Russia
'The Fate of a Man' –
T.: 1939–45
P.: Germany, and the Region of the
Upper Don, Russia

(Army – Enlistment) 6;
Bullying (by) Boys (&) Girls 2;

Children – Ambitions 1; Communism 5;
Death (of) Father 3; (Death (in) War) 3;
Escape – Second World War – 8;
Prison (of) War 2;
Russian Revolution 4, 5;
Second World War – Russia 1; (Selfish-
ness) 9;

SHUTE, Nevil

On the Beach
F.P. Wm. Heinemann 1957
Pan Books
T.: 1963
P.: Melbourne

Suicide 11–13;
War – Nuclear 1–4;

SHUTE, Nevil

A Town like Alice
F.P. Wm. Heinemann 1950
(i) HEB (New Windmill Series)
(ii) Pan Books
T.: 1930's, 1940's, principally 1942
P.: London, Malaya and Australia

Charity 13, 14;
(Hospitality) 3;
(Prison (of) War) 3;
Religion – Rites 2;
Second World War – Evacuation 4;
Second World War – Malaya 1, 2;

SILLITOE, Alan

*The Loneliness of the Long-distance Run-
ner*
F.P. W.H. Allen 1959
(i) 'A Sillitoe Selection' (Ed. Michael
Marland) Longman (Imprint Books)
(ii) Pan Books Ltd.
T.: the 1930's
P.: in and around Nottingham

(Assault (by) Husbands) 2;
(Boredom) 6; Borstal 1;
Escapades 10;
Fairs (&) Fêtes 7, 8; Family 11;
Marriage — Quarrels 7;

(Nottingham) 2;
(Rebels) 3, 4; Running 1;
Stealing 10; Suicide 14;
Wealth 3;

SILLITOE, Alan

Saturday Night and Sunday Morning
F.P. W.H. Allen 1958
Longman (Heritage of Literature Series –
   Modern Classics)
T.: 1950's
P.: Nottingham

Abortion 1;
(Baths) 2;
Factories 3; Fairs (&) Fêtes 9; Family 12;
   Fighting (by) Men 4;
Gambling 8;
(Monday) 1;
Neighbours 1; (Nottingham) 3;
Pranks 13;
Rebels 5;
(Sweets) 2;
Teasing 6;
Women 2; (Work) 7;

SOLZHENITSYN, Alexander

One Day in the Life of Ivan Denisovich
F.P. in Soviet Union 1962
HEB (New Windmill Series) (trans. by
   Ralph Parker)
T.: the early 1950's
P.: Northern Kazakhstan, USSR

Prison – Russia 1–4;
Second World War – Russia 2;

SOUTHALL, Ivan

Ash Road
F.P. Angus and Robertson Ltd. 1965
HEB (New Windmill Series)
T.: the recent past
P.: Australian bush-country

(Camping) 2;
Fear (of) fire 1, 2; Forest – Fires 3–6;
   Freedom 7
Rescue (from) Fire 2, 3;

344

SOUTHALL, Ivan

Josh
F.P. Angus and Robertson Ltd. 1971
HEB (New Windmill Series)
T.: the present
P.: Ryan Creek, a village in the Aus-
   tralian outback 100 miles from Mel-
   bourne

Animals – Trapping 2;
Daring 3;
Morning 4;
(Rabbits – Catching) 2;

SPERRY, Armstrong

The Boy Who Was Afraid
F.P. The Bodley Head Ltd. 1942
HEB (New Windmill Series)
T.: pre-colonial past
P.: Polynesian Islands

(Animals – Slaughter) 6;
Cannibals 2; Castaways 11; Courage
   15–18;
Daring 4;
Fear (of) Sea 1; Fire – Lighting 3;
(Hunting) 4;
(Killing (of) Animals) 2;
(Octopus) 5; Outsiders 6;
(Religion – Primitive) 4;
Sea – Diving 1; Sharks 10; Storms (at)
   Sea 8, 9; Survival (on) Islands 3; Sur-
   vival (at) Sea 7;

SPYRI, Johanna

Heidi
F.P. 1880
Penguin Books (Puffin) (trans. by Eileen
   Hall)
T.: 1870's
P.: Switzerland and Frankfurt

Etiquette 7;
Holidays 3; Home 7; Homesickness 1;
Mountains 2;
Pranks 14;
Reading 5; Revenge 22;

STEINBECK, John

The Grapes of Wrath
F.P. Wm. Heinemann 1939
(i) HEB (Modern Novel Series)
(ii) Penguin Books (Penguin Modern Classics)
T.: late 'thirties
P.: Oklahoma, across the USA to California

Animals – Slaughter 7; Automation 2;
Buying (&) Selling (by) Dealers 4;
Capitalism 5–7; Courage 19;
Death (of) Grandparents 1; Drought 4;
Eviction 3, 4;
(Farming) 8;
(Hatred) 3; Hiding 3; Home – Leaving 8; Hunger 10;
Loneliness 5;
Police 7, 8; (Poverty) 16; (Prayer) 4; Prison 7, 8; Protest 9; Punishment 14;
(Rain) 4; Religion – Puritan 1; Religion – Rites 3; Rules 6;
Selfishness 10;
Turtles 1;
Work 8;

STEINBECK, John

Of Mice and Men
F.P. Wm. Heinemann 1937
(i) HEB (New Windmill Series)
(ii) Penguin (as 'Of Mice and Men and Cannery Row')
T.: the recent past
P.: by the Salinas River south of Soledad, California USA.

Authority 9;
Fighting (by) Men 5; Friends – Men 3;
Killing 11;
(Respect) 3;

STEINBECK, John

The Pearl
F.P. Wm. Heinemann 1948
HEB (New Windmill Series)
T.: the recent past
P.: Central America

Buying (&) Selling (by) Dealers 5;
Dawn 5; Determination 7;
Escape 4;
Fear (of) Thieves 2; Fishing (for) Pearls 1;
Honesty 5;
(Illness) 6;
Killing 12;
Manhunt 5;
Racism – Central America 1;
Scorpions 3; Seaside 5; (Stealing) 11;
Wealth 4–6;

STEINBECK, John

The Red Pony
F.P. in England Wm. Heinemann 1938
HEB (New Windmill Series)
T.: the recent past
P.: a farm near Salinas, in southern California, USA

Boredom 7;
(Cruelty (to) Animals) 6;
Gifts 5; Grief 10;
Horses – Birth 1; Horses – Illness 1; Horses – Mating 1; Horses – Training 4;
(Killing (of) Animals) 3, 4;
Old Age 15;
(Revenge) 23;
(Surgery) 5;

STEVENSON, R.L.

Treasure Island
F.P. 1882
Penguin Books (Puffin)
T.: second half of the 18th century
P.: West Country and Treasure Island

(Boats (&) Boating) 4;
(Fear (of) Pursuers) 1;
Horror 14–16;
Killing (in) Self-defence 1;
Mutiny 2, 3;
Pirates 1, 2;
Sieges 6, 7;

STOLZ, Mary

Ready or Not
F.P. in America 1953
HEB (New Windmill Series)
T.: the present
P.: New York

Christmas (in) Church 1; Christmas –
    Gifts 2; Christmas – Nativity Plays 1;
    Courtship – Dating 3;
(Dances) 6;
Fathers 8;
Home – Removal 4; (Hotels (&)
    Restaurants) 3;
Parties 8;
School – Leaving 4;
Teaching 3;
Work 9;

STOREY, David

This Sporting Life
F.P. Longmans 1960
Penguin Books
T.: the 1950's
P.: a northern industrial city

(Ambitions – Wealth) 3;
Hotels (&) Restaurants 4;
Materialism 4;
(Parents) 6;
Rugby Football 3–6
(Sport) 1;

STREATFIELD, Noel

Ballet Shoes
F.P. 1936
Penguin Books (Puffin)
T.: early 1930's
P.: London

Acting 2; Acting – Auditions 1; Adoption
    4;
Christmas 10;
Education 3;

346

SUTCLIFF, Rosemary

The Eagle of the Ninth
F.P. O.U.P. 1954
Penguin Books (Puffin)
T.: the second century A.D.
P.: Roman Exeter, Silchester, and the
    wilds of Caledonia (Scotland)

Battles 4;
Escape (from) Pursuers 2;
Games – Roman 1;
Home 8; (Hospitality) 4;
(Initiation) 4;
Religion – Primitive 5; Roman Empire 1;
Sieges 6; (Sport) 2;

TATE, Joan

Clipper
F.P. Macmillan Education Ltd. 1969
Macmillan Education Ltd. (Topliner)
T.: the present
P.: London

Babies 3;
Courtship – Proposals (of) Marriage 14;
Home – Removal 5;
Memories (of) Childhood 9;

TATE, Joan

Sam and Me
F.P. Macmillan Education Ltd. 1968
Macmillan Education Ltd. (Topliner)
T.: the present
P.: Manchester to London

(Family) 13;
(Happiness) 5; Home 9;
Love 16;
Marriage – Disillusionment 4;
(Police) 9;
Sex 4; Stealing (of) Babies 1;
Work – First Day 5;

TATE, Joan

Whizz Kid
F.P. Macmillan Education Ltd. 1969
Macmillan Education Ltd. (Topliner)

T.: 1960's
P.: the Midlands

Assault 6;
Fear 8;
(Injuries – Head) 1;
Love 17;
Work 10;

THACKERAY, William

Vanity Fair
F.P. 1848
(i) J.M. Dent and Sons Ltd. (Everyman's Library)
(ii) Penguin Books (Penguin English Library)
T.: first quarter 19th century
P.: London, Hampshire and Brussels

Auctions 2;
Battles – Waterloo – 1815 1–3;
Courtship 15;
Fathers (and) Sons 2;
Gambling 9; Grief 11;
Hunting – Foxes 6;
Leavetaking 12; Love 18;
Social Class – Climbing 2;

THOMAS, Dylan

A Portrait of the Artist as a Young Dog
F.P. J.M. Dent and Sons Ltd. 1940
J.M. Dent and Sons Ltd. (Aldine Paperback)
T.: the years between the two world wars
P.: South Wales

Adolescence – Boys 6;
(Boys) 3;
Challenges 9;
Fighting (by) Boys 5;
Grandparents 5;
Hiking 1; Holidays 4;
Meals – Teas 2;
Night 5, 6;
School – Subjects – Art 3; Seaside 6;

THOMAS, Dylan

A Prospect of the Sea
F.P. J.M. Dent and Sons Ltd. 1955
J.M. Dent and Sons Ltd. (Aldine Paperback)
T.: the years between the two world wars
P.: South Wales

Christmas 11;
Easter 4; Excursions 5;
(Religion) 11;
(Seaside) 7; (Snow) 4;

THOMAS, Dylan

Quite Early One Morning
F.P. J.M. Dent and Sons Ltd. 1954
J.M. Dent and Sons Ltd. (Aldine Paperback)
T.: the years between the two world wars
P.: South Wales

(Boys) 4;
Christmas 12;
Holidays 5;
Memories (of) Childhood 10–12;
School – Report 1; (Seaside) 8;

THOMAS, Leslie

This Time Next Week
F.P. Constable 1964
Pan Books
T.: during and after the Second World War
P.: Dr Barnardo's, Kingston upon Thames, and elsewhere

Accidents 4; Ambitions – Writing 2;
(Christmas (in) Church) 2; (Concerts) 2;
    Courtship – Dating 4, 5;
Escapades 11;
(Fathers) 9; (Fighting (by) Boys) 6;
    (Freedom) 8;
Goats 1;
Happiness 6; (Humiliation) 15;
Initiation 5;
(Organ) 1; Orphans 9;
Piano – Playing 3;

347

Sailors 2; Second World War – Bombing 4; (Social Class – Snobbery) 8; (Truancy) 7;

THOMPSON, Flora

Lark Rise to Candleford
F.P. O.U.P. 1945
(i) O.U.P. (World's Classics)
(ii) Penguin Books (Penguin Modern Classics)
T.: 1880's
P.: a hamlet in the N.E. corner of Oxfordshire, and Candleford Green

Animals – Catching 1; Animals – Slaughter 8; (Assault (by) Husbands) 3;
Birth 9; Bullying (by) Boys 7; Bullying (by) Girls 2;
Celebrations – Royal Jubilee 2; Church – Services 6; Country – Life 6; Courtship 16, 17; Cycling 3, 4;
(Dawn) 6; (Death (in) Old Age) 3;
Entertainments 4; Excursions 6;
Fairs (&) Fêtes 10, 11; Family – Reunions 2, 3; Farming 9; Farming – Harvest 2; Fashion 2; Fear (of) Ghosts 3; Food (&) Drink 5; Friends – Girls 3; Funerals 10;
Games 11, 12; Ghosts 4; Gossip 4; Grandparents 6; Gypsies 6;
Holidays 6; Home 10; Home – Coming 7; Home – Leaving 9, 10; Hunting – Foxes 7;
Ice – Skating – Accidents 2; Interviews 7; Learning 6;
Madness 5; Marriage – Quarrels 8; Methodists 1;
Old Age 16–18; (Outsiders) 7;
Pride 6;
Reading 6;
Salesmen 3–5; School – Inspection 2; Schools – Elementary 2; Servants 6, 7; (Sex – Education) 5; Social Class 14–17; Songs (&) Rhymes 4;
Teaching – Discipline 5, 6; Telepathy 1; Tramps 3;
Winemaking 2; (Winter) 3; Work 11; Work – Pay Day 5;

348

TOLKIEN, J.R.R.

The Hobbit
F.P. George Allen & Unwin 1937
(i) Longmans (Heritage of Literature Series)
(ii) Unwin Books
T.: 'long ago'
P.: far away

Competitions 3;
Dragons 1, 2;
(Encounters) 4; (Escape) 5;
(Horror) 17;
Parties 9;
Riddles 1;
(Treasure – Seeking) 3;

TOWNSEND, John Rowe

Gumble's Yard
F.P. 1961
Hutchinson Educational Ltd. (Unicorn Books)
T.: the present
P.: a northern industrial town
Crime – Detection 2;
Family – Quarrels 8;
Home – Leaving 11;

TOWNSEND, John Rowe

The Intruder
F.P. O.U.P. 1969
O.U.P. (Paperback)
T.: the present
P.: Westmorland

Ambitions – Property Developing 1;
Crime – Detection 3;
Escape (from) Pursuers 3;
Fear (of) Strangers 2, 3;
Quarrels 3;
Sea – Tides 2–4; Storms 11;

TREASE, Geoffrey

Cue for Treason
F.P. Blackwell 1940
Penguin Books (Puffin)
T.: the end of the 16th century

.: Lonsdale, Cumberland, and Elizabethan London

Hiding 4;
Robbery 6; Running Away 8;
Sieges 7;
Unemployment 8;

TREECE, Henry

Hounds of the King
F.P. The Bodley Head 1955
Longmans (Pleasure in Reading)
T.: 11th century. The last years before the Norman Conquest
P.: Saxon England

Battles 5; (Battles – Hastings – 1066) 1;
(Encounters) 5;
Fighting (by) Men (with) Sticks 2;
(Hastings, Battle) 1;
Initiation 6, 7; Invasions – Norsemen 1;
Invasions – Normans 1;
Kings 5;
(Normans) 1;

TREVOR, Elleston

The Flight of the Phoenix
F.P. Wm. Heinemann 1964
HEB (New Windmill Series)
T.: the present
P.: the Central Libyan Desert

Army – Discipline 5;
Deserts 3–6; (Determination) 8;
Flying – Accidents 4, 5;
(Killing (of) Animals) 5;
(Lost (in) Deserts) 2;
Survival (in) Deserts 1, 2;

TROLLOPE, Anthony

Barchester Towers
F.P. 1857
J.M. Dent and Sons Ltd. (Everyman Paperback)
T.: 1850's
P.: 'Barsetshire'

Ambitions 3;
Courtship – Proposals (of) Marriage 15;
(Death (of) Father) 4;
Eccentrics 6;
(Humiliation) 16, 17;
(Marriage) 7; Marriage – Quarrels 9, 10;
Parties 10;
Revenge 24;
Social Class 18; Social Class – Climbing 3, 4;
Women – Rights 2;

TROLLOPE, Anthony

The Warden
F.P. 1855
New American Library (Signet Classics)
T.: 1850's
P.: Barchester and London

Newspapers 2, 3;
Parties 11;
Social Reform 1;
(Writing (&) Writers) 3;

Twain, Mark

The Adventures of Huckleberry Finn
F.P. 1884
(i) HEB (New Windmill Series)
(ii) Penguin Books (Penguin English Library)
T.: the 1830's and 1840's
P.: the Mississippi River, and towns and villages on its banks

(Boys) 5, 6;
Circus 2; Confidence Tricksters 1;
(Education) 4; Escape (from) Slavery 1;
Fathers 10;
Games 13; Gangs – Boys 5;
Killing 13; Kings 6;
Language 6;
Slavery 1; (Superstition) 10;
Teasing 7;

TWAIN, Mark

The Adventures of Tom Sawyer
F.P. 1876
(i) HEB (New Windmill Series)

(ii) Penguin Books (Puffin)
T.: the 1830's and 1840's
P.: St. Petersburg, Missouri, a village on the banks of the Mississippi River

(Camping) 3; Caves 3, 4; (Challenges) 10; Children – Ambitions 2; Children (in) Love 2–4;
Dawn 7; (Daydreams) 4;
(Encounters) 6;
(Fear (of) Death) 1; (Fighting (by) Boys) 7;
Games 14;
(Illness) 7; (Insects) 2;
(Jealousy) 12;
Killing (by) Partners (in) Crime 1;
Lost (in) Caves 1;
Medicine – Primitive 3; (Monday) 2;
Rivals – Boys 3; (Robbery – Graves) 2;
Smoking 1; Storms 12; Sunday School 1;
Teeth 1;
Work 12;

WATERHOUSE, Keith

Billy Liar
F.P. Michael Joseph 1959
Penguin Books
T.: late 1950's
P.: Stradhoughton, Yorkshire

Courtship 18; Courtship – Proposals (of) Marriage 16;
Death (of) Grandparents 2;
Embarrassment 9; Entertainments 5;
Family – Quarrels 9;
Morning 5;
(Public Houses) 1;
Work 13;

WATERHOUSE, Keith

There is a Happy Land
F.P. Michael Joseph 1957
Longmans (Longman Imprint Books)
T.: 1930's
P.: Leeds, West Yorkshire

Bullying (by) Boys 8;
Fairs (&) Fêtes 12; Fighting (by) Boys 8;
Games 15;

Interrogation 3;
Quarrels 4;
Showing Off 7;

WAUGH, Evelyn

Scoop
F.P. 1938
Penguin Books (Penguin Modern Classics)
T.: the late 1930's
P.: London, a house in the West Country and Ishmaelia, a fictional East African republic
Embarrassment 10;
Newspapers 4–6;
Railways 4;
(Travel (by) Train) 1;

WELLS, H.G.

The History of Mr Polly
F.P. Thomas Nelson and Sons Ltd. 1910
Longmans (Heritage of Literature Series)
T.: the end of the 19th, and the beginning of the 20th centuries
P.: Fishbourne, and other pseudonymous towns and villages between London and the S. Coast, principally Kent

(Boredom) 8;
Courtship 19; Courtship – Proposals (of) Marriage 17; Cousins 1;
Dismissal 7;
Fighting (by) Men 6–8; Fire – Fighting 2; (Fire – House) 3; Friends – Men 4; Frustration 7; Funerals 11;
Happiness 7;
(Life) 2;
Neighbours 2;
Quarrels 5, 6;
(Relatives) 2; Rescue (from) Fire 4; Running Away 9;
School – Elementary 3; (Shops) 1; Suicide 15, 16;
(Unemployment) 9;
Weddings 15, 16; Work – Seeking 4;

WELLS, H.G.

Kipps
F.P 1905
Longmans (Heritage of Literature Series)
T.: the 1890's
P.: New Romney and Folkestone, on the Kent Coast; and briefly, London

Adolescence – Boys (in) Love 1;
Birth 10;
Courtship – Proposals (of) Marriage 18, 19; (Dreams) 3;
Etiquette 8–11;
Fathers) 11; Friends – Boys 6; Future 3;
(Hotels (&) Restaurants) 5; (Humiliation) 18;
Injuries – Wrist 1;
Language 7;
Marriage – Quarrels 11; Misfortune 6;
Schools – Secondary 3; (Shops) 2; (Social Class – Climbing) 5–7; Socialism 3, 4;
Wealth, 7, 8; Work – Apprenticeship 2;

WELLS, H.G.

The Time Machine
F.P. 1895
Pan Books
T.: late 19th century and the remote future
P.: the time-traveller's Smoking-room and fields and shores of his imagination

(Escape (from) Monsters) 1;
Future 4, 5;
Horror 18;
Inventions 2;
(Magic) 5; (Monsters) 4;

WELLS, H.G.

The War of the Worlds
F.P. Heinemann 1898
(i) HEB (New Windmill Series)
(ii) Penguin Books
T.: the end of the 19th century
P.: North East Surrey and London

(Fear (of) Monsters) 2, 3;
Horror 19, 20;

(Invasions – Martians) 1, 2;
(London) 7;
Monsters 5–8; Mysteries 6;
Panic 2, 3;
(Refugees) 5; (Running Away (from) Monsters) 1;
Survival 10;

WILDE, Oscar

The Happy Prince and Other Stories
F.P. 1888
(i) Pub'd in 'Oscar Wilde: Selected Writings' O.U.P. (World's Classics Series)
(ii) Penguin Books (Puffin)
T.: the past
P.: everywhere and nowhere

(Fireworks) 2; Friends 4;
Pride 7;
Self-sacrifice 3, 4;
Selfishness 11, 12;

WILLIAMSON, Henry

Tarka the Otter
F.P. G. Putnam's Sons 1927
(i) Longmans (Pleasure in Reading)
(ii) Penguin Books (Puffin)
T.: 1920's
P.: Devon

Animals – Trapping 3, 4;
Hunger 11; Hunting – Otters 1–4;
Initiation 8, 9;
Otters 1–4; Otters – Courtship 1;
Poaching 4;
Rivers 2;
Winter 4, 5;

WOOD, James

The Rain Islands
F.P. Gerald Duckworth Ltd. 1957
HEB (New Windmill Series)
T.: early 1950's
P.: Scotland, Iceland and surrounding sea

(Animals – Slaughter) 9; Assault 7;
Escape (from) Kidnappers 2;

(Fog) 3;
Manhunt 6;
Rescue (from) Islands 2; Rescue (from) Sea 3;
Storms (at) Sea 10; Spying 4;
Trials – Inquest 1;
Whales (&) Whaling 1;

WOODHOUSE, Martin

Tree Frog
F.P. Wm. Heinemann 1966
HEB (New Windmill Series)
T.: the present
P.: London, Lincolnshire, the Austrian Alps, and the Libyan Sahara

Accidents – Road 5;
Escape 6; Escape (from) Prison 2;
Interrogation 4;

WOOLF, Virginia

Orlando
F.P. 1928
Penguin Books
T.: the end of the 16th century, and the last years of Elizabeth 1, until 1928
P.: principally England, London and a provincial estate

Frost 2, 3;
London 8, 9;
Poetry 3, 4;
Social Class 19;
Wealth 9;

WRIGHT, Richard

Black Boy
Longmans (Longman Imprint Books)
T.: 1912–1927
P.: Mississippi/Tennessee, USA

(Baptism) 4; Boredom 9; (Boys) 7, 8;
(Bullying (by) Boys) 9;
(Christianity – Evangelism) 5; Courage 20; (Cowardice) 3; Cruelty (to) Animals 7;
Faith 8; (Fathers) 12; (Fear) 9; (Fear (of)

Bullying) 1; Fighting (by) Boys (at) School 6, 7; (Fire – House) 4;
(Gangs – Boys) 6;
Hatred 4–6; Home – Leaving 12, (Humiliation) 19; Hunger 12;
Initiation 10–12;
Jews 5;
(Killing (of) Animals) 6;
Learning 7, 8;
Methodists 2; Mothers 12;
Punishment – Corporal – School 8;
Racism – America 6–10; Reading 7; (Respect) 4, 5; Running Away (from) Orphanage 1;
Shyness 4; (Stealing) 12;
(Work) 14; Writing (&) Writers 4;

WYNDHAM, John

Chocky
F.P. Michael Joseph 1968
Penguin Books
T.: the present
P.: a village in Surrey

Kidnapping 1;
Resources 2;

WYNDHAM, John

The Day of the Triffids
F.P. Michael Joseph 1951
Penguin Books
T.: the 'present'
P.: London and the South of England

Conditioning 6;
Disasters 1–3;
(Honesty) 6;
(Learning) 9; London 10, 11;
(Mysteries) 7;
Plants 1–3;
(Stealing) 13; Survival 11;

WYNDHAM, John

The Kraken Wakes
F.P. Michael Joseph 1953
Penguin Books

T.: an imaginary reconstruction of the
    recent past, present and future
P.: London and elsewhere

Floods 11, 12;
Horror 21–23;
(London) 12;
Monsters 9;
Mysteries 8–11;
Sea – Diving 2; Survival 12;

ZINDEL, Paul

The Pigman
F.P. Harper and Row Inc. N.Y. 1968
Macmillan Education Ltd. (Topliner)
T.: the present
P.: New York

Eccentrics 7;
Parties 12; Pranks 15;
Sex – Encounters 4;
Zoos 1

Anthologies Index